MINUTES

OF THE

Fourth Biennial Convention

OF

The United Lutheran Church in America

CHICAGO, ILLINOIS
October 21-29, 1924

THE UNITED LUTHERAN PUBLICATION HOUSE
PHILADELPHIA, PA.

THE UNITED LUTHERAN CHURCH IN AMERICA

CALENDAR, 1924-1926

OFFICERS

President—Rev. F. H. Knubel, D.D., LL.D.,
437 Fifth Avenue, New York City.
Secretary—Rev. M. G. G. Scherer, D.D.,
437 Fifth Avenue, New York City.
Treasurer—Mr. E. Clarence Miller, LL.D.,
410 Chestnut St., Philadelphia, Pa.

EXECUTIVE BOARD

Term Expires 1928

Rev. F. F. Fry, D.D., 110 Westminster Road, Rochester, New York.
Rev. W. D. C. Keiter, D.D., 1228 Spruce Street, Philadelphia, Pa.
Rev. A. R. Wentz, D.D., Ph.D., Gettysburg, Pa.
Robbin B. Wolf, Esq., 424 Frick Building, Pittsburgh, Pa.
George E. Neff, Esq., 29 S. Duke Street, York, Pa.
Hon. John F. Kramer, 3-5 Blymyer Building, Mansfield, Ohio.

Term Expires 1926

Rev. E. B. Burgess, D.D., 23 Chestnut Street, Crafton, Pa.
Rev. W. H. Greever, D.D., Drawer 300, Columbia, S. C.
Rev. A. H. Smith, D.D., 259 Sandusky Street, Ashland, Ohio.
Hon. C. M. Efird, Lexington, S. C.
Mr. William H. Hager, Lancaster, Pa.
Mr. Frederick Henrich, 69 Northampton Street, Buffalo, N.Y.

Members Ex-Officio

Rev. F. H. Knubel, President.
Rev. M. G. G. Scherer, Secretary.
Mr. E. Clarence Miller, Treasurer.

Place of next Convention—Richmond, Virginia.

Minutes of the Fourth Biennial Convention of the United Lutheran Church in America

THE SERVICE—INTRODUCTORY

WICKER PARK LUTHERAN CHURCH,

Chicago, Illinois.

Tuesday, October 21, 1924, 8 P. M.

· Preparatory to the Opening of the Fourth Biennial Convention of The United Lutheran Church in America, delegates-elect from the Constituent Synods, a large number of visitors and many members of the churches of the Convention City assembled to participate in The Service, at Wicker Park Lutheran Church, Chicago, Ill., on Tuesday evening, October 21, 1924, at eight o'clock. Those who took part in The Service, the Public Confession and the administration of the Sacrament of the Altar, were the Reverends J. A. Clutz and H. A. Weller, retiring members of the Executive Board, and the President and Secretary.

The text of the sermon, which was preached by the President, was John 20: 21-23; the theme, "Forgiveness of sins, the message of the Church."

FIRST MEETING

Morning Session

CONVENTION HALL, EDGEWATER BEACH HOTEL,

Chicago, Ill.

Wednesday, October 22, 8:45 A. M.

Matins were conducted by the Rev. J. L. Morgan.

The President called the Convention to order and, after the use of the Order for the Opening of Synods, declared the Fourth Convention of The United Lutheran Church in America open for business.

The President asked that by general consent the announcement of the completed list of delegates be deferred, and that the Convention proceed to business.

As a special order the President asked for the item of the

5

report of the Executive Board relating to the merger of synods (III, B, 2).

The recommendation of the Executive Board in regard to this item was adopted.

The roll as corrected follows:

ROLL OF DELEGATES BY SYNODS

1. Ministerium of Pennsylvania

Clerical Organized August 15, 1748 *Lay*

Clerical	Lay
Rev. H. A. Weller, D.D.	E. Clarence Miller, LL.D.
Rev. J. C. Seegers, D.D.	Prof. G. T. Ettinger, Ph.D., Litt.D.*
Rev. W. D. C. Keiter, D.D.	D. D. Fritch, M.D.
Rev. Adolph Hellwege	Capt H. M. M. Richards, Litt.D.
Rev. J. A. W. Haas, D.D., LL.D.	Mr. G. W. Smith
Rev. N. R. Melhorn, D.D.	Mr. F. D. Bittner
Rev. A. T. W. Steinhaeuser, D.D.	Mr. James M. Snyder
Rev. E. P. Pfatteicher, Ph.D., D.D.	Mr. P. P. Hagan
	Mr. M. L. March
Rev. F. M. Urich, D.D.	G. E. Schlegelmilch, Esq.
Rev. G. Gebert, D.D.	Mr. W. M. Mearig
Rev. G. W. Sandt, D.D., LL.D.	Mr Albert Broadmeyer
Rev. J. H. Waidelich, D.D.	Mr. John L. Potteiger
Rev. W. L. Stough, D.D.	Mr. A. Raymond Bard
Rev. I. B. Kurtz, D.D.	F. O. Ritter, M.D.
Rev. I. F. Frankenfield	Mr. F. E. Schall
Rev. A. B. MacIntosh, D.D.	Mr. Charles F. Mosser
Rev. J. C. Mattes	Mr. Luther R. Shearer
Rev. P. G. Sieger, D.D.	Mr. P. T. Lambach
Rev. F. K. Fretz, D.D., Ph.D.	Mr. Oscar C. Schmidt
Rev. G. F. Gehr, D.D.	Mr. D. F. Yost
Rev. L. D. Ulrich	Hon. F. M. Riter LL.D.
Rev. P. A. Laury, D.D.	Mr. Harry Hodges
Rev. G. C. Rees, D.D.	Mr. John Greiner, Jr.
Rev. C. M. Jacobs, D.D.	Mr. Frank L. Brown
Rev. F. T. Esterly	Mr. Chas. H. Esser
Rev. W. C. Schaeffer, D.D.	Mr. S. W. Deininger
Rev. R. B. Lynch	Mr. John M. Snyder
Rev. H. Offerman, D.D.	Mr. Harry G. G. Querns
Rev. F. O. Evers	Mr. J. H. Bonawitz
Rev. J. F. Lambert, D.D.	J. F. Trexler, M.D.
Rev. C. T. Benze, D.D.	Mr. W. H. Hager
Rev. W. Z. Artz	Mr. Henry Schneider
Rev. A. M. Mehrkam, Ph.D.	Mr. Grant Hultberg
Rev. H. S. Kidd	Mr. W. J. Daub
Rev. J. H. Orr	Hon. B. F. Miller
Rev. I. C. Hoffman, D.D.	

2. Ministerium of New York

Clerical Organized October 23, 1786 *Lay*

Clerical	Lay
Rev. F. H. Bosch	Mr. G. Bohrer
Rev. T. O. Posselt	Mr. H. Kruse

Clerical	Lay
Rev. J. A. W. Kirsch	Mr. H. Brandes
Rev. A. Holthusen, D.D.	Mr. W. Gaskell
Rev. F. Sutter	R. Moldenke, Ph.D.
Rev. J. J. Heischmann, D.D.	Mr. F. Stuessy
Rev. H. Brezing	Mr. E. Muncke
Rev. O. Krauch	Mr. T. Roehrs
Rev. G. A. Bierdemann, D.D.	Mr. E. H. R. Vogel
Rev. J. F. Holstein, Ph.D.	Mr. C. Froehlich
Rev. G. Doering	Mr. M. Wulff
Rev. S. von Bosse	Mr. A. Becker
Rev. H. C. Wasmund	Mr. F. Greiner
Rev. B. Mehrtens	Mr. J. Schantz
Rev. Paul Kirsch	Mr. W. Intemann

3. United Synod of North Carolina
Organized May 2, 1803

Clerical	Lay
Rev. J. L. Morgan, D.D.	Mr. James D. Heilig
Rev. A. G. Voigt, D.D., LL.D.	Mr. W L. Dixon
Rev. J. F. Crigler, D.D.	Mr. W. K. Mauney
Rev. J. C. Dietz	Hon. B. B. Miller
Rev. E. H. Kohn, Ph.D.	Mr. A. R. Rhyne
Rev. L. A. Thomas	Dr. R. W. Leiby
Rev. A. R. Beck	Prof. G. F. McAllister*
Rev W. J. Finck, D.D.	Hon. L. M. Swink
Rev. P. J. Bame	Mr. J. V. Sutton

*Date of organization of the Evangelical Lutheran Synod and Ministerium of North Carolina which, on March 2, 1921, with the Evangelical Lutheran Tennessee Synod (organized July 17, 1820) merged into the United Evangelical Lutheran Synod of North Carolina under an amended charter of the former of the two synods which merged.

4. Maryland Synod
Organized October 11, 1820

Clerical	Lay
Rev. J. Weidley, D.D.	Mr. W. W. Doub
Rev. W. G. Minnick	L. R. Alden, Esq.
Rev. John B. Rupley	Mr. M. P. Moller
Rev. F. R. Wagner, D.D.	Mr. A. H. Weaver
Rev. S. J. McDowell, D.D.	E. W. Young, Esq.
Rev. William A. Wade	Mr. F. W. Kakel
Rev. M. L. Enders, D.D.	H. T. Domer, Litt.D.
Rev. J. C. Bowers, D.D.	Mr. E. H. Sharretts
Rev. A. R. Wentz, Ph.D., D.D.	Wm. J. Showalter, Sc.D.
Rev. J. L. Hoffman	Mr. M. H. Buehler

5. Synod of South Carolina
Organized January 14, 1824

Clerical	Lay
Rev. H. J. Black, D.D.	Prof. S. J. Derrick, LL.D.
Rev. M. G. G. Scherer, D.D.	Hon. C. M. Efird
Rev. C. A. Freed, D.D.	Mr. R. C. Counts
Rev. H. A. McCullough, D.D.	Geo. B. Cromer, LL.D.
Rev. W. H. Greever, D.D.	Mr. H. B. Snyder
Rev. P. D. Brown	Mr. F. W. Seegers

6. Synod of West Pennsylvania

Organized September 5, 1825

Clerical	Lay
Rev. Geo. W. Nicely, D.D	Geo. E. Neff, Esq.
Rev. H. B. Stock D.D.	Mr. W. L. Gladfelter
Rev. Geo. E. Bowersox	Mr. P. A. Elsesser
Rev. G. A. Getty, D.D.	Hon. E. P. Miller
Rev. L. B. Wolf, D.D.	Mr. W. H. Menges
Rev. A. R. Steck, D.D.	Mr. A. R. Nissley
Rev. Henry Anstadt, D.D.	Mr. Alexander Diehl
Rev. S. L. Hench	Mr. I. L. Taylor
Rev. W. A. Kump	Mr. Geo. W. Hafer

7. Synod of Virginia

*Organized August 10, 1829

Clerical	Lay
Rev. C. Brown Cox, D.D.	Hon. R. W. Kime
Rev. J. J. Scherer, Jr., D.D.	W. T. Stauffer, Esq.
Rev. R. H. Anderson	Hon. H. L. Bonham
Rev. J. Luther Sieber, D.D.	Mr. Harry E. Pugh
Rev. Geo. H. Rhodes	Mr. A. D. Smith
Rev. J. A. Huffard, D.D.	Mr. Harry L. Snyder
Rev. C. L. Miller, D.D.	Mr. E. L. Keiser

*Date of organization of the Evangelical Lutheran Synod and Ministerium of Virginia which, on March 17, 1922, with the Evangelical Lutheran Synod and Ministerium of Southwestern Virginia (composed of the former Evangelical Lutheran Synod and Ministerium of S. W. Va., organized September 20, 1842, and the Evangelical Lutheran Holston Synod, organized September 29, 1860), merged into the United Lutheran Synod of Virginia.

8. Ohio Synod

*Organized November 7, 1836

Clerical	Lay
Rev. Paul W. Koller, D.D.	Mr. I. F. Mellinger
Rev. R. E. Tulloss, Ph.D., D.D.	Hon. John L. Zimmerman, LL.D.
Rev. A. H. Smith, D.D.	C. G. Shatzer, Sc.D.
Rev. Jos. Sittler, D.D.	Mr. J. W. Kahler
Rev. C. E. Rice, D.D.	Mr M. W. Lutz
Rev. M. L. Wagner, D.D.	Mr. G. A. Mayer
Rev. A. O. Becker, D.D.	Mr. Ira C. Albert
Rev. E. C. Herman	Mr. C. J. Mitchel
Rev. H. C. Brillhart	Mr. C. F. Wassenberg
Rev. H. B. Ernsberger, D.D.	Mr. H. A. Sloneker
Rev. Wm. Buchholtz	Mr. Wm. H. Schaus
Rev. A. J. Hall	Mr. A. W. Ulrici
Rev. R. A. Halverstadt	Mr. R. N. Heist
Rev. Geo. W. Miley	Mr. E. J. Young
Rev. B. W. Ziegler, D.D.	Mr. J. L. Clark

Clerical	Lay
Rev. F. E. Strobel	Mr. R. E. Sawyer
Rev. J. W. Kapp, D.D.	Mr. James Porter
Rev. T. B. Birch, Ph.D.	Mr. L. F. Palmer
Rev. L. H. Larimer, D.D.	Mr. F. W. Albrecht

*Date of organization of East Ohio Synod, which, on November 3, 1920, with the Synod of Miami (organized October 16, 1844), Wittenberg Synod (organized June 8, 1847) and the District Synod of Ohio (organized August 26, 1857) merged into the Synod of Ohio of the United Lutheran Church.

9. East Pennsylvania Synod

Organized May 2, 1842

Clerical	Lay
Rev. S. Billheimer, D.D.	Dr. Croll Keller
Rev. Luther De Yoe, D.D.	Mr. George C. Baum
Rev. R. H. Stover, D.D.	Mr. A. H. Durboraw
Rev. A. Pohlman, M.D., D.D.	Mr. E. G. Hoover
Rev. E. H Delk, D.D.	Mr. Romanus Esterly
Rev. J. D. Krout	Mr. J. E. Miller
Rev. E. A. Chamberlin	Wm. H. Emhardt, Esq.
Rev. Wm. J. Miller, Jr.	C. M. Stine, Ph.D.
Rev. G. Z. Stup	Mr. Harvey C. Miller
Rev. C. E. Rice	Mr. H. C. Smeltzer
Rev. E. E. Schantz	Mr. J. H. Brandt
Rev. J. A. Richter	Mr. J. H. Wagner
Rev. Wm. C. Ney	Mr. C. A. Good

10. Alleghany Synod

Organized September 9, 1842

Clerical	Lay
Rev. S. N. Carpenter, D.D.	Prof. H. S. Fleck
Rev. A. J. Rudisill, D.D.	Mr. Isaac Harpster
Rev. L. P. Young, D.D.	Mr. C. Luther Lowe
Rev. Wm. I. Good	Mr. W. E. Dickey
Rev. John B. Kniseley	Mr. H. W. Thompson
Rev. M. S. Kemp, Litt.D., D.D.	Mr. S. Z. Miller
Rev. Geo. N. Lauffer, D.D.	Mr. A. J. Harter

11. Pittsburgh Synod

Organized January 15, 1845

Clerical	Lay
Rev. E. B. Burgess, D.D.	Robbin B. Wolf, Esq.
Rev. S. G. Dornblaser, D.D.	Prof. O. F. H. Bert
Rev. C. P. MacLaughlin, D.D.	Hon. A. E. Reiber
Rev. J. J. Myers	Mr. J. W. Hunter
Rev. E. M. Gearhart, D.D.	Judge J. Frank Graff
Rev. A. J. Turkle, D.D.	Judge George A. Baldwin
Rev. A Hering	Mr. C. F. Stifel
Rev. B. F. Hankey	Hon. Chas. Young

Clerical	Lay
Rev. J. B. Baker, D.D.	Mr. J. L. Frederick
Rev. G. A. Benze, D.D.	Mr. C. L. Herbster*
Rev. G. W. Englar, D.D.	Dr. H. C. Hoffman
Rev. E. A. Tappert, D.D.	Mr. C. J. Mensch*
Rev. F. W. Kohler	G. F. Greiner, Esq.
Rev. J. E. Bittle, D.D.	Mr. Peter Leemhuis
Rev. H. H. Bagger	Mr. Wm. E. Yeager
Rev. C. A. Dennig	Mr E. R. Sheldon
Rev. T. Buch	Mr. Jesse Martsolf
Rev. W. H. Hetrick, D.D.	Dr. C. E. Miller
Rev. A. P. Lentz	Mr. Peter Graff
Rev. L. J. Baker	Mr. J. A. A. Geidel
Rev. J. J. Hill, D.D.	Mr. J. M. Bash
Rev. J. I. Shaud	Mr. A. M. Hartzell

12.   Indiana Synod

Organized October 28, 1848

Clerical	Lay
Rev. F. A. Dressel, D.D.	Mr. A. H. Kornfeld
Rev. J. B. Gardner	Mr. J. E. Spiegel
Rev. R. H. Benting	Mr. A. G. Renau
Rev. I. W. Gernert	Mr. M. L. Zerkel
Rev. C. H. B. Lewis, D.D.	Mr. O. W. Cromer

*Date of organization of the Olive Branch Synod which, on June 24, 1920, with portions of the Chicago Synod (organized 1896), united to form the Indiana Synod of the United Lutheran Church in America.

13.   Illinois Synod

Organized September 8, 1851

Clerical	Lay
Rev. J. M. Bramkamp, D.D.	Mr. C. J. Driever
Rev. J. Allen Leas, D.D.	Mr. C. W. Howe
Rev. S. P. Long, D.D.	Mr. Nels Jensen
Rev. C. J. Rockey	Mr. C. G. Swanson
Rev. E. C. Harris, D.D.	Mr. C H. Boyer
Rev. W. F. Rex	Mr. A. Clawson
Rev. H. D. Hoover, Ph.D. D.D.	Mr. John P. Beckman
Rev. H. Allen Leader, D.D.	Mr. Henry Denhart
Rev. F. M. Hanes	Mr. Harvey Miller
Rev. H. L. McGill, D.D.	Dr. C. R. Walser

*Date of organization of the Northern Illinois Synod which, on June 10, 1920, with the Central Illinois (organized 1862), portions of the Chicago (organized 1896) and the Southern Illinois (organized 1901) Synods, formed the Illinois Synod of the United Lutheran Church in America.

14.   Texas Synod

Organized November 10, 1851

Clerical	Lay
Rev. E. A. Sievert	Mr. C. C. Zirjacks

15. Susquehanna Synod of Central Pennsylvania

Organized February 21, 1855

Clerical	Lay
Rev. M. S. Cressman, D.D.	Mr. Joseph Dreese
Rev. L. S. Spangler	Hon. C. L. Gramley
Rev. J. G. C. Knipple	Mr. Wm. E. Benner
Rev. W. P. Ard	Mr. W. C. Garber
Rev. O. E. Sunday	A. M. Hall, D.D.
Rev. I. S. Sassaman D.D.	Prof. G. E. Fisher, Ph.D.
Rev. B. F. Bieber	Mr. J. F. Daugherty
Rev. H. W. Miller	G. B. Reimensnyder, Esq.
Rev. F. P. Manhart, D.D.	Mr. David Wardrop

*Date of organization of the Synod of Central Pennsylvania which, on September 5, 1923, with the Susquehanna Synod (organized November 5, 1867) merged under the name of the Susquehanna Synod of Central Pennsylvania of the Evangelical Lutheran Church. The newly organized synod held its first session May 22, 1924.

16. Mississippi Synod

Organized July 25, 1855

Clerical	Lay
Rev. J. B. Guiney	Mr. Ed. Kreucher

17. Synod of Iowa

Organized September 3, 1855

Clerical	Lay
Rev. C. N. Swihart, D.D.	Mr. J. L. Berger
Rev. H. Dysinger, D.D., LL.D.	Mr. J. S. Sawyer
Rev. S. M. Lesher, D.D.	Mr. L. D. Koser

18. Michigan Synod

Organized October 27, 1855

Clerical	Lay
Rev. A. H. Keck	Mr. W. W. Anderson
Rev. R. D. Wheadon	Mr. J. B. Franke
Rev. H. G. Miley	Dr. H. G. Merz
Rev. L. S. Keyser, D.D.	Dr. B. F. Teters
Rev. D. R. Huber, D.D.	Mr. C. E. Baker

*Date of organization of the Northern Indiana Synod which, on June 10, 1920, with portions of the Chicago Synod (organized 1896), formed the Michigan Synod of the United Lutheran Church in America.

19. Synod of Georgia and Adjacent States

Organized July 20, 1860

Clerical	Lay
Rev. W. E. Pugh	Mr. H. C. Lorick*
Rev. T. W. Shealy	Mr. W. B. Clarke

20. Synod of Canada

Organized July 21, 1861

Clerical	Lay
Rev. O. C. D. Klaehn D.D.	Mr. Louis Peine
Rev. O. Stockmann	Mr. Wm. Peppler
	Mr. H. Pauli

21. Synod of Kansas

Organized November 5, 1868

Clerical	Lay
Rev. R. J. Wolf	Mr. F. A. Isern
Rev. Wm. E. Wheeler, D.D.	Mr. Wm. H. Guenther
Rev. E. E. Stauffer, D.D.	Mr. E. W. Holden
Rev. J. A. McCulloch, D.D.	Mr. L. T. Bang

22. Synod of Nebraska

Organized September 1, 1871

Clerical	Lay
Rev. W. F. Rangeler, D.D.	Mr. O. A. Keyser
Rev. C. G. Aue, D.D.	Mr. M. M. Martin
Rev. G. Dorn, A.M.	Mr. G. Hahn
Rev. K. de Freese	Mr. I. N. Augustine
Rev. R. W. Livers	Mr. E. G. Sandberg

23. Wartburg Synod

Organized 1875

Clerical	Lay
Rev. R. Neumann, D.D.	Mr. Hermann Oertel
Rev. G. Schulz, D.D.	Mr. C. Hummel
Rev. B. Garten, D.D.	Mr. E. Mueller
Rev. E. Ortlepp, D.D.	Mr. C. Scholz
Rev. E. T. Fink	Mr. William Buslap

24. German Synod of Nebraska

Organized July 24, 1890

Clerical	Lay
Rev. C. Goede	Mr. G. F. Beschorner
Rev. E. Walter	Mr. G. Hilzen*
Rev. O. Hausman	Mr. Carl Laseke
Rev. P. Waldschmidt	Mr. John Rohrig
Rev. R. Kuehne, D.D.	Mr. Arthur Deichman
Rev. J. Bahnsen	Mr. Carl Goll*
Rev. G. H. Michelmann	Mr. Henry Romeiser
Rev. G. Duehrkop	Mr. H. Busselman*

25. Synod of California
Organized April 2, 1891

Clerical	Lay
Rev. H. Gehrcke	Mr. S. F. Walck
Rev. Wm. E. Crouser, D.D.	Mr. E. A. Morrison
Rev. D. J. Snyder	Mr. W. J. Gram

26. Rocky Mountain Synod
Organized May 6, 1891

Clerical	Lay
Rev. M. F. Troxell, D.D.	Mr. G. W. Fogelman
Rev. J. C. Jacoby, D.D.	Mr. A. F. Sittloh

27. Synod of the Northwest
Organized September 22, 1891

Clerical	Lay
Rev. G. K. Rubrecht, D.D.	Mr. J. K. Jensen
Rev. W. P. Christy	Mr. W. E. Black
Rev. P. W. Roth, D.D.	Mr. G. Hemsing
Rev. L. W. Steckel	C. N. Hill, Esq.
Rev. J. Stump, D.D.	Mr. J. W. Jouno
Rev. A. J. Soldan	Mr. Wm. Siegmann
Rev. P. H. Roth	Mr. G. A. Kersten

28. Manitoba Synod
Organized July 16, 1897

Clerical	Lay
Rev. G. C. Weidenhammer	
Rev. H. W. Harms	
Rev. E. Tuerkheim	

29. Pacific Synod
Organized September 26, 1901

Clerical	Lay
Rev. A. Engeset	Mr. J. Hartman
Rev. J. C. Kunzmann, D.D.	Mr. O. J. Olsen*
Rev. W. I. Eck	Mr. H. E. Turner*

30. New York and New England Synod
Organized September 23, 1902

Clerical	Lay
Rev. Samuel Trexler, D.D.	Mr. Wm. H. Stackel
Rev. F. A. Kahler, D.D.	Mr. Frederick Henrich
Rev. F. F. Fry, D.D.	Mr. Robert F. Bowe
Rev. H. F. Miller	Mr. H. M. Ungerer
Rev. A. Steimle, D.D.	Mr. P. J. Kuhn*
Rev. Wm. M. Horn	Mr. Rodney T. Martinsen
Rev. P. E. Scherer, D.D.	Mr. C. A. Rockwell

31. Nova Scotia Synod

Organized July 10, 1903

Clerical	Lay
Rev. F. D. Smith	Mr. C. B. Conrad*

32. Synod of New York

Organized October 7, 1908

Clerical	Lay
Rev. C. W. Leitzell, D.D.	Mr. C. P. Waterstreet
Rev. F. H. Knubel, D.D., LL.D.	Hon. E. F. Eilert, C.S.D.
Rev. F. E. Oberlander, D.D.	Mr. Frank Grumbach
Rev. C. Zinnsmeister, D.D.	Mr. Henry Streibert
Rev. Frank Wolford, D.D.	Mr. A. J. Grushaw
Rev. A. J. Traver	Mr. T. Coon
Rev. A. W. Baker	Mr. E. Southard
Rev. W. G. Boomhower	Mr. H. Greenwald
Rev. A. L. Dillenbeck	Mr. K. B. Schotte
Rev. A. S. Hardy, D.D.	Mr. J. O. Hagberg
Rev. T. W. Keller	Mr. C. J. Behling
Rev. W. H. Stutts, D.D.	Mr. W. P. Elson
Rev. W. E. Pierce, B.D.	Dr. Herbert Yeckel
Rev. G. J. Reumann	Mr. Fred Wefer

33. Central Canada Synod

Organized November 11, 1908

Clerical	Lay
Rev. J. Maurer, D.D.	Mr. J. C. Klaehn

34. Synod of West Virginia

Organized April 17, 1912

Clerical	Lay
Rev. C. E. Butler	Mr. John C. Lynch
Rev. Simon Snyder	Mr. W. W. Wolfe

35. Slovak Lutheran "Zion" Synod

Organized June 10, 1919

Clerical	Lay
Rev. Paul A. Putra	
Rev. John Body	

* Absent.

The reports of the boards and committees as printed in the Bulletin were received.

The program printed in the Bulletin was adopted as the established order of business for the Convention.

PROGRAM OF THE CONVENTION

The opening service will be held at Wicker Park Church, Rev. S. P. Long, D.D., pastor. Thereafter all sessions and services will be held in the large hall of the Edgewater Beach Hotel.

The Convention of the Lutheran Brotherhood precedes as usual the Convention of the Church. It begins October 20th. Special meetings of the General Synod, the General Council, and the United Synod in the South have been arranged for Tuesday afternoon, October 21st.

The offerings at all evening services will be given to the Board of Ministerial Relief.

TUESDAY, OCTOBER 21—Night, 8 o'clock.

The Service. President's Sermon. Sacrament of the Altar.

WEDNESDAY, OCTOBER 22—Morning, 8:45 to 12 o'clock.

1. Devotions. (Matins will be used. The Committee on Church Music will appoint those who are to conduct all devotions. A quartette from the Gettysburg Theological Seminary will always be present as a choir. The members thereof are, T. Benton Peery, Ralph C. Robinson, Felix G. Robinson, Carl R. Simon. The accompanist is J. Herbert Springer, organist of St. Matthews Church, Hanover, Pa.)
2. Formal Opening of the Convention.
3. Organization—Roll. New and Merged Synods. (See report of Executive Board, III B 2).
   Receipt of Reports as printed in the Bulletin. Order of Business. Appointment of Special Committees. General rules of procedure. Rules as to elections. (See report of Executive Board, II 3).
4. Approval of minutes of last Convention.
5. Reading of proposed amendments to the By-Laws (see report of Executive Board, II 2).
6. Reports of President and of Secretary.
7. Election of the President and of the Secretary.
8. Treasurer's Report, with Audit.
9. Election of the Treasurer.
10. Report of the Executive Board.
    Includes action on resolutions concerning Dr. Tressler; constitutional amendments; eligibility of synodical presidents as members of the Executive Board; time for biennial conventions and for meetings of synods; fiscal year; visitation of

synods by secretaries; reports of membership by synods; Pacific Theological Seminary; educational co-operation; next convention; combination of boards; port work; home mission co-operation; campaign by Board of Ministerial Relief; change of title for that Board; external relation of Parish and Church-School Board; co-ordination of that Board with Common Service Book Committee; annual booklet; every member canvass; budget for 1926-7; plan for 100 per cent apportionment; special appropriations of the convention; uniform division of synodical and United Lutheran Church in America apportionment funds; payments for boards; offerings of the convention; Lutheran World Convention; agreement with Church in Czecho-Slovakia; students from Europe; Federal Council; Y. M. C. A.; Conferences on Faith and Order and on Life and Work; Commission on theological education; offices of president and secretary.

(After the close of the morning session the chairmen of synodical delegations must secure ballots in the voting room for those elections which are to be held this afternoon. Each chairman will distribute the ballots to his delegation).

WEDNESDAY, OCTOBER 22—Afternoon, 2 to 5 o'clock.

1. Reports of Nominating Committees as to members of the Executive Board, of the Commission of Adjudication, of the Church Paper Committee, and of the Executive Committee of the Laymen's Movement.
2. Continuation of action on the Executive Board's report.
3. At 4 o'clock—Report of the Laymen's Movement (including several addresses by laymen).

(Immediately after the close of the session, the election is to take place for membership on the Executive Board, the Commission of Adjudication, the Church Paper Committee, and the Executive Committee of the Laymen's Movement. Each delegate must deposit his own ballot, giving his name to the tellers. Polls will close at 7 o'clock).

WEDNESDAY, OCTOBER 22—Evening, 6 o'clock.

Banquet for all laymen arranged by the Laymen's Movement.

THURSDAY, OCTOBER 23—Morning, 8:45 to 12 o'clock.

1. Devotions.
2. Minutes.
3. Report of tellers upon Wednesday afternoon's elections.

4. Action upon proposed amendments to the By-Laws.

5. Continuation of action on the Executive Board's report.

(In connection with the statements concerning the Lutheran World Convention, an address will be made at 11 o'clock by the Rev. J. A. Morehead, D.D., LL.D., chairman of the Executive Committee of that Convention).

THURSDAY, OCTOBER 23—Afternoon, 2 to 5 o'clock.

1. Representatives and General Resolutions (as arranged by the Committee on Reference and Counsel for this place and for stated places on following days).

2. Continuation of action on the Executive Board's report.

THURSDAY, OCTOBER 23—Night, 8 o'clock.

Three addresses upon the theme, "The Lutheran Church in American History."

1. "In the Foundations of America." (Noting the 300th anniversary of first Lutheran services in New York). Prof. A. R. Wentz, Ph.D., D.D.

2. "In Colonial Times." (Noting the 175th anniversary of the Pennsylvania Ministerium). Rev. H. A. Weller, D.D.

3. "Since the Establishment of the United States of America." (Noting the 100th anniversary of the South Carolina Synod). Prof. S. J. Derrick, LL.D.

FRIDAY, OCTOBER 24—Morning, 8:45 to 12 o'clock.

1. Devotions.

2. Minutes.

3. Continuation of action on the Executive Board's report.

4. At 10:30—Report of the Commission of Adjudication.

5. Report of the Church Paper Committee.

6. Report of the Board of Foreign Missions.

(After the close of the morning session the chairmen of delegations must secure ballots for this afternoon's election).

FRIDAY, OCTOBER 24—Afternoon, 2 to 4:30 o'clock.

1. Representatives and General Resolutions.

2. Report of Nominating Committee for this afternoon's elections.

3. Continuation of action on the Foreign Mission Board's report.

(Adjournment at 4:30 for the election of members to all Boards and elective Committees not included in the Wednesday elections. Polls will close at 7 o'clock).

FRIDAY, OCTOBER 24—Night, 8 o'clock.

Two addresses upon the theme, "Religion in Education."
The Civic Aspect—The Hon. J. A. O. Preus, Governor of Minnesota.
The Church Aspect—Rev. J. A. W. Haas, D.D., LL.D., President of Muhlenberg College.

SATURDAY, OCTOBER 25—Morning, 8:45 to 12 o'clock.

1. Devotions.
2. Minutes.
3. Report of tellers upon Friday afternoon's elections.
4. Report of the Board of Home Missions and Church Extension.
5. If there be time remaining, this afternoon's program will be taken up.

SATURDAY, OCTOBER 25—Afternoon, 2 to 5 o'clock.

1. Representatives and General Resolutions.
2. Report of the Board of Northwestern Missions.
3. Report of the Board of Immigrants Missions.
4. Report of the Board of West Indies Missions.
5. Report of the Jewish Mission Committee.
6. Report of the Committee on Evangelism.

SATURDAY, OCTOBER 25—Night, 8 o'clock.

Addresses on "Our Allies in Foreign Work."
Augustana Synod—President G. A. Brandelle, D.D.
United Danish Synod—Rev. V. W. Bondo, D.D.
Icelandic Synod—Rev. S. O. Thorlaksson.
Women's Missionary Society—Mrs. Syndney Kepner.
Indian Lutheran Church—Mr. Manikam.
Japan Lutheran Church—Mr. K. Hirai.
Liberia Lutheran Church—Mr. John Ziegler.
South America and China—Rev. L. B. Wolf, D.D.

SUNDAY, OCTOBER 26.

Special services in the Chicago churches, as arranged and announced by the Chicago committee. In the afternoon at 3 o'clock Unity Lutheran Church Girls' Home will be dedicated. Unity Lutheran Church is near the Edgewater Beach Hotel. The service is arranged by the pastor of that congregation, Rev. D. A. Davy, D.D., and Secretary W. Freas of the Inner Mission Board.

MONDAY, OCTOBER 27—Morning, 8:45 to 12 o'clock.

1. Devotions.
2. Minutes.
3. Report of the Board of Education.
(In connection with the report special addresses will be made on a
    Woman's College by Rev. J. H. Harms, D.D., and on
    University Student Work by Rev. H. R. Gold).
4. At 10:45—Report of the Parish and Church-School Board.
5. At 11:30—Report of the Committee on Boys' Work.

MONDAY, OCTOBER 27—Afternoon, 2 to 5 o'clock.

1. Representatives and General Resolutions.
2. Report of the Board of Publication.
3. Report of the Committee on Common Service Book.
4. Report of the Committee on Church Music.
(In connection with the report an address will be made by the Rev.
    G. C. Rees, D.D., on the 400th anniversary of the first Pro-
    testant hymnal).
5. Report of the Committee on Statistics and Church Year Book
    (including reports of the Statistical Secretary and of the
    Editor of the Year Book).
6. Report of the Committee on Publicity.
7. Unfinished Business.

MONDAY, OCTOBER 27—Night, 8 o'clock.

Home Mission Talks on Present-Day Opportunities.
    In Florida and the Southland—Rev. W. E. Pugh, D.D.
    In Canada's Prairie Provinces—Rev. G. C. Weidenhammer.
    In Our Growing Cities—Rev. James Berg.
Illustrated Talk on Achievements and Possibilities—Rev. J. S.
    Herold.

TUESDAY, OCTOBER 28—Morning, 8:45 to 12 o'clock.

1. Devotions.
2. Minutes.
3. Report of the Board of Inner Missions, with Inner Mission
    Institutions.
4. Report of the National Lutheran Home for the Aged.
5. At 10:20—Report of the Board of Deaconess Work.
6. At 11:10—Report of the Board of Ministerial Relief.

TUESDAY, OCTOBER 28—Afternoon, 2 to 5 o'clock.
1. Representatives and General Resolutions.
2. Conclusion of the morning's program.
3. At 2:45—Report of the Committee on Moral and Social Welfare.
4. At 3:45—Report of the Committee on President's Report.
5. Report of Committee on Memorials from Constituent Synods.

TUESDAY, OCTOBTR 28—Night, 8 o'clock.
Address: "Spirituality and Morality—How Related."—Rev. E. P. Pfatteicher, Ph.D., D.D.
Address: "Seventy-five Years of American Deaconess Service."— Rev. G. A. Getty, D.D.

WEDNESDAY and THURSDAY, OCTOBER 29 and 30.
Sessions at the regular hours, morning, afternoon, and night, continuing so as to cover the following items:
1. Report of Commissioners to the National Lutheran Council, addresses by the chairman, President H. A. Weller, D.D., and by Commissioner C. T. Benze, D.D.
2. Report of Committee on Lutheran Brotherhood. Hearing of representative of the Brotherhood.
3. Report of Committee on Women's Work. Hearing of representative of the Women's Missionary Society.
4. Report of Committee on Associations. Hearing of representative of th Luther League of America.
5. Report of Committee on Necrology.
6. Report of Committee on Church Architecture.
7. Report of Committee on Army and Navy Work. Address by Chaplain John Hall, representing the Chief of Chaplains' Office in Washington.
8. Report of Committee on Special Linguistic Interests.
9. Report of Committee on Transportation.
10. Report of Representative to American Bible Society.
11. Report of the Archivist.
12. Report of the Church Paper Committee, as newly constituted by the election.
13. Report of the Lutheran Historical Society.
14. Report of the Lutheran Church Book and Literature Society.
15. Report of the Committee on Leave of Absence.
16. Unfinished Business.
17. General Business.
18. Printing of Minutes.
19. The next Convention.
20. Appointment of Standing Committees.
21. Final Minutes.
22. Formal close of the Convention.

The President appointed the following special committees:

Committee of Reference and Counsel

This Committee is appointed to consider all general resolutions before they are submitted to the Convention; to arrange with the President for the hearing of representatives sent to the Convention; generally to assist the President in the daily program.

Rev. R. E. Tulloss, Chm.
Rev. A. T. W. Steinhaeuser
Rev. G. A. Bierdemann
Rev. A. R. Steck
Rev. G. Z. Stup
Rev. J. J. Myers
Rev. J. Allen Leas
Rev. R. J. Wolf
Rev. A. Engeset
Rev. L. W. Steckel

Dr. R. Moldenke
Hon. B. B. Miller
L. R. Alden, Esq.
W. T. Stauffer, Esq.
Judge J. Frank Graff
Mr. A. F. Sittloh
Mr. W. E. Black
Mr. John C. Lynch
Dr. Herbert Yeckel
Mr. I. N. Augustine

Committee on President's Report

Rev. P. W. Roth, Chm.
Rev. W. C. Schaeffer
Rev. S. Von Bosse
Rev. F. R. Wagner
Rev. H. C. Brillhart
Rev. G. N. Lauffer
Rev. O. Stockmann
Rev. E. Tuerkheim
Rev. C. E. Butler
Rev. A. S. Hardy
Rev. R. Neumann

Capt. H. M. M. Richards
Dr. W. J. Showalter
Mr. J. W. Kahler
Prof. A. J. Harter
Mr. Nels Jensen
Mr. J. B. Franke
Mr. R. T. Martinsen

Committee to Nominate Executive Committee of Laymen's Movement No. 1

Rev. A. J. Rudisill, Chm.
Rev. S. M. Lesher
Rev. B. Garten

Mr. I. F. Mellinger
G. B. Reimensnyder, Esq.
Mr. Louis Peine
Mr. J. Hartman

Committee to Nominate Members of Executive Board, Commission of Adjudication and Church Paper Committee No. 2

Rev. A. Steimle, Chm.
Rev. G. F. Gehr
Rev. B. Mehrtens
Rev. J. C. Bowers
Rev. H. A. McCullough
Rev. H. B. Stock
Rev. L. H. Larimer
Rev. C. J. Rockey
Rev. J. F. Crigler

Mr. A. Raymond Bard
Mr. J. W. Jouno
Mr. W. J. Gram
Mr. G. F. Beschorner
Prof. O. F. H. Bert
Prof. H. S. Fleck
Dr. Croll Keller
Hon. H. L. Bonham
Mr. J. C. Klaehn

Committee to Nominate Members of All Other Boards No. 3

Rev. J. J. Scherer, Jr., Chm.
Rev. J. W. Kapp
Rev. E. H. Delk
Rev. E. A. Tappert
Rev. F. A. Dressel
Rev. W. E. Pugh
Rev. F. E. Oberlander
Rev. G. Gebert
Rev. L. S. Keyser

Mr. M. Wulff
Hon. L. M. Swink
Mr. F. W. Kakel
Mr. R. C. Counts
Mr. W. H. Menges
Mr. C. W. Howe
Dr. H. G. Merz
Mr. R. F. Bowe
Mr. F. W. Wefer

Committee on Devotional Services

The Standing Committee on Church Music. Its duties being to name and secure men to conduct opening and closing devotions at the several sessions of the Convention.

Committee on Leave of Absence

Rev. A. J. Traver, Chm.
Rev. J. H. Waidelich
Rev. W. J. Finck
Rev. P. D. Brown
Rev. E. A. Sievert
Rev. J. B. Guiney
Rev. D. J. Snyder
Rev. P. A. Putra

Rev. E. Walter
Mr. I. L. Taylor
Mr. A. G. Renau
Mr. J. L. Berger
Mr. W. B. Clarke
Mr. C. H. Wilsnack
Mr. John P. Beckman

Committee on Memorials From Constituent Synods

Rev. F. P. Manhart, Chm.
Rev. A. B. MacIntosh
Rev. T. O. Posselt
Rev. G. H. Rhodes
Rev. A. Hering
Rev. M. S. Cressman
Rev. C. G. Aue
Rev. G. H. Michelmann
Rev. M. F. Troxell
Rev. J. Maurer

Hon. J. L. Zimmerman
Dr. J. F. Trexler
Mr. P. A. Elsesser
Mr. A. H. Durboraw
Hon. A. E. Reiber
Hon. C. L. Gramley
Mr. W. H. Stackel
Mr. Henry Streibert
Mr. O. W. Cromer

Tellers of Ballots for President and for Secretary and for Wednesday Afternoon's Election

Mr. P. P. Hagan, Chm.
Mr. Harry E. Pugh
Mr. F. D. Bittner
Mr. A. H. Weaver
Mr. A. R. Nissley
Mr. G. A. Mayer
Mr. J. E. Miller
Mr. H. M. Thompson
Mr. A. H. Kornfeld

Mr. C. C. Zirjacks
Mr. L. D. Koser
Mr. Wm. Peppler
Mr. A. O. Keyser
Mr. Arthur Deichmann
Mr. H. Brandes
Mr. G. C. Baum

Tellers of Ballots for Treasurer and for Friday Afternoon's Election

Mr. G. Hemsing, Chm.
Mr. F. Stuessy
Mr. H. A. Sloneker
Dr. H. C. Hoffman
Mr. Wm. E. Benner
Mr. A. R. Rhyne
Mr. R. C. Counts
Mr. Romanus Esterly
Mr. E. L. Keiser

Mr. Ed. Kreucher
Mr. Wm. H. Guenther
Mr. Hermann Oertel
Mr. E. A. Morrison
Mr. G. W. Fogelman
Mr. C. A. Rockwell
Mr. H. Greenwald
Mr. D. F. Yost
Mr. F. W. Seegers
Mr. W. B. Clarke
Mr. J. V. Sutton

It was moved and carried, That all general resolutions shall be submitted to the Convention through the Committee of Reference and Counsel, and that applications for the presentation of causes and of greetings take the same course.

It was moved and carried, That the privilege of the floor be given to members of the Executive Board, members of the Commission of Adjudication and the officers of all other Boards, when their reports are under consideration, even though they be not delegates to the Convention.

It was moved and carried, That the reports as printed be not read, but that an opportunity be given to the officers of boards and committees to explain and emphasize important items in their reports at the proper time; the length of such presentations not to exceed one half hour.

It was moved and carried, That in debate speeches shall not exceed five minutes in length.

At this point the Chairman of the Committee of Reference and Counsel introduced the Rev. Clyde F. Armitage who, upon being recognized, said, "Mr. President, it gives me great pleasure as representing the Near East Relief to present to you this gavel, which is made from the heart of an olive tree by the boys of our Orphan Training School, just across the street from where, tradition says, Jesus as a boy learned to push the plane and drive the saw."

The President accepted the gavel with thanks, on behalf of the United Lutheran Church, to Mr. Armitage, the Near East Relief and the boys of the Training School referred to.

Following the order of business, the item of the Executive Board's report concerning nominations and elections (II, 3) was taken up. On motion to adopt sub-item a., the President ruled that it would be necessary first to rescind the ruling concerning ad interim elections adopted at Washington.

It was moved and carried, That the ruling referred to be rescinded.

Thereupon, sub-item a. was adopted.

Sub-items b., c., d., e. and f. adopted.

The item of the Executive Board's report concerning Minutes (II, 1) was received as information.

In connection with this item a printed copy of the Minutes of the Buffalo Convention, certified by the Secretary and attested by the President, was submitted and approved. The President thereupon declared it to be the official record of the proceedings of the Third Biennial Convention of the United Lutheran Church.

The item of the Executive Board's report concerning the revision of the Constitution and By-Laws (II, 2), being the next order, the Secertary read Article IX, Section 1 of the Constitution of The United Lutheran Church in America and the proposed amendment thereto.

It was moved and carried, by unanimous vote, That the proposed amendment to Section 1 of Article IX be submitted to the Synods in the form presented by the Executive Board.

Amendments to certain sections of the By-Laws (see report of the Executive Board, II, 2) were then presented to be acted upon tomorrow.

At this point the President announced that he had received a letter of greetings to the Convention from the President of the United States of America. The Convention rose and stood while the President read these greetings as follows:

October 16, 1924.

To the President,
United Lutheran Church in America in Convention
Assembled at Chicago:

I extend my greetings to the fourth biennial convention of The United Lutheran Church in America.

Made up in such large degree of the descendants of that sturdy Lutheran stock which played such an important part in the development of the colonies and in the success of the Revolutionary War, the United Lutheran Church has a proud heritage.

As I study the three great movements of humanity into the American colonies, the Puritans into New England, the Lutherans and Quakers into Pennsylvania, and the cavaliers into Virginia, and examine the history of their amalgamation in blood and unity in spirit, I realize that this amalgamation and union form one of the foundations of America's greatness.

Muhlenberg and his men from Pennsylvania and the Lutheran soldiers from western Maryland, the Shenandoah Valley of Virginia, western North Carolina and South Carolina made glorious history for the patriot cause during the Revolutionary War. Their descendants, spreading out over the Mississippi Valley, had a leading role in the development of that great granary of the world.

During the Civil War, such organizations as the Iron Brigade were on every battlefield upholding the unity of the States.

It is little wonder that with such traditions to inspire their sons and grandsons, six per cent of the Lutherans in America were in the service of their country during the World War, as compared with four per cent for the general population.

The sons of Scandinavia who have come to America in more recent times have shown the same sturdy spirit and represent a contribution of vast value to the human assets of our country's future.

I am happy to recognize that the United Lutheran Church and its related bodies, all partaking of the Americanism implanted in their ancestry and traditions, are nurturing the same in the hearts of those of their faith who now leave Europe and cast their fortunes with our people.

(Signed)   CALVIN COOLIDGE.

After the reading the Convention sang the first stanza of "America." Thereupon the Rev. Prof. C. M. Jacobs offered the following resolution:

"The United Lutheran Church in America gratefully acknowledges the greetings of the President of the United States. Planted in this land in colonial days, and growing with the development of the nation, the Lutheran Church in America has stood, and still stands, for the principle of the separation of Church and State. Living under a government to which that principle is fundamental, it holds and teaches that loyalty to civil government is a Christian duty, and that to fail in that duty is to sin against God. It also holds and teaches that the only true ideals, for individuals and for nations, are those which be derived from the Gospel of Jesus Christ, and that a Church, separate from the State, which preaches Christ and the Christian way of life, is the strongest support of national existence and the surest guide to true national greatness; and it rejoices when this truth is recognized.

"The United Lutheran Church in America prays that the God and Father of our Lord Jesus Christ may bless the President of the United States, and that He may guide the nation, by His Spirit into the ways of service and into paths of peace."

The resolution was adopted by a rising vote and was forwarded by telegram to President Coolidge.

The President read a telegram from Count de Pourtales conveying greetings from the French Lutheran Church. Also a letter of greetings from the Rev. N. Astrup Larsen, President of the General Council of the Lutheran Church of China conveying the greetings of that body to The United Lutheran Church in America:

Paris, October 20, 1924.

Knubel, Lutheran Convention,
  Edgewater Beach Hotel,
    Chicago, Ill.

French Lutheran Church sends greetings, thanks, best wishes.

POURTALES.

Kikungshan, Honan, China.
May 21, 1924.

Rev. F. H. Knubel, D.D., LL.D.,
President, United Lutheran Church,
437 Fifth Avenue,
New York, U. S. A.

Dear Doctor Knubel:—

The recent (2d) General Assembly of the Lutheran Church of China has instructed me to send a cordial greeting to The United Lutheran Church in America.

The Chung Hwa Sin I Hwei (the Lutheran Church of China) is still a small organization and in its infancy. But we have a tremendous field and great tasks confront us. It is therefore with rejoicing we have heard that the strong United Lutheran Church in America has decided to enter the China field. We hope we may soon be privileged to welcome the

Mission of the United Church into full membership in the Chung Hwa Sin I Hwei.

The churches which in 1920 organized the Lutheran Church of China are those founded by the Norwegian Missionary Society, the Finnish Missionary Society, the Church of Sweden Mission, the Norwegian Lutheran Church of America (Lutheran United Mission), and the Augustana Synod Mission. At this year's General Assembly the churches of the Lutheran Board of Missions (Norwegian Lutheran Free Church in America) and the Breklum Mission were received into membership.

The Breklum Mission is the southernmost Lutheran mission in China. In South China we also have the old and strong Berlin and Basel Missions. There is good reason to believe that the Berlin Mission, at least, will link up with the Chung Hwa Sin I Hwei. From the field of the Berlin Mission it is not very far to the field of the Norwegian Missionary Society. And going on northward through Huan, Hupeh, and Honan, one comes to the fields of the various synods constituting the Chung Hwa Sin I Hwei. When the United Church takes up its work in Shantung, we trust you will from the start, be with us in the Chung Hwa Sin I Hwei thus making it much more probable that the Lutherans shall be able to make their distinctive contribution to the future Christian life of China. With the Lutherans in Shantung an integral part of the Lutheran Church of China, we shall also feel that we are a long step nearer the strong Danish Lutheran Mission in Manchuria, from which we are already drawing students to our theological seminary at Shekow, near Hankow.

With sincere greetings, and with an earnest prayer that the United Church may be privileged to do a great and blessed work in China, I am,

Faithfully yours,

N. ASTRUP LARSEN.

It was moved and carried, That proper responses be made to these greetings.

The President submitted his report to the Convention as follows:

PRESIDENT'S REPORT

It is no repetition of vain words when this report like previous ones records personal heartfelt thankfulness to God and to the membership of the Church. It would seem as though the Lord's sustaining and guiding grace has been greater than ever. As regards the entire Church, the past biennium has marked even greater help to the officers than previous ones.

Four years ago, at the convention of 1920, it was a sad necessity that the president's report include statement of the death of the Rev. Dr. T. E.

Schmauk, who had been president of the General Council. There is similar and double sadness to record in this report. During the last biennium the Rev. Dr. V. G. A. Tressler and the Rev. Dr. M. M. Kinard died. The former was president of the General Synod when the merger of the three general bodies took place in 1918. The latter became president of the United Synod in the South immediately after the merger convention. While our Necrological Committee will give fitting recognition to them, recommendation is hereby made that in the devotions which close the session when this report is made we include special memorial thought of these leaders among us.

————————

There is no difficulty in making report as to the work of the president, which the by-laws require, since only a brief statement is required. It is naturally a necessity that he shall keep himself acquainted with all activities within the Church and with tendencies, both religious and otherwise, without our own Church. This involves constant and sometimes burdensome reading of reports and minutes and current literature of all kinds from many parts of the world. A determined effort is made to keep informed.

Helpful contacts are maintained with individuals and movements outside of the Church, without surrender of too large an amount of time to the same.

Every effort is made that our constitution and by-laws, along with all declarations and resolutions, shall be observed throughout the Church. It is here above all that the loyal spirit of our membership is pronouncedly manifest. The clear desire of all is only to understand aright.

Through ex-officio membership in all of the Church's agencies and through relationship with the officials of Constituent Synods it is possible to exercise advisory help in many directions. The possibility of such advice to any agency arises simply from the contacts with all of the others.

All executive and initiative plans are carried on in constant and close conference with the other officers and members of the Executive Board. This policy, undertaken in the first biennium, has been consistently followed. As a consequence the largest part of the president's activities finds report through the report of that Board.

The above generalized statements, with the travels and correspondence and conferences involved therein, cover the work of the president. Only a few special items remain to be mentioned.

The required committees for the biennium were appointed and are listed in the minutes of the 1922 convention, pages 524 to 527. The only resignation from these committees during the biennium was that of Mr. W. H. Stackel from the Committee on Evangelism. In Dr. Tressler's place as a commissioner to the National Lutheran Council the Rev. Dr. P. W. Koller was appointed. The Rev. Dr. J. M. Bramkamp was appointed as an additional member to the Transportation Committee.

Two noted Lutheran visitors came to America during the biennium, Bishop H. Ostenfeld, Primus of Denmark, and Archbishop N. Soderblom of Sweden. They were officially welcomed on behalf of The United Lutheran Church in America.

In closing this portion of the report, it is desirable that we remind ourselves of the high importance of the 400th anniversary of the presentation of the Augsburg Confession in 1530. It is the primary and fundamental Protestant confession of faith. There are many conditions at the present time affecting humanity in general and Roman Catholicism and Protestantism and Greek Catholicism, which make desirable a prominent recognition of the anniversary. I recommend that either the Executive Board or a special committee be instructed to consider this matter and be empowered to proceed with plans.

The by-laws further require that the president shall in his report summarize the general situation of the Church. In previous biennial reports this has been done through an effort to portray general world conditions and the general religious situation, to point out the consequent obligation of the Church, and thus to ascertain our own situation by an estimate of the degree in which we were measuring up to the Church's obligation. That form of presentation was naturally somewhat theoretical in character, although it led to practical considerations which have more or less influenced our actual procedure. If for no other reason than the idea of a change in method, it seems worth while in this report to proceed at once to a practical estimate of the situation of the United Lutheran Church in America today, aiming to avoid both boastfulness and depreciation.

As a plain fact we may easily recognize that the Lutheran Church here in America receives at present far more public recognition and respect than was true in the past. Of this the United Lutheran Church in America has a generous share. It is no longer true that a man must explain to his neighbor that a Lutheran Church exists. There was a time when here one might speak emphatically of the lackluster of Lutheranism. Such is not the case now. Some of us believe that quality to inhere in Lutheranism and do not wish it to be altogether lost. However that may be, we can rightly be thankful that our wider reputation includes the fact of our fidelity to evangelical faith. Let us hope it is also because of our works and that they may always be known to be founded in Christian love. Above all, as our strength brings us public recognition, let us soberly ask ourselves whether we can stand becoming public and strong. It is recorded of a certain one, "His name spread far abroad; for he was marvelously helped, till he was strong. But when he was strong, his heart was lifted up to his destruction."

There are further encouraging facts to be noted in our situation. People are hearing the noise of our operations more widely because we have been working more intensely and more determinedly. Six years of test as to our organization have revealed its admirable adaptedness to the work to be done. Likewise the various parts are more fully grooved to their functions. Let us briefly make note of both items, the organization as a whole and the functioning of the individual parts.

As regards the first it is truly wonderful that so harmonious, well understood and well merged an organization has developed and continues to develop, especially when one considers our youth, the size and spread of the Church, and the fact that three previous General Bodies united in each of which different methods of operation existed. It is only the grace of patience with one another and the readiness for concession in unessential things which have brought about the result. Many discussions as to changes in our methods and organization continue to be heard. These are good, so long as the weightier matters of the Church's life are not interfered with. Furthermore, the time has now come when we must be on our guard against the two extremes of traditionalism and radicalism when changes are proposed. A method of operation is not necessarily good for us today just because it has existed in the long past or because other Christian groups use it. On the other hand radical overturnings in organization are not to be accepted just because a fine theory seems to commend them. Our surest test as to the value of changes will always be the question as to whether or not they will help in the production of ideal working congregations. All Christian organizations must concentrate upon these units. The Church must be made strong in the thousands of communities, otherwise it is not strong at all.

The entire item as to the organization in the previous paragraph cannot be passed by without mention of a cause for great thankfulness in that we are free from the baneful influence of what is commonly known as ecclesiastical politics.

Turning now to the individual parts of the organization we can recognize the generally satisfactory situation in our constituent synods. Here there exists conscious effort at improvement. Each one knows and acknowledges its shortcomings, and has the will for better things. The number of strongly efficient synods is constantly increasing. Supervisory helpfulness to congregations is practised more and more. Synodical officials are prayerfully seeking to fulfill what they now all know is their great responsibility. It is to be believed that the biennial conferences of synodical presidents have contributed something of value.

Our Church's boards and committees and auxiliary organizations for men and women and young people constitute the established forces for the promotion of evangelistic, educational, and merciful endeavor. When we contemplate these three general divisions of our work, every thoughtful observer is compelled to acknowledge that while we may feel reasonable satisfaction with the situation as to our evangelistic or missionary endeavor, we cannot do the same as to our educational or merciful operations. This implies no idea of criticism of special agencies. It is the failure of the Church as a whole, and includes the failure of our congregations. No suggestions of change in our educational and merciful polices are intended. No implication is made that definite advances have not taken place. Evidence to the contrary will be given a little later. There is no desire to speak adversely concerning a host of faithful pastors. However, we all need to recognize that from any true educational point of view confusion exists in most of our congregations and that the bare beginnings of merciful work are to be seen in them. In some degree the same is true of the general educational and merciful work of the Church. We are far from measuring up to the responsibilities of the Church and the needs of the times. Let it be remembered that this report is prepared as required by the by-laws, and states the situation of the Church in these educational and merciful respects as the writer sees it. Specifications of our lack were partly given in the same report four years ago and two years ago. Similar pleas are found in numerous printed articles. The cure will come from the resolute will of the whole Church that the situation must be better. To arouse that will we must call upon all of our educational and merciful agencies, along with the auxiliary organizations, for an even more thoroughgoing study of the problems, for practical plans of harmonious orderliness and advance, and for persistent information to the whole Church. It is desirable that the appropriate groups of agencies hold joint meetings of representatives for the accomplishment of such ends. It is also to be hoped, in this connection, that the resolution to come before this convention concerning a special commission on theological education will find approval. That resolution seeks only a better educational day for our Church in the matter of theological training.

Continuing our consideration of the individual parts of our organization and speaking quite in contrast with the previous paragraph, the past biennium is noteworthy for the number of new developments in our work. One thinks of the new field of foreign mission operation in China, the publication building in Philadelphia, the work of the Committee on Evangelism, the magnificent attainments of the Women's Missionary Society, the woman's college, the home mission developments including plans of the Home Mission Board with the Manitoba Synod for Western Canada, etc. This report had intended to itemize all of them. It was realized, however, that this could not be done effectively until all reports to this convention were in and until the actions of the convention were complete. It is recommended, therefore, that the editors of our official Church papers be instructed to prepare an itemized statement of these new developments and to give full publicity to the same, not for vainglory, but as an encouragement and a stimulus to the entire Church. Mention should be included therein of the significantly increasing number of intelligent and devoted laymen who are giving themselves in the Church's service.

Thus far in the attempt to describe the present situation of our Church attention has been given first to our reputation and then to our organization, both as a whole and in its parts. In referring to our organization the consideration was one, so to speak, as to our internal relations. It is proper next to consider our external relations.

No change has taken place in our formal relationships to those groups of Christians who are not Lutherans. It is always to be hoped that our honest and practical love for other Christians will grow stronger and that our readiness to re-examine the necessity of assumed relations to them will be prompt. No reasons have appeared, however, to justify any changes in our Washington Declaration nor in the consequent definite relations which were established. Indeed the confessional situation outside of Lutheranism has grown even more sadly confused than it was. Controversy reaches ever nearer to the very center of Christianity in Christ and His redemption. It would be a positive betrayal of and danger to our allegiance to Gospel principles for us to take any further steps at this time in these relationships. It is good to note that our attitude has generally received most friendly respect from these other Christians. Naturally it is always possible for us to enter into worth-while conferences with them, if only in such conferences there will be mutual and open recognition of confessional differences and if therefore such conferences will not be proclaimed as being in themselves manifestations of Christian unity.

Greater hopefulness exists in our relationships with other Lutherans. Let us enumerate our formal co-operations. We are associated with the Augustana Synod in some branches of our foreign mission, educational, and West Indies work. The United Danish Church works with us in Japan. So also does the Icelandic Synod, and a proposition for educational co-operation with them will come before the present convention. We co-operate with the Suomi Synod in home mission operations. Our Home Mission Board and Board of Education are aiming to open wide and helpful general relationships in their special tasks. Definite bonds of association exist with a number of Lutheran bodies through the common support of our common agency the National Lutheran Council. We have definite agreements with the Lutheran Churches in Hungary and Czecho-Slovakia. The past biennium witnessed a Lutheran World Convention, with the wide contacts and the promising outlook which have resulted.

The enumeration just made is of course highly pleasing, and yet it is not enough. It is not the sphere of this report to discuss the situation of world Lutheranism, but a reference thereto must be made in order to emphasize our own responsibility. In all whose hearts are sensitively devoted to the strength and beauty of truth as our Church knows it, there exists as a supreme longing the desire that that truth shall prevail among men. We know that we must sacrifice everything unessential which may interfere with that end. Everywhere today, it would seem, Lutherans are wistfully looking towards one another. Everywhere, when they meet, they are conscious of the possession of common principles and of the desire to reassert them more winningly. Nowhere is anybody aiming at forced unions, or at coalitions which might prove detrimental to truest ends, or at an organized Lutheran Church of the world. Yet everywhere obstacles seem to arise which prevent even the most harmonious development of our common aims. I am not aiming to state the sources of those interferences. Every careful student of the situation becomes conscious of them. Furthermore, all Lutherans in America are conscious that the situation here is a very critical part of the entire problem, and yet here also obstacles to harmonious development are found. The human element of fault which exists in those obstacles does not belong to only one or two bodies. The United Lutheran Church in America is, however, not truly responsible for others' faults. Primarily it is responsible only for its own. Wherever such exist we ought to correct them. When the human faults have been eliminated we may see more clearly what elements of a more serious nature remain, which are creating the obstacles. My only suggestion for the present is that we practise truest respect and love for other groups of American Lutherans, and that we make the difficulties in our Lutheran situation a matter of frequent, prayerful meditation. One thing is certain, words of unloving and nagging criticism of one another, wherever practised, are of the devil.

We come now to the final and most important factor in our situation as a Church, namely, our inner, spiritual life. The difficulty, the practical impossibility of a just estimate in this respect must be manifest to all. Some indication thereof is nevertheless given if we can have a true view of conditions as to our pastors and congregations. Even this seems unattainable. There are thousands of both and no one man can truly know them. Furthermore, outward appearances are not always sure indications of inner realities. However, an effort has been made to secure the facts from informed and reliable sources in all parts of our Church. An attempted summary of the information is given herewith.

As to our pastors, though thousands in number, there are only rare exceptions to a complete fidelity to the principles of the Gospel as our Church confesses them. Loving patience has corrected the few exceptions, and instances of discipline are lacking. There is, however, objection to the archaic form of some sermons, and to the failure of application of the Gospel to present day needs. Most serious is the complaint as to real knowledge of the Bible, as to the lack of spiritual, biblical culture. It would be well if the proposed commission on theological education would take this information into consideration, along with the popularity of modern Bible schools. Turning to the morality of the ministry, the testimony is clear that they are clean, upright, honorable men who command the respect of their parishioners, their brethren, and their communities. Occasional references are found, however, to doubtful statistical methods; to questionable financial operations; to the tendency of ministers to criticise and be jealous of one another; and to the advantage sometimes taken of an opportunity which comes to ministers as to no other class, to shirk. One source of information laconically expressed the last named item thus: Where men are their own masters, some are indolent, most are not. As a final fact concerning our pastors, their efficiency may be considered. It is altogether clear that here, as everywhere in life, men of every caliber are to be found. The percentage of efficiency is unquestionably higher than in other walks of life, especially in these days when war has taught millions of men to act merely under orders and has taken from them the inspiration of personal initiative. There is frequent testimony, however, as to the failure of pastors to train members for active Christian work. In connection with this, statements are found as to a failure to understand the value of organization, as to pitiful programs for congregations, as to lack of concern for the Church at large.

We come now to the congregations of the United Lutheran Church in America. Some indications as to their condition have been given above in what was said concerning our pastors. There is truth in the statement, "Like pastor, like people." Unquestionably the number of truly great and influential congregations among us is definitely increasing. Furthermore, the inner development of congregational life in general is on the steady upgrade. Naturally none of our congregations have attained the ideal.

In that last statement a suggestion is implied—a suggestion of a form of presentation whereby we may view our congregations as they are and as they should be. We need congregations which are aiming for the ideal. The philosopher Kant gave an excellent rule of conduct when he said, "So act that the law of thine action may be made universal." Our congregations would do well to consider whether they would wish all congregations to model after their own. It would be very helpful to us all if one of our best pastors or one of our professors of practical theology would write a book with the title, "The Ideal Congregation." It would add to our Church's life if our congregations would keep that phrase in mind.

Such a book would in no sense be a mere summary of cut and dried methods for all pastors and people to put into operation. Indeed, one section of the book would deal especially with the individuality of congregations. Each congregation has its own special problem and problems, the like of which exist fully nowhere else. To copy others will not provide solutions. Congregations must work out their own salvation with fear and trembling.

Another chapter would tell about the true temple. The possession of greater properties and beautiful structures do not in themselves mean the attainment of the ideal for congregations. The buildings are but the symbols of the true temple of God, in which the people are living stones. In their worship and in their work they must aim to make real in themselves the wonderful life of the people of God.

An entire division of the book would point out the congregation's full task. The necessities in Church operation are to learn to save, to study, and to serve. The evangelistic, educational, and merciful work of every congregation must be considered and ordered. Evangelism is the winning for ideals. Education is the cultivation of ideals. Mercy is the manifestation of ideals. All congregations of fair size genuinely need three leaders, one for each of these great sections of the full task.

An ideal congregation is also one which recognizes its responsibilities to the community where it exists. If it is merely a sort of spiritual club for the interests of its members, if its people do not recognize that they are banded together in order that they may serve others, then after all such a congregation has a corporate soul marked purely with the desire for personal profits. It possesses a sort of high grade selfishness. An important question for every congregation is the one as to the reputation it bears among the people immediately around its doors. For what kind of works is it known? In this matter of community responsibilities, furthermore, great stress needs to be laid upon the necessity that in cities and towns where two or more of our congregations exist the joint operations of those congregations form a large part of their task. Inner Mission operations alone are suffering greatly today because so many of our congregations are not aiming at the ideal in this respect of joint activity in our cities and towns.

A number of other topics should be considered in that book. Let us note only one more, the denominational relationship of an ideal congregation. It is inconceivable, even from a practical standpoint, that a congregation should in good conscience maintain itself independent of vital participation with other congregations in a general Church body. This practical impossibility pertains both to the faith and the work of a congregation. As to the *faith* first of all, a congregation exists as a group of Christians under obligation to confess and to proclaim the truth of the Gospel. The essential Christian desire in such belief is to seek the greatest possible fellowship of all who confess the same faith. There is necessary cohesion in faith and its confession. Where the faith exists, the fellowship will follow. The desire for the triumph of the truth also impels to the establishment of the wider relationship. When the denominational establishment in faith has thus taken place, the ideal congregation no longer knows merely its own separate existence. It realizes its responsibility for the common faith of the whole. Its loyalty to its Church as a whole is a loyalty to the principles professed by all. Its people, its minister, its pulpit, its font, and its altar are all witnesses only for the truth confessed by the whole Church.

From the standpoint also of its *work* an ideal congregation must partake completely in a general Church body. A tremendous responsibility is laid upon every Christian, personally to go into all the world and evangelize all nations. Christ has definitely laid the whole world on my soul. I cannot escape, but am responsible to serve in love all the need of all men, especially their need of the Gospel. It makes no difference that I cannot be everywhere at once and that I am not fitted for all kinds of service. It is when I realize that I cannot do it and that even my congregation cannot do it, that the necessity of identification with the great Church becomes apparent. It is then also that my congregation knows that all the work of the whole Church is not some burden laid upon it in the form of books to study and apportionments to give. It is that congregation's own required service. My personal Christian responsibility cannot be fulfilled excepting as my congregation has full part in a Church's operations. When then the whole Church feeds the hungry in Europe, meets the immigrant, follows students to their universities, prepares pastors, writes books and church papers, etc., it is my work which is being done, it is I personally who am doing it. The Church is a Christian man's opportunity for the fulfillment of his life's responsibility.

The President asked for immediate action on the second paragraph of his report.

The recommendation was approved by a standing vote. The report of the President was then referred to Committee.

The Convention proceeded to the election of a President under the direction of the proper committee of tellers.

The Secretary submitted his report as follows:

SECRETARY'S REPORT
I. MEMORIALS

There are in the hands of the Secretary a number of memorials addressed to the Convention of the United Lutheran Church. Some of them came too late for inclusion in the Bulletin. A complete list of the letters and memorials received with a brief indication of their contents is here given:

1. From the Susquehanna Synod of Central Pennsylvania concerning affiliation and co-operation with the International Council of Religious Education.

2. From the Illinois Synod concerning the basis of apportionment.

3. From the Synod of the Northwest concerning (a) the preparation of an order for the reception of new members; (b) the elimination of all special appeals and the exclusive use of the Duplex envelope; (c) membership statistics and the basis of apportionment.

4. From the Pittsburgh Synod concerning (a) a book of Ministerial Acts in pocket size; (b) percentage table of apportionments; (c) forms for the reception of new members from other Churches; (d) the translation and printing of the Occasional Acts in German; (e) a study of what ought to be the Church's attitude toward war.

5. From the East Pennsylvania Synod concerning (a) the basis of apportionment; (b) the invitation to hold the 1926 convention in Philadelphia.

6. From the Synod of New York concerning constitutional provisions. The Executive Board has given consideration to this memorial in accordance with action of the Buffalo convention and with the consent of the President of the Synod. See Report of Executive Board II, 2.

7. From the Synod of Texas concerning (a) time of conventions of the United Lutheran Church; (b) time of holding the conference of Presidents.

8. From the Wartburg Synod concerning time and frequency of conventions of the United Lutheran Church.

9. From the Kansas Synod concerning basis of apportionment.

10. From the New York and New England Synod concerning (a) the attitude of the United Lutheran Church toward war and related subjects; (b) literature for the Week-day Religious and Daily Vacation Bible Schools; (c) education program for the congregation.

11. From the Ministerium of Pennsylvania concerning a declaration by the United Lutheran Church on the subject of war.

12. From the California Synod concerning time of the convention of the United Lutheran Church and the fiscal year.

13. From the Rocky Mountain Synod concerning Tabitha Home and the basis of apportionment.

14. From the Synod of Iowa concerning (a) the resolution on war to be offered by the Committee on Social and Moral Welfare; (b) apportionment for the Luther League.

15. Letters from the Rev. E. M. Gearhart, D.D., and from the Executive Lutheran Council and the Lutheran Pastoral Association of Erie and Vicinity inviting the United Lutheran Church to hold its 1926 convention in Luther Memorial Church, Erie, Pa.

16. From the West Pennsylvania Synod concerning divorce and remarriage.

17. From the Indiana Synod concerning (a) basis of apportionment; (b) actions of the United Lutheran Church, whether binding or not; (c) budgets of Constituent Synods.

18. From the German Synod of Nebraska concerning (a) time and

frequency of conventions of the United Lutheran Church; (b) an apportionment to Tabitha Home; (c) merging of the Northwestern Mission Board with the other Boards, etc.; (d) the question of war.

Copies of these memorials have been handed to the chairman of the Committee on Memorials from Constituent Synods.

II.   TREASURERS' REPORTS

An examination of the Reports of Treasurers as printed in the Bulletin will show the desirability of some action whereby these reports may be submitted to the convention in satisfactory form. The following facts are noted concerning the reports to this convention:

1. In five cases there is a report for each of the two years of the biennium, each of them signed by the treasurer and having the certificate of the auditors attached. These are the Reports of the Treasurer of the United Lutheran Church, the Board of Foreign Missions, the Board of Education, the Immigrants' Mission and the Board of Deaconess Work.

2. The other nine reports differ more or less in form from the foregoing and of them no two are exactly alike.

RECOMMENDATIONS

1. That a regulation be provided explaining the requirements of the United Lutheran Church concerning reports of treasurers, the signatures of treasurers thereto and the certificates of the auditors.

2. That instruction be given for the guidance of the secretary in determining whether or not a treasurer's report that comes into his hands shall be printed in the Bulletin issued for the convention.

3. That the above two resolutions be referred with approval to the Executive Board with instruction to bring about a harmonization of treasurers' and auditors' reports.

The Bulletin for this convention was printed and distributed by our own publication house.

(Signed) M. G. G. SCHERER.

Part I was received as information.

The recommendations concerning Treasurers' Reports and Auditors' Certificates (Part II) were adopted.

The Report of the Secretary was adopted as a whole.

The Rev. Dr. Whitteker was recognized by the President and presented an invitation to the Convention to visit the Chicago

Theological Seminary on Saturday, October 25th. It was moved and carried, That the convention accept this invitation and that it adjourn at three o'clock on Saturday.

Dr. E. Clarence Miller, Treasurer of the United Lutheran Church, presented his report and called attention to special items therein. On motion the report was accepted as follows:

REPORT OF THE TREASURER OF THE UNITED LUTHERAN CHURCH

For the Fiscal Year Ended July 31, 1923

APPORTIONMENT AND SPECIALLY DESIGNATED FUNDS

Synod	Synodical Apportionment	Paid on Apportionment	Paid on Specials
Ministerium of Pennsylvania	$317,477.00	$212,310.29	$16,259.00
Ministerium of New York	144,988.00	31,383.15	3,273.94
North Carolina	45,750.00	24,600.77	4,630.32
Maryland	79,306.00	64,607.55	561.19
South Carolina	26,407.00	16,830.65	4,164.60
West Pennsylvania	75,353.00	61,487.72	8,839.73
Virginia	26,827.00	16,163.43	6,086.68
Ohio	123,963.00	106,000.00	18,374.11
East Pennsylvania	96,294.00	69,285.18	14,661.23
Alleghany	56,767.00	43,953.00	7,267.00
Pittsburgh	139,521.00	109,578.07	3,006.63
Indiana	21,445.00	16,881.82	1,917.10
Illinois	60,131.00	55,000.00	16,691.15
Texas	4,878.00	1,613.59	424.56
Central Pennsylvania	23,127.00	18,449.00	720.17
Mississippi	1,009.00	265.31	170.46
Iowa	16,231.00	7,500.00	221.05
Michigan	25,818.00	14,554.43	1,246.55
Georgia	9,335.00	9,335.00	694.12
Canada	25,818.00	4,229.49	2,772.20
Susquehanna	42,302.00	29,381.00	1,090.00
Kansas	17,240.00	12,464.94	160.00
Nebraska	22,875.00	17,897.27	1,154.41
Wartburg	11,689.00	3,500.00	1,261.75
German Nebraska	21,950.00	2,777.86	20.00
California	11,774.00	7,104.00	41.50
Rocky Mountain	4,541.00	3,598.20	209.00
Northwest	37,424.00	14,590.19	2,675.83
Manitoba	10,007.00	400.00	750.00
Pacific	5,214.00	3,157.37	195.57
New York & New England	63,916.00	44,500.00	4,112.36
Nova Scotia	5,382.00	1,044.14	1,508.39
New York	77,624.00	40,842.17	2,205.87

Synod	Synodical Apportion-ment	Paid on Apportion-ment	Paid on Specials
Central Canada	5,466.00	1,398.48	153.75
West Virginia	9,755.00	7,503.00	1,736.52
Slovak Zion	10,007.00		
Women's Missionary Society			300,550.14
Miscellaneous			1,574.41
		$1,074,187.07	$431,381.29

Paid on Apportionment $1,074.187.07
Undistributed Balance of July 31, 1922 .... 1,722.25

Total $1,075.909.32

Distributed in accordance with the United Lutheran
Church Budget $1,040,000.00

Balance $35,909.32
Advance Payment to Jewish Mission Board.................. 2,000.00

Undistributed Balance of July 31, 1923 .... $33,909.32

THE UNITED LUTHERAN CHURCH TREASURY
RECEIPTS:

Proportion of Apportionment	$33,850.00
Indiana	2.00
West Pennsylvania	9.00
Pittsburgh	2.00
Board of Publication	500.00
Interest to 5-31	1,595.84
Total	$35,958.84

EXPENDITURES:

Salaries, President	$6,000.00
Salaries, Secretary	4,000.00
Salaries, Clerks	4,333.00
Traveling Expense, President	255.50
Traveling Expense, Secretary	161.59
General Expense	574.53
Printing and Stationery	443.00
Postage	150.66
Rent	3,435.63
Treasurer's Expense	568.13
Telephone	208.53
Executive Board Expense	948.18
Common Service Book Committee	48.85
Necrology Committee	133.12
Statistical and Year Book Committee	669.66
Woman's Work Committee	220.57

Convention Expense		18,946.31
Brotherhood Committee		235.20
Church Paper Committee		18.00
Special Commissions		192.58
Work Among Boys Committee		249.18
Committee of Adjudication		407.00
Church Music Committee		15.40
Committee on Moral and Social Welfare		173.09
Church Architecture Committee		111.09
Parish and Church School Board		237.80
Committee on Evangelism		101.75
Publication of Minutes		3,295.78
National Lutheran Council		5.70
Committee on World Convention		4,874.60
Committee on Army and Navy Work		3,125.93
Young Peoples Associations Committee		268.68
Committee on Co-ordination		10.21
Conference of Presidents		198.27
Federal Council of Churches		2,000.00
Loan to Saskatoon	$6,500.00	
Less Repayment	4,300.00	
		2,200.00

Total	$58,817.52
Deficit	$22,858.68
Overdraft, July 31, 1922	734.57
Overdrawn, July 31, 1923	$23,593.25
Balance of Apportionment Fund	$33,909.32
Balance of Specials	9,597.76
Balance of Sotter Trust	223.25
Balance of Sotter Trust Income	164.25
Balance of Swygert Trust Income	78.00
Balance of Endowment Fund	200.00
Total	$44,172.58
United Lutheran Church Treasury Overdraft	$23,593.25
Balance on Hand, July 31, 1923	$20,579.33

In Hands of Treasurer	$18,317.83
In Hands of Secretary	2,261.50
	$20,579.33

Respectfully submitted,

E. CLARENCE MILLER, *Treasurer.*

PHILADELPHIA, August 28, 1924.

We have audited the accounts of the Treasurer of the United Lutheran Church in America for the year ended July 31, 1923, and we certify that,

in our opinion, the foregoing statements of Apportionment and Specially
Designated Funds Receipts and Expenditures, etc., are in accordance with
the books of account and are correct.

LYBRAND, ROSS BROS. & MONTGOMERY,
Accountants and Auditors.

REPORT OF THE TREASURER OF THE UNITED LUTHERAN CHURCH

For the Fiscal Year Ended July 31, 1924

APPORTIONMENT AND SPECIALLY DESIGNATED FUNDS

Synod	Apportionment for 1924	Paid on Apportionment	Paid on Specials
Ministerium of Pennsylvania	$341,525.00	$223,826.80	$93,037.18
Ministerium of New York	129,482.00	33,262.86	33,398.51
North Carolina	50,334.00	34,490.42	15,638.20
Maryland	88,892.00	75,070.60	2,029.35
South Carolina	32,461.00	23,500.00	7,315.94
West Pennsylvania	81,416.00	69,837.63	9,287.11
Virginia	28,741.00	17,152.39	6,992.20
Ohio	137,031.00	98,000.00	31,327.21
East Pennsylvania	108,434.00	88,539.12	22,422.76
Alleghany	61,538.00	60,117.00	12,910.03
Pittsburgh	155,756.00	117,536.03	27,021.77
Indiana	26,491.00	16,907.75	1,981.07
Illinois	69,205.00	52,602.00	16,145.36
Texas	5,098.00	1,691.51	1,666.47
Central Pennsylvania	24,150.00	19,806.00	2,852.74
Mississippi	943.00	458.94	307.22
Iowa	18,671.00	9,250.00	215.84
Michigan	31,953.00	17,211.74	2,842.66
Georgia	10,923.00	8,118.82	3,250.13
Canada	28,070.00	3,966.69	2,951.65
Susquehanna	40,808.00	37,773.00	3,040.88
Kansas	18,598.00	11,078.45	11.00
Nebraska	26,600.00	15,858.93	4,737.98
Wartburg	9,653.00	2,800.00	5,371.85
German Nebraska	15,913.00	2,245.21	
California	13,717.00	6,507.68	32.50
Rocky Mountain	5,697.00	3,743.81	1,404.97
Northwest	48,447.00	24,927.64	1,572.28
Manitoba	11,540.00		1,800.90
Pacific	5,915.00	5,093.56	1,454.09
New York and New England	68,533.00	40,000.00	19,725.37
Nova Scotia	4,808.00	949.98	1,412.32
New York	80,327.00	36,292.34	12,743.64
Central Canada	5,225.00	1,587.38	815.52
West Virginia	10,778.00	5,875.02	3,493.26
Slovak Zion	10,415.00	475.00	
Miscellaneous		560.84	1,783.51
Women's Missionary Society			289,480.57
	$1,167,115.14		$642,474.04

Paid on Apportionment $1,167,115.14
Undistributed Balance of July 31, 1923 .... 33,909.32

Total $1,201,024.46
Distributed in accordance with the basis of the United
    Lutheran Church Budget $1,196,000.00

Balance $5,024.46
Repayment of Loan to Jewish Mission Board $2,000.00

Undistributed Balance of July 31, 1924 .... $7,024.46

THE UNITED LUTHERAN CHURCH TREASURY

RECEIPTS:

Proportion of Apportionment	$44,144.60
Ohio	3.00
East Pennsylvania	60.00
Board of Publication	500.00
Interest to 5-31	1,700.65
Repayment on Loan to Saskatoon	200.00
Total	$46,608.25

EXPENDITURES:

Salaries, President	$6,000.00
Salaries, Secretary	4,958.34
Salaries, Clerks	4,317.00
Traveling Expense, President	412.58
Traveling Expense, Secretary	97.08
General Expense	492.66
Printing and Stationery	83.70
Postage	125.22
Rent	3,242.40
Treasurer's Expense	542.95
Telephone	248.72
Executive Board	1,301.12
Common Service Book Committee	32.12
Necrology Committee	50.27
Statistical and Year Book Committee	471.44
Woman's Work Committee	67.40
Special Commissions	349.69
Work Among Boys Committee	87.75
Church Music Committee	18.46
Committee on Moral and Social Welfare	51.88
Church Architecture Committee	30.86
Parish and Church School Board	205.97
Committee on Evangelism	905.92
Committee on World Convention	196.87
Committee on Army and Navy Work	1,525.00
Conference of Presidents	105.55

Federal Council of Churches	2,000.00	
Committee on Linguistic Interests	485.18	
Total		$28,406.13
Balance		$18,202.12
Overdraft of July 31, 1923		23,593.25
Overdrawn, July 31, 1924		$5,391.13
Balance of Apportionment Fund		$7,024.46
Balance of Sotter Trust		223.25
Balance of Endowment Fund		200.00
Total		$7,447.71
United Lutheran Church Treasury Overdraft		5,391.13..
Balance on hand, July 31, 1924		$2,056.58
In hands of Treasurer	$1,556.58	
In hands of Secretary	500.00	
Total	$2,056.58	

TRUST FUNDS
EMMA KIRMSE SOTTER TRUST

Income for Home Missions and Church Extension.
$2,000 Chesapeake & Ohio Equipment 6's.
 4,000 Baltimore & Ohio Secured 6's.
 3,000 Altoona & Logan Valley First Mortgage 4½'s.
 500 U. S. Liberty 4th 4¼'s.

Respectfully submitted,

E. CLARENCE MILLER, *Treasurer.*

PHILADELPHIA, August 28, 1924.

We have audited the accounts of the Treasurer of the United Lutheran Church in America for the year ended July 31, 1924, and we certify that, in our opinion, the foregoing statements of Apportionment and Specially Designated Funds, Receipts and Expenditures, Trust Funds, etc., are in accordance with the books of account and are correct.

LYBRAND, ROSS BROS. & MONTGOMERY,
Accountants and Auditors.

According to order the Convention proceeded to ballot for Treasurer under the direction of the proper committee of tellers.

The committee of tellers reported that, in the first ballot for President, Dr. F. H. Knubel had received 418 votes out of a total of 448 votes cast. No one having received a unanimous vote the tellers were ordered to proceed to take a second ballot.

The report of the Executive Board was regularly taken up.

REPORT OF THE EXECUTIVE BOARD

I. CONCERNING THE EXECUTIVE BOARD

For the second time in its history the Executive Board is called upon to report the death of one of its members, who was also one of the twelve first elected to membership in the Board. The reference is to the Rev. Dr. V. G. A. Tressler, who entered into rest September 1, 1923. The funeral services were held in the Fourth Lutheran Church, of Springfield, Ohio, the Executive Board being officially represented by the Hon. John L. Zimmerman, LL.D. The following message was sent from the office in New York: "The United Lutheran Church mourns the loss of Dr. Tressler, a faithful servant and trusted counselor." Thus two of the Presidents who signed the official documents, whereby the merger of the General Synod, the General Council and the United Synod in the South was effected (see Minutes, 1918, pp. 90-92), have joined the multitude of the Church triumphant.

As the senior member on the Executive Board from the former General Synod the Rev. Dr. J. A. Clutz was requested to prepare a minute to record our appreciation of the man and his work and our sense of loss in his removal from us. Dr. Clutz presented the following at the opening of the meeting of the Executive Board in October, and in approval thereof the members of the Board stood while Dr. F. F. Fry read from the eighth chapter of the Epistle to the Romans, verses 31-39, and led in prayer.

Minute on the Death of Dr. Tressler

Since the last meeting of the Executive Board our ranks have been invaded by death for the second time. September 1, 1923, Prof. V. G. A. Tressler, Ph.D., D.D., Dean of Hamma Divinity School, Springfield, Ohio, and an honored and beloved member of this Board, passed to his eternal reward after an illness of several months.

Dr. Tressler was born April 10, 1865. He had, therefore, completed the fifty-eighth years of his life. He was a son of the Rev. John W. Tressler, and a grandson of Col. John Tressler, the founder of the Tressler Orphans' Home at Loysville, Pa. Prof. David L. Tressler, D.D., the first President of Carthage College, was his uncle. He thus came of a prominent family in our Church, to which he gave added distinction by his own rich gifts of mind and heart, his genial personality, his fine scholarship, and his many and arduous labors in and for the Lutheran Church.

Dr. Tressler graduated from Gettysburg College in 1886 with the highest honors. He then began the study of Law, but later decided to enter the Ministry. For reasons of convenience in residence, he pursued his theological studies in the McCormick Presbyterian Seminary in Chicago, from which he graduated in 1891. He was ordained as a Lutheran minister in 1892. After serving for several years as a home missionary in San Jose, California, he went to Germany for further study. From 1897 to 1900 he was a student in the University of Leipsic, from which he received the degree of Doctor of Philosophy. In 1905 the honorary degree of Doctor of Divinity was conferred upon him by Susquehanna University, Selinsgrove, Penna.

In 1903 Dr. Tressler was called to Wittenberg College as Professor of Greek and Principal of the Academy. In 1905 he was elected Professor of Greek and New Testament Philology in Hamma Divinity School connected with Wittenberg College. This position he filled with great success and honor up to the time of his death. After the death of Dr. Bauslin he was also made the Dean of Hamma Divinity School.

At the meeting of the General Synod in Chicago, in 1917, Dr. Tressler was elected President. By action of the body he was made a member of the Joint Committee on Ways and Means, to which was committed the task of arranging all the details for the Merger meeting and the organization of the United Lutheran Church at New York in 1918. As such he proved himself a wise counselor and an active worker. At this first convention of the United Lutheran Church he was elected as a member of the Executive Board. He was re-elected for a second term of four years at the Buffalo Convention. He also filled many other positions of influence and responsibility. In all of these he faithfully served the Church he so much loved.

Dr. Tressler was deeply interested in all the work of the Executive Board and of the Church and all her Boards and Institutions. He was always ready and eager to serve them. He belonged to the pietistic type of Lutherans, and was always especially concerned for the development of the spiritual life and interests of the Church. Such men are greatly missed when they die, and their memory is long and fondly cherished. It will be so with our friend and brother, and though we bow in humble submission to the divine will we cannot but regret his going from us just in the midst of his greatest usefulness.

As a mark of respect the Secretary of the Board is directed to make this Minute a part of the record of this meeting, and also to send a copy of it to Mrs. Tressler, with the assurance of our deepest sympathy in her sore bereavement. It shall furthermore be printed in *The Lutheran* and be made a part of our report to the convention of The United Lutheran Church in America.

The vacancy caused by the death of Dr. Tressler was filled by the election on October 24th of the Rev. A. H. Smith, D.D., of Ashland, Ohio.

The following Committees of the Executive Board have been active in digesting matters referred to them severally preparatory to consideration by the Board.

Committee on Constituent Synods

Rev. J. A. Clutz, D.D., LL.D.   Rev. E. B. Burgess, D.D.
Rev. W. H. Greever, D.D.

Committee on Boards and Committees

Rev. F. F. Fry, D.D.   Rev. M. G. G. Scherer, D.D.
Rev. H. A. Weller, D.D.   Rev. A. H. Smith, D.D.
Mr. F. Henrich

The Rev. V. G. A. Tressler served as a member of the above Committee until the time of his death. Dr. Smith was appointed to fill the vacancy.

Finance Committee

Mr. E. Clarence Miller, LL.D.   Mr. Wm. H. Hager
Mr. H. C. Miller

Legal Committee

Hon. J. L. Zimmerman, LL.D.   Hon. C. M. Efird
Robbin B. Wolf, Esq.

During the biennium the Board held eight meetings, the attendance at the several meetings being indicated by the following figures: 14, 11, 13, 15, 11, 12, 13, 12.

It seems proper to note that, of the six members of the Executive Board whose terms expire at this convention, four of them are ineligible for re-election, each of them having served for a term of two years and having succeeded himself for a term of four years. These are the Revs. Jacob A. Clutz and H. A. Weller, Hon. John L. Zimmerman, and Mr. Harvey C. Miller. The Rev. F. F. Fry and Robbin B. Wolf, Esq., are the eligibles, they having served each one term of four years. It is also noteworthy that of the twelve members of the Board elected thereto in 1918 only three remain for the ensuing term: namely, the Hon. C. M. Efird, Mr. William H. Hager and Mr. Frederick Henrich, and that from this time forth, at each convention, one-half of the members of the Board elected by the Convention will necessarily retire.

The Board's nominations to fill vacancies are as follows: For term expiring 1928, Rev. F. F. Fry, Robbin B. Wolf, Esq., Rev. W. D. C. Keiter, Rev. A. R. Wentz, Hon. John F. Kramer, and George E. Neff, Esq.; for term expiring 1926, Rev. A. H. Smith.

II. MATTERS REFERRED

1. *Approval of Minutes, Printing and Distribution.* See Minutes, Third Convention, 1922, pp. 495, 507, 509. The Minutes of the two sessions of the Buffalo Convention, Wednesday, October 25th, were approved by the Executive Board. Four thousand copies of the Minutes were ordered printed. They came from the press on January 11, 1923. They were

mailed to all ministers of the United Lutheran Church, to lay delegates to the Buffalo Convention, colleges and seminaries, members of Boards and Committees, Public and State Libraries, prominent Lutheran Church officials in Europe, and others. The cost of printing, wrapping and mailing was $2856.63.

A reprint pamphlet containing the Statement in Regard to Relations with the Federal Council, an Extract from the President's Report, Report of Committee on Evangelism, Declarations on National Life and International Relations, Relations with Interdenominational Agencies, Weekday Schools for Religious Instruction and Christian Citizenship, was mailed to all Lutheran ministers in the United States and Canada, numbering over ten thousand.

2. *Study and Revision of Constitution and By-Laws.* See Minutes, 1922, pp. 308, 420. In accordance with the instructions of the Buffalo Convention, the Executive Board secured from its individual members and from other sources, including a Memorial from the Synod of New York, many suggestions for possible amendments to the Constitution of the United Lutheran Church in America. The Board considered these, meeting as a Committee of the whole. In view of the fact that the organization is but six years old and has, therefore, not had sufficient experience to test in practical manner the provisions of the Constitution as a whole and in view of the fact that none of the suggestions made commended themselves to the hearty support of the Board, unanimous decision was reached that the Church should not for the present undertake to amend its Constitution, excepting in the one minor item presented herewith.

The Article to be amended reads: Article IX, Section 1. The officers of The United Lutheran Church in America shall be a President, a Secretary and a Treasurer, who shall be elected by ballot at each regular Convention and shall serve until their successors are elected. The President, who shall be an ordained minister, and the Secretary, shall be chosen from the delegates present.

Proposed amendment: Stop after the word "Treasurer." Insert the sentence: "The President shall be an ordained minister of the Church." Then the following sentence: "The officers shall be elected by ballot at each regular Convention, but shall not take office until the first day of the third month after their election."

So amended the Article would read: The officers of The United Lutheran Church in America shall be a President, a Secretary and a Treasurer. The President shall be an ordained minister of the Church. The officers shall be elected by ballot at each regular Convention, but shall not take office until the first day of the third month after their election.

Proposed amendments to By-Laws: (All references are to the first printed copies of the Constitution and By-Laws adopted 1918 except as otherwise indicated in the report.)

Section II, Item 3. Omit all to and including the word "but" in the fourth line. Change "sessions" in the sixth line to "session." The item as amended would read:

In the absence of a quorum the delegates present may adjourn from time to time and postpone the session of the Convention until a quorum shall appear.

Section III, Item 1. After the word "presented" in the third line strike the remaining words of the sentence and substitute the words "to the Executive Board together with a copy of the Synod's Constitution." Strike lines 4, 5 and 6 to and including "recommendation" and insert the words: "Upon recommendation of the Executive Board" and conclude the item with the words: "The Synod may be received, etc." The item as amended would read:

The application of a Synod desiring to be received into The United Lutheran Church in America shall be presented to the Executive Board together with a copy of the Synod's Constitution. Upon recommendation of the Executive Board the Synod may be received in accordance with the Constitution, Article IV, Section 2. The delegates of such Synod upon the approval of their credentials shall at once be seated in the Convention and their names entered upon the roll.

Section IV, Item 2. Strike the words "the Standing Committee on Church Papers" and substitute the words: "all elective Committees." The item as amended would read:

Election of officers, members of the Executive Board and of the other Boards, including the Commission of Adjudication and all elective Committees, shall be by ballot. The Secretary shall prepare printed ballots for the use of voters in the Convention.

Section IV, Item 3. In the second and third lines omit: "On the first ballot—election." In the third line strike "second" and insert "first." In the fifth line strike "third" and insert "second." In the sixth line strike "three" and insert "two." In the seventh line strike "fourth" and insert "third." In the eighth line strike "third" and insert "second." In the tenth line strike "fourth" and insert "third." The item as amended would read:

In the election of a President, the following rules shall obtain: On the first ballot, three-fourths of all the votes cast shall be necessary to an election. On the second ballot, two-thirds of all the votes cast shall be necessary to an election. If two ballots fail to result in an election, the third ballot shall be confined to the two persons who in the second ballot receive the highest number of votes and no vote cast for any other shall be counted. In the third ballot a majority of the votes shall elect.

Section IV, Item 4. Strike "or" in line 1 and substitute "and." Strike "any" and insert after the words "regular Boards" the words "and elective Committees." The item as amended would read:

In the election of the Secretary, Treasurer and members of regular Boards and elective Committees, a majority of the votes cast shall be necessary for an election.

Section V, A. The list of Boards and Elective Committees as amended at Washington (See Minutes, 1920, pp. 24, 79, 102, 106f, 510f) stood as follows:

1. An Executive Board.
2. A Commission of Adjudication.
3. A Foreign Mission Board.
4. A Home Mission and Church Extension Board.
5. A Board of Northwestern Missions.
6. An Immigrants Mission Board.
7. A West Indies Board.
8. A Committee of Jewish Missions.
9. A Board of Education.
10. An Inner Mission Board.
11. A Board of Publication.
12. A Board of Ministerial Relief.
13. A Parish and Church School Board.
14. A Board of Deaconess Work.
15. A Board for the Home for the Aged.
16. A Committee on Church Papers.
17. An Executive Committee of the Laymen's Missionary Movement.

Section V, A. 17. Strike the word "Missionary" in order to make it conform to the present Constitution of the Movement. The list of Boards and Elective Committees will remain unchanged except as for this Item 17 which, as amended, would read:

17. An Executive Committee of the Laymen's Movement.

Section V, B. Item 8. In line four strike the word "Missionary" and the words "to twenty-five if" and for the latter substitute "as." The item as amended would read:

The President shall appoint a Committee of three ministers and four laymen to nominate a Standing Committee of ten laymen which shall be known as the Executive Committee of the Laymen's Movement and shall have charge of its development and administration. It shall have power to increase its membership as deemed expedient.

Section V, B, Item 9, (2). In the second line strike the words "Federal Council of" and in their place insert "work of Lutheran." The item as amended would read:

A Standing Committee to have the supervision of the work of Lutheran Brotherhoods.

Section V, C, Item 5. In the first line strike "reports" and substitute the word "accounts." In the second sentence strike "report of the auditor" and substitute the words "report of the Treasurer certified by said accountant." In the sixth line strike "third" and insert "fourth." The item as amended would read:

The financial accounts of the several Boards and Commissions shall be submitted for audit to an accredited accountant. In connection with its report each Board shall present to the Convention the report of the Treasurer certified by said accountant. The fiscal year of all Boards shall close on the last day of the fourth month preceding the one in which the Convention of the United Lutheran Church shall meet.

Section VI, Item 2. Strike out the item and substitute the following:

"Item 2. Robert's Rules of Order Revised shall be the governing parliamentary law except where not in harmony with the Constitution and By-Laws."

Section VI, Item 3. Strike out "situation of" and substitute the words "conditions in." The item as amended would read:

Item 3. He shall prepare a biennial report which shall briefly summarize the general conditions in the Church and his own work during the biennium and which shall be read and assigned to Committees prior to the Convention's entering into the election of a successor.

Section VI, Items 4, 5 and 6. Strike out these items. Section VI as amended would read:

Item 1. The President shall conduct all business according to the Constitution, By-Laws, and Order of Procedure of The United Lutheran Church, and insist upon the observance of the same on the part of every member. He shall appoint all committees unless otherwise provided for.

Item 2. Robert's Rules of Order Revised shall be the governing parliamentary law except where not in harmony with the Constitution and By-Laws.

Item 3. He shall prepare a biennial report which shall briefly summarize the general conditions in the Church and his own work during the biennium and which shall be presented and assigned to Committees prior to the Convention's entering into the election of a successor.

Section VII, A. The list of Special Committees as amended at Washington (See Minutes, 1920, pp. 24, 79, 102, 106f, 512) stood as follows:

1. Committee to conduct the opening and closing services of each session.
2. Committee on Leave of Absence.
3. Committee on Proceedings of District Synods.
4. Committee of Reference and Counsel. (Its duties shall include the consideration of all general resolutions before they are submitted to the Convention, arrangements with the President for the hearing of representatives sent to the Conventions, and general assistance to the President in the daily program.)

5. Committee to Nominate Executive Committee Laymen's Missionary Movement.
6. Committee to Nominate Members of Boards.
7. Committee to Nominate Members of Executive Board, and all elective Commissions or Committees.
8. Committee of Tellers.

Section VII, A. Item 5. In second line strike the word "Missionary." The list of Special Committees as amended would read as above except for Item 5 which would read:

5. Committee to Nominate Executive Committee of Laymen's Movement.

Section VII, B. The list of Standing Committees as amended at Washington (See Min. 1920, pp. 24f, 79, 102, 106f, 437, 511) and Buffalo (See Min. 1922, pp. 169, 308, 513) stood as follows:

The following Standing Committees shall be appointed by the President before the close of each Convention:
1. Statistical and Church Year Book Committee.
2. Committee on Common Service Book.
3. Committee on Church Music.
4. Committee of Conference on Special Linguistic Interests.
5. Committee on Lutheran Brotherhoods.
6. Committee on Women's Work.
7. Committee on Associations of Young People.
8. Committee on Work Among Boys.
9. Committee on Army and Navy Work.
10. Committee on Moral and Social Welfare.
11. Committee on Evangelism.
12. Committee on Church Architecture.
13. Committee on Publicity.
14. Committee on Necrology.
15. Committee on Transportation.   (Its duties shall include all transportation interests, including the mileage and transportation arrangements for the Conventions.)
16. An Archivist.
17. Such other Standing Committees as may be provided for from time to time.

Strike from the sentence at the head of this list the words "before the close of each Convention." The sentence as amended would read:

The following Standing Committees shall be appointed by the President: (List of Standing Committees as above.)

3. *Revision of System for Nominations and Elections at Conventions.* See Minutes, 1922, pp. 132, 472.
The Executive Board recommends the following as a series of standing resolutions upon the subject:

a. Although the 1920 Convention in Washington ruled that ad interim elections of members of Boards are to be effective only until the next Convention thereafter, further study of the Constitution and By-Laws reveals that it would be thoroughly in harmony therewith if such elections are made effective for the entire remainder of the term concerned. It is therefore recommended, particularly in the interest of a simplification of records and of elections, that the above-mentioned action in 1920 be rescinded and that all ad interim elections apply for the entire remainder of the terms of office concerned. This new ruling is to apply to all such elections during the present biennium and therefore to all elections at the 1924 Convention in Chicago. It is to be understood under this decision that such an ad interim election for an unexpired term is to count as one of the two successive terms for which a member of a Board is eligible.

b. In the preparation of ballots for an election, the nominations made by the Board concerned are to stand first, arranged in alphabetical order. Also an asterisk shall be used to indicate nominations made by a Board; in case of a renomination, a double asterisk. Then will follow the nominations, arranged alphabetically, made by the Nominating Committee. In the case of each nominee the Synod of which he is a member shall be indicated.

c. In all elections, including those for officers of the Church, identifying initials must be used for all individuals. A vote for an individual not carrying his initials is not to be counted.

d. The election of officers of the United Lutheran Church in America will ordinarily take place during the sessions of the first Wednesday of a Convention. No election of a Secretary is to take place until after the President has been chosen. In the election of an officer of the Church only the regular method shall be used whereby each delegate has the opportunity to cast an individual ballot.

e. The elections for membership on the Executive Board, the Commission of Adjudication, the Church Paper Committee, and the Executive Committee of the Laymen's Movement shall ordinarily take place at the close of the first Wednesday afternoon session of a Convention.

f. The elections for membership on other Boards and other elective Commissions and Committees shall ordinarily take place at the close of the first Friday afternoon session of a Convention.

4. *Eligibility of Synodical Presidents as Members of Executive Board.* See Minutes, 1922, pp. 424, 457.

There is no conceivable constitutional ground against such membership. Statements in Article XIV, Section 3, are not sufficient ground.

The question is therefore reduced to the desirability of such membership and the consequent desirability of a By-Law making such membership impossible. On any fair consideration probably as many reasons could be advanced which distinctly favor such membership as those which render it undesirable. The Executive Board's work is one which rarely if ever has to do with the relation of Synods one to another, but more especially with the relation of Boards one to another and to the Church as a whole. Wherever it deals with the work of Synods it is dealing with that which is the work of them all, that is, the work of the Church as a whole.

As a result of the above statements the Executive Board cannot find sufficient considerations to favor the proposition submitted to it by the Buffalo Convention and therefore recommends its rejection.

5. The action of the Executive Board on certain other matters which were referred to it will be reported under other heads as here indicated:

a. Work among the Siebenburgers. Minutes, 1922, pp. 424, 457. (See IV, B. 2.)

b. Asiatics on the Pacific Coast. Minutes, 1922, p. 309. (See IV, B. 4.)

c. Survey of field for work among Negroes. Minutes, 1922, pp. 452, 456. (See IV, B. 5.)

d. (1) Conventions of the United Lutheran Church, time of holding. Minutes, 1922, pp. 425, 457. (See III, A, 3, a.)

(2) Synodical meetings, time of. Minutes, 1922, pp. 425, 457. (See III, A, 3, b.)

(3) Fiscal Year, date for closing. Minutes, 1922, pp. 336, 337. (See III, A, 3, c.)

e. Boards, Combination or Reorganization of. Minutes, 1922, pp. 65, 111, 472. (See IV, A. 2.)

f. Boards, representation of at Synods. Minutes, 1922, pp. 425, 457. (See III, A, 4.)

g. The Saskatoon Institutions. Minutes, 1922, p. 504. (See V, 1.)

h. Special Appropriation for Army and Navy Work. Minutes, 1922, p. 131. (See IV, C, 4.)

i. Request of Committee on Work Among Boys for $2000. Minutes 1922, p. 296. (See IV, C, 5.)

k. Lutheran World Convention, appointments to. Minutes, 1922, pp. 66, 315, 321, 323, 421. (See X.)

l. Agreement with the Evangelical Lutheran Church in Czecho-Slovakia. Minutes, 1922, p. 111. (See XI, 1.)

III.   SYNODS

A.   In General

1. *Conference of Synodical Presidents*: It having been ascertained through correspondence that the Presidents of the Constituent Synods of the United Lutheran Church in America were favorable to the holding of a Conference of Presidents, such a Conference was called to meet at Harrisburg. Pa., January 29th and 30th, 1924. In response to this call the personnel of the Conference was composed of 29 Presidents, one Vice-President and the three officers of the United Lutheran Church. The Presidents who were absent expressed by letter their regrets at not being able to attend. A number of subjects of a practical character vitally affecting the life and work of the Church were freely and fully discussed. A consensus of opinion taken before adjournment was to the effect that the Conference had been one of much profit.

2. *Apportionments*: The apportionments proposed by the Finance Committee and approved by the Executive Board were as follows:

For the year 1923:

Synod	Apportionment
Ministerium of Pennsylvania	$317,477.50
Ministerium of New York	144,988.40
North Carolina	45,750.40
Maryland	79,306.30
South Carolina	26,407.40
West Pennsylvania	75,353.60
Virginia	26,827.90
Ohio	123,963.40
East Pennsylvania	96,294.50
Alleghany	56,767.50
Pittsburgh	139,521.90
Indiana	25,314.10
Illinois	60,131.50
Texas	5,382.40
Central Pennsylvania	23,127.50
Mississippi	1,009.20
Iowa	16,231.30
Michigan	25,818.70
Georgia	9,335.10
Canada	25,818.70
Susquehanna	42,302.30
Kansas	17,240.50
Nebraska	22,875.20
Wartburg	11,689.90
German Nebraska	21,950.10
California	11,774.00
Rocky Mountain	4,541.40
Northwest	37,424.50
Manitoba	10,007.90
Pacific	5,214.20
New York and New England	63,916.00
Nova Scotia	5,382.40
New York	77,624.30
Central Canada	5,466.50
West Virginia	9,755.60
Slovak Zion	10,007.90

$1,682,000.00

A revision of this apportionment resulted in reducing the amount apportioned to the Indiana Synod to $21,445.10 and that apportioned the Texas Synod $4,878.40.

For the year 1924:

Synod	Confirmed Membership	Current Expenses	Apportionment
Min. of Penna.	175,093	$1,177,105	$341,525.19
Min. of New York	67,155	439,583	129,482.72
North Carolina	23,606	192,786	50,334.23
Maryland	40,701	349,153	88,892.36
South Carolina	17,445	104,886	32,461.41
West Pennsylvania	39,090	303,860	81,416.62
Virginia	13,863	105,937	28,741.68
Ohio	51,752	634,609	137,031.04
East Pennsylvania	42,534	488,369	108,434.52
Alleghany	32,589	250,982	67,571.98
Pittsburgh	68,573	635,883	155,756.68
Indiana	9,966	123,119	26,491.70
Illinois	25,201	328,758	69,205.03
Texas	2,855	15,448	5,098.75
Central Pennsylvania	12,618	81,201	24,150.99
Mississippi	624	2,117	943.54
Iowa	5,357	101,385	18,671.20
Michigan	11,902	149,426	31,953.34
Georgia	4,422	48,022	10,923.29
Canada	15,240	89,328	28,070.31
Susquehanna	22,164	129,741	40,808.11
Kansas	5,672	97,997	18,598.63
Nebraska	11,047	114,431	26,600.57
Wartburg	4,169	40,152	9,653.14
German Nebraska	6,735	67,325	15,913.16
California	4,583	68,726	13,717.62
Rocky Mountain	1,910	28,521	5,697.53
Northwest	19,773	211,336	48,447.15
Manitoba	6,205	37,229	11,540.22
Pacific	2,368	29,048	6,278.17
New York and New England	28,441	294,899	68,533.67
Nova Scotia	2,639	15,085	4,808.42
New York	31,695	360,077	80,327.91
Central Canada	2,052	23,455	5,225.76
West Virginia	4,244	48,468	10,778.13
Slovak Zion	7,161	20,000	10,415.23
	821,444	$7,208,447	$1,814,500.00

The amount apportioned to the Alleghany Synod was later reduced to $61,538.98. The apportionment for the Pacific Synod was likewise reduced to $5,915.17.

For the year 1925:

Synod	Confirmed Membership	Current Expenses	Apportion-ment
Min. of Pennsylvania	175,093	$1,177,105	$339,846.78
Min. of New York	67,155	439,583	128,847.65
North Carolina	23,606	192,786	50,107.42
Maryland	40,701	349,153	88,493.17
South Carolina	17,445	104,886	32,298.10
West Pennsylvania	39,090	303,860	81,035.57
Virginia	13,541	118,767	29,766.87
Ohio	51,752	634,609	136,468.55
East Pennsylvania	42,534	488,369	107,989.97
Alleghany	32,589	250,982	67,254.44
Pittsburgh	68,573	635,883	155,067.17
Indiana	9,966	123,119	26,391.90
Illinois	25,201	328,758	68,923.78
Texas	2,870	16,887	5,271.12
Susquehanna Synod of Central Penna...	34,782	210,942	64,632.49
Mississippi	624	2,117	952.61
Iowa	5,357	101,385	18,607.70
Michigan	11,902	149,426	31,817.26
Georgia	4,566	32,701	9,108.79
Canada	15,240	89,328	27,934.23
Kansas	5,672	97,997	18,526.05
Nebraska	11,047	114,431	26,491.70
Wartburg	8,708	54,510	16,394.01
German Nebraska	9,332	67,325	18,689.35
California	4,583	68,726	13,663.19
Rocky Mountain	1,910	28,521	5,079.39
Northwest	19,773	211,336	48,229.41
Manitoba	5,364	39,241	10,805.38
Pacific	2,300	26,850	5,897.13
New York and New England	28,441	294,899	68,234.27
Nova Scotia	2,639	15,085	4,790.28
New York	31,695	360,077	79,983.16
Central Canada	2,052	23,455	5,198.54
West Virginia	4,244	48,468	10,741.79
Slovak Zion	7,161	20,000	10,360.80
	827,505	$7,221,567	$1,814,500.00

The apportionment to the Alleghany Synod was reduced to $61,248.44.

3. *Times of holding Conventions and Synodical Meetings, also dates for closing Fiscal Year*:

a. Time for Biennial Conventions of the United Lutheran Church: Through correspondence it was ascertained that either by synodical action, or through their officers, in most cases the latter only, fourteen Synods would prefer the holding of the Convention the latter part of Summer or in the Fall as at present; twelve would prefer the Spring or early Summer. Some seemed to have no preference, others were not heard from.

A majority of the larger Synods seem to favor the Fall as the time of meeting.

The Executive Board recommends that until there is manifested a more decided preference for another time of meeting of the general Conventions no change be made.

b. Time of meeting of Synods: In connection with the consideration of the time for holding the conventions of the United Lutheran Church it became evident that no time could be found that would be agreeable to all unless all of the Constituent Synods could be induced to meet either in the Spring or Fall. Such an arrangement would also make it more convenient for representatives of the Boards and other agencies of the Church to be present. Yet, however desirable such an arrangement might be, the Executive Board deems it impracticable, at least for the present.

c. Close of the fiscal year: In regard to this matter there was found to be great confusion. Most of the Synods determine the end of their fiscal year by the time of their meetings. These run through nearly all the months of the year. While it may not be vitally important, it does seem to be very desirable to have the fiscal year of all the Synods, and, if possible, of all the congregations to harmonize. We believe that the best time for this would be the close of the calendar year, which is also the close of the apportionment year of the United Lutheran Church. We recommend, therefore, that the Convention take action requesting all the Constituent Synods to work to this end.

4. *The Visitation of Synods by Board Secretaries, etc.*: This matter was under consideration during the greater part of the biennium. It was before the Executive Board, the Conference of Synodical Presidents, and the Conference of Secretaries. Finally, a plan was worked out, largely by the Executive Committee of the Secretaries' Conference, consisting of the officers of the same. This plan, submitted herewith, covers all the Synods meeting during the latter half of 1924 and the first half of 1925. It provides for the attendance of at least one Secretary or Representative of the general work of the Church at each Synod, and not more than five at any Synod.

The plan follows:

SYNODS

One Representative   *Confirmed Members*

1.	Slovak Zion	7161
2.	Manitoba	6205
3.	Rocky Mountain	2495
4.	Mississippi	816
5.	Central Canada	3125
6.	Nova Scotia	2818

Two Representatives

1.	West Virginia	4276
2.	Kansas	7949

		Confirmed Members
3.	Iowa	5329
4.	Wartburg	9094
5.	Texas	6200
6.	Pacific	2386
7.	California	5260
8.	Georgia	4422

Three Representatives

1.	South Carolina	13615
2.	Virginia	13863
3.	Indiana	10139
4.	Nebraska	10468
5.	German Nebraska	9094
6.	Michigan	11816
7.	Canada	14900

Four Representatives

1.	North Carolina	26140
2.	Northwest	18306
3.	New York and New England	27843
4.	Alleghany	27000
5.	Illinois	25000
6.	Susquehanna Synod of Central Penna.	34655

Five Representatives

1.	Ministerium of Pennsylvania	171000
2.	Ministerium of New York	67000
3.	Maryland	39000
4.	West Pennsylvania	38000
5.	Ohio	51000
6.	East Pennsylvania	51000
7.	Pittsburgh	68000
8.	New York	36000

Presentation of Causes to Synods

a. *By One Representative*—All phases of the work of the United Lutheran Church.

b. *By Two Representatives*—

First

Missionary
Foreign
Home Missions and Church Extension
Immigrant
West Indies
Jewish
Northwestern

Educational
Board of Education
Parish and Church School
Publication

Promotional
Laymen's Movement
Brotherhood
Luther League

Second

Ministerial Relief
Deaconess Work
Inner Missions
National and Tabitha Homes

c. *By Three Representatives—*

First

Missionary
Foreign Missions
Home Missions and Church Extension
Northwestern
Immigrant
West Indies
Jewish

Second

Educational
Parish and Church School
Board of Education
Publication

Promotional
Brotherhood
Laymen's Movement
Luther League

Third

Ministerial Relief
Inner Missions
Deaconess
National and Tabitha Homes

d. *By Four Representatives—*

First

Foreign Missions
Home Missions and Church Extension
Immigrant
West Indies
Northwestern
Jewish

Second

Education
Parish and Church School
Publication

Third

Ministerial Relief
Deaconess
Inner Missions
National and Tabitha Homes

Fourth

Brotherhood
Luther League
Laymen's Movement

e. *By Five Representatives—*

First

Home Missions and Church Extension
Northwestern
Immigrant
West Indies
Jewish

Second

Foreign Missions
Deaconess
Laymen's Movement

Third

Publication
Educational
Parish and Church School

Fourth

Inner Missions
Deaconess
National and Tabitha Homes

Fifth

Ministerial Relief
Luther· League
Brotherhood

This plan was approved by the Executive Board and referred back to the Executive Committee of the Secretaries' Conference to be put into effect with such changes as might be found necessary.

We recommend that all the Synods, Boards and Board Secretaries and other Representatives of the general work of interests of the Church be urged to co-operate heartily with said Committee in its efforts to carry out this plan of visitation.

5. *Concerning Reports of Memberhip by Synods*: There was brought to the attention of the Executive Board a "very striking and unusual" drop in the number of confirmed members reported by one of the Constituent Synods in 1923 as compared with the report made in 1922. Inquiry as to the reasons for this elicited the following answer: "The reason for

the decrease of confirmed members is the fact that a good number of reports failed to appear, and that according to a resolution of our last meeting only those have to be counted as confirmed members who contribute towards the support of the congregation."

Examination of the minutes of the Synod referred to showed that thirty-one congregations had not made any report as to their membership. Twenty-seven congregations reported more communing members than confirmed members which is out of harmony with the rubrics of the official Parochial Report.

Inasmuch as the United Lutheran Church is given power under its Constitution to lay apportionments on its Constituent Synods for benevolent work and has defined the basis on which these apportionments can be equitably distributed, namely, "current expenses" and "confirmed members"; and inasmuch as it is made the duty of the Executive Board of the United Lutheran Church to "co-ordinate the work of the entire body," the Executive Board therefore instructed the Secretary to call the attention of the officers of the Synod in question to the facts recited above and ask them to have the resolution quoted rescinded at its next meeting, to use all diligence to have every congregation connected with the Synod to report fully each year in accordance with the rubrics of the official Parochial Blank and to instruct its Statistical and Historical Secretary to insert the figures of the last report presented, where these are lacking in the membership columns.

In view of the great importance of securing more accurate statistics and especially fuller and more complete reports as to our membership, the Executive Board also formally instructed the Statistical Secretary of the United Lutheran Church, in case of incomplete reports from Constituent Synods, to correct them in accordance with the rubrics found on the blanks for Parochial Reports.

We recommend that this action be endorsed and that it be brought to the attention of all Constituent Synods.

6. *Concerning Uniformity of Method in Division of Funds as between the Synod and the United Lutheran Church*: (See VII, 5.)

7. *Certificates of Ordination and other important documents*: A letter came to the Executive Board from the Secretary of one of the Constituent Synods setting forth that a certain ministerial member of that Synod had deposited his Certificate of Ordination with the officers of another Synod of the United Lutheran Church several years ago, that this certificate had been lost and that he, desiring to resume work as a pastor and wishing to have a Certificate of Ordination as evidence of his right to do so, was seeking advice as to the method of procedure under such circumstances. The letter also suggested that it might be well to have all Certificates of Ordination deposited with Synods by ministers not engaged in pas-

toral work, placed in the keeping of the officers of the United Lutheran Church so as to guard against their being lost.

The Executive Board took the following action:

a. That in case a Certificate of Ordination has been lost, a duplicate copy of such certificate may be given by the Synod which originally granted the ordination; or if this should be found impracticable, a certified copy of the official record of the ordination may be furnished.

b. That the Executive Board offer to receive and deposit with the archives of the United Lutheran Church any Certificates of Ordination or other important documents, that may be placed in its keeping by Constituent Synods, and that it recommend that this offer be accepted by all Synods that do not have an official depository for the safe keeping of such documents.

B. In Particular

1. At the meeting of the South Carolina Synod in November, 1922, the pastors and congregations of the South Carolina Conference of the North Carolina Synod, formerly connected with the Tennessee Synod, were received into the Synod of South Carolina.

2. The Evangelical Lutheran Synod of Central Pennsylvania (organized February 21, 1855) and the Susquehanna Synod (organized November 5, 1867) met in joint session in Zion Lutheran Church, Sunbury, Penna., September 5, 1923. At this meeting a series of resolutions, presented by the two Synods, were unanimously adopted, whereby a merger of the two Synods was formally effected, under the name and title of the Susquehanna Synod of Central Pennsylvania of the Evangelical Lutheran Church. Though it was decided that each of the Synods should carry on its own work until May, 1924, an election of officers was held resulting as follows: President, Rev. F. P. Manhart, D.D.; Secretary, Rev. W. M. Rearick, D.D.; Treasurer, Mr. Wm. T. Horton.

The newly organized Synod held its first session May 22, 1924, in Zion Lutheran Church, Sunbury, Pa., at which time the charter was approved and the interests of the two Synods officially merged. The Synod adopted the Constitution for Constituent Synods recommended by the Executive Board, including the doctrinal basis, making only such minor changes as seemed called for by certain local conditions.

The Executive Board recommends that this merger be approved and that the Susquehanna Synod of Central Pennsylvania of the Evangelical Lutheran Church be enrolled in the place occupied by the older of the merging Synods as has been done in other cases.

3. *Actions concerning Pacific Synod and its work:*

a. Pacific Theological Seminary: The Executive Board was officially notified through the Secretary of the Pacific Synod that on January 19, 1923, the said Synod took the following action:

"In view of the action of the United Lutheran Church in regard to our Pacific Theological Seminary at Seattle, as reported by our delegation to the Buffalo Convention,

"Be it unanimously resolved, by the Pacific Synod of the Evangelical Lutheran Church:

"1. That we sincerely rejoice in the hearty recognition given by the Church to the historical fact that in projecting the plans for the location of the Pacific Seminary at Seattle and in the work there attempted the Pacific Synod proceeded entirely within its rights and under the specific sanction of the United Lutheran Church; but that we again respectfully remind the Church that those plans and the inauguration of that work were a *fait accompli* before the organization of The United Lutheran Church in America;

"2. That we are deeply grateful for the warm commendation given by the Church of our hearts' desire to the sacrifice and devotion of our people in behalf of the Seminary at Seattle, and that we cherish the hope that our hearts may be gladdened, our hands strengthened and our love requitted by the due reward of devoted fidelity;

"3. That we humbly give expression to our sincere conviction that the safest, most trustworthy and most effective method of arriving at a correct view of facts such as are involved in our Seminary matter is through the instrumentality of those who have devoted their lives to the study and development of these facts:

"4. That, after earnest reconsideration, we solemnly declare that we can not do otherwise than adhere to the decision unanimously reached by the Synod in the Tacoma Convention in favor of a permanent location of the Pacific Seminary at Seattle, the reasons for which are fully stated in our Statement of Position presented to the Church in Convention assembled at Buffalo;

"5. That our hearts are cheered and our loyalty deepened by the renewed assurance that we have not been mistaken in our sure confidence and trust that our great Church would not in any way infringe upon the rights accorded as under its Constitution; and

"6. That we earnestly petition the United Lutheran Church in America and its constituted authorities to devise ways and means whereby the pledges made to us in the New York Convention may now begin to bring forth fruit."

(1)   The Executive Board expressed the judgment that in view of this action there is no desirability for the appointment of an Eastern Advisory Committee as was done prior to the Buffalo Convention. (See Minutes, 1922, pages 54, d., and 56, d.)

(2)   In answer to Item 6 of the action of the Pacific Synod it was

Resolved that with our report to the Washington Convention (see Minutes, 1920, page 59f) which was adopted by the United Lutheran Church, we fully discharged our responsibilities so far as the resolution of the New York Convention is concerned.

This is submitted for your consideration and action.

b. Co-operation: The Pacific Synod requested the Executive Board "to present to the coming Convention of the United Lutheran Church a plan for co-operation with the Norwegian Lutheran Church in educational work and home missions."

A plan for co-operation in Home Missions had been adopted by the Board of Home Missions and Church Extension and approved by the Executive Board. The matter of co-operation in education was referred by the Buffalo Convention to the Board of Education of the United Lutheran Church with "full power, subject to the approval of the Executive Board," and, as we were informed, was in process of adjustment.

The Executive Board was of the opinion that further action should not be taken at this time and so recommends to the Convention.

4. *Synod of the Northwest*: In answer to a request of the Rev. G. K. Rubrecht, D.D., President of the Synod of the Northwest, for an interpretation of the Buffalo resolutions concerning the location of the Northwestern Seminary (see Minutes, 1922, page 470) the President sent by wire the following statement which was approved by the Executive Board:

"Buffalo resolutions seem plain. Synod's action is upheld as constitutional. The Church disagrees with the Synod's judgment, deplores its action as taken and frankly says so. It wishes the Synod could agree with it. The Church, however, does not wish to promote division in the Synod. It desires unified support within a Synod of constitutional synodical action. To make my interpretation complete the Church similarly expects complete support from all Synods for all work the Church constitutionally undertakes."

5. The Executive Board received a letter from a joint committee of representatives of the Ministerium of Pennsylvania and the East Pennsylvania Synod renewing the invitation extended by the Ministerium of Pennsylvania (see Minutes, 1922, pages 426 and 457) to hold the 1926 Convention of the United Lutheran Church in Philadelphia.

The Executive Board recommends that this invitation be accepted.

IV. BOARDS AND ELECTIVE COMMITTEES

A. In General (*Where two or more are concerned*)

1. *Effort to Stimulate Response to Apportionment*: The Executive Board adopted the following and officially brought it to the attention of all Board Secretaries:

Resolved, That the attention of all Boards be called to the importance of increasing the interest of our Synods and congregations in their response to apportionment obligations and that all Secretaries be requested to add a strong appeal that each congregation shall meet at least its full apportionment when presenting the particular causes which they represent.

2. *Combination or Reorganization of Boards*: At the organization of the United Lutheran Church in America the Joint Committee on Ways and Means, in order to provide for the prosecution of the work previously carried on by the several General Bodies with as little disturbance as possible to its continuity and effectiveness, felt itself under the necessity of recommending the creation of several Boards and Agencies to carry on the work of Home Missions. The United Lutheran Church adopted the recommendation of the Joint Committee on Ways and Means and thus five several agencies were established for the prosecution of what might properly be called the Home Mission work of the Church. (See Minutes, 1918, p. 49.)

At the same time, however, the Convention requested several of these Boards "to meet together during the interim and endeavor to arrange for the unification of their work under one Board." (See Minutes, 1918, p. 57.) Although the completion of the work of merging was committed by the Convention to the Executive Board with instructions to act (see Minutes, 1918, p. 55), which again was reaffirmed at Washington (see Minutes, 1920, p. 61), no effort was made on the part of the Executive Board to bring about such unification of the Home Mission work until there came an appeal from the West Indies Mission Board asking for a statement as to its sphere of operations. It was found that this would involve certain interests of the Board of Foreign Missions. Representatives of these two Boards met with the officers of the Executive Board for conference on this matter. No final conclusion being reached, the two Boards themselves held a further conference and adopted a resolution in which they give it as their "deliberate judgment that the question of the spheres of the activities of these two Boards could not be properly determined until the United Lutheran Church had given further consideration to the question of the reallocation of the work at present assigned to its various Boards." The Executive Board then took action instructing its Committee on Boards and Committees to begin a study of the question of the determination of the spheres of operation of the Boards and requested the Convention of the United Lutheran Church in Buffalo to instruct all Boards to give their fullest co-operation. This action of the Executive Board was approved. (See Minutes, 1922, pp. 65, 105, 108.) Also at the Buffalo Convention the Executive Board asked for instructions and power to effect a merger of Boards of the United Lutheran Church if found practicable. This request was recommitted to the Executive Board. (See Minutes, 1922, p. 111.) A resolution submitted to the Convention through the Committee of Reference and Counsel instructing the Executive Board to investigate and consider in what ways it might be possible to combine or reorganize the Boards and Committees of the United Lutheran Church so as to make the work of administration more economical and to report findings with recommendations to the next Convention was adopted. In connection with that resolution, upon suggestion of the President, the Convention also adopted the following: "Resolved, That the Executive Board be empowered to effect such mergers wherever satisfactory to the Boards concerned." (See Minutes, 1922, p. 472.)

At its meeting in May, 1923, the Committee on Boards and Committees recommended to the Executive Board the creation of a single Board to be known as the Board of American Missions of The United Lutheran Church in America. The Committee also submitted a constitution which had been drafted for the governance of such Board. This constitution will be found in the Minutes of the Executive Board for May 9, 1923. The Board took no action except that it authorized the Committee on Boards and Committees to call, at the earliest convenience, a conference of representatives of the Boards which would be affected and to present this matter to such representatives.

Such a conference was held in the Church of the Holy Trinity, New York, October 23, 1923. At this conference were present, besides the Committee on Boards and Committees, the following Boards: Board of Home Missions and Church Extension, Northwestern Mission Board, Immigrants Mission Board, West Indies Mission Board and the Jewish Mission Committee. The following action was taken which was reported to the Executive Board and approved: We recommend that each of the five agencies here represented be requested to appoint a committee of three members to act in conjunction with the Committee on Boards and Committees in the further consideration of the question of merging.

It is proper to state that the constitution that had been drafted by the Committee on Boards and Committees did not seem to commend itself to the Boards. In fairness it may also be said that doubt was expressed as to the wisdom of the proposed merger and that there were some who expressed themselves very strongly in that sense.

During the next three months the matter dragged slowly along. On February 14, 1924, the Committee on Boards and Committees reported to the Executive Board that it had requested the several agencies to submit for themselves a constructive plan of merger, that two of the Boards had appointed committees to confer with a view to presenting a plan for the merging of these two Boards. The Committee thought it undesirable that any two of the Home Mission agencies should merge, inasmuch as this would probably delay the larger merger which the Convention at New York in 1918 recommended and which the Convention at Buffalo also evidently had in mind. This was approved by the Executive Board. At the same time, however, the Executive Board, upon recommendation of the Committee, expressed its willingness, in case two of the Boards should wish to arrange a merger of their own, to submit the proposition to the next Convention of the United Lutheran Church.

On April 24, 1924, under the call of the Committee on Boards and Committees, a conference of representatives of the five Home Mission Boards was held at 437 Fifth Avenue, New York. As expressing the sense of this conference the following was adopted and was reported by the Committee on Boards and Committees to the meeting of the Executive Board held May 8, 1924:

(a) "There shall be a General Board of the United Lutheran Church which shall function through the synodical authorities and shall have the power of determining the general policy, and be given such general administration as may be necessary for the harmonious co-ordination of the various Home Mission interests and Church Extension work.

(b) "It was further resolved,
"That this body of representatives appoint a sub-committee of five, one from each agency of the Church, to condense into a statement the sentiment of this meeting, and to submit this to the several Boards together with a recommendation that each Board or Committee appoint not more than two men to work out a missionary policy for the work of the United Lutheran Church. This missionary policy to be submitted to the Executive Board and through it to the Chicago Convention.

"Immediately after the adjournment of the conference, the committee of five met and adopted the following:

"Your Committee reports that during the discussions, and the various opinions expressed on the resolutions adopted, it developed that the general sentiment of the members present indicated that the adoption of section 'a' is to be considered as the simplest statement of a definite principle, the policy to be worked out later as suggested in the second resolution.

"It was also definitely understood that in the administration, by the proposed General Board, of the work now carried on by the five interested Boards to be amalgamated or merged, the Church Extension work is to be included.

"It was further brought out that by 'synodical authority' is meant a specially constituted body or committee for the carrying on of the missionary work on the territory of the Synod.

"The sentiment expressed with regard to the various missionary operations now carried on by the several Boards was that their character as causes was to be carefully preserved.

"It was definitely agreed that one of the desirable objects to be attained by this plan is the stimulation and energizing of the missionary spirit in all the Synods of the United Lutheran Church in America and to encourage and promote missionary initiative and activity.

"It is to be noted that there was an inspiring unanimity of agreement on the general principles of the plan proposed."

This was received as information.

The action above quoted was subsequently considered by the several Boards, and a committee of ten, consisting of two members from each of the Boards, met in Philadelphia, July 8, 1924, and drew up a missionary policy as requested, which was reported to the Executive Board at its meeting on July 9th and 10th by the Committee on Boards and Committees. This missionary policy thus drafted is herewith submitted in full:

"Whereas, the United Lutheran Church at its Convention in Buffalo approved the instructions given by the Executive Board to its Committee on Boards and Committees to study the question of the determination of the spheres of operation of the Boards, and also instructed all Boards to give their fullest co-operation in this work (Minutes, Third Convention of U. L. C., p. 66) and

"Whereas, the Executive Board has approached the five Home Mission agencies concerning the possibilities of a reorganization of their work, and

"Whereas, the work of the Boards thus affected by such reorganization covers a distinctive field and some of the work, though restricted to the boundaries of a Synod, is, because of its nature, the obligation of the entire Church so that such reorganization demands the guarantee that each work shall be maintained as a distinctive cause that its appeal may not be lost to the Church at large, and

"Whereas, various conferences have been held resulting in the Boards concerned appointing a Committee of Ten to formulate a policy under which the work now being done by the five Boards might be reorganized without loss to the causes represented,

"Be it resolved, that we present to the Executive Board the following suggestions:

"(1) There shall be a General Board of the United Lutheran Church which shall function through the synodical authorities and shall have the power of determining the general policy and shall be given such general administration as may be necessary for the harmonious co-ordination of the various Home Mission interests and Church Extension work.

"(2) This Board shall be organized according to Article XIII, Sections 1 to 6 of the Constitution of the United Lutheran Church, and it shall have charge of the mission operations in the Western Hemisphere.

"(3) The Constituent Synods, under the direction and authority of the General Board, shall have charge of the missionary operations and Church Extension work on their territory, carrying on the same through a specially constituted body or committee chosen by the Synod for this purpose. Missions not organically related to a Constituent Synod shall be under the control of the General Board of the United Lutheran Church until such time as a Constituent Synod shall be organized.

"(4) This Board shall have as a special object the stimulation and energizing of a missionary spirit in all the Constituent Synods of the United Lutheran Church in America and the encouragement and promotion of synodical missionary initiative and activity.

"(5) This Board shall be charged with the promotion of new work, especially in such localities as may not be covered by Constituent Synods, and shall for the sake of preserving the several causes as causes of the entire United Lutheran Church, and of promoting their growth, call general secretaries, qualified by special knowledge of the cause which they represent, who shall advise with synodical mission authorities, present the various causes to the Church, and supervise the mission activities where no Synods exist, and these secretaries shall have the privilege of meeting with the General Board to present on an equality with all other interests the work of the agencies entering into this reorganization, and for the further protection and development of the causes represented, this Board shall have the power to departmentalize its work.

"(6) This Board, with the approval of the Executive Board, shall be authorized to receive advisory members from other Lutheran bodies co-operating in the work under its supervision.

"(7) Inasmuch as the Home Mission work of the United Lutheran Church would require time for a successful change from the present methods of operation to the plan proposed under the reorganization, we request the Executive Board to recommend to the United Lutheran Church that the present Home Mission agencies, known as the Board of Home Missions and Church Extension, the Northwestern Mission Board, the West Indies Mission Board, the Immigrants Mission Board and the Jewish Mission Committee, be empowered by the Convention at Chicago to adjust their work to the missionary policy here proposed, and be instructed to constitute the Board thus created by the Home Mission Board nominating six members, the Northwestern Mission Board nominating four, the West Indies Board nominating four, the Immigrants Mission Board nominating four, and the Jewish Mission Committee nominating three, which shall be submitted to the Executive Board as the twenty-one members of the new Board, and when so elected by the Executive Board shall, when a Constitution, Charter and Plan of Operation have been prepared by said Board and approved by the Executive Board, take over the work not later than January 1, 1926, and serve until the United Lutheran Church at its Convention in 1926 elects the membership of this Board according to the usual rules for election of Boards.

"(8)   In harmony with the linguistic policy adopted at Washington and in order to preserve representation of the various interests in the future, the new Board shall be charged in making its nominations to the biennial conventions to include nominations that will represent the various interests.

"(9)   The Church Extension funds now in the possession of the Boards, except such funds as are held under special conditions, shall be placed in the general fund and used without discrimination for Church Extension purposes."

The Executive Board approved suggestions (1) and (2) subject to a conference with the Board of Foreign Missions, the special reason for this being that the work of that Board in South America would be affected by the proposed new arrangement.

In place of (7) the Executive Board recommends the following as a substitute:

Inasmuch as the Home Mission work of the United Lutheran Church would require time for a successful change from the present methods of operation to the plan proposed under this reorganization, we request the Executive Board to recommend to the United Lutheran Church that the present Home Mission agencies, known as the Board of Home Missions and Church Extension, the Northwestern Mission Board, the West Indies Mission Board, the Immigrants Mission Board and the Jewish Mission Committee, be empowered by the Convention at Chicago to adjust their work to the missionary policy here proposed, and be instructed to constitute a Joint Commission by the Home Mission Board nominating six members, the Northwestern Mission Board nominating four, the West Indies Mission Board nominating four, the Immigrants Mission Board nominating four, and the Jewish Mission Committee nominating three, which shall be submitted to the Executive Board as the twenty-one members of a Joint Commission, functioning for the Boards, and when so elected by the Executive Board shall, when a Constitution, Charter and Plan of Operation have been prepared by said Joint Commission and approved by the Executive Board, take over the work not later than January 1, 1926, if possible, and serve until the United Lutheran Church at its Convention in 1926 elects the membership of this Board according to the usual rules for election of Boards.

Likewise the Board recommends the following as a substitute for 8:

In harmony with the linguistic policy adopted at Washington, and in order to preserve representation of the various interests as necessary, in the future, the new Board shall be charged, in making its nominations to the biennial conventions, to include nominations that will represent the various interests.

With these slight changes the proposition and plan receives the approval of the Executive Board and is recommended to this Convention of The United Lutheran Church in America.

3. *The Visitation of Synods by Board Secretaries, etc.* (See III, A, 4.)

4. *Concerning Church Extension Funds:*

(a) In November, 1922, the Board of Northwestern Missions, having before it "many urgent and legitimate requests for loans" which that Board found itself unable to entertain because of lack of Church Extension funds, took action requesting the aid of the Executive Board in approaching the Board of Home Missions and Church Extension with a view to making the Church Extension funds of the latter Board available for congregations under the jurisdiction of the Board of Northwestern Missions. At the same time the Northwestern Mission Board authorized its Executive Committee to take whatever steps might be found necessary in the premises.

The Executive Board through its Committee on Boards and Committees approached the Board of Home Missions and Church Extension with reference to two needy and worthy missions under the jurisdiction of the Board of Northwestern Missions, giving an itemized statement of the membership, finances and amount of loan required, with reference to each of the mission congregations. As a result the Board of Home Missions agreed to grant a loan of $5000 to satisfy a mortgage upon the church property at Edmonton, Alberta, Canada, provided the application should come to them in regular form. The Board of Home Missions and Church Extension further agreed to grant a loan of $5000 to the mission in Guttenberg, Iowa, also under the jurisdiction of the Northwestern Mission Board, with the understanding that a first mortgage on the property should be given them.

(b) In the spring of 1923 at a conference of a special committee of the Board of Northwestern Missions with the officers of the Church, it was discovered that the financial conditions of the said board were embarassing and the committee asked that some relief be provided.

Upon the suggestion of the officers, the Executive Board requested the Board of Home Missions and Church Extension to take over, from the Board of Northwestern Missions, certain extension loans amounting to about $20,000, which would return that sum to the treasury of the Board of Northwestern Missions and make it available for current expenses. The Executive Board has received no information of compliance with this request.

5. *Port Work Transferred:* The port work, so important in connection with immigration, was temporarily placed in the hands of the Immigrants Mission Board subject to final arrangements with the officers of the Church. There was some misunderstanding as to the exact character and scope of these operations. The Immigrants Mission Board, however, operated to the best of its ability, especially when consideration is given to that Board's lack of funds for such work.

After conference of the officers with the Boards concerned and with individuals, it was recommended that the Inner Mission Board be requested to take present charge of the port work, the officers of the Church continuing a watchful interest in the development thereof. The Inner Mission Board was thus recommended because such work is quite generally regarded as a part of Inner Mission activity and because that Board seemed in a better position financially to take charge of this work. Full understanding was reached with the Inner Mission Board that the activities must have regard for the chief ports of entry, other United States ports, Canadian interests, information to pastors at the destination of immigrants, care for those immigrants in whom the Immigrants Mission Board is especially interested, and helpful contacts with European operations of a similar character.

The Executive Board recommends your approval of this arrangement for the present.

B—In Particular

1—*Foreign Mission Board:*

(a) In view of the fact that an appeal of the National Lutheran Council for world service was approved, which appeal was set for the early part of the year 1924, the Executive Board requested the Board of Foreign Missions to bring to a close its special appeal for $300,000, to remove the deficit of their current fund and extend their work in the mission field, on or before December 31, 1923.

(b) The Executive Board, upon request of the Board of Foreign Missions, gave its approval to a special appeal for Japan Earthquake Relief.

(c) Vacancy filled: On nomination of the Board Paul Van Reed Miller, Esq., was elected ad interim to fill a vacancy in this Board.

2—*Board of Home Missions and Church Extension:*

(a) In accordance with the recommendation of the Committee on Proceedings of Constituent Synods (see Minutes 1922 p. 424) the work among the Siebenburgers was transferred by the Executive Board from the jurisdiction of the Immigrants Mission Board to the Board of Home Missions and Church Extension.

(b) The following statement of policy concerning co-operation with other Lutheran bodies was submitted by the Board of Home Missions and Church Extension and received the approval of the Executive Board:

Whereas, in our Home Mission Work, a number of instances calling for adjustment or co-operation with other Lutheran Bodies have arisen,

Whereas, the United Lutheran Church has left the details of such a policy of adjustment and co-operation with the Board,

Whereas, the Board of Home Missions and Church Extension as a result of this action has a standing Committee on Co-operation with other Lutheran Bodies,

Whereas, it is very desirable that a uniform policy be adopted for the approach of all instances demanding adjustment or co-operation, therefore

Resolved, That the Board favors the appointment of synodical sub-committees subject to the Board's Committee on Co-operation with other Lutheran Bodies.

The Executive Board recommends the approval of the same by this convention.

(c) Vacancies filled: The following were duly elected ad interim to fill vacancies in the Board of Home Missions and Church Extension: Mr. A. Raymond Bard, Mr. G. F. Greiner, Mr. John F. Kramer, Prof. S. J. Derrick.

3—Northwestern Mission Board:

Upon recommendation of the Finance Committee the income from the Sotter Fund of nearly $10,000 (see Minutes 1922, p. 94) was appropriated to the Northwestern Mission Board for the year 1923.

4—Immigrants Mission Board:

(a) In accordance with the action of the Buffalo Convention the Executive Board called attention of the Immigrants Mission Board to the problem of undertaking missionary operations among the Asiatics on the Pacific Coast. That Board replied that no work could be taken up by it for the present because of lack of funds.

(b) There was reported to the Executive Board in December, 1922, that there existed some misunderstanding between the Immigrants Mission Board and the Synodical Board of Missions of the Ministerium of Pennsylvania relative to supervision of the Italian mission work in the city of Philadelphia, formerly established and maintained by the Ministerium of Pennsylvania but latterly yielded, by action of the Ministerium, to the direct oversight of the Immigrants Mission Board. The Executive Board was asked to define the relation of the Italian work to the Ministerium of Pennsylvania. The Board took action as follows:

Concerning the relation of the Italian Mission Work in Philadelphia to the Home Mission Board of the Ministerium of Pennsylvania, the Executive Board regards as ideal the relationship existing between the Home Mission and Church Extension Board of the United Lutheran Church and the Synodical Mission Boards and would recommend a similar relationship on the part of the Immigrants Mission Board.

(c) Vacancies filled: Mr. Grant Hultberg and Mr. J. Ruzicka were elected ad interim to fill vacancies in this Board.

5—*West Indies Mission Board:*

(a) The material of a comprehensive survey of Negro work in the United States, prepared by the Executive Secretary of the West Indies Mission Board, was referred to the Executive Board by the Buffalo Convention with authority to publish such parts of the survey as might be considered helpful in arousing and informing the Church upon this subject. In view of the proposed merger of home mission agencies of the United Lutheran Church, which would materially affect the solution of this problem, the Executive Board thought it best to defer action for the present.

(b) Vacancies filled: On nomination of this Board the Rev. Dr. W. D. C. Keiter and G. E. Neff, Esq., were duly elected to fill vacancies which occurred ad interim.

6—*Board of Education:*

(a) At the request of this Board permission was given to circularize Kropp and Breklum graduates in this country for special gifts for those institutions.

(b) Vacancy filled: Wm. J. Showalter, Sc. D,. was duly elected ad interim to fill a vacancy in this Board.

7—*Inner Mission Board:*

(a) The report on lay service in the Church adopted by the Buffalo Convention (Minutes, pp. 99-104) was referred to the Inner Mission Board with the request that they give practical effect to the recommendations in that report as far as possible.

(b) Vacancies filled: The Reverends J. J. Scherer, Jr., and F. B. Clausen were elected to fill vacancies in this board.

8—*Board of Publication:*

Vacancy filled: Mr. Otto W. Osterlund was elected to fill a vacancy in this board.

9—*Board of Ministerial Relief:*

(a) The Committee on Boards and Committees held a conference with a special committee of the Board of Ministerial Relief to discuss the time for the campaign for a $3,000,000 endowment for that board, which was authorized by the United Lutheran Church in Convention at Buffalo. It was agreed by all that the firm establishment and development of our apportionment system is most important at the present time to the welfare of the Church and that nothing should be done by any of the boards that would interfere with this endeavor. An agreement was reached which was reported to the Board of Ministerial Relief by its own special committee and to the Executive Board by its Committee.

The terms of this agreement as adopted by the Executive Board are as follows:

(1) That no other campaign shall be authorized prior to the one of the Board of Ministerial Relief.

(2) That it shall be made to mark the tenth anniversary of the organization of the United Lutheran Church, and

(3) That a period of one year preceding said anniversary and six months succeeding shall be given to the Board for campaign purposes.

The Executive Board recommends the adoption of this by the Convention.

(b) The Executive Board was requested by the Board of Ministerial Relief to approve the change of its corporate title to "Board of Ministerial Pensions and Relief of the United Lutheran Church in America." The request seemed to be based upon an interpretation of the words "Pensions" and "Relief" as used by this board in the administration of its work, the interpretation being that the two forms of help represented by these two terms are essentially different.

This request is reported to the Convention with the recommendation that it be not granted.

(c) Vacancy filled: Mr. Peter Hagan was duly elected to fill a vacancy in this board.

10—*Parish and Church-School Board:*

(a) The Executive Committee of the Parish and Church-School Board requested consent of the Executive Board to the establishment by said Parish and Church-School Board of a relationship with the International Sunday School Council of Religious Education. The Parish and Church-School Board could not report itself as satisfied with the method of organization and representation of this Council. Accordingly the Executive Board took the following action:

"Whereas, the Parish and Church School Board has made certain presentations and requests with respect to its work and its relations to the International Sunday School Council of Religious Education;

"Therefore, (1) Resolved, that we approve the existing relationship which consists in membership on the International Lesson Committee;

"(2) *Resolved,* That any further relationships for the development of our general educational program and the safeguarding of the spiritual welfare of our constituency shall require the approval of the Executive Board before established by the Parish and Church-School Board.

"(3) *Resolved,* That they use their influence to correct any irregularity in the organization of the Council so that the principle of proper representation shall be preserved.

"(4) *Resolved,* That while agreeing to Resolution 1, we request the Parish and Church-School Board to use its influence against promiscuous affiliation with general organizations and the use of literature not immediately prepared or promoted by our own Parish and Church School Board;

"(5) *Resolved,* That we suggest to the Parish and Church-School Board as rapidly as possible to develop and provide adequate literature for Sunday Schools, Week-Day Schools and Daily Vacation Bible Schools, which in method and content is in complete harmony with Lutheran teaching and practice."

The Executive Board also authorized the Parish and Church-School Board to appoint a Friendly Visitor on the Committee of Week-Day Religious Education of the Council. The Board recommends the approval of this action.

(b) A question was raised by the Parish and Church-School Board as to the spheres of authority of that Board and the Common Service Book Committee in regard to the matter of the preparation of Sunday School Hymnals. Committees representing these two agencies respectively were convened under the auspices of the Committee on Boards and Committees and agreed upon the following statement which was approved by the Executive Board:

"The action of the United Lutheran Church establishes the principle of joint responsibility by the Parish and Church-School Board and the Common Service Book Committee in the matter of determining the character and approving the details of Sunday School Hymnals.

"The duty of initiative and active preparation is committed to the Parish and Church-School Board, limited by the specific requirement of 'consultation with the Common Service Book Committee' whose general authority 'in all matters pertaining to the worship of the Church' is thus recognized, with the specific authority in the matter of Sunday School Hymnals as an item definitely 'referred to it by the Church.' (Min. 3d Convention, p. 293).

"The question is, therefore, one of method. In the interest of successful co-operation and best results, it is agreed that preliminary plans covering the scope, character, arrangement and general contents of a Sunday School Hymnal or Hymnals and with respect to services and hymns and their music shall be prepared by a sub-committee of the Parish and Church-School Board and discussed in full with a sub-committee of the Common Service Book Committee.

"The details of the plan which may jointly be agreed upon shall then be completed by the sub-commitee of the Parish and Church-School Board in occasional consultation with the sub-committee of the Common Service Book Committee and after agreement by the joint sub-committee shall be submitted to the Parish and Church-School Board and the Common Service Book Committee meeting in joint or separate session as may later be determined."

This is recommended to the Convention for adoption.

(c) A request that it be recognized as the function of the Parish and Church-School Board to supervise all programs for use in the schools of the United Lutheran Church was answered by the following action: That in the preparation of special programs for use in the Sunday schools the several boards confer with the Parish and Church-School Board.

(d) Vacancy filled: Prof. Gilbert P. Voigt was elected ad interim to fill a vacancy in this board.

11—*Board of Deaconess Work:*

(a) A request of the Deaconess Board that Septuagesima Sunday of each year be appointed as a day for special appeal by pastors for the enlistment of candidates for the deaconess calling was answered by the Executive Board as follows: "In order to avoid a multiplication of special days we recommend that the Deaconess Board seek co-operation with the Board of Education in the matter of a general appeal concerning life callings."

(b) Vacancy filled: Rev. J. F. Crigler was elected ad interim to fill a vacancy in this board.

12—*Board of the National Lutheran Home for the Aged:*

(a) The relation of this institution to the United Lutheran Church has not yet been determined.

(b) Vacancy filled: Mr. Harry L. Snyder was elected ad interim to fill a vacancy in this board.

13—*Laymen's Movement:*

(a) In accordance with the provisions of the Constitution of the Laymen's Movement adopted at Buffalo (see Min., p. 111) the President, with the approval of the Executive Board, appointed as members of the Executive Committee, Treasurer E. Clarence Miller, Mr. H. C. Miller, Mr. W. H. Hager, Mr. F. Henrich, Hon. J. L. Zimmerman and as members of the Administrative Committee, Treasurer E. Clarence Miller, Mr. H. C. Miller and Mr W. H. Hager.

(b) The Executive Board has authorized the Every Member Canvass by the Laymen's Movement for this fall, has instructed the Laymen's Movement to seek the co-operation of synodical commiteees in the development of the canvass, and approved the publication of a booklet, as has been done for several years, with the request that all boards co-operate in the preparation of material and in the bearing of expenses.

The Executive Board asks authority of the Convention to have issued annually, in connection with the Every Member Canvass, a booklet, such as has been previously issued, descriptive of the work of such boards as it believes should be included, the expense to be borne proportionately by these boards.

(c) In order to aid the Every Member Canvas conducted by the Laymen's Movement the Executive Board recommends the adoption of the following resolution:

Resolved, First, That in view of the great importance of securing full information governing the annual Every Member Canvass, all pastors and church officials be urged to make prompt and full reply to all official communications addressed to them by the Laymen's Movement of the United Lutheran Church.

Second, That the passing of a similar resolution and the planning of means necessary to assure prompt replies to such communications be commended to the Constituent Synods.

(d) The Laymen's Movement was requested to take into consideration the support of such students, as are not otherwise provided for, upon recommendation from the President of The United Lutheran Church in America.

C—STANDING COMMITTEES

1—Common Service Book Committee:

Its part in the preparation of Sunday School Hymnals. (See IV, B, 10, b).

2—Committee on Evangelism:

Suggestions of the inauguration of a campaign whereby the indifferent in our Church membership might be reclaimed and the faith which we confess might be set before the unchurched were referred to the Committee on Evangelism by the Executive Board with an expression of a deep conviction of the vital importance of this matter to the life and work of the Church. Special emphasis was laid upon the importance of providing suitable literature on this subject for our pastors and people. The Committee on Evangelism actively assumed the responsibility laid upon them and labored diligently in the prosecution of its task, at the same time exercising great care to guard the Church against the dangers which might easily arise in connection with the emphasis which it gave to the subject of evangelism.

3—Women's Missionary Society:

(a) The Executive Board records its appreciation of an appropriation of $2,000 per annum for two years to the Inner Mission Board by the Women's Missionary Society of the United Lutheran Church, the special object being to assist in the port work under the direction of the Inner Mission Board.

Subject to the approval of the Executive Board this Society appropriated $10,000 for the Margaret Mehring Annuity toward the establishment of a mountain school in Virginia to be known as the "Margaret Mehring School." The Society also included in its budget sufficient funds for the maintenance of the work to be paid through the Inner Mission Board.

The Executive Board cordially gave its approval to this new line of work and rejoices in the wide and helpful view which the Women's Missionary Society takes of its sphere of operations.

(b) Upon petition to the Executive Board for consent to closer counsel and co-operation between the Women's Missionary Societies of the various Lutheran bodies in America, the Board expressed its appreciation of the loyalty of the Women's Missionary Society to the organized work of the United Lutheran Church and answered their petition with its approval.

(c) In connection with the Lutheran World Convention at Eisenach the group of Lutheran women there assembled met to consider the possibility of forming an international committee which shall include the Lutheran women's groups all over the world. Those present assumed the responsibility of carrying this message to their own home groups, asking them to appoint from their number one who shall represent them in this international committee. Where the women's groups are already organized, as is the case in America, it was agreed that such a representative might be nominated by her own board; and it was recommended that, where no organized group exists, a committee of about fifteen women be selected who shall choose one of their number to represent them. The following preliminary resolutions were adopted by the women assembled at Eisenach.

To select a small working committee from those here assembled to help to form the basis for an international committee of Lutheran women which shall include the Lutheran women's groups in every country.

To select a committee in every country to inaugurate a movement to establish relations between Lutheran women's groups in all lands. These committees shall select their members for the standing international committee.

The task of this international committee shall be to call together the Lutheran women of all countries for a gathering in connection with the next Lutheran World Convention.

The Executive Board of our Women's Missionary Society accepted these preliminary resolutions and reported their action to the Executive Board of the United Lutheran Church.

The Executive Board of the United Lutheran Church approved this step on the part of the Women's Missionary Society, instructing them, however, to take no steps whatsoever excepting in conference with the Committee which plans the next Lutheran World Convention.

4. *Committee on Army and Navy Work*:

(a) Having been officially notified by the President of the Ministerium of Pennsylvania of an action of that body concerning the discontinuance by it of the work at League Island Navy Yard and provision made whereby work might be taken up and carried forward by the proper agency of the United Lutheran Church, the Executive Board requested the Committee on Army and Navy Work to make every effort to resume the work at League Island Navy Yard.

(b) The special appropriation of $4,500 for Army and Navy Work authorized by the United Lutheran Church at Buffalo (see Minutes, 1922, page 131) was paid in full to the Committee.

5. *Boys' Work Committee*:

The resolution of the Buffalo Convention, requesting the Executive Board to reserve for the use of this Committee the sum of $2,000, together with a ruling of the President to the effect that the resolution would practically mean that the Executive Board should grant the amount asked if the state of the treasury would permit (see Minutes, 1922, p. 296), was referred by the Executive Board to the Finance Committee. The expenses incurred by the Boys' Work Committee have been paid, as have the expenses of other committees, on order of the President and Secretary.

6. *Committee on Associations of Young People*:

The Committee on Associations of Young People requested the Executive Board to set apart the Sunday nearest to Luther's birthday as Young People's Day. It was proposed that the Luther League of America provide and distribute a program to be used at the evening service of the churches and that the offering received at said service be given to the Luther League of America. In regard to this request the Executive Board took the following action:

That the Church has already set apart the Reformation Season for a presentation of the cause of Home Missions;

That the Executive Board has no authority delegated to it to set apart days for such special purposes and offerings; the Church in Convention should act upon such request;

That, having knowledge of the fact that the Luther League in America is aiming to secure a number of sustaining members whose contributions are to further the purposes of the League, we strongly endorse this effort.

7—*Committee on Publicity:*

(a) Inasmuch as we have two agencies for the service of our Church in the matter of publicity, namely, our standing Committee on Publicity and the Publicity Department of the National Lutheran Council, the Committee on Boards and Committees was requested to undertake the co-ordination or harmonious adjustment of these two agencies. Both of these agencies showed a readiness in every way to meet the desire of the Church. With the sole intention to secure the best possible publicity for the Chicago Convention by the co-ordination of these agencies under a direction with means and facilities for effective service, the Executive Board, upon recommendation of its Committee, adopted the following:

That for the publicity purposes of the Chicago Convention the heads of these two publicity agencies be requested to establish a partnership in the direction of these operatinos.

That the Executive Director of the National Lutheran Council be given the general direction of these operations with authority.

That in the matter of expenses consultation be held with the officers of the Church.

(b) A suggestion that during the Convention a daily bulletin be printed was submitted for consideration to those in charge of the matter of publicity.

8—*Archivist:*

For documents and materials forwarded to the Archives, see report of the Archivist.

9—*Statistical Secretary*:

The Reverend G. L. Kieffer was re-elected by the Board as Statistical Secretary for the term of two years at a salary of $500 per annum.

10—*Transportation Committee:*

(a) Upon the recommendation of this Committee the Executive Board requested the Chairman of the Committee to inform Presidents of all Constituent Synods, Secretaries of Boards and others concerned that, in the interest of better transportation facilities, the Executive Board earnestly desires that all persons seeking passes apply for them through the Transportation Committee of the United Lutheran Church.

(b) In accordance with action of the Executive Board, the Rev. John M. Bramkamp, of Chicago, was appointed by the President as an additional member of the Committee on Transportation and was appointed by the Committee as Transportation Secretary for the West. Dr. Bramkamp accepted his appointment and has been active in the service of the Church.

(c) Under instruction of the Executive Board a sub-committee of the Committee on Transportation took up, in the spring of 1923, with the Federal Council of Churches, the question of a co-operative effort to secure annual passes in a limited number from the eastern railroads. Several conferences were held under the auspices of the Federal Council and were attended by transportation representatives of a number of the larger denominations, including our own United Lutheran Church. It was agreed that a special effort should be made and in the fall of 1923 a small committee was appointed to lay the matter before the railroad authorities. As yet we have had no report from that committee.

V.   INSTITUTIONS

1—*Saskatoon Seminary:*

The Convention at Buffalo having approved of the recommendations of the Board of Education concerning provision of funds for the completion of the Saskatoon Seminary and having authorized the Executive Board to arrange for the funds immediately necessary (see Min. 1922, p. 504), the Executive Board made a loan of $5,000 to this institution soon after the Convention. The Board of Education undertook to secure through the synods, gifts from the congregations to make up the amount of this loan. Within a few months $3,500 had been returned to the treasury leaving $1,500 still due on the loan. The necessities of the Saskatoon Institution, because of their building operations, being very great they appealed for a reloan of $2,500 of the $3,500 which they had paid back. Since it was learned, that, subsequent to the request for an additional loan of $2,500, the Board of Education had remitted about $1,000 to the Saskatoon Institution, the Executive Board authorized its officers to reloan $1,500 provided promise of repayment during the present biennium be made.

2—Chicago Seminary:

The Chicago Seminary reported to the Executive Board its readiness to arrange in 1924 to have its directors chosen from such synods of the United Lutheran Church as are ready to assume and promote the moral and financial trust now committed to the Board of said Seminary. It was further asked that the Executive Board request said synods to appoint committees which shall in conjunction with the Board of Directors of the Seminary formulate plans by which the directors from the various synods may be elected.

The Executive Board requested its President to act on its behalf for the ends above stated. On April 19, 1923, the President held an informal conference at Cleveland, Ohio, with the Presidents of the Illinois, Indiana, Michigan, Northwest, Ohio and Pittsburgh Synods, which synods are now represented on the Board of Directors of the Chicago Seminary.

As a result of that conference and with the concurrence of the synodical Presidents mentioned President Knubel reported to the Executive Board that there seemed to be a reasonable hope that sufficient synodical consent might be secured in order to carry out the readiness expressed by the Board of Directors of the Chicago Seminary. For this purpose it did not seem desirable to approach formally the Ohio and Pittsburgh Synods for the appointment of committees to confer with the Chicago Seminary Board. The Executive Board might, however, so approach the Illinois Synod; similarily a request might be addressed to the Indiana and Michigan Synods, asking the appointment of such a committee, the understanding being that any ultimate formal relationship of those synods to the Chicago Seminary is not to interfere with their former relationship to Wittenberg College and Hamma Divinity School. A request might likewise be addressed to the Synod of the Northwest for an expression of its good will and the appointment of a committee to confer on that basis.

The Executive Board thereupon took the following action:

Resolved, That we approve of the steps so far taken, but believe that the point has now been reached when any further steps should be taken by the Chicago Seminary Board itself and that we report to said Board that as a result of the recent conference held in Cleveland, Ohio, it is our judgment that the Chicago Seminary Board might now properly approach such contiguous synods as they may think likely to co-operate with them, leaving it to these synods to determine their relation to the Chicago Seminary.

This action was promptly communicated to the Board of Directors of the Chicago Seminary by the Secretary.

The following letter was received from the Secretary of the Board of Directors and submitted to the Executive Board at its meeting October 24, 1923:

October 16, 1923.

The Rev. M. G. G. Scherer, D.D.,
    437 Fifth Avenue,
        New York City.
Dear Sir and Brother:

Replying to your communication of May 18th in re the matter of synodical control of the Chicago Seminary, would say that the Board of Directors of the Seminary at the meeting on October 3d passed the following action:

"*Resolved,* That we reply to the Executive Board of the United Lutheran Church and restate our willingness to co-operate as per our action of April, 1922, and that we again suggest that we are ready to receive overtures from such synods as are ready to assume the necessary moral and financial obligations and that the Executive Committee is hereby authorized to receive any such overtures."

On motion it was further resolved, to send a copy of this report to the synods mentioned in your report of May 18th.

An additional resolution was also passed that copies should be sent to the Ohio and Pittsburgh Synods as a matter of information and courtesy.

Permit me here to restate the action of April, 1922:

"*Resolved,* That the Chicago Seminary accepts the principle enunciated by the United Lutheran Church in America at its convention at Washington

"*Resolved,* That according to the action of the Executive Board, the Chicago Seminary is ready in 1924 to have its directors chosen from such synods of the United Lutheran Church as are ready and willing to assume and promote the moral and financial trust now committed to the Board of Directors of said Seminary.

"*Resolved,* That in order properly to consummate this change in the policy of our institution, we suggest that the Executive Board of the United Lutheran Church in America request said synods to appoint commitees, which in conjunction with the Board of Directors of the Seminary shall formulate plans by which the directors of the various synods may be elected. I might state that the board regretted exceedingly that your communication was too late for action at the spring meeting.

Very sincerely,
(Signed) J. ALLEN LEAS,
Secretary.

The Executive Board then took the following action: *Resolved,* That we note the fact that the Board of Directors of the Chicago Seminary has sent a copy of its action, as given in the letter of October 16, 1923, to the synods concerned, and that we regard the matter thereby concluded.

3—*Pacific Seminary:* (See III, B, 3)

4—*National Lutheran Home for the Aged:* (See IV, B, 12)

5—*Feghtley Home:*

The title to this institution is vested in the General Synod which body elected directors at its last meeting. The question as to whether or not the title might be transferred by the General Synod to one of the Constituent Synods of the United Lutheran Church was referred to the Legal Committee of the Executive Board and the General Synod was instructed to take, at its meeting in Chicago, action upon this matter for the guidance of the Legal Committee.

VI.   CO-ORDINATIONS

1—*Of Agencies Working With the Children and Young People of the Church:*

After numerous conferences of representatives of the Women's Missionary Society, the Luther League and the Parish and Church-School Board, an agreement was reached which was submitted to the Executive Board in the following form:

"Whereas, It is our judgment that the work of the Luther League and that of the Women's Missionary Society are of a different character in the development of their programs, Therefore, Be It Resolved, That we request the Executive Board of the United Lutheran Church to permit the work among the children in the United Lutheran Church to remain in statu quo for the time being and a committee be appointed of equal representation from the Parish and Church-School Board, the Women's Missionary Society and the Luther League by the respective agencies to co-ordinate programs.

"Young People: The Young People's question having been definitely and conclusively settled when the United Lutheran Church in America made the Luther League of America its official young people's organization, the Luther League of America at the same time realizing the need of young women's missionary societies therefore waives its right to dispute the question of the missionary training of the young women, there really existing no conflict between the young women's missionary societies and Luther League, and the Women's Missionary Society waives the right that is given to it by its Constitution to organize Young People's Societies and in accord with the policy of co-ordination reports that it has changed its Young People's Department to Young Women's Department."

In connection with these statements the conference adopted also the following:

"That we have in this paper a basis which, while not entirely satisfactory, may be accepted as a basis on the lines of which the two organizations may seek to reach a complete understanding and solution of the problem of work with the children and young people."

As a matter of interpretation the committee agreed by the words "in statu quo" it is to be understood that the field of the Light Brigade is from birth to confirmation; that the Women's Missionary Society is at liberty to work among girls and young women of any age, and that the Luther League is at liberty to continue its work through its Junior, Intermediate and Senior Departments, train its members in accordance with the constitution of its several departments.

The Executive Board approved of these propositions and directed the President of the Parish and Church-School Board to call the committee together and put the plans agreed upon into operation as soon as possible.

2. In relation to the preparation of Sunday School Hymnals. (See IV, B, 10).

VII. FINANCE

1. In accordance with the instructions of the United Lutheran Church the Treasurer has given bond in the sum of $50,000, with the United States Fidelity and Guaranty Company of Baltimore, Md., as security.

2—Auditors:

The firm of Lybrand, Ross Brothers and Montgomery was appointed as Auditors of the Boards for the years 1923 and 1924.

3—Budget:

(a) The Executive Board submits the following budget for the years 1926 and 1927:

Board of	Amount	Percentage
Foreign Missions	$600,000	30.00
Home Missions and Church Extension	538,000	26.90
Northwestern Missions	75,000	3.75
Immigrants Missions	52,000	2.60
West Indies Missions	77,000	3.85
Jewish Missions	19,000	.95
Education	175,000	8.75
Parish and Church School	17,000	.85
Inner Missions	25,000	1.25
Ministerial Relief	235,000	11.75
Deaconess Work	42,000	2.10
National Home for the Aged	20,000	1.00
Tabitha Home	13,000	.65
Lowman Home	4,000	.20
National Lutheran Council	23,000	1.15
American Bible Society	5,000	.25
United Lutheran Church Treasury	80,000	4.00
	$2,000,000	100.00

4. The Board recommends the adoption of the following as a standing resolution:

Resolved, That the Convention shall not finally vote appropriations in addition to and above those budgeted until they have first been referred to the Budget Committee for report to the Convention.

5—*Concerning uniformity of method in division of apportionment funds:*

Believing it to be highly important that uniformity of method obtain among our synods in their division of apportionment funds as between the synod and the United Lutheran Church, that the same basis of good faith and fairness may prevail, the Executive Board recommends:

(a)   That each of the synods be requested to prepare annually a budget which shall include all payments to be made by it; and that money received for the joint budgets of synod and the United Lutheran Church be proportionately divided between them.

(b)   That where any department of work of a synod is under the supervision of one of the Boards of the United Lutheran Church and supported by it, no additional place be given on the budget of the synod.

6.   The Board recommends that the United Lutheran Church authorize its Treasurer to make such payments on behalf of boards as have been or shall be approved by it, whenever such payments have not been made by the boards themselves, and to deduct same from the apportionment distributions to boards.

7—*The Sotter Trust:*

With the approval of the Executive Board $3,000.00 Constantin Refining Company First Mortgage Bonds belonging to the Sotter Trust (see Min. 1922, p. 94) have been exchanged for $3,000 Altoona & Logan Valley First Mortgage 4½'s.

8—*The Swygert Fund:*

Hon. C. M. Efird, Treasurer of the Southern Lutheran Theological Seminary handed to the Treasurer of the United Lutheran Church a certified copy of the decree of the Court of Common Pleas of the County of Richland, State of South Carolina, appointing the said Seminary as the new trustee for the S. C. Swygert bequest. Accordingly the Treasurer delivered to the said Seminary the investments and all papers belonging to said Trust.

The Executive Board approved of this action.

9—*The Cover Fund:*

Likewise Judge Efird presented a decree from the Virginia Court appointing the Bank of Salem, Va., as trustee for the Cover Fund and requested that the Treasurer transmit this fund to the newly appointed trustee.   In accordance with instructions of the Executive Board, the Treasurer stated all the securities and cash belonging to the Cover Trust were delivered to the Bank of Salem, Va., and took a proper receipt.

10.   The Executive Board recommends that the offerings taken at this Convention be given to the Board of Ministerial Relief.

VIII. NATIONAL LUTHERAN COUNCIL

1. The Executive Board approved of an appeal to the churches by the National Lutheran Council for $1,500,000 for World Service and designated the early part of the year 1924 for such an appeal.

2. Our Commission to the National Lutheran Council reported that at its meeting in Pittsburgh in January, 1924, the Council had taken action concerning the publication of the Lutheran World Almanac. It was decided (a) That it be given the character of a condensed book of reference, giving summarized facts concerning the Lutheran Church in America and in the world. (b) That it be issued biennially, provided approximately $5000 to cover probable deficit be assumed by publication houses or by the general bodies themselves, in the form of an addition to the budget.

When it had been ascertained that the Publication Boards were not willing to assume the responsibility in view of the fact that a sufficient number of advance subscriptions could not be secured to insure publication without a serious deficit, a meeting of the Budget Committee of the Council was held and the Executive Director of the National Lutheran Council was instructed to appoint a Committee on Almanac, with himself as chairman, and appeal to the general bodies for a subsidy sufficient to make possible the issuance of the Lutheran World Almanac.

The request for a subsidy was for one year only.

The Executive Board took action acceding to the request up to the stipulated amount, on condition that care be given, as the Council itself directed, to the condensed character of the book and, on the further condition, that this subsidy is to provide merely for any lack in the publishing cost of the book and not for the editing thereof.

3. *Correction*:

In the Minutes of the Buffalo Convention (page 456) a cablegram was reported as having been received from Dr. Larsen. This cablegram was forwarded to Buffalo from the office of the National Lutheran Council with the statement that it came from Dr. Larsen who was then in Russia. It was discovered later that the cablegram was sent by the Rev. W. L. Scheding who was also in Russia in the service of the National Lutheran Council.

IX. RELATIONS WITH OTHER LUTHERAN CHURCH BODIES IN AMERICA

The Rev. J. A. Singmaster was appointed as official visitor to the Augustana Synod in 1923, and the Rev. F. G. Gotwald to the Augustana and Icelandic Synods in 1924. They reported that they had been most cordially received and given assurances of appreciation of the friendly relations manifested by the United Lutheran Church.

X. LUTHERAN WORLD CONVENTION

A. *Arrangements*:

The Joint Committee on Lutheran World Convention representing several different bodies of Lutherans in America, reported to the Executive Board in February, 1923, that the Convention would meet at Eisenach in Thuringia, August 20th to 26th, of that year. That a call for the meeting had been issued, signed by the Presidents of the National Lutheran Council and the Allgemeine Konferenz. This call was sent to all the Lutheran Church bodies in America, those outside the National Lutheran Council as well as those within it. The representation of American bodies was fixed at one for every 100,000 communicants, the European representation at approximately one for every 500,000 baptized members, making the membership of the Convention 175 to 200. The European invitations were issued, not to Churches, but to individuals and free organizations. Invitations were extended to representative men in the following countries: (1) Germany, including the following States: Bavaria, Brunswick, Bremen, Hamburg, Hanover, Hesse, Danzig, Hesse-Nassau, Luebeck, Oldenburg, Saxony, Schleswig-Holstein, Schwerin, Strelitz, Thuringia, Wurttemberg; a few invitations also in Prussia; (2) Czecho-Slovakia, (3) Jugo-Slavia, (4) Hungary, (5) Rumania, (6) Austria, (7) Poland, (8) Lithuania, (9) Latvia, (10) Esthonia, (11) Russia, (12) Finland, (13) Sweden, (14) Norway, (15) Denmark, (16) Holland, (17) France. Members were to be invited from India, China, Australia, Iceland and Brazil. It was planned that Bishop Ihmels, of Saxony, should preside over the opening session; the Presidents of other sessions to be chosen by the Convention.

A program had been tentatively fixed consisting of three chief topics, namely, (1) The Ecumenical Character of Lutheranism; (2) The Confessions as the Indispensable Basis of the Lutheran Church; (3) "That They May All Be One"—What can the Lutheran Church contribute to this end? Other subjects that were chosen for discussion were: (1) Foreign Mission Problems; (2) The Support of the Lutheran Churches by One Another; (3) The Diaspora; (4) Inner Mission Problems. It was decided that the official languages of the Convention should be German and English. At the opening of the Convention commissions were to be appointed which would frame the resolutions of the Convention on any subjects that might require such action.

This program having been adopted by the International Committee and by that of the National Lutheran Council, subject to slight modifications, was approved also by the committee of representatives of the United Lutheran Church.

Drs. J. A. Morehead and C. T. Benze were asked to act as the American representatives in the International Committee.

The National Lutheran Council was requested to advance such sums of money as might be necessary to finance the preliminary arrangements of the Convention, these sums to be repaid by the bodies participating in the ratio of their communicant membership. These requests received the approval of the Council.

As regards the selection of speakers the American Joint Committee took the following action: (1) It expressed its earnest wish that Bishop Ihmels consent to prepare the paper on the subject, "The Ecumenical Character of Lutheranism"; (2) That it urge Dr. Morehead to accept the invitation of the International Committee to speak on the subject, "The Support of the Lutheran Churches by One Another"; (3) It asked Dr. F. H. Knubel to prepare and present the paper on the subject, "That They All May Be One."

The United Lutheran Church having authorized the Executive Board to appoint representatives to attend the Lutheran World Convention and having chosen President Knubel to be the Chairman of the delegation (See Minutes, 1922, pp. 322 and 421) the Board elected eight delegates, making the complete list as follows:

Principals

Rev. F. H. Knubel, D.D., LL.D.
Rev. C. M. Jacobs, D.D.
Mr. E. Clarence Miller, LL.D.
Rev. J. A. Morehead, D.D., LL.D.
Rev. J. L. Neve, D.D.

Rev. A. G. Voigt, D.D., LL.D.
Rev. A. R. Wentz, Ph.D., D.D.
Rev. F. F. Fry, D.D.
Rev. E. Hoffman, D.D.

The following were elected as alternates, the first to serve as alternate for the first on the list of principals; the second for the second, etc.:

Alternates

Rev. M. G. G. Scherer, D.D.
Rev. H. Offerman, D.D.
Hon. F. M. Riter, LL.D.
Rev. C. T. Benze, D.D.

Rev. V. G. A. Tressler, D.D., Ph.D.
Rev. J. F. Krueger, D.D., Ph.D.
Rev. J. A. Clutz, D.D., LL.D.
Rev. E. C. J. Kraeling

The sum of $600 was fixed as a maximum amount for each of the delegates to the Lutheran World Convention and the officers of the Church were constituted a committee to adjust the amount in each case. All of the principals named attended the Convention in Eisenach.

B. *Report of Delegates:*

The report of the delegates is herewith presented in full:

As delegates we have been in doubt as to whether our report should be made directly to a Convention of the United Lutheran Church or to the Executive Board. Our appointment was authorized by the Buffalo Convention, but was made through instruction of that Convention by the Executive Board. We have decided to make report to and through the

Executive Board, especially because we believe that tentative approval by the Executive Board of the recommendations we make is desirable.

It would easily be possible for us to report at great length, describing the Lutheran World Convention and commenting upon it. However, the Washington and Buffalo Minutes of the United Lutheran Church and Minutes of the Executive Board for several of its meetings fully recorded the preliminaries of this World Convention. The Church papers have described the event itself at length. An official book of the Convention will soon be published in both the English and German languages. For these reasons we content ourselves with the following admirable judgments or impressions of the Convention, taken from an address which was made by Professor Wentz at the closing meeting.

"1. The distinct impression that the Convention by the grace of God has achieved success. Beyond the most sanguine hopes of those in whose hearts the idea of a Lutheran World Convention was born, beyond the most delightful dreams of those who have labored for years at the preparations for the convention, and beyond the fondest expectations of the great multitude of those who have been praying these days for the prosperity of the Church of the Reformation, the first Ecumenical Council of the Lutheran Church has been a success. In the number of those who accepted the invitation to attend the convention, in the high degree of unanimity with which the appointed delegates were permitted to be present in person, in the devout spirit that characterized our services of worship, in the high grade of scholarship and churchmanship that characterized the prepared addresses of the convention, in the many personal contacts that were formed and in the general spirit of brotherly love and Christian fellowship that prevailed throughout, and in the high significance of the practical conclusions reached in this afternoon's session, the first Ecumenical Council of the Lutheran Church has been a distinct success. For this we lift our hearts in sincere gratitude to God and pledge anew our loyalty and our energy to the great Head of the Church, our Lord Jesus Christ.

"2. The distinct impression of the manifold character of the Lutheran Church. From many lands we came, and with many tongues. So that the convention itself set forth in very concrete form the ecumenical character of Lutheranism, even before the excellent address of the Convention President on that subject. Varied as the nations of earth themselves, varied as the clouds that from day to day passed over this beautiful city in which we were met, but stable as the hills that are crowned by the Wartburg, our sitting down together at the convention table and our daily deliberation in common on these themes so vital to our faith gave forceful expression to the truth that the sun never sets upon Lutheran soil, that around the globe there stretches a glorious belt of Lutheranism, and that wherever there are human beings capable of worshiping God, irrespective of their race or language or color, there the Lutheran Church may flourish.

"3. The distinct impression of the essential unity of the Lutheran Church. That such a representative gathering of Lutherans from all lands, setting forth so concretely the manifold character of the Lutheran Church, representing such a variety of church government and embodying genuine differences of opinion on questions of practice, could sit for five days and in brotherly love discuss the common problems of Lutheranism and together plan for the future prosperity and extension of the Lutheran faith, was possible only because beneath the superficial and external differences there is genuine unity of spirit. This essential unity of Lutherans in all lands was profoundly felt throughout the convention and more than once filled our hearts with songs of praise. This essential unity of the Lutheran Churches throughout the world, so manifest during the past week, is far more important than any external union of those Churches. It rests primarily upon our common faith in Christ as our Saviour, our common acceptance of the Bible as God's Word and the only infallible rule of faith and practice, and upon our common acceptance of the confessions of the Church.

"4. The distinct impression that a glorious future lies before our Lutheran Church. Not the smallest element in the success of the convention that has just closed must be seen in the fact that the convention did not rest with a consideration of abstract themes but definitely addressed itself to practical problems and so directed its eyes to the future. The resolutions that were adopted with such a high degree of unanimity at the business session today gave assurance that the first Lutheran World convention shall not be the last one. Henceforth the Lutheran Church of the world will be able to speak as a unit. The strength of the whole will be made the strength of each several part. Many of us go away from this first Lutheran World Convention with high hopes that what has here been done is really the beginning of a new period in the history of the Evangelical Lutheran Church. In millions of hearts that hope will find an echo, and millions of prayers will ascend to the throne of grace that these hopes may be realized and that the Lutheran Church with all her glorious history may, through this first Lutheran World Convention, be granted a still more glorious future."

There were several definite decisions of the convention which we submit. Other resolutions adopted may be consulted in the books to be published. These we believe require official record and approval by the United Lutheran Church. Until so approved they are not binding upon any Church body which sent delegates.

(1) The following doctrinal statement. "The Lutheran World Convention acknowledges the Holy Scriptures of the Old and New Testaments as the only source and the infallible norm of all Church teaching and practice; and sees in the Lutheran Confessions, especially the Unaltered Augsburg Confession and Luther's Small Catechism, a pure exposition of the Word of God."

(2) The following form of organization as a practical continuation of the purposes for which the Convention was held. (We give the gist of the proposals.)

Two committees are to be established, a large Standing Committee and a small Executive Committee.

The Executive Committee is to make preparations for another Lutheran World Convention. It shall aim to harmonize all Lutheran activities which are carried on for works of serving love (Liebestaetigkeit), for the care of emigrants (Diasporapflege), and for Foreign Missions. It shall consider the suggestions made by Dr. Morehead in his paper at the convention, such as an exchange of visitors (professors and others), an exchange of news, an exchange of literature. It shall voice the attitude of the whole Lutheran Church when that is necessary or for grave reasons desirable. Until the next convention this committee is to consist of six members. The following are nominated, two each from the Scandinavian countries, Germany and America: Dr. Jorgensen, of Denmark; Dr. Rundgren*, of Sweden; Dr. Ihmels and Dr. Freiherr von Pechmann, of Germany; Dr. Morehead and Dr. Boe, of America. It is contemplated that this committee will in the course of time establish a central office.

The Standing Committee is to be more generally representative of the Lutheran Church in all lands and of groups in those lands. They will serve for counsel and reference to the Executive Committee. They will also be advocates in their lands for the purposes of the Convention. From seven to ten members of this committee are to be appointed from America, and will be as far as possible representative of the various Church bodies which approve and support the entire plan.

Vacancies in both committees are to be filled by co-option.

As delegates we unanimously recommend

1. The approval of the doctrinal statement.

2. The approval of the organization as planned in the appointment of the two committees.

3. A temporary appropriation for the expenses of these committees until a settled budget can be determined and recommended.

C. *Recommendations of the Executive Board:*

The Executive Board recommends the approval of

1. The doctrinal statement of the Lutheran World Convention.

2. The approval of the form of organization as stated in item 2 of the report of the delegates.

3. The adoption of the following:

Resolved, That in the choice of a place for a central office, the United Lutheran Church express its clear conviction and desire that it should not be located in any of the countries or group of countries represented by the three pairs of members of the Executive Committee.

4. That the action of the Executive Board appropriating $500 on our share in a budget, which is to be determined and reported later, be approved.

5. That the Executive Board be authorized to sanction the budget when submitted.

6. The Executive Committee of the Lutheran World Convention having suggested that for the present eight be named for the Larger Committee, and notified us that the United Lutheran Church would be entitled to four of these eight, the Executive Board chose Prof. J. A. Clutz,

---

* The Executive Committee of the Lutheran World Convention reported later that Dr. Rundgren was unable to act and that it had named in his place the Rev. Dr. Per Pehrsson.

D.D., LL.D.; Rev. E. C. J. Kraeling; E. Clarence Miller, LL.D.; Prof. A. G. Voigt, D.D., LL.D., to serve on the Larger Committee until the present Convention, and now recommends that they be elected for the coming biennium.

XI. RELATIONS WITH LUTHERAN CHURCHES IN EUROPE

1. Agreement between the United Lutheran Church in America and the Evangelical Lutheran Church of Czecho-Slovakia:

This matter was referred by the Buffalo Convention to the Executive Board. The agreement has been completed and signed as follows and is submitted for the approval of the Convention.

Proposition for an Agreement between the Evangelical Lutheran Church in Slovakia (Aug. Conf.), represented by its regularly elected bishops, general inspector, district inspectors, party of the first part; and the United Lutheran Church in America (Aug. Conf.), represented by Rev. Prof. J. A. Morehead, D.D., Chairman of the European Commission of the National Lutheran Council of America, party of the second part.

It is first noted, mentioned, that the proposition was prepared as the result of conferences in the city of Prague, December 8 and 9, 1920, and the representatives continued to exchange opinions and views by correspondence.

Inasmuch as the Evangelical Lutheran Church in Slovakia (Aug. Conf.) and the United Lutheran Church in America have attained unity of faith, evidenced by their common acceptance of the Holy Scriptures and the historic confessions of the Lutheran Church, serving and preaching the same Gospel of Christ for the glory of God and the advancement of His Kingdom, they do agree to co-operate in brotherly love for the accomplishment of the following purposes:

(1) Each body shall observe with warm interest the plans and work of the other and, to this end, approves of the exchange of official representatives as frequently as practicable.

(2) The Church of each country will accept for the services of its congregations regular pastors from the other, under the requirements of the Constitution or regulations for receiving them which are customary in the synods or districts concerned, and if they are provided with proper letters of recommendation from the constituted authority of the body from which they come.

(3) In estimating the amount of pension or stipend to which a pastor is entitled, the years of service devoted to the regular ministry of the Gospel in the related bodies of both America and Slovakia shall be included. Should a Pension Association or Pastors' Fund Society find the admittance of a new member a burden because of the extent of his previous service it is understood that reasonable special financial compensation therefor shall be made by the body in which the greatest term of service has been rendered.

(4) The contracting Church of each country shall recognize the validity of the diplomas (pastors) under conditions of Article Two.

(Term "diploma" refers to status of a completed pastor, repeats par. 2; credit for study par. 5).

(5) The Church (seminaries of the Church). of each country may fix the minimum number of semesters during which the students shall attend its institutions in order to graduate (before they are admitted to examination for pastors). Students of theology, who would leave a theological seminary before completing the prescribed number of semesters, shall receive credit (svedectvo) for work (study) done in the seminaries of both countries.

(6) In the interest of the uninterrupted care of souls and the conservation of the material of the Church (believers), these contracting bodies of both countries do agree to adopt measures for the systematic preparation of statistics of emigration and immigration. Information thus secured shall be promptly exchanged for the mutual aid of the co-operating Churches of America and Slovakia.

(7) This agreement, on the part of the Evangelical Lutheran Church in Slovakia (Aug. Conf.), becomes binding (valid) when it is approved by the general assembly (of the two districts) (generalny knovent).

> Za Cirkve Evanj. A. B. na Slovensku,
> Geo. Janoska.
> Biskop, duchovny predseda.
> D. John Vanovic,
> Gener. Dozoru.
> The United Lutheran Church in America,
> F. H. Knubel,
> President.

2. In the course of our developing relationships with Lutheran Church bodies in Europe, the necessity arose for some regulated methods whereby provision and supervision could be established for students from Europe, some of whom may remain and others return to their native lands after the completion of their educational courses. As suggestions towards such regulation the following recommendations, concerning only such students as are not supported by boards of the Church, are offered:

(a) That the Laymen's Movement be requested to take into consideration all such students as need support upon recommendation to them from the President of the United Lutheran Church in America.

(b) That the choice of institutions for attendance by these students be decided by the official head of the Churches from which they come and the Officers of the United Lutheran Church.

(c) That supervision of their work shall be committed to the officers of the United Lutheran Church.

(d) That in the case of those students who are to remain in this country, the plans for their ultimate service are to be determined by the officers of the United Lutheran Church.

XII. RELATIONS WITH INTERDENOMINATIONAL AGENCIES

1—*American Bible Society:*

The American Bible Society having suffered great loss by the earthquake in Japan, the Secretary, as instructed by the Executive Board, requested the Church papers to call this to the attention of our pastors and congregations and to ask that contributions for this purpose be sent through the regular channels.

2—Federal Council:

(a) The Rev. Dr. E. B. Burgess, Dr. John L. Zimmerman and the Rev. Dr. A. H. Smith, were appointed as friendly visitors to the annual meeting of the Executive Committee of the Federal Council of Churches which was held at Columbus, Ohio, December 12-14, 1923. They attended the meeting and submitted to the Executive Board a comprehensive report of their impressions and observations favorable and otherwise. The substance of the report may be summed up in the following words quoted therefrom: "Many thing were said during the course of the convention that met with the hearty approval of your delegation; many other things only served to deepen our conviction that the United Lutheran Church was wise in sharply defining her relations to the Council."

(b) For each of the years of the biennium, by authorization of the Executive Board, the Treasurer has paid to the Federal Council of Churches $2,000, the same amount as was contributed in 1922. (See Min. 1922, p. 87).

(c) Our consultative representatives of the general Commissions and Committees of the Federal Council submitted their reports to the Executive Board as provided for in our agreement with the Federal Council. (See Min. 1922, p. 86, 2d item). These reports show a careful study of the operations of the Federal Council and of what it is doing and proposes to do in the development and prosecution of its work.

As these representatives of ours meet with the agencies of the Federal Council only in a consultative capacity and consequently have offered no recommendations, we recommend that the Executive Board be instructed to consider the reports in connection with the conduct of relations with the Federal Council during the coming biennium.

(d) Concerning transportation matters. (See IV, C, 10).

3—Young Men's Christian Association:

An official request came for the appointment by the United Lutheran Church of a Standing Committee on Young Men's Christian Association for purposes of conference on matters of mutual concern to the two bodies. It also asked for the naming of one member of a general counseling commission to confer at least annually with the Y. M. C. A.'s International Committee or its Executive Committee and officers on such problems of relationship as are national in scope and pertain to all the Churches. The following was the action of the Executive Board in regard to this matter:

"Resolved, That the Executive Board of the United Lutheran Church in America accepts the invitation of the International Committee of the Young Men's Christian Association:

"(1) To appoint a committee of three persons, one clerical and two lay, to confer with the International Committee on matters that concern the Y. M. C. A. and the Evangelical Lutheran Church.

"(2) To ask the chairman of the above-named committee to serve as a member of a general counseling commission with whom the International Committee or its Executive Committee and officers may hold annual conferences on such problems of relationship as pertain to all the churches.

"This action is taken with a desire to help the Y. M. C. A. in its declared purpose to establish itself more firmly on a sound evangelical basis."

The President, in accordance with this action, appointed the following as a Committee of Conference with the Y. M. C. A.:

Rev. Paul E. Scherer, D.D., Mr. W. H. Hager, Robbin B. Wolf, Esq.

The Chairman, Dr. Paul E. Scherer, was named as the special representative for general counsel as requested.

XIII.   MISCELLANEOUS

1—*Commission to Study and Report on Theological Education in The United Lutheran Church in America:*

President Knubel reported that at the informal conference concerning the Chicago Theological Seminary held at Cleveland, Ohio, April 19, 1923 (see V. 2), the discussion of all who took part in that conference was constantly found to be entering upon the consideration of the whole theological problem of The United Lutheran Church in America. As a result of that conference and again with the concurrence of all who participated in it, he recommended that the Executive Board appeal to the next convention of The United Lutheran Church in America for the appointment of a special commission which shall undertake a complete study of theological education in the United Lutheran Church for report to the next succeeding convention. This recommendation was adopted. He also suggested that the commission be ten in number consisting of three members of theological seminary faculties, two laymen, three members of the Board of Education and two pastors.

The Executive Board approved these suggestions and recommends

(a) The appointment of a commission to study the subject of theological education in the United Lutheran Church and to report to the next convention.

(b) That the appointment of this commission be committed to the Executive Board.

2—*Arrangements for the Chicago Convention:*

(a) After correspondence on the part of the President with those in charge of arrangements in Chicago it was decided that the opening date of the convention be Tuesday, October 21, 1924. It was further determined that all sessions of this convention should be held in the Edgewater Beach Hotel with the exception of the Opening Service on Tuesday evening. The place chosen for the Opening Service was the Wicker Park Church, N. Hoyne Avenue and Le Moyne Street, Chicago, Rev. S. P. Long, D.D., pastor.

(b) In accordance with action of the Executive Board the Secretary authorized the Presidents of the three General Bodies to call meetings for Tuesday, October 21, at two o'clock P. M. Arrangements were made for these meetings as follows: The General Synod in Holy Trinity Church, corner Addison Street and Maple Square Avenue, Chicago, the Rev. J. A. Leas, pastor. The General Council in Unity Church, corner Balmoral and Magnolia Avenues, Chicago, Rev. D. A. Davy, D.D., pastor. The United Synod in the South in the Rogers Park Church, corner Morse Avenue and Paulina Street, Chicago, Rev. Luther Hogshead, pastor.

3—*Church Paper Week:*

A request from the editors of *The Lutheran* and Mr. Grant Hultberg that the Executive Board designate the week of October 5th as Church Paper Week was sanctioned.

4—*Offices of the President and Secretary:*

Inasmuch as the offices of the President and Secretary of the United Lutheran Church are held under a lease which expires in May, 1925, we recommend that the matter of the location of the offices and provision for their proper establishment and equipment be referred to the Executive Board with power.

Respectfully submitted for the Executive Board,
(Signed) F. H. KNUBEL, *President.*
M. G. G. SCHERER, *Secretary.*
E. CLARENCE MILLER, *Treasurer.*

(Actions on the Executive Board's Report assembled with references.—Secretary.)

I. Approved. (Wednesday morning, October 22.)

II. 1. Received as information. (Wednesday morning, October 22.)

II. 2. Proposed amendment to Constitution, Article IX, Section 1, referred to Constituent Synods. (Wednesday morning, October 22).

Proposed amendments to By-Laws adopted. (Thursday morning, October 23.)

II. 3, a to f. Adopted. (Wednesday morning, October 22).

II. 4. Approved. (Wednesday morning, October 22.)

III. A. 3. a. Adopted. (Wednesday, October 29.)

III. A. 3. b. Adopted. (Wednesday morning, October 22.)

III. A. 3. c. Adopted. (Wednesday morning, October 22.)

III. A. 4. Adopted. (Wednesday morning, October 22.)

III. A. 5. Adopted. (Wednesday, October 29.)

III. B. 2. Adopted. (Wednesday morning, October 22.)

III. B. 3. a. Adopted in connection with Item 1 of Supplementary Report. (Monday afternoon, October 27.)

III. B. 3. b. Adopted. (Wednesday morning, October 22.)

III. B. 5. Richmond, Va., was chosen as the place for the next Convention. (Tuesday afternoon, October 28.)

IV. A. 2. For action see minutes of the afternoon session, Wednesday, October 22. In connection with this, action was also taken on Item 6 of the Supplementary Report.

IV. A. 5. Adopted. (Thursday morning, October 23.)

IV. B. 2. b. Adopted. (Thursday morning, October 23.)

IV. B. 9. a. Adopted as amended. (Thursday morning, October 23.)

IV. B. 9. b. Request of the Board of Ministerial Relief granted. (Thursday afternoon, October 23.)

IV. B. 10. a. Adopted. (Thursday afternoon, October 23.)

IV. B. 10. b. Adopted. (Thursday afternoon, October 23.)

IV. B. 13. b. Approved. (Thursday afternoon, October 23.)

IV. B. 13. c. Adopted. (Thursday afternoon, October 23.)

VII. 3. Adopted. (Thursday afternoon, October 23.)

VII. 4. Adopted. (Thursday afternoon, October 23.)

VII. 5. a. and b. Referred to Constituent Synods with the Memorial from the Indiana Synod. (Friday morning, October 24.)

VII. 6. Adopted. (Thursday afternoon, October 23.)

VII. 10. Adopted. (Thursday afternoon, October 23.)

X. C. 1, 2 and 3. Adopted. (Thursday morning, October 23.)

X. C. 4. Adopted in connection with Item 4 of the Supplementary Report. (Thursday morning, October 23.)

X. C. 5 and 6. Adopted. (Thursday morning, October 23.)

XI. 1. Approved. (Thursday afternoon, October 23.)

XI. 2. Adopted. (Thursday afternoon, October 23.)

XII. 2. c. Adopted. (Thursday afternoon, October 23.)

XII. 3. Adopted. (Thursday afternoon, October 23.)

XIII. 1. Substitute adopted. (Monday afternoon, October 27.)

XIII. 4. Adopted. (Wednesday, October 29.)

Items 2 and 3 of the Supplementary Report approved. (Thursday afternoon, October 23.)

Item 5, A and B of the Supplementary Report adopted. (Wednesday, October 29.)

Item 7 of the Supplementary Report adopted. (Wednesday, October 29.)

Report adopted as a whole, Wednesday, October 29th.

Amendment to Section VII, B, 4 of By-Laws adopted. (Friday morning, October 24th.)

Amendment to Section VII, B, 14 of By-Laws adopted. (Wednesday, October 29th.)

The Minute on the death of Dr. Tressler (I) was approved by a rising vote.

Item 4 of Matters Referred (II) approved.

III, A, Item 3, (a) was deferred until after the report of the Committee on Memorials from Constituent Synods.

III, A, Item 3, (b) and (c) adopted.

III, A, 4, adopted.

The tellers in charge of the election of Treasurer reported. Dr. E. Clarence Miller, having received 421 votes out of a total of 426, was declared elected.

The tellers having charge of the ballot for President reported that on the second ballot 401 votes were cast, 382 of which were for Dr. F. H. Knubel. Dr. Knubel having received more than the required three-fourths of the ballots, the Secretary declared him elected as President of The United Lutheran Church in America. On motion of Dr. S. P. Long the Convention united in voluntary prayers for God's blessing on the leadership of the newly elected President. Prayers were offered by Drs. J. C. Seegers, A. Pohlman and S. P. Long.

The Convention proceeded to the election of a Secretary.

The consideration of the report of the Executive Board was resumed.

III, A, 5 was read and action thereon was deferred.

III, B, 3, a., concerning the Pacific Theological Seminary, was taken up. The Secretary stated that there was an item in a supplementary report to b esubmitted by the Executive Board relating to this matter. Consideration of the matter deferred until the submission of the supplementary report.

III, B, 3, b. was adopted.

III, B, 5. Consideration of the invitation to the United Lutheran Church to hold its next convention in Philadelphia was deferred, in view of the fact that other invitations are to be reported by the Committee on Memorials.

The tellers appointed to conduct election of Secretary reported that 393 votes had been cast, 383 of them for the present secretary. The President declared Dr. M. G. G. Scherer elected.

The Convention adjourned until two o'clock P. M.   Prayer was offered by the Rev. L. H. Larimer.

Afternoon Session

Wednesday, October 22, 2 : 00 P. M.

The President called the Convention to order.

Prayer was offered by the Rev. W. M. Horn.

The Rev. A. Steimle, Chairman of Nominating Committee No. 2, reported nominees for the Executive Board, Commission of Adjudication and the Church Paper Committee:

For Executive Board: Rev. F. F. Fry, Rev. W. D. C. Keiter, Rev. A. R. Wentz, Mr. R. B. Wolf, Hon. J. F. Kramer, Mr. George E. Neff, Rev. M. J. Kline, Rev. Jacob Maurer, Rev. J. S. Simon, Mr. Frank D. Bittner, Mr. J. K. Jensen, Mr. Louis Swink.

For Commission of Adjudication: Rev. H. E. Jacobs, Rev. R. E. Tulloss, Hon. H. W. Harter, Rev. F. A. Kaehler, Rev. C. P. MacLaughlin, Hon. F. M. Riter.

For Committee on Church Papers: Rev. J. A. Singmaster, Rev. C. E. Gardner, Mr. H. L. Snyder, Rev. J. W. Horine, Rev. A. T. W. Steinhaeuser, Mr. W. J. Showalter.

The Rev. A. J. Rudisill, Chairman of Nominating Committee No. 1, reported nominees for the Executive Committee of the Laymen's Movement:

For Executive Committee of the Layman's Movement: Mr. J. L. Clark, Mr. P. A. Elsesser, Mr. E. J. Young, Mr. E. Clarence Miller, Mr. F. W. Albrecht, Mr. H. C. Miller, Mr. P. P. Hagan, Mr. W. H. Hager, Mr. W. L. Glatfelter, Hon. C. Steele, Mr C. H. Boyer, Mr. H. Buehler, Mr. C. J. Driever, Mr. E. G. Hoover, Mr. F. S. Hock, Mr. M. P. Moller, Mr. R. G. Rose, Mr C. F. Stifel, Mr. I. A. Shaffer, Jr., Mr. F. H. Wefer.

The reports of these nominating committees were accepted and announcement was made that the election would take place today from 5 to 7 P. M., according to the order adopted.

Consideration of the report of the Executive Board was resumed. The Secretary read the item concerning combination or reorganization of Boards (IV, A, 2). The suggestions submitted to the Executive Board by the Committee of Ten referred to in the item of the report and submitted with the approval of the Executive Board were considered seriatim.

Suggestion (1) was adopted.

Suggestion (2). On motion this item was divided. The first part was then adopted. Under the consideration of the second part the Secretary submitted an item (No. 6) from the supplementary report of the Executive Board consisting of two recommendations. These recommendations were adopted, thus disposing of the second part of Suggestion 2.

Suggestions (3), (4), (5) and (6) were adopted.

Suggestion (7). On motion the form suggested by the Executive Board was substituted for the original form and was adopted.

Suggestion (8). A motion to adopt (8) in the form recommended by the Executive Board was lost. Thereupon suggestion (8) in its original form as proposed by the Committee of Ten was adopted.

Suggestion (9) was adopted.

The entire series of suggestions was then adopted.

The President at this point introduced the Rev. J. A. O. Stub, D.D., who appeared as the representative of the Norwegian Lutheran Church by appointment of his father, Rev. H. G. Stub, D.D., Litt.D., President of that body. Dr. Stub conveyed the greetings of the Norwegian Lutheran Church, and, at the request of the President of the United Lutheran Church, Dr. C. M. Jacobs responded.

At this time also the President introduced the Rev. Dr. H. J. Urdahl, Vice-President of the Lutheran Free Church. Dr. Urdahl emphasized the need of unity and co-operation among Lutherans in America. To his greetings Dr. E. B. Burgess responded at the request of the President.

Dr. C. G. Shatzer, Secretary of the Laymen's Movement, commented upon the report of the Laymen's Movement submitted by him, calling attention to the principles and practice of stewardship and appealing to the men of the Church to assist in carrying out the program.

REPORT OF THE LUTHERAN LAYMEN'S MOVEMENT

The Lutherans Laymen's Movement herewith presents its first report under the present organization, commission and constitution.

I. ORGANIZATION

1. *Executive Committee*:

The Buffalo Convention of the United Lutheran Church elected the following members of the Executive Committee:

Mr. J. L. Clark	Mr. Harvey C. Miller
Mr. A. P. Elsesser	Mr. Wm. C. Stoever
Mr. E. J. Young	Mr. Wm. H. Hager
Mr. E. Clarence Miller	Mr. W. L. Glatfelter
Mr. F. W. Albrecht	Mr. Charles Steele

At the meeting of June 19, 1923, the following men were added by the elective members of the Committee:

Mr. I. A. Shaffer	Mr. Raymond Bard
Mr. M. P. Möller	Mr. Fred Wefer
Mr. E. G. Hoover	Mr. Frederick Henrich
Mr. M. H. Buchler	Mr. Wm. J. Gram
Mr. F. D. Bittner	Mr. B. T. Steiner
Mr. P. P. Hagan	Mr. George E. Neff

Executive Committee Meetings: The Executive Committee met June 19, 1923, and May 21, 1924.

2. *Administrative Committee*:

A regularly constituted Administrative Committee consisting of Mr. W. H. Hager, chairman, Mr. E. Clarence Miller, Mr. W. L. Glatfelter, Mr. Harvey C. Miller and Mr. E. G. Hoover has held meetings and directed the work of the movement as defined by the Constitution and outlined by the Executive Committee.

Regular reports of the work of the Executive Committee and Administrative Committee have been submitted to the Executive Board of the United Lutheran Church.

II. Membership

The present membership is composed of some of the finest laymen of the United Lutheran Church.

The membership is distributed in nine states and fifty-two cities.

A far-reaching and influential piece of work is done by members of the Laymen's Movement when they leave their business, and at their own expense, visit various cities and address groups of laymen upon the work of the Church.

Fourteen cities have been visited by members of the Laymen's Movement during the past eighteen months. The men have presented the financial needs of the Church and the necessity of recruiting men for the ministry. In each city men have become members of the Laymen's Movement.

III. Secretaries

Four Secretaries have been employed during the past year.

Mr. A. D. Chiquoine, Associate Secretary, in charge of the office from October, 1922, to April, 1923, resigned in June, 1923.

C. G. Shatzer, General Secretary.

Rev. E. C. Cronk, D.D., Associate Secretary.

Mr. A. R. Brane, Associate Secretary for the months—December, 1923, to June, 1924.

In June, 1923, the office was removed from Philadelphia, Pa., to Springfield, Ohio, and the work placed under the direction of the present General Secretary.

IV. Work Undertaken

The Lutheran Laymen's Movement has completed the first two years of activity. It has endeavored to carry out the commission presented to it by the Buffalo Convention of promoting Christian Stewardship and assisting in securing an adequate ministry for the church.

1. *Interpretation of Function*:

Christian Stewardship involves the proper disposition of life and material possessions. The initial efforts of the Laymen's Movement in its work in Stewardship has been to assist the Church in financing its local, national and foreign program. The deficits reported by the Boards have attracted the attention of the members of the Laymen's Movement and naturally, their first efforts in Stewardship have been to devise means for raising the apportionment in full.

It was decided that if the members of the congregation could be brought into possession of more intimate knowledge of what the tasks are before our Church and what is being done to complete those tasks, it would be possible to stimulate all congregations to meet the apportionment more fully, if not in full.

2. *Program*:

A program was devised to carry out this idea. It consisted of two addresses and the showing of 45 minutes of moving pictures.

The first address called to mind the fact that the Church has made a tremendous contribution to civilization. It was presented by a representative of the Synod in which work was being done. It was followed by the moving pictures showing some of the work the Church is now doing. These two parts of the program gave a Secretary of the Laymen's Movement an opportunity to discuss the Efficient Church and advocate good systems whereby the work of the Church could be financed.

The whole program was built about the idea of stimulating the people to greater enthusiasm for the work of the Church and at the same time demonstrating to them effective methods of expressing a measure of their stewardship of material possessions.

Splendid co-operation has been given the Laymen's Movement by the synodical officers, committees and pastors in this work.

3. *Field Covered*:

It was deemed desirable to touch the greatest number of congregations in the shortest possible time and at the same time give an effective presentation of the work. To accomplish the results, synodical officials and synodical stewardship committees in the various Synods were asked to co-operate with the Laymen's Movement in organizing the churches of the Synods in groups whereby each group could send their strong church-workers and key men to the centers to hear the program and see the pictures. The effort was made to make the centers sufficient in number that the distance any one congregation would have to travel would not exceed ten miles. 222 meetings were held, 530 congregations of a possible 998 were represented and 21,026 adults heard and saw the program. Adults are represented in this count, which in most cases represented actual counts and not estimates, and not the children, although many children were present. Probably the most hopeful side of the promotional work lies with the children. The percentage of attendance for any Synod varied from six to thirty-four per cent.

The following Synods were visited:

Ohio—covered in full.

Indiana—covered in full.

Michigan—covered in full.

Pittsburgh—covered in full.

New York—covered in full.

New York and New England—covered in greater part.

New York Ministerium—part of New York Conference.

West Virginia—covered in full.

It is difficult to cite the tangible results of such a piece of work. All that can be said is that the comments upon the whole program have been very satisfactory. All the agencies of the Church that are concerned in promoting the payment of the benevolence of the Church have contributed materially to increasing the amount paid during the present year as compared with the year 1923. The Laymen's Movement has certainly contributed something to the advance.

4. *The Program—Applied Stewardship:*

The work is looked upon as supplementary to the work of the synodical organization and the pastors. The program is a path-finding program and is only a beginning along lines that should be more thoroughly developed. The time is here when a combination of agencies should be undertaken which will make it possible to cover the whole United Lutheran Church each year with a program devised to give the Lutheran people a greater vision of the whole work of the Church and the obligation each member of a congregation has to Christianity to carry out the Christian program.

The philosophic principles of Stewardship are fairly well defined. People must be brought to understand these principles of Stewardship and develop a heart-desire to work upon the basis of that understanding. A field that needs exploration is that of methods and practice in the field of Applied Stewardship.

5. *Every-Member Canvass—A Method in Stewardship:*

The effective and efficient use of the Every-Member Canvass and its associated features of Budget, Duplex Envelope, Quarterly Statements of individual and congregational financial standing, and simple accounting systems must be urged upon the congregations.

Two canvasses have been conducted since the Buffalo Convention.

The canvass of 1922 was under the direction of the former Secretary, A. D. Chiquoine. In 1923, the pastors were approached directly and urged through correspondence to undertake or continue the use of the Every-Member Canvass. In addition, each Synodical Committee was communicated with and asked to urge upon the pastors and congregations the conduct of an efficient Every-Member Canvass. The plan as evolved, permitted the Laymen's Movement and the Synodical Committees to use their influence and render possible personal service without overlapping or interference.

In 1922, 300,000 copies of a Booklet of Information, financed by the Boards and Agencies of the Church, to be distributed in connection with the Every-Member Canvass, were distributed by the Laymen's Movement. These were accompanied by 500,000 Pledge Cards.

In 1923, 322,000 copies of a booklet, "Your Church at Work," published by the Boards and Agencies of the Church, were distributed, accompanied by the usual Pledge Cards.

The Lutherans are not supporting their Church enterprises commensurate with their financial ability. Denominations no more able than our own are doing much more per capita to carry on their world work. Our people must be stimulated to proportionate giving not only because it will finance the work of the Church, but because through such giving comes a large, personal, spiritual blessing. Several denominations report fine results from the use of the Every-Member Canvass and its associated systems. There are two facts that suggest that our people are not employing it effectively:

1. The report of the Treasurer of the United Lutheran Church indicates a large difference between the Benevolence Budget adopted by the Buffalo Convention and the amounts actually paid to the Treasurer.

2. Fifty per cent of the congregations fail to report to the Laymen's Movement concerning the Every-Member Canvass, the use of the Duplex and the amounts pledged for Church and Benevolence maintenance. The fact is interpreted as meaning that a large percentage of these congregations are not conducting canvasses or do not finish the canvass and reduce the results to a definite statement which makes available definite information. Coupled with this fact must be the fact that many of the congregations reporting are carrying deficits to Benevolence, suggesting that this business method is not being employed effectively.

The system is not an end in itself, but if it is effectively used, in all its educational and accounting details, it will lend tremendous assistance toward eliminating the deficits in the accounts in the Church.

The number of replies received to official requests for simple reports upon phases of the Church's work is extremely discouraging. A first request received about a 25 per cent reply and to get a final 50 per cent to 60 per cent reply requires two or three requests; all of which incurs needless expense and consumes resources that might be used to decided advantage in other work. These reports form the basis for projecting work and are necessary.

6. *Ministerial Education*:

In accord with the spirit of Article 2b of the Constitution, the Laymen's Movement has been assisting sixteen men in their educational preparation for full-time service in the Church. Fourteen of these men are preparing for the ministry and two of them are preparing in the Medical Schools to enter Foreign Mission service.

The men chosen for this aid were recommended by the Recruiting Department of the Board of Education. The amount given them was determined upon the basis of the cost of a year's training in the various institutions as reported by the President of the institution or some other agent authorized by him to report. In every case aid was granted upon the basis of very great need.

An effort was made to correlate the methods of assistance of the Laymen's Movement with that of the various Synods. A measure of success was attained. The work is being continued. It is hoped that such students as are being helped by the Synods will not apply to the Laymen's Movement and that all students assisted by the Laymen's Movement will receive aid from that source alone.

There are some cases in which aid in addition to that rendered by the Synod is necessary. In such cases assistance should be rendered, but only with the knowledge and sanction of the Synod already assisting.

7. *Theological School Lectures*:

Lectures on Church Financial Systems and the Merits and Methods of Conducting the Every-Member Canvass were delivered in the Theological Seminary, Gettysburg, Pa., the Seminary of Susquehanna University and Hamma Divinity School.

8. *Summer Assemblies*:

The Summer Assemblies of the various Synods have made possible the presentation of the Principles of Stewardship both from the platform and in the classroom.

Four Assemblies were participated in during the summer of 1923, and nine during the summer of 1924.

It is the desire that Stewardship class study may be undertaken among the adult members of the congregations and among the young people.

V. An Objective

The Lutheran Church has a large number of laymen who have demonstrated their unusual ability in the business and professional world. This ability is available to the Church and can be utilized in similar fields in the Church. These men are in the habit of thinking and then acting quickly and forcefully in accord with their judgment. Every effort should be made to secure their attendance at and participation in the deliberations of the meetings of the District Synods.

It is a question of giving them the opportunity to develop along normal lines and presenting a program for them that does not consider merely the stewardship of money, but keeps ever in mind utilizing this ability, personality, organizing and administrative skill in the interests of the Church. The great demand is for genuine leadership and the definition of a concrete task.

RECOMMENDATIONS: 1. It is recommended that in so far as the work and the plans of the Lutheran Laymen's Movement have commended themselves to the United Lutheran Church, it is desired that this Convention sanction the continuance and development of the work.

2. Representatives of the Synodical Committee on Stewardship, Secretaries of Beneficence and the Laymen's Movement respectfully recommend that the United Lutheran Church, in convention assembled, consider the

advisability of setting aside the month of November of each year as a stewardship month.

3. That the convention recommend to the congregations through district synods that the pastors be urged to emphasize stewardship during the said month:

(a) Through sermons.
(b) Through the Sunday School: Class instruction and discussion and specially organized discussion groups.
(c) Through the young people's organizations by pageants, playlets and study groups.
(d) In the women's organizations, through the presentation of topic studies and discussion.
(e) In the Brotherhood (as in (d) above).
(f) Through the distribution of suitable literature.

4. That the Parish and Church School Board, Women's Missionary Society, the Luther League, the Brotherhood and other organizations be asked to insert in their programs or supplement the outline program, so far as possible, with suggestions for stewardship studies.

Respectfully submitted for the Committee,
J. L. CLARK, *Chairman,*
C. G. SHATZER, *General Secretary.*

Recommendations. Item 1 adopted. Item 2 with its recommendation, adopted. Item 3 with its divisions adopted. Item 4 adopted.

In connection with Item 1, the Convention adopted the following:

"*Resolved,* That we express to this earnest group of laymen our appreciation of the work which they are doing for the Church without any charge and with liberal expenditure of time and means."

Upon invitation of President Knubel, Mr. J. L. Clark, Chairman of the Laymen's Movement, made a brief address, presenting an earnest plea for co-operation of the men in the work of the Laymen's Movement.

The report of the Laymen's Movement was adopted as a whole.

At 5:15 P. M., after closing prayer by Dr. Pohlman, the Convention adjourned for the day.

Laymen's Banquet

The annual dinner of the Laymen was held at 7:00 P. M. Wednesday, October 22d, in the Black Cat Room of the Edgewater Beach Hotel, with 151 present.

Invocation was offered by Dr. F. H. Knubel.

Mr. W. H. Hager was Toastmaster.

Dr. Ross Stover led the Laymen in general singing of popular songs.

After dinner, the program was continued as follows:

Mr. E. Clarence Miller, LL.D., "Our Church Finance."
Mr. C. G. Shatzer, Sc.D., "The Laymen's Movement."
Mr. W. A. Granville, Ph.D., LL.D., "The Responsibilities of Stewardship."
Mr. J. L. Clark, "The Laymen's Task."

A number of short impromptu speeches were made, after which the gathering adjourned.

————•◆•————

SECOND MEETING

Morning Session

CONVENTION HALL, EDGEWATER BEACH HOTEL,
Chicago, Ill.

Thursday, October 23d, 8:45 A. M.

Matins were conducted by the Rev. H. H. Bagger.

The Convention was called to order by the President.

The Minutes of Wednesday morning and afternoon sessions were read and approved.

The Tellers Committee, Mr. P. P. Hagan, Chairman, reported that each of the following persons had received a majority of votes cast in the election for members of the Executive Board:

Rev. F. F. Fry   Mr. R. B. Wolf
Rev. W. D. C. Keiter   Mr. G. E. Neff
Rev. A. R. Wentz   Hon. J. F. Kramer

The President thereupon declared them elected.

The Tellers Committee reported that each of the following had received a majority of the votes cast in the election for Executive Committee of the Laymen's Movement:

Mr. F. W. Albrecht	Mr. W. H. Hager
Mr. J. L. Clark	Mr. E. C. Miller
Mr. P. A. Elsesser	Mr. H. C. Miller
Mr. W. L. Glatfelter	Mr. C. J. Driever
Mr. P. P. Hagan	Mr. M. P. Moller

The President declared them elected.

The Committee of Tellers reported that each of the following had received a majority of the votes cast in the election for the Commission of Adjudication:

Rev. H. E. Jacobs
Rev. R. E. Tulloss
Hon. H. W. Harter

The President declared them elected.

The Tellers Committee reported that the Rev. J. A. Singmaster and Dr. W. J. Showalter had received a majority of the votes cast in the election of the Committee on Church Papers.

The President thereupon declared them elected.

The committee having reported that there was one clergyman yet to be elected on the Committee on Church Papers, the President instructed the tellers to proceed to take the ballot.

The President announced that the next order of business would be the consideration of amendments to the By-Laws as proposed by the Executive Board. (Report II, 2.)

The proposed amendments to Section II, Item 3, of the By-Laws were adopted.

Proposed amendments to Section III, Item 1, were adopted.

Proposed amendments to Section IV, Item 2, were adopted. Proposed amendments to Item 3 were adopted. Proposed amendments to Item 4 were adopted.

Proposed amendment to Section V, A, 17 was adopted.

Proposed amendment to Section V, B, Item 8 was adopted.
Proposed amendment to Section V, B, Item 9 (2) was adopted.

Proposed amendments to Section V. C. Item 5, were adopted.

Proposed amendment to Section VI, Item 2. The amendment in the form of a substitute was adopted.

The proposed amendment to Section VI, Item 3, was adopted.

The recommendation to strike out Items 4, 5 and 6 of Section VI was adopted.

Proposed amendment to Section VII, A, 5 was adopted.

Proposed amendment to Section VII, B. The proposed amendment to the heading of the list of standing committees was adopted.
At this point the Secretary presented the following:

"In view of the action of the Convention yesterday afternoon concerning the reorganization of the Home Mission work of the United Lutheran Church, the following amendment to the By-Laws, Section VII, B, 4, is proposed by the Executive Board:

"Change the name of the Committee hitherto known as the Committee of Conference on Special Linguistic Interests and make it the *Committee on German Interests*. Add the following as a definition of the Committee's sphere: It shall arrange, in conference with the Executive Board, for any meetings of a German Conference required. It shall also be a place of counsel for any agencies of the Church when they are dealing with matters which concern especially the German-speaking portions of the Church. It shall, furthermore, have the privilege to approach any agency of the Church upon matters which are for the interest of that portion of the Church."

The President announced that this would be considered tomorrow.

Tellers Committee reported that no one had received a majority of the votes cast in the second ballot for the Committee on Church Papers. The tellers were instructed to pass the ballots.

The consideration of the report of the Executive Board was resumed.

The item concerning Port Work (IV, A, 5) was adopted.

The item concerning co-operation in Home Mission Work (IV, B, 2, (b)) was adopted.

The item concerning the proposed campaign of the Board of Ministerial Relief (IV, B, 9 (a)) was next considered.

Moved and carried, That Item (2) of the terms of agreement reported, be amended by striking out the words "it shall be made" and substituting the words "a campaign for the Board of Ministerial Relief shall be authorized."

It was further moved and carried, That the order of the terms of agreement be changed so that (2) shall become (1), that (3) shall become (2), and that (1) shall become (3). As thus amended the recommendation reads as follows:

(1) That a campaign for the Board of Ministerial Relief shall be authorized to mark the tenth anniversary of the organization of the United Lutheran Church.

(2) That a period of one year preceding said anniversary and six months succeeding shall be given to the Board for campaign purposes.

(3) That no other campaign shall be authorized prior to the one of the Board of Ministerial Relief.

As amended the entire recommendation was adopted.

The Committee of Tellers reported that on the third ballot in the election for member of the Committee on Church Papers, no one had received a majority of the votes cast. The President instructed the tellers to distribute ballots.

It was moved and carried, That in case the ballot about to be taken should not result in an election, in the next succeeding ballot the nominations be confined to the two persons having received the highest number of votes.

Resuming consideration of the report of the Executive Board, the item IV, B, 9 (b) concerning change of the title of the Board of Ministerial Relief was taken up.

The recommendation of the Executive Board was discussed and action deferred.

The Committee of Tellers reported that in the fourth ballot for a member of the Committee on Church Papers no person had received a majority of the votes cast. The tellers were instructed to distribute ballots, the President stating that the two persons who had received the highest votes in the former ballot were the Revs. C. E. Gardner and A. T. W. Steinhaeuser.

The special order being the report on the Lutheran World Convention, Section X of the Executive Board's Report was taken up.

The Secretary read the "several definite decisions" of the Convention reported by our delegates, and the action of the Executive Board thereupon, together with recommendations of the Executive Board. At this point the Rev. Dr. J. A. Morehead, Chairman of the Executive Committee of the Lutheran World Convention, addressed the United Lutheran Church.

The recommendations of the Executive Board (X, C) were then taken up.

Item 1, the Doctrinal statement, was adopted.

Item 2, the form of organization, was adopted.

Item 3, together with the resolution of the Executive Board, was adopted.

Item 4 adopted.

At this time the Secretary presented Item 4 of the supplementary report of the Executive Board, to the effect that the Board had authorized a further advance of $300 on behalf of the United Lutheran Church toward a budget for the Executive Committee of the Lutheran World Convention. This was adopted.

Items 5 and 6 were adopted and the President declared the persons named in Item 6 to have been elected as members of the Larger Committee of the Lutheran World Convention for the present biennium.

The Committee of Tellers reported that in the fifth ballot for a member of the Committee on Church Papers, the Rev. C. E. Gardner had received a majority of all the votes cast. The President thereupon declared Dr. Gardner elected.

The Convention adjourned with prayer by the Rev. William J. Miller, Jr.

Afternoon Session

Thursday, October 23d, 2:00 P. M.

The President called the Convention to order.

Prayer was offered by the Rev. O. Krauch.

The Committee of Reference and Counsel submitted the following which was adopted:

Resolved, That the Biennial Convention of the United Lutheran Church reaffirms its approval of the constructive care and training being given the orphans of the Bible lands who were orphaned by war and deportation. With food, clothing and shelter they are also receiving preparation of hand, head and heart to prepare them for self-support, citizenship and leadership. Our pastors and other officials are encouraged to continue their co-operation with the Near East Relief in its plans for the support of its work.

With reference to the request for the appointment of a committee to advise with the Near East Relief regarding its policies and to co-ordinate its plans with other Lutheran activities, it was thought wise to suggest to the Near East Relief that the Executive Board of the United Lutheran Church is always available for service of this kind.

The Rev. A. J. Traver, Chairman of the Committee on Leave of Absence, submitted the following through the Committee of Reference and Counsel:

Resolved, That the Chairmen of Synodical Delegations shall be responsible for keeping the attendance roll of their members for each session, receive excuses for absence and report to the Chairman of the Committee on Leave of Absence, with their recommendations, at the opening of the morning session of the concluding day of the Convention.

The resolution was adopted.

Dr. Holmes Dysinger presented the report of the Commission of Adjudication.

REPORT OF THE COMMISSION OF ADJUDICATION

The Commission of Adjudication met in Pittsburgh, Pennsylvania, April 5, 1923, and transacted the regular routine business. No special matters requiring action on the part of the United Lutheran Church have been before the Commission during the biennium. Appeals of various kinds have been presented, but they were so clearly outside the jurisdiction of the Commission, as defined by the Constitution of the United Lutheran Church, that no meeting was needed to consider them. Accordingly only one regular meeting of the Commission was held during the biennium. In the meantime question has been raised within the Commission as to the right to defer meetings informally that are prescribed in the Constitution of the United Lutheran Church, when there is no special business requiring action. This matter will be considered by the Commission at its next meeting to be held in Chicago in connection with the convention of the United Lutheran Church, and the findings will be reported to that body at that time.

HENRY E. JACOBS, *President.*
HOLMES DYSINGER, *Secretary.*

Dr. Dysinger also submitted the following:

Supplementary Report of the Commission of Adjudication

In regard to meetings to which reference is made above, it is the judgment of the Commission that the plain implications of the Constitution make it unnecessary to hold a meeting of the Commission when no matters are before it for consideration.

The officers of the Commission for the next biennium are:

President—Rev. Henry E. Jacobs, D.D., LL.D., S.T.D., Lutheran Theological Seminary, Mt. Airy, Philadelphia, Pa.

Vice-President—Rev. A. G. Voigt, D.D., LL.D., Lutheran Theological Seminary, Columbia, S. C.

Secretary: Rev. Holmes Dysinger, D.D., LL.D., Western Theological Seminary, Fremont, Nebr.

Clerk—Judge E. K. Strong, Columbia City, Ind.

Judge H. W. Harter was recognized and explained the reasons for the judgment of the Commission as set forth in the Supplementary Report.

Resuming consideration of the report of the Executive Board (IV, B, 9 (b)) the request of the Board of Ministerial Relief for a change of its corporate title was again taken up.

A motion to adopt the recommendation of the Executive Board was put and lost.

Moved and carried, That the Convention grant the request of the Board of Ministerial Relief to change its corporate title to "Board of Ministerial Pensions and Relief of the United Lutheran Church in America."

IV, B, 10, (a) and (b) adopted.

IV, B, 13, (b) approved.

IV, B, 13, (c) adopted.

VII, 3, adopted.

VII, 4, adopted.

VII, 5, with its recommendations was read and action deferred.

It having been stated that there was a memorial referring to the latter part of this item, it was moved that the convention dismiss the Committee on Memorials from action on this particular memorial. Action on the motion was deferred until a copy of the memorial might be obtained.

VII, 6, adopted.

VII, 10, adopted.

XI, 1, approved.

XI, 2, adopted.

XII, 2, (c) adopted.

XII, 3, adopted.

The Secretary submitted Item 2 of the Supplementary Report of the Executive Board concerning participation in the World Conference on Faith and Order. (See Supplementary Report, Wednesday, October 29th.)

It was moved and carried, That the conditions of our taking part in the conference as recommended by the Executive Board be approved.

Moved and carried, That this matter be referred back to the Executive Board with power to act as to the proposed conference of 1927.

The Secretary next submitted Item 3 of the Supplementary Report concerning participation in the Universal Conference on Life and Work. (See Supplementary Report.)

It was moved and carried, That the Convention approve the conditions under which we might enter the conference as stated in the report of the Executive Board.

Moved and carried, That the question of entering the Conference on Life and Work be referred back to the Executive Board with power to act.

The Chairman of the Committee on Memorials from Constituent Synods produced, at this point, a memorial from the Indiana Synod relating to VII, 5, (b) of the report of the Executive Board.

The memorial submits that in the judgment of the Indiana Synod the action proposed would be "an encroachment upon the autonomy of the District Synods."

It was then moved and carried, That the Convention dismiss the Committee on Memorials from Constituent Synods from consideration of this memorial.

Prayer was offered by the Rev. Paul H. Roth and the Convention adjourned.

———————•———————

Evening Service

A service was held at eight o'clock P. M., the theme of which was "The Lutheran Church in American History."

The Vespers were conducted by the Rev. H. C. Wasmund.

The Rev. John C. Seegers presided.

Addresses were delivered as follows:

1. "In the Foundations of America."   (Noting the 300th anniversary of first Lutheran services in New York.)   Prof. A. R. Wentz, Ph.D., D.D.

2. "In Colonial Times."   (Noting the 175th anniversary of the Pennsylvania Ministerium.)   Rev. H. A. Weller, D.D.

3. "Since the Establishment of the United States of America." (Noting the 100th anniversary of the South Carolina Synod.) Prof. S. J. Derrick, LL.D.

THIRD MEETING

Morning Session

CONVENTION HALL, EDGEWATER BEACH HOTEL,
Chicago, Ill.

Friday, October 24, 8:45 A. M.

Matins were conducted by the Rev. A. Engeset.

The Convention was called to order by the President.

The President requested and obtained general consent for the hearing of the Report of the Common Service Book Committee immediately after that of the Church Paper Committee.

By general consent it was also ordered that the afternoon session today continue until five o'clock.

Minutes of the morning and afternoon sessions of Thursday were read, corrected and approved.

The Secretary reported that the roll had been completed and that there were 500 delegates present representing all Constituent Synods.

The amendment to By-Laws, Section VII, B, 4, as proposed at yesterday morning's session was adopted.

Consideration of the report of the Executive Board was resumed.

VII, 5, (a) and (b) referred to the Constituent Synods. Along with them also was referred the memorial from the Indiana Synod touching paragraph (b).

Under Section XIII, 1, motion was made and seconded to adopt the recommendations of the Executive Board. Various suggestions were made, among them that the investigation embrace not only the subject of theological education but that it extend also to college and secondary education.

The following substitute was moved and seconded:

Resolved, first, that the Executive Board appoint a commission to make a scientific survey of the educational institutions in the United Lutheran Church, and that it consider the relation of our educational work to the whole status of religious education in our country. Second, that this commission, with the approval of the Executive Board, be empowered to employ impartial educational experts outside of the Lutheran Church. Third, that this commission be asked to report at the next convention.

Moved and carried that a special committee be appointed to which the item and all of the resolutions relating thereto shall be referred and that the committee report recommendations to this convention.

The following were appointed on the committee: Drs. J. A. W. Haas, H. Offermann, F. P. Manhart, P. W. Koller, J. L. Zimmerman, J. A. Clutz.

The Rev. J. A. Singmaster presented the report of the Standing Committee on Church Papers.

REPORT OF THE STANDING COMMITTEE ON CHURCH PAPERS

The United Lutheran Church may well congratulate herself on the possession of two excellent, official weekly church papers—*The Lutheran* and the *Lutherischer Herold*. In appearance they are handsome, in contents interesting, and in price reasonable. The circulation of the former is about 30,000 and of the latter about 7,000. With the faithful co-operation of the pastors these figures can be doubled.

The editors of the *Herold,* elected at your last Convention, resigned some months ago, and the Rev. C. R. Tappert was elected by your Committee as the sole editor. He has had charge of the paper since July 1st.

The Committee hereby nominates the Revs. Drs. George W. Sandt and Nathan R. Melhorn as the editors of *The Lutheran,* and the Rev. C. R. Tappert as the editor of the *Lutherischer Herold* for the coming biennium.

J. A. SINGMASTER, *Chairman.*

Upon motion to adopt, the Rev. N. R. Melhorn and Dr. W. J. Showalter were heard in the interest of the Church papers. The report was adopted.

The Common Service Book Committee reported, Dr. Singmaster presenting the report.

REPORT OF THE COMMON SERVICE BOOK COMMITTEE

The Committee respectfully submits the following report:

NEW HYMNAL FOR CHURCH SOCIETIES.

Since the last meeting of the United Lutheran Church the collection of

"Hymns and Prayers for Church Societies and Assemblies" prepared by the Committee, has been issued by the Publication House. The collection contains 150 hymns, a large number of special Collects and Prayers—many of them new—a selection of Psalms, and several Orders of Service.

The favorable response already accorded this compact and inexpensive hymnal indicates that it will prove generally serviceable in the work of Women's Missionary Societies, Luther Leagues, Brotherhoods, Men's Bible Classes, Sunday Schools, Assemblies, etc. The Luther League of America has officially commended the collection to all its societies and has discontinued its own Hymnal.

The Family Service Book.

The sub-Committee charged with the completion of the Family Service Book (the Rev. Drs. Strodach, Steinhaeuser and Bell) report that the work is progressing, and it is hoped that the book will soon be ready for publication.

New Sunday School Books.

Representatives of the Committee met with representatives of the Parish and Church School Board in a conference at which the Rev. F. F. Fry, D.D., Chairman of a Sub-Committee of the Executive Board presided, to discuss the preparation of Sunday School Hymnals and to define the spheres of authority of the Board and of the Committee respectively. It was agreed that the action of the United Lutheran Church itself had established the principle of joint responsibility and that the question was one of method. It was further agreed that preliminary plans for such a Hymnal or Hymnals should be prepared by the Sub-Committee of the Parish and Church School Board and discussed in full with the Sub-Committee of the Common Service Book Committee, and that after joint agreement on details had been reached and the work completed, it should be submitted for final approval to both the Board and the Committee before publication.

Acting under this agreement the Chairman appointed the Rev. Drs. Reed, Ohl and Strodach as the representatives of the Committee on the Joint Sub-Committee, which organized by electing the Rev. C. F. W. Hoppe, D.D., Chairman, and the Rev. Luther D. Reed, D.D., Secretary. A great deal of preliminary work was done by the Chairman, and the Sub-Committee itself has held three lengthy meetings of four or five days each, blocked out the plans for two books, completed the first draft of the selection of hymns, and made a substantial beginning in the choice of tunes and the preparation of Orders of Service.

Foreign Translations of the Common Service Book

At the request of the Foreign Mission Board and also of the West Indies Mission Board some attention has been given in a preliminary way to the preparation and authorization of Japanese and Spanish translations of the Common Service Book. The work of translation is in process, and the Committee expects to receive thoroughly prepared briefs covering the principles and methods employed, which, as well as the completed translations themselves, will be carefully considered before authority is given the Boards to publish the books.

The Committee presents no recommendations.

JOHN A. SINGMASTER, Chairman,
LUTHER D. REED, Secretary.

The report was adopted.

The President announced the following additional members of the Tellers Committee for today's election: Messrs. F. W. Seegers, A. R. Rhyne, R. C. Counts, W. B. Clarke, Romanus Esterly, J. V. Sutton, E. L. Keiser.

The Rev. L. B. Wolf, Secretary of the Board of Foreign Missions, presented the report of that Board.

REPORT OF THE BOARD OF FOREIGN MISSIONS

Fathers and Brethren:—Your Board of Foreign Missions presents its third biennial report and asks a most careful study of its various fields of operation. The congregations and the constituent Synods have shown an increasing interest in this great department of the Church.

BOARD ORGANIZATION

At the November meeting, 1922, the Secretary of the United Lutheran Church reported that at the Buffalo Convention the following members were elected, whose terms would expire in 1928:

Rev. August Steimle, D.D.	Rev. Jacob S. Simon, D.D.
Rev. Lewis C. Manges, D.D.	Rev. Paul W. Koller, D.D.
Henry P. Boyer, M.D.	Mr. H. D. Bonham
Mr. Mathias P. Moller	

Prof. C. W. Foss was also elected to fill out an unexpired term till 1924.

In November, 1922, Dr. Henry P. Boyer resigned his membership on the Board. At the January meeting, 1924, Mr. Paul Van Reed Miller was elected to fill the vacancy.

At the November meeting, 1922, the following officers were elected for the biennium:

President, REV. EZRA K. BELL, D.D., LL.D.
Vice-President, REV. PROF. C. THEO. BENZE, D.D.
Recording Secretary, REV. GEORGE DRACH, D.D.
Treasurer, REV. LUTHER B. WOLF, D.D.

On March 13, 1924, at Winston-Salem, N. C., Dr. M. M. Kinard passed away. He was a member of the Board's Executive Committee and had a long connection with our foreign cause.

At the March meeting of the Board, Rev. J. Luther Sieber, D.D., was elected to fill the vacancy.

At the same meeting the following nominations were made, to be voted on at the Chicago Convention:

Name	Address

I. For term expiring 1930:

Rev. Ezra K. Bell, D.D.	821 W. Lanvale St., Baltimore, Md.
Rev. J. A. Singmaster, D.D.	Gettysburg, Pa.
Rev. M. J. Epting, D.D.	1413 Bull St., Savannah, Ga.
Rev. Prof. C. Theo. Benze, D.D.,	7304 Boyer St., Mt. Airy, Phila.
Rev. R. C. G. Bielinski	Delanco, N. J.
Mr. James M. Snyder	111 S. 4th St., Philadelphia, Pa.
Prof. C. W. Foss, Ph.D.	3808 8th Ave., Rock Island, Ill.

II. For term expiring 1928:

Paul Van Reed Miller, Esq.	Widener Bldg., Philadelphia, Pa.

III. For term expiring 1926:

Rev. J. L. Sieber, D.D.	352 Church Ave., Roanoke, Va.

GENERAL SUMMARY

The enterprise of Christian Missions does not need motive power, rather does it call for a fuller and clearer apprehension of the main purpose. We cannot restate more clearly that purpose than to emphasize the world or mankind's chief need. This, without doubt, is found in the time-honored words—regeneration and conversion. The essential aim of the missionary is not many-sided. It is one and single, though many elements may contribute to bring it to fruition. It is clearly in Christ's words: "Ye must be born again." Nor can it set before men more definitely the plight of humanity and how to escape therefrom, than to look at mankind as St. Paul did, as in need of a new creation, for "if any man is in Christ there is a new creation; old things are passed away; behold all things are become new." The high end of the missionary movement is to lead men and women into a knowledge of God and the way to God and the new creation is the way of the cross.

The cross and the love, for which it is the symbol, are humanity's and civilization's high need. It cannot be fulfilled but in one way and it is idle to hope to realize it except the world address itself to the divine plan, which is conditioned on "a change of heart." History and human experience meet in admitting that our Easter message is the world's only sure way out. The missionary has this supreme purpose "with the world under his feet, with heaven in his eye, with the gospel in his hand and with Christ in his heart."

The missionary enterprise dares not disregard the certain contributions of the oriental civilizations of past times. It must keep itself "open-minded." It will help much to discover the highest truths found in non-Christian faiths. It should grant something, but hardly dare claim that a golden rule is found in: "What you do not like when done unto yourself, do not do unto others." It is fine to contemplate that Love that fills all and ponder the poet's words about it:

"Thine is the mystic life great India craves,
        Thine is the Parsees' sin-destroying beam,
    Thine is the Buddhist's rest from tossing waves,
        Thine is the Empire of vast China's dreams."

But it will take more than poetry to transform ethnic faiths. They need more than the coloring of Christianity. Jesus Christ must indeed permeate India and all oriental thought. Much more is needed for the human mind than to free itself from "conflicting dogmas and a mind that wars against science." Every ethnic faith must bow to the Nazarene. This must be Christianity's task before it can become "the bridge between East and West." New storm-centers will appear above the horizon in the future as in the past, unless Christ gets his rightful place among men and nations. The thinking of the East must become grounded in the plan of deliverance, revealed by the Lord, before it will meet with that of the West at the foot of the cross. But the West needs to practise the way of the cross perfectly. Well should it weigh the words: "the crowning service" that the West can render to the East is the conversion of the West to Christianity. In fine, "all Western contact" must be Christian and then Christ shall dominate the East.

Our United Lutheran Church has some humble share in the great enterprise. It is neither as large, nor as efficient as it ought to be, but since our merger in 1918, our foreign work has made commendable progress.

In our congregations there are evidences that we are more fully sharing in Christ's great purpose for the nations.

We started our Mission in 1842 in India. We have now assumed responsibility in Liberia, Japan, South America and China. We dare not say, as another great communion does in definite terms, that we have accepted a definite number of people in the non-Christian world as our responsibility, but it may be a good idea if every member of our communion were to accept in his plan, thought and prayer his share of the unreached and unevangelized. In India we have our work among the Telugus and the Oriyas in the Madras Presidency and within that area we touch a large Mohammadan population, which has penetrated the whole of South India. In Africa for 64 years our contacts have been with the aboriginal tribes, chiefly among the Pfessi on the St. Paul River and the adjacent parts of Liberia, though in our schools we teach Gola, Grebo, Bussa, Vay and Mai and other tribal dialects. In the Japan Empire for 30 years our activities have been in school and evangelism and our contacts have mainly been in the Island, Kyushu, though we are setting up stations in the great cities of Tokyo, Osaka, Kobe and smaller centers besides, in evangelistic, educational, rescue and other forms of endeavor. Our new Girls' School to be erected at a cost of $175,000, is our most notable advance in education. In the metropolis of South America, Buenos Aires, the mission began a forward march in 1920, and while it suffered a serious loss in the death of Dr. Mueller, in the strengthening of the foreign staff by the transfer of Rev. Ralph J. White and his wife from British Guiana, and the sending of Rev. and Mrs. Armbruster, the opening of the new church in Villa del Parque in Buenos Aires, the whole plan of the Mission has been greatly enlarged for efficiency. If our Lutheran Church unites with the La Plata Synod, which now we are willing to help financially in the gift of $2,000, and it becomes part of the enterprise, the future prospects will be much brightened.

On the north coast of the Southern Continent in British Guiana, the sending of Rev. and Mrs. Harlow Edgar Haas has met the needs due to withdrawal of Rev. Ralph J. and Mrs. White, and the progress of all parts of the Mission has been insured.

On the home base our hold on the Church seems to be growing, notwithstanding the failure to meet our appeal to raise our Foreign Mission Forward Fund. At the last convention the Board was voted permission to raise $300,000 to meet the indebtedness of the Board of $100,000, and to provide for some much needed advance in our fields, especially in Japan and South America. The Board invited the co-operation of the Presidents of the District Synods and the pastors of the congregations, but the response to the effort was rather disappointing. Up to date the amount raised in cash and pledges is shown as follows:

Cash $114,133.76
Pledges 75,790.84

Total in Cash and Pledges $189,924.60

The total receipts of the Board from all sources for the biennium have been encouraging:

Our apportionment for 1922-23 and 1923-24................ $699,256.40
From Women's Missionary Society 415,425.72
From Augustana Synod 45,646.46
From Danish Synod 20,162.34
From Icelandic Synod 2,400.00
From other sources on current account 204,117.15
From specials not included in current account 182,059.77
From interest on investments 32,462.85
From Legacies and Annuities 25,054.37
Other miscellaneous sources and publications 9,791.33

Total $1,636,376.39

The expenditure on various accounts is summarized as follows:

Budgets to the fields $688,403.48
Salaries of Missionaries 203,773.23
Traveling of Missionaries to and from fields 66,303.45
Medical and other expenses of Missionaries on furlough
    and Candidates 22,903,02
Home Base Expenses and Publications, including secretaries'
    salaries, Board representatives and publicity 86,633.77
Special to various objects on fields 165,246.70
Women's Missionary Society 409,202.90

Total $1,642,466.55

The Board rejoices that it has for the first time since the merger been able almost to balance its budget for the biennium and with the many calls from all the fields to meet some of the most pressing. Its current receipts from all sources amounted to $1,038,890.90 and the disbursements to $1,068,016.95, leaving a deficit of $29,126.05. The totals of receipts and disbursements are exclusive of the Women's Missionary Society and Specials, not included in current account, which together amount to $597,485.49.

It is difficult to estimate the tasks which confront the foreign missionary. The influence, on a great nation, of two methods of missionary operation, the school and the hospital, is not easily estimated. It does not lend itself to tabulation, but it is enough to remember that through them, as well as through all other methods of missionary work, the Kingdom of God is coming, even though it is not so obvious to impatient human eyes. In all our fields we have been steadily reaping a harvest of baptized members, numbering at least 125,000 and in addition to this it is safe to say that the community surrounding these, reached and influenced, is more than four times as large as is represented by these figures. Through school and hospital, and other institutional work, as well as by the direct preaching of the Gospel, our impact is being made on the great non-Christian community in all lands.

We have added in the biennium to our foreign missionary body thirty-six new recruits. We have lost among others from each field those whom the Church could hardly afford to lose—three veterans. Dr. Mueller in South America, the Rev. Frank Traub of Africa and Miss Jessie Brewer in India, were called from their labors here to their eternal reward.

One laid down his active participation in the great India Mission after a connection of fifty years, during which he saw the Christian community grow from a handful of 1300 to its present proportions of 110,000. The Rev. L. L. Uhl, Ph.D. (Johns Hopkins), D.D., has retired to his home in Cambridge, Mass., where he is spending his time with his books and rejoicing as he marks the rapid pace at which things now move in the "land of Ind."

The rest of the representatives of our United Lutheran Church in America, who serve their Church and Lord, are faithfully standing at their posts, and are surely working and waiting for the coming of Christ's Kingdom.

The Christian Church, on the Mission field, has been showing signs of self-conscious life, especially in India, Japan and South America. The body of national pastors, thirty-six in number, and about 3,400 Christian workers, encourage the hope of great advancement in the future in all our fields.

The great World War called us of the United Lutheran Church to extend our operations and embrace the task thrown on us by the almost forcible collapse of the Germany Missionary Societies. Our National Lutheran Council, at first largely in war work service for our boys at the front, so reorganized as to continue its loving service, and assumed large financial responsibilities on behalf of our distressed German Lutheran Missions in the continents of Asia and Africa.

In connection with our Board the Gossner field in Chota Nagpore in the Central Province of India, a territory occupied by our Lutheran Missionaries since 1845, and a most fruitful mission, was financially aided by the National Lutheran Council. After the war, the question was raised whether a united Church, composed of Anglican and Lutheran elements, could not be organized. The members of the Gossner Mission voted to become an autonomous Lutheran Church, the British Government assuming the trusteeship of all property belonging to the German Mission and the Christian bodies through the National Missionary Council of India, appointing a committee to direct the internal affairs of the national Lutheran Church thus organized. Some of our missionaries assisted in the superintendence of the Church and Mission, one of its members becoming the Secretary of the Advisory Committee. During the biennium, Rev. Isaac Cannaday has been Secretary of the Advisory Committee, and with him in the work of the Mission and autonomous Church, Rev. O. V. Werner and wife have been associated.

In South India, in the Jeypore country, and in the Oriya area in the northern part of the Madras Presidency, our Board continued to superintend and support the Schleswig-Holstein (Brecklum) Mission, furnishing men and means in the amount of from $25,000 to $30,000 annually. This field alone has a considerable baptized and communicant membership and is being reorganized and will eventually form part of the United Lutheran Church in India. Two of the old missionaries, Revs. Andersen and Toft, and their families, have been permitted to return to their former fields and have reached the Mission. They are taken over as our missionaries and will work under the guidance of our Mission Council.

From the beginning of our India Mission the Augustana Synod has always been deeply interested in the evangelization of the Telugu country. Although they did not enter the merger in 1918, they have furnished devoted men and women and given generously toward the various developments of work. They have continued their relation with us in the Foreign Board and are represented by Prof. C. W. Foss, who sits as a regular member, and by Dr. Brandelle, the President of the Augustana Synod, and Rev. Dr. Abrahamson, as associate members. All departments, school and hospital, evangelistic and philanthropic, appeal to this vigorous Synod and its great foreign missionary spirit. At present there are 12 missionaries at work, and some on their way to India, and the amount contributed toward the current expenses during the last biennium was $45,646.00. Besides this, they are erecting the Swenson Memorial at a cost of $20,000.

The unity of the Foreign Mission's spirit has also manifested itself in the Danish and Icelandic Synods.

The Danish Synod co-operates with our Foreign Board, of the United Lutheran Church, in all their foreign mission endeavor and are setting an apportionment among their membership on something of the same basis as ours. The Danish Foreign work is incorporated in our Japan Conference, and at the home base all funds are sent to the field through our Board. Their missionaries are among our oldest and most honored and their home organization is represented by two associate members, the Rev. V. W. Bondo and Rev. E. R. Anderson, and on the Japan field by six missionaries.

The Icelandic Synod has also for years united in our Japan work and supported our Foreign Mission operations with men and means. This body of American Lutherans, though not large, has furnished one of the stations of the Japan field. During the biennium they have contributed

$2,400.00 to the funds and the recent visit of the missionary, Rev. S. O. Thorlaksson, among the churches has been most effective in awakening a deeper interest among the church members.

We rejoice in this cooperation and hope it will increase more and more and become the means to draw all our Lutheran bodies, by thus uniting us all in the common task, into closer bonds in our home land. We join forces on the foreign field and thereby increase our effectiveness in world-evangelization.

The next ally to be noted is our Women's Missionary Society. While the Constitution of our United Lutheran Church refers to it as a valuable "auxiliary," this does no more than give it a place among the foreign forces of the Church, and in a way indicates its service. This Society has its own organization among the women of the Church, which functions through its Executive Board. It raises large sums of money to support missionaries in the Church's fields, where are assigned to it departments of work under Mission direction. The major effort is in India, where its missionaries carry on three hospitals and a High School and many schools of lower grade for girls, and a vast work in the Christian community by the maintenance of the Boarding Schools for girls training for Christian work. In Japan the Society is not less effective among women and girls, their last effort being to raise $175,000 to found a Girls' High School. The Society supports 44 missionaries and makes large grants of money to the budgets of India, Japan, Africa and South America. The sum total of their financial output for foreign work during the biennium was $415,425.72. All money raised by them, through their congregational and general organization must be in excess of the church apportionment and under the new organization since the merger of their Societies in 1918, they have made rapid advance in all departments of the Foreign Movement.

Death claimed their efficient Executive Secretary, Mrs. Helen C. Beegle in March last, and a new secretary has been elected in the person of Miss Amelia Kemp, the grand-daughter of Dr. Kemp who for many years was Board member and physical adviser of one of the Foreign Boards of our United Church.

Since our merger in 1918 we have increased from 112 missionaries to over 200 foreign workers. These men and women have met the vast responsibilities of our foreign enterprise in the trying times of the last decade.

No adequate tribute can be paid to those who incarnate the missionary idea of the Church. It is well to call attention to this body of Christian workers in the fine statement of one who is not a missionary or secretary of a Board, but who has lived in the same country with some of them and seen them at their work. Nathaniel Peffer, editor of the *Shanghai China Press* and correspondent of the *New York Tribune*, has this to say of them as a class in an article under the title, "The Uniqueness of the Missionaries:" "To the missionaries in their purely personal aspect, only the prejudiced and ignorant will refuse an abundant meed of admiration. I have never met any other class anywhere so little moved by personal ambition or desire for gain. I doubt whether another exists. They have found an ideal for themselves and they serve it alone and for its own sake. How heavy a sacrifice it demands is known only to those, who like me, have been much with them and seen them in their daily activities and even in some part have shared their experiences." The home church does deeply appreciate the missionary body, as a class, and many of them are so related to individuals and congregations that they are, not excepting our home pastors, remembered in thought and prayer more than any other body of Christians.

Our missionaries have continued to labor diligently and successfully in the Lord in all our fields. Their organized association shows that they are of one heart and one mind in their effort to build up and extend a strong and aggressive Lutheran Church in the world.

In a special manner we must bear testimony to the devoted and faithful efforts of our women missionaries in all branches, evangelistic, educational, medical, merciful and industrial work. Without doubt we owe to our single and married women missionaries much of the spirit of harmony, good will and co-operation which has characterized all our missions during the past two years.

As the missionaries go to, and come from, these distant fields, it is well for the Church to know that they are bid "Godspeed" from the ports of departure, and "welcome home" from the ports of entry. In New York, Board member, Dr. Steimle, has organized a committee to speed them on their way and, if possible, when they return to welcome them home again. On the Pacific Coast our pastors have been most thoughtful in their efforts to meet and say "good-bye" to those who sail through Pacific ports.

The expansion of our work calls for the deepest concern on the part of the Board and Church leaders.

Four years ago we determined, on the recommendation of the Executive Board of the Church, to enter the field of Argentina and take over the work begun in the metropolis city, Buenos Aires. Our missionaries have been richly blessed in their endeavor and now a new situation presents itself which contains much promise for our Lutheran Church. The La Plata Synod has shown itself most friendly to our Mission and steps are being taken with in by our Mission, approved by the Board, to unite in the founding, in the future, of a United Lutheran Church in the Argentina. The plan in contemplation is to work for a German-Spanish Lutheran Church. To further the effort in some practical way, the Board voted $2,000.00 for school and other work among the churches of the La Plata Synod. This convention will be asked to approve of this co-operation.

Since then, through correspondence and conferences, negotiations have progressed in connection with the Berlin Missionary Society so that the Shantung Mission of this organization has been definitely handed over by its Advisory Board to our Board for a consideration of the property of $185,500.00, to be paid in ten annual installments, the transfer to be completed January 1, 1925. With the transfer, the Board will also take over several missionaries of ripe experience and the Chinese congregations, schools and hospital. The Chinese church has a membership of 1,000 communicants.

We need not do more than draw the Convention's attention to these proposed new missions. Our missions in India, Africa and Japan are loudly calling for expansion. We must not deny them, in this high day of opportunity, anything which their rapidly advancing progress demands. Our education prospects should be furthered at once in India, Africa and Japan. Not less than $500,000 should be raised within the next two years, if we are to measure up to our responsibilities in this department.

The last Convention voted for a United Christian College in India:

That the Board of Foreign Missions be authorized to co-operate with other Evangelical Missionary Societies and Boards at work in the Telugu area, India, for the establishment and maintenance of a United Christian College, provided that our Mission in India is proportionately represented in the College Council (Board of Directors) and faculty, and that the unrestricted spiritual care of the Lutheran Students is committeed to our Missions in India.

All indications are now pointing toward the establishment of this College in our Telugu area, in which our Church has been asked to take a leading part. This mighty evangelizing force must be heartily supported. Our Church must not fail here. Of the $500,000 named, not less than $300,000 should be raised for this high endeavor, to dominate education in our part of India by Christianity. We dare not be cold or faint-hearted in these days. Our plans must be backed by consecrated gifts.

While the Board has been considerably relieved by the Foreign Mission Forward Fund, though it fell short in our expectations, a glance at our financial statement must convince all that we have not, as a Church, met (simply mended a bit) our condition. The Board asks every member of the Church to consider the Treasurer's report with deep and prayerful thought. The apportionment laid $1,090,000, for the biennium has been realized only in about 64 per cent of the total asked, or $699,256.40. If all moneys raised be added to this amount, which can be spent on our current work, we have secured through other Synods, specials from churches and individuals, $339,634.50, or almost enough to close this year's work without any deficit, so far as this year's expenditure goes.

We need not be discouraged. But every member of our church should ask himself—"Is this at all an adequate showing of our faith in the 'one only and perfect plan' of world redemption?"

World-peace, world-safety, can be found in the divine way, to meet future problems and heal the hurt of humanity.

INDIA

The statistics of the year 1923 are very encouraging. The net increase in the Christian community for that year was 5,450, raising the total membership to 106,500 in the Rajahmundry and Guntur fields. The work in the Jeypore field has been conducted with increasing vigor during the past two years and there are now five ordained married and two single, women missionaries in that field. It is especially gratifying to be able to report that our Board, as a missionary society recognized by the British Government, has succeeded in securing the return of two former German missionaries, now Danish citizens. Rev. Anders Andersen and Rev. Hans Toft, who with their families sailed from London on September 16, 1924. They will serve under the appointment of our Board in that part of the Jeypore field which belongs to the Madras Presidency. These two are the first Lutheran missionaries formerly in the employ of a German Missionary Society to be allowed to return to India after the great war. It is confidently expected that others will follow soon.

In February, 1923, our Mission celebrated the eightieth year of its history, the fiftieth year of the missionary service of Rev. L. L. Uhl, D.D., and the thirty-third year of the service of Dr. and Mrs. John Aberly. Drs. Uhl and Aberly have returned to the United States, the former as an emeritus missionary, now living in Boston with his wife and daughter, the latter as professor of Missions in the Lutheran Theological Seminary at Chicago.

Two veteran missionaries have entered life. Their names are held in honored and grateful remembrance both in India and in America. Miss Susan E. Monroe served for twenty years at Rajahmundry as an honorary missionary. After a few years in retirement at Mt. Airy, Philadelphia, Pa., she died on May 17, 1923. Miss Jessie Brewer, of Guntur, at the time of her death there on February 12, 1924, was in charge of the Bible Training School at Mangalamandiram.

Of the ninety missionaries in our India fields forty-three are serving their first term of service and fifteen new missionaries are being sent out this year. This indicates to what extent the home Church has been supplying the Mission with new workers since the merger. Of the 3,220 Indian Christian workers in the two fields there are now 31 ordained pastors and a total of 610 men and women who are engaged in evangelistic and pastoral work. The multiplication of this class of workers insures more rapid progress in church life, organization and activity.

The departments of the mission's educational work have enlisted the special interest and thought of the Board. One of these is the Vocational

School on the Lam Reserve near Guntur, where the mission is establishing an industrial middle school which will have far-reaching influence for the economic development of the Christian communities.

The other is the United Christian College. The financial inability of the other Protestant missions in the Telugu area to co-operate for the present in this college on the basis of equal contributions, makes it necessary for our mission to strive to secure enough to begin this great educational enterprise in the hope that later others may furnish their proportionate shares of financial support. The presence of Rev. J. Roy Strock in the United States on furlough undoubtedly will awaken wide-spread interest in this project, because he is the first principal of the Andhra Christian College now temporarily located in Noble College, Masulipatam. An intial $300,000 for site, buildings, equipment and endowment is to be secured by private solicitation, principally through the efforts of our newly appointed field secretary, Rev. J. Frank Heilman, D.D., and Rev. J. Roy Strock. The constitution which is the basis of co-operation for this college has been approved by the Indian mission and the Board, and has been printed in the Annual Report of our Missions. The doctrinal basis, as defined in this constitution, is that of the Declaration of the United Lutheran Church in 1920 at Washington, D. C.

Other developments of primary importance are the Reading Room at Rajahmundry, for which a fine building near the bazaar was purchased and equipped for $13,000; the appointment of a Telugu Lutheran pastor to serve in Rangoon, Burma; the growth of general medical work at Rentichintala and Tarlupad; the increase of the salaries of Indian workers; the transfer of more responsibility in administration to our Indian synods; the successful conduct of a theological school at Luthergiri from which seventeen men were graduated on April 22, 1924. All of them were called and are now serving in definite fields of pastoral work in different parts of the mission.

For those who desire more detailed information concerning the various missionaries, districts, departments and institutions, we refer to the Annual Report, distributed free of charge, and the monthly magazines, "The Foreign Missionary" and "Der Missionsbote."

LIBERIA, AFRICA

THE REPORT OF THE MUHLENBERG CONFERENCE

The Mission has passed the years of this biennium with little change in the methods of work, but with many marks of substantial progress.

At the request of the Mission the Board transferred the name "Muhlenberg" from the Mission to the Conference, and has named the Mission, the American Lutheran Mission in Monrovia. The Conference has ceased to function quarterly and has voted to hold only an annual meeting in the month of January. The work of administration has been handed over to an Executive Committee with power to act under such limitations as the Muhlenberg Conference shall set from time to time.

The health of our missionaries has continued fair. The Board has, after long deliberation, determined to set the uniform limit to each term of service at 27 months, to be followed by six months furlough to America. In doing this it is following the length of service required of those who work in other services on the West Coast of Africa. During the biennium our Mission Staff has been augmented by the following missionaries: Rev. and Mrs. Roy L. Yund, Mr. and Mrs. E. D. Ireland, Rev. Paul M. Counts, Mr. and Mrs. Homer C. Leonard, Miss Mary E. Bauer, Dr. H. L. Worrall, Miss Bertha Klein, Miss Bertha Dierolf, Miss Dora Hahn, Miss Mariam Treon, Mr. and Mrs. George Cope, Rev. and Mrs. Fred Bloch, Dr. and Mrs. E. A. Lape and Rev. Knud Jensen. The missionaries who withdrew from the field and severed their relations were Rev. and Mrs. Frank Traub, Rev. and Mrs. C. H. Brosius. The Rev. Frank Traub passed away on May 7, 1923, in Philadelphia.

Our staff totals 37 at the close of this report, including the wives of our missionaries.

The Mission has been strengthening the various departments of its operations, especially the medical and educational, though it has also pressed into the "hinterland" and opened up new stations as school and evangelistic centers. The health of our missionaries has been safeguarded by the employment of Drs. Worrall and Fuszek. With the latter who has had many years of experience on the West Coast a contract has been made to be continued as needs require. A laboratory has been in operation. New sub-stations are being opened and Zorzor has been occupied as a station at which the gift of the Gettysburg Assembly is to be used to furnish all needed buildings and equipment. Dr. Worrall is conducting the medical work with success at Zozo.

The old Wuodi station, which has been superintended for some years by Rev. E. A. Ayers, who was formerly one of our missionaries, has been, on his retirement from mission work, transferred to our Mission as one of our stations with all property rights and work.

The Board has called to its service Mr. George Cope, a graduate of Pennsylvania State College. He goes out as the first Agricultural Missionary. He will especially interest himself in our industrial mission work. He has taken special courses in agriculture in the South. Africa needs help in every way and our Mission has fostered its physical needs as well as its spiritual.

We are pressing on toward the interior and are endeavoring to occupy that part of Liberia in which Pfessi and allied dialects are spoken.

Our educational work continues to prosper. A Commission under friends interested in Africa's and Liberia's education recently made an extended visit and report on West Africa and the schools thereof. As the result heard by Dr. Jones of the Phelps-Stokes Foundation in New York, an Advisory Committee has been formed on Education to survey and report on the needs of education in Liberia with a view to improvement of system and schools. The Committee is backed financially by the American Colonization and New York Colonization Societies, the Protestant Episcopal, Lutheran and Methodist Foreign Boards and the Phelps-Stokes Fund. The Committee contemplates sending a specialist to Liberia to make a careful study and survey of the whole education system and are calling for a suitable man for this work.

The Mission now conducts, including its boys and girls boarding schools, 10 schools in which are 584 pupils. The Boarding Schools are intended primarily for the training of Christian boys and girls for future work in the Mission. A Girls' School has been opened at Sanoghie.

The building operations under Mr. Miller have been carried on with success. A doctor's house and an extra house for general and the builder's use have been built. The Mission's house in Monrovia has been found most convenient in the work of transportation of goods and travel of missionaries to and from the field. The new building at Kplopele for use of the Theological Institute and the Reading Room at the Boys' School, all mark advance in our work.

The church membership is growing and while it is a matter of slow growth in the interior, the number increases at every station, and our communicant members numbers 188.

JAPAN

As we look back upon the work of our Japan Mission during the past two years our minds are still filled with thoughts of the great disaster which befell Yokohama and Tokyo on September 1, 1923, when after several severe earthquake shocks, fire destroyed so many lives and so much property in the afflicted area. Our Lutheran Church in America was quick to respond to the Board's appeal for relief funds, which enabled the Board to place $35,000 at the disposal of our missionaries in Tokio, where they concentrated on the relief of the suffering and distress of old people and of widows and children, housed in hastily constructed barracks. The Japanese people were filled with gratitude and friendship for America and Americans, after the outpouring of sympathetic goodwill whereby $10,000,000 flowed into Japan through the Red Cross Society.

Little progress has been made during the past two years in supplying the Japan Mission with adequate material equipment for its work. A lot was purchased in Tokio for $21 640, on which a chapel and a parsonage for the Japanese pastors will be erected at once. A lot was bought also in Shimonoseki for $7,000. of which the United Danish Church furnished $4,705. No new buildings have been erected; but the next biennium should witness great activity in building operations. Plans and estimates have been approved for an additional wing of the Kyushu

Gakuin dormitory, for which the United Lutheran Church Brotherhood has raised $5,000. The Luther League of the State of New York has in hand $5,600 for a professor's home on the grounds of the theological seminary in Tokio. The Brown Memorial Chapel at Kyushu Gakuin will be erected at an estimated cost of $35,000, and a second missionary's home will be built for $5,000 on the campus of Kyushu Gakuin. With funds borrowed from a member of the Lutheran Church in Shimonoseki, amounting to about $4,000 a chapel is to be erected on the site recently purchased. The erection of a chapel and parsonage on the Tokio lot has been authorized at an approximate cost of $5,000. It is hoped that chapels in Osaka and Kobe may be erected although adequate financial provision for them has not yet been made.

Undoubtedly the most significant feature of the development of our work in Japan during the past two years is the return of three Japanese, Rev. I. Miura, Rev. H. Inadomi and Rev. N. Asaji, who completed their studies in America. Within the next two years two others, K. Hirai and C. Kishi, will join this group. Rev. S. Sato who spent several months in study in Germany, England and the United States, also returned to the mission last year. Other members of our Lutheran Church in Japan are taking courses in American colleges. Thus there will gradually be formed a strong nucleus of trained and qualified Japanese Lutherans, from which must grow a sturdy and flourishing Japanese Lutheran Church.

By the purchase of a large tract of land at Kumamoto for $35,000, a good beginning has been made in the establishment of the proposed Girls' School.

There are now 34 missionaries in Japan, of whom 14 are ordained men and six single women missionaries. They all are zealously engaged in evangelistic or educational work in co-operation with the Japanese Lutheran Church (Nihon Fukuin Ruteru Kyokwai), and the next few years should bring abundant fruit (in the harvest of souls and rapid progress in every direction of mission work).

THE SOUTH AMERICAN MISSIONS
British Guiana

In British Guiana the most marked change has been the transfer of Rev. and Mrs. Ralph White to our Buenos Aires field in Argentina at the close of 1923 and the call and appointment of Rev. and Mrs. Edgar Haas to take charge of the field in British Guiana. They are getting acquainted gradually with the Mission and report progress in the schools and churches.

Missionary White was in charge of the Mission since 1916 and left it in good condition and well organized in all branches. The field while limited, contains most interesting spheres of influence. The old historic church in New Amsterdam, established in 1748, the more recent development along the Berbice River, the work in the interior, the congregations among the Arrowak Indians, and the last effort to organize a mission among the East Indian people in the Hindi tongue—all combine in making a most interesting field of Foreign Missions. With our large work in India it is easy to see how our British Guiana Mission links up with future possibilities among that large population of Hindus, who have settled on the soil of South America to help work out the labor problems in the colony. Our Hindi Mission among these people is growing and we should give more attention to it.

Our schools in New Amsterdam and on the Berbice River continue to flourish under the generous aid received from colonial authorities. A vocational and commercial school has been opened and bids fair to be a new center of influence and helpfulness to all classes.

The evangelistic work has been extended into the interior and a new station beyond Ituni has been organized among the Arrowaks. All our old congregations are flourishing and our Sunday schools are growing in size and efficiency, that one in connection with the New Amsterdam Church being the largest in the colony.

The invested funds administered by the colonial authorities meet a good part of the mission upkeep. The total expenditure of the mission last year was $5,485.00, of which grants from the Government amounted to $1,197.00, income from endowments and property $1,499.00, benevolence $866.00 and from the home church $1,975.00. The ordinary repairs on all church property was borne by the congregations. Extensive improvements were paid for by the Board.

The statistics of the Mission for last year show 8 Christian workers, 4 congregations and Luther Leagues, 3 Primary Schools, 112 pupils, and a baptized membership of 505, and a confirmed membership of 347.

Buenos Aires, Argentina

This Mission has passed through a great trial and loss in the death of Dr. E. H. Mueller on November 22, 1923. This event, however, called special attention to this last Mission of the Board. It was deemed wise to send one of the secretaries to make a closer inspection of what had been done since the reorganization under our Board in 1920. In every way the visitation has been beneficial, and a new interest has been aroused in the field. The Board's Secretary spent two months in his visitation, looked into the plans of the Mission and helped to introduce the Rev. Ralph J. White, who had answered the Board's call in British Guiana to become a missionary in the Argentina field, and who arrived in Buenos Aires in February to enter this most important work, where so much was to be done and so large a field of operation opened up to our church.

Our property interests in Buenos Aires are considerable and all these were duly studied by the Board's representatives. We now have purchased land, a site in Villa del Parque, 350 ft. front and from 120 to 160 ft. deep; on it we have two mission houses and a fine church building and the whole will cost the Church not more than $85,000.

The congregation work at Villa del Parque, Caseros, San Miguel, Jose C. Paz has grown and the day schools and Sunday schools are well attended and promise well for the future.

THE LA PLATA SYNOD

While in Buenos Aires the Secretary of the Board became interested in the operations of the La Plata Synod. For several years our Mission and the representatives of the Synod have carried on correspondence and were on frindly terms. They have approached each other with a view to learning the nature of the church life and work, and also to ascertain whether they might not be mutually helpful. Some sort of co-operation seemed possible, which might eventually lead to the establishment of a permanent, self-governing Lutheran Church. A conference was held between the representatives of the La Plata Synod and the Mission on February 21, 1924, in the German Church in Buenos Aires.

There were present representing the Mission, Rev. L. B. Wolf, Rev. Ralph J. White and Rev. Paul O. Machetzki, and on the part of the Synod, Rev. Wick, Rev. Shuler, Rev. Detterborn and Rev. Ohlert. Full and unhurried discussion of the nature of the work to be done, the ground of co-operation and the aim in view to be attained, was held.

The two groups of representatives arrived unanimously at certain agreements, chief of which are:

(1) That all work in school and church should be conducted bilingually, or linguistically as needs require.

(2) That the ultimate goal is the establishment of a national Lutheran Church in South America.

These representatives signified their willingness to present these agreements to their respective bodies at as early a date as possible, so that practical operations might begin.

It was agreed (1) That the field for work be the section of the Republic of Argentina known as the Entre Rios, between the Parana and La Plata Rivers, with Urdenarrain, as a probable center, and

(2) That for the first year the starting of four schools on the new basis and the employment of two additional pastors for church expansion, one to be chosen by the Mission and one by the Synod, should be attempted.

(3) That an estimate of the cost involved be left to members of the La Plata Synod for subsequent report to the Mission as a basis for consideration.

The following estimate, as promised by the representatives of the

Synod and approved tentatively by our Mission has been submitted, under date of March 11, 1924.

Two pastors .... $m/n	7,200
Rent	1,200
Travel	800
4 schools—salaries	7,000
Rent	2,000
Enlargement for additional classes	1,000

$m/n 18,200 or $6,500

It was also suggested that parsonages be built at an estimated cost of about $6,500.

All agreements entered into by your representatives and our Mission Board of Foreign Missions of the United Lutheran Church in America.

The following action was taken by the Board:

Voted I. That our Board approves the steps taken by their representatives and their Mission in Buenos Aires looking toward the ultimate formation of a Lutheran Church in Argentina.

Voted II. That as a basis of co-operation, the Board submits the following to the La Plata Synod:

(1) That Luther's Small Catechism be taught in all the schools and Sunday schools of the churches.

(2) That the doctrinal basis of the Spanish speaking, self-governing church is to be that of the United Lutheran Church in America, as follows:

(a) The United Lutheran Church in America receives and holds the Canonical Scriptures of the Old and New Testaments as the inspired Word of God, and as the only infallible rule and standard of faith and practice, according to which all doctrines and teachers are to be judged.

(b) The United Lutheran Church in America accepts the three ecumenical creeds, namely, The Apostles' The Nicene and the Athanasian, as important testimonies drawn from the Holy Scriptures and rejects all errors which they condemn.

(c) The United Lutheran Church in America receives and holds the Unaltered Augsburg Confession as a correct exhibition of the faith and doctrine of the Evangelical Lutheran Church, founded upon the Word of God; and acknowledge all churches that sincerely hold and faithfully confess the doctrines of the Unaltered Augsburg Confession to be entitled to the name of Evangelical Lutheran, and

(d) The United Lutheran Church in America recognizes the Apology of the Augsburg Confession, the Smalkald Articles, the Large and Small Catechisms of Luther and the Formula of Concord, as in the harmony of one and the same pure Scriptural faith, and

Voted III. That upon the La Plata Synod's acceptance of this basis the Board of Foreign Missions will begin the proposed co-operative work in Argentina and elsewhere, as the Mission and Synod shall agree, provided this plan of co-operation is approved by the United Lutheran Church in America.

Voted IV. That pending further negotiations with the La Plata Synod, the Board makes an appropriation of $2,000 towards the support of Spanish-speaking and Spanish-German-speaking schools, provided the teachers shall be amenable to the Mission.

CHINA

At the last biennial Convention of the United Lutheran Church the following resolution was passed:

China Mission.—*Resolved,* That when opportunity is offered and funds are made available, the Board of Foreign Missions be authorized to begin a Mission in China.

Early in 1923 Missionsdirektor Knack in conversation with the Board Secretaries remarked how heavy the Berlin Society found its load financially and intimated that it might be possible for his Society to hand over the Shantung, China, Mission, if our Board was disposed to consider such a proposition. He made it clear that this was his own suggestion and could not bind his Society to any course of action. It was mutually agreed that he should present the whole matter to his Executive Committee on his return to Germany. It was also pointed out that such a transfer, if negotiated, would involve the purchase of mission property by the Board at a fair price and this would enable the Berlin Society to carry on their Canton Mission with more success and without financial embarrassment.

The whole matter was left to further consideration. After Dr. Knak's return to Germany in March, 1923, he conferred with his Committee and on the 5th of May wrote to our Board the result of his conference with his Executive Committee. He found the sentiment to be very much in favor of handing over the Mission and asked a cable concerning our Board's position. The conditions on which the Executive Committee of the Berlin Society would transfer the Shantung Field to the United Lutheran Church were as follows:

(1) Our property (land and buildings) is to be purchased for a sum fixed by an impartial estimate. We would suggest that the Norwegian Missionary, Rev. Mr. Larsen, brother of the late President of the National Lutheran Council, or another suitable member of a friendly Lutheran Society be requested to make the estimate. The payments might be made in installments during a period of ten (10) years.

(2) Inasmuch as the transfer of our work would be justifiable only if our older and greater work in Canton would thereby be strengthened, the Committee would expect the United Lutheran Church to continue to do all in its power to help us to preserve our work in the South.

(3) A number of our missionaries in Shantung would be transferred and serve the United Lutheran Church, namely Superintendent Voskamp of Tsingtau, Missionary Scholz of Kiautschou and Sister Kæthe Voget of Tsingtau. Missionaries Miller and Matzat and Sister Frieda Strecker would be used by the Berlin Mission in its other field.

(4) Corresponding with the agreement between the Augustana Synod and the Leipsic Mission in East Africa, an arrangement might be made for the Berlin Mission to again take a part of the work in Shantung should favorable circumstances arise. This point is not so important as 1 to 3.

The Berlin Mission has been at work in Shantung since 1898. There are now three main stations:

(1) Tsingtau. Work in two sections of the city. (a) Dabaudau and (b) Tai-Dungschen.

The Mission house in Tsingtau is located on a hill overlooking the city with a view of the bay and the open sea. Built for two families and roomy. A garden surrounds the house.

The High School building in the garden was destroyed when the city was captured.

In the city the Mission owns a well-located and rather good-sized property on which the Girls' School and dormitory are erected.

Dabaudau and Tai-Dungdschen each have a chapel with residential quarters for a married pastor.

(2) Kiautschou. Here there is a missionary's home for two families and single woman missionary. The surrounding garden is very large. There is a well-built chapel, home for helper and school.

(3) Tsimo, north of Tsingtau, reached by railway and mule-cart in two or three hours. Like Kiautschou a country seat. The mission station is located outside of the city on property containing a building for two small missionary families, chapel, pastor's house and outbuildings. Five minutes distant is a small, well-built hospital with rooms for a woman missionary. Chinese doctor and an unmarried coolie. The lot is 10 Chinese or 5 Prussian acres large.

With Tsingtau eight out-stations are connected; with Kiautschou 9, with Tsimo 14. In sixteen of these out-stations are chapels on lots belonging to the Mission. The other chapels are rented. The number of Christians has shrunken to 1,000 on account of the war and its aftermath.

At each station is a primary school. The higher schools for boys and the Theological Seminary, as well as the Hospital were not reopened after the war. The Girls' School was reopened. In Tsingtau and Kiautschau the women missionaries have trained a number of Bible-women. Four students are being sent to the Joint Lutheran Seminary in Shekow. The industrial schools for agricultural work and the young men's societies in Dabaudau, Tai Dunghschen and Tsimo have not been resumed.

Other missions in and around Tsingtau are American Presbyterians, who started their work before the Berlin Society and have been friendly.

In Dr. Knak's judgment the following points of view should be considered in regard to the transfer:

(1)   Shantung is one of the densely populated provinces of China, as densely populated as parts of Germany.

(2)   The people are quiet, reliable, true-hearted, sincere, conservative, slower than those in the South but more serious.

(3)   The people are poor and live simple lives. The salaries of Chinese pastors and helpers are comparatively low, approximately $10.00 Mex. per month and lower. The development of the city will increase salaries. Tsingtau will become an important international center. Nearly half of the property of the city remains in the hands of the Japanese, despite the transfer of the province to China in September, 1922.

(4)   The language of the people is Mandarin. As a consequence there is much missionary literature available, much more than in Pakhoi, where the Punti Dialect is spoken.

(5)   For the development of Christianity in China, and therefore, for the Lutheran Church in China, Shantung is far superior, strategically than Pakhoi.

(6)   From Tsingtau Shekow, where the Joint Seminary of the Lutheran Church in China and a center of church government is located, is easily reached by rail, over the Tsingtau-Tsinanfu-Hankow Railroad.

(7)   It would be advantageous to continue the development of the Berlin Mission. The main stations are well located far enough apart and yet form a complete whole. The work may be readily developed northward, where the Iai-Jang, a country seat, an out-station has been started with an active congregation. The work may also be extended westward by way of Kiautschau and beyond.

The pioneer work has been done by the Berlin Mission. An organization of the native Church, discussed while I was there, embraces the established work. But the work is still new and conditions plastic, awaiting further development. Lack of funds has held the work back. The aftermath of the war threatens stagnation.

Capable and earnest missionaries and a number of pious and efficient helpers have given work the character of sound piety as the basis of Lutheran teaching. Luther's Small Catechism, which some farmers are known to have tied to their plows in order to prepare themselves for holy baptism, has proven its value in the work.

The retention of the services of missionaries Voskamp and Scholz would insure the continuation of the prestige won by the Berlin missionaries. Voskamp ranks above the average intellectually and is regarded as an outstanding China missionary. He is conversant with the classical Chinese, a good evangelist, an earnest pastor (Seelsorger), and a talented author. He would be invaluable to the New Board in control. His interesting mission reports in American papers are said to have been the incentive which led the Missouri to begin its work in China. He speaks and writes English fluently, having been acquainted with it since childhood.

Missionary Scholz has been in charge of the training of native pastors. His pupils have distinguished themselves as clear thinkers and good preachers. It would be well to locate a preparatory theological school at his station, Kiautschau and then send the students for final work to Shekow.

Yours sincerely,

(Signed) MISSIONSDIREKTOR KNAK.

Our Board's action on receipt of this letter was as follows:

Voted 1. That the following cablegram, as suggested by Missiondirektor Knak of the Berlin Society, be sent by Secretary Dr. Wolf: ACERVATE BOARD. This means that the Board is willing to enter into further negotiations with the Berlin Missionary Society for the transfer by purchase of the Shantung field to our Board.

2. That as a basis for these negotiations our Board accepts conditions one, two and three, as stated in Missionsdirektor Knak's letter of May 5th.

3. That the fourth condition be left for further discussion and correspondence.

4. That Secretary Dr. Wolf be directed to seek a conference with Missionsdirektor Knak in Berlin this summer, before or after attending the meeting of the International Missionary Council, and report to the Board.

On July 21, 1923, Dr. Benze and Dr. Wolf met the Committee. Out of this meeting the following proposals were agreed to:

1. That the Board of Foreign Missions of the United Lutheran Church in America will purchase outright all the property and good-will of the Shantung Mission Field of the Berlin Society, paying for it in ten equal installments (or less if possible), and will pay interest at 3 per cent on balances due.

2. That the value of the Mission property shall be fixed by a committee of three, one to be Rev. N. Astrup Larsen, or any one chosen, one to be chosen by the Berlin Society and these two to choose the third member.

3. That upon the first annual payment the Board of Foreign Missions of the United Lutheran Church in America will assume control of the Mission and be wholly responsible for the entire force of native Christian workers as well as the missionaries named in the letter of Missionsdirektor Knak dated May 5, 1923, namely, Missionaries Voskamp, Scholz and Sister Kæthe Voget, provided that the native Christian Church is in sympathy with and agrees to the transfer.

4. That the Board of Foreign Missions of the United Lutheran Church will retain the services of Missionaries Voskamp, Scholz and Sister Kæthe Voget so long as they are willing to work under the Board in control, it being understood that their salaries and allowances are to remain as they are at present until the Board fixes its own scale.

The question most discussed was as to the future, and two proposals were left for the Berlin Society to consider as follows:

"(1) It is agreed that the question of the future of the Berlin Society in Shantung shall be considered with prayerful sympathy, should the way open for their return to the former field.

"(2) An additional statement re the future of the Berlin Society in Shantung: Inasmuch as the Berlin Society has expressed a most earnest desire, if its ability allows in future, to be permitted in some way, to resume mission work in its present Shantung field, by a transfer of some part thereof or by some plan of co-operation: It is further agreed that future negotiations concerning this matter be left an open question to be dealt with by the two Societies (Viz. the Board of Foreign Missions of the United Lutheran Church in America and the Berlin Society) should circumstances be favorable to such negotiations as the situation may call for."

It is understood that, if part of the field should be transferred by the Baltimore Board to the Berlin Society, it would be after an agreed price has been fixed as in this case; or should co-operation in work seem best, it shall be of such a nature as shall be fully agreed to by the two parties to this present transfer, or by their successors.

Under date of February 9, 1924, Rev. N. Astrup Larsen writes a report of the Appraisement Committee, consisting of Rev. C. I. Voskamp, Chas. F. Johnson and himself, as follows:

Valuation Berlin Mission Property.—The Committee appointed to appraise the property of the Berlin Mission in Shantung, met Wednesday to Saturday, January 30th to February 2, 1924.

The first day was spent in viewing the property in Tsingtao, Taitungchen, Litsun, and the out-station, Tangyao. The second day the Committee went to Kiaochow and viewed the property there. The third day the property at Tsimo was reviewed.

In all these places disinterested parties, Chinese as well as foreigners, were consulted as to values.

The last day the Committee again met in Tsingtao and hereby submit the following as their findings:

Tsingtao Mission house	$140,000
" Girls' School	50,000
" Church	20,000
Taidungchen chapel, school, etc.	15,000
Litsum church, dwelling and land	12,000
Kiaochow mission house, chapel, school, land, etc.	85,000
Tsimo dwelling, church, hospital and land	40,000
Out-stations in Tsimo district	5,400
" " " Kiaochow district	2,600
" " " Tsingtao district	2,600
Total	$372,600
Deduction for repairs	20,000
Total Mex.	$352,600

At present rate of exchange(U. S. $1.00 about Mex. $1.90).

Total U. S.	$185,500

Committee:

C. I. Voskamp.
Chas. F. Johnson.
N. Astrup Larsen.

The following letter accompanied the above estimate:

Dear Dr. Wolf:—

In compliance with the request of the United Church Board of Foreign

Missions I have now been in Tsingtao for the purpose of helping to appraise the property of the Berlin Mission. And I hereby submit the Committee's report in connection with which I wish to make a few remarks.

In your letter of August 20th, 1923, you intimated that you would prefer the third member of our Committee to be chosen from the Presbyterian Mission in Shantung. We are very fortunate in securing the Chairman and Secretary of that Mission, Dr. Chas. F. Johnson (M.D.). Dr. Johnson has been in China more than thirty years, and is universally recognized as one of the wisest and best informed missionaries in North China.

As to the Girls' School and Church in Tsingtao we felt that in view of their central location and undoubted value from a business point of view, the estimate of the Berlin Mission was by no means unreasonable. The Presbyterian Mission has recently sold a piece of property less favorably located than the Tsingtao church, and smaller, for the sum of $15,000. Pastor Voskamp reports that a Chinese sometime ago offered him $18,000 for the church property and when Mr. Voskamp intimated that he would not think of selling for that price, the Chinese immediately raised the offer to $20,000. The Girls' School is almost as centrally located, and all inquiries led us to believe that $50,000 was a very fair price.

Time would not allow us to visit the out-stations. We saw only one out-station in the Tsingtao district. The buildings here were substantial and solid, and upon being assured by Pastor Voskamp that the other out-station buildings owned by the Mission were equally substantial we felt that the estimate for out-stations were very conservative.

But as the buildings are nearly all in need of extensive repairs, we felt that a further cut of $20,000 for repairs was not unreasonable. By making this deduction for repairs the total sum was reduced to Mex. $352,600. At present the rate of exchange in Shantung and also in Honan, is about Mex. $1.90 to U. S. $1.00. Figuring on this basis we have therefore placed the sum total to be paid in United States currency at $185,500.

Although we had not been asked to do so, Dr. Johnson and myself thought we might save time for your Board and the Berlin Mission by seeing the American Consul in Tsingtao as to the transfer of property held by former German subjects on the strength of deeds given by the German Government. When the Japanese took possession they compelled Pastor Voskamp to give up most of the deeds given him by the German Government. But the Japanese authorities gave him certain papers to indicate his ownership of all property in question. Now that the Kiaochow territory has been receded to the Chinese Government, it was thought that perhaps complications might arise in a case of transfer. The Consul stated, however, that he thought there would be no difficulties if the German Mission would be able to show clear title of the property as by the Washington Agreement the Chinese authorities have bound themselves to respect and safeguard the legitimate vested interests of the different powers within the leased territories. He expressed himself as very much interested in the matter and promised to take it up with the legation at Peking and thus make preparations for the contemplated transfer. He declared that in order to facilitate matters, after the transfer is ultimately decided upon, the Berlin Mission ought to give full power of attorney to Pastor Voskamp, and your Board likewise appoint some person with full power of attorney to represent you in the matter. The property in Kiaochow and Tsimo districts is all held on the strength of regular Chinese deeds and should present no difficulties whatever.

I cannot refrain from saying a word or two as to the importance of Tsingtao. I had heard about the beauties of the place and the splendid city laid out by the Germans. I had therefore expected much, but must nevertheless say that the reality surpassed my expectations. Tsingtao is a thoroughly modern and up-to-date city, well laid out with broad streets, and most beautifully situated upon what has by some been expressed as the best deep-water harbor on the Chinese coast. If some day the plans of the Germans are realized, and Shantung railway continued westward through western China, Tsingtao should automatically become a far more important port than at present. For these and other reasons, I am very eager to see the United Church come to Shantung and build up a strong Lutheran Church at Tsingtao and surrounding territory.

Dr. Johnson asked me as to your Board's plans for the future, whether you intended to retain the German missionaries, etc. He expressed a very definite hope that you would decide to retain the present missionaries, especially Pastor Voskamp who is well and favorably known not only in Shantung, but also in other parts of China, and has won universal respect and confidence of all who know him. I cannot but say that I fully share Dr. Johnson's views of the matter. But though I hope that you will decide, in case of transfer, to retain the present German missionaries, I also hope that you will be able to send a large staff of well-prepared young men and women at an early date to join them and put the now very much under-staffed work upon its feet again.

Hoping that the contemplated transfer may be made, and that we may soon have the joy of welcoming the United Church in China, I am

Yours very sincerely,
(Signed) N. Astrup Larsen.

The Board's action was as follows:

In view of the action taken by our Board on May 24, 1923, and in view of agreements made at the Berlin Conference with Dr. L. B. Wolf, July 20-23 1923, the following resolutions were adopted as the terms of settlement for the transfer of the Shantung field to the United Lutheran Church in America:

(1) That the Board of Foreign Missions accepts the estimate of the value of property in the Berlin mission field, Shantung Province, as fixed by the special appraisement committee at $353,600 Mexican, or $185,500 United States.

(2) The sum of $10,000 be paid by July 1, 1924, to the Berlin Missionary Society as a first installment for the purchase of its mission property in the Shantung field, and that on or before January 15th of each year subsequent to that date, an annual payment of at least one-tenth of the principle with interest at 3 per cent shall be made on account of this purchase until the entire purchase price of $185,000 shall have been paid provided that the Berlin Missionary Society shows clear title to the property and makes transfer of the same to the Board of Foreign Missions of the United Lutheran Church on or before January 1, 1925.

(3) That the Board of Foreign Missions of the United Lutheran Church appoints Rev. J. Astrup Larsen with full power of attorney on

its behalf, and requests the Berlin Missionary Society likewise to appoint someone with full power of attorney to act for it in this transfer.

(4) That on and after January 1, 1925, the Board of Foreign Missions of the United Lutheran Church will assume full authority financially and administratively, of the Shantung mission work, retaining for the present the services of Missionaries Voskamp, Scholz, and Sister Kæthe Voget.

(5) That in order to consumate this transfer and conduct this Mission in China the Board of Foreign Missions requests the United Lutheran Church to add to its present budget $50,000 annually for the China mission.

Action was somewhat delayed due to some questions raised on the last point, viz., the return of some part of the field, or the question of future co-operation. The Board made its final answer in the following:

1. That our Board is prepared, if the Berlin Society agrees, to take over the Shantung Mission on the terms indicated at the original Conference held in Berlin in July, 1923.

2. That the Board is satisfied and willing to stand by a sympathetic interpretation of the statements contained in its representative's report, and that under the conditions pointed out, the question of the Berlin Society resuming work and the conditions under which it shall be resumed, is left open for future determination on the same conditions under which our Board now is willing to assume the responsibility of the Shantung field.

3. That in regard to any further missionaries than the ones named, it is quite willing to give sympathetic consideration, but would call the Berlin Society's attention to the fact that the matter was left an open question to be determined when the time comes, the appointment of such missionaries to be settled by the consideration of each case on its merits as our Board settles appointments of its own missionaries.

Voted, That the present negotiations cover the transfer of the entire Shantung field to our Board, but our Board agrees to reopen negotiations for the return of a part of this field to the Berlin Society should the society present a request to resume mission work in this field within ten years from the date of the transfer.

The final letter from the Berlin Society reads as follows:

Berlin, July 9, 1924.

Reverend and dear Brethren:—

It is now a little over a year that negotiations have been carried on between your and our Board, with reference to the transfer of our Mission property in Shantung in North China.

We have also received a letter from Dr. Wolf of your Board informing us of your resolution of March 27, 1924, and we hasten to inform you of our decision in this matter.

We are convinced that this is the way appointed by God's wise providence, consequently we accept your proposition as the proper and only way out of the difficulties.

We herewith declare ourselves to be in full accord with the four items of your resolution of March 27, 1924.

1. That the value of our property in Shantung is fixed at the sum of $185,500.

2. That a payment of $10,000 United States currency be made during 1924, that further, the remaining balance be paid by annual installments

of at least 1-10 of the principal—besides 3 per cent interest, on or before
the 15th day of January of each year, until the total or $185,500 be paid
in full. It is understood that we deliver the deeds of the property in
Shantung to your Board by January, 1925.

3. That the United Lutheran Church and the Berlin Mission appoint
each one commissioner who shall act as their representative at the transfer
of the property. We welcome the appointment of the Rev. Astrup Larsen
and reserve the right to appoint a competent commissioner after consultation with our missionary superintendent, Dr. Voskamp.

4. That beginning January 1, 1925, your Board assume full control of
the Shantung field, including financial responsibility, as well as the support of the missionary superintendent, Dr. Voskamp, Theo. Scholz and
Sister Kæthe Voget.

We take for granted that your Board will carry out certain resolutions
communicated by Dr. Wolf on May 14, 1924, and repeated since; namely,
first—the possibility of an eventual return by the Berlin Mission to the
old field; second, the support of additional missionaries by your Board.
Both tentative propositions have been the result of a conference in Berlin
in which Dr. Wolf and Dr. Benze participated. We understand this
verbal agreement is not binding for the present, but we reserve the
privilege for our Berlin Mission to reopen the matter, if request is made
before January 1, 1935, in case we should be strong enough to assume
the work, partially at least.

In making a transfer of real estate from your Board to ours the present appraised value will be considered as a basis for negotiations.

The probabilities of renewing as stated above are very small under
present conditions.

In addition to the support of above-named missionaries we would kindly
ask you to support the following workers also: Missionary W. Matzat in
Tsimo and Sister Frieda Strecker in Kautschu. . . We believe it would be
a great calamity for the field at Shantung to remove our workers, or
to be compelled to call them home, especially as there is a lack of
workers, to say nothing of efficient workers on the field. To demonstrate this lack of workers we just wish to mention a few items.
The great competition on the field, which is caused by the work of
the Adventists, Presbyterians and Swedish Baptists, aiming at the
complete isolation of our work. Had we sufficient means we would
now, as soon as possible, create new stations, main stations, in
Dschuidschong where we had a station in former years, in Gaijini, where
the liberal German Missionsverein (protestant) did some medical work
until the war, eventually also in Gingdschi, and especially in Laiyang, to
the north of Tsimo, the country seat, where one of our most vigorous
congregations under the able leadership of a consecrated, active, forward
pushing young preacher flourishes. That is the work that should be done
—but probably better than that the fact that before he war we had alone in
Shantung 7 workers (Missionaries) where we today have only 3, demonstrates the lack of able workers. Even after the transfer of the present
working staff it will be necessary to add American missionaries to the
force.

We also would like to point out the necessity of opening a station in
the capital—Peking, for the good of the work as a whole. The prere-
quisite for this is a strong mission field in the Hinterland. Our work
in Shantung would furnish this. We have been forced by lack of means
only to decline all invitations to go to Peking.

We are forwarding a letter to our superintendent, Dr. Voskamp, asking him to convey to you in proper form the title of our property there. Also in proper form to ask our congregations if they have any objections to the change of supervision. We shall point out that difficulties regarding finances will be alleviated by the kindness of the American friends which are better able to care for the work financially than we, for as we trust you understand fully, there is no other reason whatever that caused our withdrawal.

Finally we ask you to consider the following proposition. During our conference in Berlin we spoke of the advisability of employing additional German missionaries in Shantung, but the matter was not fully settled. Should you fail to win men in your own home church, we would gladly recommend candidates who have taken the preparatory course over there. Any inquiry concerning this proposition would be gladly received by us.

At this time we call attention to the fact that we have a large number of medical men, efficient doctors, for the service. These cannot be sent by German Mission Societies for lack of funds.

For instance some time ago our Berlin Society for Medical Mission work advertised for medical men. Among 50 applications there were especially two, one from a physician in Southern Germany and another from a Dr. Buhre of the Balticum.

We have in Tsimo a hospital under the supervision of Mrs. Matzat, but the work had grown too great for her. If you should decide to send more medical missionaries we would gladly recommend Dr. Buhre, or other applicants.

We would have sent you an outline of the contract between you and ourselves, had we not believed that we should wait for an expression of your opinion toward these our wishes.

We do not doubt that our wishes will be met in a brotherly manner and we look upon the matter as if a decision regarding the future of our Shantung work has already been made. With a sad heart we relinquish the work of this field and we praise the grace of God which has moved a great Lutheran Church to come to the rescue of our Chinese work at this hour of perplexity and danger to save the work for the Kingdom of God, for the pure gospel and for the Church of Luther.

We are confident that as we have endeavored to bring the gospel to the heathen and Christians, so will also your Board and missionaries. We promise always to uphold with our prayers the work that was ours and that now is about to become yours.

In Christian service cordially yours,
(Signed) MULLER.

CHINA

Estimate for 1925

Budget	$25,000.00
Initial payment to Berlin Mission Society	10,000.00
Second payment to Berlin Mission Society, Jan. 1, 1925	10,000.00
5 Missionaries taken over from the German Society	5,000.00
3 Missionaries to be sent out from America	6,000.00
2 single Missionaries	1,800.00
Travel expenses and outfit	2,200.00
Total	$60,000.00

HOME BASE

LITERATURE

Because nothing is more essential to the cultivation of the home base than the publication and distribution of interesting and inspiring missionary literature, the Board has given much attention to the department of publicity. The annual report of our missions is an established feature of this department. Another is the publication of two monthly magazines. The *Foreign Missionary* has increased its circulation to over 10,000 and is highly commended wherever it is read because of its interesting contents and attractive appearance. *Der Missionsbote* has a subscription of 4,000.

The literature published and distributed in connection with the Foreign Mission Forward Fund appeal and the observance of the annual Foreign Mission Day at the close of the Epiphany season, has greatly stimulated the cause of foreign missions in the home Church.

We may be permitted in this connection to draw attention to Dr. George Drach's book on "Forces in Foreign Missions," published by the United Lutheran Publication Board, as one of a contemplated series of study books planned by the Conference of Secretaries and to be prepared under the general editorship of Drs. M. G. G. Scherer and F. H. Knubel. It should be widely used in study classes throughout our Church during the next few years.

The twenty-one stereopticon lectures of the Board have been extensively used and have given excellent satisfaction.

PATRON AND PROTEGE

It is remarkable how many individuals, societies, Sunday schools and congregations desire to undertake special work in our foreign fields. The outstanding feature of this department is the list of patrons supporting foreign missionaries, as follows:

Patron	Pastor	Missionary	Field
Allentown, Pa., St. John's	W. C. Schaeffer, Jr.	Oscar V. Werner	India
Altoona, Pa., 2d Church	G. N. Lauffer	Harry Goedke	India
Ashland, Ohio, Trinity	A. H. Smith	J.M. Armbruster	B.Aires
Baltimore, St. Mark's	R. D. Clare	T. Cannaday	India
Baltimore, St. Paul's	P. A. Heilman	J. D. Curran	Liberia
Brooklyn, N. Y., Redeemer	S. C. Weiskotten	A. Neudoerffer	India
Canton, Ohio, Trinity	E. C. Herman	A. C. Knudten	Japan
Canton, Ohio, Trinity	E. C. Herman	H. E. Haas	B. Guiana
Canton, Ohio, Trinity	E. C. Herman	G. Rupley	India
Chambersburg, Pa., First	H. Anstadt	J. W. Miller	Liberia
Charleston, S. C., St. Andrew's	J. H. Worth	C. K. Lippard	Japan
Dayton, Ohio, First	M. H. Krumbine	V. McCauley	India
Dayton, Ohio, First	M. H. Krumbine	G. N. Schillinger	Japan
Dayton, Ohio, First	M. H. Krumbine	L. G. Gray	Japan
Dixon, Ill., St. Paul's	L. W. Walter	C. B. Caughman	India
Ft. Wayne, Ind., Trinity	P. H. Krauss	L. A. Gotwald	India
Greensburg, Pa., Zion's		A. Schmitthenner	India
Greensburg Conf. S. S. Association		W. F. Adolphsen	India
Hagerstown, Md., Trinity	J. S. Simon	H. F. Miller	India
Harrisburg, Pa., Zion's	S. W. Herman	J. K. Linn	Japan
Harrisburg, Pa., Zion's	S. W. Herman	R.M. Dunkelberger	India
Harrisburg, Pa., Memorial	L. C. Manges	G. R. Haaf	India

Pastor		Pastor	Missionary	Field
Hummelstown, Pa., Zion's	C. G.	Leatherman....	R. J. White	B. Aires
Huntingdon, Pa., St. James'	E. L.	Manges	Not Yet Assigned	
Icelandic Synod			S. O. Thorlaksson.	Japan
Johnstown, Pa., First	H. W.	Snyder	A. J. Stirewalt	Japan
Kitchener, Ont., St. Peter's	H. A.	Sperling	L. Irshick	India
Mansfield, Ohio, First	H. C.	Roehner	C. E. Norman	Japan
Mansfield, Ohio, First	H. C.	Roehner	J. C. Finefrock	India
New York State Luther League			F. W. Heins	Japan
Norristown, Pa., Trinity	P. Z.	Strodach	E. Neudoerffer	India
Perkasie, Pa., Hilltown	C. A.	Miller	George Cope	Liberia
Philadelphia, Pa., Tabernacle	W. J.	Miller, Jr	M. L. Dolbeer	India
Philadelphia, Pa., Messiah	J. R.	Stover	R. L. Yund	Liberia
Philadelphia, Pa., John E. Miller	John E.	Miller	J. E. Graefe	India
Philadelphia, Pa., Temple	A.	Pohlman	J. Larsen	India
Philadelphia, Pa., Nativity	J. C.	Fisher	H. H. Sipes, Jr	India
Pittsburgh, Pa., N. S., Mt. Zion	G. E.	Swoyer	J. A. Linn	Japan
Pittsburgh, Pa., First	C. P.	McLaughlin	F. L. Coleman	India
Pottstown, Pa., Emmanuel	I. B.	Kurtz	F. J. Fiedler	India
Princeton, Ill., English	K. E.	Irvin	H. C. Leonard	Liberia
Reading, Pa., Trinity	E.	Pfatteicher	E. T. Horn	Japan
Rockford, Ill., Trinity	H. M.	Bannen	C. W. Hepner	Japan
Rockford, Ill., Trinity	H. M.	Bannen	F. H. Bloch	Liberia
Shippensburg, Pa., Memorial	R. S.	Bowers	J. R. Strock	India
Springfield, Ohio, First	J. B.	Markward	G. C. Leonard	Liberia
Sterling, Ill., St. John's	E. C.	Harris	H. E. Dickey	India
Wilkensburg, Pa., Calvary	C. B.	Foelsch	C. P. Tranberg	India
Wilmington, Del.	Dr. Chas. M.	Stine	J. J. Raun	India
Winchester, Va., Grace	A.	Kelly	L. S. G. Miller	Japan
York, Pa., Zion's	G. A.	Getty	J. R. Fink	India
Zanesville, Ohio, St. John's	W. L.	Dowler	P. M. Counts	Liberia

NATIVE WORKERS SUPPORTED

The following congregations and societies are contributing $200 or more annually:

Place	Church	Patron	Protege	Field	Amount
Rockford, Ill.	Trinity	H. M. Bannen	V. Ch. John	India	$1,000
Arendtsville, Pa.	Lutheran	A. R. McCauslin	N. Asaji	Japan	800
Huntingdon, Pa.	Lutheran	A. B. Van Ormer	I. Guzman	Argentina	600
Y. P. Societies	United Danish Church		N. Asaji	Japan	400
Y P. League	United Danish, N. Dak. Dist		Kawase	Japan	300
Philadelphia, Pa.	Scherer Family	E. C. Cronk	Ishimatsu	Japan	250
Steelton, Pa.	St. John's	C. N. Shindler	A. Turkle	Liberia	250
Philadelphia, Pa.	Holy Communion	Blanche E. Henniger	S. Kawagiri	Japan	200
Y. P. League	United Danish, Minnesota Dist		A. Kazunami	Japan	200

Others are being supported by smaller annual payments.

Those who make annual payments ranging from $25 to $800 a year for the support of proteges in our foreign fields constitute a list of about seven hundred names and addresses.

The Board expects to inaugurate a new and most interesting plan of special objectives in the near future. It has asked the India mission to prepare a list of stations and out-stations with estimates of the approximate sums required for their support by patrons in America. Already a number of congregations have applied for assignments of such stations.

The United Danish Church continues to support its parish abroad, which includes Kurume, Amagi, Hiida, Moji and Shimonoseki. The Icelandic Synod supports Rev. S. O. Thorlaksson, one of its members, as a missionary in Japan.

FINANCIAL STATEMENT

The Board of Foreign Missions at the Buffalo Convention was voted an apportionment for the biennium of $1,090,000.00 for the general work on all fields. This amount is not supplemented by the Women's Missionary Society. This Society makes up a separate budget of its needs and raises it and besides this pays all the salaries of the single women missionaries. As will appear in the comparative statement which follows this, the Board has realized a considerable increase over the previous biennium, but it is due to the effort to raise the Foreign Mission Forward Fund, which shows $114,133.00. The Treasurer would draw the Convention's attention, under a few simple heads, to a comparative statement of receipts and expenses of the last and present bienniums:

COMPARATIVE STATEMENT OF BOARD TREASURER OF THE
PREVIOUS AND PRESENT BIENNIUMS
RECEIPTS

	1921-22	1923-24
Received on Apportionment................	$689,942.05	$699,256.40
Received from Augustana Synod...........		45,646.46
Received from Danish Synod..............	61,745.48	20,162.34
Received from Icelandic Synod............		2,400.00
Women's Missionary Society..............	300,016.29	415,425.72
Interest	21,863.52	32,462.85
Publications, Slides and Rental, etc.........	7,360.23	9,791.33
Special Funds—F. M. F. F.; R. D. J. A. F. and Japan Relief.....................	171,755.29	182,059.77
Trust Funds	14,364.20	
General Donations, not included in apportionment	50,013.69	204,117.15
Bequests	24,141.41	15,401.56
Annuities	26,550.00	9,652.81
	$1,367,752.16	$1,636,376.39

DISBURSEMENTS

	1921-22	1923-24
Budgets	$577,267.22	$688,403.48
Salaries of missionaries	133,437.32	203,773.23
Travel to and from fields.................	64,484.17	66,303.45
Expenses of Missionaries on furlough......	1,175.00	
and Candidates	10,757.51	22,903.02
Secretaries, Treasurer, Board Representatives, Clerks, Stenographers..........	25,754.88	36,452.38
Publicity	11,179.10	10,709.60
Publicity and Slides......................	13,564.46	13,399.92

Office Expenses and Supplies, Postage, Expressage, Tel. and Tel.................	7,310.33	12,740.92
Property Expenses, Improvements, etc.— 18 East Mt. Vernon Place..............		6,098.79
Interest on Annuities......................	3,422.50	4,678.36
Contributions to Intermissionary Organizations	3,565.25	2,553.80
Special on R. D. J. A. F.—F. M. F. F.....		50,553.47
	124,954.44	114,693.23
Women's Missionary Society..............	334,443.23	409,202.90
	$1,311,315.41	$1,642,466.55

This statement shows that if you deduct the contributions of the Women's Missionary Society and the Special Funds received on the Japan Relief, Reformation Diamond Jubilee and Foreign Mission Forward Fund, amounting to $471,980.58 in previous biennium, and $597,485.49 in this biennium, the current funds amounted to $895,980.58 and $1,038,-890.90 respectively for the bienniums or, the actual amount for current funds was $142,910.32 more for the latter than the former period.

The current expenses for the former biennium were $871,318.27 and for the latter $1,067,016.95, or expenses ran $195,698.68 higher for the latter than for the former period.

REFORMATION DIAMOND JUBILEE FUND

The Reformation Diamond Jubilee Advance Fund shows receipts amounting to		$257,011.37
Expenditures on India "Specials" under this Fund amount to	$54,824.16	
Amounts allotted to the Africa Mission to date..	3,300.00	
Purchase of 18 East Mt. Vernon Place........ ($2,000 yet to be adjusted in the Books of the Board).	15,500.00	
Additional Funds invested under Endowment for higher education	60,000.00	
Total Expenses in raising Fund................	7,914.98	$141,539.14
Balance in Fund...........................		$115,472.23

Annuities

The annuities have been greatly reduced by the death of several annuitants and at present they amount to $27,452.81. During the past biennium the following were received:

Miss Mary Weaver......................	January,	1923......		$152.81
Mrs. Carrie Sypher.....................	April	"	......	500.00
Elizabeth M. Schmauck.................	May	"	......	5,000.00
Louise E. Chisolm......................	June	"	......	1,000.00
Carrie D. Stephens.....................	June	"	......	500.00
Dr. George Scholl......................	July	"	......	1,000.00
E. H. Trafford.........................	January,	1924......		1,000.00
Jas. S. and Sarah Jane Schreffler..........	June	"	......	500.00
Total				$9,652.81

Bequests

The bequests made to our Board and realized in the biennium were as follows:

Sept. 16, '22	Anna M. Lake...............................		$450.00
Sept. 23, '22	Butt & Butt, Attys., care of Shoemaker Bequest $1,000		
Sept. 26, '22	Butt & Butt, Attys., care of Shoemaker Bequest 500		
May 24, '23	Butt & Butt, Attys., care of Shoemaker Bequest 1,300		2,800.00
Nov. 25, '22	John D. Cappleman, care of J. F. Lown.......		500.00
Feb. 27, '23	Hannah M. Hankey...........................		452.50
Dec. 1, '22	Wm. H. Staake, care of Rebecca Berkheimer..		512.13
Apr. 28, '23	D. L. Gladfelter, care of Will of Frank A. Richards		100.00
May 24, '23	Annie R. Sweigard, Ex. Will of Anna Ruhl....		181.00
June 8, '23	Chas. I. McNett, Atty. Est. of Nellie S. Anderson		2,433.13
	(½ to Board of Foreign Missions)		
	(½ to Board of West Indies Missions)		
Nov. 22, '23	Philadelphia Trust Co., care of Will of Mary E. Monroe		5,000.00
	Croll Kellar a-c Gilbert Memorial Fund......		1,000.00
Apr. 17, '24	Through I. L. Taylor (party not known)......		500.00
Apr. 9, '24	Mrs. W. O. Keyser Tr. W. M. Evang. Synod of Nebraska		500.00
	Jonathan Reitz Estate.........................		4,773.44
	John C. Guether Estate.......................		220.86
June 7, '24	Lehigh Valley Trust Co. a-c Will of Amelia Ziegler		181.00
	Total		$19,604.06

Our Board presented to the Executive Board the following budget for the years of the biennium:

Board Budget:

	1926	1927
Home Base	$50,400	
Unforseen 3 per cent	18,600	
African Mission:		
General Budget	37,800	
Salaries	12,000	
Travel	6,600	
New Missionaries	2,400	
India Mission:		
General Budget	207,700	
Salaries	50,400	
Travel	18,000	
New Missionaries	9,600	
Breklum	36,400	

Japan Mission:

General Budget	93,200
Salaries	24,000
Travel	9,600
New Missionaries	4,800

British Guiana:

General Budget	1,400
Salaries	1,200
Travel	1,200
New Missionaries	1,800

Buenos Aires:

General Budget	56,400
Salaries	6,000
Travel	1,200
New Missionaries	1,200

	$651,900	$651,900
Total apportionment asked for each year of the coming biennium	$651,900	$651,900
China Mission, Board's action March, 1924	50,000	
Russian Mission, United Lutheran Church Buffalo Convention action	20,000	
Total asked from the churches for each year of the biennium	$721,900	$721,900

RECOMMENDATIONS

The Board recommends the following resolutions, to the Convention, for adoption:

1. THANKSGIVING.—*Resolved,* That we give thanks to God, Who, during the past two years, has continued to bless and prosper our missions and missionaries in India; Liberia, Africa; Japan; British Guiana and Buenos Aires, South America.

2. PRAYER.—*Resolved,* That during the presentation of this report the President of the Board set apart a period of intercession and thanksgiving.

3. LA PLATA SYNOD.—*Resolved,* That the proposed cooperation of the Mission in Argentina with the La Plata Synod in the establishment of a United Lutheran Church in Argentina, on the doctrinal basis of the United Lutheran Church in America, be approved.

4. CHINA MISSION.—*Resolved,* (1) That the transfer of the mission of the Berlin Missionary Society in the Shantung province of China to the United Lutheran Church in America, on the agreed conditions, be ratified, and

(2) That a letter be sent by the Board of Foreign Missions to each pastor in the United Lutheran Church, describing this newly acquired China Mission and the Board's plans in regard to it, and soliciting initial

contributions in 1925 for this new mission in order that there may be money to pay the first year's expenses, for which no provision has been made in the apportionment.

5. TELUGU CHRISTIAN COLLEGE.—*Resolved,* (1) That the Board of Foreign Missions be authorized to accept the invitation of the Andhra Christian Council in India to establish a first grade college for the Telugu area, India, at a central place to be determined as soon as the location of the proposed Andhra University has been fixed, and

(2) That the Board of Foreign Missions be authorized to invite other Protestant Boards and Societies which have missions in the Telugu area, to cooperate in the establishment and maintenance of this college on a basis of cooperation in harmony with the principles laid down by the United Lutheran Church in America, in 1920, in its Washington Declaration, it being understood the majority of the Board of Directors of the College shall be members of the Lutheran Church, and

(3) That the convention commends this project to the sympathetic cooperation of the congregations and benevolent individuals in our Church.

(4) That to stimulate interest in foreign missions, and especially in this college, Foreign Mission Conferences shall be held at some center or centers in each synodical territory, after consultation with the President of the Synod.

6. MAGAZINES.—*Resolved,* That the Convention heartily commends to all our pastors and people the Board's magazines, "The Foreign Missionary" and "Der Missionsbote," as the official organs of the Church in the promotion of the cause of world evangelization.

7. *Resolved,* That the Convention recognizes the material assistance and sympathetic cooperation of the Augustana Synod, the United Danish Church, and the Icelandic Synod, and requests the election of Prof. C. W. Foss as a regular member of the Board of Foreign Missions, as provided by the action of the Washington Convention (See Minutes, page 208).

EZRA K. BELL, *President.*
GEORGE DRACH, *Secretary.*
LUTHER B. WOLF, *Secretary.*

REPORT OF THE TREASURER OF THE BOARD OF FOREIGN MISSIONS

For the Year Ended 31st July, 1924

ASSETS:

Cash in Banks and on Hand	$108.029.89
Investments, at ledger values	193,592.14
	$301,622.03

FUNDS:

Trust Funds	$164,152.46
Annuity Funds	27,452.81
Foreign Mission Forward Fund	32,921.50
Reformation Diamond Jubilee Advance Fund	91,713.85
Japan Earthquake Relief Fund	8,278.64
Women's Missionary Society Fund	21,939.37

$346,458.63

General Fund, Overdraft, borrowed from other Funds 44,836.60

$301,622.03

RECEIPTS AND DISBURSEMENTS
For the Year Ended July 31, 1924

RECEIPTS:

	General Fund	Women's Missionary Society Fund	Other Funds
United Church on Apportionment	$372,734.40		
Women's Missionary Society		$209,192.22	
Augustana Synod	22,088.15		
Danish Synod	12,668.88		
Icelandic Synod	1,200.00		
Donations (through Board Treasurer and General Treasurer)	114,846.88		
Bequests	12,175.30		
Donations for Specific Funds			$119,654.60
Annuities			1,500.00
Interest on Investments	12,782.98		
Interest on Bank Balances	1,460.93		
The Foreign Missionary	2,372.86		
Der Missionbote	2,150.67		
Rental of Slides	367.49		
Rental of Garage	200.00		
Collection of Account of Mortgage	1,000.00		
	$556,048.54	$209,192.22	$121,154.60

DISBURSEMENTS:

Budget paid to Missions	$325,181.48	$92,780.80
Specials paid to Missions	20,384,31	97,283.64
Salaries of Missionaries	93,250.32	42,892.65
Salaries of Secretaries and Board Representatives	7,475.00	
Salaries of Clerks, Stenographers, etc.	5,096.00	
Expenses of Missionaries traveling to and from fields	31,238.86	9,465.20
Expenses of Treasurer, Secretaries and Board Representatives	4,702.90	
Expenses of Missionaries on Furlough	8,387.08	2,188.56

Expenses of Candidates and Students	3,585.47	4,307.99	
Disbursements from Specific Funds....			114,693.23
Publicity	4,612.06		
The Foreign Missionary	4,058.25		
Der Missionsbote	2,140.24		
Expenses of Slides	39.98		
Office Supplies and Expenses..............	1,958.40		
Telephone, Telegraph and Cables........	477.65		
Postage and Expressage........................	949.57		
Forward	$513,537.57	$248,918.84	$114,693.23

	General Fund	Women's Missionary Society Fund	Other Funds
Receipts, Forward	$556,048.54	$209,192.22	$121,154.60
Disbursements, Forward	$513,537.57	$248,918.84	$114,693.23
Auditing	1,530.26		
General Office Expenses	1,364.99		
Contributions to Intermissionary Organizations	1,150.00		
Special Allowances and Pensions........	1,864.57		
Annuity Interest	2,126.44		
Expenses of Property	959.22		
	$522,533.05	$248,918.84	$114,693.23
Excess or Deficiency of Receipts	$33,515.49	$39,726.62	$6,461.37

RECONCILEMENT OF CASH
For the Yead Ended July 31, 1924

	General Fund	Women's Missionary Society Fund	Other Funds
Balances, August 1, 1923	$28,702.11	$58,454.40	$78,027.36
Receipts	556,048.54	209,192.22	121,154.60
	$527,346.43	$267,646.62	$199,181.96
Disbursements	522,533.05	248,918.84	114,693.23
Balances, July 31, 1924	$4,813.38	$18,727.78	$84,488.73
		$108,029.89	

Respectfully submitted,

L. B. WOLF, Treasurer.

PHILADELPHIA, August 26, 1924.

We have audited the accounts of the Board of Foreign Missions of the United Lutheran Church in America for the year ended July 31, 1924, and we certify that the foregoing Balance Sheet, Receipts and Disbursements, etc., are in accordance with the books of account and, in our opinion, are correct.

LYBRAND, ROSS BROS. & MONTGOMERY,
Accountants and Auditors.

REPORT OF THE TREASURER OF THE BOARD OF FOREIGN MISSIONS

For the Year Ended 31st July, 1923

Cash in banks and on hand	$107,779.65	
Investments, at ledger values	191,592.14	
		$299,371.79

FUNDS:

Trust Funds	$138,152.46	
Annuity Funds	48,752.81	
Miscellaneous Funds	191,829.82	
Women's Missionary Society Fund	68,088.40	
	$446,823.49	
General Fund, Overdraft, borrowed from other Funds	147,451.70	
		$299,371.79

RECEIPTS AND DISBURSEMENTS

For the Year Ended 31st July, 1923

RECEIPTS:

	General Fund	Women's Missionary Society Fund	Other Funds
United Church on Apportionment	$326,522.00		
Women's Missionary Society		$206,103.40	
Augustana Synod	22,073.15		
Danish Synod	7,493.46		
Icelandic Synod	1,200.00		
Donations (through Board Treasurer and General Treasurer	102,446.84	130.10	
Bequests	7,428.76		
Donations for Specific Purposes	2,237.00		$54,152.36
Annuities			8,152.81
Interest on Investments	16,372.45		
Interest on Bank Balances	1,846.49		
The Foreign Missionary	2,638.11		
Der Missionbote	1,557.77		
Rental of Slides	344.43		
Rental of Garage	100.00		
Trust Funds			100.00
Securities Sold or Matured	28,273.77		
Profit on Securities Sold or Matured	735.00		
	$521,269.23	$206,233.50	$62,405.17

Cash Receipts $780,282.90
Securities Received 9,625.00
Total Receipts $789,907.90

DISBURSEMENTS:

Budgets Paid to Missions	$334,925.76	$87,869.90	
Specials Paid to Missions	12,167.31	7,623.47	
Salaries of Missionaries	104,734.15	44,101.21	
Salaries of Secretaries and Board Representatives	8,525.00		
Salaries of Clerks, Stenographers, etc.	4,633.00		
Expenses of Missionaries traveling to and from Fields	36,264.59	14,828.04	
Expenses of Treasurer, Secretary and Board Representatives	4,155.61		
Expenses of Missionaries on Furlough	7,514.78	1,029.76	
Students' Allowances and Expenses..	3,415.69	2,006.68	
Disbursements from Specific Funds....	3,462.62	2,825.00	$50,553.47
Publicity	6,097.54		
The Foreign Missionary	4,672.08		
Der Missionbote	2,426.03		
Expenses of Slides	63.34		
Office Supplies and Expenses	2,026.65		
Office Rental	250.00		
Telephone, Telegraph and Cables	379.68		
Postage and Expressage	979.74		
Auditing	1,041.09		
General Office Expenses	1,420.18		
Contributions to Intermissionary Organizations	1,403.80		
Special Allowances and Pensions	3,355.88		
Forward	$543,914.52	$160,284.06	$50,553.47

	General Fund	Women's Missionary Society Fund	Other Funds
Receipts, Forward	$521,269.23	$206,233.50	$62,405.17
Disbursements, Forward	$543,914.52	$160,284.06	$50,553.47
Annuity Interest	2,551.92		
Securities Purchased	20,930.00		
Purchase of Property, 18 E. Mt. Vernon Place	15,500.00		
Improvement to Property, 18 E. Mt. Vernon Place	1,550.00		
Furnishings for 18 E. Mt. Vernon Place	855.13		
Other expenses of property, 18 E. Mt. Vernon Place	2,734.44		
	$588,036.01	$160,284.06	$50,553.47
Excess or Deficiency of Receipts	$66,766.78	$45,949.44	$11,851.70

RECONCILEMENT OF CASH
For the Year Ended 31st July, 1923

	General Fund	Women's Missionary Society Fund	Other Funds
Balances, August 1, 1922	$42,689.67	$12,504.96	$71,175.66
Receipts	516,644.23	206,233.50	57,405.17
	$559,333.90	$218,738.46	$128,580.83
Disbursements	588,036.01	160,284.06	50,553.47
Balances, July 31, 1923	$28,702.11	$58,454.40	$78,027.36
		$107,779.65	

Respectfully submitted,

L. B. Wolf, *Treasurer.*

PHILADELPHIA, 16th June, 1924.

We have audited the accounts of the Board of Foreign Missions of the United Lutheran Church in America for the year ended 31st July, 1923, and we certify that the foregoing Balance Sheet, Receipts and Disbursements, etc., are in accordance with the books of account and are correct.

LYBRAND, ROSS BROS & MONTGOMERY,
Accountants and Auditors.

On motion to adopt the first two resolutions, the Rev. J. Frank Heilman, Field Secretary of the Board of Foreign Missions, and Dr. Wolf addressed the Convention.

Resolutions (I) and (II) were adopted by a rising vote and the Rev. Paul E. Scherer led in the prayer of intercession and thanksgiving.

The Rev. O. C. D. Klaehn led in the closing prayer.

The Convention adjourned until 2:00 o'clock.

———•———

Afternoon Session

Friday, October 24, 2:00 P. M.

The President called the Convention to order.

Prayer was offered by the Rev. E. A. Sievert.

The Chairman of the Committee of Reference and Counsel offered the following resolution which was adopted:

WHEREAS, There is in the report of the Committee on Moral and Social Welfare a resolution (No. 8) with reference to which there seems to exist much difference of opinion, and

WHEREAS, the present order places the report of this committee late in the session in this Convention, and

WHEREAS, the pressure of business before the Convention requires careful conservation of time,

Be It Resolved, (1) That the report of the Committee on Moral and Social Welfare be set as a special order of business at the beginning of the session on Monday morning, October 27th.

(2) That debate upon the resolution referred to be limited to a total of thirty minutes.

(3) That all persons desiring to present substitute resolutions or to speak upon the resolution apply to the Committee of Reference and Counsel for an assignment of time.

(4) That ten minutes of the period assigned be retained for general discussion by speakers other than those so applying for permission to speak and for speeches in answer to arguments advanced.

(5) That if at the end of the thirty minutes assigned for this discussion the Convention is not ready to agree upon some resolution the whole matter be referred to a special committee which shall include in its membership a representative of each resolution proposed. This committee to prepare a resolution for recommendation to the Convention on Tuesday morning.

The Chairman also presented the following resolution from the Administrative Committee of the Laymen's Movement:

Resolved, That the United Lutheran Church in convention assembled urge upon all its Constituent Synods the importance of their giving fullest support to the Executive Committee of the Laymen's Movement in their continued vigorous organized efforts to accomplish the raising of the apportionment in full in each of the Synods of the United Lutheran Church for the biennium 1926 and 1927. Each Constituent Synod is further requested to take definite action on the matter at the next convention.

The resolution was adopted.

The Chairman of the Committee of Reference and Counsel introduced to the Convention the Revs. C. E. Norman, representative of the Church in Japan; J. D. Curran, representative of the Church in Africa; and J. Roy Strock, representative of the mission field in India, and moved that during such time as the report of the Foreign Mission Board is being considered these representatives be given the privilege of the floor.

The motion was carried.

The Rev. G. A. Brandelle, D.D., President of the Augustana Synod, was introduced and addressed the Convention conveying the greetings of that body.

Upon request of the President, Dr. F. F. Fry made the response.

The Rev. J. J. Scherer, Jr., reported for Nominating Committee No. 3 as follows:

For Board of Foreign Missions: Rev. E. K. Bell, Rev. C. T. Benze, Rev. R. C. G. Bielinski, Rev. M. J. Epting, Rev. J. A. Singmaster, Mr. James Snyder, Prof. C. W. Foss, Rev. A. O. Becker, Rev. A. MacIntosh, Rev. J. J. Schindel, Rev. H. W. Snyder, Rev. J. A. Weyl, Mr. R. F. Bowe, Mr. Harvey C. Miller.

For Board of Home Missions and Church Extension: Rev. J. M. Francis, Rev. C. J. Smith, Rev. H. B. Stock, Rev. J. E. Whitteker, Mr. A. R. Bard, Mr. J. H. Rehder, Prof. S. J. Derrick, Rev. F. A. Dressel, Rev. H. D. Hoover, Rev. A. H. Keck, Rev. C. W. Leitzell, Mr. H. Belmer, Mr. A. F. Sittloh, Hon. J. L. Zimmerman.

For Board of Northwestern Missions: Rev. G. A. Benze, Rev. E. C. J. Kraeling, Rev. H. Rembe, Sr., Rev. C. S. Roberts, Rev. H. D. E. Siebott, Prof. C. Hausmann, Mr. Ernest Muncke, Rev. F. H. Bosch, Rev. H. Offermann, Rev. T. Posselt, Rev. R. Schmidt, Rev. W. C. Veit, Mr. F. Grumbach, Mr. T. Roehrs.

For Immigrants Mission Board: Rev. F. E. Jensen, Rev. W. M. Rehrig, Mr. S. E. Long, Mr. H. E. Young, Rev. J. C. Mattes, Rev. A. J. Traver, Mr. G. M. Jones, Mr. G. B. Reimensnyder.

For West Indies Mission Board: Rev. F. H. Bosch, Rev. F. B. Hankey, Rev. H. W. A. Hanson, Rev. J. H. Meyer, Mr. J. H. Brandt, Mr. C. W. Fuhr, Mr. H. F. Heuer, Rev. J. L. Morgan, Rev. F. E. Oberlander, Rev. J. B. Rupley, Rev. L. P. Young, Mr. W. L. Glatfelter, Mr. A. D. Smith, Mr. F. H. Wefer.

For Jewish Mission Committee: Rev. A. C. Carty, Rev. J. F. Heckert, Rev. L. H. Larimer, Mr. C. J. Fite, Mr. H. F. Heuer, Rev. G. N. Lauffer, Rev. S. J. McDowell, Rev. R. W. Woods, Hon. B. B. Miller, Hon. E. M. Rabenold.

For Board of Education: Rev. R. D. Clare, Rev. W. F. Hoppe, Rev. E. P. Pfatteicher, Rev. A. Steimle, Dr. A. S. Downing, Mr. G. M. Cummings, Mr. W. H. Stackel, Rev. G. Engler, Rev. P. J. Hoh, Rev. J. A. Huffard, Rev. G. W. Nicely, Mr. J. L. Clark, Hon. G. B. Cromer, Mr. W. W. Doub.

For Inner Mission Board: Rev. E. F. Bachmann, Rev. W. H. B. Carney, Rev. W. Krumwiede, Mr. James Carr, Mr. G. B. Morehead, Rev. F. K.

Fretz, Rev. A. Hering, Rev. P. E. Scherer, Mr. W. P. M. Braun, Mr. W. K. Mauney.

For Board of Publication: Rev. C. F. Steck, Rev. F. P. Manhart, Rev. N. R. Melhorn, Mr. G. D. Boschen, Mr. D. F. Efird, Mr. E. F. Eilert, Mr. G. E. Schlegelmilch, Rev. J. W. Horine, Rev. S. Snyder, Rev. P. Z. Strodach, Mr. J. A. Alexander, Mr. A. D. Chiquoine, Mr. G. T. Ettinger, Mr. P. J. Kuhn.

For Board of Ministerial Pensions and Relief: Rev. C. L. Miller, Rev. R. H. Stover, Rev. M. H. Valentine, Mr. G. P. Tustin, Mr. J. H. Wattles, Rev. M. S. Cressman, Rev. C. Brown Cox, Rev. Samuel Trexler, Mr. M. H. Buehler, Mr. T. Hetzler.

For Parish and Church School Board: Rev. T. B. Birch, Rev. C. F. Dapp, Rev. W. L. Hunton, Prof. G. P. Voigt, Rev. F. R. Knubel, Rev. H. Moehling, Jr., Rev. A. T. W. Steinhaeuser, Mr. H. Benner.

For Board of Deaconess Work: Rev. E. F. Bachmann, Rev. J. F. Crigler, Rev. J. F. Ohl, Mr. F. C. Hassold, Hon. J. D. Cappelmann, Rev. A. E. Bell, Rev. H. F. Miller, Rev. H. J. Musselman, Mr. P. A. Elsesser.

For National Lutheran Home for the Aged: Rev. H. Anstadt, Rev. J. E. Harms, Rev. J. L. Frantz, Rev. J. T. Huddle, Rev. F. R. Wagner, Rev. R. Schmidt, Rev. J. Weidley, Mr. L. R. Alden, Dr. W. K. Butler, Mr. H. T. Domer, Mr. F. E. Cunningham, Mr. W. H. Finckel, Mr. J. H. Jones, Mr. F. W. Kakel, Mr. H. L. Snyder, Rev. J. C. Bowers, Rev. W. E. Brown, Rev. G. M. Diffenderfer, Rev. W. J. Finck, Rev. H. Manken, Jr.; Rev. W. G. Minnick, Rev. W. C. Waltemeyer, Hon. B. Capps, Mr. J. L. Fray, Mr. C. Keller, Mr. H. Pugh, Mr. F. Stuessy, Mr. J. Umlauf, Mr. A. H. Weaver, Mr. E. W. Young.

The report of the Nominating Committee was accepted.

Secretary, Dr. Wolf, presented at this time resolution (VII) submitted by the Foreign Mission Board. The resolution was adopted.

Dr. Wolf introduced Prof. R. B. Manikyam, of the Tamil Lutheran Church in India, spending a year in America in further preparation for his work as teacher in the Andhra College, and Mr. Joel Lakra, of the Gossner Church, who is taking a theological course at the Chicago Theological Seminary. These gentlemen were heard by the Convention with manifest interest. Remaining resolutions submitted by the Board of Foreign Missions were then taken up.

On motion to adopt the third resolution (III) Secretary, Dr.

Drach, was heard in support of the motion. The resolution was then adopted.

Resolutions (IV), (V) and (VI) were adopted.

The Secretary read the following cablegram: "Greetings. Christ's work in Japan needs emphasis. Japan Mission."

At this point the Revs. C. E. Norman, Missionary to Japan on furlough, and J. D. Curran, Missionary in Liberia, Africa, on furlough, were heard.

The Rev. L. L. Uhl, Ph.D., D.D., of Cambridge, Mass., was introduced as a veteran who had served in the India mission field for a period of fifty years. Mr. K. Hirai, student at Mount Airy Seminary, was also introduced to the Convention.

Upon motion the report was adopted as a whole.

The Rev. J. Elmer Bittle presented the report of the Immigrants Mission Board:

REPORT OF IMMIGRANTS MISSION BOARD

The Immigrants Mission Board presents with grateful hearts the record of its labors during the biennium just ending. With a field covering the United States and Canada and a constituency of many nationalities and tongues some work that pressed for immediate attention had to be put off for some future time. The Board gave serious consideration to all problems as they were presented.

The Board deplores that with the utmost economy the treasury shows a deficit. Besides this some work that should have been done had to be postponed. The survey of the Asiatics on the Pacific Coast could not be undertaken as planned because of the lack of means. The work of the Port Entry Pastor at New York City had again to be postponed although fully planned and prepared for. Candidates seeking the office of the holy ministry to labor among their own nationality had to be refused assistance. Help to missions sadly needed and urgently asked for had to be declined because of an empty treasury.

The Board records with grateful recognition the liberal assistance of the Women's Missionary Society which made it possible to undertake so much. Further mention should be made of the help rendered by neighboring pastors and congregations to some of our work. The Board is anxious to interest a larger number to encourage the work with word and gift.

In its extensive and varied field the Board administers its work under three departments with a superintendent over each. The story of achievements, with an inspection of needs and an outlook of prospect, follows.

I. SLAV-HUNGARIAN—A. L. RAMER, PH.D., SUPERINTENDENT

In presenting the report of our Immigrants Mission Board we are conscious of the fact that the substance of our report deals with a specialized form of mission work, and that the general principles of mission operation do not always apply to our constituency. We are dealing with a class of people whose church experience and antecedent environment before their arrival in America were quite different from that of the purely American people. Were it not for the fact of the frequent errors in judgment and valuation of methods, that must of necessity be pursued, it would be superfluous to refer to this condition. In general association with American people, there is a marked contrast between the native and immigrant population, but this difference is far more pronounced, for example, in the sphere of the family circle and church affiliation. Many a prominent project miscarried in mission enterprise, because this distinction was underestimated.

When the Lutheran Church entered upon this sphere of mission activity in 1904, it embarked on a new venture. A plan of operation and adequate policy for dealing with this field of mission work had to be evolved. It is no vain presumption to express the hope that the situation is well understood by the Board and that the perplexing problems are handled as efficiently as the circumstances permit. In the course of development of the mission field, racial consciousness is manifested sometimes not in harmony with our conception, but charitable consideration usually finds a solution of the difficulty.

The field is constantly growing. Frequently new communities are found who look to us for administration. The Macedonian cry goes up in our day "Come and help us, we are spiritually perishing." Many of the immigrants have learned by sad experience, in spite of the alluring conditions of living in America, that "Man does not live by bread alone, but by every word that proceedeth out of the mouth of God." Our immigrants are scattered over the entire area of the United States. Those in the eastern portion of the country are more readily reached to receive services, while those in the far west are seldom visited. The superintendent makes strenuous efforts to extend his itinerary clear across the country and for the twelve years has succeeded in visiting once a year those on the Pacific Coast. The immigrants are not yet permanently established in their abode, but are influenced by industrial conditions and frequently move about. This presents a serious problem to follow up members. There is also a growing tendency to leave the mines and industrial centers and engage in agricultural pursuits. In this manner many families will be lost to the Church unless special attention is given to follow up these immigrants.

A growing demand is made for local pastors. Years ago when mission operations were first begun, the people felt satisfied with an occasional service. As an immigrant colony becomes more thoroughly established, families securing their own homes, and men engaging in definite spheres of industry, there arises a desire to have a pastor and a church home. The occasional itinerant mission service at long intervals does no longer meet the needs of the community. This condition has forced the necessity of preparing a capable ministry for the immigrants, who should serve as pastors. Under the circumstances the academic training had to be of a shorter course than was desirable in order to meet the urgent need for pastors. We are doing our utmost to prepare men for the ministry for all the different nationalities who look to us for assistance. This is a problem! Sometimes young men present themselves for a course of training who have excellent qualifications, but are weak in knowledge of English. Special instruction is needed in such cases to meet the requirements. On the other hand, young men present themselves who were born in America and passed through the public schools of the land. In their case special instruction is needed in their own mother tongue to qualify these as acceptable pastors. The Board engages an instructor who meets especially the Slovak students and supervises their training along the line of linguistic preparation. Such a special training is absolutely necessary for our class of students. It should be observed, however, that this instruction takes into view the work of the students as supply pastors during the summer vacation, and that great attention is devoted to prepare the students to render efficient service in this sphere. The Board had seventeen beneficiary students during the past year. Many of the students render services in vacant congregations throughout the year. During the summer months ten students were in charge of congregations.

A gratifying evidence of the permanent development of our work among the immigrants is the fact that they are endeavoring to secure their own houses of worship. Until a foreign congregation is conscious that it has its own place of worship, the work languishes. While the more earnest souls will attend the services conducted in other churches, a large number are indifferent to contribute support to the mission congregation and its pastor. It is indeed laudable to observe the liberality of the people when once the project of church building is launched. It may be of interest to mention some of the progress that has been made during the past biennium. The Slovak congregation in Philadelphia remodeled its church edifice. The Slovak congregations in Detroit, Muskegon Heights, Mich., Grassflat, Pa., and Port Clinton, Ohio, erected new churches. The Slovak congregation in East Pittsburgh recently laid the cornerstone of a new church edifice. The Hungarian congregation in Buffalo, N. Y., and the Slovak congregation at Northampton, Pa., have built new parsonages. The congregations at Mahanoy City and Freeland, Pa., have installed large pipe organs. The Slovak congregation in Youngstown, Ohio, placed a bell on its church. The Sts. Peter and Paul Slovak congregation in Chicago made a number of extensive improvements in its church property. The Hungarian congregation in Perth Amboy has secured church lots and building operations will soon begin. There is a great need for assistance to congregations engaged in these building operations in the form of church extension loans. In many congregations the building operations are delayed for a long time and thus the development of the congregation retarded for lack of funds to finance the project.

Notable progress has been made during the biennium in establishing parishes with resident pastors. We may mention the new work among the Assyrians in the city of Philadelphia with Rev. Yaure Abraham as pastor. Many of the Assyrians were refugees and together with their. pastor, Rev. Yaure Abraham, have located in Philadelphia. Mission work has been begun in Chicago among the Lithuanians. A new Hungarian-Windish parish was organized in Perth Amboy and Newark, N. J., with Rev. Stephen Smodis as pastor. The Slovak Mission field in Garfield, N. J., has called its first pastor. A new Slovak English congregation was organized in Minneapolis, Minn., with Rev. Paul Chropuvka pastor. The Slovak congregation in Akron, Ohio, has united with a newly organized Hungarian congregation and both are served by Rev. John Ormai. The Hungarian-English congregations in Martin's Ferry, Ohio, have recently become self-sustaining. New Slovak mission congregations have been added to the superintendent's itinerary at Lynch, Ky., Triadelphia, W. Va., and Perth Amboy, N. J. The city of New York, where thousands of immigrants of all nationalities are located, has been sorely neglected. Efforts have been made on several occasions to engage in work, but for unavoidable reasons failure was the result. Recently the Immigrants Mission Board in conjunction with the New York and New England Synod called the Rev. L. Sanjek to this promising field. The work undoubtedly will assume partly the character of Inner Mission work in visiting the numerous eleemosynary institutions. Rev. Sanjek is well qualified for this position, speaking all the Slavic dialects including those that use the Cyrillic alphabet. The Board has also succeeded in entering upon the sphere of social work by having a young Slovak lady taking the full course for deaconess to engage in parish work in the large Slovak centers. This department of the Board's activity has been delayed for lack of suitable personnel, but since the beginning has been made, it is hoped that more young women will offer their services. Through the assistance of the Board the Sunrays have been translated into the Slovak language and published. This is a valuable contribution to the meager Sunday school literature now extant in foreign languages.

The question has been asked how the restricted immigration would affect our mission work. Undoubtedly with the very small quota assigned to all our racial groups there will be a standstill as far as new arrivals are concerned. But this does not indicate that our sphere of activity is crippled. There is abundant work still to be done with the nationalities who are here now. It would be a mistake to presume that, with the limited number of arrivals, our task were finished. There is much territory unoccupied, and more intensive work is needed to gather in the various racial groups still without regular spiritual ministration.

The question of Americanization is stressed on all occasions. Our pastors are all conscious of the great advantage it is, that their constituency should be thoroughly in sympathy with American institutions and strive for the goal of American citizenship. Every effort is put forth to make all our immigrants a loyal law-abiding citizenry. We hold forth the apostolic vision: "Now therefore ye are no more strangers and foreigners, but fellow-citizens with the saints, and of the household of God."

II. Italian Department. Rev. F. Scarpitti, Superintendent

It has been only a few years since the United Lutheran Church took up the work among the Italian people. There was an effort made many years ago, which resulted in the work of St. Peter's Italian Lutheran Church of Philadelphia, Pa., but in 1917, a greater effort was made to expand this work all over the counrty by the former General Synod, but after the merger was effected this work passed into the hands of the Immigrants Mission Board which has conducted it with great results. But to do better work there are certain things which are needed.

1. *Lutheran Ministry*

In order to conduct this work efficiently, the first thing required is a Lutheran Ministry. By this is meant that young Italian men must pursue their studies in Lutheran educational institutions in order that they may form a Lutheran consciousness. Up to the present time we have been compelled to send our students to other denominational institutions in order that they may receive instruction in the Italian language; but in the next biennium, an Italian department with an Italian professor should be placed in one of our colleges. We are already corresponding with one of our Lutheran schools with the purpose of opening such a department in this school.

We must have an educated ministry, at least, one versed in their own language, and also a fairly good knowledge of the English language. What a miserable spectacle it is today to see in the pulpit men trying to preach to their people without a knowledge of their mother tongue, and it is pitiable to see Italian pastors unable to speak the English language.

A new call has come to the Church today, to work among the children of foreign parentage. The new generation is growing rapidly. They are attending public schools and high schools in our towns and cities. This

new generation is out of the American congregations as well as the
Italian churches. A means of approach must be found. The Immigrants
Mission Board is trying a new method by which we may get to work
among these people. We are employing an English-speaking girl in the
city of Erie, in connection with the Italian Mission, under the supervision
of the Italian pastor, aiming to bring this new generation, through the
Italian and American efforts, into the Church of Christ. These girls
must come from Lutheran institutions and must be consecrated with the
love of the Church in their hearts. This kind of ministry of men and
women can be made complete and efficient in a Lutheran institution. They
must have the English as well as the Italian viewpoint.

2. Church Buildings

Another imperative need is church buildings. The great mistake made
by the Protestant Church in the past has been to open Italian Missions
in storerooms, which were in many instances filthy, inadequate and unsani-
tary. There we have placed our missionaries to preach the blessed Gospel
of Jesus Christ, forgetting that these people are accustomed to worship in
ancient and artistic cathedrals and churches. They come from a land
where church architecture and beauty is unsurpassed in all the world.
This is true of the cities as well as of the small towns in Italy.

In order that we may do efficient work in the United Lutheran Church
we must build churches for these people. Other denominations are spending hundreds and thousands of dollars for church extension, and the
United Lutheran Church must do its share in order to reap greater fruitage in this field of labor.

We were compelled to begin our work in English-speaking churches,
but such arrangements have been very unsatisfactory, both on the part
of the Americans as well as on the part of the Italians. At the present
time we have only one church building for the exclusive use of the
Italian people. Our other Italian churches and missions are worshiping
in American churches. This does not permit the use of the church building
every day in the week as it should be in the Italian Mission, for the conducting of religious, educational and vocational classes. Neither are they
able to conduct their services during Lent, at Easter time nor the Christmas
season when our efforts bring much fruitage. It is very imperative then
that we provide church buildings for the Italian people.

3. Co-operation:

Another need which is manifesting itself now is the co-operation of
Enlgish churches in towns where the population is small and does not
justify the employment of an Italian pastor. There are quite a few Italians
where an Italian Sunday school could be started if we could have the
co-operation of the local English congregations. These congregations

should provide Sunday school teachers and officers, workers for sewing school classes as well as teachers for Americanization classes. The Immigrants Mission Board, through the superintendent, could supply such centers with preaching services at intervals. We feel that our mission work should not only be centered in large cities but also in small communities, and this is the only feasible plan to work the small centers.

4. *Local Committees*:

The need which is most important to my mind is the organization of local committees wherever Italian missions are instituted. These committees are to be composed of representatives from all Lutheran churches. The aim of these committees should be to co-operate with the Superintendent of Italian work of such a mission. They should be responsible for the securing of volunteer helpers, and also raise funds for local needs. More than this, the representatives should be connecting links between the English congregation and the Italian Mission. Two such committees have already been organized—one in Erie, Pa., and one in Philadelphia, Pa., and both are functioning with great satisfaction.

Such arrangements are undoubtedly beneficial to the local Lutheran constituency, for that would give them a part in the work which the United Lutheran Church is performing in their community.

5. *Larger Appropriations*:

At the present time many applications are coming to us from Synods and churches, requesting us to open Italian Missions in their territories and communities. We would like to open these new Missions in the next biennium, if a larger appropriation is granted us by the United Lutheran Church.

6. *Its Future*:

A great field is before us. There are nearly five millions of Italians in this country. Of this number there are sixty per cent out of the Church, indifferent and uncared for. These people are waiting for the Bread of Life, tired of the old religious affiliations. They are looking toward the new dawn which will bring peace and understanding to their hearts and which will bring them more closely to God and the Cross of Jesus Christ. Thousands and thousands of Italians in large cities and small communities are waiting for our Church to go and preach the Gospel of Jesus Christ to them. It is the mission that Jesus Christ has entrusted to us: "Go into all the world and preach the Gospel." What will be our answer?

At present we have five Italian pastors, three organized churches and two missions that will be organized before the meeting of the United Lutheran Church to be held in Chicago, Ill., with a membership of over two hundred adults, one lady mission-worker and one student; and six

Sunday schools with an enrollment of nearly five hundred children and thirty-five teachers. In connection with the Philadelphia Mission there is the Martin Luther Neighborhood House with a staff of three workers, not including the Italian pastor, who conducts the kindergarten work, Bible studies and Americanization classes.

The membership of these Italian Missions is growing steadily, presaging a great future of service in the Kingdom of our Lord. Men, women and children are coming to us to receive the light of Jesus Christ. Men who once upon a time lived wretched live, have been rehabilitated to noble purposes and good citizenship. Women who never set foot inside a church, who lived in indifference to all problems of life, today have been aroused through our efforts, to a better understanding of life. Men and women of high character and of good standing in the community are being added to our churches, to form a community of saints. If we could only print the stories of the various conversions which are happening daily in our churches, they would indicate again and again the great love of God for His children.

The work of an Italian Mission cannot be judged or measured by the extent of its few members, but should be judged by the light of the service which it renders in the community, for, after all, the missionary has adopted the entire Italian colony as his parish, and he performs a service of love among all.

One of the most important items to be reported to the United Lutheran Church is the first Italian Lutheran Missionary Conference which was held in Holy Trinity Italian Lutheran Church, Erie, Pa., July 16-18, 1924. By it has been written another glorious page of the history of the United Lutheran Church. I have never read in the history of our Church that there has ever been a Missionary Conference of Italian pastors; but we are making history, and when the Church has the outlook of faith and the vision to do the work of the Lord Jesus Christ throughout the world, that Church is bound to write history.

This Conference was opened on Wednesday evening, July 16th, with confession and communion service, with a sermon preached by the Rev. F. Scarpitti, Superintendent of the Italian Missions of the United Lutheran Church, and who was also the presiding officer of the Conference. His theme was "The Outlook of Faith and Its Promises," taking for his text Genesis 12:1, 2. It was a missionary sermon, setting forth the great work that lies before us in America. All the missionaries were present, a lady mission worker, a student, and wives of two of the ministers. There were also present the President of the Immigrants Mission Board, Rev. J. Elmer Bittle, D.D., of Pittsburgh, Pa., and the Secretary of the Board, Rev. George Gebert, D.D., of Tamaqua, Pa., Mr. Frank L. Fox, another member of the Board, and pastors from the Erie churches. Harmony, unanimity and loyalty marked the utterances of the conference.

III. FINNISH DEPARTMENT. REV. V. KOIVUMAKI, SUPERINTENDENT

This department is conducted in co-operation with the Suomi Synod. This Synod numbers 51 ministers, 177 congregations, 18,440 confirmed members and a baptized membership of 33,161, and if the missions are considered, there are no less than 80,000 souls who come under the influence of the Gospel through its ministrations. When we contemplate that there are between four and five hundred thousand Finns in this country, it will be readily seen what a large task lies upon this little Synod of loyal Lutherans.

Rev. Koivumaki, the Superintendent, is doing a wonderful work and splendid progress marks his labors. The Synod maintains a College and Theological Seminary in Hancock, Michigan, in which there are in all departments 104 students. The Board assisted in supporting 7 students in 1922-1923, and 5 students in 1923-1924. The Board assists in supporting 5 missionaries: Rev. Herman Matero, Newfield, N. Y., Rev. Bruno Vuormos, Sandwich, Mass., Rev. J. Isaac, Brantwood, Wis., Rev. K. V. Mykkanen, Lead, S. Dak., Rev. Niilo Korhonen, Fort Bragg, Calif. The Synod has vacancies in Butte, Mont., Reedley, Calif., Seattle, Wash., and Copper Cliff, Ont. New openings in the making: Alberta, Sask., Chicago, Ill., and the States of Wyoming, Colorado, Utah, Minnesota, North Dakota and Idaho. These fields are ripe for work with a promising harvest. It will be unnecessary to multiply words to show the vastness of the work done, work doing and work waiting to be done.

In this rapid survey the Immigrants Mission Board presents its report and prays for the serious consideration of its contents.

J. ELMER BITTLE, *President,*
GEORGE GEBERT, *Secretary.*

IMMIGRANTS MISSION BOARD TREASURER'S REPORT

Balance Sheet, July 31st, 1923

ASSETS:

Cash in Bank	$1,120.23	
United States Third Liberty Loan 4¼'s	100.00	
Loan to St. Matthew's Slovak Lutheran Congregation, Mt. Carmel, Pa.	500.00	
Option on Property at Erie, Pa.	1.00	
		$1,721.23

LIABILITIES:

Loans Payable:		
Bethlehem Trust Co.	$1,000.00	
H. E. Young, Treasurer	500.00	
		$1,500.00
Funds:		
Church Extension Fund	829.71	
General Fund	608.48	
		$1,721.23

RECEIPTS AND DISBURSEMENTS

For the Year Ending July 31st, 1923

RECEIPTS:

	General Fund	Church Extension Fund
United Lutheran Church on Apportionment............................	$24,904.00	
United Lutheran Church General and Branch Synods......	97.13	
United Lutheran Church, Women's Missionary Society..	6,001.00	
Pittsburgh Synod for expenses of Student Del'Osso........	200.00	
Suomi Synod, One-half Finnish Missionaries' Salaries and Traveling Expenses......................................	2,372.16	
Miscellaneous Contributions for Students' Expenses........	196.31	
Missionaries' Collections	1,246.55	
Donations	143.75	
Sale of Slovak "Sunrays"...	508.50	
Interest on Bank Deposits.....................................:..............	6.19	$6.62
Interest on investments...		4.25
Certificate of Deposit, redeemed..	2,400.00	
Loans:		
Bethlehem Trust Co. $1,000.00		
H. E. Young 500.00		
	1,500.00	
	$39,575.59	$10.87

DISBURSEMENTS:

Superintendents' and Missionaries' Salaries and Allowances	$20,893.22
Superintendents' and Missionaries' General Expenses......	4,217.22
Missionaries' Moving Expenses...	213.14
Education of Students	10,811.51
Expenses of Board Members..	703.90
Secretary's Office and Traveling Expenses..........................	253.48
Treasurer's Salary	75.00
Treasurer's Office and Traveling Expenses........................	31.84
Salary of Music Director, Erie, Pa., Mission....................	360.00
Salary of Janitor, Erie, Pa., Mission.................................	200.00
Expenses of Mission, Erie, Pa.	65.00
Bibles, Text-Books, Literature, etc., for Missions..............	324.44
Salaries of Teachers in Martin Luther Neighborhood House, Philadelphia, Pa..	212.50
Slovak "Sunrays"	489.40
Printing	157.25
Auditing	125.00
Apportionment, Home Mission Council................................	100.00
Interest on Loans	44.78
Miscellaneous	16.80
	$39,294.48

Excess of Receipts	$281.11	$10.87

RECONCILEMENT OF CASH
For the Year Ending July 31st, 1923

Balance, August 1st, 1922	$828.25
Add, Receipts as above	39,586.46
	$40,414.71
Deduct, Disbursements as above	39,294.48
Balance, July 31, 1923	$1,120.23

RECONCILEMENT OF GENERAL FUND
For the Year Ending July 31st, 1923

Balance, August 1st, 1922		$3,010.41
Add, Receipts as per Statement annexed..................	$39,575.59	
Less, Certificates of Deposits Redeemed..	$2,400.00	
Loan from Bethlehem Trust Co.....	1,000.00	
Loan from H. E. Young, Treas......	500.00	
	3,900.00	
		$35,675.59
		$38,686.00
Deduct, Disbursements as Statement annexed..............		39,294.48
Deficit, July 31st, 1923		$608.48

Respectfully submitted,

H. E. YOUNG, *Treasurer.*

PHILADELPHIA, 28th November, 1923.

We have audited the accounts of the Board of Immigrants' Missions of the United Lutheran Church in America for the year ended 31st July, 1923, and we certify that the foregoing report of the Treasurer is in accordance with the books of account and is correct.

LYBRAND, ROSS BROS. & MONTGOMERY,
Accountants and Auditors.

Balance Sheet, July 31, 1924
ASSETS:

Cash in Bank	$2,471.86	
United States Third Liberty Loans 4¼'s......................	100.00	
Option on Property at Erie, Pa..	1.00	
		$2,572.86

LIABILITIES:

Loans Payable:		
Bethlehem Trust Co.....................................	$2,000.00	
H. E. Young, Treasurer...............................	900.00	
		$2,900.00
Funds:		
Church Extension Fund	837.12	
General Fund	1,164.26	
		$2,572.86

RECEIPTS AND DISBURSEMENTS
For the Year ended July 31, 1924

RECEIPTS:

	General Fund	Church Extension Fund
United Lutheran Church on Apportionments	$30,456.40	
United Lutheran Church, Branch Synods	1,149.43	
United Luther Church, Women's Missionary Society..	5,000.00	
Suomi Synod, One-half Finnish Salaries and Traveling Expenses	2,771.12	
Missionaries' Collections	1,592.85	
Donations	828.64	
Martin Luther Neighborhood House:		
Profit on Cards $1,262.75		
Contributions 565.00		
	1,827.75	
Missionary Students' Traveling Expenses refunded by Congregations	135.00	
Interest on Bank Deposits		$7.41
Repayment of Loan made August 3, 1920		500.00
Transfer of Funds	700.00	700.00
Loans:		
Bethlehem Trust Co. $5,000.00		
H. E. Young 900.00		
	5,900.00	
	$50,361.19	$192.59

DISBURSEMENTS:

	General Fund	
Superintendents' and Missionaries' Salaries and Allowances	$29,002.37	
Superintendents' and Missionaries' General Expenses..	3,300.59	
Education of Students	6,981.03	
Expenses of Board Members	1,263.16	
Secretary's Salary and Office Expenses	67.73	
Treasurer's Salary and Office Expenses	87.05	
Expenses of Mission, Erie, Pa.	270.00	
Expenses of Mission, Dunkirk, N. Y.	60.00	
Expenses of Mission, New York City	70.00	
Martin Luther Neighborhood House:		
Salaries $2,220.00		
Expenses 202.28		
Interest on Mortgage 153.90		
	2,576.18	
Printing	231.06	
Auditing	125.00	
Apportionment, Home Missions Council	100.00	
Interest on Loans	182.80	
Loans Liquidated:		
Bethlehem Trust Co. $4,000.00		
H. E. Young 500.00		
	4,500.00	
	$48,816.97	
Excess or Deficit of Receipts	$1,544.22	$192.59

RECONCILEMENT OF CASH
For Year ended July 31, 1924

Balance, August 1, 1923 .... $1,120.23
Add, Receipts, as above 50,168.60

$51,288.83
Deduct, Disbursements, as above 48,816.97

Balance, July 31, 1924 .... $2,471.86

RECONCILEMENT OF GENERAL FUND
For the Year ended July 31, 1924

Deficit, August 1, 1923 .... $608.48
Add, Receipts as per statement annexed $50,361.19
Less, Transfer from General Fund............ $700.00
  Loans 5,900.00
                                                                        6,600.00

                                                                        $43,761.19
Deduct, Disbursements as per statement an-
  nexed $48,816.97
Less, Notes Liquidated 4,500.00
                                                                        $44,316.97 $555.78

Deficit, July 31, 1924 .... $1,164.26

Respectfully submitted,
H. E. YOUNG, *Treasurer.*

PHILADELPHIA, September 10, 1924.
We have audited the accounts of the Board of Immigrants Missions of
the United Lutheran Church in America for the year ended July 31, 1924,
and we certify that, in our opinion, the foregoing Balance Sheet, Receipts
and Disbursements, etc., are in accordance with the books of account and
are correct.
LYBRAND, ROSS BROS. & MONTGOMERY,
Accountants and Auditors.

In connection with the consideration of this report, the Rev.
A. L. Ramer presented the work of the Slav-Hungarian Department; the Rev. V. Koivumaki that of the Finnish Department;
and Dr. Bittle spoke briefly of the work of the Italian Department.
The report was thereupon adopted.

The report of the Jewish Mission Committee was presented by
the Rev. F. O. Evers.

REPORT OF THE COMMITTEE ON JEWISH MISSIONS

The two years elapsed since the last convention of the United Lutheran Church have helped to establish the cause of Jewish Missions more firmly in the hearts and minds of the pastors and members of the Church. Gradually, but surely, this great task of Christendom is winning the recognition it deserves and the interest and intercession it needs. This is not due to the great results and outstanding accomplishments. There is no work within the Christian Church which is so completely a work of faith, toiling and trusting as the work of Jewish Missions.

The awakening of the Church's interest rather indicates a fuller acceptance of our obligations as laid upon us by our Lord, the Messiah of Israel, and a clearer vision of the opportunities of evangelizing an entire race in our very midst which is still without the knowledge of the Christ and His redemption. Your Committee heretofore has patiently waited and prayed for this day to come. Unlimited strength is bound to be unfolded as soon as the Christians in our congregations throughout the land will take hold of this work and whole-heartedly, obediently and enthusiastically enter the active missionary forces of Jewish Missions. It would be ridiculous to think that the task of bringing the Gospel to a people, numbering between three and four millions and spread over the entire territory of our Church, could be attempted with any hope of even an impressive showing by four scattered mission stations, or for that matter, by tenfold that number. The cause of Jewish Missions will only then become the task of the Church, when every congregation will accept its field as Jewish Mission territory and with prayer and aggressiveness lay plans and make attempts to win their Jewish neighbors for Christ. The counsel and assistance of our experienced missionary force is at the disposal of any congregation courageous enough to enter upon this task.

Perhaps the special plight in which your Committee found itself immediately after the Buffalo Convention and the urgent appeal for a larger support carried through the congregations by Pastor Paul I. Morentz, as general representative of this work during the year 1923, is largely responsible for this awakening of a large host of friends. The indebtedness of the Committee has been greatly reduced through these efforts. The Committee was enabled to carry on its work with an increased number of missionaries and mission stations without curtailment of any branch of its activities. The friends in need proved friends indeed, and to them we wish to acknowledge our debt of gratitude publicly on this occasion.

The missionary staff suffered an irreparable loss through the untimely death of our veteran worker, Pastor John Legum, of Pittsburgh, the pioneer of Jewish Missions of the United Lutheran Church. It was John Legum who founded our first mission station in Pittsburgh twenty years ago. He succeeded in convincing and converting the Lutherans on that territory. Out of this acorn the oak has grown. Without funds, but with an unshakable faith, with every thinkable personal sacrifice, with untiring devotion, with holy zeal for Christ's reign over Israel, and with a profound understanding of his own people and a burning love for their salvation, he laid down his life for his brethren in the flesh. His wholly original personality, his keen insight into Jewish psychology, his invaluable counsel and his shining example are sorely missed by the Committee. To the list of her pioneers in missionary enterprise from Muhlenberg to Heyer and to Passavant the Lutheran Church must gratefully add the name of her first Jewish Missionary, John Legum.

There are at present four mission stations through which the work of your Committee is being carried on. Christ's Mission to the Jews at Pittsburgh, in charge of Rev. S. Paul Lapidos; Messiah Hebrew Lutheran Mission at Philadelphia, in charge of Rev. Paul I. Morentz; Salem Hebrew Lutheran Mission at Baltimore, in charge of Rev. Henry Einspruch; Emmanuel Lutheran Mission at Toledo, in charge of Rev. Isadore Schwartz. The character of the work is as uniform as local conditions permit. Every mission is kept open at regular stated hours every day for visits of inquirers; regular Bible Study classes are maintained, missionary meetings and services are held at regular hours. Every mission has a visiting list of interested Jews, whose homes are visited by the missionary. In Baltimore and Toledo there are weekly outdoor meetings during the summer season at which thousands of Jews are brought within the hearing of the Gospel. The Lutheran Churches of both cities are giving splendid support to this enterprise by sending their choirs to help in the singing, and often the local pastors mount the chair at the street corner and demonstrate by their words that our missionaries are doing their work in the name of and with the whole-hearted support of the Christian Church of the community. Daily Vacation Bible Schools are a regular feature of the summer work at Philadelphia and Toledo. The Philadelphia Mission up to this time is the only station where systematic work among the children in daily classes and a Sunday school is being done, thanks to the special support granted for this work by the Women's Missionary Society. In Mrs. Agnes Herter, a well-trained and experienced worker has been found for this particularly difficult field. Forceful tracts are being distributed by the missionaries on an average of one hundred a week. Old Testaments and New Testaments, both in their native tongue and in English are given to every one who shows a desire to read them. A multitude has thus been reached, hundreds have been deeply and lastingly impressed, and four have, during this past biennium, come to the final decision and accepted Jesus as their Saviour publicly in Holy Baptism. These men and the many who are near the truth, but cannot for obvious reasons take the last decisive steps, and all who are earnestly seeking the truth under the guidance of the Holy

Spirit through our missionary pastors, we lay upon the praying hearts of the Church. May the Great Shepherd of Israel, who has not cast away His people, hasten the day when the veil shall be lifted from their eyes and all Israel shall be saved.

The work of every mission station is being supervised by a local committee of pastors and laymen. All the stations are increasing the number of their local friends. The large constituency of the Philadelphia Luthera Association for Jewish Missions after the consolidation of the directorate of this body with the Philadelphia Committee has loyally continued its support of the Philadelphia station. The Lutheran Churches of Baltimore, of Pittsburgh and Toledo are chiefly responsible for the healthy growth of the work in their cities. The Maryland Synod has assigned the eighteenth Sunday after Trinity as Jewish Mission Sunday. The Pittsburgh Synod is appealing for the Easter offerings of the Sunday schools in behalf of the Pittsburgh work. Standing Committees of the Pittsburgh Synod and the Pennsylvania Ministerium are co-operating with the local committees on their territory in the building up of strong local support around their mission stations.

Greater attention must be given in the future to the important work of literature. We must be enabled to publish our own tracts. The proposed handbook on Jewish missions will be of great help to every one interested in the salvation of the Jewish people. A regular missionary publication to be used in the intercourse with inquiring Jews should be issued. Lack of funds has prevented the realization of these hopes heretofore. The *Hebrew-Lutheran* has been made a medium of information for the Christian friends of the work. The Committee has officially taken over this quarterly which was formerly published as a private enterprise of the missionaries.

The Committee had to refrain from carrying out its plan of two years ago of entering the city of New York with its fifth and most important mission station. After the death of Pastor Legum, the number of our ordained missionary pastors is only sufficient for the four stations now in existence. Appeals coming from other cities with large Jewish populations and an eager flock of Lutherans to support such a work in their community had to remain unanswered for the same reason. The field truly is white for the harvest. Pray the Lord that He may give us the men to send into His fields!

Two events of outstanding importance in the development of Jewish Missions must yet be recorded. On Whitsunday, 1923, the William P. M. Braun Memorial Chapel in the building of the Philadelphia Mission was solemnly dedicated. The regular Sunday services can now be held among appropriate surroundings. Such a sanctuary within a mission building contributes in a remarkable degree to the creation of a spiritual atmosphere and proves of incalculable value. In the fall of 1923, Miss Margaret

Mehring, of Bruceville, Md., created a memorial of her deceased brother, Frederick Mehring, by a gift of $20,000 for the purpose of Christian Mission work among the Jews of Baltimore and elsewhere. This fund is to be used for the acquisition of a permanent mission home at Baltimore, and it may be reported in this connection, that the Baltimore Committee has recently purchased a very suitable property. The Baltimore Committee is to consider this fund as a loan to be used without interest until such time that the Committee can repay the same partly or in full. The repayment must be made to the Jewish Mission Committee of the United Lutheran Church, which, keeping the principal intact, shall use the same in the purchase of permanent mission homes at other stations under the same conditions. Thus by this generous gift the work of Jewish Missions throughout its extent will be strengthened and helped.

These two gifts are the first large contributions coming to our cause. Both are of a constructive character adding possibilities which otherwise would have been unobtainable to our workers. We are confident that they are but the forerunners of even greater things.

In conclusion, your Committee wishes to emphasize its appreciation of the services rendered by the kindest of treasurers, Mr. Charles J. Fite, and also to speak with sincere commendation of the faithful labors of our missionaries. May God imbue them with continued wisdom and strength and bless their work that they may bring much fruit and that their fruit may abide.

Respectfully submitted,

F. O. EVERS, *President,*

A. C. CARTY, *Secretary.*

REPORT OF THE TREASURER OF THE COMMITTEE ON JEWISH MISSIONS

for the year ended 31st July, 1923

Balance in bank, 1st August, 1922....... $988.45

RECEIPTS

Treasurer, United Lutheran Church:
Apportionment, year ended July
   31, 1923 .... $6,798.00
Advance on Apportionment, year
   ended July 31, 1924............ 2,000.00
United, General & Branch Synods.. 672.97
Women's Missionary Society....... 1,155.00
Church of the Reformation, Milwaukee, for Student Support... 150.00

$10,775.97
1,500.00

Loans ....

Donations, etc.:
Rev. Paul I. Morentz, Collections..	1,167.80	
Sunday Schools, Luther Leagues, Churches, etc.	179.00	
Ministeriums and Synods...........	943.90	2,290.70

Interest on bank balance...............   8.06

                                                          $14,574.73

                                                          $15,563.18

DISBURSEMENTS

Salaries of Missionaries, Helpers, etc....		$10,096.00

General Expenses of Missions:
Rent	$1,020.00	
Janitors	50.00	
Interest on Mortgages on Philadelphia Mission	360.00	
Gas and Electricity	11.99	
Telephone	18.05	
Furniture, Janitors' Supplies, etc....	112.45	
Moving Expenses, Rev. Isadore Schwartz	211.50	1,783.99

Educational and Charitable:
Expenses of Missions: Charity......	93.00	
Literature ..	91.54	
Student Aid.	73.35	257.89

Unexpended Balance, contribution for student support refunded.......	76.65
Loans Repaid	600.00
Administrative and Traveling Expenses.	952.63
Mimeographing	38.15
Stationery and Postage	10.60
Auditing	50.00
Philadelphia Chapel Fund..............	40.00
Miscellaneous Work	10.00
Interest on Loans.....................	230.56

	$14,146.47
Balance July 31, 1923..................	1,416.71

                                                          $15,563.18

LIABILITIES

Notes Payable to Bank................	$3,900.00
United Lutheran Church, Advance on Apportionment	2,000.00

Special Building Fund — Pittsburgh Mission	109.00	
Special Fund for work in New York City	5.00	
	$6,014.00	
Less Cash in Bank......................	1,416.71	
General Fund Deficit...................		$4,597.29

Respectfully submitted,

CHARLES J. FITE, *Treasurer.*

for the year ended 31st July, 1924

Balance in bank, 1st August, 1923...... $1,416.71

RECEIPTS

Treasurer, United Lutheran Church:			
Apportionment, Year ended July 31, 1924	$9,535.80		
Synods	1,675.01		
Women's Missionary Society.......	1,380.25		
For Mission in Toledo.............	24.00		
Father Heyer Mis. Soc., Mt. Airy, Phila., Pa.	25.00		
First Church, Mansfield, Ohio......	100.00		
		$12,740.06	
Donations, etc.:			
Rev. Paul I. Morentz, Collections..	3,166.42		
Donations	21.00		
Rent from Pittsburgh Mission......	125.00		
Ministeriums and Synods...........	1,190.82		
		4,503.24	
Interest on bank balance...............		9.62	
			$17,252.92
			$18,669.63

DISBURSEMENTS

Salaries of Missionaries, Helpers, etc...			$9,892.85
General Expenses of Missions:			
Rent of Missions...................	1,135.00		
Rent allowance to Missionaries.....	349.86		
Interest on Mortgages on Philadelphia Mission	540.00		
Special donations for Missions......	136.43		
Moving Expenses, Rev. Samuel P. Lapidos	150.00		
		2,311.29	

Educational and Charitable:
    Expenses of Missions: Literature... 203.58
    Student Aid .....·............. 25.00   228.58

Loans Paid 3,900.00
Administrative and Traveling Expenses.   799.10
Mimeographing 49.00
Expenses of General Representative....   400.57
Auditing 50.00
Interest on Loans 165.34

     $17,796.73
Balance July 31, 1924.................   872.90

                                    $18,669.63

LIABILITIES

Notes Payable to Bank................. $2,000.00
Special Building Fund — Pittsburgh
        Mission 109.00
Special Fund for work in New York City   5.00

     $2.114.00
Less Cash in Bank 872.90

General Fund Deficit.................. $1,241.10

Respectfully submitted,

CHARLES J. FITE, Treasurer.

The following reports were received from the Auditors after the Convention.—Secretary.

September 7th, 1923.

Mr. Charles J. Fite, Treasurer.

Dear Sir:

We have audited the accounts of your Committee for the year ended July 31, 1923, and submit the following report:

General Fund Deficit: During the year the general fund deficit increased $2,471.74, viz.:

Deficit, August 1, 1922 .... $2,125.55
Add:
    Advance from United Church on apportionment for
        the year ended July 31, 1924 .... 2,000.00
    Increase in Notes Payable 900.00

                                           $5,025.55
Deduct, Excess of Cash Receipts 428.26

Deficit, July 31, 1923 .... $4,597.29

The details of the receipts and disbursements for the year are annexed.

Cash: We traced the cash received by the Treasurer, as shown by the cash book, into the bank deposits and compared the paid checks and invoices with the entries in the cash book.

The balance on deposit at the Diamond National Bank, Pittsburgh, as shown by the bank's statement was reconciled with the books and found to be correct.

Notes Payable: We confirmed with the Diamond National Bank of Pittsburgh, the notes payable which, at July 31, 1923, totaled $3,900.

Annexed we submit:

Balance Sheet of the General and Special Funds, July 31, 1923;
Statement of Receipts and Disbursements, and
Summary of Cash Account, for the year ended July 31, 1923.

Very truly yours,
LYBRAND ROSS BROS. & MONTGOMERY,

August 13, 1924.

Mr. Charles J. Fite, Treasurer.
Dear Sir:

We have audited the accounts of your Committee for the year ended July 31, 1924, and report thereon as follows:

General Fund Deficit: During the year the general fund deficit decreased $3,356.19, viz.:

Deficit, August 1, 1923		$4,597.29
Deduct:		
Repayment of advance received from United Church during the year ended July 31, 1923	$2,000.00	
Decrease in Notes Payable	1,900.00	
		3,900.00
		$697.29
Add, Excess of Cash Disbursements		543.81
Deficit, July 31, 1924		$1,241.10

The details of the receipts and disbursements for the year are annexed.

Cash: We traced the cash received, as recorded in the cash book, into bank, examined the paid checks and supporting invoices and compared the amounts with the entries in the cash book.

The balance on deposit at the Diamond National Bank, Pittsburgh, as shown by the bank's statement was reconciled with the books and found to be correct.

Notes Payable: We confirmed with the Diamond National Bank, Pittsburgh, the notes payable which, at July 31, 1924, totaled $2,000.

Annexed we submit:

Balance Sheet of the General and Special Funds, July 31, 1924;
Statement of Receipts and Disbursements, and
Summary of Cash Account for the year ended July 31, 1924.

Very truly yours,
LYBRAND ROSS BROS. & MONTGOMERY,

The Revs. Paul I. Morentz, H. Einspruch and I. Schwartz, Missionaries under the jurisdiction of this Committee, addressed the Convention.

The report of the Jewish Mission Committee was adopted with the understanding that the Auditors' Certificate should. be secured.

It was ruled that all reports which do not bear auditors' certificates, when adopted, are adopted with the proviso that such certificates be secured.

The closing prayer was offered by the Rev. J. B. Guiney. Convention adjourned at 5.00 P. M.

Evening Service

A service was held at eight o'clock P. M., the theme of which was "Religion in Education."

The Vespers were conducted by the Rev. E. P. Pfatteicher and the Rev. A. Steimle read the Scripture Lessons.

The Rev. A. J. Turkle presided and introduced the speakers.

Addresses were delivered as follows:

"The Civic Aspect"—The Hon. J. A. O. Preus, Governor of Minnesota.

"The Church Aspect"—Rev. J. A. W. Haas, D.D., LL.D., President of Muhlenberg College.

FOURTH MEETING
Morning Session

CONVENTION HALL, EDGEWATER BEACH HOTEL,
Chicago, Ill.

Saturday, October 25, 8:45 A. M.

Matins were conducted by the Rev. R. Neumann.

The Convention was called to order by the President.

Minutes of the morning and afternoon sessions of Friday were read, corrected and approved.

Mr. G. Hemsing reported for the Committee of Tellers as follows:

In the election for

Board of Deaconess Work

Votes cast, 427; necessary to election, 214. The following received a majority:

Rev. E. F. Bachmann
Rev. J. F. Crigler
Rev. J. F. Ohl
Mr. J. D. Cappelmann
Mr. F. C. Hassold

The President declared the foregoing the duly elected members of the Board of Deaconess Work.

Board of Education

Votes cast, 424; necessary to election, 213. The following received a majority:

Rev. R. D. Clare
Rev. W. F. Hoppe
Rev. E. P. Pfatteicher
Rev. A. Steimle
Mr. G. M. Cummings
Mr. W. H. Stackel
Mr. J. L. Clark

The President declared the foregoing the duly elected members of the Board of Education.

Board of Foreign Missions

Votes cast, 430; necessary to election, 216. The following received a majority:

Rev. E. K. Bell
Rev. C. T. Benze
Rev. R. C. G. Bielinski
Rev. M. J. Epting
Rev. J. A. Singmaster
Mr. C. W. Foss
Mr. James M. Snyder

The President declared the foregoing to be duly elected members of the Board of Foreign Missions.

Board of Home Missions and Church Extension

Votes cast, 421; necessary to election, 211. The following received a majority:

Rev. J. M. Francis   Rev. J. E. Whitteker
Rev. C. J. Smith   Mr. A. R. Bard
Rev. H. B. Stock   Mr. S. J. Derrick
          Mr. J. L. Zimmerman

The President declared the foregoing to be duly elected members of the Board of Home Missions and Church Extension.

Immigrants' Mission Board

Votes cast, 407; necessary to election, 204. The following received a majority:

Rev. F. E. Jensen   Mr. S. E. Long
Rev. W. M. Rehrig   Mr. H. E. Young

The President declared the foregoing to be duly elected members of the Immigrants' Mission Board.

Inner Mission Board

Votes cast, 426; necessary to election, 214. The following received a majority:

Rev. E. F. Bachmann   Rev. W. Krumwiede
Rev. W. H. B. Carney   Mr. J. Gear
          Mr. G. B. Morehead

The President declared the foregoing to be duly elected members of the Inner Mission Board.

Committee on Jewish Missions

Votes cast, 428; necessary to election, 215. The following received a majority:

Rev. A. C. Carty   Rev. L. H. Larimer
Rev. J. F. Heckert   Mr. C. J. Fite
          Mr. H. F. Heuer

The President declared the foregoing to be duly elected members of the Committe on Jewish Missions.

Board of Ministerial Pensions and Relief

Votes cast, 427; necessary to election, 214. The following received a majority:

Rev. C. L. Miller

Rev. R. H. Stover

Rev. M. H. Valentine

Mr. G. P. Tustin

Mr. J. H. Wattles

The President declared the foregoing to be duly elected members of the Board of Ministerial Pensions and Relief.

National Lutheran Home for the Aged

Votes cast, 418; necessary to election, 210. The following received a majority:

Rev. H. Anstadt

Rev. J. L. Frantz

Rev. J. E. Harms

Rev. J. T. Huddle

Rev. R. Schmidt

Rev. F. R. Wagner

Rev. J. Weidley

Mr. L. R. Alden

Mr. W. K. Butler

Mr. F. E. Cunningham

Mr. H. T. Domer

Mr. W. H. Finckel

Mr. J. H. Jones

Mr. F. W. Kakel

Mr. H. L. Snyder

The President declared the foregoing to be duly elected members of the Board for the National Lutheran Home for the Aged.

Board of Northwestern Missions

Votes cast, 427; necessary to election, 214. The following received a majority:

Rev. E. C. J. Kraeling

Rev. G. A. Benze

Rev. H. Rembe, Sr.

Rev. C. S. Roberts

Rev. H. D. E. Siebott

Mr. C. Hausmann

Mr. E. Muncke

The President declared the foregoing to be duly elected members of the Board of Northwestern Missions.

Parish and Church-School Board

Votes cast, 405; necessary to election, 203. The following received a majority:

Rev. T. B. Birch

Rev. C. F. Dapp

Rev. W. L. Hunton

Mr. G. P. Voigt

The President declared the foregoing to be duly elected members of the Parish and Church-School Board.

West Indies Mission Board

Votes cast, 399; necessary to election, 200. The following received a majority:

Rev. F. H. Bosch   Rev. J. H. Meyer
Rev. B. F. Hankey   Mr. J. H. Brandt
Rev. H. W. A. Hanson   Mr. C. W. Fuhr
                  Mr. H. F. Heuer

The President declared the foregoing to be duly elected members of the West Indies Mission Board.

Board of Publication

Votes cast, 415; necessary to election, 208. The following received a majority:

Rev. F. P. Manhart   Mr. G. D. Boschen
Rev. N. R. Melhorn   Mr. D. F. Efird
Rev. C. F. Steck   Mr. E. F. Eilert

The President declared the foregoing to be duly elected members of the Board of Publication and announced that one layman was still to be elected. The tellers were instructed to distribute ballots.

Moved and carried, That if there be no election on this ballot, in the next succeeding ballot the nominations be confined to those two receiving the highest number of votes.

Following the regular order the Rev. John F. Seibert, General Secretary of the Board of Home Missions and Church Extension, presented the report of that Board.

REPORT OF THE BOARD OF HOME MISSIONS AND CHURCH EXTENSION

FOREWORD

Home Missions is the response of the Church to the Saviour's command to Christianize the nation. It has always pioneerd. It strengthens the work of every agency. The size and influence of this Convention would have been impossible had there been no Home Mission interest in the United Lutheran Church and in groups that preceded it. Many of our strongest churches, fruitful in all denominational good works, were once Home Mission congregations. Entire synods are the result of Home Mission planting and most of them have been greatly strengthened by this blessed agency. Without Home Missions our United Lutheran Church would be a provincial organization, and a small one at that, along the Atlantic seaboard. The Board, therefore, submits this the third biennial report with a deep sense of gratitude for the substantial achievements it is privilege to record. It is not the complete record, for many results, some of them the most spiritual, cannot be tabulated. It is, however, sufficiently informing to indicate that the Board has earnestly striven to administer the work in accord with the spirit and purpose of the trust committed to it.

THE WORK OF THE BIENNIUM

New Missions Received and Congregations Organized:

Sixty-two new missions have received regular budgeted appropriations. Thirty additional ones have been organized and are still served by Field Missionaries, Theological Students or other stated supplies. This marks a creditable advance over previous bienniums. Had the congregations actually organized been in one state and formed into a new synod they would have constituted a body of more parishes than sixteen of the thirty-six synods in the United Lutheran Church. The total appropriation for those placed on the budget was $54,885 for the first year. To preserve the unity of the report the names, with date of reception or of organization and location by synods are given in Appendix A.

Self-supporting:

It has been said that one of the most significant and satisfactory marks of progress and successful Home Mission work is the proportionately large number of churches that assume self-support in a reasonable time. Congregations usually begin their work in great weakness and it is a delight to missionaries, missions and Board alike to note their development into sufficient strength to assume entire support. Forty-nine missions were thus added to the self-sustaining list and arrangements were made to take care of several others without continued aid from the Board, thus releasing an appropriation of $20,148.00. In only three instances was further appropriation withheld because of unpromising conditions. The names, dates and synodical connection of missions assuming self-support are given in Appendix B.

Aid Granted to Secure Lots and Churches:

It is not the appropriation for maintenance alone that must be considered in founding a mission. Proper equipment must be provided and it is the exception for a mission to procure it unaided. The Board cautions against contractual obligations that will hopelessly involve a mission in debt and insists upon proper financing as a condition to aid, but it also recognizes the necessity of a choice location and of an attractive edifice. The biennium has witnessed remarkable activity in the purchase of lots and in building operations, the latter in part due to inability longer to wait for a drop in building cost. At the beginning of the biennium *13* unpaid loans totaling $55,100 were subject to call; *87* additional ones were promised aggregating $367,341.59, a total liability of *100* loans, and $422,441.59. Of these *75* in whole or in part were called for and paid at a total of $282,-091.59. $140,000 was therefore subject to call at the close of the biennium, $50,000 of which is for missions of, and will be paid by, the Women's Missionary Society. Three loans were made to missions supported by the Northwestern Mission Board and another subject to call is to a mission supported by the Immigrants Board. Assistance, due to unusual conditions, was given to several additional congregations not under the care of the Board, to provide suitable churches at educational centers. Donations to assist in payment of interest and other small grants were made to *206* churches in a total of $130,148.67. An itemized list of churches aided by loan or donation is noted under Appendices *C* and *D*.

Evangelism:

It is proper to mention the Home Mission contribution to the growth of the Church. The ultimate object of planting churches is to win souls for Christ. Perennial evangelism has been stressed continuously by office and superintendents. Pastors of mission congregations meet every situation that makes kingdom building difficult anywhere. Probably more than others they feel the need of trained leadership, have inadequate equipment, must devote energy to financial matters, encounter prejudice or meet ignorance concerning their Church, yet, as a body they have been aggressive in conducting adult catechetical classes, organizing their people for community visitations and otherwise seeking to reach the unchurched. The result is inspiring. The average adult addition per congregation for the year for the self-supporting congregations in the synods functioning in Home Mission work through our Board according to the 1923 Minutes was 9.9 per cent.; for our mission congregations it was 17.5 per cent. With the Easter accessions as a criterion the record for the current year will be fully maintained. The statement of the Board of another denomination, substituting only our name, would seem to apply with equal force to us "The average Home Mission Church is the most consistently effective Evangelistic force the United Lutheran Church has."

Expansion:

The call to advance has come from every district. A few illustrations from some of the less familiar sections, in addition to the well-known appeal from the cities indicate the almost unlimited extent of the Home Mission field.

Alaska—This territory has been entered. Field Missionary Baisler has driven the first stakes at Juneau, a town of 5,000, with over half of the Protestant population Lutheran. Sixty have signed a petition for an

English Lutheran congregation and call for a pastor. Other towns visited were found ready for Lutheran occupancy. The gateway was Prince Rupert, in far Northwestern British Columbia, where the Field Missionary has organized a substantial congregation.

Prairie Provinces of Canada—Here the Northwestern Board, through successful missionating in Manitoba, Saskatchewan and Alberta, has developed the Manitoba Synod. In this vast territory of the richest farming lands and growing cities the Lutheran population has largely increased in the last census period. With only one English congregation, the call has come for a Field Missionary to occupy.

Texas—The Lone Star State is quite a distance, even by airplane, from Alaska and Northwestern Canada. The call for advance in English work here has come from our Texas Synod, itself largely German or bilingual. Nobody could be more ardent in its desire to see the many growing cities occupied. The successful planting at Houston and Dallas by Field Missionary Gillison with San Antonio, the next point of attack, indicates the wonderful possibilities of this great state.

Florida—This Mecca of winter tourists has been having remarkable growth in population. A large percentage of the immigration is from New York, Pennsylvania, New Jersey, Ohio, Indiana and Michigan, where the United Lutheran Church is strong. This spells opportunity for us and calls for aggressive missionary endeavor.

North Carolina—Cotton mills by the score, a goodly number owned by Lutherans, are displacing those in New England. With new towns springing up and with congregations in less than one-third of the counties of the state, the call to plant the Church is sounded loud by the synod which has manifested its faith by its works in raising a large Home Mission Endowment Fund.

The Great Cities—The opportunities in the great centers of population were never more insistently challenging. The drift suburbanward has intensified. The most remarkable housing program of a generation calls for energetic Home Mission effort to minister to hosts that are so rapidly moving from the old church neighborhoods. Were the Church justified in limiting her missionary operations, every dollar of the Board's income could be expended and every available man used for the next biennium in metropolitan sections where the United Lutheran Church has reasonably strong representation.

In its endeavor to meet this responsibility for advance, the Board uses various agencies:

Pastors and professors on vacation, or ministers temporarily without a charge, have been available for a limited period and have rendered effective service making surveys or organizing congregations.

Seminary students, in increasing numbers, with profit to themselves and with advantage to the Board, spend their vacations in similar activity or in supplying pastorless missions. Thirty-two young men from nine seminaries were thus located in eighteen synods during the 1924 vacation.

Field Missionaries regularly called, with territory defined, give their entire time to organizational work and to such other duties as may be assigned. In planting the Church in communities removed from the Theological Seminaries or other available source of supply, the Field Missionary is invaluable. He surveys the field, organizes the congregation, frequently guides in selection of lot, securing of funds and erection of chapel and remains in charge until a pastor can be located. This field staff now numbers twenty-one, an increase of eight during the biennium. The names and territory of the new men are:

Rev. E. B. Keisler, Georgia Synod, who will give special attention to Florida.

Rev. N. D. Yount, Western Section Synod of North Carolina, working at Asheville and Shelby.

Rev. G. C. Weidenhammer, Manitoba Synod with the first work at Prince Albert and Shellbrook.

Rev. E. P. Schuler, D.D., Southern Conference of the California Synod, which includes the State of Arizona.

Rev. H. C. Gans, Northern Conference of the California Synod.

Rev. F. E. Strobel, Toledo, Ohio.

Rev. W. D. Sharritt, Cleveland, Ohio.

Rev. C. S. Foust, Southern Conference, Synod of Ohio.

With one exception, the synods cooperate in whole or in part in providing for the support of these new men.

Cooperation:

The Board rejoices in the fine spirit of cooperation that has been manifested in carrying on our common task. It appreciates the contribution of every agency to the success of its work and is glad for any service it has been able to render. Under this heading we note the following:

Other United Lutheran Church Boards—The Board of Education, through its Department of Universities, has cooperated with our Board in twelve centers, in ten of which it has made an appropriation toward the salary of the missionary for services rendered in caring for Lutheran Students. Conference is had in regard to pastors proposed for such missions. The Inner Mission Board has been granted an annual appropriation of $2,500 for 1924 and 1925 to enable it to undertake Port of Entry work at New York—a type of missionating that annually will conserve hundreds of families to the Lutheran Church. The Northwestern and Immigrant Boards, as stated elsewhere, were assisted in their work by loan of $13,000 to three of their missions.

The Women's Missionary Society—This efficient organization has continued its cooperation in a substantial manner. The presence of Miss Flora Prince and Mrs. H. D. Hoover at the Board meetings as Advisory Members has been beneficial. Four missions supported by the Society have become self-sustaining, Pasadena and Riverside, California; Indianola, Columbus, Ohio, and North Austin, Chicago. The support of six others has been assumed, University, Seattle, Kelso, Wash., and Victoria, B. C., in the Pacific Synod, and Boulder, Colo., Casper and Laramie, Wyo., in the

Rocky Mountain Synod. The support of the Parish Worker for the Watauga Mission is also provided. The total receipts for loan, interest, gifts and salary was $80,060.46. An increased budget for the new biennium, particularly for Church Extension, has been assumed.

Synodical Boards—The policy of the Board to function largely through Synodical Boards in its administration of the mission work is being better understood. The salary budgets and the requests for Church Extension aid must receive their recommendation. Synodical authority is recognized in the calling of pastors, recommendations, if any, being presented through the proper channel. As a result, there is an increased assumption of synodical responsibility and a growing feeling of good will.

Overlapping Synods—The mission authorities of certain overlapping synods—the New York Ministerium, the New York and the New York and New England—meet at stated times to survey the field and to determine occupancy. The spirit of competition here has yielded to the spirit of cooperation.

Our Church Papers—The Board deeply appreciates the support which the work has received in the pages of *The Lutheran,* in *Lutheran Boys and Girls,* and *Woman's Work.* Many parish papers have been furnished with missionary news items and illustrations. Through the Luther League Topics an interest in missions has been quickened as evidenced by the increased number of inquiries which have come to the office during the past months.

Promotion:

Home Mission Conferences—A Conference of the Secretaries, Superintendents and Field Missionaries was held with the Board at its headquarters September 18, 1923. The purpose was to make a thorough survey of the field and to study the plan of operation. Thirty-one of the thirty-two workers and fifteen Board members were present. The following resolutions were adopted:

Whereas, The Secretaries, Superintendents and Field Missionaries of the Board of Home Missions and Church Extension, have profited greatly from and by attendance at the sessions of this Special Conference, be it

Resolved, That we extend our sincere thanks and grateful appreciation to the Board for this special and inspirational privilege, feeling convinced that the results of this Conference are of lasting value to all the field forces and to the mission fields and churches which are our fields of labor.

Resolved, That it is our judgment that the Home Mission and Church Extension Board will advance the work of Missions by devising some plan whereby they may assist Mission congregations in securing parsonages and we recommend that they make such arrangements.

Resolved, That we recommend to the Board the publication of a small paper, issued quarterly or monthly, in which shall be given items of Home Mission and Church Extension information. This publication to be sent to members of the Board, all missionaries, secretaries, superintendents and ministers of the United Lutheran Church in America. The expense of the publication to be paid by the Treasurer of the Board.

Resolved, That the Board secure, in such ways as they deem best, a wider presentation of the cause of Home Missions and Church Extension in our congregations.

Resolved, That the Board take under consideration the isuing of a program for Reformation Day in our Sunday schools, beginning with 1924, in which the needs of the Home Mission and Church Extension cause shall be stressed.

Resolved, That in view of the splendid Home Mission work which has been and is being accomplished by some congregations in supporting a Home Mission pastor, we request the Board to publish in pamphlet form and give to the Church a list of the congregations supporting or helping to support a Home Missionary, hoping thereby to inspire other congregations to do likewise.

Resolved, That we earnestly request the Board to adopt an effective method to collect overdue loans.

Resolved, That we rejoice that the Board is uniting with the Committee on Evangelism of the United Lutheran Church in its nation-wide mission for souls and promise our most cordial cooperation.

Resolved, That the review of the entire Home Mission field of the United Lutheran Church as outlined by the General and District Superintendents, the Synodical Superintendents and the Field Missionaries at this conference, has presented such unusual opportunities for immediate occupation of important fields, that we bring to the attention of the Church the imperative need for a larger proportion of the benevolences of the Church for the important agency of Home Missions and Church Extension.

A conference, under the auspices of the Home Missions Council, was held December 8th-10th at Rochester, N. Y., to promote a city-wide interest in Home Missions. Board representatives presented their work in all the churches of their denomination. Drs. Hartman, Hoffman, Seibert and Superintendent Berg represented our Board. One or more cities will be selected for similar conferences this year.

Home Mission conferences have been held by a number of synods at which the local opportunities and problems particularly were stressed. Others are contemplated.

The Accelerator—This is a news letter, containing messages from field and office that is sent out monthly with salary vouchers to missionaries and also to the members of General and Synodical Boards. It seems to be well received and to have an inspirational effect.

Illustrated Lecture—A beginning has been made in this method of presentation of Home Missions by the preparation of a lecture with slides giving a general survey of the whole field. It is available at the office of each of the District Superintendents. We trust the demand for it will justify the speedy preparation of others illustrating the work of each district and of different types of Home Missions.

Reformation Day Service—A Home Mission Service for the use of Sunday schools at the Reformation season has been prepared for the Board by Rev. I. Chantry Hoffman, D.D., the Eastern District Superintendent, with the cooperation of the representatives of the other Home Mission agencies. The use of such services in the past had a fine inspirational and educational value. The present generation is considerably indebted for its knowledge and interest in the work of the Boards to the training thus received. It is a custom well worth reviving.

An Awakened Interest:

Lutherans are becoming more profoundly convinced that Christ is calling every member of the Church to join Him in a conquering crusade that shall bring the Gospel to every soul in the Homeland. During the year a number of names have been added to the growing list of congregations that are supporting their own Home Mission pastor.

First Church, Altoona, Pa., Rev. M. J. Kline, D.D., pastor, assumed the support of Emmanuel Mission, Rochester, N. Y. Mt. Zion, Pittsburgh, Rev. C. E. Swoyer, pastor, assumed the support of Grace Church, Tarentum, Pa. Unity, Terre Haute, Ind., has been assigned to the First Church, Indianapolis, Rev. W. C. Davis, D.D., pastor. Hundreds of our strong congregations should not be content until they are represented in the Home Field by one or more missionary pastors.

A consecrated layman, Mr. J. B. Franke, a member of the Board, has made provision by means of an Endowment Policy through which the support of one or more missions will be assured for many years.

The Brotherhood of Indiana took the initiative in establishing the mission at Terre Haute and the Brotherhood of Illinois has assumed the support of Reformation, St. Louis. The Luther League of Minnesota has pledged a thousand dollars towards the support of a traveling missionary for the neglected rural sections of that state. Individual pastors, supported by a consecrated membership, are reaching out into outlying communities, conducting Sunday schools and establishing preaching points.

Finances:

Just a few items need be mentioned here, as the Treasurer's report is given under Appendix *F.*

Returned Loans—Forty-eight churches returned loans in whole or in part amounting to $58,586.50. (For itemized list see Appendix *E.*) This is an increase of $25,000 over the preceding biennium. However, with outstanding loans amounting to $928,355.60 this increase should have been much larger. The Board has adopted a follow-up policy which we hope will bring decided results. Synodical officers and Boards can render a great service to other needy missions by urging a prompt return of loans when due.

Bequests—Twenty-seven legacies were received as follows:

Anna M. Lake	$720.00
Wm. Ashmead Schaeffer	34,805.28
Anna M. Leidigh	400.00
Anna M. Trittle	76.41
Miller Estate	119.04
Hannah M. Haney	905.00
Emma Koch	259.16
J. F. Lowry	500.00

Wm. P. Huffman	329.29
Ida Kate Fite	466.94
Sarah Shuster	2,426.59
Rebecca Bernheimer	512.13
Francis A. Richard	100.00
Anna Van Axte	450.00
Anna Ruhl	362.00
Adam Miller	178.57
Mary Mintz Fithian	1,750.00
Augusta Young	905.00
Samuel Brecker	270.00
Lavina Kennedy	100.00
Amelia Ziegler	181.00
Chas. Diehl	50.00
Mrs. Kate Wolf	142.50
Jonathan Reitz Estate	9,687.89
Frederick Van Axte	1,000.00
Bridenbaugh Estate	13.06
In Memoriam	100.00
Total	**$ 56,809.86**

Unless otherwise stipulated by the testator, this amount has been added to the Permanent Loan Fund, and will thus perpetuate the memory of the donors by helping continuously in the erection of churches.

Annuities—$24,000 was received on the annuity basis. The annuity plan offers an opportunity to many who could not otherwise give large amounts, to make a safe investment and at the same time to further the cause of the Master.

Assets—It is well to keep in mind that the available resources are limited to the cash on hand. The securities, with few exceptions, represent gifts for endowment, the interest of which only can be used. The $928,355 reported as Class "A" loans are assets but only become available as the loans are repaid. Thus the Board in the prosecution of the work during the new biennium will be limited to the cash on hand, receipts on budgeted apportionment, special gifts, legacies and amounts received on outstanding loans.

The Retirement of Dr. Weber:

For some years, Rev. H. H. Weber, D.D., had expressed a desire to be relieved of the responsibility he had carried as Executive of the Board of Home Missions and Church Extension. His deep interest in and intelligent zeal for the cause to which he had with marked ability devoted many years restrained him from making his resignation effective until the Board had been relocated and a successor secured. He retired April 20, 1923, at which time the Board placed on record a minute of appreciation, from which the following paragraph is taken:

"For more than thirty years, with patient planning, courteous conduct and prayerful perseverance, he enhanced the conduct of Home Missions and Church Extension. He stirred the Church to a larger liberality for and to an increasing interest in this vital work. His gifts and his talents were consecrated to the work to which the Church called him and the effect of his labors will remain. The fruitage of long service will be enjoyed and participated in by many congregations in this country as the Church goes forward in establishing new congregations throughout the land."

In Memoriam:

A deep loss was sustained by the Board in the death of E. Augustus Miller, Esq. For many years Mr. Miller was one of the outstanding men in the work of the Home Mission Board of the former General Council. When the Boards of the three General Bodies were merged it was but natural that he should become a member of the new Board. As a legal adviser he rendered valuable service to the cause of Home Missions. A suitable memorial was adopted and spread upon the Minutes, which closed with this beautiful tribute:

"The intense earnestness with which he entered into every issue, the tempered zeal with which he followed out the lines of conviction inspired by a sense of right; the sympathetic spirit with which he approached every enterprise that claimed the Board's attention or called for his endorsement— in this, and all else, a frank, open, unbiased attitude, on his part, was ever in the ascendent. While we shall keenly feel the loss of his manly and masterful service we rejoice that the Lord gave us so capable a co-worker in the Home Mission cause and that by God's good grace he has now entered into his heavenly rest. With all sincerity of heart, we can inscribe in the page that records his mission activities, the commending words of the Master: 'Well done, thou good and faithful servant'."

The working force also sustained a deep loss in the departure of Rev. H. A. Ott, D.D., Rev. C. W. Stoever and Rev. M. H. Wickman.

Dr. Ott gave the greater part of his ministry to the work of Home Missions. As missionary pastor at Freeport and Quincy, Ill., and as Superintendent of Missions of the Kansas Synod, he gladly made many sacrifices. During the winter of 1922 while engaged in an exhaustive canvass in the development and organization of St. John's Church, Kansas City, Mo., because he could not be prevailed upon to spare his strength he contracted a fatal disease. He died at Topeka, Kans., March 28, 1923.

Rev. C. W. Stoever rendered faithful and successful service as pastor of several mission churches on the Pacific Coast. At the time of his tragic death, and that of his daughter, March 4, 1924, in an automobile accident he was pastor of the mission at Redlands, Calif.

Rev. M. H. Wickman was privileged to serve only a few years in the active ministry, being called to his reward at the age of thirty-four years. His first labors were in the Northwest Synod. June 1, 1921, he became pastor of our mission at Lakeland, Florida, which he served with great zeal until his death, October 12, 1923.

THE ADMINISTRATION.

At the Buffalo Convention, the Board was constituted as follows:

Terms to expire in 1924: Revs. H. B. Stock, D.D., J. M. Francis, D.D., J. E. Whitteker, D.D., Chas. J. Smith, D.D., G. E. Holtzapple, E. Augustus Miller, J. H. Rehder.

Terms to expire in 1926: Revs. J. B. Markward, D.D., J. C. Seegers, D.D., J. M. Bramkamp, D.D., G. K. Rubrecht, D.D., W. L. Glatfelter, J. B. Franke, F. D. Bittner.

Terms to expire in 1928: Revs. G. F. Gehr, D.D., O. D. Baltzly, D.D., C. E. Gardner, D.D., O. S. Gruver, D.D., C. H. Boyer, C. J. Driever, Geo. E. Neff, Esq.

During the biennium E. Augustus Miller, Esq., Geo. E. Neff, Esq., W. L. Glatfelter and Dr. G. E. Holtzapple resigned. Mr. A. Raymond Bard was nominated to succeed Mr. Miller, Pres. S. J. Derrick to succeed Dr. Holtzapple, Hon. John F. Kramer to succeed Mr. Glatfelter and George H. Greiner, Esq., to succeed Mr. Neff. These nominations were approved by the Executive Board of the United Lutheran Church.

Organization:

The organization of the Board during the biennium has been as follows:

President—Rev. J. E. Whitteker, D.D., LL.D.
Vice-President—Rev. J. C. Seegers, D.D.
Treasurer—Mr. C. J. Driever.
Recording Secretary—Rev. J. M. Bramkamp, D.D.
General Secretary—Rev. J. F. Seiber, D.D.
Educational Secretary—Rev. A. Stewart Hartman, D.D.
Supt. Eastern District—Rev. I. Chantry Hoffman, D.D.
Supt. Southern District—Rev. A. D. R. Hancher.
Supt. Central District—Rev. J. S. Herold, D.D.
Supt. Western District—Rev. Geo. H. Hillerman, D.D.
Executive Committee—Revs. J. E. Whitteker, D.D., LL.D., J. M. Bramkamp, D.D., J. B. Markward, D.D., G. Keller Rubrecht, D.D., C. J. Driever, J. B. Franke and C. H. Boyer.
Attorneys-General—Theodore Johnson, Chicago.
Special—E. Augustus Miller, Philadelphia, Pa.; Geo. E. Neff, York, Pa.; Robbin B. Wolf, Pittsburgh, Pa.; Hon. C. M. Efird, Lexington, S. C.; Henry Alberts, Jr., New York City; Louis V. Lundberg, Portland, Ore.; Clarence Runkle, Los Angeles, Calif.

Upon the death of E. Augustus Miller, his son, Paul Van Reed Miller, was elected to succeed him.

At the April, 1923, meeting of the Board, Rev. J. F. Seibert, D.D., Superintendent of the Central District, was elected to succeed Dr. Weber as General Secretary. Rev. G. H. Hillerman, D.D., December, 1922, was elected Superintendent of the Western District, and Rev. J. S. Herold, D.D., September, 1923, Superintendent of the Central District.

Removal of Headquarters:

At the organizational meeting action was taken to carry into effect the decision of the Buffalo Convention to remove the Headquarters to Chicago. The Treasurer's office was transferred March 6, 1923, and that of the General Secretary April 20, 1923. The offices are at 860 Cass Street in the building purchased by the Board of Publication. It is located in the rapidly developing office building section of the near northside. Since

December, 1922, all meetings of the Board and its Executive Committee have been held in Chicago.

Nominations:

The Board desires to place in nomination the following names to fill the vacancies occasioned by the expiration of their terms of office:

To serve for six years: Revs. H. B. Stock, D.D., J. M. Francis, D.D., J. E. Whitteker, D.D., LL.D., Chas. J. Smith, D.D., A. Raymond Bard, J. H. Rehder and S. J. Derrick.
To serve for four years: George H. Greiner.
To serve for two years: J. H. Kramer.

REPORTS OF THE DISTRICT SUPERINTENDENTS

These reports give in greater detail the work, opportunities, problems and statistical exhibit of the entire mission field and emphasize the challenging call that comes from every section.

EASTERN DISTRICT
I. Chantry Hoffman, Superintendent.

The "Big Business" of the kingdom has been carried on in the Eastern District, through the biennium, under the guidance of the Great Head of the Church and with the most cordial cooperation of all officially related to the work.

Stimulating Statistics—The number and amounts of Church Extension Loans and Donations of Interest, the increased salaries, the purchase of strategically located lots and the building of commodious and churchly edifices, the spirit of consecration shown by pastors in accepting calls to fields that challenge faith and demand Christian courage; the organization of thirty new congregations, the assumption of self-sustenation by nineteen, the reductions made in the appropriations received by thirty, the investigation of sixty prospective fields and the very large offerings for the local and especially for the work of the United Lutheran Church; these show that God is doing great things for us and in us and through us.

Invaluable Information—Knowledge of conditions enables the Board to take proper action. General and generous help along this line has been contributed by contiguous congregations, Conference Committees and Synodical Boards. The determination of a field's strategic importance and of its absolute needs is dependent upon the invaluable information gotten and given by all related even remotely to the administration of our Home Mission and Church Extension operations. Great cities, the centers of civilization, have been surveyed and the results studied. Towns and smaller communities which are rarely the halting places of "the caravans of commerce" have not been neglected. Facts solve difficult problems.

Constructive Cooperation—Competition has been eliminated; constructive cooperation has been established between overlapping synods. The domination of this Christian method of missionating is not only encouraging, but is positively productive of efficiency and economy. Outstanding illustrations of this better way are found in Canada and are eventuating in the merger of these two synods, and in that vast territory covered by the New York Ministerium, the New York Synod and the Synod of New York and New England. It has been a real joy to sit with the representatives of the Synodical Boards of these Synods, at their bimonthly meetings, and join in giving careful and unbiased consideration to the many fields (now numbering 40) and assigning these to the synod best fitted to make fullest investigation as to prospects for development and report for final allocation. God has blessed this order of procedure and the work of the King has prospered wonderfully.

Modern Macedonias—They are here, in America. The very cosmopolitan character of our population is the Macedonian cry. "Come over and help us" is the appeal from the Dominion of Canada; from "Old New England," with its great cities of cultural and commercial importance; from the dominating middle section—New York, the Empire State; Pennsylvania, the Keystone State; New Jersey, the Garden State; Delaware, the Blue Hen State. As Muhlenberg, Heyer and the Passavants and Barnitz and the Fathers heard and answered in their day, so must we in our day. We will pray and God's power will come; we will give our men and our money and our talents that these modern Macedonias may know Him whom to know is life eternal. From the lakes to the sea, from the rivers and the mountains; from the warm South and the frozen North comes the appeal. May God give us the spirit of Paul, the Great Missionary, that these modern Macedonias may hear the Gospel.

Effective Evangelism—Emphasis has been placed upon Scriptural Evangelism. Every opportunity has been seized to urge the importance of pastoral visitation and the fulfillment of the obligation of the Divine Commission to evangelize the unevangelized of all nations. The splendid record of accessions, in our mission congregations, is proof positive of the earnest effort put forth to win the souls of the unsaved and to woo unfaithful saints to faithfulness. This "Big Business" is appealing to men as well as to women and the telling of "the old, old story of Jesus and His love," is being done as never before. There is an appreciation of the obligation of the Christian to be witnesses (martyrs) of the Saviour to sinners. The realization of this responsibility has meant much in the winning of souls and the deepening of the spiritual life of the Church. Our mission congregations have cooperated heartily with the Committee on Evangelism and are prepared to go even farther in the Christlike service of saving the unsaved.

Our Optimistic Outlook—During the biennium splendid advance has been made. The past is prophetic of mightier victories in the future. The promise of greater things than these will be redeemed by Him whose command is to go in His name to do His work. Through consecration, coordination, and cooperation His confessors will be more than conquerors

STATISTICAL REPORT—EASTERN DISTRICT

SYNODS	Missions, July 31, 1922	Appropriations, July 31, 1924	Missions, July 31, 1924	Appropriations, July 31, 1924	Missions Received since July 31, 1922	Appropriation for Same	Number Receiving increased Appropriations	Amount of Such Increase	Self-sustaining since July 31, 1922	Amount Released by Same	Number Reducing Appropriations	Amount of Such Reductions	Missions Increasing Salaries	Amount of Such Increase	Number of Parsonages, 1924	Vacancies, July 31, 1924
1 Allegheny	7	$2,750	6	$2,400					1	$200	1	$150			6	2
2 Central Canada	5	3,200	5	3,425	4	2,700	2	225	5	1,850	3	600	2	225	2	1
3 East Penna.	21	10,760	20	11,260	6	800	1	250	1	300	5	1,200	3	800	12	2
4 Min. of Penna.	12	7,180	*17	6,730			2	250	2	1,800	3	400	4	450	9	6
5 Nova Scotia.	3	1,100		1,300	5		1	200					1	200	3	
6 N. Y. and N. E.	10	8,200	13	7,400	9	900	2	500					8	2,100	9	6
7 New York.	17	9,050	21	9,700	4	3,800	3	500	5	2,450	7	1,200	6	1,115	13	6
8 Pittsburgh.	32	17,660	32	20,960		3,780	7	2,500	4	1,540	11	1,440	1	500	1	5
9 Susquehanna.	2	950			2											
10 West Penna.	4	1,780	6	2,250		350	1	120	1	250	1	100	4	1,730	6	1
Totals....... Average	113	$62,630 / 554	124	$65,025 / 532	30	$12,330	19	$4,545	19	$8,390	31	$5,090	29	$6,120	64	23

*Five of these are new congregations to which no definite appropriations for pastoral support have been made.

through Christ, the Conqueror. The standards of the Saviour are being set up and America is being possessed for the King, who is to reign from sea to sea and from pole to pole.

SOUTHERN DISTRICT
A. D. R. Hancher, Superintendent.

The Southern District has made progress during the biennium. Some sections have made more than others due in part to local conditions. One had had poor crops for two successive years, another suffered curtailment of mill operations to half-time and even three days a week. These conditions had their effect.

Church buildings have been erected as follows: two in the city of Baltimore, one in East Riverdale, Md., one now under construction in Hendersonville, N. C., also in Cullman, Ala., one at Saxa Gotha, S. C., one at Ridge Spring, S. C., Jackson, Miss., and Louisville, Miss. The mission at Chattanooga, Tenn., purchased a fine building centrally located, as did the mission in Dallas, Texas. The church in St. Petersburg, Fla., has been completed and has a seating capacity of 700. Lots have been secured for St. Stephen's, the second new work in Washington, D. C., Rocky Mount, N. C., Shelby, N. C., Durham, N. C., Greenville, Tenn., and Laurel, Miss. The initial steps have been taken for a second church in Atlanta, Ga.

Additions to the working forces have been made in the Field Missionaries for the western section of the North Carolina Synod and for the Georgia Synod.

The missionary pastors entered heartily into the program of the Committee on Evangelism with the result that the accessions were gratifyingly large—one mission has doubled its membership in two years, 72 per cent. of the increase coming from non-Lutheran sources. Two pastors reported eleven adult baptisms each in their quarterly report.

The youngest work in this District is in the oldest city in the United States, St. Augustine, Fla. It is expected that an organization with a membership of at least twenty-five will be effected.

All over the district opportunities for new work exist. Especially appealing are those in the Muscle Shoals territory, Florida, Memphis, New Orleans, and the vast state of Texas. The opportunities for Home Mission work are the greatest challenge ever made to the Church.

CENTRAL DISTRICT
J. S. Herold, Superintendent.

The Central District comprises that great sweep of country from Ohio in the East to Montana in the West and Oklahoma in the South across the international boundary to the Arctic Circle, that has rightfully been called the granary of the world. In this mighty Empire a remarkable change is taking place with which the Church must reckon in determining the Home Mission program of the future. Westward the course of another Empire

STATISTICAL REPORT—SOUTHERN DISTRICT

SYNODS	Missions, July 31, 1922	Appropriations, July 31, 1922	Missions, July 31, 1924	Appropriations, July 31, 1924	Missions Received Since July 31, 1922	Appropriations for Same	Number Receiving Increased Appropriations	Amount of Such Increase	Self-sustaining or Discontinued Between July 31, 1922, and July 31, 1924	Amount Released by Same	Number Reducing Appropriations	Amount of Such Reductions	Missions Increasing Salaries	Amount of Such Increase	Number of Vacancies, July 31, 1922	Number of Vacancies, July 31, 1924	Number of Parsonages
1 West Virginia	6	$4,150	7	$4,690	1	$400	3	$550	1	300	4	$410	5	$1,020	4	2	3
2 Maryland	12	7,250	16	10,650	5	3,800	4	550	1	400	4	300	7	1,000	1	2	7
3 Virginia	11	7,860	10	8,525	1	750	2	200	1	558	6	695	12	2,035	4	5	3
4 North Carolina	15	10,353	20	14,425	6	4,920	3	320	2	450	9	635	14	2,747	2	2	10
5 South Carolina	11	5,200	9	5,485	2	1,650	1	75	1	900	6	340	8	775	4	2	7
6 Georgia	6	5,720	8	6,120	3	1,580	2	200			1	100	3	650	1		3
7 Mississippi	6	2,600	5	1,675							1	25					2
8 Texas	1		2	750	1	750			1								
Totals	68	$43,133	77	$52,320	19	$13,850	15	$1,895	6	$2,608	31	$2,505	49	$8,227	16	14	35

takes its way—the Empire of Industry. In 1910 almost 75 per cent. of the population of the Central States was found in the country. In this same territory, ten years later, according to the census of 1920, urban and rural population was equally divided.

Lutheranism predominates in the life of this district. But all to often it is a Lutheranism which not only speaks a foreign tongue, but which manifests a foreign spirit and finds its strongest centers in the rural communities. When the forward looking sons and daughters of the sturdy Lutheran races have become thoroughly Americanized and throng our city streets will Lutheranism still dominate the life of the Middle West? An aggressive missionary policy will help to answer the question in such a way that future generations of American Lutherans need not hang their heads in shame. Every available dollar and every available man could profitably be used by the Board in the extension of the kingdom in this Central District.

The Field Force—Four of the synods are served by Synodical Superintendents, in three synods full-time presidents supervise the mission work. Eleven Field Missionaries are exploring new fields and doing pioneer work for the Church. More than one hundred missionaries with intense zeal and true consecration are carrying the standards of the Church to new battle fronts. The percentage of increase in the confirmed membership reported by the missions of this territory averages 24.51 per cent.—an eloquent testimony to the missionary spirit of our mission pastors.

Neglected Opportunities—One of our Field Missionaries reports a territory of one hundred miles square without a single church of any kind. It is true, this territory is sparsely settled, but the government has thought it worth while to erect a school building every four miles. Should the Church do less in spiritual matters for these widely scattered pioneers? The Northern Peninsula of Michigan with a score of cities with a population from five to fifteen thousand is an unknown land to the United Lutheran Church. In Montana there are two lone missionaries of the United Lutheran Church holding the field and eagerly awaiting reenforcements. Oklahoma with its rapidly growing cities has but two English United Lutheran churches. In the great industrial centers, in the neglected rural communities, in the lumber camps of the North and the irrigation farms of the West, the unchurched multitudes present an opportunity which comes as a challenge to test the faith and the courage of the Lutheran Church of America. The fields are white unto harvest, but the laborers are few.

WESTERN DISTRICT
G. H. Hillerman, Superintendent.

Its Size—Ten states of the Rocky Mountain and Pacific Coast territory, together with British Columbia, Alaska and El Paso, Texas, represent the field, which covers, in round figures, two million square miles, with a population of over 10,000,000.

Its Material Prospects—Two aspects alone can convey some idea of the

STATISTICAL REPORT— CENTRAL DISTRICT

SYNODS	Mission Parishes, July 31, 1922.	Appropriations, July 31, 1922.	Mission Parishes, July 31, 1924.	Appropriations, July 31, 1924.	Missions Received Since July 31, 1922.	Amount Appropriated for the Same.	Number Receiving Increased Appropriations.	Amount of Such Increase.	Missions Assuming Self-support during the Bi-ennium.	Amount Released by the Same.	Number Reducing Appropriations.	Amount of Such Reductions.	Missions Increasing Salaries.	Amount of Such Increase.	Number of Vacancies, July 31, 1922.	Number of Vacancies, July 31, 1924.	Number of Parsonages.
1 Ohio	22	$16,490	23	$15,375	4	$3,000			3	$1,480	12	$3,355	6	$1,100		3	9
2 Indiana	11	7,575	14	9,350	3	3,000			1	425	9	1,475	4	750	1	1	7
3 Michigan	8	11,290	10	13,850	3	4,100			1	360	8	1,700	4	550	1	1	6
4 Illinois	19	17,690	18	16,200	5	7,200	5	1,560	8	4,400	11	2,200	7	1,300	3	2	5
5 Northwest	21	23,930	26	24,635	6	4,900			1	240	14	5,710	3	250	1		5
6 Iowa	11	7,225	10	8,080	1	1,400			1	150	5	315	3	470	1	1	11
7 Nebraska	6	4,250	7	3,500		900			2	750	3	600	2	300	1	1	5
8 Kansas	11	5,700	8	6,350	3		4	1,675	3	575	2	365	1	400		1	3
Totals	109	$94,150	116	$97,340	25	$24,500	9	$3,235	20	$8,380	64	$15,720	30	$5,120	8	10	52

future possibilities. Government officials have shown that the eleven states (includes Montana) alone have close to 75 per cent. of the available hydro-electric power of the country; and that the land possible for irrigation in the same district can support two hundred million people, or more than twentyfold the present population.

The Religious Situation—It is distinctly pioneer work, laboring with what is largely a migratory population, beset on all sides by the concentrated manifestations of all the isms and fads of mankind. And in its separation from the main body of our Church it faces the added and serious difficulty of securing readily and quickly men of the proper caliber to care for its activities.

The Synods—Three synods are at work in this territory, separated from each other by a day and a half or two days' railroad travel. One of these synods is a string of congregations 1,100 miles in length, as far as from New York City to Florida, and the other synods have already entered terri-tory of that length, but having more breadth than the first named.

The Field Force—Six Field Missionaries and fifty-one pastors are allotted to the oversight of the missionary operations of the United Lutheran Church in this district, under the direction of the three Synodical Boards and the District Superintendent.

Some Outstanding Results of the Biennium—Eleven new missions have been organized, four of which have not yet received an appropriation from the Board; four assumed self-support, while seventeen made increases in the salaries of pastors, and twenty made reductions in appropriations from the Board.

The Outlook—A few facts will be sufficient to emphasize the importance of the field and the possibilities of the future. In the state of Arizona we have but one congregation, with growing cities like Tucson, Prescott and Bisbee bespeaking the need of a Field Missionary; New Mexico has but one functioning congregation, while there is not even one in Idaho, Nevada or Utah, and Wyoming has but two. In this district there are thirty-one cities of 10,000 or over population which have no English Lutheran work; and it has been estimated that the entire Lutheran force has not gotten into its congregations more than about 6 per cent. of the Lutheran material. Cities like Los Angeles, San Francisco, Seattle, Denver, San Diego and others could use the entire service of a Field Missionary immediately and keep him busy for years on the material already there. The opportunity is shown in one case where a Field Missionary in 500 consecutive calls found fifty Lutheran families.

The Need—Aside from the conventional work of missions, there is a preeminent call for our Church to enter the field of the Community Church, which shall meet the needs of the entire community, and not of a Lutheran clientele alone, yet under direct Lutheran control. Men with a vision, men ready to "endure hardship as good soldiers," men who will put service above remuneration, men ready to lay foundations for another's building, men

STATISTICAL REPORT—WESTERN DISTRICT

SYNODS	Missions, July 31, 1922.	Appropriations, July 31, 1922.	Missions, July 31, 1924.	Appropriations, July 31, 1924.	Missions Received Since July 31, 1922.	Amount of Appropriation for the Same.	Number Receiving Increased Appropriations.	Amount of Such Increase.	Self-sustaining to July 31, 1924.	Amount Released by the Same.	Number Reducing Appropriation.	Amount of Such Reduction.	Missions Increasing Salaries.	Amount of Such Increases.	Number of Vacancies, July 31, 1922.	Number of Vacancies, July 31, 1924.	Number of Parsonages.
1 California	17	$14,015	19	$18,080	5	$3,450	1	$300	2	$550	10	$855	8	$1,525	1	6	5
2 Pacific	16	14,800	20	18,660	5	3,900	.....	.....	1	900	2	240	6	1,600	2	4	13
3 Rocky Mountain	12	7,250	12	9,685	1	1,620	1	240	1	300	8	725	3	980	2	3	4
Totals	45	$36,065	51	$46,425	11	$8,970	2	$540	4	$1,750	20	$1,820	17	$4,105	5	13	22

willing to be all things to all men in order to accomplish the salvation of some of them. Money sufficient to start our missions on a self-respecting basis. We have entered the field in most cases long after the other denominations have obtained a strong foothold, and what would have been sufficient when they began, today is only a trifle, and subjects our congregations to extreme embarrassment, to say the least, before the eyes of a critical community. But one slogan fits the situation and the need, "Occupy, occupy, occupy!"

Conclusion

With heartfelt appreciation of the untiring labors of the devoted missionaries and in grateful recognition of the many blessings which the great Head of the Church has bestowed upon the work of the biennium, the Board continues to look to Him for wisdom and guidance as we go forward.

Respectfully submitted,

J. E. Whitteker, *President,*
J. F. Seibert, *General Secretary.*

APPENDIX A.

New Missions Received and Organized

East Pennsylvania Synod

Palmyra, New Jersey	First	October,	1921
Narberth, Penna.	Holy Trinity	January,	1922
West Chester, Penna.	Calvary	March,	1923
Drexel Hill, Penna.	Grace	April,	1923
Woodbury, N. J.	Trinity	February,	1924

Ministerium of Pennsylvania

Laureldale, Penna.	Calvary	February,	1921
Frankford, Phila., Pa.	Covenant	April,	1924
Pleasantville, N. J.	Epiphany	February,	1924
Vineland, N. J.	Redeemer	April,	1924
Ocean City, N. J.	St. John's	June,	1923
Manasquan, N. J.	Holy Trinity	September,	1923
Somers Point, N. J.	Grace	April,	1924

New York and New England Synod

Woodhaven, L. I., N. Y.	St. James'	October	1921
Rochester, N. Y.	Emmanuel	November,	1922
Flushing, L. I., N. Y.	Messiah	May,	1924
Queens, L. I., N. Y.	Redeemer	December,	1923
Franklin Square, L. I., N. Y.	Ascension	October,	1923
Hollis Circle, L. I., N. Y.	Hollis Circle	May,	1924

New York Synod

Springfield Gardens, L. I., N. Y.	Bethany	September,	1922
Hillside, N. J.	Calvary	June,	1922
Howard Beach N. Y.	St. Barnabas'	July,	1922
Gerrittsen Beach, N. Y.	St. James'	February,	1924
Hillside, L. I., N. Y.	Our Saviour	October,	1923
Baisley Park, N. Y.	Incarnation	February,	1924
Pelham Park, N. Y.	Calvary	July,	1924

Pittsburgh Synod

Arnold, Penna.	Calvary	November,	1922
Cleveland, Ohio	St. John's	July,	1922
Sharon, Penna.	Holy Trinity	September,	1921

West Virginia Synod

New Milton, W. Va.	St. Johannis	January,	1924

Maryland Synod

Lansdowne, Md.	Our Saviour	February,	1923
Mt. Winans, Md.	St. Paul's	February,	1923
Washington, D. C.	St. Stephen's	September,	1923
East Riverside, Md.	St. John's	February,	1924
Cordova, Md.	St. Paul's	February,	1924

Virginia Synod

Danville, Va.	Ascension	January,	1923

North Carolina Synod

Shelby, N. C.	Ascension	June,	1923
Asheville, N. C.	St. Mark's	June,	1923
Rocky Mount, N. C.	Trinity	April,	1923
Durham, N. C.	St. Paul's	June,	1924
Rockingham, Va.	Parish	January,	1924
Boone, N. C.	St. Mark's	March,	1924

South Carolina Synod

Lexington Co.	Bethlehem	January,	1923
Rock Hill, S. C.	Grace	June,	1923

Georgia Synod

Weirsdale, Fla.	St. John's	January,	1923
Cullman, Ala.	Christ	May,	1924

Mississippi Synod

Winston, Miss.	Parish	January,	1923

Texas Synod

Dallas, Texas	Luther Memorial	May,	1923

Ohio Synod

Columbus, Ohio	Redeemer	April,	1923
Oak Harbor, Ohio	Grace	April,	1923
Toledo, Ohio	Reformation	February,	1923
Bowling Green, Ohio	First	June,	1923

Indiana Synod

Indianapolis, Ind.	Bethany	October,	1923
Indianapolis, Ind.	Bethlehem	October,	1923
Terre Haute, Ind.	Unity	June,	1924

Michigan Synod

Lansing, Mich.	Redeemer	October,	1922
Windsor, Ont.	Trinity	September,	1922
Sault Ste. Marie, Ont.	Zion	July,	1923
Detroit, Mich.	Unity	November,	1922
Detroit, Mich.	Hope	November,	1923
Saginaw, Mich.	Resurrection	May,	1924

Illinois Synod

Chicago, Ill.	St. Mark's	October,	1922
Elmhurst, Ill.	Elmhurst	April,	1923
St. Louis, Mo.	Reformation	September,	1923
Brookfield, Ill.	Brookfield	December,	1923
Yorkville, Ill.	Bethesda	September,	1923

Synod of the Northwest

West Bend, Wis.	Trinity	September,	1922
Oxboro, Minn.	St. Luke's	September,	1922
Jefferson, Wis.	St. Mark's	November,	1923
Marshfield, Wis.	Trinity	June,	1923
Morris Park, Minn.	Resurrection	May,	1923
Milwaukee, Wis.	Pentecost	May,	1924
Argonne, Wis.	Trinity	May,	1924

Iowa Synod

Des Moines, Iowa	Unity	February,	1924

Nebraska Synod

Elkhorn, Neb.	Elkhorn	September,	1923
Sidney-Gurley, Neb.	Parish	November,	1923
Paxton-Sutherland, Neb.	Parish	April,	1924

Rocky Mountain Synod

Casper, Wyo.	Grace	October,	1922

Pacific Synod

American Lake, Wash.	American Lake		
Tacoma, Wash.	Grace	June,	1923
Kelso, Wash.	Trinity		
Portland, Ore.	St. Mark's	July,	1924

Total, 92.

APPENDIX B.

SELF-SUPPORTING OR DISCONTINUED FROM BUDGET

EASTERN DISTRICT

New York Synod

Hicksville, N. Y. ....St. Stephen's
Hollis, N. Y. ....Holy Trinity
South Ozone Park, N. Y. ....Good Shepherd
Dolgeville, N. Y. ....Zion
Jersey City, N. J. ....Calvary
Brooklyn, N. Y. ....St. Paul's

New York and New England Synod

Merrick and North Bellmore, L. I..................St. John's and Grace
Brooklyn, N. Y. ....Mediator

Ministerium of Pennsylvania

Philadelphia, Pa. ....Immanuel

East Pennsylvania

Camden, N. J. ....Trinity
Collingswood, N. J. ....St. Paul's
Fort Washington, Pa. ....Trinity
Oreland, Pa. ....Christ
Reading, Pa. ....St. Peter's
Ambler, Pa. ....St. John's

Alleghany Synod

Woodbury Parish

Pittsburgh Synod

Pittsburgh, Pa. ....Memorial
Smithton, Pa. ....Memorial
North East, Pa. ....St. Peter's
Rural Valley Parish

Susquehanna Synod

State College, Pa. ....Grace

SOUTHERN DISTRICT

Maryland Synod

Baltimore, Md. ....Holy Comforter

Virginia Synod

Vinton Parish

North Carolina Synod

Greensboro ....First

South Carolina Synod

Saluda, S. C. ....Mt. Pleasant and Trinity
Silver Street, S. C. ....Silver Street

Mississippi Synod
Greenville, Miss. ....Greenville

CENTRAL DISTRICT
Ohio Synod
Cleveland, Ohio ....Trinity, Lakewood
Columbus, Ohio ....Indianola
Lorain, Ohio ....First

Indiana Synod
Batesville, Ind. ....Batesville

Michigan Synod
Butler, Ind. ....Butler

Illinois Synod
Chicago, Ill. ....North Austin
Chicago, Ill. ....Advent
Chicago, Ill. ....Atonement
Chicago Heights, Ill. ....Trinity
Cicero, Ill. ....Gethsemane
St. Louis, Mo. ....Reen Memorial
Peoria, Ill. ....Grace
Webster Grove, Mo. ....Webster Grove

Northwest Synod
Marinette, Wis. ....St. James'

Iowa Synod
Princeton and Pleasant Valley ....Parish

Nebraska Synod
Leigh, Neb. ....St. John's
Gretna, Neb. ....Gretna

Kansas Synod
Whitewater, Kans. ....Whitewater
Greenleaf, Kans. ....Greenleaf
Tulsa, Okla. ....First

WESTERN DISTRICT
California
Pasadena, Calif. ....Trinity
Riverside, Calif. ....Trinity

Rocky Mountain Synod
Albuquerque, N. Mex. ....St. Paul's

Pacific Synod
Seattle, Wash. ....St. Paul's

Total, 49.

APPENDIX C.

Loans Paid

EASTERN DISTRICT

 1. Arnold, Pa. ....Calvary
 2. Butler, Pa. ....Trinity
 3. Cleveland, Ohio ....St. John's
 4. Hamilton, Ont. ....Trinity
 5. Hasbrook Heights, N. J. ....Holy Trinity
 6. Hillside, N. J. ....Calvary
 7. Mountainville, Pa. ....Trinity
 8. Philadelphia, Pa. ....Gloria Dei
 9. River Edge, N. J. ....Grace
10. Schenectady, N. Y. ....First
11. Sharon, Pa. ....Trinity
12. Syracuse, N. Y. ....Atonement
13. Trenton, N. J. ....Bethel
14. Wilkes-Barre, Pa. ....Holy Trinity

SOUTHERN DISTRICT

 1. Baltimore, Md. ....All Saints
 2. Baltimore, Md. ....Ascension
 3. Chattanooga, Tenn. ....Ascension
 4. Cullman, Ala. ....Christ
 5. Dallas, Texas ....First
 6. Easton, Md. ....Grace
 7. East Riverdale, Md. ....St. John's
 8. Goodman, Miss. ....St. Mark's
 9. Hendersonville, N. C. ....Grace
10. Laurel, Miss. ....Grace
11. Lynchburg, Va. ....Trinity
12. Mt. Pleasant, N. C. ....Watauga Mission
13. Raleigh, N. C. ....Trinity
14. Rock Mount, N. C. ....Trinity
15. Statesville, N. C. ....St. John's
16. Jackson, Miss. ....Trinity

CENTRAL DISTRICT

 1. Billings, Mont. ....First
 2. Bowling Green, Ohio ....First
 3. Broadview, Ill. ....Broadview
 4. Chicago, Ill. ....Immanuel
 5. Chicago, Ill. ....Norwood Park
 6. Chicago, Ill. ....North Austin
 7. Chicago, Ill. ....St. Thomas
 8. Cleveland Heights, Ohio ....Messiah
 9. Columbus, Ohio ....Redeemer
10. Des Moines, Iowa ....Unity
11. Detroit, Mich. ....Hope
12. Detroit, Mich. ....Luther Memorial
13. Detroit, Mich. ....Unity
14. Elmhurst, Ill. ....Elmhurst
15. Evanston, Ill. ....St. Paul's

16. Evansville, Ind. ....Christ
17. Flint, Mich. ....Holy Trinity
18. Indianapolis, Ind. ....Bethlehem
19. Kansas City, Kans. ....Trinity
20. Lansing, Mich. ....Redeemer
21. Lincoln, Neb. ....
22. Marshfield, Wis. ....Incarnation
23. Milwaukee, Wis. ....Resurrection
24. Minneapolis, Minn. ....Luther Memorial
25. Madison, Wis. ....Grace
26. Muscatine, Iowa ....Trinity
27. Ottumwa, Iowa ....St. Mark's
28. St. Louis, Mo. ....Advent
29. Superior, Wis. ....Holy Trinity
30. Terre Haute, Ind. ....Unity
31. Toledo, Ohio ....Redeemer
32. Walters, Minn. ....Faith
33. Waukesha, Wis. ....St. Luke's
34. Williston, N. Dak. ....Trinity
35. Windsor, Ont. ....Trinity

WESTERN DISTRICT

1. Casper, Wyo. ....Grace
2. Huntington Park, Calif. ....First
3. Los Angeles, Calif. ....Hollywood
4. Oakland, Calif. ....St. Johannes'
5. Seattle, Wash. ....St. James
6. Seattle, Wash. ....University
7. Victoria, B. C. ....Grace

NORTHWESTERN MISSION BOARD:

1. Edmonton, Alta. ....St. John's
2. Chicago, Ill. ....Friedens
3. Guttenberg, Ia. ....St. Paul's

Total, 75 .... $ 282,091.59

APPENDIX D

Donations

EASTERN DISTRICT

1. Altoona, Pa. .... Temple
2. Ambler, Pa. .... St. John's
3. Ashtabula, Ohio .... First
4. Athol, Pa. .... St. Paul's
5. Baden, Pa. .... Christ
6. Beechview, Pa. .... St. Stephen's
7. Berwick, Pa. .... Holy Trinity
8. Bethlehem, Pa. .... St. Stephen's
9. Bethlehem, Pa. .... Rosemont
10. Bridgeport, Ohio. .... Trinity
11. Brooklin, Pa. .... Temple
12. Brooklyn, N. Y. .... Advent
13. Brooklyn, N. Y. .... Covenant
14. Brooklyn, N. Y. .... St. Paul's
15. Brooklyn, N. Y. .... St. Phillip's
16. Buffalo, N. Y. .... Zion
17. Butler, Pa. .... Trinity
18. Charleroi, Pa. .... Christ
19. Chester, Pa. .... Nativity
20. Cleveland, Ohio .... St. John's
21. Coatesville, Pa. .... Our Saviour's
22. Cold Springs, Pa. ....
23. Cogan Station, Pa. .... St. Michael's
24. Conneaut, Ohio .... Grace
25. Dolgeville, N. Y. .... Zion
26. Drexel Hill, Pa. .... Grace
27. Eberta, Pa. .... St. James'
28. Elmwood, Pa. ....
29. Emigsville, Pa. .... Parish
30. Erie, Pa. .... Christ
31. Farmingdale, L. I. .... St. Luke's
32. Ghent, N. Y. .... Christ
33. Glen Morris, L. I. .... St. Andrew's
34. Guelph, Ont. .... St. Paul's
35. Halifax, N. S. .... Resurrection
36. Hamilton, Ont. .... Trinity
37. Harmony Grove, Pa. ....
38. Harrisburg, Pa. .... St. Paul's
39. Hellam, Pa. ....
40. Herkimer, N. Y. ....
41. Homstead, Pa. .... Messiah
42. Jersey City, N. J. .... Calvary
43. Jersey City, N. J. .... Holy Trinity
44. Jersey City, N. J. .... Our Saviour's
45. Johnson City, N. Y. .... St. Paul's
46. Le Moyne, Pa. .... Trinity
47. Logansville, Pa. .... Christ
48. Milvale, Pa. .... Christ
49. Mountainville, Pa. .... Trinity
50. Montreal, Ont. .... Redeemer

51. Mohawk, L. I. ....
52. Narberth, Pa. .... Holy Trinity
53. Newark, N. J. .... Advent
54. Mt. Wolf, Pa. .... Parish
55. Newberry, Pa. .... St. Matthew's
56. New Cumberland, Pa. .... St. Paul's
57. New York, N. Y. .... St. Thomas
58. New York, N. Y. .... Holy Trinity
59. Ocean City, N. J. .... St. John's
60. Philadelphia, Pa. .... Advocate
61. Philadelphia, Pa. .... Christ
62. Philadelphia, Pa. .... Luther Memorial
63. Philadelphia, Pa. .... Mediator
64. Philadelphia, Pa. .... Muhlenberg
65. Philadelphia, Pa. .... St. Simeon's
66. Philadelphia, Pa. .... Temple
67. Pitcairn, Pa. .... St. Paul's
68. Pittsburgh, Pa. .... Holy Trinity
69. Pittsburgh, Pa. .... Luther Memorial
70. Reading, Pa. .... Redeemer
71. Reading, Pa. .... St. Peter's
72. Reynoldsville, Pa. .... Reynoldsville
73. Ridgefield Park, N. J. .... Christ
74. River Edge, N. J. .... Grace
75. Sewickley, Pa. .... St. Paul's
76. Shrewsburg, Pa. .... Grace
77. Schenectady, N. Y. .... First
78. Scranton, Pa. .... Grace
79. Smithton, Pa. .... Memorial
80. Starview, Pa. .... Parish
81. Syracuse, N. Y. .... Atonement
82. Tinicum, Pa. .... Holy Trinity
83. Trenton, N. J. .... Bethel
84. Trenton, N. J. .... St. Mark's
85. Toronto, Ont. .... St. Paul's
86. Upper Darby, Pa. .... Christ
87. West Chester, Pa. .... Calvary
88. Wesleyville, Pa. .... Messiah
89. West Collingswood, N. J. .... St. Luke's
90. Wilmington, Del. .... Holy Trinity
91. Wilkes-Barre, Pa. .... Holy Trinity
92. Woodlawn, Pa. .... House of Prayer
93. Wyomissing, Pa. .... Atonement
94. York, Pa. .... Augsburg
95. York, Pa. .... Good Shepherd
96. York, Pa. .... Messiah
97. York, Pa. .... St. James'
98. York, Pa. .... Salem

CENTRAL DISTRICT

1. Benson, Nebr. .... First
2. Billings, Mont. .... First
3. Bowling Green, Ohio .... First
4. Broadview, Ill. .... Broadview
5. Cambridge, Ohio .... Christ

6. Centralia, Ill. .... Redeemer
7. Champaign, Ill. .... Grace
8. Chicago, Ill. .... Advent
9. Chicago, Ill. .... Belmont Park
10. Chicago, Ill. .... North Austin
11. Chicago, Ill. .... Reformation
12. Chicago, Ill. .... Tabor
13. Columbus, Ohio .... Hilltop
14. Columbus, Ohio .... Indianola
15. Council Bluffs, Iowa .... St. John's
16. Covington, Ky. .... First
17. Cleveland, Ohio .... St. James'
18. Davenport, Iowa .... St. Mark's
19. Dayton, Ohio .... Westwood
20. Des Moines, Iowa .... Unity
21. Detroit, Mich. .... East Jefferson Ave.
22. Detroit, Mich. .... Hope
23. Detroit, Mich. .... Reformation
24. Detroit, Mich. .... St. Paul's
25. Detroit, Mich. .... Unity
26. Dubuque, Iowa .... St. Mark's
27. Elkhorn, Neb. .... United Evangelical Lutheran
28. Evansville, Ind. .... Christ
29. Evansville, Ind. .... St. Mark's
30. Flint, Mich. .... Holy Trinity
31. Hutchinson, Kans. .... Zion
32. Indianapolis, Ind. .... Gethsemane
33. Indianapolis, Ind. .... Reformation
34. Iowa Falls, Iowa .... English
35. Joliet, Ill. .... St. John's
36. Kansas City, Mo. .... St. John's
37. Lakewood, Ohio .... Trinity
38. Lincoln, Neb. .... Grace
39. Livingston, Mont. .... Redeemer
40. Madison, Wis. .... Luther Memorial
41. Manly, Iowa .... Manly
42. Marinette, Wis. .... St. James'
43. Milwaukee, Wis. .... Incarnation
44. Milwaukee, Wis. .... Washington Park
45. Muncie, Ind. .... Holy Trinity
46. Muscatine, Iowa .... Grace
47. Ottumwa, Iowa .... St. Mark's
48. Omaha, Neb. .... Redeemer
49. Paducah, Ky. .... St. Matthew's
50. Park Ridge, Ill. .... St. Luke's
51. Peoria, Ill. .... Grace
52. Phillips, Wis. .... St. John's
53. Saulte Ste. Marie, Ont. .... Zion
54. St. Louis, Mo. .... Advent
55. Toledo, Ohio .... Augsburg
56. Toledo, Ohio .... Olivet
57. Tulsa, Okla. .... First
58. Wilmette, Ill. .... Wilmette
59. Windsor, Ont. .... Trinity

SOUTHERN DISTRICT

1. Baltimore, Md. .... All Saints'
2. Baltimore, Md. .... Bethany
3. Baltimore, Md. .... Holy Comforter
4. Baltimore, Md. .... Luther Memorial
5. Baltimore, Md. .... Salem
6. Baltimore, Md. .... Zion
7. Brunswick, Md. .... Parish
8. Charleston, S. C. .... St. Barnabas
9. Charlotte, N. C. .... Holy Trinity
10. Columbia, S. C. .... Incarnation
11. Concord, N. C. .... Calvary
12. Dallas, Texas .... First
13. Easton, Md. .... Grace
14. High Point, N. C. .... Emmanuel
15. Lenoir, N. C. .... St. Stephen's
16. Lexington, S. C. .... St. James'
17. Linthicum Heights, Md. .... St. John's
18. Lynchburg, Va. .... Holy Trinity
19. Macon, Ga. .... Redeemer
20. Mississippi Missions
21. Parkville, Md. .... St. John's
22. Raleigh, N. C. .... Holy Trinity
23. Ridge Spring, S. C. .... Immanuel
24. Salem, Va. .... College
25. Sands, N. C. .... Mt. Pleasant
26. Saxa Gotha, N. C. .... St. James'
27. Silver Run, Md. .... St. Mark's
28. Sparrow's Point, Md. .... St. John's
29. Statesville, N. C. .... St. John's
30. Walkersville, Md. .... Walkersville
31. Washington, D. C. .... Columbia Heights
32. Washington, D. C. .... Incarnation
33. Washington, D. C. .... St. Mark's
34. Wheeling, W. Va. .... Edgewood

WESTERN DISTRICT

1. Casper, Wyo. .... Grace
2. Denver, Colo. .... Messiah
3. Denver, Colo. .... St. Paul's
4. El Paso, Texas .... St. Paul's
5. Fresno, Calif. .... St. Paul's
6. Glendale, Calif. .... First
7. Huntington Park, Calif. .... St. Luke's
8. Oakland, Calif. .... St. Johannes
9. Portland, Ore. .... Redeemer
10. Sacramento, Calif. .... Temple
11. San Bernardino, Calif. .... First
12. Seattle, Wash. .... St. James'
13. Seattle, Wash. .... St. Paul's
14. Seattle, Wash. .... University
15. Tacoma, Wash. .... Grace

Total, 206 .... $ 130,148.67

APPENDIX E
LOANS RETURNED

EASTERN DISTRICT
1. Brooklyn, N. Y. .... Advent
2. Brooklyn, N. Y. .... Covenant
3. Homstead, Pa. .... Zion
4. Brooklyn, N. Y. .... Calvary
5. New York City .... St. Thomas
6. Narberth, Pa. .... Holy Trinity
7. Oswego, N. Y. .... St. Matthew's
8. Reading, Pa. .... St. Peter's
9. Ridgefield Park, N. J. .... Christ
10. Scranton, Pa. .... St. Paul's
11. Scranton, Pa. .... Grace
12. South Ozone Park, N. Y. .... Church of the Good Shepherd
13. Stony Creek Mills, Pa. .... Christ
14. Philadelphia, Pa. .... Luther Memorial
15. Philadelphia, Pa. .... Our Saviour
16. Philadelphia, Pa. .... Resurrection
17. Weehawken, N. J. .... Good Shepherd
18. Wilmington, Del. .... Holy Trinity

SOUTHERN DISTRICT
1. Brookside, N. C. .... Mt. Pleasant
2. Charlotte, N. C. .... Holy Trinity
3. Greenville, S. C. .... First
4. Lenoir, N. C. .... St. Stephen's
5. Spencer, N. C. .... Calvary

CENTRAL DISTRICT
1. Appleton, Wis. .... Trinity
2. Batesville, Ind. .... Bethany
3. Chicago, Ill. .... Advent
4. Chicago, Ill. .... Austin
5. Chicago, Ill. .... Marquette Manor
6. Chicago, Ill. .... St. Stephen's
7. Chicago, Ill. .... Tabor
8. Duluth, Minn. .... St. John's
9. Evansville, Ind. .... St. Mark's
10. Fargo, N. Dak. .... St. Mark's
11. Gary, Ind. .... Grace
12. Joliet, Ill. .... St. John's
13. Neenah, Wis. .... St. Paul's
14. Newark, Ohio .... Holy Trinity
15. Norfolk, Neb. .... St. Johannes
16. Omaha, Nebr. .... Redeemer
17. Park Ridge, Ill. .... St. Luke's
18. Pittsfield, Ill. .... Pittsfield
19. Racine, Wis. .... Atonement
20. Spring Brook, N. D. .... St. James'
21. Waterloo, Iowa .... St. Luke's

WESTERN DISTRICT
1. El Paso, Texas .... St. Paul's
2. Fresno, Calif. .... St. Paul's
3. Sanger, Calif. .... Grace
   Total, 48 .... $ 58,586.50

TREASURER'S REPORT OF THE BOARD OF HOME MISSIONS AND CHURCH EXTENSION

RECEIPTS AND DISBURSEMENTS

For the Year ended July 31, 1923

RECEIPTS:

Balance on hand, August 1st, 1922	$99,765.60	
United Lutheran Church, on apportionment, less amount transferred to Northwestern Board	359,440.83	
Returned loans, class "A"	31,831.50	
Bank interest	1,265.27	
Interest on investments and certificates of deposit	7,915.09	
Interest on class "A" loans	98.38	
Donations	44,484.01	
Annuity gifts	1,000.00	
Proceeds from sale of securities	250.00	
Rentals of land, etc.	105.40	
Sunday schools	5.00	
Ministerium of Pennsylvania, in trust	2,284.09	
		$548,445.17

DISBURSEMENTS:

Donations to churches	$63,369.98	
Class "A" loans	143,135.59	
Salaries, Missionaries	237,346.76	
Salaries, Secretary and District Superintendents	16,632.75	
Salaries, Office	3,215.00	
Expenses, Missionaries	3,144.21	
Expenses, Secretary and District Superintendents	9,393.33	
Expenses, Officers and Board Members	4,607.28	
Printing and stationery	525.88	
Office supplies and expenses	237.23	
Office rental	736.00	
Telephone and Telegraph	54.03	
Postage and Express	40.16	
Light	35.58	
Legal auditing and system	1,760.21	
United Lutheran Church of America handbook	1,614.00	
General expenses	1,369.81	
Annuities paid	1,351.00	
Certificates of deposit purchased	500.00	
Office furniture and fixtures	1,594.25	
Balance on hand, July 31, 1923	57,782.12	
		$548,445.17

Respectfully submitted,

C. J. DRIEVER, *Treasurer.*

RECEIPTS AND DISBURSEMENTS
For the Year ended July 31, 1924

Balance in Banks and in transit, July 31, 1923		$57,782.12

RECEIPTS:

United Church on apportionment	$321,970.80	
Women's Missionary Society	34,818.37	
District Synods	5,984.54	
	$362,773.71	
Less amount transferred to Board of Northwest Missions	1,000.00	
Less amount returned to United Church Treasurer	62.50	
		$361,711,21
Returned loans, class "A"		26,455.00
Returned loans, class "B"		300.00
Bank interest		2,201.73
Interest on investments and certificates of deposit..		9,223.01
Rental from Properties		18.00
Donations		13,673.77
Annuity gifts		18,000.00
Proceeds from sale of securities		36,286.50
Certificates of deposit collected		102,000.00
Total Receipts		$569,869.22
		$627,651.34

DISBURSEMENTS:

Donations to churches	$44,807.04	
Loans to churches	140,000.00	
Salaries to Missionaries	227,805.74	
Salaries to Secretary, Treasurer and District Superintendents	20,567.19	
Salaries to Clerks, Stenographers, etc	1,490.00	
Expenses of Missionaries	5,276.07	
Expenses of Secretary, Treasurer and District Superintendents	8,655.04	
Expenses of Board Members and Other Officers	2,967.61	
Printing and Stationery	639.36	
Office supplies and expenses	202.78	
Office rent	2,100.00	
Telephone and Telegraph	92.79	
Legal and Auditing	516.00	
Publishing "Your Church at Work"	895.74	
General expenses	1,341.19	
Annuity interest paid	2,301.50	
Securities purchased	70,000.00	
Office fixtures and furniture	468.57	
Total Disbursements		$530,126.62
Balance in banks, July 31, 1924		$97,524.72

Respectfully submitted,

C. J. DRIEVER, *Treasurer.*

PHILADELPHIA, September 12, 1924.

We have audited the accounts of the Board of Home Missions and Church Extension of the United Lutheran Church in America for the two years ended July 31, 1924, and we certify that in our opinion the foregoing statements of Receipts and Disbursements for the years ended July 31, 1923, and July 31, 1924, are in accordance with the books of account and are correct.

LYBRAND, ROSS BROS. & MONTGOMERY,

Accountants and Auditors.

BALANCE SHEET—JULY 31, 1924

ASSETS

Cash in Banks:

The Chicago Trust Co.	$ 66,875.12	
State Bank of Chicago	30,649.60	
		$ 97,524.72
Certificates of Deposits		14,000.00
Outstanding Loans to Churches, represented by Class "A" Notes and Mortgages		928,355.60
Securities at Par Value		176,450.00
Real Estate at Book Values		19,975.00
Building Lots and Unimproved Properties at Book Values		8,185.00
		$ 1,244,490.32

Notes and Mortgages Held in Trust for the Women's Missionary Society	121,463.05	
Properties Held in Trust for Various Congregations, Transferrable to the Board in the Event of the Dissolution of the Congregation	25,800.00	
		$ 147,263.05

LIABILITIES

Due Women's Home and Foreign Missionary Society		600.00
Excess of Assets Over Liabilities, Represented by the Following Accounts:		
Home Mission Treasury	28,368.20	
Church Extension Treasury	1,070,704.92	
Annuity Account	47,550.00	
Permanent Loan Account	121,071.14	
Endowment Fund Account	27,294.78	
General Fund Account	51,098.72	
		1,243,890.32
		$ 1,244,490.32

We have examined the accounts of the Board of Home Missions and Church Extension of the United Lutheran Church in America as at July 31, 1924, and certify that, in our opinion, the above balance sheet sets forth correctly the financial position of the Board at that date.

LYBRAND, ROSS BROS. & MONTGOMERY,
Accountants and Auditors.

Chicago, Illinois, August 21, 1924.

Dr. Seibert called attention to special items of the report and made appreciative mention of the services of Dr. H. H. Weber, who for so long served the Church in the capacity of Secretary of the Board of Home Missions and Church Extension, and of Dr. H. A. Ott, who was called to his eternal reward in March, 1923.

After Dr. Seibert's presentation the Revs. I. Chantry Hoffman, A. D. R. Hancher, G. H. Hillerman and J. S. Herold, District Superintendents, and the Rev. A. S. Hartman, Educational Secretary, addressed the Convention.

The Revs. S. G. Trexler and John Weidley led the Convention in prayer in behalf of the Home Mission work and those who are directing, and those actively engaged in, the work.

On motion to adopt the report of the Board of Home Missions and Church Extension, Mr. George E. Neff spoke, urging that the apportionment be paid in full and also that Church Extension loans be promptly repaid.

The Rev. J. C. Kunzmann presented briefly the needs on the Western Coast.

The motion was then put and carried and the report adopted.

Mr. Hemsing reported for the Tellers Committee that the second ballot for the Board of Publication resulted in no election.

The President directed the tellers to distribute ballots. Also the names of the two who received the highest number of votes were announced.

The time for adjournment not having arrived, the second item in the order scheduled for the afternoon was taken up; namely, the report of the Board of Northwestern Missions. This report was presented by the Rev. G. A. Benze, Secretary of the Board.

REPORT OF THE BOARD OF NORTHWESTERN MISSIONS

The Board of Northwestern Missions is to be "photographed" on these and the following pages. Let no one, however, imagine that it is to be dressed up especially for this occasion. Given a field so vast that its boundary lines are limited only by the Atlantic and Pacific Oceans, a work so great that even a modest description sounds like vain boasting, and an opportunity so wonderful that it surpasses the fondest hopes and expectations of its promoters, the Board of Northwestern Missions does not have to employ artificial means and devices to make its report attractive, nor can it be satisfied with a half-hearted attention and consideration of its needs on the part of the Church and miserly, stingy allowances, such as have been handed out to it too often in the past.

What the Government of the United States has done in years gone by and what the Canadian Government is doing at the present time—inviting foreign immigration, especially from German and Scandinavian lands, offering such immigrants homesteads and a certain acreage of fertile land as well as giving them financial assistance for procuring livestock, farm implements, seeds and other necessities—that the Church must do for the Lutheran immigrants coming to our shores and to Canada. It must send them missionaries who can speak to them in their own tongue and gather them into the fold; it must render them financial assistance in establishing churches, schools and colleges, and take care of all their spiritual wants.

To neglect this most important work, to fail to provide the necessary men and means, and to make insufficient provision, is a very short-sighted policy and will be the cause of deep regret to the Church in coming years. If the Lutheran Church has lost thousands and tens of thousands of young people born and reared on American soil through its failure of commencing English home mission work amongst them at the psychological moment, it has lost many more through its neglect of the immigrant who was left to shift for himself and fell an easy prey either to diverse sects or to secret and other societies.

All this was probably unavoidable, as the Church was then in a formative stage, confronted with numerous problems pressing for solution, and as the necessary means were not always available. But with our present increased resources, we should be able to take care of the vast numbers coming from Lutheran lands and arriving on every steamer. One hundred thousand are coming from Germany, Russia, Austria and other States where German is spoken, from July to December of the present year, according to the official quota, and that is lower even than last year's or of the years before and since the war.

To give a faint idea of the opportunities awaiting our Lutheran Church if it avails itself of them, I may be permitted to cite just one instance of a German Lutheran Church in Greater New York, which added to its communicant list more than three hundred Lutheran immigrants in one year, i. e., from April, 1923, to April, 1924.   What would have become of them and where would they be if that Lutheran congregation had not taken care of them?

In the Board of Northwestern Missions the Church has just the machinery it needs for this work, and through its efforts great things have been accomplished, and in the face of conditions, circumstances and obstacles that seemed at times almost insurmountable. Is it any wonder then that those hitherto charged with this work and representing the Synods most concerned and also the sentiment of those Synods—men of high standing in their own community and of ripe experience—have been averse to the attempts that are being made to dissolve the Board that has forty years of a most successful history to its credit, and to turn the work over to a Board such as is planned by the Merger Committee (whose report will engage the attention of this Convention), where a sub-committee of two or three members is expected to accomplish the same or get even better results than the twenty-one members of the present Board, especially when they are assured that by such an arrangement the overhead charges will not be reduced but greatly advanced?

At the last meeting of the Board of Northwestern Missions on May 14, 1924, the following resolutions were passed (Sec. 21a) :

"That the Board of Northwestern Missions is still of the same opinion as expressed last year, viz., that it believes that the German Mission interests can best be conserved and developed by a continuance of the Board of Northwestern Missions.
"That it can take action on the newly submitted plan only after it has been carefully considered and also submitted to the different District Synods affected by it."

At the Washington Convention of the United Lutheran Church, the mission work of the German Nebraska Synod, the Wartburg Synod, and the Canada Synod was transferred to the Board of Northwestern Missions. Through an oversight, however, no appropriation whatsoever was made to enable the Board to do this extra work, which required an annual expenditure of about $18,000. For two whole years the Board carried this heavy burden, hoping that at the next convention to be held at Buffalo, this matter would be investigated, the Board reimbursed to this amount, and the needed appropriation made. But the Convention came and passed into history without taking any action in the matter. And what is the result? Not only has the Board of Northwestern Missions spent all the surplus it brought to the United Lutheran Church from the General Council, amounting to about $15,000, but it had to make one appeal after another to our German Lutheran Churches for special donations, had to borrow thousands and thousands of dollars from the bank, paying a high rate of interest, retrench on all sides and cutting down its expenses in such a way that the work is suffering greatly and many requests for commencing new work have to be turned down.

If this state of affairs continues much longer the Board may find it necessary to reduce all salaries of missionaries, small and meagre as these salaries are, by twenty per cent or even more. That, however, would not only be a great injustice and be accompanied with untold suffering, but would be ruinous and disastrous in its ultimate results.

In its report two years ago, the Board has given the Church a detailed account of its activities, the names of all parishes on the territory of each Synod, and a statistical survey of the communicant membership of all these parishes, together with the number of Sunday schools and church societies. Instead of repeating and reprinting these figures, we will confine ourselves this time to the reports of the Superintendents of Missions, of which there are three, and to the reports of the Synodical Mission Committees in those Synods, which so far have no superintendent. Before we give them a hearing, however, we would like to say a word about the man who stands at the head of all the active mission workers and who is the personal representative of the Board of Northwestern Missions before the Synod, on whose territory we labor and before the Church at large, our General Secretary, the Rev. P. Ludwig. He visits the Canada, Manitoba, Wartburg and German Nebraska Synods annually, at the time of their meetings, when he consults with the Synodical Mission Committees about the work on their respective fields, and arranges with them the budget for the coming year. As a rule, he also visits at that time the individual missions and missionaries, so that he is personally acquainted with almost all the missions and missionaries under our Board. This enables him to give useful information to the Board at its meetings. Before the Church in general he represents the Board by visiting and addressing as many other Synods, Conferences and congregations as he possibly can, and by writing occasionally for *The Lutheran* and *Lutherischer Herold,* and regularly for our mission monthly, *Siloah.* He also conducts a good deal of missionary correspondence, issues all general letters and special appeals of the Board, and has charge of the statistical matters. In the performance of his duties he is often away from home and family, sometimes for weeks and months, and has traveled about thirty thousand miles during the past biennium.

Condensed Summary

In the Manitoba Synod, with its three conferences named after the three provinces, Manitoba, Saskatchewan and Alberta, the Board has thirty mission congregations served by twenty pastors.

In the Canada Synod we have twenty-three mission congregations served by twelve pastors.

In the German Nebraska Synod there are twenty-six mission congregations served by twenty pastors.

In the Wartburg Synod we have fifteen mission congregations and a number of preaching places served by fifteen pastors.

In the Texas Synod we have nine mission congregations with a number of preaching places served by five pastors.

In the Pacific Synod we have three mission congregations served by three pastors.

Grand Total: 106 mission congregations with a number of preaching places. 75 pastors.

Mission Work in the Manitoba Synod
By Rev. H. Becker, Superintendent of Missions

The territory of the Manitoba Synod is no longer an unknown district to the members of the United Lutheran Church. Much has been said and written about Western Canada, its immense areas, its richness in fertile soil, its hidden treasures in minerals, its great dormant possibilities; very little, however, about the drawbacks of this country, its long winters, its often inclement weather, and the many hardships that confront the settler. This is only natural; but it is absolutely necessary to consider both sides equally well in order to get the right impression of the work our Church is doing there.

Though Western Canada made splendid progress during the first years of this century, it almost came to a stand-still during the last few years. Lately, however, the signs are increasing that a new period of prosperity is ahead of us. This has been noticeable in all our mission work. Hardly any new fields could be opened up, and of the thirty-three congregations and preaching stations that were taken care of by the Northwestern Mission Board in 1922, only one parochial district, that of Rosthern-Bergheim in Saskatchewan, has become self-supporting.

But we have no reason to complain. Through the grace of God our work is not going backwards, but slowly and steadily progressing. Though we are unable to boast of great numerical increases, our congregations are gaining, if not from outside then from within. And as far as the outside growth is concerned, there is very good prospect that this will come in the near future. Great numbers of immigrants, amongst them many Lutherans, are starting to come into this country. A Lutheran Immigration Board has been formed by members of the different Lutheran

Synods working here, and from its activities great results are expected.

Saskatoon College and Seminary reports a very successful year. It obtained its highest number of students since its foundation, that is, forty-seven. The Parliament of the Province of Saskatchewan, at the suggestion of and in agreement with the City of Saskatoon, has granted it exemption from taxation. If only the financial situation of our institution, that is causing us some alarm, could be improved!

According to a notice we read in a Winnipeg paper, the Manitoba Synod is ready to spend $175,000 on a proposed college in Edmonton, Alberta, Canada. Comparisons are odious; but would it not be possible for the United Lutheran Church to give us the $50,000 promised us at Washington, of which we have received so far a little more than half of the total amount?

Here is an opportunity for a well-to-do Lutheran layman in the United Lutheran Church to invest his money in such a way that it will be an everlasting credit to himself and firmly establish the Church we love so dearly in this part of the Western Hemisphere.

Mission Work in the Evangelical Lutheran Synod of Canada, in Ontario and Quebec

By Rev. G. Brackebusch, Secretary, Canada Mission Committee

The Canada Synod has always been very active in all kinds of missionary enterprises, as is best shown by the fact that up to the time of the Washington Convention of the United Lutheran Church all mission work in its territory was carried on by the Synod itself, without any help from the General Council, to which it formerly belonged, or the United Lutheran Church, with which it has been affiliated from the time of the merger.

Though the individual congregations were not very large, the parishes were in some instances exceedingly so and spread over a wide area, making it necessary for the missionaries to travel great distances in all sorts of conveyances and in all kinds of weather, spending days and nights in the saddle or the buckboard, sleeping in shacks, barns, district school houses, and what not.

These men were so poorly paid that they could not leave their field in Canada even if they wanted to, and they shared all the privations of their poor parishioners, mostly immigrants, who cleared the land, cut roads through the forests and swamps, and wrung a bare living from the newly broken soil for themselves and their families. Though conditions have changed a good deal in the last ten or twenty years, and for the better in many ways, it must not be forgotten that prices have gone up, too. If the Board of Northwestern Missions wants to keep step with the progress Canada is making, it must send men into the field, whenever there is a vacancy, who are able to preach both in the German and English languages, must enable them financially to meet the high cost of living, and must divide the work that was formerly carried on by one man, between two or even three.

Canada is making great strides forward and we must not lag behind, especially in the face of the great number of German immigrants pouring into that country.

REPORT OF MISSION WORK IN THE GERMAN NEBRASKA SYNOD

Rev. G. K. Wiencke, Superintendent of Missions

Missions Already Organized:

There were under my supervision during the biennium, sixteen mission parishes with twenty-two congregations and four preaching points, served in all by seventeen pastors, who often labored under greatest difficulties and in a self-sacrificing spirit. The mission congregation Salem, at Stillwater, Okla., lost their church building by fire. A new church was erected last year. September, 1923, Christus congregation at Salem, South Dakota, dedicated a new parsonage, valued at $5000. The small mission deserves great credit for completing this building. They refused the offer made by the Board of Northwestern Missions to pay the interest on the money still owed, in order to save the Board this expense. St. John's Mission at Lipscomb, Texas, remodeled their parsonage at a cost of $1100. The mission work in Valley County, Montana, begun in 1922, has made good progress. Our missionary, Rev. Mr. Urban, has been stationed at Larslan, Montana, from where he serves four mission points, namely, Herman, Grain, Avondale and Westfork. He serves, at present, twenty-five Lutheran families on widely scattered homesteads.

New Work:

Five new congregations were received, namely, Zion, at Wakeeney, Kan., March, 1923, with 203 communicants, 397 baptized members; Grace Lutheran Church, at Bird City, Kan., organized August, 1923, with 14 members. This congregation subscribed $1200 toward the pastor's salary. When Rev. Mr. Diekhoff took charge of this field, the congregation paid him half of his annual salary in advance and rented a parsonage. East La Junta, Colo., a preaching point under the care of Rev. Juttner, our missionary at Rocky Ford, Colo., was organized by him in September, 1923, as St. Paulus Congregation, with 43 communicant and 99 baptized members. Immanuel's, at Hoisington, Kan., organized March, 1924, with 25 members. This mission has bought a church building which is to be remodeled, valued at $3000. A minister has been called. St. Paulus, at McDonald, Kan., organized May, 1924. This new field has been affiliated with our congregation at Bird City, Kan.

During the biennium, I made 185 trips to the widely scattered mission points of the German Nebraska Synod, conducting divine services, presiding at congregational meetings, and collected $518.25 for mission purposes.

MISSION WORK OF THE WARTBURG SYNOD
Rev. O. Doering, Missionary Superintendent

The mission work of this Synod on the home-field has made good and substantial progress. For another period of two years the good Lord has permitted us to sow the Word and see some fruits ripen unto the harvest.

A good deal of the work done by the missionaries of this Synod is bilingual. The missions are to be found in the States of Illinois, Iowa, Wisconsin and Michigan; another mission at Cullman, in the State of Alabama, was transferred to the Georgia Synod. There are now in this field nine ordained mission pastors, with the Missionary Superintendent, Rev. Otto Doering, and two licensed candidates taking care of twelve mission parishes, with a total membership of about 2,000. Of these missions, seven are located in the city of Chicago, or in suburbs. This city, with its teeming population, will remain for years to come the center of our activities. Within the last few years many new additions and subdivisions have been made and opened up great opportunities for the primary efforts of every Synod doing Home Mission work.

Another field of great promise, that recently has been taken over, is to be found in the Iron Ridge territory of Northwestern Michigan. At this writing there are two parishes served by our missionaries with marked success. By the bilingual work of our missionaries under the Lord's providence, a door of great opportunity has been opened for the United Lutheran Church. Oh, that we could give to these fields the best of men and liberal support! Blessed results would then be seen before long. We find many Lutheran people here in these great mining and milling towns, who must be gathered into the Church. St. Paul's, at Guttenberg, Iowa, erected and dedicated a beautiful church edifice and entertained the Synod before the congregation had attained the second anniversary of its existence. Frieden's church at Chicago also built and dedicated a new church and parish house at a cost of $23,500. St. Paul's, at Chicago, acquired by purchase from another Lutheran church a very fine property consisting of a church and a parsonage. Wartburg Church, at Berwyn, remodeled and enlarged its chapel and greatly enhanced its usefulness. Two other missions are making plans for building operations. Frieden's Church as Chester and Tabor Church at Chicago were permitted to cancel their debts. The membership gain in these missions for the period of two years amounts to over 600 souls.

The Synodical Home Mission Board as well as the missionaries were greatly encouraged in their efforts by the sympathetic attitude shown by the Northwestern Mission Board and its generous financial support, as well as by the greatly needed aid toward church building operations liberally and promptly rendered by the Board of Home Missions and Church Extension. The annual budget of the Synodical Mission Board calls for over $10,000.00.

Home Mission work in the German and English tongues, as carried on by this synod, has the promise of great success, providing it receives the proper support. The United Lutheran Church must not neglect the Middle West.

MISSION WORK IN THE TEXAS SYNOD

By Rev. E. A. Sievert, President of Synod

The mission work on the territory of the Evangelical Lutheran Texas Synod of the United Lutheran Church in America, carried on with the aid of the Board of Northwestern Missions, returned satisfactory results during the last biennium.

Noticeable progress was made in the local development of the established mission congregations. This consists in increased membership, increased local financial support, and property development.

Territorial expansion could not be undertaken though opportunities were many, because of the lack of funds and the difficulty to secure suitable men. Even vacancies could not be filled at all times, which reduced our force from five to two missionaries for nearly one whole year. Fortunately, no loss of established work had to be recorded, thanks to the readiness of the pastors of synod to supply in the vacant charges whenever possible, and to the people's patience.

Trinity Lutheran Church, Miles, Texas, owns a church and parsonage, debt free. It has 95 baptized and 86 communicant members. It has voted to raise $800 of the pastor's salary this year.

Church of Peace, Vernon, Texas, owns a church and parsonage with some encumbrance. It has 71 baptized and 39 communicant members, and has resolved to raise $600 toward the pastor's salary this year.

St. John's, Goliad, Texas, owns a church free of debt, and offers parsonage if pastor will dwell there. It has 167 baptized and 103 confirmed members. St. John's, together with Emmanuel, Inez, Texas, with 45 baptized and 31 confirmed members, and First Lutheran, Tivoli, Texas, with 53 baptized and 25 confirmed members, have asked for $100 less support from the Board of Northwestern Missions for this year.

St. Paul's, George West, Texas, organized 1922, has erected a neat chapel with the aid of the Synodical Educational and Missionary Fund, dedicated June 29, 1924. It numbers 25 baptized and but 10 confirmed members.

In Alice moneys are being collected at this writing for the building of a church, about $300 having already been received.

From Mission, Texas, has come a request, addressed to the Mission Committee of the Synod, signed by six parties, asking for service from the Texas Synod.

We have been able to collect but 500 baptized and about 350 confirmed members in this vast field thus far. It is largely rural work, with new settlements opening up on all hands. It is therefore largely follow-up work of the present generation, and, to a large extent, the gathering in of the churchless. Mission work, pure and simple.

Respectfully submitted,
E. C. J. KRAELING, President.

REPORT OF THE TREASURER OF THE BOARD OF NORTHWESTERN MISSIONS

BALANCE SHEET, JULY 31, 1924

ASSETS

Cash: in banks and on hand......................	$9,006.92
Loans to congregations and to Saskatoon College, as annexed	18,234.33
Building Lot, Harriman, Tenn...................	180.00
	$27,421.25

LIABILITIES

Loans from Bank	$7,000.00

FUNDS

Mission Fund	$13,072.71	
Saskatoon College Campaign Fund...............	40.75	
Annuity Fund	200.00	
Church Building Fund	8,596.54	
	$21,910.00	
Less Siloah Fund Deficit	1,488.75	
		$20,421.25
		$27,421.25

H. D. E. SIEBOTT,
Treasurer.

Philadelphia, September 12, 1924.

We have audited the accounts of the Board of Northwestern Missions of the United Lutheran Church in America for the two years ended July 31, 1924, and we certify that in our opinion the foregoing Balance Sheet, July 31, 1924, Cash Receipts and Disbursements, Loans to Congregations, etc., are in accordance with the books of account and are correct.

LYBRAND, ROSS. BROS. & MONTGOMERY,
Accountants and Auditors.

CASH RECEIPTS AND DISBURSEMENTS
for the Year ended 31st July, 1923

RECEIPTS

	Missions Fund	Church Building Fund	Siloah Fund	Annuity Fund
United Church, on apportionment	$32,134.84			
United Church, Specials..........	4,610.89			
United, General and Branch Synods	231.85			
Bd. of Home M. & Ch. Ext. for Wartburg and Nebr. Missions	12,000.00			
Bd. of Educ. for Sask. Coll. Camp. Fund	10,574.00			
Exec. Bd., Loan for Sask. Coll...	5,000.00			
Donations:				
For Saskatoon College $14.50				
For Waterloo College 12.50				
General 30.00	57.00			
Repayment of Loans:				
Church Bldg. Fund... 5,079.13				
Missionaries .,....... 160.00	5,239.13			
Mortgages and Notes Receivable		$920.00		
Interest on Mortgages and Notes.		136.67		
Subscriptions for Siloah..........			$266.24	
Bank Interest	49.39			
Annuity				$200.00
Miscellaneous Receipts	178.45			
	$70,075.55	$1,056.67	$266.24	$200.00

DISBURSEMENTS

Salaries of Missionaries..........	$27,192.13
Salaries of Dis. Superintendents..	4,400.00
Salary of General Secretary......	2,200.00
Expenses of Miss. in the Field....	298.55
Expenses of Missionaries Moving.	476.50
Expenses of District Supts.......	251.31
Expenses of General Secretary...	561.02
Expenses of Officers and Board Members	1,264.71
Manitoba Syn. for Coll. Prof.....	3,666.67
Aid to Students preparing for Mission Field	2,630.00
Special Donations forwarded.....	25.00
Legal and Auditing Expense..........	227.62
Printing and Stationery..........	100.00
Interest: On Mission Church Mortgages $708.00	

	Missions Fund	Church Building Fund	Siloah Fund	Annuity Fund
On Bank Loans....... 285.25	993.25			
Bank Charges, Exchanges, etc....	43.96			
Printing and Mailing Siloah......			$762.00	
Editorial and Office Expenses....			15.68	
Loan to Missionary..............	100.00			
Mission Handbook	221.25			
Saskatoon Coll. Cam. Funds fwd.	21,205,25			
Refund of Loan, Mission Fund...		$5,079.13		
	$65,857.22	$5,079.13	$777.68	
Excess of Receipts, July 31, 1923..	$4,218.33			
Deficiency of Receipts, July 31, 1923		$4,022.46	$511.44	
Balances, July 31, 1922..........	3,097.78	3,980.63		
Deficits, July 31, 1922............			644.31	
Balances, July 31, 1923..........	7,316.11			200.00
Deficits, July 31, 1923............		41.83	1,155.75	

CASH RECEIPTS AND DISBURSEMENTS

for the Year ended 31st July, 1924

RECEIPTS

	Missions Fund	Church Building Fund	Siloah Fund	Annuity Fund
United Church, on apportionment	$38,125.60			
Women's Missionary Society......	1,812.50			
United, General and Branch Synods	4,800.89			
Executive Board, Sotter Trust Income	545.50			
Donations:				
For Saskatoon Col.. $2.50				
For Rev. C. W. Sterzer				
Fire Loss 1,017.95				
General 299.75	1,320.20		$10.00	
Collections of Mortgages and Notes Receivable		$1,170.67		
Interest on Mortgages............		132.50		
Subscriptions for Siloah..........			429.50	
Bank Interest	64.61			
	$46,669.30	$1,303.17	$439.50	

DISBURSEMENTS

	Missions Fund	Church Building Fund	Siloah Fund	Annuity Fund
Salaries of Missionaries..........	$24,282.10			
Salaries of District Supt..........	4,400.00			
Salary of General Secretary......	2,600.00			
Expenses of Miss. in the Field....	149.00			
Expenses of Mssionaries Moving.	245.00			
Expenses of District Supt........	284.97			
Expenses of General Secretary...	250.97			
Expenses of Officers and Board Members	1,693.70			
Manitoba Synod for Coll. Prof...	3,666.67			
Aid to Students preparing for Mission Field	2,840.00			
Special Donations forwarded.....	2,551.20			
Legal and Auditing Expense......	200.00			
Printing and Stationery..........	159.04			
Special Appropr. for Rev. Sterzer's Fire Loss	200.00			

Interest on Mission Church Mortgages	$922.00			
Interest on Bank Loans..	428.17			
Int. on Annuity Bond....	10.00			

	Missions Fund	Church Building Fund	Siloah Fund	Annuity Fund
	1,360.17			
Bank Charges, Exchange, etc.....	68.26			
Printing and Mailing Siloah.....			$745.00	
Editorial and Office Expense......			2.50	
Agent's Commission			25.00	
	$44,951.08		$772.50	
Excess of Receipts, July 31, 1924.	$1,718.22	$1,303.17		
Deficiency of Receipts, July 31, 1924			$333.00	
Balances, July 31, 1923..........	7,316.11			$200.00
Deficits, July 31, 1923............		41.83	1,155.75	
Balances, July 31, 1924..........	9,034.33	1,261.34		200.00
Deficits, July 31, 1924............			1,488.75	

LOANS TO CONGREGATIONS, Etc., July 31, 1924

Trinity, Saskatoon, Mortgage......................	$2,700.00	
Paid on account Jan. 29, 1924.................	100.00	
Balance		$2,600.00
Trinity, Strathcona, two notes:		
$1,000 due Nov. 15, 1916....................	$1,000.00	
Paid on account	416.67	
	583.33	
Ten installment notes, due annually Apr. 1st, four paid, six left, one overdue, balance..	1,200.00	
		$1,783.33

St. Johns, Edmonton, Mortgage.................		$1,500.00
St. Johns, Harts Hill: two installment notes, due annually on Jan. 2d....................	200.00	
Paid on account, Jan. 23, 1923......... $70.00		
Paid on account, Jan. 29, 1924....... 100.00	170.00	
Balance		30.00
Gartenland, Esk.: two notes:		
$200 due Nov. 24, 1924		
Paid on account, Dec. 28, 1915.... $75.00		
Balance	$125.00	
Paid on acc., Sept. 30, 1923........... 25.00		
Paid on acc., Nov. 27, 1923........... 54.00	79.00	
Balance	46.00	
$100 due March 25, 1916....................	100.00	
		$146.00
Friedens, Kindersley, Cornfield, one note:		
$100 due Apr. 24, 1917, paid on acc. Apr. 30, 1918	$25.00	
Balance		$75.00
St. Paul's, Friedensfeld:		
Ten installment notes of $50 each, due annually on July 1st, four paid, six left, one overdue, balance		300.00
Brightholme, Sask.:		
Ten installment notes of $50 each due annually on Sept. 1st, one paid, three overdue, balance..		450.00
Golden Bay, Man.:		
Ten installment notes of $100 each, due annually on July 1st, one paid, three ovrdue, bal		900.00
Saskatoon College, two notes:		
$1,000 due March 22, 1916, paid on acc. Apr. 3, 1918	300.00	
Paid on acc. July 14, 1919....................	225.00	
Balance	475.00	
$6,000 dated July 15, 1920, term indefinite......	6,000.00	
Mont Clare, Chicago:		
Ten installment notes of $200 each, payable annually on Sept. 6th, two paid, eight left, bal.	1,600.00	
Ten installment notes of $100 each, payable annually on Oct. 24th, two paid, eight left, bal.	800.00	2,400.00
Rosenthal, Leduc:		
Note, dated Jan. 1, 1922, payable two years after date, overdue		75.00
Immanuel, Lodge Pole, Nebr.:		
Ten installment notes of $150 each, due annually on March 15th, first one due March 15, 1925		1,500.00
		$18,234.33

The Convention then heard the Rev. Paul Ludwig, General Secretary of the Board, the Rev. Otto Doering, Missionary Superintendent of the Wartburg Synod, and the Rev. O. C. D. Klaehn.

The report of the Board was adopted.

Mr. Hemsing reported for the Tellers Committee the result of the third ballot for

Board of Publication

Votes cast, 370; necessary to election, 186. Mr. G. E. Schlegelmilch received the majority of the votes cast and was thereupon declared duly elected a member of the Board of Publication.

A motion that the Convention reconvene at 1:30 instead of 2:00 o'clock this afternoon, as previously determined, was adopted by common consent.

The Rev. W. J. Finck led in prayer and the Convention adjourned.

Afternoon Session

Saturday, October 25, 1:30 P. M.

The President called the Convention to order.

Prayer was offered by the Rev. Simon Snyder.

The Chairman of the Committee of Reference and Counsel submitted the following resolution which was adopted:

Resolved, That the Executive Board be instructed to consider and define the relation between the work of the Laymen's Movement and the Lutheran Brotherhood to the end of avoiding duplication of effort and removing uncertainty as to the field and function of each; and for the purpose of making possible the co-operation of all of the laity of the United Lutheran Church in the Stewardship and Canvass program.

The Chairman of the Committee read a petition received from the Synod of Nebraska as follows:

WHEREAS, We believe that giving to the Church would be more liberal and less burdensome if efficient methods were adopted:

"Be it resolved, That the United Lutheran Church in America be petitioned to refer the whole matter of Church finance to a special committee or to the Laymen's Missionary Movement Committee for the purpose of

working out and putting into practice an ideal system of raising and handling the moneys of the Church, to which end we make the following specific suggestions

"1. That a standard, authorized system or form of congregational finance be devised and put into print, and that the published form be then distributed among the congregations.

"2. That, as soon as the above system or form is ready for exploitation, all the field secretaries of the various Boards and all other employees of the General Church (in so far as practicable) be put under the jurisdiction and direction of the said special committee or Laymen's Missionary Movement Committee to propagate and organize the standard, authorized financial system in each congregation of the United Lutheran Church in America, it being understood that all the promotional efforts and expenditures of the United Lutheran Church in America for a sufficient period shall be diverted from other causes and concentrated upon the effort to put the finances of the United Lutheran Church in America upon a rational, ethical, efficient (in short, a Scriptural) basis.

"Respectfully,

"K. DE FREESE, *Chairman.*"

In connection with the foregoing petition the Chairman of the Committee moved the following recommendation in regard thereto:

After consideration of this petition, it was resolved to recommend to the Convention that this petition be transmitted through the Executive Board to the Executive Committee of the Laymen's Movement, with the request that they give consideration to the matter of working out a standard system of congregational finance, and such forms for record keeping, receipting and accounting as would be desirable in connection with the use of the suggested system.

The recommendation of the Committee was adopted.

The Chairman moved the following additional resolution for the Committee:

Resolved, That the request for the concentration of all promotional efforts and expenditures upon this one matter for a stated period be referred to the Executive Board, with the suggestion that action in this direction may be possible in connection with the observance of Stewardship Month in November of each year.

The resolution was adopted.

The Chairman moved, on behalf of the Committee, that

speeches in favor of a place for the 1926 Convention be limited to five minutes for each place.   Motion adopted.

The Chairman also moved that the report of the Committee on the proposed commission to study the educational problem be set as a special order immediately following the report of the Board of Education.   Motion adopted.

By special permission the Rev. F. Scarpitti, Superintendent of the Italian Department of the Immigrants' Mission Board, addressed the Convention at this time.

The Rev. H. W. A. Hanson presented the report of the West Indies Mission Board.

REPORT OF THE WEST INDIES MISSION BOARD

As a matter of conscience, the West Indies Mission Board places at the beginning of its report an emphatic contradiction of the impression that seems to be current in the Church that a merger of its work with the other Home Mission Agencies will result in a more economic administration of the field assigned this Board.   We know that not only the cost of administration but the expenses on the field will be increased rather than diminished by the proposed merger.   We have reason to think that this will be true also of some of the other Boards affected by the reorganization.

The West Indies Mission Board, however, gladly co-operated in the discussions concerning the reorganization of home mission work, and if the Church believes that there will be an economy of men and money in other departments, sufficient to compensate for the increased expense in administering the work now being done by the West Indies Mission Board, we stand ready to do our part in making such reorganization a success. But we would not be true either to ourserves or to our workers if we permitted to pass uncontradicted the statement that the merger would save the Church men or money as far as the West Indies Mission Board is concerned.

We also record our conviction that the proposed reorganization will not remove the dissatisfaction in the Church which has been expressed in this demand for a merger unless the vital point raised by the Foreign Mission Board and the West Indies Mission Board at Buffalo be first given due consideration.

The importance of a clear definition of the spheres of the various agencies of the United Lutheran Church is evident in the present close intermingling and frequent duplication of activities whereby some Boards are doing work which fundamentally belongs to the sphere of another. We firmly believe that no satisfactory co-ordination of the varied interests of the United Lutheran Church can be secured unless the Foreign Mission Board, the Inner Mission Board, the Deaconess Board and the Board of Education are called into conference with the Boards now participating in the present movement.

Increased Support. We have been greatly encouraged by the increased support which the Church has given the work assigned our Board. This was very noticeable in the special gifts from congregations and individuals and in the liberal grants from the Women's Missionary Society. This money has made possible the purchase of property, the erection of a greatly needed church building, and the sending out of additional missionaries to relieve the overburdend workers of our undermanned field. If this extra support had not been received, it would have been impossible to hold certain important fields for our church.

We regret that matters over which we had no control and against which no protection can be secured, prevented us commencing work in Santo Domingo, Cuba and Mexico. During the past biennium over half our American missionaries returned to the States because of illness. As a result, their unexpected traveling and moving expenses as well as the additional expense of sending new workers to the field went far beyond the amount budgeted for this purpose, and consumed the funds which otherwise would have been available for new work. We rejoice, however, that our prayers for laborers were answered so that we can report more workers sent to the field in the last eight months than in the previous eight years.

EXPANSION

Santo Domingo and Cuba. Because of the deplorable economic conditions in the Virgin Islands many natives have sought employment in Santo Domingo and Cuba. These people, cut off from their church, have for years been petitioning our congregations in Porto Rico and the Virgin Islands to send them pastors. It is unnecessary to state that the religious condition of these two islands is more deplorable even than in most Roman Catholic countries. In large sections the Roman Church makes no attempt, even in its superficial way, to reach the people. It is our earnest hope that the income during the next two years will permit us to enter these fields.

Mexico. After the turmoil of the past years, a stable government seems to be forming in this republic, and while the last constitution is revolutionary in many respects, especially in its relation to the church, it, nevertheless, opens an opportunity for Protestant work that has seldom been equaled in this Western world. The large German colonies being formed in this country also add emphasis to the obligation of our

Church to establish missions in Mexico. Some of our pastors along the Texas border have attempted to do something for the people and have made earnest pleas that the church enter this promising field.

Spain. Our Lutheran Church in Porto Rico has been for years in touch with the Evangelical Church in Spain, hoping from that source to secure literature for our Spanish people. But since practically nothing was available, our contact with the church in Spain gradually lessened until in the early part of 1923, when a representative from Spain came to Porto Rico appealing for assistance. Reports from our missionaries led to correspondence with Pastor Fliedner, and after consultation with the National Lutheran Council and the United Church officers, arrange‑ ments were made to send Dr. Ostrom to Spain to investigate the sit uation with the hope that by assisting the work there we might, through such co-operation, secure men for our Spanish work in the West Indies. The illness and death of Mrs. Ostrom on the eve of Dr. Ostrom's de parture for Spain prevented the immediate execution of this plan, but arrangements have been made for Dr. Ostrom to go to Spain the first of the year, and it is our sincere belief that the co-operation that may result will be as helpful to the Church in Spain as it will be to our Church in Porto Rico and the Spanish fields under our jurisdiction.

The American Negro. The interest of our Board in work among this group which numbers one-eighth of the American population, and of which more than one-half are untouched by the Christian Church, is such that we have been prepared to co-operate with synods which de sired to carry out the resolution of the United Lutheran Church at Buffalo. In one instance, namely, the work in Charleston, S. C., active steps have been taken looking toward the establishment of a mission among American colored people, and the enterprise was placed upon our budget and submitted to the Finance Committee of the Executive Board of the United Lutheran Church. However in conformity with the reso lution of the United Lutheran Church our Board resolved to co-operate in this work only on the following basis:

"Be It Resolved, That hereafter when any work is undertaken within the bounds of a constituent synod of the United Lutheran Church in which the West Indies Mission Board is expected to co-operate

"a. It shall have the official approval of the proper synodical author ities.

"b. It shall continue under the jurisdiction of the synod in whose boundaries it is located.

"c. It shall be supervised by the West Indies Mission Board only in such matters as require the specialized knowledge of the Board and its representatives, the West Indies Mission Board co-operating also in all other matters necessary for co-ordination of the work with similar work in other synods.

"d. It shall be supported by the West Indies Mission Board only from such funds as may be placed in its budget for this special purpose and so approved by the United Lutheran Church."

We would recommend that the United Lutheran Church approve of this, especially in view of the fact that it is in harmony with the plans proposed for the reorganization of the Home Mission work in America.

The Common Service Book and Hymnal in Spanish

For many years our missionaries have been hampered by the lack of a Spanish hymnal and service book, as well as literature which the missionaries could use with a clear conscience in our Spanish Lutheran Churches. Much work has been done by the men on the field and the various services have been translated and furnished in typewritten form for our American ministers, but the growth of the field demands a printed book. With over two thousand Spanish people regularly attending our church services, it is unwise to continue the use of interdenominational literature, and under instructions from the Board, Dr. Ostrom has given much time to the careful compilation of hymns and a complete translation of the Common Service Book. When the final report came to the Board, revealing such remarkable painstaking attention to every detail, giving a translation which under ordinary circumstances would not have been produced until after several revised editions had gone to press, the book was deemed so valuable by the Board that it was felt it should be given to the Church for official publication. Therefore, the entire matter has been referred to the Committee on Common Service Book with the request that a church book be prepared and issued for our Spanish speaking Lutherans, offering this Committee the free use of the results of the months of labor given the subject by Dr. Ostrom, with the assurance of our hearty co-operation in securing the early publication of the Common Service Book and Hymnal in Spanish.

We present a brief summary of the work done by the Board in the past biennium commencing with the field in

Porto Rico

Our Mission celebrated this year the twenty-fifth anniversary of the beginning of the Lutheran Church in Porto Rico. While the work often presents a discouragingly slow growth, nevertheless, a review of the quarter century just past, in which, starting with nothing, we have come to a point where we have a goodly number of congregations and excellent church buildings and active orginzations occupying the Porto Rican field, we believe the Church has every reason to feel encouraged. The last two years have been exceptionally trying because of illness among our American missionaries. The Rev. Dr. Knoll shortly after arriving on the field was taken seriously ill so that, accompanied by his wife, he returned to the States for an operation. For ten months he was utterly incapacitated and at the end of that time, feeling it would be unwise to go back to the tropics in his weakened condition he resigned to accept a call as Superintendent of Missions in the New York Ministerium. The Rev. Mr. Lindke was taken ill with a tropical disease and compelled to come to the States, where he spent several months recovering his health, returning to the field because of the great need when there was every inducement to accept a call and remain in the States.

The Rev. Gustav K. Huf, a graduate of Mt. Airy Seminary this year, and his wife, who studied at the Baltimore Motherhouse, accepted a call to fill the vacancy caused by Dr. Knoll's resignation. The Rev. J. C. Pedersen has been transferred from the Virgin Islands to Porto Rico because of his wide missionary experience and knowledge of Spanish.

I. *San Juan District*. In this section the first Lutheran work was established twenty-five years ago. The Rev. Dr. Alfred Ostrom is in charge. This year, his wife, who had labored with him for nineteen years, was called to her eternal reward. Although she was aware some time ago when operated upon for cancer that she could not live long, she preferred to spend her remaining years among the people for whom she had given so much of her life. Only at the last when the physicians knew the time was short did she return to the States, and then too late to reach her people, dying in the Lutheran Hospital in New York on April 11th. For such self-sacrifice and devotion there could be no more fitting tribute than the words of the Holy Scriptures: "Blessed are the dead who die in the Lord from henceforth; yea, saith the Spirit, that they may rest from their labors; and their works do follow them."

This district covers the capital city of San Juan and its suburbs and because of its importance has hitherto had the larger staff of workers. Here Dr. Ostrom and his faithful wife labored during the past two years; Miss Sofia Probst was in charge of the educational work, assisted by Miss Cataline Zambrana. The Rev. J. C. Pedersen is also located in this section in charge of the English congregation and assisting in the Spanish work. Native helpers are Mr. Demetrio Texidor and Mr. Sergio Cobian, and his wife, who has had charge of the industrial classes. The principal center is Puerta de Tierra with its beautiful church property where two congregations worship—San Pablo's Spanish Lutheran Church, and the only English Lutheran Church in Porto Rico. The other stations are the preaching points and Sunday schools at Gandul, in old San Juan and La Perla, and the new station at Monte Flores.

II. *Cataño District*. During the greater part of the biennium this district has been supplied by the pastors from the neighboring districts on account of the illness of Dr. Knoll. The vacancy has now been filled by the arrival of the Rev. Gustav K. Huf. In spite of handicaps the work has made progress under the direction of the native helper, Mr.

Salustiano Hernandez, located in Cataño proper, and Mr. Frank Colon at Palo Seco. Mr. Colon was a Porto Rican who had been in Government service during the war and had been brought to the States, where after the war he had a position at a good salary which he sacrificed in order to serve the Church. Mis Bertha Casos has been teaching the kindergarten and vacation schools in this district with volunteer assistance from members of the congregation. There are two organized congregations, Divino Salvador at Cataño, and Betesda at Palo Seco. The outlying stations are at San Tomas, Sabana and Amelia.

III. *Bayamon District.* This large country district has been in charge of the Superintendent, Rev. F. W. Lindke, who would not have been able to care for it, in addition to his other duties, had he not been furnished with an automobile. Mrs. Lindke is also a commissioned missionary actively engaged in the work. The native teachers are Miss Rosa Gonzàlez, Miss Carmen Rosario and Miss Saldaña. They have done exceptionally good work, their qualifications being shown in their possession of Public School Teachers' certificates. The native preachers in this district are Mr. Guillermo Marrero in the Bayamon parish, Mr. Juan Zambrana in the Dorado-Toa Baja parish, Mr. German Vazquez in the Monacillo parish. The Bayamon parish has two organized congregations, Santisima Trinidad and Sion's. There is an out-station at Pajaros. The other organized congregations are: San Pedro's in Toa Baja, with an out-station at Campanilla; Gethsemani in Dorado, and Betel in Maracyo; with out-stations at Higuliar and Santa Rosa; in the Monacillo parish, Betania at Monacilo proper and Nuestro Salvador at Juan Domingo, with out-stations at Monacillo Arriba and Juan Velez.

In this district there was erected this summer at Dorado a beautiful church facing the public plaza. This meant much to the congregation which has for years worshiped in an unseemly shack. Sion's congregation, Comerio Street, Bayamon, also greatly improved their property by the addition of a tower with practically no cost to the Board.

VIRGIN ISLANDS

The work in this field has been very difficult not only because of vacancies created by sickness but also because economic conditions are so bad that the population is leaving as fast as passage can be secured. Nevertheless, the congregations have not only held their own but in some instances shown an increase. There are three parishes including five organized congregations.

I. *Frederiksted-King's Hill,* which was served by Pastor J. C. Pedersen until he was called to Porto Rico. The assistant here is Clerk Reginald McFarlane.

II. *Christiansted.* Pastor A. E. Jensen came here at the beginning of the biennium but on account of the illness of his wife and daughter suddenly left the field. He was succeeded by Pastor J. P. Christensen, who after his furlough took the St. Croix work in place of the parish at St. Thomas. But one of his children contracting a tropical disease, he also has resigned and left the field, to be succeeded in October of this year by the Rev. D. E. Rupley, of Philadelphia, who with his wife and two daughters will enter enthusiastically upon the task of building up the work in St. Croix.

III. *St. Thomas-St. John.* These two organized congregations were supplied by Dr. Ostrom and Pastor Pedersen until the Rev. N. T. Nesgaard and wife arrived on the field. Clerk Carl E. Francis is the assistant on the Island of St. John. The congregation has been greatly affected by the steadily diminishing shipping upon which the people depend for support. This is the result of the Government taking from St. Thomas its status as a free port.

IV. *Works of Mercy.* The Board has been constrained to continue our charitable institutions but with the establishment of a civil government it is expected that much of this work will be assumed by the civil authorities.

Children's Homes. This charity, supported by the Women's Missionary Society, has done much to relieve the suffering among the sick and neglected babies of the poor. They are known as the Queen Louise Homes, having been originally established by the Danish Societies under the patronage of the Dowager Queen Louise. One Home is located in Christiansted and the other in Frederiksted, and each has a capacity of sixty children. Three departments are maintained,. a sick ward, where neglected infants receive proper care; a day nursery where little ones are cared for whose mothers are working in the fields; and the kindergarten. Sister Maren Knudsen is in charge at Frederiksted, arrangements having been made with the Motherhouse at Copenhagen whereby she was permitted to return to the field for another term of service. She has spent sixteen years in this field and her devotion to the cause has won for her a lasting place in the hearts of the people. Sister Clara Smyre, of the Baltimore Motherhouse, is in charge of the Home at Christiansted. Her work in the Home as well as in the parish has been noteworthy and has obtained the recognition of the government authorities.

Ebenezer Orphanage. In the last two years this institution has been thoroughly organized on an American basis and is accomplishing fine work among the group of girls which it shelters. Miss Nanca Schoen has been in complete charge of the work and the results attained, as well as the kindergarten established in the parish, has won the commendation of the school commissioners and of the courts. Miss Schoen's furlough being due, Miss Florence Hines accepted a call to the field after having spent a year in preparation at the Baltimore Motherhouse. She was entered enthusiastically upon the work. Miss Schoen will be received into

the Milwaukee Motherhouse and be consecrated a deaconess before returning to the field to continue her important labors.

Lepers. In justice to our workers, mention must be made of the part
which they take in the care of the lepers in the two colonies, one located
on the Island of St. Croix, and the other in Porto Rico on a little island
in the harbor of San Juan. These poor unfortunates are ministered
to by the various Protestant denominations who take their turn holding
services and bringing gifts to supplement the supplies furnished by the
Government. The Christmas boxes which the congregations in the States
send yearly in such liberal amount for the poor in the parishes and for
gifts to the children in the kindergartens and Sunday schools always
furnish ample supplies for our missionaries in ministering to the lepers.

V. *Industrial.* In all our stations there are people who have been
brought up amid such environments and in such ignorance as to make
their earning of a livelihood a problem. Many hundreds never know
what is is ever to have enough to eat, for their earnings seldom exceed a
few pennies a day. To reach this class successfully, they must be aided
in improving their living conditions. Other denominations have established well-equipped industrial schools but with our limited income it is
impossible to attempt to equal the magnificent work that others have
accomplished. However, our missionaries for a long time have been
planning for something that would solve this problem. Mrs. Ostrom
and other missionaries established small classes to train the poor people
in making baskets and lace work, so that they could add somewhat to
their income. In the meantime, the articles made by those in the classes
and others made by their poor relatives and neighbors were purchased
by Mrs. Ostrom and sent to the States for sale. This work grew until
it became a large enterprise, but it is at present severely handicaped by
the death of Mrs. Ostrom. Nevertheless, her labors have already resulted in a goodly sum which is being held as a trust fund until we
establish an industrial school. We are not asking the Church for an
apportionment for this as we believe in a short time the special gifts
and the profits from the sales by the Women's Missionary Societies
will permit something to be done that will be a credit to the Lutheran
Church.

NEW YORK CITY

In order to put an end to the great losses that our Church was suffering among the West Indians who had emigrated to New York City,
the West Indies Board in 1920 established a mission in the heart of
Manhattan. In three years it grew to such an extent that no hall large
enough could be secured to hold the people, and while Lutheran churches
were willing to give other people practically free use of their churches Sunday after Sunday, our West Indians, on account of the color which God put
in their skin, were without a home. Although prices were abnormally
high, yet to save the congregation, the Board was compelled to buy a

property at almost twice its pre-war value. It was the only available location adapted to our work, and so on the first of January, 1923, $57,000 was paid for the property at 74 West 126th Street. This structure had originally been a clubhouse but three successive congregations had owned it and rebuilt it until it was a modern church with a beautiful auditorium on the first floor, a Sunday school room and kitchen on the second floor, janitor's quarters on the third floor, offices and rooms for the workers on the first and second floors, and a bowling alley in the basement, giving a complete church equipment seldom found in so small a compass. That the West Indians appreciate the Board's action is shown by the fact that out of their poverty, the first year they were in their own church building, they contributed toward the expenses of the work the sum of $4,500. The congregation has shown a growth of 100 for each year of its life and now numbers over 430 communicants and is today the largest colored Lutheran congregation in the country.

The work is well organized in every department, its Boy Scouts being recognized as the best disciplined and the largest of any colored church. The parish is cared for by Mr. Paul E. West, one of our students for the ministry, now in Wagner College, and by Deaconess Sister Emma Francis. The pastoral oversight as well as the services are under the direct charge of the Executive Secretary, assisted by missionaries on furlough. The name chosen, the Church of the Transfiguration, is the same as that of a famous New York church of another faith and in time will become as well known in its way as the other "little church around the corner."

The only local support worthy of mention was received from the Church of the Atonement, 140th Street and Edgecomb Place, of which the Rev. Dr. Knubel was the former pastor, which congregation, although surrounded by the colored section, generously contributed almost a thousand dollars for this work.

Spanish Work. After securing a church property, it was possible to give attention to the Spanish Lutherans in New York City. These people being white were, of course, welcomed in the Lutheran churches, but not understanding the English language and greatly scattered over the city, they were drifting from the Lutheran fold. After a year of effort put forth in searching out the people and ministering to them, holding services regularly in the church, an organization was effected with twenty-five charter members. These people during the past year have maintained a larger average of attendance at the church services than Spanish congregations of other denominations in New York which have been organized for twenty years with their own church property. The loyalty of these people to the Lutheran Church is a credit to the labors of our missionaries as well as an evidence of the power of the Lutheran faith. Student of Theology Eduardo Roig, of Porto Rico, now at the Mt. Airy Seminary, is in charge of this work. Credit should be given to the New York and New England Synod for their co-operation in receiving Mr. Roig on their Student Aid Fund during his Seminary course.

Education of Men for the Ministry and Theological Seminary. The demand for men trained in the Spanish language impressed itself upon our missionaries from the very start. The men on the field zealously put forth efforts to establish a seminary, giving part of their time each week to teaching. Their prayers for help were answered by the Rev. H. L. McMurray, who left his property, after the death of his wife, for the founding of a theological seminary. Through the large-hearted vision of Mrs. McMurray, and the advice of the Rev. B. F. Hankey, the life-long friend who interested Pastor McMurray in this work, the property was made available for use at once. A contract of sale has been made which when carried out will provide about $30,000 for the erection of a Memorial Seminary.

In the meantime, the Board has been compelled to make provision for the education of students and has at present, in addition to the seven native helpers who are being educated in the islands, Mr. Paul E. West studying at Wagner College, and Mr. Eduardo Roig at Mt. Airy Seminary; there is another student available for Spanish work who will enter an American college this fall if supported by the Board; in the island three high school graduates are ready if supported, to enter the University of Porto Rico. While this is a heavy drain upon the resources of the Board, yet the importance of educating men for the Spanish work is so great that we feel the expenditures are justified.

Statistics. Only a general summary of statistics will be possible in the brief limits of this report. During the past biennium seven American pastors were on the field the whole time and four others part time. Seven women missionaries also labored the full period and six others part time. Mr. William Arbaugh and Mr. Eduardo Roig, students at Mt. Airy Seminary, labored acceptably during their vacation in Porto Rico. There are four deaconesses working on our fields, and twenty native assistants, eleven men and nine women; making fifty full-time workers in all. Under our Board are nineteen organized congregations with eleven additional preaching points and twenty-six Sunday schools. The baptized membership is 3,841, and the confirmed 2,158. In the Sunday schools are enrolled 2,386 children. The congregations raised over $9,000 for their support. The property, most of which is held by the Board, is valued at over $400,000, half of which came from the Danish National Church at the time of the transfer of the Virgin Islands to the United States.

CO-OPERATION

Augustana Synod. We rejoice in being privileged to report the continued interest of the Augustana Synod in the work in Porto Rico, where for so many years before the merger they had provided the larger amount of the support and furnished most of the missionaries. In this connection we would also report that the United Danish Synod is co-operating to the extent of furnishing pastors for the work in the Virgin Islands, the Rev. N. T. Nesgaard coming from that Synod.

Deaconess Motherhouses. The Motherhouse in Copenhagen, Denmark, kindly made arrangements whereby Sister Maren Knudsen could remain on the field. The Baltimore Motherhouse not only furnished Deaconess Sister Clara Smyre but also generously co-operated in preparing missionaries for the field, having already trained two of our young women, and expects this year to train more who are considering our field. The Motherhouse in Milwaukee has also arranged for the return of Sister Nanca Schoen to the field in order that she may continue her efficient labors. The Mary J. Drexel Motherhouse in Philadelphia has not only received Sister Emma Francis as a member of the Motherhouse but also is preparing West Indians for the diaconate. Miss Edith Prince was the first candidate to receive the garb. It is hoped that others will soon be found willing and qualified to receive training so that the Deaconess Board may be able to establish a Motherhouse for Colored Deaconesses.

The Women's Missionary Society. We cannot close our report without paying tribute to the generous support of the Women's Missionary Society, which has not only provided for the Children's Homes but also undertaken the support of all our unmarried women missionaries and deaconesses. The Society has cordially co-operated in the sale of products from the islands, and, in its literature, brought the Church a new insight into the needs of our field. Sufficient words of praise cannot be found to express our appreciation of what the Women's Societies are doing for us.

ORGANIZATION

The annual election of officers required by the charter resulted in the election of: President, the Rev. H. W. A. Hanson, D.D., Gettysburg, Pa.; vice-president, the Rev. C. A. Freed, D.D., Newberry, S. C.; secretary Mr. H. F. Heuer, Philadelphia, Pa.; treasurer, Mr. S. F. Telleen, Chase National Bank, New York City. The other members are: Rev. E. Belfour, D.D., Rev. F. M. Bosch, M. S. Boyer, M.D., Mr. J. H. Brandt, Rev. S. N. Carpenter, D.D., Rev. F. B. Clausen, Mr. A. H. Durboraw, Mr. C. W. Fuhr, Mr. R. E. Gaskell, Rev. F. U. Gift, D.D., Rev. B. F. Hankey, Rev. W. M. Horn, Rev. J. H. Meyer, E. J. Mosser, Esq., Rev. W. C. Schaeffer, D.D., Rev. J. J. Scherer, D.D., Mr. H. M. Schmitt; representing the Augustana Synod, Rev. J. A. Eckstrom, D.D., Rev. J. A. Anderson, D.D.; representing the Women's Missionary Society, Mrs. F. F. Fry and Mrs. B. S. Copenhaver; executive secretary, Rev. Z. M. Corbe.

During the biennium death called home two of our members. The Rev. Dr. E. Belfour was a prominent figure in the life of the General Council and from the beginning of the Lutheran Mission in Porto Rico was associated with the Boards having control of that work. Being of Danish birth, his interest in the new work in the Virgin Islands received from the Danish National Church was equal to his interest in Porto Rico. His long years of usefulness speak for themselves and need no additional tribute.

Mr. Robert E. Gaskell was called away from a life of activity, and he is greatly missed not only in the councils of our Board, but in the Church of the Holy Trinity, New York, and all the Lutheran activities of the city in which his cheerful labors played so important a part.

While mourning these losses, we would at the same time express our gratitude that we were permitted to have the valued counsel of these men during the past six years.

RECOMMENDATION

We would recommend that the United Lutheran Church approve of the following policy, especially in view of the fact that it is in harmony with the plans proposed for the reorganization of the Home Mission work in America.

"Be It Resolved, that hereafter when any work is undertaken within the bounds of a constituent synod of the United Lutheran Church in which the West Indies Mission Board is expected to co-operate

"a. It shall have the official approval of the proper synodical authorities.

"b. It shall continue under the jurisdiction of the synod in whose boundaries it is located.

"c. It shall be supervised by the West Indies Mission Board only in such matters as require the specialized knowledge of the Board and its representatives, the West Indies Mission Board co-operating also in all other matters necessary for co-ordination of the work with similar work in other synods.

"d. It shall be supported by the West Indies Mission Board only from such funds as may be placed in its budget for this special purpose and so approved by the United Lutheran Church."

HENRY W. A. HANSON, *President.*

C. A. FREED, *Vice-president.*

HENRY F. HEUER, *Secretary.*

S. FREDERICK TELLEEN, *Treasurer.*

ZENAN M. CORBE, *Executive Secretary.*

TREASURER'S REPORT OF THE BOARD OF WEST INDIES MISSIONS

STATEMENT OF RECEIPTS AND DISBURSEMENTS FOR THE YEAR ENDING
JULY 31, 1923

RECEIPTS

United Church on Apportionment through Treasurer Miller	$37,356.00	
Synods, Churches and Individuals through Treasurer Miller	918.47	
Women's Missionary Society through Treasurer Miller	5,175.00	
Churches, societies and individuals, direct.......	4,572.62	
Augustana Synod	1,350.98	
Danish Grants	6,095.88	
Loans	37,450.00	
Calada Fund	1,035.00	
Proceeds from Sale of Securities...............	14,079.50	
Interest on Investments	185.25	
Discount refunded	124.50	
		$108,343.20

DISBURSEMENTS

Salaries of Missionaries and Native Workers....	$19,838.83	
Salary of Secretary	2,000.00	
Salaries of Clerks, Stenographers, etc..........	1,074.00	
Expenses of Missionaries and Native Workers ..	3,318.70	
Expenses of Secretary and Board Members......	888.32	
Expenses of Missionaries on Furlough..........	1,385.90	
Mission Literature and General Expenses on the Field	702.43	
Donations to Homes, etc.......................	4,016.79	
Interest on Loans	1,543.49	
Real Estate and Property Purchased............	42,252.06	
Real Estate Maintenance, Taxes, Insurance, etc...	1,327.24	
Rental of Office	265.00	
Office Supplies and Expense	121.23	
Postage and Telegrams	83.97	
Publicity	738.00	
Auditing	200.00	
Bank charges for exchange, discount, etc........	385.06	
Designated funds transmitted through Treasurer.	91.41	
Danish Grants	528.54	
McMurray Estate	90.37	
Loans Repaid	14,000.00	
Securities Purchased	10000.00	
To Emergency Fund, Field Treasurer...........	1,000.00	
		$105,851.34

Excess of Receipts $2,491.86

S. F. TELLEEN, *Treasurer*

Balance Sheet, 31st July, 1923
ASSETS

Cash	*$8,702.47
Real Estate and Buildings at appraised values or cost	361,500.14
House and Office Furniture and Fixtures and Automobile at cost	2,580.68
	$372,783.29

LIABILITIES

Loans	$31,478.00	
Mortgage Payable	22,000.00	
Accounts Payable	377.02	
Interest Accrued on Loans and Mortgage........	603.22	
Special Funds	12,935.75	
General Fund	305,389.30	
		$372,783.29

*Includes $3,235.75 apportionment for July, 1923, received and deposited 1st August, 1923.

Philadelphia, Pa., 17th September, 1923.

We have audited the accounts of the Board of West Indies Missions of the United Lutheran Church in America, Inc., for the year ended 31st July, 1923, and we certify that the foregoing Balance Sheet, in our opinion, correctly sets forth the financial condition of the Board at 31st July, 1923.

The aggregate of the receipts as recorded in the cash book for the year ended 31st July, 1923, is $108,343.20, which includes $3,235.75 apportionment for July, 1923, and the aggregate of the disbursements is $105,851.34.

LYBRAND, ROSS BROS. & MONTGOMERY,   *Accountants and Auditors.*

TREASURER'S REPORT OF THE BOARD OF WEST INDIES MISSIONS

STATEMENT OF RECEIPTS AND DISBURSEMENTS FOR THE YEAR ENDING JULY 31, 1924

RECEIPTS

United Church on apportionment through Treasurer Miller	$ 44,918.60
Synods, Churches and Societies through Treasurer Miller	398.93
Women's Missionary Society through Treasurer Miller	5,839.39
Augustana Synod through Treasurer Miller	124.26
Augustana Synod—direct	2,291.86
Synods, Churches, Societies, Schools and Individuals direct	4,776.66
Nellie S. Anderson Estate	240.00
H. L. McMurray Estate	2,449.83
Danish Grants	924.43
Calada Fund	1,010.11

Interest on Investments	174.22	
Loans Made	1,500.00	
		$ 64,648.29

DISBURSEMENTS

Salaries of Missionaries and Native Workers	$ 19,140.00	
Salary of Executive Secretary	2,350.00	
Salary of Stenographer, etc.	1,130.00	
Expenses of Missionaries and Native Workers	6,632.95	
Expenses of Missionaries on Furlough	703.06	
Expenses of Secretary and Board Meetings	732.26	
Donations to Homes	3,658.45	
Real Estate Maintenance, Taxes, Insurance, etc.	2,009.59	
Real Estate and Other Property Purchased	1,513.48	
Danish Grants	886.00	
Office Rent, Supplies, Postage and Publicity	206.26	
Loans Paid	6,060.00	
Interest on Loans	2,935.08	
McMurray Estate	8,246.53	
Designated Funds Transmitted through Treasurer	680.85	
Exchange	3.33	
Investments Purchased	8,126.88	
Auditing—Lybrand, Ross Bros. & Montgomery	175.00	
		$ 65,189.72
Excess of Disbursements		$ 541.43

BALANCE SHEET, JULY 31, 1924
ASSETS

Cash	$ 7,161.04	
Investments: U. S. Certificates 4½s, 1927	8,126.88	
Real Estate and Buildings at appraised values of cost	402,252.62	
House and Office Furniture and Fixtures and Automobile at cost	3,074.68	
		$ 420,615.22

LIABILITIES

Loans	$ 27,358.00	
Mortgage Payable	21,560.00	
Accounts Payable	462.98	
Interest Accrued on Loans and Mortgage	526.55	
Special Funds	44,773.35	
General Fund	325,934.34	
		$ 420,615.22

Philadelphia, Pa., September 3, 1924.

We have audited the accounts of the Board of West Indies Missions of the United Lutheran Church in America for the year ended July 31, 1924, and we certify that the foregoing balance sheet, in our opinion, correctly sets forth the financial condition of the Board at July 31, 1924.

The aggregate of the receipts as recorded in the cash book for the year ended July 31, 1924, is $64,648.29, and the aggregate of the disbursements is $65,189.72.

LYBRAND, ROSS BROS. & MONTGOMERY,
Accountants and Auditors.

The Rev. Z. M. Corbe, Executive Secretary, addressed the Convention and read the recommendation of the Board. The recommendation was adopted.

On motion that the report be adopted as a whole, the Rev. F. W. Lindke, one of our missionaries in the Virgin Islands, was introduced and addressed the Convention. The motion to adopt as a whole was put and carried.

The Rev. J. C. Seegers presented the report of the Committee on Evangelism and addressed the Convention.

REPORT OF THE COMMITTEE ON EVANGELISM

The Committee on Evangelism, composed of the Rev. S. G. Weiskotten, D.D., F. Wolford, D.D., O. Krauch, A. Pohlman, D.D., M.D., P. W. Roth, D.D., E. A. Tappert, D.D., John F. Crigler, D.D., C. J. Rockey, S. D. Daugherty, D.D., Secy., J. C. Seegers, D.D., and Messrs. W. H. Stackel and F. Stussy, Jr., presents this report with a feeling of gratitude and appreciation: Gratitude to God for his favors and blessings; appreciation of the Church's cordial attitude toward, and deep interest in, the plans we have submitted, and the efforts we have made. There has been a steady and marked increase of interest in the subject of Evangelism. Synods, Conferences, Schools for the training of church workers, Summer Assemblies, have had the subject discussed and studied. Discussion has led to action, and action has resulted in an increased ingathering of souls.

At this time, and in this manner, we desire to acknowledge our indebtedness to the editors of The Lutheran for the generous support they have given us. Their frequent reference to the work of the Committee, their hearty endorsement of our plans and purposes, their constant urge upon the Church for a sympathetic and hearty co-operation contributed, in no small measure, to the effective prosecution of our work.

It is proper, also, at this time, to record, in an appreciative manner, the courteous and uniformly cordial attitude of the Presidents of the Distrist Synods. We sought and secured their co-operation. Through them, and the committees they appointed, the task of conveying our plans to, and making them operant in, the congregations, was facilitated and the more generally accomplished.

During the biennium your Committee endeavored, above everything else, to create an atmosphere favorable to, and a spirit which will be active in, the promotion of Evangelical Evangelism. We presented a program which aimed to increase church attendance, intensify church activity and imbue the members of the congregations with a sense of their responsibility to preach the gospel to every creature. We placed the emphasis upon the *Congregation* in action. We urged the necessity of stressing the *Primacy of the Spiritual,* and suggested that every congregation adopt the motto, "The whole Congregation at work all the Year for Souls."

The stress was laid upon that which belongs to a congregation's abiding effort. We attempted no evangelistic campaign, but urged a constant flow of evangelical life. We believe this to be the only safe and sound course to follow. The sporadic and spasmodic never prove permanently beneficial to the life of a congregation. A permanent spirit manifesting itself constantly in evangelistic effort is what we need.

To this end the celebration of the Festival of the Reformation in 1923 was directed. In every section of the Church the celebration emphasized evangelism. We rejoiced in our privilege and heritage, but we recognized also our duty to the times in which we live. We looked backward, but we did not fail to face forward. The keynote of the celebration was "This Country for Christ through Us."

To conserve the interest created through this celebration a nation-wide follow-up movement was proposed, suggesting as the first step the deepening of the spiritual life of the church, an awakening to a keen sense of responsibility and realization of the obligation resting upon the congregation to present the claims of Christ to every creature.

We recommended that the efforts of the congregations, throughout the whole United Lutheran Church, during the months of November and December, 1923, be directed towards the reclamation of lapsed members, the retrieving of losses sustained, and the securing of unattached Lutherans in every community. The seasons of Epiphany, Lent, and post-Easter were set apart as the opportune time for seed sowing and harvesting.

During the biennium the Committee issued a leaflet setting forth, in popular form, some of the fundamental facts characterizing the Lutheran Church. The entire edition of one hundred thousand was distributed, upon order, to the pastors of the church.

How effective our plans have proven cannot be stated. Spiritual influences and forces cannot be measured in terms of statistics. We planted and watered, and believe God, in His own time and way, will give the increase. Whatever results were accomplished, we attribute to the working of the Spirit of God through Whom alone souls are brought to, and kept in union with, Jesus Christ in true faith. We give Him the praise. We pray for His guidance and blessing as we plan for the future.

EDUCATIONAL EVANGELISM

This reveals the character of the program we submit for your ratification at this time.

The starting point in this program is the Festival of the Reformation. There is no more appropriate time to inaugurate a program of this character than at the celebration of this festival. It brings to mind precious memories. It recalls courageous faith, undaunted zeal, unflagging fidelity, untiring effort in behalf of truth. It flashes before us, in a striking way, the essential factors of a great spiritual movement growing out of the experience of an individual soul which had been led to freedom and life through faith in Jesus Christ. It demonstrates to us the liberating power of the Gospel. It records tremendous conquests of a spiritual nature. It marks the acquisition, as well as the declaration, of principles whose powers are eternal, and which can meet and, therefore be applied to the problems confronting the church of the twentieth century.

With these principles we want the people acquainted, and we want to stir our own people to a deeper appreciation of them. The gospel which made the Reformation must be made known. It must be brought in contact with souls. The object of the celebration is to begin an aggressive forward movement which will affect the church throughout our entire territory.

Through the proclamation of the gospel souls will be saved. With these souls the second feature of our program deals. It aims at

THE CONSERVATION OF OUR FORCES

Souls awakened must be conserved. Converts must be cared for. New members must be nurtured. Those who have been added must be anchored. Inquirers must be instructed. We urge, therefore, definite and positive instruction on all questions connected with faith and life. Religious instruction should follow, as well as precede, confirmation or profession. In the public and private ministrations of the Word the element of instruction should find a definite place. In giving this religious instruction

THE ADULT CATECHETICAL CLASS

must not be overlooked. It is an outstanding feature in this program of Educational Evangelism. It is recommended most heartily to the congregations. It offers a positive opportunity to bring the soul to, and build it up in, Christ. It is, perhaps, the best way to do constructive work. Four to six weeks in an earnest effort to gather material for such a class, together with direct, heart to heart instruction of those gathered, will yield a more fruitful harvest than energy expended in any other way. We stress this as an indispensable item in the congregation's program of evangelism.

THE DEVELOPMENT OF THE DEVOTIONAL LIFE

of our people must loom large in a program such as we are presenting. We are endeavoring to accomplish this through our church papers, *The Lutheran* and *Lutherische Herold*. We have arranged to give to the Church during Advent, Epiphany and Lent a series of daily devotional meditations. The central thought running through these meditations will be APPROPRIATING, ADVERTISING AND ADVANCING THE KINGDOM. The meditations will be practical and popular in their character. Daily Scriptural readings, together with a Collect for each day, will be suggested. We ask the pastors to bring this important phase of our program to the attention of our people, and to urge them to a faithful use of these aids to devotion.

CHURCH COUNCILS

are asked to devote some time in their monthly meetings to an intensive study of the subject of evangelism from a local viewpoint. To make this study the more possible and helpful our Committee will publish monthly in *The Lutheran* and *Lutherische Herold* articles treating subjects vitally related to the growth and development of the congregation.

We plan also to prepare and publish, as early as possible, literature which will be adapted for study by church councils and other groups in the congregation.

To avoid the duplication of literature and to co-ordinate, in a measure the work of our Committee with that of the Commitee on Social and Moral Welfare, we take the privilege of directing the serious thought of our people to the series of articles which will be given the Church by that Committee in the columns of *The Lutheran*.

THE STEWARDSHIP OF LIFE

must be emphasized in its relation to evangelism. It is inseparably connected with evangelism. It logically finds a place in a program aiming at Educational Evangelism. It has been said: "The Stewardship of Life depends upon evangelization. A life is evangelized only when it is begotten through the gospel, and is lived according to the principles and spirit of the gospel. This means that Christ is accepted as Saviour and Lord and that the life is lived not simply after his example, but as the expression of the indwelling Christ. When a life is evangelized in such a manner and degree the supreme purpose of that life is service, and the supreme motive is love." Evangelism aims to bring about a right relationship between the individual and Christ, and a living expression of that relationship. It deepens the sense of stewardship. It spells consecration, and consecration means a recognition of the fact that we belong to Christ, as well as a manifestation of a willingness to spend and be spent for Him. Educational Evangelism, therefore, leads to a recognition of the Stewardship of Life, and the Stewardship of Life expresses itself in an evangelical service.

Only as we realize that we are not our own, that we have been bought with a price, will we consecrate ourselves wholly to the service of Christ, but such a consecration will manifest itself in what is known and called

Personal Evangelism

For personal evangelism is nothing more than the outgoing of a consecrated personality to testify for Christ and to bring His claims to bear upon the non-Christian. It is individual witness-bearing. It grows out of a motive, and that motive is love, love for Christ and the soul. It is not dependent upon methods. Methods will vary. They will be determined by the person approaching and the person approached. The motive remains the same. It always is found in the soul of a consecrated personality.

The chief feature of personal evangelism is attestation. It is not argumentation. People are not argued into an acceptance of Christ, but are led to Christ.

But this personal witness-bearing and individual seeking of souls will not take place unless there is an appreciation of what Christ is in Himself, and what He has done for us; an appreciation of the value of the soul; an appreciation of the means of grace as administered by the Church. Educational Evangelism aims to produce this personal effort through constant instruction. When this appreciation is established there will be personal effort on the part of the members of the congregation. It will result in the congregation in action, and not merely one individual making an isolated attempt and an independent effort. Not only will the individual members of the congregation become active, but their activity will be related to the life of the congregation. It will make a congregation as a whole a spiritual force in the community.

We submit this program with the confident belief that its execution will result in an increased attendance upon the services of the church, an enlarged membership, and an intensifying of the church's influence.

Respectfully submitted for the Committee,

J. C. Seegers, Chairman.

On motion to adopt the report, the Revs. P. W. Roth, A. Pohlman and Dr. A. R. Steck spoke in advocacy of the work of Evangelism.

The report was adopted.

On motion of the Rev. A. Engeset, the item of the report of the Executive Board concerning the Pacific Theological Seminary was made a special order for Monday afternoon, immediately following the report of the Committee of Reference and Counsel.

The Rev. H. W. A. Hanson led in prayer, and the Convention adjourned until Monday morning.

FIFTH MEETING

Morning Session

CONVENTION HALL, EDGEWATER BEACH HOTEL,
Chicago, Ill.

Monday, October 27, 8 : 45 A. M.

Matins were conducted by the Rev. P. D. Brown.

The President called the Convention to order and announced the special orders for the day.

The Minutes of the Saturday sessions were read and approved.

Moved and carried, That the Secretary be authorized to make such changes in the code of By-Laws as are required by amendments, submit the result to the Executive Board for approval, and have the By-Laws, as amended, printed together with the Constitution of the United Lutheran Church.

The special order being the report of the Committee on Moral and Social Welfare, the Rev. E. P. Pfatteicher, Chairman of the Committee, reported as follows:

REPORT OF THE COMMITTEE ON MORAL AND SOCIAL WELFARE

I. THE WORK OF THE PAST BIENNIUM. SURVEY.

A. THE STUDY OF MORAL AND SOCIAL WELFARE PROBLEMS

Introductory Statement: The work of the past biennium has been preeminently the stupendous task of seeking to know something about the society in which we live and the problems which confront it. In this, our earnest quest, we are not alone nor do we feel that we are very far behind those who have been functioning longer than we have. Practically every worth-while moral and social welfare agency in the religious and secular world is seeking, as we are, for a clearer conception of things as they are. The agencies of today are compiling statistics, diagnosing conditions, seeking ever more light. This is being done by the agencies with a religious background, not because they have lost faith in the Gospel of our Lord, but because they are convinced they must understand the needs of the hour in terms of the hour and must be able to apply the Gospel of Jesus Christ as He would have us apply it. The direction of our studies is indicated for the benefit of those who are interested in the social problems of the day sufficiently to carry on a bit of personal investigation.

(a) *Copec*: This name has been applied to an English Conference on Christian Politics, Economics and Citizenship which was held at Birmingham, England, April 5-12, 1924. The Lord Bishop of Manchester was chairman of the Conference and Miss Lucy Gardner, 92 St. George's Square, London, S. W. 1, its secretary. The Conference itself did not turn out to be as valuable as was the carefully planned preparation for it. Pamphlets on the separate social problems of the day, intended as questionnaires, were sent out broadcast and certainly acted as proper propaganda. They were preceded by a pamphlet indicating the purpose, scope and character of the Conference. It contained among other things of real value the following platform:

"The basis of this Conference is the conviction that the Christian faith rightly interpreted and consistently followed, gives the vision and the power essential for solving the problems of today, that the social ethics of Christianity have been greatly neglected by Christians with disastrous consequences to the individual and to society, and that it is of the first importance that these should be given a clearer and more persistent emphasis. In the teaching and work of Jesus Christ there are certain fundamental principles—such as the universal Fatherhood of God with its corollary that mankind is God's family, and the law that 'whoso loseth his life, findeth it'—which if accepted, not only condemns much in the present organization of society but show the way of regeneration. Christianity has proved itself to possess also a motive power for the transformation of the individual without which no change of policy or method can succeed. In the light of its principles, the constitution of society, the conduct of industry, the upbringing of children, national and international politics, the personal relations of men and women, in fact, all human relationships must be tested. It is hoped that through this Conference the Church may win a fuller understanding of its Gospel and hearing a clear call to practical action may find courage to obey."

(b) *The Inquiry*: Following along the lines of the English Conference there is an American Conference, planned by "The National Conference on the Christian Way of Life." The Commission on International Relations of this National Conference has prepared a comprehensive syllabus of questions for use by forums and discussion groups on "International Problems and the Christian Way of Life." In addition to the questions there are selected readings. The pamphlet impresses us as being more popular and perhaps less searching than the English pamphlets. The latter are irreconcilably Christian. The American pamphlet seeks to be conciliatory. Contrast the platform of Copec with the following statement taken from the introduction of "International Problems and the Christian Way of Life":

"Those of us who profess to follow Him may have formally accepted His teachings, yet today we find ourselves sometimes wondering either whether they are true, or, if true, whether we are sufficiently intelligent to search out the way of life to which they seem to lead. . . .

"From the beginning it has been hoped that the Conference might be an even broader basis than that of the Federal Council of Churches, including not only members of churches not affiliated with the Federal Council, but also those who, though not regarding themselves as members of any particular Church believe that the following of Jesus' way of life might transform industrial, racial and international relations. . . ."

If Copec split on the rock of radicalism as was reported, what will happen to The Inquiry?

(c) *The Commissions of the Federal Council*: The Federal Council of the Churches of Christ in America, Dr. Robert E. Speer, President, the Revs. Charles S. MacFarland and Samuel McCrea Cavert, Secretaries, with offices at 105 E. 22d Street, New York, has two commissions which are active in moral and social welfare work. One of these is the "Commission on International Justice and Good Will," of which Dr. John H. Finley is chairman and the Rev. Sidney L. Gulick, secretary. The Commission seeks to act as a co-ordinating body of the many agencies at work upon this world problem. It is conducting an effective campaign in the interests of the World Court and seeks to stress the international obligations of America. It is interested in world relief and seeks to co-ordinate and prevent duplication in appeals. Dr. F. H. Knubel is the chairman of its Committee on Mercy and Relief, a fine bit of tribute to the splendid relief work of the Lutheran Church. The Commission is also seeking to bring about a new attitude on the part of America toward Mexico and Latin America.

The second of these commissions of the Federal Council is the "Commission on the Church and Social Service," of which the Rev. Worth M. Tippy is the secretary. This Commission seeks to be helpful to the churches in pointing the way in matters of social welfare. The Commission has held a series of conferences on the Church and Community Co-operation in Ohio, the Ohio Federation of Churches co-operating in the movement. "The Commission is interested at this time in the development of religious work for prisoners in local jails." A survey of the American jail is being prepared and is announced for publication in October. A pamphlet on Child Labor in the United States helped to pave the way for the recent enactment of legislation on that subject by Congress. There are other pamphlets on "The Coal Controversy," "The Wage Question," etc., that have provoked discussion.

(d) *The Denominational Literature*: It is manifestly impossible in this report to indicate even a bit of the wealth of material which has been prepared by the denominations through their respective agencies and their publication houses. Some of the denominations, *e. g.*, the Presbyterians, have a separate paper devoted to "Moral Welfare." We are inclined to the opinion that it is better not to detach these questions from their proper consideration in the church papers, or granting this is done also, we believe that our plan of study books plus enlisting the members of our committee as students of special subjects will prove more fruitful in the end. To ascertain the scope of the literature of any denomination we suggest consultation with a leader of that denomination in your community or correspondence with our committee.

(e) *The Kirby Page Pamphlets*: Under the editorship and direction of Mr. Kirby Page, 311 Division Avenue, Hasbrouck Heights, New Jersey, several series of pamphlets have been published by the George H. Doran Company, of New York. These pamphlets, intended for study groups and for individuals, have had a very large circulation. They are as follows:

The Christianity and World Problems Series to date consists of:
(1) War: Its Causes, Consequences and Cure, by Mr. Page.
(2) Russia: A Warning and a Challenge, by Sherwood Eddy.
(3) France and the Peace of Europe, by Mr. Page.
Pamphlets to appear in the near future: "World Problems of Today," "The Near East," "Latin America."
The Christianity and Industry Series consists of:
(1) Industrial Facts, by Mr. Page.
(2) Collective Bargaining (Trade Unionism and the Open Shop), by Mr. Page.
(3) Fellowship (and the Christian Social Order), by Messrs. Mathews and Bisseker.
(4) The Sword or the Cross (Jesus' Way of Life), by Mr. Page.
(5) The U. S. Steel Corporation (Modern Business Policies), by Mr. Page.
(6) America: Its Problems and Perils, by Sherwood Eddy.
(7) Incentives in Modern Life (Are Jesus' Principles Workable?), by Mr. Page.
(8) Industrial Unrest, A Way Out, by B. Seebohm Rowntree, Employer.
(9) The Economic Order: What is it? What is it worth? By Prof. J. H. Gray.
(10) Why Not Try Christianity? By Samuel Zane Batten.

(f) *The Foundations for Social Service*: Foremost among these is the Russell Sage Foundation, 130 East 22d Street, New York; a $15,000,000 foundation, incorporated by the Legislature of New York in 1907, "for the improvement of social and living conditions in the United States of America." There are eight departments:

(1) Charity Organization—Aim, to study, teach, publish and advise in questions affecting case work and administration, etc.
(2) Child Helping—Provides counsel for agencies interested in dependent, neglected, delinquent and defective children.
(3) Industrial Studies—Constructive Research.

(4)   Recreation—To aid in constructive social organization of leisure time.

(5)   Remedial Loans—To conduct a campaign of education regarding the evils of the small loan business and to secure protection and legislation.

(6)   Statistics—Furnishes statistics to other departments.

(7)   Surveys and Exhibits—To assist communities in the preparation of exhibits.

(8)   The Library—Contains about 22,500 books and 69,000 pamphlets on social subjects.   Carries 250 periodicals.   Open to the public; weekdays, 9 to 5.

(g)   Other libraries in New York which can profitably be consulted by students of social problems are:

The New York Library, Forty-second Street and Fifth Avenue.
Missionary Research Library, 25 Madison Avenue, 9 to 5, weekdays.
Columbia University Library, Broadway at 116th.
Union Theological Seminary Library, Broadway at 120th.
American Association for Labor Legislation Library, 131 East 23d.
American Social Hygiene Association Library, 105 West 40th.
Municipal Reference Library, 512 Municipal Building.

It is needless to add that practically every city in the United States has a library or libraries specializing in this subject.   It is also true that the great State Universities both East and West have departmental libraries on sociology.

B.   The Publications of the Committee

(a)   Perhaps the most important work assigned to the Committee has been the preparation of Study Books for individuals and groups, especially for the young people of our Church.   The first of these little books appeared two years ago and is entitled "The Sunday Problem." In it, the Christian Lord's Day is contrasted with its ancient predecessor and its more modern substitutes.   One of the high points in the argument is reached when it is said: "The modern Sunday is constantly pictured as a better, finer thing than the Puritan Blue Law Sabbath, but it is not fair to compare the modern Sunday with the Puritanic Blue Law Sabbath.   It is essential to compare and contrast the modern Sunday with the Christian Lord's Day."   And again it is asserted: "As a matter of fact, the Lord's Day becomes the type of what every day should be, for every day is holy unto God and His Christ."

(b)   Our second Study Book, prepared by the Secretary of the Committee, is on the vital subject, "The Family."   This book will not be ready until 1925.   It is an admirable little book on a most timely subject.   We desire to say for the benefit of those who do not know it that the author has been awarded his Doctorate in Philosophy by the University of Pennsylvania for post-graduate work in sociology.   Hence he was specially fitted for the preparation of this book.   The table of contents is here given to indicate to our constituency what may be expected: Ch. 1, The Family; Ch. 2, Marriage; Ch. 3, Factors in an Ideal Marriage; Ch. 4, Factors in an Ideal Marriage, con.; Ch. 5, Divorce; Ch. 6, Causes of Divorce; Ch. 7, Divorce Laws; Ch. 8, The Home; Ch. 9, The Training of the Child in Church and School; Ch. 10, The Family in Industry. We believe that a careful study of this little book will help our young people to a much saner appraisement of the whole subject than they are getting in current magazine articles.

(c) The compass of this report is too limited to indicate the many articles written by members of the Committee and by those co-operating with them, articles which have appeared during the biennium in the various weekly and more infrequent publications of the Church. In the third part of our report, paragraph 3 of section C, we say: "We shall be glad to transmit any information we may have to those who may care to know about literature on specified subjects."

(d) The members of our Committee, distributed over a wide territory, men whose vocational pursuits bring them into direct and constant contact with audiences, have taken themselves seriously as propagandists of the right sort. They have had many opportunities and have availed themselves of these opportunities to speak in no uncertain language in terms of the stewardship committed to them. We have had abundant testimony to the fact that an ever larger group of our pastors and laymen have endeavored to interpret the Word of God as it applies to the age in which we live and the problems which confront us.

(e) Church calendars have been used effectively in many parishes to bring to the attention of the constituency questions and facts in matters of moral and social welfare which need to be stressed repeatedly. A purely spiritual sermon with an intelligent use of printer's ink in its moral application to the needs of the hour has proved more effective than the not infrequent purely moral harangue of the reformer.

II. THE PROBLEMS IN THE FOREFRONT. DIAGNOSIS

A. The International Problems

One of the healthiest signs of the times is the fact that international problems are no longer viewed as questions which belong for settlement to a small group of diplomats, but as questions which must sooner or later be answered by every honest citizen interested in the brotherhood of man through Christ. No one who would think intelligently of world problems can do so without perusing the splendid July, 1924, number of the "Annals of the American Academy of Political and Social Science." There is a compact little "Handbook of the League of Nations" published by the World Peace Foundation, 40 Mt. Vernon Street, Boston, Mass., which can be had at five cents and is very helpful. We shall limit ourselves in this statement to three phases of the one international problem.

(a) *War and Peace*: The first of the international problems now in the public eye and mind concerns the question of war and peace. Wherever conventions are being held this year, whether their background be religious or secular, national or provincial, this question is discussed and an expression of sentiment on it is injected into platforms and utterances. There is a healthy longing in all of these statements for a firmer understanding of the brotherhood of man, and for a share in this experience. It is quite natural that the expressions should vary greatly in their approach to the problem. Here, on the one hand, is the pronouncement of the ultrapacifist who believes that there must be the immediate and complete renunciation of the entire war system and the immediate overthrow of our economic social order, which is asserted to be the real reason for wars. The pacifist point of view is well stated by Mr. Kirby Page in "War, Its Causes, Consequences and Cure," and "The Sword or the Cross—An Examination of War in the Light of Jesus' Way of Life," both of which are published by the George H. Doran Company. As over against the literature of Mr. Page, we have the pamphlet by the Rev. James M. Gray, D.D., of the Moody Bible Institute, of Chicago. Mr. Page says: "We believe in the latent goodness of all peoples everywhere." Dr. Gray, in his pamphlet on "What the Bible Teaches About War," says: "War is a consequence of sin and a punishment for sin." Mr. Page says: "We will never again sanction or participate in any war." Dr. Gray says: "It sometimes becomes the duty of nations to declare war."

It is because war is a consequence of sin rather than sin in its incipiency that it leaves the patient prostrate and convalescent for many years. It is because the sin is that of the people and not that of the drafted soldiers only that the people cannot escape the more remote consequences of the sin. To declare unequivocally that "war is sin" is to declare that the powers that declare war are not ordained of God and have acted against conscience in their declaration. To assert that the pulpit, having espoused the cause of the nation during times of war, is hypocritical, if in subsequent times of peace it lends its voice to the destruction of war and the perpetuation of peace, is an unwarranted indictment of the consciences of Christian ministers. There is no greater paradox in this apparent inconsistency than there is in the entire paradoxical Gospel of Jesus Christ. We believe that we are morally bound to prevent war with all the strength that is ours. We cannot abolish war until we shall have found and started to apply its moral substitute. A World Court and other legal agencies are crutches which are needed to sustain the patient. The Christ alone can bid the patient discard the crutches.

(b) *Emigration*: Immigration is the national phase of the larger international problem of emigration. Emigration deals with the source. It deals also with the goal of national world service. How can any nation best serve the commonwealth of nations? We believe that as nations arrive at a greater consciousness of world service and consequent world stewardship, as they come to realize that nations cannot live unto themselves alone, but must live for the larger brotherhood, there must be born the conviction that certain immigration regulations are needed as at least temporary expedients to weld a national sense of unity of purpose. We believe, therefore, that restraints placed upon immigration are not only justifiable but necessary means to the end of world service and that the unrestricted permission of immigration is unworthy of the ideals of a nation which seeks to be Christian. Even the Old Testament makes clear the disapproval of unrestricted migrations and unrestricted matrimonial intercourse such as Israel at times practiced contrary to the commands of God. We are, therefore, in accord with the principle that restrictive laws must be passed, not from selfish or haughty or un-Christian motives, but because of what we believe to be our Christian duty and our Christian obligation toward the brotherhood of man. The nations abroad are naturally seeking at this juncture to hold their better nationals at home. We can and we ought to say to them the spirit of America is religious. Those who come to our shores must come as those who are loyal to this spirit, as those who will not antagonize this spirit, as those who will not seek to overthrow this spirit. The American Lord's Day is, for instances, a heritage, the value of which America alone seems to understand. It is peculiarly American, different from the Continental Lord's Day, different from the Scotch Sabbath, different from Sovietism's day of license. America is peculiarly a spirit, not a letter. America will never be saved through mere law enforcement. The Americanization program must be a program of America for world service through loyalty to the spirit of the·fathers and their God.

(c) *Race*: What has just been said about emigration and immigration may help us to arrive at a sane estimate of the race problem. The Bible is very explicit in its teaching about the one blood of the brotherhood of man. It is also explicit in its survey of the manner in which differences have arisen among tribes and nations and have branded us with marks of descent from Shem, Ham and Japheth. Commerce in its sweeping, ruthless, onward march, unmindful of any reign but that of Mammon, has ignored both the rights and the limitations of race and has sought to solve the problem on the anvil of talking money. War, in its frenzy and in its inability to take time to solve the problem, has further complicated it. The Christian missionary, heroic and ready to make large sacrifices, has at times been forced into difficult positions on the field by fellow nationals whose only dream has been that of exploitation. The problem of race can be solved only by those who believe absolutely in the brotherhood of man in Christ and who view brotherhood as something more than a melting pot, something more than a melange, something that possesses tremendous supplementary potentialities. The solution of the race problem, as for instance it affects the white man and the negro, does not necessitate the mixed marriage as some would have us believe; it necessitates spiritual, not carnal, oneness. The world is ever in a state of flux. It needs the various races to lend it that completeness and that supplementary character which shall best serve to fulfill its manifold mission. The world needs more than a mongrel civilization, and this statement is made with no assumption that the white man always brings the blue blood to a mixed union. We believe, therefore, that nations do not act counter to the plans and purposes of God in writing an ennobling race legislation, which does not contradict the ideal of brotherhood, into their statute books.

B. The Domestic Problems

(a) *Law Enforcement*: The foremost of our domestic problems right now is that of law enforcement. Prohibition enforcement is simply one phase of a complicated and nasty situation, complicated because law enforcement has broken down all along the line, nasty because disclosures have implicated government officials and have shaken the confidence of the people in their government. The drastic measures assumed by the government have had a beneficial effect, but it is nevertheless true that we are not enforcing the law in our nation as it ought to be enforced. And it is equally true that much lawlessness that has nothing whatever to do with prohibition is being made to masquerade behind a bugaboo which has been created by friends of liquor. The need for more drastic enforcement of the law is a crying need of the hour. It is also true as suggested by one of our Judges in an Associated Press news item that we have carried the thought of pardon too far and have given the low-browed politicians a leverage which they are using with a vengeance. A careful examination of the record of pardons in your own State will prove a most revealing study in sociology, clearly indicating some of the channels of present-day lawlessness. The thing most needed today is a sane and Christian reaction from the abuses of a wrongly applied parole system. The police officer of today has every reason to be discouraged, if he is an honest official, sincerely desiring to serve his community. What we need is a higher regard for the law by lawyers themselves, a more rapid and more heroic functioning by many of our courts, and a willingness on the part of Christian citizens to cease being deliberate law breakers in business, in clubs and in their homes.

(b) *Morality Enforcement*: Of no less importance than the question of law enforcement. in fact, of much greater importance to every Christian, is the problem of morality enforcement—the enforcement of moral standards through no legal enactments, but solely through the conscience. Perhaps the average Christian would resent being charged with an immoral attitude toward society because of his willingness to let hands off or to let well enough alone. It is certainly true that far too many Christians are absolutely unmoral in their perspective of life. Somehow they have divorced spirituality and morality as social forces and the divorce has invariably led to a complacent and easily satisfied attitude toward personal morality. We cannot be true Christians unless we are willing and ready to smite our breasts as we say: "God be merciful to me a sinner." We are suffering today from an inability to get sufficiently relentless self-examinations.

The home is unquestionably directly responsible in the majority of instances for the startling lack of morality enforcement. Mothers must be held responsible, not Parisian modistes, for the kind of dresses their daughters wear. Mothers must be held responsible for painted and powdered faces and the unearthly hours their daughters are allowed to keep. Fathers must be held responsible for the gambling instincts of their sons, and the many "secret faults" which might have been anticipated through companionship and better example.

The big problem in industry now as ever is not that of rights, we have deliberately made it that; nor that of economics, we have made it that; the big problem in industry is how to secure morality enforcement. Industry will not be what it ought to be until both employers and employees shall be brought to see that they have both been too much interested in the wrong starting point. "The Acquisitive Society" is the very appropriate title of an English scholar's social findings. The employer and the employee must be persuaded to substitute the word "ought" based upon a worthy conception of brotherhood for the word "grab" based upon an unworthy conception of "the survival of the fittest." Public opinion must insist upon morality enforcement in industry.

(c) *Church and State*: The spiritual life of the Church must contribute in such an unconscious and spontaneous way to the legal life of the nation as to produce the moral welfare of the State. We believe wholeheartedly in the separation of Church and State. We also believe wholeheartedly in the exercise of the franchise by Christian citizens as citizens who have the highest welfare of the State at heart. Consciously or unconsciously, the Christian must have, subscribe to and practice a Christian creed in civics. The State is groping for light on the subject of its sovereignty and its authority, its limitations and its reaches. Social experts are today approaching a solution of the problem from the legal, the economic, the socialistic and false ecclesiastical points of view. Have we nothing to add to the solution of the problem?

(d) *Marriage and Divorce*: In 1916, there was one divorce for every 9.3 marriages. The most recent figures show one divorce for every 7.6. This increase becomes even more startling when we bear in mind that during the same period there has been a decided falling off in the number of marriages. Judge J. D. Harvey, of Houston, Texas, recently established a new record by granting 212 divorces in 243 minutes. A New York attorney who "has not made a specialty of divorces, but divorce cases have made a specialty of him," has published a pamphlet in which he advocates a divorce law so liberal we wonder why some people advocate marriage at all. The pamphlet contains a complete compilation of the marriage and divorce laws of the States and territories of the United States. Judge J. Willis Martin, of Philadelphia, calling attention to the 300 per cent increase in divorces in his city since 1913, issues a strong indictment of "the divorce mania." He says, among other things: "In many instances both parties to the divorce have other partners in wait for them, so that there are cases where husbands and wives are merely exchanged." In one instance recently, a manufacturer conceived the idea of stealing a body, placing it in his bungalow, setting fire to the bungalow and eloping with his stenographer without so much as the semblance of a divorce, to gratify his low impulses. The charred skeleton found in the bungalow was actually buried as his body and he eluded detection for several years. Here again we are compelled to return to our premise concerning morality enforcement. The problem of marriage and divorce is infinitely more than a legal problem and can never be adjudicated or settled as a legal problem. Marriage is more than a civil contract. The civil contract is not the first step in marriage. Before marriage is a civil contract, it is a covenant. In this covenant God is either recognized or ignored. In Christian marriage God must be recognized. In marriage we covenant to subordinate individual rights to mutual helpfulness and forbearance. The marriage covenant is an agreement on the part of both man and woman "for better or worse." Love and happiness are ideals to be sought in marriage, rather than realities, the absence of which voids marriage. The marriage ceremony is the sealing of the original covenant with the authorization of the State and the benediction of the Church. There can be but one cause for more than a separation and the deliberate connivance of unscrupulous mismated individuals to produce that one cause has raised the question in the minds of the High Church party in England whether divorce is ever justifiable.

(e) *Motion Pictures*: The motion picture has become a tremendous factor for weal or woe in our modern social complex. The saloon was often characterized as "the poor man's club." The motion-picture house has gotten to be "the universal club." It reaches men, women and children of every social station and holds and grips them. It gives them new ideas and ideals. It descends from the mountain top of Sinai with its "Ten Commandments" and the University Heights with splendid series of educational and historical pictures to the frolicking of the prodigal son and his wallowing among the swine. One and the same picture is oftentimes sublime and stupid, moral and immoral, chaste and lewd. To those who are interested in studying the subject we commend the "Catechism on Motion Pictures," by Canon William Sheafe Chase, D.D., of Brooklyn, N. Y., or the recent investigations conducted by "Collier's Weekly," finding expression in a series of articles, the concluding article asserting that "the greater and all-enveloping evil of the movies is that they are teaching our children false ideas and ideals." The Citizens' League of Maryland for Better Motion Pictures, has issued a pamphlet entitled, "Principles of Film Censorship," by the President of the British Board of Film Censors. There is pending in Congress the so-called "Upshaw Motion Picture Regulation Bill, H. R. 6821," a copy of which can be secured from your Congressman. This bill justly seeks to deal with the motion picture at the source of production, and not as a censorship of the finished product. It seeks to free the industry from the stranglehold of a few men with purely commercial instincts who are even now charged by the Federal Trade Commission with conspiring to form a trust, contrary to law.

We would urge our constituency whenever it sees a really good picture to write about it in commendatory terms to the local management and also to the producers, and on the other hand, we would urge our people whenever they see a picture that contains immoral features to protest to the management and the owners of local houses at which the picture is shown and also to convey their protest in writing to the producers. The specious argument of the local management, "We must take what they send us," must be met with the counter-argument of personal responsibility. We believe that the overwhelming majority of American citizens desire clean pictures and helpful pictures, pictures that present worthy ideals. We also believe that this majority is too slothful to state its desires, hence the ability of immoral men to foist immoral pictures upon the youth of the land.

III. THE WORK OF THE COMING BIENNIUM. PROGNOSIS

A. Intensified Study: Systematized and Apportioned

Our report thus far has sought to show what has been accomplished and what are the problems in the forefront. There is, of course, very much to be accomplished in the new biennium. Our efforts thus far have very necessarily been rudimentary. We are now ready to ask those who are specially interested in one or the other of the great moral and social welfare problems to join, with members of the Committee to whom special research is to be delegated, in the intensive study of these problems. It is our earnest hope and desire that a meeting of the Committee shall be held as soon after this convention as possible, at which time the subjects to be studied contemporaneously and the leaders of the various groups will be decided upon. It is furthermore hoped that a somewhat detailed minute of this meeting will be printed by The Lutheran in order that our entire constituency may be informed where to turn for definite information on questions which need solution.

B.   Proposed Publications

(a)   The Committee has keenly felt the need of a study book which shall be the first of a series of study books, because of its treatment of the entire question of "The Christian Life." This book is to set forth in a nutshell the relationship between the spiritual and the moral life and the relationship between individual questions and the whole problem of life. The Rev. Dr. E. E. Fischer, Professor of Apologetics and Ethics at the Philadelphia Seminary, has been asked to proceed with the preparation of this book. The tentative outline indicates its great scope: Ch. 1, The Beginning of the Christian Life; Ch. 2, The Development of the Christian Life; Ch. 3, The Characteristics, Content, and Manifestations of the Christian Life; Ch. 4, Christian Self Love; Ch. 5, The Love of Others; Ch. 6, The Christian in the Family; Ch. 7, The Christian in the Church; Ch. 8, The Christian Citizen; Ch. 9, The Christian in Industry; Ch. 10, The Christian and the Kingdom of God.

(b)   The intensified study indicated above is to bear fruit in various series of articles, among them a series for *The Lutheran,* which will place at the disposal of our constituency valuable material long before such material can be made available in the form of study books.

(c)   In this series and in all our research work we shall seek to interest others than members of the Committee, recognizing the vastness of the field and the intelligent interest in it of many who are not members of the Committee. We welcome individual effort and invite suggestions.

C.   The Christian Conference on Life and Work

There is to be held in the city of Stockholm, Sweden, in 1925, a Christian Conference on Life and Work. Archbishop Soederblom is the sponsor of the Conference. We believe that the time is ripe for such a conference, but in order that it may be truly worth while we must indicate a real interest in its outcome. We believe that the Committee on Moral and Social Welfare can bring a very real contribution to the Conference, and we also believe that the Conference will be helpful to our Committee in its work as that work projects itself into the new biennium.

D.   The Office of the Secretary a Clearing House

Your Committee has no salaried Secretary. It has, however, requested the Secretary, in so far as possible, to permit his office to become a clearing house in matters pertaining to its work.

(a)   We need a constantly revised list of names of persons in the various parts of our territory who are qualified to speak on social questions and willing to do so without thought of compensation other than their legitimate expenses.

(b) We need as complete as possible a file of local church calendars which stress moral and social problems in pithy paragraphs. We desire from time to time to supply our pastors with helpful suggestions and in order to do so, we must have the co-operation of those who have tried out suggestions and won out in their presentation.

(c) We shall be glad to transmit any information we may have to those who may care to know about literature on specified subjects.

Conclusion: Resolutions Proposed by the Committee

(1) Our recognition of the sinfulness of the human heart in every age must not deter us, but rather stir within us the holy purpose of re-studying the Word of God, the better to apply its principles to ourselves and to the age in which we live.

(2) We recognize the importance of mutual study and conference and hence welcome the announcement of the holding of a "Christian Conference on Life and Work" at Stockholm in 1925.

(3) We petition the United Lutheran Church to send representatives to this Conference, of whom the President of the United Lutheran Church shall be one.

(4) We gratefully acknowledge the co-operation of the Publication Board in making possible the study books which are being furnished the Church by the Committee and ask that our pastors note the appearance of these books in their calendars and use their best endeavors to introduce the study books in such ways and through such channels as may to them seem most fitting.

(5) We believe the constant inculcation of the Christian standard of morality to be peculiarly the task of the Christian Church. We would, therefore, urge an unsparing self-examination on the part of parents, employers and employees, and Christian citizens in the discharge of their civic responsibilities.

(6) We believe that the time has come when the United Lutheran Church should express itself clearly upon the relationship of Church and State, to offset false ideas and ideals, and, therefore, recommend that the United Lutheran Church authorize the President thereof to appoint a committee which shall prepare a statement on this important subject.

(7) In the matter of prohibition enforcement, we repeat and reprint the resolution passed by the United Lutheran Church in convention at Buffalo in 1922:

"Concerning the problem which has been created by those who in an unlawful way are seeking to invalidate the law of the United States in the matter of prohibition enforcement, we would call attention to the constant necessity of enforcement laws on the part of Congress to render all constitutional provisions effective. It is the duty of loyal citizens everywhere within the United States to abide by constitutional provisions and the laws passed by Congress relating to their enforcement."

(8) We believe that the time has come when it is necessary to stress the fact that nationalism and internationalism are not mutually exclusive terms, that patriotism and the love of other nations and races are complementary, that the processes employed by and within the nation to secure justice, peace and stability must be employed in an ever-increasing measure in the intercourse between nations, that the arbitrament of arms must yield in an ever larger degree to the arbitrament of reason, of law and of Christian love, and that to this end Christian citizens are pledged as such to exert every effort, through the establishment of some effective agency, to further justice and good will in their own country and in the commonwealth of nations. We believe that the Lutheran World Convention can contribute materially to the furtherance of world peace and petition it to consider this problem.

Holding these fundamental principles we recognize the fact that sin is still in the world and that nations might be unwarrantably incited to attack and invade our nation and therefore we believe that in accordance with the teaching of Article XVI of the Augsburg Confession and Article I of the Constitution of the United States, Christians may engage in just war and act as soldiers.

(9) In reference to the statement concerning motion pictures, we recognize the evil that is produced by suggestive, lewd and immoral pictures, and we believe that it is the duty of the Christian Church to protest against the same. In order to make such protest effective, we recommend that careful surveys be made in various centers and where such a survey shows conditions such as are referred to, that protests, with the facts secured, be presented to the Governor of the State in which such surveys shall have been made. We recommend, that the Committee on Moral and Social Welfare be hereby authorized to act in accordance with this resolution.

Respectfully submitted,
E. P. Pfatteicher, *For the Committee.*

Items 1 and 2 of the report were adopted.

Item 3 was referred to the Executive Board in conjunction with other matter so referred bearing on the same subject.

Item 4 was adopted.

Moved and carried, That Item 5 be amended by substituting the words "the Christian standard" for the word "standards." The item was then referred back to the Committee for further consideration and report.

Items 6 and 7 were adopted.

It was moved and carried to reconsider the resolution adopted Friday afternoon relating to Item 8 of the report of the Committee on Moral and Social Welfare.

It was then moved and carried to amend the resolution of Friday so as to read as follows: That if at the end of the thirty minutes assigned for the discussion of Item 8, the Convention is not ready to agree upon some resolution, the whole matter be referred back to the Committee on Moral and Social Welfare and that a representative of each resolution proposed shall have the privilege of a hearing.

The resolution was adopted as amended.

The Chairman of the Committee on Moral and Social Welfare then requested the privilege to withdraw Item 8 in its original form and to substitute the following:

"We believe that the time has come when it is necessary to stress the fact that nationalism and internationalism are not mutually exclusive terms, that patriotism and the love of other nations and races are complementary, that the processes employed by and within the nation to secure justice, peace and stability must be employed in an ever-increasing measure in the intercourse between nations, that the arbitrament of arms must yield in an ever larger degree to the arbitrament of reason, of law and of Christian love, and that to this end Christian citizens are pledged as such to exert every effort, through the establishment of some effective agency, to further justice and good will in their own country and in the commonwealth of nations. We believe that the Lutheran World Convention can contribute materially to the furtherance of world peace and petition it to consider this problem.

"Holding these fundamental principles we recognize the fact that sin is still in the world and that nations might be unwarrantably incited to attack and invade our nation and therefore we believe that in accordance with the teaching of Article XVI of the Augsburg Confession and Article I of the Constitution of the United States, Christians may engage in just war and act as soldiers."

Dr. Manhart, Chairman of the Committee on Memorials from Constituent Synods, read, for the information of the Convention, memorials received from the Synod of New York and New England, the Iowa Synod and the Ministerium of Pennsylvania.

Several resolutions were then proposed as substitutes for the resolution of the Committee. The discussion which ensued followed the arrangement adopted Friday afternoon.

The time for discussion having passed, a motion to adopt the substitute Item 8, as proposed by the Committee, was carried.

By request of the Chairman of the Committee on Moral and Social Welfare, permission was given to Mr. W. H. Hager to present the following which was adopted as Item 9 of the Committee's report:

"In reference to the statement concerning motion pictures, we recognize the evil that is produced by suggestive, lewd and immoral pictures, and we believe that it is the duty of the Christian Church to protest against the same. In order to make such protest effective, we recommend that careful surveys be made in various centers and where such a survey shows conditions such as are referred to, that protests, with the facts secured, be presented to the Governor of the State in which such surveys shall have been made. We recommend that the Committee on Moral and Social Welfare be hereby authorized to act in accordance with this resolution."

The Rev. A. J. Turkle presented the report of the Board of Education.

REPORT OF THE BOARD OF EDUCATION

Fathers and Brethren: Your Board of Education takes great satisfaction in presenting the subjoined report of its work for the past biennium. This satisfaction grows out of the consciousness of the manifold blessings of the great Head of the Church, upon the Fundamental, educational department of the Church's activities, with the serving of which this Board is charged by the Church. A perusal of the details of the departmental reports will at once convince of the gracious leadership and benediction of Him who said: "Go—Teach."

By increased support may His Church enable our Board still further to enlarge and strengthen its blessed services to the schools and the youth of the Church in the coming biennium.

I—MATTERS OF RECORD
Organization

The Advisory members for the past biennium have been:
From the Women's Missionary Society:
Miss Sarah Van Gundy, Washington, D. C.
Mrs. W. F. Morehead, Salem Va.

From the Augustana Synod:

Prof. George M. Stephenson, of the University of Minnesota, Minneapolis.

The following officers were elected by the Board for the biennium:

> President, Rev. Alonzo J. Turkle, D.D.
> Vice-president, Rev. George J. Gongaware, D.D.
> Recording Secretary, Rev. Howard R. Gold.
> Treasurer, Mr. John M. Snyder.

The Executive Staff for the work of the Board is as follows:

Departmental Secretaries

Miss Mary E. Markley, Women Students,
> 437 Fifth Avenue, New York City.
Assistant, Miss Mathilde Peper.
Rev. Carolus P. Harry, Students in State Universities,
> 210 W. Fornance St., Norristown, Pa.
Rev. Charles S. Bauslin, D.D., College Secretary,
> Evangelical Building, Harrisburg, Pa.
Rev. Frederick G. Gotwald, D.D., Executive Secretary,
> 47 E. Market Street, York, Pa.

In addition to the officers the following were elected members of the Executive Committee:

> Rev. A. Steimle, D.D.
> Rev. J. H. Harms, D.D.
> W. T. Stauffer, Esq.

To take the place of Mr. E. Hokanson, Milwaukee, Wis., who declined his election by the Buffalo Convention, the Board nominated and the Executive Board elected William J. Showalter, Sc.D., Associate Editor of *The Geographic Magazine*, Washington, D. C., as a member of the Board for the term expiring in 1928.

On June 20, 1924, the Board suffered a great loss in the death of one of its most capable, zealous and distinguished members, Rev. Dr. Huber Gray Buehler, Headmaster of the Hotchkiss School, Lakeville, Conn.

The nominations of the Board for the terms which expire at this Convention are the following:

To fill the unexpired term of William J. Showalter, Sc.D.

> William J. Showalter, Sc.D.

To fill the unexpired term of four years of the late Dr. Buehler:
Rev. Prof. Hugo C. M. Wendel, Ph.D., New York City.

For the full terms of six years:
Rev. R. D. Clare, D.D.
Rev. W. F. Hoppe, D.D.
Rev. E. P. Pfatteicher, D.D.
Rev. A. Steimle, D.D.
Mr. W. H. Stackel
G. M. Cummings, Esq.
Augustus S. Downing, LL.D.

The Saskatoon Building Appeal

During the biennium several appeals by correspondence were made in the hope of completing the $50,000 authorized by the Washington Convention. The result has not been all that was desired, but receipts of over $19,000 have been added to this greatly needed fund. The beautiful new building is now completed and in use, but at least the balance of nearly $11,000 of the desired amount is still most imperatively needed for adequate equipment and the removel of the remaining $8,000 debt on the property.

The Women's College

Since the last Convention further steps have been taken toward the establishment of a College for Women under the auspices of our Church. The Board of Education has been co-operating with the ten Synods interested in the enterprise and since the inception of the movement has kept in touch with the sentiment for a Women's College, lending every possible encouragement and aid. The following will be of interest and will show that definite progress has been made:

As a result of investigations referred to in our last report the Joint Committee decided, March 20, 1923, to report its findings to the several interested Synods, and to make certain recommendations. Briefly, the findings of the Committee were to the effect that a Women's College ought to be founded as soon as possible, and it recommended to the Synods that they approve the founding of such an institution, the college to be of standard grade, to be controlled by a Board of Directors to be elected by the Synods co-operating, and to be located in the best place available in the judgment of the Board. The Committee also recommended that the Synods agree that, in view of the delay which would probably occur before attaining the goal which had been set, namely, a College for Women built according to the most modern methods of construction, grouping, and adaptability for college uses, and in view also of the present great demand for the organization of such a college for women as soon as possible and the possibility of immediate patronage by the Lutheran young women on the territory named, and elsewhere, the Board of Directors be authorized to rent or purchase an existing institution or property and proceed at once to organize a college for the education of our young women. The Committee also recommended the laying of an apportionment for the support of the institution and suggested a basis for the election of directors.

Several Synods responded promptly and a Board of Directors was organized in Philadelphia February 7, 1924. At this meeting it was decided that "the permanent location of the proposed college should be in a metropolitan district." A form of charter and a constitution for the college were also adopted, and these are now being submitted to the Synods for approval. The following Synods, representing a confirmed membership of about five hundred thousand are interested: East Pennsylvania, West Pennsylvania, Maryland, Ministerium of Pennsylvania, Virginia, West Virginia, New York, New York and New England, Alleghany and Susquehanna of Central Pennsylvania. It is expected that during the coming biennium the Board of Directors will be able to take definite action on the location of the college and to adopt measures to organize and finance it in a manner worthy of its object.

Co-operation in Education

Little progress has been made in the plan for co-operation in education with the United Norwegian Lutheran Church in the Northwest and on the Pacific Coast. Plans are now pending for such co-operation at Parkland College.

Co-operation in University Student Work with the Augustana Synod has continued happily, with ever increasing possibilities for mutual service. The recent Augustana Convention graciously renewed their annual appropriation of $2,000 for our Board for this department. The University Student Department has also reached a working understanding with the United Norwegian Lutheran Church.

Plans are practically completed for co-operation with the Icelandic Synod of America in its Academy at Winnipeg, Manitoba, through an annual appropriation of $2,000 toward its budget.

Gifts

Special appeals for annuity gifts have been made during the biennium with considerable success, the splendid result of $38,000 having been achieved for this laudable form of benevolence.

A bequest of $500 was received from the late Mrs. Hannah Hankey, of New Kensington, Pa., widow of the late Rev. Dr. Hankey, to be used for Ministerial Education. In accepting this gift the Board made

it the nucleus of a permanent trust fund for this purpose and decided
to apply to this fund all future gifts not designated for other purposes.

Literature

The departments have, of course, issued their specific literature for
their respective objectives. In addition the Board has published for
free circulation throughout the Church the following:

Report of Joint Committee on Women's College.

Annuity Appeals.

Service and Teachers' Bulletin, No. 3.

"Christian Theology and Modern Science"—Dr. L. F. Gruber.

"Value of the Observance of the Church Year"—Secretary Gotwald.

"History of Higher Education for Lutheran Women"—Secretary
Markley.

"Aims in College Education"—Pres. R. E. Tulloss.

"Science and Revelation: Do They Conflict?"—Dr. L. F. Gruber.

"Your Church at Work," in collaboration with the other Boards.

Breklum-Kropp Graduates

The report of Director Rohnert of Kropp Seminary conveys the
gratifying information that during the past biennium there have been
realized the first fruits of the Washington Convention Agreement, on
the basis of which we have been aiding the Breklum-Kropp schools.
In view of their desperate financial needs, caused by the disorganized
economic state of Germany and the consequent falling off in gifts to
these schools from German sources, the Board has increased its appropriation for the year beginning June 1, 1924. An appeal for aid
toward this increase has recently been issued jointly with the Northwestern Mission Board to all graduates of these two schools who are
now laboring in the United Lutheran Church in America. In addition
to the six graduates who have come during the biennium three more
will probably come in September. Thus, in four years, there will have
been nine recruits in our American Seminaries for the last two years of
their training for bilingual work in this country.

The six students and their Seminaries are as follows:

Karl Schindler, Mt. Airy.

Hans Simoleit, Gettysburg.

Kurt Molzahn, Susquehanna.

Otto Heick, Wittenberg (Hamma)

Karl F. Schultze, Saskatoon.

William Kraft, Saskatoon.

The three to come here in September have been assigned as follows:

Rudolph Krey, Wittenberg (Hamma).

Otto Zbinden, Gettysburg.

Gustav Kupse, Chicago.

The transportation expenses have been shared by the Board and the Seminaries. The Washington agreement contained no provision for this item of the plan.

Northwestern and Pacific Seminaries

The Buffalo Convention adopted the report of the Survey Commission, approving its findings, among other matters, relative to the locations of the Northwestern Seminary and the Pacific Seminary.

Since that Convention the Synod of the Northwest has taken no further action on this matter.

The Pacific Synod has, however, taken action to the effect that it could not do otherwise than adhere to the position unanimously adopted by the Synod in the 1922 Convention in favor of a permanent location of the Pacific Seminary at Seattle, the reasons for which are fully stated in their Statement of Position presented at Buffalo.

II—Reports of Departments

A—Department for Women Students

Correlation and Co-operation.—This Department functions wherever women students of our Church are found. It, therefore, co-operates with the Department of Institutions on United Lutheran campuses and with the University Department of non-Lutheran co-educational campuses. Only in women's colleges located in places without a Lutheran Church has this Department no direct contact with other phases of our student work. And even on such campuses the co-operation with the Lutheran Student Association of America helps to bind our work into one unified whole.

To the Women's Missionary Society of the United Lutheran Church this Department is much indebted for most generous financial assistance on the annual budget. Still more valuable has been the assistance given through the annual census-taking of students in the local congregations which this year gave us, through the Synodical Student Secretaries, the names of 2,200 women students and 2,300 men students. The most valuable contribution has been the general and growing interest aroused by these Student Secretaries in all questions relating to the student and the Church in local congregations, local Student Commitees, Lutheran Women's Leagues, as well as in Conference and Synodical Missionary Conventions. At the latter the secretaries of this Department have frequently been invited to speak to large audiences of women.

The fact that since April, 1922, the Secretary for Women Students has been a member of the Candidate Committee of the Executive Board of the Women's Missionary Society makes her work more challenging. The appeal for Christian service in homeland and foreign countries can be made in person to the young women who, because of increasing educational requirements, can alone undertake such service. The women students who in the past few years have offered themselves to their Church have been educated in State and denominational colleges and universities, as well as in Lutheran Colleges.

Advisory Group.—The committee of the Board of Education which is especially charged with the work of the Department for Women Students will soon have available the thinking of a group of women educators who are closely in touch with the Church. The group will include deans of women at a State university and a Lutheran college, faculty members at a normal school and a municipal college, and a woman nationally known in student work.

Scholarship and Loan Fund for Women.—This fund goes back to May, 1921, when the first gift of a $1,000 bond was received. A second gift of the same amount has since been invested and smaller gifts have been available for immediate use. Several girls preparing for Church work have been assisted according to their pressing needs. If the fund grew more rapidly it would be possible to remove some of the present necessary restrictions and to serve more students.

Student Conferences.—To the summer conferences held by College Y. W. C. A. students at Silver Bay, N. Y., Eagles Mere, Pa., Blue Ridge, N. C., and Lake Geneva, Wis., this Department has sent its secretaries, or representatives, who have in several cases taken integral parts in the programs. Among the students of our Church met at these conferences are some of the leaders in Christian activities on their respective campuses. The Secretary for Women Students, as the delegate from the Council of Church Boards of Education, in April, attended the National Student Assembly of the Y. W. C. A. To this convention the Lutheran Student Association of America, upon invitation, sent as a delegate a student at Barnard College.

The Department has been privileged to be part of the regional conferences for Lutheran students held the past two years at Gettysburg College, at Wittenberg College, at the University of Pennsylvania, and at Newberry College. The opportunity to help arrange for the student Conference held at Augustana College, at which time approximately 75 men and women students from 45 different institutions formed the Lutheran Student Association of America, was much appreciated. This conference marks a distinct advance on the part of students in regard to their responsibility to their Church.

Student Volunteer Convention.—The ninth international convention of the Student Volunteer Movement for Foreign Missions held at Indianapolis, December, 1923, was attended by all of the Secretaries of the Board of Education. The gatherings of Lutheran students at the First Lutheran Church on Sunday afternoon, and again on Monday evening at the supper hour, were the largest and most representative church student meetings ever held. The entire group of Lutheran men and women numbered more than 300 and came from 109 different academic institutions, 37 of them Lutheran. In the group there were secretaries of the Boards of Foreign Missions, missionaries on furlough, missionaries under appointment, and student volunteers from practically every great body of the Lutheran Church. In addition to the meetings referred to above, at which invited Church speakers were heard, there was a well attended early Sunday Communion. Many students had personal interviews with secretaries with whom they have since been corresponding.

Visits.—During the past biennium the Secretary of this Department and her associate, Miss Peper, have visited groups of students from 256 campuses in 20 different States—Massachusetts, Connecticut, Rhode Island, New York, Pennsylvania, New Jersey, Maryland, Virginia, West Virginia, North Carolina, South Carolina, Ohio, Indiana, Illinois, Michigan, Wisconsin, Minnesota, Nebraska, Iowa and Kansas. The number of different student groups that have been personally visited since the beginning of the work of this Department, in 1919, is close to 300. In the case of large middle western State universities and the large colleges for women in the east the visits were made conjointly with student secretaries of other denominations. In such visits the coordinating agency for the men secretaries is the Council of Church Boards of Education, and for the women secretaries the Federated Student Committee, which is composed of women working with students under the direction of any of the denominations belonging to the Federation of Women's Boards of Foreign Missions, Council of Women for Home Missions, and Council of Church Boards of Education, or under the direction of the Young Women's Christian Association, Student Volunteer Movement, and Student Fellowship of Christian Life Service. In all visits the method is much the same; every effort is made to meet the local pastor and a church group and to have a group meeting of our Church students which is followed by as many personal calls and interviews as time will permit. In many cases individual correspondence concerning problems connected with the Church result and regular follow-up messages are sent annually to all students who have evinced a desire to enter Christian service and to those who are graduating.

B—Department of Religious Work in State Universities

Regional Organization.—The Regional Organization reported at the last meeting of the United Lutheran Church functioned with great satisfaction to the Board. The busy pastors who so generously helped us to get into touch with the groups of students in their regions did their work very efficiently. Several of them have asked to be relieved of this additional burden. As the University Secretary is now in touch with practically the whole field, it is possible to relieve these men without injury to the work. Two regions west of the Mississippi will be continued under the direction of the Regional Secretaries, namely:

Kansas-Nebraska-Oklahoma-Missouri region, Rev. N. D Goehring, University of Kansas, Lawrence, Kansas.

Colorado-Wyoming-New Mexico region, Rev. O. F. Weaver, University of Colorado, Boulder, Colorado.

With other parts of the country the University Secretary himself will keep in direct touch.

Western Trip.—In order to become thoroughly acquainted with the entire field, the University Secretary spent the autumn months of 1923 in visiting the universities and colleges in the far west. The results of the trip have justified the time spent. It has made possible far more effective work by our pastors in the University of Washington and the University of California than had been done up to that time. It has also revealed that the primary responsibility for student work in the northern tier of States lies with the pastors of the Augustana Synod and of the Norwegian Lutheran Church.

Synodical Committees.—At the suggestion of a group of pastors doing student work in colleges and normal school towns, the Board of Education has requested the Synods of the United Lutheran Church to appoint standing committees on Lutheran students in non-Lutheran educational institutions. In general the purposes of these committees are:

1. To see to it that the names of students are forwarded to the secretaries or the pastors through the proper channels.
2. To make recommendations to Synod for assistance to weak congregations in student communities.
3. To co-operate with the University Department and the Department for Women Students of the Board of Education and the Student Department of the Synodical Women's Missionary Society, especially in
   (a) planning and executing plans for work with students on the territory of Synod;
   (b) suggesting suitable pastors for congregations in student centers through the proper authorities of Synod.
4. To secure special contributions from congregations or individuals for student work on the territory of Synod

Pastors of other Lutheran Synods not officially connected with the United Lutheran Church are working with students at a number of points. The Secretary of this Department has been in correspondence with many of them.

Seminary Visits.—Through the courtesy of the Presidents of the Seminaries of the United Lutheran Church in America, it was possible for the Secretary, or a representative of this Department, to visit almost all of the Seminaries. Opportunity was given to speak to the senior classes in most instances and in some instances to the entire student body on the nature and methods of work among students and its place in the Church. The courtesy with which these visits were received is deeply appreciated. The Secretary personally visited the following seminaries: Philadelphia, Susquehanna, Gettysburg, Hamma, Waterloo, Chicago, Southern, Northwestern and Pacific.

Extent of the Work.—The Department for Women Students and this Department, working together, are in correspondence with the colleges and State normal schools listed in the Educational Directory of the United States Bureau of Education and with all university and provincial normal schools in Canada.

We are co-operating with one hundred and fifty local pastors, assisting them in discharging their responsibilities to students in their communities.

Conferences.—1. A Conference of pastors working with students was held in Chicago in January, 1923, attended by our pastors from the Mississippi Valley. A similar conference was held in Philadelphia in January, 1924, attended by pastors in the eastern States, beginning with Virginia. Both conferences went on record endorsing the following theses:

The primary agent in ministering to students is the congregation.

We do not seek primarily to render to students pastoral service, but to relate them to the life of the local congregation

The pastor must have the co-operation of the members of the congregation in receiving students from sister congregations into the fellowship of their worship, their work and their families.

The primary responsibility for Lutheran students in any community rests upon the Lutheran congregation or congregations in the community.

The Synod, of which the congregations are a part, is responsible for assisting the congregations in ministering to the students in the community.

The entire United Lutheran Church has recognized its responsibility for Lutheran students and through the Board of Education is prepared to render assistance to Synods and congregations in discharging their responsibilities to the students on their territories.

2. The Secretary attended the Conference of the Lutheran Student Association of America, the first general conference of which was held at Rock Island, Ill., April 13-15, 1923. This Association is the outgrowth of an invitation extended the Lutheran students of America by the Brotherhood of America in connection with their Convention held in Toledo in May, 1922. The students, while there, organized the Association and called their first conference at Rock Island.

The Secretary attended the following Regional Conferences of the Lutheran Student Association of America:

Ohio Valley, Springfield, Ohio;

Mississippi Valley, University of Wisconsin, Madison;

North Atlantic, Gettysburg, 1923; University of Pennsylvania, 1924;

Southern, Newberry College, Newberry, S. C.;

A Conference was also held at the University of Kansas, where our Regional Secretary, Rev. N. D. Goehring, was present.

Regional Conferences were held, one at Fargo, North Dakota, 1923, and one at the University of North Dakota, Grank Forks, 1924; both were attended by our Regional Secretary and pastors in that region.

The Lutheran Student Association of America is an autonomous student movement. The Board's Secretaries have been glad to respond to the students' requests for advice and help in carrying on their work.

3. Student Volunteer Quadrennial Convention, Indianapolis. A full account of the Convention will be found under the report of the Department for Women Students. All the Secretaries of the Board were present and had a fine opportunity for meeting students and working with them.

4. Y. M. C. A. Summer Conferences. During the past two years the Board of Education has sent its Regional Secretaries or Student Pastors to the various Y. M. C. A. Conferences where Lutheran students are in attendance. The general trend of these conferences is ethical rather than evangelical. They have been dealing very largely in social-economic problems. They are very stimulating to students. It is highly important that our representatives be present to assist our students in properly relating the inspiration they gather there to the work of the Church.

International Y. M. C. A. Convention, Atlantic City, November, 1922.— The Secretary was the official visitor of the University Committee of the Council of Church Boards of Education at that Convention. He is glad to report that the Convention was outspokenly in favor of larger co-operation with the churches, particularly in student work, and that in general the attitude of the majority of the delegates was evangelical.

Literature Published.—During the biennium, this Department of the Board has published the following literature:

Living the Life;
Bill-to-Bob;
Bill-to-Bob Again;
The Lutheran Church and Modern Religious Life;
Why Lutherans Should Do Religious Work Among Students;
Devotional Folders—Christ is Risen;
     Go Ye Into All the World;
     The Iniquity of Us All;

What to Do;
Helping the Student.

Better Churches Needed.—The Board would call the attention of the Church to the need for greatly increased equipment at certain important centers. The Board has already authorized its University Committee to proceed, in co-operation with Synodical authorities and the Home Mission Board, in an attempt to secure more adequate Church buildings and equipment which shall more truly represent the United Lutheran Church to the thousands of students of our Church and other churches in attendance at these universities and colleges. It is a striking fact that, with few exceptions, Lutheran Churches have been planted apparently without regard to the necessity of ministering to Lutheran students and that, in many instances, their equipment is entirely inadequate and fails to represent the great Church of which they are a part. A list of seven places most needing this improvement was brought to the Board's attention at its last regular meeting.

The Secretary.—The Secretary of this Department during the biennium has been privileged to meet nearly five hundred Lutheran students in personal interviews. He has addressed in convocations, or other large gatherings, between four and five thousand Lutheran students. He has met in committee meetings and other small group conferences approximately one thousand Lutheran students. During the same period, he has been in personal consultation with two hundred and fifty pastors and other Lutherans interested in working with students.

The Department would like to call attention to the fact that the work of its Secretary is not merely administrative but, in a very real and broad sense, a pastoral office in which intimate contacts are formed with students in many parts of the country and skilled guidance given both in personal problems and in those relating to the work of groups of students and their faithfulness to Christ and the Church.

C—Department of Recruiting for the Ministry

Keeping the Church reminded of its sacred duty to provide a continuing stream of youth offering themselves for the holy office of the gospel ministry and rendering personal service to scores of these prospective youth has engaged the thought and energy of this Department and its special committee. Every part of its program which has been developed and expanded is receiving minute attention year by year, with a broad definite goal of an adequate ministry, both in quantity and quality, always in sight.

Letters, leaflets, programs, pageants, articles and advertisements sent out from the headquarters of this Department clearly set forth the scope, the purpose and the urgency of the work and appeal for interest, prayers, active assistance and co-operation.

A survey of the United Lutheran Churh to determine the vacant pastorates was conducted in April, 1924. This survey has disclosed vacant pastorates to the number of 236, approximately. Estimates here are based on the latest Minutes of Synod and also on the official reports of officers of Synods. While there are at present but 236 vacancies as over against 243 in the former biennium, the net gain is so small as to be practically negligible. The loss in the ministry by death during the biennium was 121. We also record herewith the death rate for the past two bienniums by years, which has never before been shown:

For 1920	49
For 1921	46
For 1922	41
For 1923	56
For 1924 (to July)	24
	216

This demonstrates that the loss by death per year approximates 50, with a continuing number retiring from active service by reason of disability, age, etc. The Home Mission Board has indicated that on a very conservative basis they should enter at least one hundred new fields annually for the next five years. A survey by districts shows than an average of 65 new missions should be established per year reasonably to meet the challenge; and that a minimum of 45 must be planted to measure up at all to the most pressing opportunities. Illustrative figures for the five-year period are as follows—the first column indicating what should be done and the second is almost mandatory:

Eastern District	110	80
Southern District	70	40
Central District	110	80
Western District	35	25
	325	225

Our Board of Foreign Missions states that 39 persons are needed in the foreign fields immediately, as ordained ministers, evangelists, educators, physicians and nurses.

It is evident that the paramount need of the Church today may still be said to be "Men for the Ministry"—a sufficient number of able young men to take the place of the faithful veterans who have been promoted to higher service and to overtake the vast destitution that abounds on every hand.

It has been surprising to some and gratifying to all to know to what an extent different quarters of the Church and different organizations have become interested in the various phases of this work. The program itself in conducting the work of life enlistment has embraced the plan as here follows:

(A) Letters and leaflets to thousands of choice youth.

(B) Arousing the Church to pray the Lord of the harvest, by preparing literature for addresses, programs, etc.

(C) Providing worthy literature for parents, pastors, teachers, etc., as vocational counsellors.

(D) Sending out Board Secretaries and "Recruiting Agents"—

(a) To assist boys and girls in schools colleges and universities to discover God's plan for their lives.

(b) To improve the conditions surrounding our student growth, such as encouragement of and guidance in student religious organizations, etc.

(c) To assist in conferences of young people.

(E) Enlisting the interest, prayer and active assistance of the Women's Missionary Society, Luther League, Brotherhood, Laymen's Movement, etc., in solving by prayer and interest the great problems of life work as faced by our youth and of laborers so greatly needed by our Church.

(F) Co-operating with pastors, Sunday school officers, teachers, etc., in making their leadership in the work of vocational guidance more effective.

In connection with the observance of the Day of Prayer for Colleges a Life Service Day program was offered the Church in both years of the biennium; in 1923, "What Shall I Do?" and in 1924, "Faith of Our Fathers." These are being very extensively used.

That the inherent right of pageantry and dramatics as the handmaids of religion has been manifest is evidenced by the approval of the Church in receiving the new life service pageant of this Board, entitled, "The Reply of Youth." This in itself and by reason of its very wide use in the Church has become a valuable asset in intensifying the thought of the youth on the subject of the investment of life in full-time Christian service.

During the biennium this Department has co-operated with the Laymen's Movement in giving financial assistance to 16 young men in preparation for the gospel ministry in our colleges and seminaries. This is a matter which has engaged the attention of this Department during the entire biennium and is the occasion of great satisfaction that a beginning has been made. The worth and wisdom of this policy, we believe, has revealed itself so clearly to the laymen that an increased number is expected to be taken on their funds in the near future. The special motive of the laymen in this objective is to supply adequate financial resources to a number of worthy students of "parts and piety" so as to enable these students to secure their education upon a basis which will enable them to command their entire time during college and seminary days for high ideals of scholarship and other activities that are conducive to scholarly attainments; the premise here being that many of our students for the ministry are upon an insufficient financial footing to enable them to give their utmost to student development. Further thought suggests that when young men are forced to remain out of the seminary to earn money for their theological course or forced as college students to vitiate their study period by manual labor to earn a livelihood, the Church is the greater loser in the end.

This Department has co-operated with the Laymen's organization in seeking out and investigating the candidates for these benefits, in most cases upon personal acquaintance and observance, sometimes upon the recommendation of the college authorities, always in consultation with the college administration.

During the past biennium there has been the largest offering of life for the ministry and mission service on the part of the young men and young women in the history of the Church. There are on the rolls of the Synods in our colleges and seminaries a total of approximately 800 men for the ministry.

D—Department of Institutions

This has been a memorable biennium in the work of the Department of Institutions. There has been the largest offering of money the Church has ever recorded for Christian education. In the past seven years the amount of money contributed has been seven millions; three millions of this has come within the biennium. Our schools, colleges and theological seminaries have been richly blessed during the past two years and are more firmly rooted in the hearts of Lutherans than ever before.

There has been the largest number of youth of the Church enrolling in our institutions to "get wisdom—and with all their getting to get understanding."

Referring again to the contribution of the Church in the past seven years, and particularly during the biennium, to the endowment and equipment of our colleges it should further be said that this is by no means a finished task. Practically all institutions have shared in this advance movement, but there is every indication that it will be necessary for the Church to continue to give even larger appropriations for our institutions if they are to be put upon a permanent basis of efficiency. Only in recent years have we begun to realize the unparalleled demands upon modern educational institutions. The time has come when colleges must furnish equipment never dreamed of in an earlier day. Proving this point, we would show that in the year 1830 the total annual income from endowment and all other sources of Yale University was only $17,856. Not so very many years ago a certain famous institution, now known as Brown University, changed its name in recognition of a gift of $5,000.

To keep at all abreast of the times our colleges must enlarge their curricula remodel old plants, erect and equip new buildings, employ more professors and pay them more. There is another reason we wish to set forth for this as a talking point to the unfinished task of the Church in higher education. The need for larger endowments especially is manifest when we recall that every student pays on the average scarcely one-third of the cost of his education. State institutions make this so by appropriations derived from taxation; our institutions must depend upon income from endowments. They cannot raise the price of the tuition without shutting out many able and deserving students. They cannot reduce the cost of instruction without seriously impairing their standards; they must rather increase it.

Some time ago a careful study of the report of the United States Commissioner of Education revealed that the average cost of education in tax supported institutions of higher learning was $383 per student, in secondary schools $192 per student. In order to have a like amount for expenditure on the education of each student in Lutheran institutions we would need an annual income of $3,000,000 as against $1,135,947.

These figures emphasize the immense economy and the simply tremendous sacrifice made in the administration of our colleges as well as the large increase we must make if we would give them anything like fair and adequate relative support.

The Board of Education is distributing practically $65,000 annually to 24 institutions, which in all cases is applied merely to current expenses, but is an aid that is greatly appreciated by every institution and considered indispensable. The unfinished task of the Church in its responsibility to the schools and the necessity for increased appropriations from the Board of Education is clear and commanding.

The Department of Institutions has sought to keep the Church reminded of its sacred duty to provide for its colleges, and thoroughly believes that it has had a share in creating a church consciousness which has been productive of more generous giving to the cause.

The movement for funds to meet the serious crisis to which our institutions have come, by securing additional equipment and endowment, has staged itself most prominently during the biennium in the case of Muhlenberg College, where the total goal sought—one million dollars—has been realized. A very unique feature of this campaign worthy of mention is the fact that there were no extremely large gifts, but the total number of subscribers approximated 100,000. Again, in the case of one of our youngest institutions, Midland College, and on much more pioneer territory, a total objective of $400,000 seems assured. Roanoke and Lenoir have also greatly strengthened their resources and equipment.

During the biennium there was an increase in enrollment in the colleges of nearly 2,000. This indicates the necessity for additional income simply to care for the increase of students.

Complying with the action of the United Lutheran Church Convention at Washington, October, 1920, we wish to report that Marion Junior College, Marion, Va., has very recently amended its Charter as follows:

"(1) That two-thirds of the members of the Board of Trustees and the President of the College shall be members of congregations in organic connection with the Lutheran Synod of Virginia.

"(2) That the present members of the Board shall be retired at the rate of five members per year until all the present members have been retired.

"(3) That all vacancies shall be filled by election by the Lutheran Synod of Virginia or its Executive Committee."

The institution at Saskatoon, Saskatchewan, Canada, has been chartered by the Provincial Assembly as "The Lutheran College and Seminary." The act provides that the Trustees "shall be appointed or elected by the Evangelical Lutheran Synod of Manitoba" or its successors.

The set-up of the program for the Day of Prayer for Colleges and Universities, came under the particular supervision and direction of the Department of Institutions; all departments of this Board, however, co-operated in promoting the observance of this day, the last Sunday in February of each year. There has been with each recurring year since the organization of the United Lutheran Church a more general recognition of the day on the part of the churches, and co-operation of the Synods and institutions of our constituency reveals a marked advance. We call attention to the increase particularly of the last two years, reaching on Sunday, February 24, 1924, a total of 850 congregations, Sunday schools, Young People's Societies, observing this occasion. Doubtless a goodly number of other congregations kept the day, from whom no report was received.

This day is invaluable to the cause of the Church college and student life in our institutions. A United Church united in prayer—"the hand that moves the world to bring salvation down."

Vocational features were also combined in the observance of the Day of Prayer for Colleges. Excellent results in this work are at once apparent in the cordial co-operation of the churches, which has been most gratifying.

DISBURSEMENTS TO INSTITUTIONS

The following amounts were paid to Institutions during the biennium, ending July 31, 1924:

Breklum	Budget	$5,000.00	
"	Increased Budget	416.65	
"	Transportation of 7 students		
"	to American Seminaries..	1,185.00	$6,601.65
Carthage	Budget	10,000.00	
"	Special	20.00	10,020.00
Chicago Seminary	Budget	———	2,000.00
Gettysburg College	Budget	3,600.00	
" "	Special	146.00	3 746.00
Hartwick Seminary	Budget	———	2,400.00
Lenoir College	Budget		3,600.00
Marion College	Budget		5,000.00

Martin Luther Sem...	Budget	....		1,000.00
Midland College......	Budget	....	24,000.00	
" "	Special	....	163.33	24,163.33
Mt. Amoena Sem.....	Budget	....................———		2,000.00
Mt. Pleasant Inst.....	Budget	....		4,000.00
Muhlenberg College...	Budget	....	3,600.00	
" " ...	Special	....	25.00	3,625.00
Newberry College.....	Budget	....................———		7,200.00
Pacific Seminary......	Budget	....	5,400.00	
" "	Special	....	591.43	591.43
Roanoke College......	Budget	....................———		6,000.00
Saskatoon College.....	Budget	....	3,000.00	
" "	Special	....	283.75	
" "	Building Fund (including			
" "	$4,500 repaid Ex. Board			
	on loan)	....	11,626.09	14,909.84
Southern Seminary....	Budget	....................———		5,000.00
Sumerland College....	Budget	....		3,600.00
Susquehanna Univ....	Budget	....		3,600.00
Thiel College........	Budget	....		3,600.00
Wagner College.......	Budget	....	5,000.00	
" "	Special	....	10.00	5,010.00
Waterloo College.....	Budget	....	5,000.00	
" "	Special	....	2,124.66	7,124.66
Weidner Institute.....	Budget	....	2,000.00	
" "	Special	....	9.00	2,009.00
Wittenberg College....	Budget	....................:		3,600.00

Total for Biennium....... $135,800.91

III—Reports of Institutions

The following are reports from the twenty-seven educational institutions of the United Lutheran Church, arranged according to their respective types, in the order of their establishment. They depict a biennium of considerable achievement.

A—Theological Seminaries

Hartwick Seminary, New York

Founded 1797

Rev. J. H. Dudde, *Principal*

Hartwick Seminary is the oldest Lutheran school in America, founded in 1797 for the preparation of young men for the ministry. Its works falls into two departments: Preparatory and Theological.

The Preparatory Course consists of the usual classical subjects in preparation for college, with an additional year of college rating. This department is co-educational.

During the past year the 25 girls have enjoyed the comforts of a new cottage dormitory under the supervision of a matron.

Of 37 male boarding students during the past year 25 were students for the ministry.

There has been a steady increase of enrollment during the biennium; the last year exceeded the previous by 60 per cent. The scholarship standards of the biennium were the best in more than a decade.

The Theological Department offers a standard course of three years; graduates receive a theological diploma, and, if their work meets certain requirements, they are granted the degree of B. D.

The Board of Trustees recently authorized and set in operation a post-graduate course of study which can be taken *in absentia* and which leads to the degree of S.T.D. Many pastors have availed themselves of this opportunity of continuing their studies.

At the present writing, the school is being reorganized with the election of Rev. Charles R. Myers of Mount Carmel, Pa., as President.

THE THEOLOGICAL SEMINARY AT GETTYSBURG, PA.

Founded 1826

Rev. J. A. Singmaster, D.D., LL.D., *President*

The Seminary is a high-grade theological institution founded by the General Synod ninety-eight years ago. It occupies a commanding site of forty acres on the great battlefield. Its buildings are ample and its property is unencumbered. The endowment amounts to $425,000.

The Faculty consists of five regular professors and three instructors. The enrollment of students during the past year was 41, all resident undergraduates. No effort has been made to build up a Graduate Department. The Constitution provides, however, for a Post Graduate Course, leading to the B. D. degree. This course may be taken *in absentia*.

The regular courses of study have a broad scope under the two general heads: namely, the Biblical Literature Group in which Hebrew and Greek are required, leading to the B. D. degree; and the English Historical Group. Much attention is given to the English Bible. All the courses, Classical and Scientific, in Gettysburg College are open to students of the Seminary. The establishment of a Chair of Religious Education has been authorized. During the first week of August of each year an inspiring Summer Assembly has been held at the Seminary.

The government of the Seminary is vested in a Board of Directors, elected by such district synods of the United Lutheran Church, as support and patronize it.

SOUTHERN SEMINARY, COLUMBIA, S. C.

Founded 1830

Rev. A. G. Voigt, D.D., LL.D., *President*

The charter name of this institution is now Evangelical Lutheran Southern Seminary. All through its long history as a Theological and Classical Institute in early days, as a department of Newberry College, as the Seminary of the Southern General Synod, later as the Seminary of the United Lutheran Synod in the South, and, since the formation of The United Lutheran Church. in America, as the Seminary of the separate synods that composed the United Synod, until 1921, this institution had no charter. This year the Seminary availed itself of the powers conferred upon it by its charter and conferred the degee of Bachelor of Divinity for the first time.

The past biennium has been marked by a new aggressiveness. A movement to raise enough funds to erect two professors' houses and make repairs was entirely successful. The two houses have been built. A larger movement to raise $300,000 has been inaugurated with auspicious prospects. Meanwhile sufficient funds have been contributed by the synods to increase professors' salaries.

The Seminary has a faculty of four professors, one of whom also serves as Executive Secretary.

In 1921 the attendance of students reached the lowest ebb. There was no junior class. Gradually the attendance has been improving, and the prospect for the coming session is very good. In 1921-22 the attendance was thirteen; in 1922-3 it was eleven, with five graduates; in 1923-4 it was sixteen, but no graduates. Of the students enrolled in 1923-4 two were from Virginia, eight from North Carolina, three from South Carolina, one from Georgia, one from Mississippi, and one from Japan. The men who go from the Southern Seminary are for the most part absorbed by the Church in the South Atlantic States. Some go to the foreign field.

This Seminary has been an important part of the life of the Lutheran Church in the South and it must remain an important part of its life in the future. Its existence is vital to the development of this section of the United Lutheran Church. The Lutheran constituency in the South Atlantic and Gulf States is not large, but it is growing with the increasing industrial and agricultural development of the South. An old part of the nation and of the Lutheran Church, it is still a large mission field. The Southern Synods are exerting themselves to provide the necessary churches and the necessary men. It is not a light burden and with noble efforts it is still difficult to secure adequate endowment for an up-to-date theological seminary. But in spite of all drawbacks the Seminary is steadily increasing its permanent resources.

It has a beautiful granite building and three professors' houses on its campus of six acres, the whole property worth not less than $80,000. The endowment has grown to $72,000.

The Seminary is the property of the synods that formerly composed the United Synod in the South. All of these synods have representation on the Board of Trustees.

THE LUTHERAN THEOLOGICAL SEMINARY AT PHILADELPHIA

Founded 1864

Henry E. Jacobs, D.D., LL.D., *President*

The Theological Seminary at Philadelphia endeavors to provide a center of consecrated scholarship, in the interest of the entire Lutheran Church, for the thorough cultivation of all branches of theology. In addition to a school for necessary practical elementary instruction for the Christian ministry, its well-furnished and catalogued library, open every day of the year, except Sundays and holidays, and, in session time, by night as well as by day, affords ample apparatus for research work, not only to its own students, but to all scholars. While supported by four synods of The United Lutheran Church in America, its advantages are not restricted to students of any synod or denomination. Nor does attendance at the Seminary place any limitation upon the freedom of the student in the acceptance of a call to any part of the Church. The presence during the past year of 101 students, prepared at 48 colleges, universities and seminaries, representing 18 synods, 16 States and 4 foreign countries, living and studying together with one heart and one mind, is a gratifying indication of God's blessing. The great diversity of homes and churches whence students come, besides contributing important educational influences in their daily intercourse, cultivates Christian fellowship, enlarges the vision and forms bonds of permanent interest and affection for their future ministry. But, in the very nature of the case, all this brings increased responsibilities.

A distinctive feature, recently introduced with great success, has been the flexibility of the curriculum, enabling an adjustment of a portion of the time of each student according to his previous preparation and attainments. In some branches the unity of each class is preserved; in others, there are separations into groups, particularly of the more advanced students, with special tasks assigned for the scholarly work of every individual. Every effort is made to maintain a just balance between the various departments of theological science; so that the specializing process is constantly offset by attention to Biblical and practical courses.

The limits of capacity, so far as buildings are concerned, have been reached. The lecture rooms are uncomfortably crowded; every room for the accommodation of students has been filled. Every indication points to steady growth. In response to this clear call, plans have been prepared by a distinguished architect for extensive changes on our grounds, which have been recently enlarged by the purchase of neighboring properties. The first building to be erected will be a Lecture Hall; and, after that a second Dormitory. Provision to fulfill these plans will, doubtless, be made in due time.

The Faculty are a unit in their sense of responsibility for the trust committed them, and in their purpose, together with their colleagues in other seminaries of The United Lutheran Church, to abide, firmly, amidst the conflicts and confusion of the present day, by the simple faith which has given our beloved Church its name and its sole right to exist.

BREKLUM-KROPP SEMINARY

Preparatory Department, Breklum

Founded 1885

Prof. Petersen, *Director*

Theological Department, Kropp
Founded 1882

Rev. Prof. Ernst Rohnert, *Director*

Schleswig-Holstein, Germany

The Preparatory Department

We wish to begin the report of the pro-Seminary with twofold thanks. First of all we thanks to the Lord whom we desire to serve with our work, who during these last two years has been kind to us above asking and thinking and has graciously helped us through all needs and difficulties. Then we feel ourselves irresistibly compelled also to thank with our whole heart the Board of Education of the United Lutheran Church for its ready and friendly willingness which has been shown to us at all times, and for the vigorous assistance given to us, which made it possible to maintain and to continue our work without any harmful restrictions.

During the past two years our school laid special emphasis upon the instruction in languages, according to the plan of instruction agreed upon. In the main the instruction was given by the Director of the Institution. His assistant at first was Dr. S. Kahlke who left us already in October, 1922, in order to take up the study of theology in the university at Kiel. We owe him sincere thanks for his zeal and faithfulness and were truly sorry for his departure. His place was taken by Mr. Erich Pohl, candidate of Philology, who likewise did his work here faithfully and successfully. But he too left us Easter, 1923, in order to finish his studies at Kiel. His successor was the candidate for the ministry. Mr. Egon Pascholke, who has been active as teacher in our school from May, 1923, until now. The instruction in the English language has been given by Mission inspector Pastor Pohl.

At the end of every semester the usual semi-annual examinations were conducted by the commission called for this purpose. Two final examinations were held during the last two years; on March 20, 1923 three students of our school were promoted to the Seminary in Kropp and one on April 1, 1924.

At the beginning of the biennium the number of students was 9, to which 9 others were added in the course of the two years. Of these 18 few went to Kropp, 2 were dismissed as unsatisfactory, 1 left of his own accord, in order to study theology at a German university. Accordingly the number of students in each semester was as follows:

```
End of 1st semester, 1922...........................   9
Beginning of 2d semester, 1922, additions............   5
                                                      ——
End of 2d semester, 1922, total......................  14
Beginning of 1st semester, 1923, addition............   1
                                                      ——
Beginning of 1st semester, 1923, total...............  15
   Left school ......................................   4
                                                      ——
End of 1st semester, 1923.... .......................  11
Beginning of 2d semester, 1923, additions............   3
                                                      ——
   Total ............................................  14
   Left school ......................................   1
                                                      ——
2nd of 2d semester, 1923, total......................  13
   Left school ......................................   2
                                                      ——
End of 1st semester, 1924............................  11
```

At the beginning of August of this year 5 new students will be received, we shall, therefore, be able to start the new semester with 16 students. The average age of our students was 21 years; the condition of their health was quite pleasing, with very few exceptions. Nothing detrimental can be said as to their conduct excepting one case, where dismissal was ordered.

May I here speak briefly about the economical situation of our institution during the last two years. This was more or less determined by the bad economical condition of Germany. It became really critical in the second half of the year 1923, and in the beginning of August, 1923, we were confronted by the question, whether we should be able to continue our work at all. The prices went up by leaps and bounds. The buying value of the German mark sank day by day in a threatening manner. The treasury was completely exhausted in a very few days. At this very time of our highest need and our heaviest sorrow the Board of Education of the United Lutheran Church sent us the large amount of $400 and thereby relieved us from all our difficulties. This was verily and truly help in need; we were again able to breathe freely and to continue our work in joyful trust. This instance alone shows that the friends and brethren in America have saved our work from destruction through their contributions. For this we shall be everlastingly grateful to them. And we are particularly thankful, because upon our request these contributions have been sent to us monthly, punctually and in the full amount promised to us by the Board of Education. The monthly payments preserved us from the necessity to contract large debts and to pay high interests.

Since the end of last year the stabilization of money has been introduced in Germany. This has brought more quietness and steadiness into the economical life of Germany, but has caused at the same time a great scarcity of money, the detrimental results of which we feel more and more in our work. On account of this scarcity the support and gifts from our friends in Germany have been considerably reduced; they are now only about one-tenth of what they were before the war, and it is to be expected that they will steadily continue to decline. This disadvantage is the more noticeable as the prices for all the necessities of life surpass those before the war. Such unfavorable circumstances compel us to consider, whether we shall be able to maintain our work in the above mentioned modest limits and with the most stringent restrictions. But we put firm confidence in the United Lutheran Church and trust, that she will grant us also in the future the necessary means for our work, with which we wish to serve her gladly.

The Theological Department

The Seminary has continued its work in the past biennium in the same manner as before. No great changes have been made, either as regards the plan of instruction nor the faculty. Unfortunately the so-called "American Professorship" is still vacant, as a result of which the Director must still teach those branches which were formerly taught by the American professor. The other professors are: Pastor Hansen, the pastor loci of Kropp, Pastor Fliedner, the pastor of the Deaconess Motherhouse in Kropp, and Miss Sager, the teacher of English.

The number of students varied between 15 and 20; at present there are 15. The instruction, comprising all theological branches and philosophy and English besides, is given in three courses according to old custom; the old and tried Kropp plan of instruction having been retained.

The curriculum goes from Easter to Easter. Examinations are conducted in spring and fall. Since July 1, 1922, eight candidates have successfully passed their final theological examination, and six of these have since then gone to American Seminaries of the United Lutheran Church for their post graduate studies.   Carl Schindler to Mt. Airy, Otto Heick to Springfield, Wilhelm Kraft and Friedrich Schultze to Saskatoon, Curt Molzahn to Selinsgrove and Hans Simoleit to Gettysburg.   All of them feel at home in their new surroundings and are grateful for the kind reception and the vigorous assistance they found. Two candidates remained in Germany.   One of these is studying for another year in the Theological School at Bethel-Bielefeld and will then go to an American seminary, the other one continues his studies at a university and intends later to devote his services to the Church at home.

The moral conduct and the spirit of our students was good and gave us joy.   Friends from the United Lutheran Church who visited our seminary have testified to this.   Thanks to God, the health of our students was not seriously disturbed.

The collaboration with our brother-seminary at Breklum proceeds not only without friction but after the ideal of the psalmist: "Behold, how good and how pleasant it is for the brethren to dwell together in unity."

Great difficulties were caused by the financial conservation of the seminary.   The rapidly rising scarcity in its casual connection with the really catastrophic devaluation of money brought about one disturbance after the other.   Our situation became worst when the German money was stabilized by the introduction of the Rentenmark, November, 1923. For then it became horribly manifest, how ridiculously small our buying power was.   The dollar, which up to that time had been admired as a world power, henceforth had a value of only 410-420 Pfennige. The Seminary was for months in constant danger of bankruptcy and destruction.   We owe our salvation, after God, to the energetic help of a few, a very few, old and faithful friends in America and above all to the assistance of the Board of Education, which upon our appeals has adapted its contributions to the changed conditions as quickly as possible.   For this we wish to express our heartfelt thanks also in this place.   A very appreciable special contribution of the Board of Education, of which we just lately have received the first installment, shall put us in a position to free us from the burden of debt that has been pressing upon us since winter.   We honestly and earnestly strive to soon again get on a sound financial basis of which we need not be ashamed before God and men.

That our Seminary has not been swallowed up by the abyss of the "German Misery," "this is the Lord's doing, it is marvelous in our eyes." Soli Deo Gloria!

Account of the Contributions

which have been paid to the Kropp department of the united Germany Seminary by the Board of Education within the last biennium since August 1, 1922.

We received from the Board of Education through the treasurer, Mr. Herman Jenssen, Breklum:

Sept. 11, 1922	88,651	Papier-Mark
Nov. 18, 1922	666,664	" "
Apr. to Oct., 1923	878,556,436,750	" "
Nov., 1923	33,472,370,220,400	" "
Dec., 1923	947,770,663,000,000	" "
Jan., 1924	21,000,000,000,000	" "
Feb., 1924	448,400,000,000,000	" "

1451,521,590,412,465	Papier-Mark
1451,52	Renten-Mark

Besides these regular contributions we have received on June 23, 1924, $416.67 as a special contribution (1st installment). The regular contributions have been used for the current expenses of the Seminary; the special contribution shall serve us to pay off the debt, which the Seminary treasury has had to contract on account of the special difficulties of the last months since November, 1923.

We express also in this place our sincere thanks to the United Lutheran Church.

CHICAGO SEMINARY, MAYWOOD, ILL.

Founded 1891

Rev. J. E. Whitteker, D.D., LL.D., *President*

The Chicago Seminary, founded by the General Council with a self-perpetuating Board, was transferred to the United Lutheran Church under the same form of government. When a sufficient number of synods are ready to assume all the obligations of the Seminary and will undertake to carry out its original plans in the ways of endowment and equipment, the Board of Directors have pledged themselves, in harmony with the action of the United Lutheran Church, to transfer the entire control to the synods uniting in the Seminary's support.

Since our last report the curriculum has undergone a radical change. There are now two distinct courses: (a) The regular Standard Course leading to the degree of B. D.; (b) An all-English Course, which brings a diploma without a degree and in which the English Bible and special Mission studies take the place of Hebrew and Greek. In addition, there is a Post Graduate Course of one year, in residence, leading to the degree of B. D. to college graduates or S. T. M. to those who have the B. D. degree; and the course in the Extra-mural Department leading (by correspondence) to the degrees of B. D., S. T. M., and D. D.

The regular course of theological studies is supplemented by various features so essential to the proper conduct of the pastoral offices:

1. The Department of Music is in charge of one of the professors,

who has made a special study of church music and is most capable in imparting instruction in the art.

2. The Course of Public Speaking and Voice Culture, in which the students are drilled by classes as well as in private. The professor of this department has more than a local reputation, his books being used in a large number of American colleges and universities.

3. The devotional side of student life receives more than ordinary notice. The day begins with Matins, when one of the professors preaches a short sermon, with a student in charge of the service; the day closes with Vespers, when a student preaches the sermon and conducts the service. The constant aim is to cultivate the churchly spirit. Hence the chapel appointments are of the most approved order, while the liturgical parts of each service are carefully observed.

4. The spiritual estate of the students is a constant care. Heart and mind must move as one, the motive power being centered in the spiritual nature. To this end, the dean is in constant touch with the student in all his life, with personal conferences and devotional moments to give the true heart tone.

During the year 1923-24, the student body numbered 132. Of these, there were 35 resident students, one special student, three *in absentia* in the regular course, and 93 in the Extra-mural Department. In this department, five men received the B. D. degree and four the degree of S. T. M. The Post Graduate Department, in residence, had four graduates—two with the B. D. degree and two with the degree of S. T. M. There were in residence ten candidates for graduation—two receiving the degree of B. D., four the diploma of the Standard Course, and four the diploma of the English Course.

The Student Help Fund now totals $34,320 in endowment, with special gifts aggregating last year $300. The income of this fund is disbursed to students according to certain conditions specified by the donors and by the regulations given in the by-laws of the Seminary. During the past year, fourteen students received help through this fund—$100 each being the maximum amount.

The same needs are urgent today as two years ago—a greatly increased endowment, a library building, a chapel, and a gymnasium. Along all other lines, abundant provision has been made. The church has nobly rallied to our support; the Seminary deeply appreciates its loyalty and love. The Lord has greatly blest our work; to His Name be the praise.

PACIFIC THEOLOGICAL SEMINARY
Founded 1911

Rev. J. C. Kunzmann, D.D., *President*

Up to 1919 the Seminary had but one resident professor in the person of Prof. P. W. H. Frederick, D.D. Then Dr. Kunzmann was called to the presidency. In October of the same year Rev. T. W. Kretsch-mann, D.D., began his labors as the second professor.

There were graduated in the 1922-23 session four and in the 1923-24 session one candidate for the ministry. The Pacific Synod which is directly responsible for the Seminary's establishment, maintenance and development numbers but 2,368 confirmed members. The Seminary is located in the most Lutheran section of the coast and has prepared men for the ministry for all branches of our Church in the Far West with the exception of the Synodical Conference and enjoys their confidence. Our sister Synod, the California, has had students in continued attendance since 1919. Our hope for an adequate and efficient ministry lies in the boys and young men of the congregations of the Pacific Synod organized into Gideon Bands. These to the number of 115 or more are passing through the grade and high schools and colleges on their way to the Seminary.

Three funds have been created; first; a General Endowment Fund into which are placed all the legacies, bequests, special gifts and annuities; second, the Philadelphia Endowment Fund of $75,000, for the President's Chair; toward this $50,000 has been secured in subscriptions payable to the custodian, Bioren & Co., of which firm the Treasurer of the United Lutheran Church is President; third, the Endowment provided by the clergy, to which annual donations are being made.

All the debts on the buildings and grounds have been paid and there remains but a floating indebtedness of $2,400. As the frame structures on the grounds are poorly adapted for the work of the Seminary a program of buildings under the advice of the Committee on Church Architecture of the United Lutheran Church has been adopted. They are to be erected as the development of the institution demands. Funds are now being gathered for the erection of the president's residence temporarily to be used for the growing needs of the Seminary, until more ample provisions can be made. Thereafter will be realized the erection of a building, the basement of which will be used as a refectory; the first story with partitions moved will have library, chapel, recitation rooms and offices, and the second and third floors will be used as a dormitory. This will cost $200,000. The synod on recommendation of the Board has authorized the securing of subscriptions toward this object.

Martin Luther Seminary
Founded 1913
Rev. F. Wupper, D.D., *Director*

This institution is maintained by the German Nebraska Synod for the special purpose of training for the ministry men who shall be able to use both the German and English languages and who shall become capable leaders in a difficult transition period.

Its course consists of four years of pro-seminary work and three years of seminary work. Proper credit is given to men with college training.

During the biennium we have had our blessings and our cares. The average number of students has been fourteen. In 1923 there graduated two; in 1924 five students. One of these was commissioned to work in the Texas Synod. Our students came from the states of New York, South Carolina, Pennsylvania, Texas and Nebraska. Sixteen of our seventeen graduates are serving in the ministry of the United Lutheran Church in the states of Nebraska, Illinois, Oklahoma, Kansas, New York and Pennsylvania; this is evidence that we serve the Church beyond the limits of our own synod. Calls came also from other sections but could not be answered for lack of candidates.

The Faculty consisted of Dr. Wupper and Dr. Wellhausen as regular professors and Prof. Alexis, Ph.D., as assistant professor. Dr. Wellhausen resigned, after nine years of faithful service, on account of age. The Board contemplates calling a graduate of a Lutheran college and seminary, with the degree of Ph. D., from an American University, as successor to Dr. Wellhausen. As soon as finances permit, a third regular professor should be called.

While we were able to cover our regular expenses of about $8,000 annually, we were embarrassed by a $3,000 assessment for street paving. This amount constitutes a debt against us; but we expect a legacy coming due this fall, to off-set this debt.

We are grateful for the aid of the Board of Education, and solicit further sympathy and aid. Confident that we are doing the Lord's work, our trust is in Him.

NORTHWESTERN THEOLOGICAL SEMINARY, MINNEAPOLIS, MINN.

Founded 1921

Rev. Joseph Stump, D.D., *President*

The Seminary was founded by the English Evangelical Lutheran Synod of the Northwest to provide an adequate ministry for the English missionary work in the great Northwest. It is located in the metropolis of that vast and predominantly Lutheran territory reaching from Lake Michigan on the east to the Rocky Mountains in the west. In this rapidly anglicizing territory the need of thoroughly trained men who can preach acceptably in the English language is very great. The demand has always far outrun the supply. It is the purpose of Northwestern Seminary to train men for this field. Efforts are being made by the synod to increase the supply of men for the ministry from this territory instead of drawing them from other parts of the Church where they are needed.

The institution has been incorporated under the laws of the state of Minnesota during the past year, but its Board of Directors is elected by the Synod of the Northwest, so that the Seminary remains fully under the control of the synod. Its teaching force consists of four regular professors and two instructors.

The total enrollment of resident students during the year 1923-24 was nineteen, of whom four were in the post graduate department. Post graduate extra-mural or correspondence courses are also offered, and eleven men have enrolled in them. A class of six was graduated in 1923 and a class of seven in 1924 in the regular course, and one each year in the post graduate course. One of the graduates has gone as a missionary of the United Lutheran Church to Liberia, Africa.

The Seminary was fortunate in finding a building most excellently adapted to its purpose. This was purchased in 1922. It contains light and comfortable rooms for students, a lecture room for each of the professors, a commodious chapel, a tiled basement and kitchen, a large recreation room, two bowling alleys and shower baths.

A campaign is in progress for an endowment and equipment fund of $250,000 of which about $150,000 in cash and subscriptions has so far been raised.

This is distinctly a missionary Seminary in that it constantly keeps before the mind of the students the great missionary work of the Church as a whole and the great missionary opportunity of the Synod of the Northwest in particular.

B—Colleges
GETTYSBURG COLLEGE
Gettysburg, Pa.

For Men and Women

Founded 1832

Rev. Henry W. A. Hanson, D.D., *President*

Gettysburg College is glad to report encouraging developments in all departments. In added endowment, in the general raising of standards and in the largest enrollment in its history, the college has been augmented to a degree which enables it, as never before, to serve our Church.

A number of important changes have been made, the beneficial results of which are becoming more and more apparent.

A. A provision has been made by which all full professors are enabled to spend a full week every year in studying the work of their respective departments in other institutions. The expense connected with this college visitation is borne by the college. By this method Gettysburg College seeks to keep its professors fully informed as to the latest methods employed by the representative institutions of our country.

B. In order to enrich the student life by broader contacts a series of bi-weekly chapel addresses has been arranged. The prominent Protestant leaders of our country are brought to the campus for these addresses. Among those who have delivered important messages during the past year are Drs. John Timothy Stone, Sherwood Eddy, F. H. Knubel, S. Parkes Cadman, William F. McDowell, Harris Kirk, A. Pohlman W. C. Schaeffer and Charles L. Fry. Perhaps the most convincing evidence of the far-reaching consequences of this innovation is shown by the fact that during the entire year the Discipline Committee did not hold a single meeting.

C. Gettysburg College has introduced a special course for the young men who are looking forward to the ministry. The Monday evening meetings are addressed by the President and by prominent Lutheran clergymen. The course of lectures aims to quicken in the student a deeper appreciation of the opportunities and requirements of the present-day ministry. Each ministerial student is brought into personal contact with a large number of the outstanding ministers of our own church.

D. The greatest undeveloped field in modern college life lies in the freshman class. The first two weeks of college life are the most important in a student's career. Into these two weeks Gettysburg College seeks to compress an intensive course of Christian idealism. The student is taught at the beginning of his college life that the only man who possesses any chance for the highest success in life is the one who carries the religion of his home into every relationship of his campus life.

Gettysburg College is deeply grateful for the loyal support of the United Lutheran Church and pledges its devoted service to our beloved Church.

The enrollment has been, 1923-24, men 490, women 77.

WITTENBERG COLLEGE

Springfield, Ohio

Founded 1845

Rev. Rees Edgar Tulloss, D.D., Ph.D., LL.D., *President*

The following are the principal items in the history of Wittenberg for the biennium.

The enrollment has continued to increase. Students in the College Classes have numbered as follows:

1920-21	450
1921-22	603
1922-23	720
1923-24	801

The total enrollment in all departments of the institution for the year 1923-24 was 1,576.

For the last two years the Freshmen enrollment has been limited to 300. This limitation must continue until additional buildings and teachers are made possible by increased resources. The number of students using the library during the school year has increased from 4,785 to 22,329.

New departments have been inaugurated as follows: Art, Business administration, Industrial Chemistry, Comparative Literature, Education, Journalism, Missions, Music, Political Science, Religious Education, and Sociology. Ample provision has been made for work in physical education for both men and women. A college nurse has been regularly employed. A full-time Director of Publicity has been added to the staff.

The total budget of the institution has increased from $68,000 to $250,000. This has been accomplished without breaking the record of the college of never closing a year with a deficit.

During the summer of 1924 a gift of $40,000 on the annuity plan was made to the college by Mr. John W. Guard, of Logansport, Indiana.

Special stress has been placed upon an appeal for men for the ministry. The number of young men at Wittenberg preparing for this work is larger than ever before.

Important advancement along academic lines has been made. The "Quality-Point System" has been adopted, requiring for graduation not only a certain number of hours but also a superior quality of work. Participation in student activities has been definitely limited. Honors Courses have been installed for the special advantage of unusually promising students. The enrollment in classes has been limited to a maximum of thirty students per class or section, placing Wittenberg in this respect in the company of the best colleges of America. Entrance requirements have been raised. Definite pre-professional courses are offered to students expecting to take up a later study of theology, law, medicine, engineering or business administration. The work in education has been much strengthened. Ample provision is made for preparing young people for teaching work in any State.

Extensive property improvements have been made. The new Ferncliff Hall, a dormitory for young women, has been erected and equipped at a cost of $180,000. Through the generosity of the Hon. J. L. Zimmerman, an extensive addition has been made to the Zimmerman Library. Changes and improvements have been made in Carnegie Science Hall, Recitation Hall and Myers Hall. A new building has been purchased and equipped for the School of Music. New quarters have been provided for the new Wittenberg Academy. A pipe organ has been installed in the college chapel. Extensive improvements have been made about the campus, including a new and attractive entrance. With the help of generous citizens of Springfield a magnificent stadium has been erected.

The Summer School has increased its schedule to two terms during each summer with a heavy increase in enrollment.

The Wittenberg Academy has been completely reorganized and has been fully recognized as a school of the first grade.

The School of Music has made remarkable progress, enrolling 130 students in its second year.

The well-known Warren Military Band School has been removed to Springfield in connection with the School of Music, and is now known as the Wittenberg-Warren Military Band School.

An Extension Department has begun its work, offering courses in the afternoons and evenings in Springfield and nearby cities.

An annual Educational Conference for the benefit of the students of the Saturday School and Summer School is now being held.

Plans for the establishment of a School of Religion have been approved by the Board of Directors.

A new system of Accounting devised by Ernst and Ernst has been installed and arrangements made for an annual audit of all college books by the above firm.

A Students' Service Bureau has been established for the purpose of aiding students in finding spare-time work.

Three Graduate Scholarships have been established for aiding graduates of the College and Seminary to do graduate study.

The annual celebration of "Founders' Day" with appropriate exercises has been begun.

All student organizations have been financed through a Wittenberg Student Campaign.

Control of College athletics has been completely reorganized with the establishment of a new Board of Athletic Control directly responsible to the Board of Directors.

During the past year the college expended over $16,000 in providing aid for deserving students.

Urgent needs of the college at the present time are: An addition to Carnegie Science Hall or a second Science Building; a new building for Administration and Recitation purposes; a Gymnasium; Dormitory for young men; additional Endowment.

The great problem before Wittenberg at the present time is that of meeting the requirements of the conditional offer made by the General Education Board. A gift of $233,000 from this Board will come to Wittenberg if there can be added to the endowment of the institution before May 1, 1925, $467,000. Of this amount $325,000 is yet to be raised. This is much more than can be expected to come in by way of regular payment upon appeal pledges.

HAMMA DIVINITY SCHOOL

Springfield, Ohio

Rev. L. H. Larimer, D.D., *Dean*

This institution suffered a deep grief and loss in the taking away by death September 1, 1923, of Dean V. G. A. Tressler, Ph.D., D.D., Dr. Tressler had a large and influential place in the work of the Church.

During the biennium three new men have been elected to the Faculty— Rev. E. E. Flack, M.A., S.T.M., Professor of Old Testament Language and Literature; Rev. Allen O. Becker, D.D., Professor of Christian Missions; and Rev. John O. Evjen, Ph.D., Professor of Church History. Prof. L. H. Larimer, D.D., was transferred from the Department of the Old Testament to the Department of Homiletics and Practical Theology. In addition to these regular professors, courses of instruction are given in Public Speaking and Church Music, and special lectures on Religious Education, Sociological Problems, Modern Church Movements, and Liturgics, by different members of the Faculty of Wittenberg College. The Faculty has been reorganized by the appointment of Professor L. H. Larimer as Dean, and Professor E. E. Flack as Registrar.

The Seminary is equipped with a regular faculty, supplemented by special lecturers, so as to be able to give extensive and well-balanced courses. Each department is so co-ordinated with the other departments that the instruction given produces in an articulated way a combined and organized effect upon the mind and life of the students. Modern methods of instruction are employed, and careful, critical investigation of the problems of theological scholarship is pursued in each department. While not overlooking or undervaluing the worth of scholarly attainments, as necessary in this day to be able ministers of the New Testament, yet this Seminary judges its students not only as scholars, but also as pastors and preachers.

Without interfering with their school work, but rather contributing to it under the direction of the faculty, the students of the Middler and Senior Classes are engaged in preaching in vacant churches, and thus are helping in the practical work of the Church during their student days.

The school is committed to a whole Evangelicalism. The faculty and students work together with a zeal and fellowship of a high order.

The school will give itself in the next few years to an intensive and extensive search and finding of proper young men for the ministry, and has set for the goal in the very near future an average annual enrollment of sixty men. This Seminary pledges itself anew to the large mission and plan of the United Lutheran Church.

ROANOKE COLLEGE

Salem, Va.

For Men

Founded 1853

Rev. Charles J. Smith, D.D., *President*

The enrollment for the session of 1923-24 was as follows:

Regular Session 232
Summer Session 126
Extension Courses 181

Total 539

The enrollment represents students from fifteen different states and two foreign countries. In religious affiliation the Lutherans show the largest group, with the remainder scattered among eleven other Christian denominations.

Nineteen full-time professors and five part-time instructors compose the faculty. For the next session the enrollment will be limited to 230 students. This is in keeping with the avowed program of the college to matriculate only that number of students which can be taught in small classes where there is intimate personal contact of students with professors and with one another.

Extension and summer school work have been carried on with gratifying results.

The campus activities of the students have been most successful. Literary societies, debating teams, student publications, the fraternities, and the Y. M. C. A. have functioned on a high-minded plane, while there has been little or no disciplinary action necessary under the present student government program. Roanoke won the state collegiate championship both in football and baseball.

Upon recommendation of the facuty, the Trustees have announced the offering of a new degree course, namely, "Bachelor of Science in Education." All candidates for this degree must complete a minimum of 30 hours in summer and extension courses conducted by Roanoke College, and must spend in residence at Roanoke College at least three summer sessions or a total of eighteen weeks.

Roanoke takes pleasure in announcing that Dr. Luther A. Fox, who has given up the chair of philosophy which he has occupied with distinction for so many years, has accepted a newly created chair of Bible and Christianity to which his whole time will hereafter be given. The college congratulates both itself and its students upon commanding the ripe scholarship and the inspirational personality of Dr. Fox in this important field of Religious Education.

The Board has authorized a two-year program for financing an appeal for $700,000 which will be used to erect two new buildings and to bring the endowment funds to a total of $1,000,000.

Roanoke College is being challenged for service as never before in her history. While its church constituency is greatly limited both numerically and financially, its administrators look forward in faith that ways may be found to carry on the enlarged program made necessary by the new educational demands of these present times.

NEWBERRY COLLEGE

Newberry, S. C.

For Men and Women

Founded 1856

Prof. S. J. Derrick, LL.D., *President*

The College session of 1923-24 showed an enrollment by classes as follows: Post graduates, 3; seniors, 60; juniors, 38; sophmores, 73; freshmen, 103; sub-freshmen, 19; total, 306. Forty-five seniors received diplomas on June 10th, the largest class in the history of the College.

The total enrollment of students in the summer term of the College, July 9-August 17, 1923, was 207. Prof. Jas. C. Kinard was director of the summer school. The term of 1924 will begin July 1st and continue six weeks, with Prof. Kinard again as director. The summer term is of great value to the work of the college in the opportunity it gives students to smooth out irregularities, and for prospective students of mature age out of reach of good high schools to make the entrance requirements. The normal training work done at this term for the public school teachers is an important contribution to the educational interests of this state.

Newberry has had a good year. The order has been good, the habits of the students generally have been steady and correct; their conduct in public has been most gratifying.

Our students won the triangular debate, stood in the first division in the oratorical and the glee club contests, won the state championship in basketball and were rated one of the "big four" in the southern basketball tournament held in Macon, Georgia.

The first of January this year saw the completion of the new gymnasium, one of the very best in the state. The total cost was about $36,000, and the citizens of Newberry have promised to provide the full cost.

The standing committee, convinced that a new dormitory is a necessity in the further progress of the college, decided to proceed with the erection of one, modern in equipment and large enough to accommodate nearly one hundred students. Building is now going on and the dormitory will be ready this fall. The total cost will be about $57,000, and there will be funds available to pay this cost up to about $45,000.

The requirements set forth by the Southern Association of Colleges for a standard college can be met by Newberry College in every particular except one, namely, that a standard college, except a tax-supported college, shall have an endowment of $500,000. The time is near when this State, just as North Carolina and Virginia have already done, will reduce in rank every college unable to reach the requirements set by the Southern Assoction. The enrollment for 1923-24 has been, men, 254; women, 47.

SUSQUEHANNA UNIVERSITY AND SCHOOL OF THEOLOGY

Selinsgrove, Pa.

For Men and Women

Founded 1858

Rev. Charles T. Aikens, D.D., *President*

During the biennium Susquehanna University has enjoyed a splendid increase in enrollment, so that we are pleased to report, including the summer school of 1923, an attendance for the year closing June, 1924, of 738. The endowment has been increased and additional grounds have been purchased.

The laboratory and classroom equipment has been increased and improvements have been made to the athletic field and the running track.

A large new heating plant has been installed at a cost of more than $25,000, which provides heating facilities for double the present demands.

Building operations are now on, which will give the University a large dining hall and kitchen, a chapel to seat 500 people and dormitory rooms for 70 additional young women. We now have 50 more student applications than we are able to accommodate.

During the past year Susquehanna has sustained great loss in the death of two staunch members of the Board of Directors, Rev. A. H. Spangler, D.D., and Mr. William Decker, A.M., and one most excellent teacher in the Theological Seminary, Rev. J. B. Focht, D.D., a born teacher and a most lovable man in every respect.

The Theological Seminary is in splendid condition with 28 students enrolled for the coming year. The importance of the Theological Seminary of the Susquehanna University can not be overestimated.

Susquehanna is one of the most conveniently and beautifully located institutions of the Lutheran Church and is within easy reach of more than 350 of our congregations, located within a radius of 75 miles of Selinsgrove, one of the cleanest and best-kept boroughs of central Pennsylvania. The enrollment 1923-24 has been, men, 280; women, 147.

MUHLENBERG COLLEGE, ALLENTOWN, PA.

For Men

Founded 1867

Rev. J. A. W. Haas, D.D. LL.D., *President*

Muhlenberg College reports "still further progress"; 350 students enrolled in college, and in preparatory school 160 students. The Arts Department, in which both Greek and Latin are required, holds its own. The largest increase is in the Science Course and the Philosophy Course.

In order that the professors may have opportunity for further development the Board has again affirmed the rule of the sabbatical year.

In the problem of student government and life we have introduced a strict system of monthly control for those who are backward in their work, and a system dropping students who do not properly take care of unexcused absences.

When, recently, the Committee on Standards of the Association of Colleges and Preparatory Schools of the Middle States reported on the colleges which met the new and higher standards, Muhlenberg College was one of the colleges approved.

The State of New York has also admitted it to its list of approved colleges, and it is well known how strict are the standards of the Educational Department of New York.

The campaign for $1,000,000 begun last winter, has now gone "over the top," and the money is coming in nicely.

Ground was broken for the erection of the library and science building during commencement week. Construction of the science building will begin this summer. The enrollment, 1923-24, has been 482. Women are enrolled in the extension courses.

THIEL COLLEGE, GREENVILLE, PA.

For Men and Women

Founded 1870

Rev. Carl A. Sundberg, D.D., *President*

We are glad to report continued progress during the biennium at Thiel College materially, numerically and scholastically.

A new regime was inaugurated when the present incumbent assumed his duties as president on Founder's Day, February 2, 1923. With no president at the helm since July 1, 1921, when Dr. H. W. Elson, Litt.D., resigned, many matters needed attention, adjustment, and reorganization. This primary objective was attained in the adoption of modern business methods.

We are sorry to state that to date only one-third of the anticipated goal of $500,000 of the Semi-Centennial Campaign has been realized, so that the monetary receipts have not kept pace with our advancement along other lines. Our crying need is for an adequate endowment, or income; it is absolutely necessary to supplement the 39 per cent which the students contribute toward their education.

Our endowment is less than $108,000, while we ought to have half a million dollars at least. A friend has offered $10,000, if nine others will each contribute a similar amount.

Numerically, we have made splendid progress. With 58 freshmen and a few specials in 1922-1923, we had 102 freshmen in 1923-24, plus 16 specials, or a total of 118; and there were enough other new students entered in the upper classes so that over one-half of the entire student body was composed of new students. The total enrollment is now 484 (110 women), or a gain of 103 over last year. Last year there were 24 graduates, 15 women and 9 men; and 8 of the 9 men are students for the ministry. At our 1924 commencement we graduated 34—17 women and 17 men—the largest class in the history of the college.

And we commemorated the fiftieth anniversary of the graduation of the first class, in 1874—a class of 6, of whom 3 are still living, Mr. John M. Bott, of Greensburg; Rev. Geo. L. Rankin, of Wilkinsburg, and Dr. T. B. Roth, "Thiel's Grand Old Man." Dr. Roth also celebrated the thirtieth anniversary of his connection with his alma mater.

A feature of commencement week was the unveiling of the Alumni Association of a memorial tablet in the college chapel, in honor of Henry Warren Roth, D.D., LL.D., first president of Thiel College 1870-1887, beloved preacher, teacher, philanthropist.

Scholastically, we are happy to report that Thiel College is fully accredited. Thiel holds membership in the Association of American Colleges, and the Association of Colleges and Preparatory Schools of the Middle States and Maryland, besides being recognized by the State Departments of Education of both Pennsylvania and New York.

Thiel conducts a six weeks' Summer School for Teachers, with 120 in attendance this summer. It also conducts a Lake School of Biology at Conneaut Lake—the only Lake School of Biology in the state of Pennsylvania. Besides, there is the annual summer school for church workers, generally held the last week in July, with fine faculty and interesting, instructive and inspiring sessions.

All in all, Thiel is growing bigger and better, for the glory of God and the welfare of mankind.

CARTHAGE COLLEGE, CARTHAGE, ILL.

Founded 1870

For Men and Women

Rev. Harvey D. Hoover, Ph.D., D.D., *President*

The college advanced during the past biennium in a significant way. There were enrolled over seven hundred students. The graduates numbered ninety-three.

The Semi-Centennial Fund of $400,000 was paid in by the district synods during this biennium. This fund, together with $125,000 pledged by the people of Hancock County, and the $175,000 promised by the General Education Board, brings the endowment almost to $900,000.

There has been added to the college property a beautiful forest preserve which includes a small lake. Here the departments of botany and zoology cultivate and care for all forms of life. A ten-acre athletic field was purchased and is being improved and equipped.

During this biennium six missionaries educated in part at Carthage, were sent into the foreign field; candidates for the ministry were preparing in five different Lutheran Theological Seminaries.

The Carthage faculty has been trained in more than thirty of the leading universities and colleges in America and Europe. The president is now president of the Federation of Illinois Colleges.

Carthage is the only Lutheran College on the approved list of the Association of American Universities.

The college conducted its fiftieth commencement exercises in 1924. There were present the first graduate of the college, Rev. J. M. Cromer, D.D., of Casper, Wyo.; Prof. E. F. Bartholomew, Ph.D., L.H.D., only survivor of first faculty; first football coach, Prof. R. H. McKee, LL.D., now of Columbus University, together with many other prominent alumni. The forty years of service of Dean W. K. Hill were recognized at this commencement. The enrollment, 1923-24 has been, men, 134, women, 116.

WAGNER COLLEGE, STATEN ISLAND, NEW YORK CITY
Founded 1883
For Men
Rev. A. H. Holthusen, A.M., D.D., *President*

Wagner College is the property of the Evangelical Lutheran New York Ministerium, in the spirit of which the work is carried out. The trustees appoint the faculty and are constantly in touch and consultation with it.

With an initial capital of ten dollars, a student body of six, and a faculty of pastors of Rochester, New York, Wagner College began its work in 1883. Impressed and moved by the special need of the time, the pastors Alexander Richter, then in Rochester, and George H. Gomph, of Pittsford, New York, planned an institution which should give to prospective ministers of the Lutheran Church the preparatory training that would enable them to officiate in German as well as in English.

During the first year of its existence the institution was known as the Lutheran Pro-seminary. Its name was changed, however some years later when through the generous interest of John C. Wagner, of Rochester, it received $12,000 to purchase new quarters on Oregon Street. The new name adopted was Wagner Memorial Lutheran College.

Until 1888 the college was under the control and chiefly maintained by Zion Lutheran Church, Rochester, but in that year it was transferred to the New York Ministerium. This body has since that time pledged itself to provide the expenses of administration.

In 1918 in accordance with the desires of the New York Ministerium the college was moved from Rochester, New York, to Staten Island This was necessary in order to provide sufficient room for future expansion of the work of the college. Thirty-eight acres of property, the old Cunard estate, with four buildings, were acquired. This provided dormitory quarters, class rooms, and the basis for two professors' dwellings. These last two were remodeled and a new home built for the president.

In 1921 the ministerium voted and appropriation of $185,000, with which to build a dormitory and professors' dwellings, and to make repairs and changes. At the present time the new dormitory and three new cottages for professors are finished.

In 1922 the alumni of the college bought of the Vanderbilt property of fifteen acres adjoining our campus. This, with five additional acres which we needed, increases the acreage of the campus to fifty-seven acres.

Wagner College has the usual course of four years in the liberal arts. There is also a high school department, with a four-year general course. The faculty numbers thirteen professors and two assistants. Eighty-five per cent of the graduates enter the ministry.

Wagner College does not offer any degrees. New York State requires an endowment fund of $500,000 before it grants permission to give degrees. The institution is planning to raise this amount of money in 1925.

The healthful location of Wagner, overlooking the ocean, on one of the highest points along the Atlantic coast, is a decided advantage. The institution boasts of a campus that is rarely equaled for beauty. The enrollment for the past year has been 72.

MIDLAND COLLEGE AND WESTERN THEOLOGICAL SEMINARY
Fremont, Nebraska
For Men and Women
Founded 1887
Rev. J. F. Krueger, Ph.D., *President*

The biennium has marked the inauguration of the Greater Midland Campaign. The Board of Trustees, in June, 1923, decided to ask the constituent synods of the college to co-operate in raising the sum of $500,000, this money to be used toward wiping out the existing deficit the erecting of new buildings, and the increasing of the endowment fund. By unanimous vote the synods declared themselves in favor of this movement, the German Nebraska Synod specified that all funds collected in their congregations should be used only for endowment. The sum of $320,000 has been subscribed up to the present time. The campaign has been vigorously pursued and will be completed as soon as possible.

A definite building program has been outlined and adopted. This year the new gymnasium-commons building and the central heating plant will be completed. The foundation measurements of the building are 74x130 feet, with 40x40 feet additional for the heating plant. The building cost $125,000.

This first handsome building constitutes only the preamble in the Midland building program. It is planned to lay the foundation of the new dormitory for women this fall. The sum of $50,000, which Mr. and Mrs. Henry C. Luckey have so generously given, will be used toward the erection of this much-needed building.

Midland has had a remarkable growth in its student body since it was moved to Fremont. In all its departments Midland shows an increase of over 300 per cent within the past five years; while the college department alone has grown 165 per cent.

During the past two years special attention has been paid to strengthening the science department of the college. New equipment has been purchased and the teaching force has been increased.

Midland has always emphasized the fact that it is a Christian and a Lutheran college. The religious organizations have flourished. We are especially glad to report that scarcely ever in the history of the college have there been as many and as promising young men looking forward to the gospel ministry. More and more our young men realize the wonderful greatness of this calling. The enrollment, 1923-24 was, men, 163, women, 362.

Practically all Midland students who expect to study for the ministry enter the Western Theological Seminary. This Seminary is absolutely necessary for the development of the mission territory in the Middle West. It would have been impossible to build up the Lutheran Church in this promising section of the country without the pastors who have been sent forth from the Western Seminary. Many of the graduates of this school of the prophets serve as pastors of our bi-lingual congregations.

The teaching force of the Seminary has been materially strengthened by the acquisition of Rev. Robert L. Patterson as a member of the faculty. He entered upon his duties at the beginning of the Seminary year 1923-24. His specific work is the teaching of the English Bible and Practical Theology.

Midland College appreciates deeply the generous support which the Board of Education has again granted during the biennium. Without this appropriation it would be absolutely impossible to carry on the work of the institution.

Lenoir College, Hickory, N. C.

For Men and Women

Founded 1891

Rev. John C. Perry, D.D., *President*

The most outstanding event of the college during the biennium was the appeal for additional funds following only three and one-half years after a previous effort which had yielded over $300,000. In the last appeal the net result was $465,000 in cash and unconditional pledges. At least $200,000 of this is to be used for the erection of new buildings and the remainder is to be added to the endowment fund.

At the present time Highland Hall (a boys' dormitory erected 18 years ago) is being thoroughly renovated, and a new gymnasium is being completed. Within 30 days ground will be broken for a new $100,000 fireproof dormitory for girls.

During this biennium eighteen and one-half acres of additional land has been purchased at a cost of $30,000. This land is adjoining the old campus of eighteen acres and will make possible the future material development of the institution.

The enrollment of the institution has continued to grow. During 1923-24, 262 students were enrolled in the regular college classes. The special students and those in the summer school bring the enrollment considerably above 500, of which number 322 were women.

During the past year one new department was added and three new professors were employed. About 2,600 volumes were added to the library, and several thousands of dollars were spent for laboratory material and apparatus.

Waterloo College and Seminary, Waterloo, Ontario, Canada

For Men

Founded 1911

Rev. E. Hoffman, D.D., *President*

College commencement on May 30th and Seminary graduation on June 6th closed a very successful biennium in the history of this institution. Owing to building operations during the past year the number of students had to be restricted, the total enrollment being 50 in the College and 11 in the Seminary. The new Administration Building Annex being completed, a large increase can be cared for during the year 1924-1925. This annex, which was formally dedicated May 25th, furnishes additional dormitory accommodation, 8 modern class rooms, an up-to-date science room and laboratory, a gymnasium with complete equipment, an assembly hall with a seating capacity of 400, a new heating plant, toilet and wash rooms, fireproof vault and a number of store rooms. With the completion of this new building one of the great problems of the past has found its solution. In addition to the regular Ontario high school course, a Faculty of Arts has been created, which will furnish a four years' course equivalent to the Arts Course of the Canadian University. Dr. A. C. Potter has been appointed Dean of the Faculty of Arts.

The College has continued to furnish Seminary students; every one of the seven Seminary graduates of the past biennium has been secured through the College, and at least 50 per cent of the 49 collegians now enrolled have the ministry in view. About 20 per cent of the collegians are non-Lutheran. The combined faculty numbers nine and one instructor; seven being ordained ministers. The total number of graduates since 1911 is 31, two of whom died, while 29 are in active service in the provinces of Ontario, Nova Scotia, Saskatchewan and Alberta, and one in the foreign field.

The approximate annual expenditure required to run the institution is $22,000, of which the Canada Synod is expected to contribute 75 per cent and the Central Canada Synod 25 per cent.

SASKATOON COLLEGE AND SEMINARY, SASKATOON, SASK., CANADA

For Men and Women

Founded 1913

Rev. H. W. Harms, *President*

The enrollment for 1922-23 was 32, and that for 1923-24 was 49 (12 women). Fourteen students have the ministry in view.

The completion of our new recitation hall, which was built from the proceeds of our campaign in the United Lutheran Church, represents a big step forward. We have now at least a commodious building, where we can do our work, and in addition we have been able to buy some equipment.

Under conditions prevailing here, the preparatory work is of chief importance, and we have been able during the biennium, to bring this department up to that grade of efficiency which enables us to hold our own against the state high schools on the territory. As our classes are smaller than those in the state high schools, we have aimed to give our students a large amount of personal attention with the result, that all our high school graduates were able to pass the examinations prescribed by the provincial Department of Education. The time has come, however, when it is imperative to focus our attention on the Theological Department, and it has therefore been decided to call another professor. It seems quite possible at the present time, to get, in addition to the young men trained by ourselves, a number of students from Europe.

A very gratifying feature during the last biennium has been, that our people apparently begin to realize the value of the work done in our institution, and are sending their children in larger numbers. If this favorable attitude develops as we hope, a further expansion of our plant will soon be necessary. At the present time we may say, that fully 75 per cent of all the young people from our congregations, going in for high school education, come to our institution, and if we can bring our plant and equipment up to requirements, there is no reason why this high figure should not be maintained or even exceeded. The gain for the church accruing from her congregations can hardly be overestimated. During 1923 a new wave of Lutheran immigration to Western Canada began; almost every boat crossing the Atlantic brings its quota of Lutheran immigrants to Canadian ports. By the efforts of the Lutheran Immigration Board alone over 500 heads of Lutheran families were brought over and placed in our congregations during the last twelve months.

As Saskatoon is the only school and theological seminary of the United Lutheran Church in Canada west of the Great Lakes, its claim on the interest of the United Lutheran Church is unique. There is no doubt that the future of our Church in this part of the country to a very large degree depends on this institution and for these reasons we do not hesitate to urge on the Church at large the importance of bringing this institution to its fullest efficiency. We have asked the Church for $50,000, thereby stating the minimum amount absolutely necessary. About $20,000 are outstanding. This amount ought to be raised at an early date, as the money is most urgently needed for still further equipment.

C—Junior Colleges

COLLEGIATE INSTITUTE, MT. PLEASANT, N. C.

For Men

Founded 1854

Prof. G. F. McAllister, A.M., *Principal*

The Collegiate Institute has had gratifying patronage the past two sessions. In 1922-23 there were enrolled 161 from seven states, and in 1923-24 nine states were represented in an enrollment of 173, the largest in the entire history of the school. Fifty-four young men were graduated in these two years; an unprecedented number.

The usual large percentage of these graduates go on to the completion of their college course, and so maintain the record of institute men, Splendid reports come from the higher institutions to which our graduates go, and give evidence of the good work done at the institute.

The gospel ministry as a life-work continues to attract our students. There have been a number of definite commitments during the biennium and there are a number of others seriously considering the ministry. By the time they complete their course here, it is believed that they will have definitely decided to offer themselves for the ministry. Two factors which have undoubtedly contributed to the serious consideration of the subject during the biennium were the presentation of the claims of the gospel ministry by the appointee of synod and an address delivered by Dr. C. S. Bauslin on his visit to the institute during the past session. The goodly number of men who have gone from this institution into the ministry would seem to be an answer to the prayer expressed in the early days by the founders.

The pressing need for additional dormitory space will soon be relieved, it is hoped, thanks to the success of the campaign for funds authorized by the North Carolina Synod and now being conducted. The Executive Committee of the Board planned a campaign for $75,000 for a new dormitory and equipment. The Financial Secretary had secured pledges among the alumni, ex-students and special friends for more than one-third of the amount before the canvass of the congregations began the last of May. More than two-thirds of the amount has now been pledged, and it is confidently believed by the time all the congregations have been canvassed the full amount sought will have been subscribed. So, for session 1925-26, the institute should have a new dormitory and other much needed equipment.

With a meager endowment and with the rising cost of operation, the institute experiences increasing difficulties in current finances. The aid received from the Board of Education, therefore, means much to the institute, and the management is duly appreciative.

The outlook for the next session is encouraging. Already a large number of students have engaged rooms, and the old students are enthusiastically promoting the institute among their friends and acquaintances.

WEIDNER INSTITUTE, MULBERRY, IND.

For Men and Women

Founded 1902

Prof. M. L. Zerkel, *Acting President*

Weidner Institute had an enrollment of 45 (23 men and 22 women) for the school year 1923-24, which was an increase of 10 over that of the year preceding when the attendance had declined by about the same number. Most of the increase was in the academy classes.

The faculty consisted of seven members, of whom four were doing full-time teaching. This included the field secretary who gave part of his time to teaching during the past year.

Of the 22 men in the college and academy classes last year 11 were preparing for the ministry. Several of the girls were planning to take up work of a distinctive Christian character. Four Weidner men were in our Theological Seminaries and two others plan to enter this fall.

Indiana's new law relative to teacher training has been a severe blow to Weidner as at present our work, for teacher training, is not accredited by the State Board of Education. To secure such credit is impossible without additional funds. Since Weidner credits are accepted in Indiana institutions and schools generally in other states, it merely means that students planning to teach must complete their training in other schools. This prevents us from enrolling many young people who contemplate teaching in the elementary schools.

During the past year the income was sufficient to meet all operating expenses, but the deficit of the two previous years has not yet been covered. The net indebtedness was reduced by about $3,000 during the year.

In order to meet an annual operating deficit of about $4,000 for the past biennium about 200 underwriters throughout the Indiana Synod were secured. In nearly all cases these individuals agreed to assist for both years. From that source about $7,500 has been realized for the two years. Such support has enabled Weidner to continue operation but the time is rapidly approaching when income of a more permanent nature must be available.

The matter of relocating has been seriously considered during the year and several prospective sites seem very desirable. It is felt by many that Weidner needs more local support than is available in a small community and the possibility of securing this from other Indiana communities is favorable. Along with the matter of relocation, the plan of changing to a four-year college has also been considered. With one student in college out of every 110 persons in the state the need of a college to our people is evident but the difficulty of supplying that need with our present resources is a serious problem.

D—Institutions for Women

Mont Amoena Seminary, Mt. Pleasant, N. C.

Founded 1859

Rev. Prof. J. H. C. Fisher, A.M., *Principal*

On May 23, 1924, Mont Amoena Seminary ended her sixty-fifth year with a graduating class of 19. Three hundred and forty girls have been graduated from Mont Amoena since the present principal's connection with the school. We have just finished a good year's work with an enrollment of 94; 85 of whom are in the college classes. Mont Amoena has been noted for many years for the fine work she has done along the line of Church work in the Luther League and Missionary

Society.   She has also furnished many teachers for both elementary and high schools.

The class of 1922-23 numbered 18, one of the best classes that we have sent out.   This makes 37 young women that we have sent out during the biennium.   Mont Amoena has furnished a good Christian home and a fine school for these girls and her influence will be an inspiration and help to them through life.

MARION JUNIOR COLLEGE, MARION, VIRGINIA

Founded 1873

Rev. C. Brown Cox, A.M., D.D., *President*

Marion Junior College has had a successful biennium.   During both years there has been capacity enrollment.   Class room work has maintained a high level and campus conditions have been satisfactory.   If the serious criticisms directed against campus life in general are true, then campus conditions at Marion are a remarkable exception.   At Marion the campus life is clean and wholesome.

During the biennium two new buildings have been constructed.   One is a gymnasium, which has ample floor space to provide for all indoor games, including basketball and tennis.   The other increases the dormitory, class room and dining room space so that the college will be able to accommodate one hundred and twenty-five boarding students.   It is the purpose of the college not to increase its capacity beyond this limit.

Recently the Board of Trustees secured amendments to the college charter which bring it into conformity with the requirements of the United Lutheran Church as expressed at the Washington Convention. Under the amended charter two-thirds of the members of the Board of Trustees and the President of the college must be members of congregations in organic connection with the Lutheran Synod of Virginia.   Provision is made for retirement of the present members of the Board of Trustees, and all vacancies on Board must be filled by election by the Lutheran Synod of Virginia.   Thus Marion Junior College not only belongs to the Church, but henceforth it will be controlled by the Church through a Board of Trustees elected by the Synod.

The graduating class of 1924 consisted of 24 young women of whom 18 were Lutherans.   This answers the question as to whether the college is serving the Lutheran Church.   When diplomas were presented to the members of the graduating class of 1924, there was attached to each diploma a Virginia State Teachers' Certificate, issued by the State Board of Education, good for six years and renewable, entitling the graduate to teach in all of the public schools of the state, both grammar schools and high schools.   This indicates the standard of work which the college is doing and the value placed upon it by the state of Virginia.

The date of founding of the college is usually given as 1873, but the first charter was granted by the Virginia Legislature in 1874; therefore 1874 may be properly regarded as the date of founding. Upon this basis the college is now 50 years old, and extensive preparations are being made for celebration of the semi-centennial in the fall of 1924.

Having this background of 50 years of service to the Church, the friends of the college who have made it what it is are determined that it shall render still greater service to the Church during the next half century. Therefore they have taken action placing the college directly under the control of the Church and are giving their money for increase and development of plant and equipment. The outlook for the college is more promising than ever before.

Summerland College, Leesville, S. C.

Founded 1912

Rev. P. E. Monroe, D.D., *President*

On May 27, 1924, Summerland College ended the twelfth year of work. The past biennium was marked by growth in numbers and in the advancement of the standard work done. The number of students in the college department has increased each succeeding yeor of the institution's history.

Every member of the student body is a Christian. About 80 per cent are members of the Lutheran Church. The regular church services were well attended and every member of the student body was a member of the Mission and Bible study classes.

The finances of the institution are in excellent condition, there being no current expense debts. The new brick and stone dormitory which was erected and furnished two years ago at a cost of $75,000 has a debt of $5,365.

There is a growing interest in this college for young women in South Carolina. The Board of Trustees and President are very grateful for the assistance given us by the Board of Education of the United Lutheran Church.

President Monroe has recently resigned to accept a pastorate at Hickory, N. C.

Recommendations

The Board submits for your favorable consideration the following:

1. *Resolved*, That we renew most gratefully our acknowledgment of the guidance and blessing of the great Head of the Church in behalf of the Educational Department of our work, and that we herewith renew our pledges of fidelity to this sacred cause, the divine method of bringing to pass the coming of our Lord's Kingdom throughout the world.
2. *Resolved*, That we herewith acknowledge with particular gratitude

the generous gifts of those who have participated in the unusually large amount given during the biennium as annuity gifts for the perpetual carrying on of the various activities of the Board.

3. *Resolved,* That we have learned with gratification of the steps being taken by ten of the Eastern Synods toward the early establishment of a College for Women. We bespeak for this a successful consummation during the coming biennium and we shall rejoice in liberal gifts from friends throughout its large constituency, to make possible an ideal equipment for this greatly needed institution.

4. *Resolved,* That the authority granted at the last Convention looking toward plans for co-operation in educational work with other general bodies of Lutherans, especially in the Northwest and on the Pacific coast, be renewed for the coming biennium, upon the same terms, namely: all plans for such co-operation to be subject to the approval of the Executive Board.

5. *Resolved,* That the Synods and the Board of Home Missions and Church Extension be urged to co-operate in securing and equipping adequate church or school buildings, or other facilities, for the better service of our Lutheran students in non-Lutheran educational centers.

6. *Resolved,* That the Board proceed as soon as possible, through its University Work Department, to organize accredited Schools of Religion in the university centers.

Respectfully submitted,

ALONZO J. TURKLE, *President.*

HOWARD R. GOLD, *Recording Secretary.*

FREDERICK G. GOTWALD, *Executive Secretary.*

REPORT OF THE TREASURER OF THE BOARD OF EDUCATION

for the Fiscal Year Ended July 31, 1923

GENERAL ACCOUNT

Balance on hand August 1, 1922................ $3,800.42

RECEIPTS

Treasurer United Lutheran Church on Apportionment	$93,300.00	
Treasurer United Lutheran Church Women's Missionary Society	4,230.19	
Treasurer United Lutheran Church Waterloo Seminary Professorship	1,316.49	
Treasurer United Lutheran Church Miscellaneous	688.00	
Miscellaneous Receipts	1,897.33	
Income from Annuity Fund Investments........	728.26	
Interest on Deposits..........................	174.12	102,334.39

$106,134,81

DISBURSEMENTS

Pacific Seminary Budget	$2,700.00	
Pacific Seminary Special	296.25	
Northwestern Seminary Special	50.19	
Southern Seminary Budget	2,083.33	
Saskatoon Seminary Budget	1,250.00	
Waterloo Sem. and College Budget	2,083.33	
Waterloo Sem. and College Special	1,426.49	
Chicago Seminary Budget	833.33	
Hartwick Seminary Budget	1,000.00	
Martin Luther Seminary Budget	500.00	
Breklum-Kropp Seminary Budget	2,291.66	
Thiel College Budget	1,500.00	
Wittenburg College Budget	1,500.00	
Wagner College Budget	2,083.33	
Summerland College Budget	1,500.00	
	$21,097.91	$106,134.81
Special, Wagner College	$10.00	
Lenoir College Budget	1,800.00	
Marion College Budget	2,083.33	
Muhlenberg College Budget	1,500.00	
Roanoke College Budget	2,500.00	
Newberry College Budget	3,000.00	
Weidner Institute Budget	833.33	
Weidner Institute Special	9.00	
Susquehanna University Budget	1,500.00	
Mt. Pleasant Collegiate Institute Budget	1,999.99	
Carthage College Budget	4,166.61	
Carthage College Special	20.00	
Midland College Budget	12,000.00	
Midland College Special	163.33	
Gettysburg College Budget	1,500.00	
Mt. Amoena Seminary Budget	833.33	
Secretaries' Salaries	12,099.99	
Secretaries' Traveling Expenses	3,921.16	
Student Pastors' Salaries	6,914.47	
Students Pastors' Expenses	6,148.48	
Women Student Worker's Salary & Expenses	1,922.29	
Annuities	1,192.00	
Student Asaji Fund from St. Matthew's. Phila. Support of Japanese Student at Mt. Airy Seminary	250.00	
Printing and Publications	5,738.13	
General Expenses	2,224.57	
Office Rent	654.00	
Stenographers	2,532.15	
Telephone and Telegraph	207.50	
Postage	619.86	
Office Supplies	437.42	
Transferred to Ministerial Education Fund	126.00	
Expenses of Meetings (Board & Executive)	1,216.17	101,221.02
Balance cash on hand, July 31, 1923		$4,913.79

SASKATOON COLLEGE AND BUILDING FUND

Balance on hand August 1 1922................		$2,238.47

RECEIPTS

Treasurer United Lutheran Church........,.....	$8,514.85	
Miscellaneous ,..............................	30.00	8,544.85

DISBURSEMENTS

Northwestern Mission Board	$10,574.00	
Balance Cash on Hand	209.32	
	$10,783.32	$10,783.32

PERMANENT MINISTERIAL EDUCATION FUND
PRINCIPAL ACCOUNT

Miscellaneous Receipts	$705.08

SCHOLARSHIP AND LOAN FUND FOR WOMEN

Balance on hand August 1, 1922................	$280.00

RECEIPTS

Individuals, etc.	$1,260.00	
Interest on Deposit	27.50	
Interest on Bond of Mandon North Dakota....	60.00	1,347.50

DISBURSEMENTS

Invested (see list) Bond & Accrued Int.........	$979.27	
Cash	50.00	
Balance Cash on Hand	598.23	
	$1,627.50	$1,627.50

CALIFORNIA COLLEGE FUND

Balance on hand August 1, 1922................	$60.00

ANNUITIES ACCOUNT

Balance on hand August 1, 1922................	$12,500.00

RECEIPTS

Miss Louise E. Rehm .....:..................	$100.00	
Miss Louise E. Rehm, Additional	500.00	
Rev. Frederick Beates	1,000.00	
Sister Alice L. Ott	100.00	
H. A. Willery	1,500.00	3,200.00
		$15,700.00

DISBURSEMENTS

Invested (see list)	$15,403.19	
Accrued Interest on Investments Purchased....	228.94	
Cash on hand	67.87	
	$15,700.00	$15,700.00

INVESTMENTS
ANNUITIES ACCOUNT

5,000 Bell Telephone Co. of Pa. 1st Ref. Mtge. 5's 1948	$4,918.75	
2,000 Phila. Electric 1st Mtge 5's 1966		
1,000 Phila. Electric 1st Mtge.		
1,000 Phila. Electric 1st Mtge.		
500 Phila. Electric 1st Mtge.		
100 Phila. Electric 1st Mtge.	4,574.37	
3,000 Pa. R. R. Eq. 5's due 1938................	2,974.80	
1,000 Ches. & Ohio Eq. 5's due 1935............	969.67	
2,000 Pa. R. R. Eq. 5's due 1938...............	1,965.60	$15,403.19

SCHOLARSHIP AND LOAN FUND FOR WOMEN

1,000 City of Mandon, N. Dakota (Gift of Catherine A. Dussel)	$1,000.00	
1,000 Ches. & Ohio Eq. 5's due 1935...........	969.68	1,969.68
		$17,372.87

Respectfully submitted,

JOHN M. SNYDER,
Treasurer.

Philadelphia, 20th November, 1923.

We have audited the accounts of the Board of Education of the United Lutheran Church in America for the year ended 31st July, 1923, and we certify that the foregoing report of the Treasurer is in accordance with the books of account and is correct.

LYBRAND, ROSS BROS. & MONTGOMERY,
Accountants and Auditors.

REPORT OF THE TREASURER OF THE BOARD OF EDUCATION

for the Fiscal Year Ended 31st July, 1924

GENERAL ACCOUNT

Balance on hand August 1, 1923................	$4,913.79

RECEIPTS

Treasurer United Lutheran Church on Apportionment	$105,917.20
Treasurer United Lutheran Church Women's Missionary Society	3,000.00
Treasurer United Lutheran Church Waterloo Seminary, Special	998.96
Treasurer United Lutheran Church, Miscellaneous	522.18
Augustana Synod for Religious Work at the Universities	2,000.00
Lutheran Student's Work Committee of Phila.	1,500.00
Income from Annuity Fund Investments........	955.00
Saskatoon College and Seminary Building Fund..	998.52

Miscellaneous Receipts	795.00	
Interest on Deposits	79.87	116,766.73
		$121,680.52

DISBURSEMENTS

Pacific Seminary Budget	$2,700.00
Pacific Seminary Special	295.18
Southern Seminary Budget	2,916.67
Waterloo Seminary and College Budget	2,916.67
Waterloo Seminary and College Special	693.17
Mt. Airy Seminary Special	25.00
Gettysburg Seminary Special	69.00
Saskatoon Seminary and College Budget	1,750.00
Saskatoon Seminary and College Special	1,135.84
Breklum-Kropp Seminary Budget	3,124.99
Hartwick Seminary Budget	1,400.00
Martin Luther Seminary Budget	500.00
Chicago Seminary Budget	1,166.67
Wittenberg College Budget	2,100.00
Wagner College Budget	2,916.67
Thiel College Budget	2,100.00
Susquehanna University Budget	2,100.00
Summerland College Budget	2,100.00
Roanoke College Budget	3,500.00
Newberry College Budget	4,200.00
Muhlenberg College Budget	2,100.00
Muhlenberg College Special	25.00
Lenoir College Budget	1,800.00
Gettysburg College Budget	2,100.00
Gettysburg College Special	146.00
Mt. Pleasant Collegiate Institute Budget	2,000.00
Carthage College Budget	5,833.39
Marion College Budget	2,916.67
Midland College Budget	12,000.00
Mt. Amoena Seminary Budget	1,166.67
Weidner Institute Budget	1,166.67
Secretaries' Salaries	12,099.97
Secretaries' Traveling Expenses	4,952.72
Student Pastors' Salaries	8,434.86
Student Pastors' Expenses	6,641.53
Women Student Work Assistant, Salary and Expenses	2,108.64
Annuities Payments	1,380.50
Printing and Publications	5,216.01
Office Rent	866.00
Stenographers	3,472.67
Telephone and Telegraph	274.41
Postage	653.10
Office Supplies	647.95
General Expenses	2,083.98
Expenses of Meetings (Boards & Executive)	1,373.75

$119,170.35	$121,680.52

Woman's College Specials		$32.00	
Accrued interests on Annuity Investments......		277.24	
		$119,479.59	
Transferred to Annuity Fund.........	$228.94		
Less amount transferred from Saska- toon College Fund.............	9.32	219.62	$119,699.21
Balance Cash on hand July 31, 1924...........			$1,981.31

SCHOLARSHIP AND LOAN FUND FOR WOMEN

Balance on hand August 1, 1923................	$598.23	

RECEIPTS

Interest on Bonds	$50.00	
Interest on Deposit	26.81	
Individuals	27.50	
Treasurer United Lutheran Church............	25.00	
	$727.54	

DISBURSEMENTS

By Cash	$200.00	$527.54

CALIFORNIA COLLEGE FUND

Balance August 1, 1923	$60.00

BREKLUM-KROPP RELIEF FUND

Treasurer United Lutheran Church............	$682.20

PERMANENT MINISTERIAL EDUCATION FUND
PRINCIPAL ACCOUNT

Balance August 1, 1923.......................	$705.08	
Miscellaneous Receipts	496.91	
	$1,201.99	

DISBURSEMENTS

Invested in 1,000 B. & O. 6's 1929 @ 102¼.....	$1,022.50	
Balance on hand		$179.49

PERMANENT MINISTERIAL EDUCATION FUND
INCOME ACCOUNT

Interest on Deposit	$30.10	
Accrued Interest on Investments...............	29.00	
		$1.10

ANNUITIES PRINCIPAL ACCOUNT

Balance on hand August 1, 1923................	$67.87

RECEIPTS

Sept. 25 to Cash	$1,000.00	
1924		
Feb. 28 to Cash	1,000.00	
May 29 to Cash	5,262.33	
June 21 to Cash	12,000.00	
July 31 Transferred from General Fund........	228.94	$19,491.27
		$19,559.14

DISBURSEMENTS

Invested (see list)	$12,104.76	
Balance	7,454.38	
	$19,559.14	$19,559.14

SASKATOON SEMINARY AND COLLEGE BUILDING FUND

Balance on hand August 1, 1923................	$209.32

DISBURSEMENTS

Northwestern Mission Board	$200.00	
Balance transferred to General Fund...........	9.32	$209.32

INVESTMENTS

ANNUITIES ACCOUNT

5,000 Bell Telephone Co. of Pa. 1st Refunding Mtge. 5's 1948.........................	$4,918.75	
4,600 Phila. Electric 1st Mtge. 5's 1966.........	4,574.37	
3,000 Pa. R. R. Eq. 5's due 1938...............	2,974.80	
1,000 Ches. & Ohio Eq. 5's due 1935...........	969.67	
2,000 Pa. R. R. Eq. 5's due 1938...............	1,965.60	
1,000 Bell Tel. of Pa. 1st 5's 1948...............	970.00	
1,000 Pa. R. R. 5's due 1934....................	992.26	
5000 B. & O. 6's due 1929.....................	5,112.50	
1,000 Phila. Elec. 5½'s due 1947................	1,030.00	
5,000 Altoona & Logan Valley 1st Mtge. 4½'s due 1933	4,000.00	
		$27,507.95

SCHOLARSHIP AND LOAN FUND FOR WOMEN

1,000 City of Mandon, North Dakota (Gift of Catherine A. Dussel)	$1,000.00	
1,000 Ches. & Ohio Eq. 5's due 1935...........	969.68	$1,969.68

PERMANENT MINISTERIAL EDUCATION FUND

1,000 B. & O. 6's 1929.........................		$1,022.50
		$30,500.13

Respectfully submitted,

JOHN M. SNYDER,
Treasurer.

Philadelphia, September 2, 1924.

We have audited the accounts of the Board of Education of the United Lutheran Church in America for the year ended July 31, 1924, and we certify that, in our opinion, the foregoing report of the Treasurer is in accordance with the books and is correct.

LYBRAND, ROSS BROS. & MONTGOMERY,
Accountants and Auditors.

By common consent the following paragraphs were permitted to be substituted for corresponding paragraphs in the report as first submitted under the heading "Northwestern and Pacific Seminaries":

"The Buffalo Convention adopted the report of the Survey Commission, approving its findings, among other matters, relative to the locations of the Northwestern Seminary and the Pacific Seminary.

"Since that Convention the Synod of the Northwest has taken no further action on this matter.

"The Pacific Synod has, however, taken action to the effect that it could not do otherwise than adhere to the position unanimously adopted by the Synod in the 1922 Convention in favor of a permanent location of the Pacific Seminary at Seattle, the reasons for which are fully stated in their Statement of Position presented at Buffalo."

Permission was also given to insert the report of Wittenberg College and Hamma Divinity School in the proper place.

Miss Mary Markley, Secretary of the Department for Women Students, delivered an address on the proposed Women's College. The Rev. H. R. Gold, Chairman of the Committee on Students in State Universities, also addressed the Convention.

The Rev. J. Weidley led in prayer, and the convention adjourned until 2:00 P. M.

Afternoon Session

Monday, October 27, 2:00 P. M.

The President called the Convention to order.

Prayer was offered by the Rev. S. N. Carpenter.

The Committee of Reference and Counsel reported. First the

Chairman of the Committee read the following communication from the Chairman of the Japan Lutheran Church:

Osaka, Japan, October 1, 1924.

Rev. F. H. Knubel, D.D., LL.D., Pres.,
    United Lutheran Church in America.

Dear Brother:

It is my privilege and pleasure to carry out the action taken by the annual convention of the United Lutheran Church in Japan held at Arima, Hyogo, Japan, September 6th to 11th, 1924, to the effect that the Japan Lutheran Church send fraternal greetings to the United Lutheran Church in America in convention at Chicago. The Japan Lutheran Church herewith desires to express to you its sincere appreciation of your consecrated and sustained efforts on behalf of the work of extending the Kingdom of God in Japan. Twenty-seven years have elapsed since the first Lutheran work was established in our country. No doubt to our brethren in America the progress of the Church in Japan seems slow, and perhaps sometimes even discouragingly slow, but we witness to the fact that the Kingdom is making steady and sustained progress through your efforts, and we pray that the Lord may richly bless all that the Lutheran Church in America has done and encourage her to still larger and greater labors in the future.

We wish at this time especially to express to the United Lutheran Church in America our heartfelt gratitude for the very generous sympathy of American Lutherans toward our countrymen on the occasion of the dreadful disaster in Tokyo, Yokohama and vicinity. By your public and private expressions of sympathy, by the vast amount of money that you immediately dispatched for relief work, and in various other ways, you have given ample evidence of a brotherly solicitude and affection for us which has deeply impressed not only us but our countrymen at large, and which has done much to make us try to see, through the dark clouds that sometimes seem to threaten, the silver lining of the underlying good will of the Christian people of America.

It is our conviction that there is no power than can save individuals or nations except the power of the Gospel of Jesus Christ, which you and we preach on opposite shores of the Pacific. We believe there is no other program by which men and nations can live together in harmony, peace and prosperity except the Christian program. We believe that there is no remedy for the ills of men and nations except the application of the Gospel of forgiveness, of righteousness, of truth, of love and peace as our Divine Lord and Saviour Jesus Christ proclaimed it and applied it. To the unceasing proclamation of this Gospel have you and we consecrated ourselves. We pledge you our heartiest co-operation, and pray your continued and ever-increasing zeal in your labors for the advancement of the cause of Christ in Japan.

Fraternally,
KOKICHIRO TAKIMOTO,
Chairman, Japan Lutheran Church.

On motion the President was requested to make a proper reply.

The Chairman of the Committee read the following cablegram from Rajahmundry, India. It was received with the same request to the President.

Rajahmundry, October 23, 1924.

Dr. George Drach,
  Edgewater Beach Hotel,
    Chicago, Ill.
India Council in session at Rajahmundry sends greetings. Prays for the success of Convention, also large advance by our Church in rapidly growing world mission.   GRAEFE.

The Committee presented the following resolution which was adopted. (See Minutes, Tuesday P. M., October 28th.—Secy.)

WHEREAS, It is highly desirable that information regarding the work of this Convention, and so far as possible the inspiration of the sessions, be carried to our congregations as fully as possible,

Resolved, That the Executive Board be instructed, at their discretion, to prepare a booklet summarizing the work of this Convention, for general distribution among our members.

The following resolutions were adopted:

Resolved, That the Presidents and Executive Committees of Synods give consideration to a plan by which delegates to this Convention appear before as many congregations as possible for the purpose of describing and reporting the work of the Convention and of the United Lutheran Church during the past biennium.

Resolved, That the Executive Board be instructed to study the problem of securing a more equitable distribution of nominations among the various Synods of the United Lutheran Church and to devise some plan looking toward this end, to be used at the next Convention.

The Chairman of the Committee of Reference and Counsel moved that the report concerning the work of the Women's Missionary Society be taken up tomorrow afternoon immediately after the report of the Committee of Reference and Counsel.

The motion was adopted.

The Chairman of the Committee announced the presence at the Convention of the Revs. Dr. K. K. Olafson, President of the Icelandic Synod, and A. Haapanen, President of the Suomi Synod.

President Olafson was then introduced and addressed the Convention. The response was made by the Rev. F. G. Gotwald.

The Rev. Mr. Haapanen was then presented and after he had addressed the Convention the response was made by the Rev. J. E. Bittle.

The special order at this time being the item in the report of the Executive Board relating to the Pacific Theological Seminary (Item III, B, 3 (a)), the Secretary read the item referred to and in connection therewith Item 1 of the Supplementary Report of the Executive Board. (See Supplementary Report, Wednesday, October 29th.)

After full discussion Item III, B, 3 (a) of the Executive Board's report was adopted by a rising vote. The vote stood 174 in favor of the motion, 59 opposed.

It was moved and carried, That we commend the Pacific Theological Seminary to the hearty support and sympathy of the Church, Synods, congregations and individuals.

Resuming consideration of the report of the Board of Education, recommendations 1, 2, 3, 4, 5 and 6 were adopted.

The report was adopted as a whole.

The Rev. F. O. Evers offered the following resolution concerning Kropp-Breklum Seminary:

In view of the distressing circumstances in which, according to the report, the Seminary at Kropp-Breklum finds itself at this time, and

In view of the valuable contribution to the ranks of the ministry of the Lutheran Church in America by these institutions during a period of forty years, and

In view of the necessity of preserving and strengthening this essential source of supply of pastors for the German-speaking portion of the

Church and for the large Lutheran immigration to be expected in the nearest future,

Be it resolved:

1. That this Convention send greetings to the trustees of the Kropp-Breklum Seminary, to Director Rohnert and the faculty, and assure these brethren of the sincere interest of the United Lutheran Church in America in their work and welfare, and

2. That this Convention request the Executive Board, the Board of Education and the Board of Northwestern Missions to arrange for such an adjustment in the support of this institution as will more adequately meet the present emergency.

A division of the resolution was called for.

The first section of the resolution was then adopted.

It was moved that the following be adopted as a substitute for the second section of the resolution:

That this Convention request the Executive Board, the Board of Education and the Board of Northwestern Missions to aim to adjust the provisions for Kropp-Breklum so as more adequately to meet the needs of the institution.

The substitute was adopted.

The resolution was adopted as a whole.

The Rev. Paul Koller reported for the Special Committee to which had been referred the question of study and report upon the condition of theological education in the United Lutheran Church as follows:

1. *Resolved,* That a commission be appointed to study the subject of theological education in the United Lutheran Church and to report at the next Convention.

(a) This commission shall consist of ten members. At least two of this number shall be members of the Board of Education.
Executive Board, which Board in its appointments shall give due consideration to all sections of the Church.

(b) The appointment of this commission shall be committed to the

2. *Resolved,* That the Board of Education be asked to make a scientific survey of the educational situation in the United Lutheran Church, in those spheres not covered by the Commission on Theological Education, and that

it consider the relation of our educational work to the whole status of religious education in our country and Canada.

(a) That the Board of Education, with the approval of the Executive Board of the United Lutheran Church, be empowered to employ impartial experts outside of the Lutheran Church.

(b) That the Board of Education be asked to report, if possible, at the next Convention.

Signed:

J. A. W. Haas, Chairman,
J. L. Zimmerman,
H. Offermann,
F. P. Manhart,
P. W. Koller.

It was moved and carried, That resolution 1 (a) and (b) be adopted as a substitute for the recommendation of the Executive Board concerning the matter. (See Executive Board's report, XIII, 1.)

Resolution 2, (a) and (b), was adopted.

The report was adopted as a whole.

Dr. W. L. Hunton, Secretary of the Parish and Church-School Board, presented the report of that Board.

REPORT OF THE PARISH AND CHURCH-SCHOOL BOARD

The Problem of Religious Education

The problem of developing Religious Education in our parishes through Church Schools, Bible study and a Weekday Religious Education Program is one of the outstanding tasks of the Church. During the past biennium, the Parish and Church-School Board, realizing the importance of this problem and the magnitude of the task, has given itself especially to the development of plans, methods and material.

With this subject in mind and recognizing its importance, several conferences were held during the biennium. To these conferences, there were invited, in addition to special committees of the Board, persons who had been successful in developing various types of parish education. These conferences proved most fruitful in developing clear ideas of theory and practical plans for the application of the theory.

The Board has prepared a "Hand-Book of Weekday Religious Instruction" which presents a resume of the need, purpose and problems of this type of religious education, together with outlines of various courses in actual use and suggestions for special courses to be introduced. A "Program for Weekday Religious Schools" has been arranged, the literature available for use in the carrying out of such a program being indicated. The Board of Publication has also issued a special catalog of books published by our own Publication House, which are available for use in Weekday Religious Schools. The Junior Class Manual, a pre-confirmation textbook, by the Rev. G. J. Muller, is probably the most important piece of literature which has been published for use in Weekday Schools during the biennium. It is a practical textbook developed through actual use of the material and provides exactly what is needed for use in a school composed of those looking forward to confirmation. In addition, the Lutheran Graded Series is recommended for use in schools, especially where it is not already introduced into the Sunday school.

It will thus be seen that quite an amount of literature is available and definite work is planned. In anticipation of the greater development of this work, the Board has in contemplation the preparation of additional textbooks as part of a Weekday Religious School series of books, treating on the Bible, Church History, Faith, Worship and Work, together with its Liturgy and Hymnology.

Recognizing the importance of this subject, the Board advises that it be included in the synodical programs, and is prepared to co-operate with Synodical Religious Committees in the preparation and presentation of such programs.

For the purpose of gathering statistics and of getting a clearer and more comprehensive view of religious educational conditions in our parishes, an official Questionnaire has been prepared and will be furnished on request. It should be used by all our Synods in seeking information concerning educational work in their parishes.

The Synods are requested to make provision for an officer to be known as Parish and Church-School Secretary or Director of Religious Education. This representative should be one who is familiar with the problems and interested in the work of Religious Education and who will act as a synodical representative to co-operate with the Parish and Church-School Board in unifying and co-ordinating the work.

Teacher Training Schools

In view of the need of training schools for Church workers, this Board, in connection with the Board of Deaconess Work and the Inner Mission Board, has prepared a diploma which is issued by the Parish and Church-

School Board for the completion of definite courses in institutes for the training of Church workers.

Substantial progress has been made toward the perfection of recognized courses for these training schools. The aim is to establish uniform courses with elective subjects of required standards, in order that the diploma will stand, not only for an approved course, but a course with sufficient variation to make it useful in the several departments of teacher training for Christian Service.

1. The Life of Christ.
2. The Bible.
3. Christian Doctrine.
4. Christian Worship.
5. Christian Ethics.
6. Church History.
7. Missions.
8. Practical and Applied Christianity.
9. Pedagogics.

The establishment of such schools is urged upon the Synods, Conferences and communities and the co-operation of the officers of the Board in this work is assured.

OUR BIBLE SCHOOL WORK

Without exception the literature which has been previously published for our English Bible Schools was continued during the biennium. We believe that through the efforts of our editors decided improvements have been made in some of this literature.

In the preparation of the lessons of the uniform series, for use in our Lutheran Schools, owing to the fact that the schedule for 1924, as arranged by the International Lesson Committee, could not be harmonized with the Lutheran Church Year principle, by unanimous action of our Board, the order of the lessons was reversed, making it possible, with slight changes, to present an orderly Church Year schedule. In view of the fact that the schedules for the coming years have been made out in consultation with our own editors, this variation will not occur again and it will be possible for us to use the lessons as scheduled, with slight changes.

Our Lesson Commentary, which was begun in 1922, and which was a continuation of the Lutheran Lesson Commentary of the former General Council, from its first issue, met with a hearty response from the Church. The result is that the Commentary has been continued, and we believe from year to year improved. The Commentary for the year 1925 is already published. The existence of a Commentary of this character makes it possible for our teachers to have all the supplementary material which they may need prepared under our own editors.

The Augsburg Series of Lessons, based on the Uniform Lessons of the International Sunday School Council has steadily gained in circulation and prestige, and is recognized by others than Lutherans as of superior merit. The material furnished for our schools in this entire series has all come from Lutheran pens and passed under the eyes of our own editors. The aim is to provide systematic and intensive Bible study which will increase the knowledge and strengthen the faith of our Lutheran people.

Our Lutheran Graded Series

Our Lutheran Graded Series of Sunday School Lessons has been continued and the various grades published in bound form in new editions from time to time. The scholar's grades have also been published in quarterly or periodical form.

The basic textbook of the entire series, "In Mother's Arms," which is issued both as a bound book and as booklets for the use of the pastor, the superintendent of the school and the superintendent of the Cradle Roll (Font Roll), together with eight quarterly booklets for distribution to mothers of babes, has been issued in a new, revised edition. There is nothing in Sunday school literature of which we have knowledge which will compare with "In Mother's Arms."

For emphasis we give the following list of the official literature of the Church provided for our Bible schools:

In Mother's Arms..................................Eleven Booklets (Cradle Roll)

Primary

Wonderland ....(Scholar's Weekly)   } 4 and
Sunbeams ....(Teacher's Quarterly)   } 5 years

Workland ....(Scholar's Weekly)   } 6 and
Sunshine ....(Teacher's Quarterly)   } 7 years

Pictureland ....(Teacher's Quarterly)   8
Sunrays ....(Scholar's Weekly Picture Card)   and
Picture Charts ....(Department Lesson Chart)   9
Pictureland Weekly ..(Scholar's Weekly)   years

Intermediate Department

(Parallel Courses)

The Graded Course		The Uniform Courses
Bible Story		
10 years		The Junior Lesson Book
Bible Readings		10-12 years
11 years		
Bible History		
12 years		

Bible Facts and Scenes
    13 years
Bible Biography
    14 years
Bible Teachings
    15 years
Bible Outlines
    16 years

The Intermediate Lesson Book
13-16 years

Young People's Department

The Senior Lesson Book
17-20 years

The Adult Department

Adult Bible Class Lesson Book
21 years and above
The Home Department Lesson Book

Teachers' Helps

The Lesson Commentary (Annual Bound Volume)
The Augsburg Teacher (Monthly)

The revision of the Primary Grades of this series is now well advanced. The two years of Wonderland and of Workland have been revised, and Pictureland is now being furnished in revised form. A new revised edition of the picture charts has also been secured. The financial problem in connection with these charts was a difficult one to solve; but by making some modifications in the series, it was possible through the enterprise of the Business Manager of our Publication Board, not only to have a new edition of the charts published, but to secure them at a reduction in price. With the full equipment available for our Primary Schools in all three of the grades, we see no reason why our schools generally should not adopt this series, which is our official primary literature.

In the Intermediate Grades, Bible Story has been the largest seller, and the most popular book in the entire series. It is now issued in revised edition. A general study of the grades, with a view to improvement, is now being made. In the revision of any of the grades and of the system as such, special care is taken to serve the interests of the schools, and to make it possible for schools to use the literature they already have until a better and revised edition of the same grades shall have been provided. We publish this statement to encourage our schools to make use of the system.

PERIODICALS

Our various papers published for distribution to the children of the Church have all enjoyed an increasing circulation during the biennium, and without exception the editors are receiving constant expressions of approval of these periodicals. They are as follows:

"Lutheran Young Folks," an illustrated weekly for older pupils and adults; "Lutheran Boys and Girls," which is a combination Sunday school and Missionary paper for boys and girls, ten to thirteen years of age. The Primary papers for the three grades of the Primary Department, namely, "Sunbeams," "Sunshine" and "Pictureland Weekly," being the papers for the "Wonderland," "Workland" and "Pictureland" grades respectively. The Publication Board also publishes "Little Ones." This paper is not a part of the official literature of the Church, but is continued for those who still use the uniform international lesson for their beginners.

Our Sunday School Standard

Our Sunday School Standard which was approved at the last Convention of the United Lutheran Church has been published through our Magazine and the Church papers. It has also been issued in circular form and in poster form. The purpose is to encourage higher ideals in our schools and to spur them to work up to the standard and secure the certificate which places them in our Roll of Honor.

New Hymnals

At the last Convention of the United Lutheran Church, two hymnals were authorized, a Standard Service Book and a Popular Hymnal. In the development of these hymnals, the Committee of the Parish and Church-School Board has been in constant conference with a Committee of the Common Service Book Committee. The selection of hymns, subject to elimination and revision, has been practically completed, and the determination of the music for the hymns, together with the Order of Service, Lessons, Psalms, Prayers, etc., to be included is well advanced. The aim of the Board is, if possible, to have the text of the two hymnals completed during the present year. If our aims are realized, these official hymnals for our schools should both be issued during the coming biennium.

Libraries

Our workers in our schools and congregations will be materially aided in their work and developed in efficiency through a well established Worker's Library. With this thought in mind, a systematic effort has been made to prepare a recommended list of books for such a library. This list has been tentatively published and is subject to revisions and constant additions. It is proposed to make it available as a guide for the creation of such libraries in all our congregations.

To advance the intellectual and spiritual interests of our young people, a general reading library should be made available. This is particularly the case in congregations where there is not access to public libraries. As a guide in the establishment of these libraries, in local churches, and as a guide also in the efforts to have placed in public libraries books of a proper character which will make for the development of the young people of our congregations, a general reading or library list has been prepared.

This also has been tentatively published and its final appearance in pamphlet form authorized. It is urged that parishes and workers secure copies of these recommended lists of books and use them as guides in the establishment of parish libraries or in requesting additions to public libraries.

THE PROBLEM OF FIELD SECRETARIES

One of the special needs for the advancement of the work of the Parish and Church-School Board is closer contact with the Synods, Conferences and also wherever possible with the congregation and local communities. This contact is necessary to create interest, insure uniformity and efficiency and to inspire to greater thoroughness as well as higher ideals and aims.

To this end having secured through the action of the United Lutheran Church at Buffalo and endorsement of the Executive Board, the assurance of the support of the Church, comprehensive plans have been mapped out and a beginning has been made in the selection of a Field Secretary for the Middle West in the person of the Rev. Charles H. B. Lewis, D.D., who entered upon his duties June 15, 1924. The Board contemplates, through its editors and Field Secretaries, to establish contacts with the whole Church and to co-operate in every way possible in systematizing our educational work and developing a comprehensive religious educational program. This program, according to previous recommendations of the United Lutheran Church, has been thus far worked out to the point that we have recommended the organization of our religious educational forces along synodical and conference lines. In addition, it is the purpose and aim of the Board wherever possible, to co-operate with local communities in the development of Lutheran Training Schools and Teacher Training work and Bible School institutes.

A good beginning in this direction has been made in training schools for Christian workers and an official diploma in which the Board of Deaconess Work and the Inner Mission Board are co-operating with the Parish and Church-School Board, as explained under the item of Teacher Training Schools, has been published. The Board desires to co-operate with all Synods in this work and would recommend that the Church advise Synods wherever possible to have a Field Secretary or Religious Educational Director or at least a special Committee on this work.

OUR EDUCATIONAL MAGAZINE

The Parish and Church-School Magazine, which is now in its fourth volume, is a very helpful agency in the aims and problems of our Church. Through its columns, many of the experts of our Church are speaking and presenting both theory and experience. The pages of this magazine are regularly filled with material which is of the greatest value to every Lutheran interested in the education and development of the people of our congregations. As a technical magazine, it is essential on the table of every member of our congregations who is engaged in any phase of the Educational or Parish work in our churches. We would ask that the Church recommend to the congregations the advisability of placing · this magazine in the hands of all such workers.

CONSTITUTIONS

A series of model Constitutions for local Sunday Schools, Sunday School Institutes and Conference and Synodical Sunday School Associations are in progress of preparation. Their general use when finally approved is urged upon the Synods. By this method a uniform government and uniformity in method of administration and instruction will be assured.

NOMINATIONS

The following members of the Board whose terms expire with this Convention all of whom are active in the work of the Board are herewith nominated for re-election for the term of six years:

The Rev. W. L. Hunton, Ph.D., D.D.

The Rev. T. Bruce Birch, Ph.D.

The Rev. Charles F. Dapp, Ph.D.

Prof. Gilbert P. Voigt.

RECOMMENDATIONS

1. We recommend that the Parish and Church-School Board be authorized to develop and provide special textbooks for Weekday Religious Schools.

II. We approve the organization of training schools for Church workers and recommend that Synodical and other groups, in consultation with the Parish and Church-School Board, establish such schools.

III. We recommend that for work in our Training Schools for Church Workers, as well as in our Weekday Religious Schools, where texts from Lutheran authors are not now available, the Board be authorized to secure manuscripts and issue special textbooks.

IV. We rejoice in the progress made in the development of the Lutheran Graded Lessons and recommend that special emphasis be laid on the preparation of comprehensive helps for the use of teachers in all the grades.

V. With special gratification, we note the progress made in the publication of suitable periodicals or religious papers for the children of the Church and in view of the fact that we now have papers for the various ages, we recommend that our schools be urged to use only our own religious papers.

VI. We commend the progress made in the preparation of the two proposed hymnals for use in the schools of the Church and recommend that the Committee in charge be requested to complete and publish these hymnals at the earliest possible date.

VII. We recommend the establishment of libraries in connection with our churches, especially where public libraries are not available and in the establishment of such libraries, advise the use of the recommended lists of books arranged by the Parish and Church-School Board.

VIII. We approve the principles of employing Field Secretaries to do religious educational work in co-operation with our Synods, Conferences and congregations and recommend that the number of such Field Secretaries be increased as rapidly as possible.

In view of the great educational value of such representatives who can reach down through the Synods into the conferences and congregations and develop interest and efficiency, the Board feels that if it is to meet the expectations of the Church, it must have a large fund available for the prosecution of this work which is purely educational and largely missionary.

IX. We recommend the educational magazine of the Parish and Church-School to the favorable consideration of all our people who are in any way interested in the plans, problems and development of Religious Educational Work. As a technical magazine, it should be found in every worker's hands.   Approved by the Board.

CHARLES P. WILES, *President,*
WILLIAM L. HUNTON, *Secretary.*

TREASURER'S REPORT OF THE PARISH AND CHURCH-SCHOOL BOARD

RECEIPTS AND DISBURSEMENTS
For the Year ended July 31, 1924

RECEIPTS:

United Lutheran Church on Apportionment	$4,213.00	
United Lutheran Church, Specials	205.97	
General Donation	1.00	
Total Receipts		4,419.97

DISBURSEMENTS:

Salary of Field Secretary	$412.50	
Expenses of Field Secretary	151.55	
Expenses of Hymnal Committee	141.66	
Expenses of Board Meetings	642.01	
Stationery	8.50	
Official Seal of the Board	6.00	
Total Disbursements		$1,362.22
Cash Balance, July 31, 1924		$3,057.75

Respectfully submitted,
H. M. M. RICHARDS, *Treasurer.*

PHILADELPHIA, September 4, 1924.

We have audited the accounts of the Parish and Church School Board of the United Lutheran Church in America for the year ended July 31, 1924, and we certify that, in our opinion, the foregoing statement of Receipts and Disbursements for the year ended July 31, 1924, is in accordance with the books of account and is correct.

LYBRAND, ROSS BROS. & MONTGOMERY,
Accountants and Auditors.

The resolutions I, II, III, IV, V, VI, VII, VIII and IX were adopted.

The Rev. C. P. Wiles addressed the Convention and thereupon the report was adopted as a whole.

The Rev. C. P. Harry, Chairman of the Committee on Boys' Work, reported as follows:

REPORT OF COMMITTEE ON WORK AMONG BOYS

Meetings: The Committee held one meeting, January 23, 1923, in the Parish House of the Church of the Holy Communion. Rev. C. P. Harry was elected chairman, Rev. G. H. Bechtold, secretary and treasurer. The Committee chose an Executive Committee consisting of the officers, Rev. Stanley Billheimer, D.D., Rev. Luther De Yoe, D.D., Mr. George M. Jones, Reading, Pa., with instructions to meet as often as necessary to carry on the business of the Committee and to call another meeting of the Committee when necessary.

The Executive Committee met four (4) times during the biennium. There being no business which could not be laid before the other members of the Committee by correspondence, a second meeting of the Committee was not called.

Conference of Workers With Boys: A Conference of workers with boys was called in connection with the meeting of the Inter-Synodical Inner Mission Conference, May 17, 1923, at Toledo, Ohio, and was attended by members of the Committee and workers among boys in the Middle West. Camping, conferences, approach to boys, father and son problems and the like, were discussed fully.

Relation With the Parish and Church-School Board: In conference with the officers of the Parish and Church-School Board the following agreements were entered into:

I. A column is to be available in the Augsburg Teacher for review of Boys' Books and for articles or paragraphs on Boys' Work.

II. In the compilation of lists of Recommended Books, the Boys' Work Committee is invited to name special books for boys and on Boys' Work which may be listed under proper classification headings in these "Official Book Lists."

III. In the Field Work of the representatives of the Parish and Church-School Board representatives at institutes, conventions, summer schools, etc., literature and information concerning Boys' Work is to be furnished and the work presented. When possible for Boys' Work Committee members to do so, they may also represent the work of the Parish and Church-School Board.

IV. In the future selection of Field Secretaries of the Parish and Church-School Board, if the Boys' Work Committee determines to co-ordinate their work with that of the Parish and Church-School Board, the latter will welcome suggestions of possible Secretary and undertake to have its various editors and representatives posted on all phases of the Work Among Boys.

Investigation of Boys' Movements: The Committee has continued to carry on its survey of various boys' movements which claim the attention of our pastors and Sunday school workers in different parts of the territory of the United Lutheran Church in America. The results of these investigations are on file with the chairman, and inquiries at any time will be promptly answered.

Camps and Conferences: The Committee would like to call the attention of the United Lutheran Church in America to the large and increasing number of camps and conferences being held in the Constituent Synods through the Boys' Committees of the Synods. Conferences have been reported to the Committee in the following Synods: Alleghany, New York, New York and New England, New York Ministerium, East Pennsylvania, Ministerium of Pennsylvania, Northwest, Susquehanna, Ohio.

Camps have been reported in the following Synods: Pittsburgh, Ohio, Ministerium of Pennsylvania, East Pennsylvania, California, Kansas, Pacific.

Father and Son meetings have been reported in the following Synods: Alleghany, East Pennsylvania, Northwest, Ohio.

Literature: The Committee has revised and reissued pamphlets—one on Camps and the other on Conferences for Boys, which were published during the previous biennium. Copies are in the hands of the Secretary and may be procured by request.

Boys' Intermediate Luther League: One of the finest developments in the Work Among Boys of our Church in the past biennium is the well-considered and efficient program worked out by the Intermediate Committee of the Luther League of America. It is a well-balanced program in itself and can be readily used where other boy organizations have already been established in the Church, particularly Boy Scouts.

The Committee would take this opportunity of very heartily commending the work of the Intermediate Committee of the Luther League of

America. In view of this fact and also in view of the fact that the Luther League of America has been recognized as the official Young People's organization of the Church, the Committee is of the opinion that special assistance should be given the Luther League in order that the Boys' Work of the Church in connection with it may be carried on in the most efficient manner, and particularly because the Boys' Work Committee is convinced that the United Lutheran Church in America should have a man giving his entire time to Boys' Work—an expert always available. The Committee therefore begs leave to recommend:

Recommendation: The Committee recommends that the United Lutheran Church in America appropriate five thousand dollars ($5000.00) annually for the next biennium to the Luther League of America for the purpose of calling an Intermediate Secretary with special reference to Boys' Work, and for paying his salary and expenses.

Respectfully submitted,

C. P. HARRY, *Chairman,*
G. H. BECHTOLD,
A. E. DIETZ,
CHARLES M. TEUFEL,
H. D. HOOVER,
C. J. DRIEVER,
C. A. DENNIG,
A. B. MACINTOSH,
GEORGE BEISWANGER,
GEO. H. RHODES,
H. MANKEN, JR.,
LUTHER DE YOE,
A. T. MICHLER,
STANLEY BILLHEIMER,
GEORGE M. JONES.

On motion to adopt the recommendation of the Committee, the President ruled that according to a standing resolution adopted at a previous session of this Convention, this recommendation must be submitted to the Finance Committee before it can be brought to the Convention. The recommendation having been so referred, the report was adopted. (For action on the recommendation see Report of Finance Committee, Wednesday, October 29th.—Secy.)

Mr. Grant Hultberg, Business Manager of the Board of Publication, submitted the report of that Board.

REPORT OF THE BOARD OF PUBLICATION

DEDICATION

An outstanding event in the annals of publication work in the Lutheran Church was the dedication of the Muhlenberg Building, the new publication home in Philadelphia, on Tuesday, April 29, 1924. A large number of friends of the publication work assembled that day in the Book Room on the ground floor, where seating arrangements had been provided. The Dedication Exercises were presided over by the President of the Board, William C. Stoever, Litt.D., a veteran in the publication work of the Church. Addresses were delivered by Dr. C. M. Jacobs on behalf of the Board, and by E. Clarence Miller, LL.D., on behalf of the Church. The formal dedication of the building was by the President of the United Lutheran Church, the Rev. F. H. Knubel, D.D., LL.D. In this connection it may be mentioned that the cornerstone of the Muhlenberg Building was laid by Dr. F. H. Knubel on January 31, 1923, in the presence of the Board members and other interested friends.

NEW PUBLICATION BUILDINGS

The new Publication Building at Thirteenth and Spruce Streets, Philadelphia, known as the Muhlenberg Building, has been completed and equipped during the biennium. This building represents the investment of $520,000, exclusive of the ground, for which $150,000 was paid. The Board has occupied the building since the first of November, 1923, when we moved from the rented quarters at Ninth and Sansom Streets. Additional equipment to the amount of $64,000 has been installed in the new building. The Board's facilities for handling the publication business of the Church have thus been very materially enlarged. The manufacturing facilities alone have been increased by fully 50 per cent, enabling us to produce all but two of our periodicals, and most of our publications in our own plant at a considerable saving to the Board, and with assurance of high-grade work.

Early in 1923, a building with ground at the corner of Cass and Chestnut Streets, Chicago, was purchased to provide added facilities and more adequate quarters for the Chicago Branch. Forty-five thousand dollars were paid for this property, and alterations and additions brought the cost up to $66,000. The property consists of a corner lot 25x86 feet, facing a small park in a location undoubtedly destined soon to become a part of Chicago's main business section. On this lot there was a two-story and basement brick residence which has been remodeled and enlarged to provide a light and comfortable ground floor Book Room, and adequate office space for the Home Mission Board and other Church agencies with headquarters in Chicago.

In acquiring the Chicago property, the Board found it advisable, under the Illinois law governing corporations not for peculiar profit, to take title in the name of the business manager as trustee. The Board is, however, anxious to have the title vested directly in the name of the Board. In order that this may be done with security, and the interests of the Church and the Board may be properly safeguarded in every way, a resolution has been prepared for adoption by the Convention. This resolution is appended to this report as Recommendation 2.

The Board's indebtedness on all its property consists of a mortgage of $90,000 on the Philadelphia property and one of $8500 on the property at Columbia, South Carolina.

New Books

New books published during the biennium include the following titles: "The Way," by Charles M. Jacobs, D.D.; "I Believe," by William L. Hunton, D.D.; "Six Years in Hammock Land," by the Rev. Ralph J. White; "Gospel Truths," by J. E. Whitteker, D.D.; "Wrecks Rebuilt," by the Rev. Walter Krumwiede; "Sermons on the Gospels, Vol, II," by E. P. Pfatteicher, D.D.; "Russellism," by Joseph Stump, D.D.; "The Sunday Problem," by the Committee on Moral and Social Welfare; "The Kingly Christ, Vols. I and II," by G. A. Getty, D.D.; "The Lutheran Church in American History," by A. R. Wentz, D.D.; "The Junior Class Manual," by the Rev. G. J. Muller; "The Living Christ," by T. E. Schmauk, D.D., compiled by the Rev. A. C. R. Keiter; "Paths in the Wilderness," by the Rev. C. E. Sparks; "Jesus, Wer Er War und Was Er Wollte," by H. Offermann, D.D.; "The Story of Jesus," by M. Hadwin Fischer, Ph.D.; "Introits and Graduals," by H. Alexander Matthews and Luther D. Reed, D.D.; "Fishing for Fishers of Men," by the Rev. Carroll J. Rockey.

The total of the new books published amounts to 143,280 copies. The Year Book of the United Lutheran Church has appeared each year and Der Lutherische Kalender has been published jointly with the Lutheran Literary Board. The Crucifixion, a Good Friday Service, by the Rev. George Dorn, D.D., was published for Good Friday this year, and shortly after the Buffalo Convention, "The Heritage of the Child," by Mrs. Laura Scherer Copenhaver, came off the press. This was the pageant that was presented at the Convention. The Lutheran Lesson Commentary has been continued and each new volume has been received with increasing interest and demand. "The First Christmas," by the Rev. C. F. Steck, Jr., and "In the Light of the Bethlehem Star," by Miss Erin Kohn, two Christmas pageants, were issued for the holiday season of 1923. The Parish and Church-School Board has prepared a Handbook of Weekday Religious Instruction and also a Program for such schools. Both of these have been issued by this Board. The Church Year Calendar has been continued and the edition for 1925 is now ready.

REPRINTS

The reprints issued during the biennium total 392,500 copies. These include new editions of Golden Treasury, Life of Luther by Koestlin, Book of Concord (People's Edition), Way of the Cross, Doctrinal Theology, The Conservative Reformation, The Perfect Prayer, Elements of Religion, Book of Concord, Vols. I and II, That Man Donaleitis, Twice Born Men in America. A large number of titles in the Lutheran Graded Series have been reprinted and this applies also to the Teachers' Training Course.

PAMPHLETS AND TRACTS

A total of 198,000 new pamphlets and tracts including Christmas and Easter Services for the Sunday School have been issued during the biennium and 114,000 reprints have been published.

HYMNALS

Hymns and Prayers for Church Societies and Assemblies, compiled and edited by the Common Service Book Committee, was first published in July, 1923. This little hymnal has been very well received. It is being used by an increasing number of societies and organizations in our churches. Shortly after the Buffalo Convention, a Mission Edition of the Common Service Book with Music, known as No. 590, was put on the market. This edition of the book has been so well received that three large editions have already been printed. Of the various hymnals, there have been published since the last report, the following number of copies: Common Service Book, 55,000; Book of Worship, 22,000; Church Book, 8,000; Kirchenbuch, 7,000.

PERIODICALS

The average circulation of the periodicals during the first year of the biennium was: weeklies, 174,200; monthlies, 152,800, and quarterlies, 466,700. The average circulation of the various periodicals for the first six months of 1924 was as follows:

The Lutheran	33,000
Lutheran Young Folks	97,000
Lutheran Boys and Girls	38,000
Lutherischer Herold	7,200
Sunbeams	34,500
Sunshine	21,000
Augsburg Teacher	34,500
Pictureland Weekly	9,500
Little Ones	30,500
Lesson Leaves	20,700
Jugend Freund	4,500
Home Department Lesson Book	30,500
Adult Lesson Book	**77,000**

Senior Lesson Book 160,000
Intermediate Lesson Book 62,000
Junior Lesson Book 50,000
Parish and Church-School 2,000
Bible Outlines 1,800
Bible Teachings 3,100
Bible Biography 2,900
Bible Scenes 3,300
Bible History 4,800
Bible Readings 5,300
Bible Story 7,800
Pictureland 3,000
Workland 2,000
Wonderland 3,000
Sunrays 45,000
Sonnenstrahlen 3,500

CHURCH PAPERS

The Lutheran has been continued as a 32-page paper with the exception of one issue in 1923. An attempt was then made to reduce the size to 16 pages during the month of July. This brought so many immediate protests that the attempt was at once abandoned. The consolidation of *Der Deutsche Lutheraner* and *Lutherischer Zions Bote* was effected in October, 1923, under the name of *Lutherischer Herold*. The paper has been continued under the latter name as a 12-page paper with a 16-page issue for the last week of each month.

The report of the Committee on Church Papers deals with the policy and editorial merits of these weekly papers. The Board of Publication has consistently complimented the high literary standards of the editors by issuing these journals in the best form possible. Good paper and painstaking "make up" enable the United Lutheran Church's periodicals to rank in the first class of religious journals.

Both of these publications have required considerable financial support from the Board as the subscription receipts are not sufficient to cover the expense of publication and the advertising income is necessarily limited. With the stabilizing of the cost of production, it is hoped that the deficit can be materially decreased. Whether either or both of the papers can be made entirely self-sustaining without readjustment of size or subscription price is a question that cannot be answered at this time. A most encouraging feature is that the deficit on *The Lutheran* in particular has been materially reduced during the past year.

With the knowledge and consent of the Executive Board, the first Sunday of October and its week was presented to the congregations as Church Periodical Week. In view of the many vital questions of religion, ethics and church that demand attention, and because Lutheranism must make a definite contribution to the discussion and settlement of these questions, and since October culminates in the celebration of the date of the restoration of evangelic principles, we recommend that a similar designation of the first Sunday of October and its week be authorized and that religious reading in general as well as the periodicals of the Church be stressed.

PUBLICATION PROGRAM

The Publication Program reported to the Buffalo Convention has ever been kept in mind. Most of the manuscript for the completion of Luther's Works in English is now ready for the printer, and it is hoped that this valuable work can be completed before the next Convention.

A series of Study Books on the Church and its activities, sponsored by the Secretaries' Conference is now under way. The first volume of the series, entitled "Our Church," should be ready by the time of this Convention and other volumes should follow at regular intervals.

Two Study Books, The Junior Class Manual for use in Pre-Confirmation classes, and The Story of Jesus for use in Training Schools, Summer Assemblies and Camps have been published. The History of the Lutheran Church in this country was brought out last year, and an Outline of the History of the entire Church up to the end of the Nineteenth Century is now on the press. We further have on the press The Ecclesiastical Year, a study of the Introits, Collects, Epistles and Gospels for the Church; also an Introduction to the Epistles and Gospels of the Church Year. Considerable progress has thus been made on the program as outlined two years ago. Expansion and modification of this program is constantly being considered.

ORGANIZATION

Following the Buffalo Convention, the Board of Publication had its first regular meeting October 31, 1922. Dr. Samuel P. Sadtler was elected President; Dr. Wm. C. Stoever, Vice-President; Dr. N. R. Melhorn, Secretary; and Mr. E. G. Hoover, Treasurer. With deep feeling of the valuable services rendered by Dr. Sadtler, we have to report his death on December 20, 1923. Dr. Sadtler had served as President of this Board since its organization in 1918, and for a number of years prior thereto, had been a member and president of the General Council Board. He took a deep interest in the publication work of the Church, with which he had familiarized himself by years of devoted attention.

At the January meeting, Dr. Wm. C. Stoever was elected President, and Mr. John M. Snyder, Vice-President. The vacancy on the Board caused by the death of Dr. Sadtler was filled by the election of Mr. O. W. Osterlund by the Executive Board following his nomination by the Board of Publication. Eight meetings of the Board have been held during the biennium.

STANDING COMMITTEES

The Board's Executive Committee has held monthly meetings during the biennium. The various Standing Committees have been made up as follows:

Manufacture and Sales: E. F. Eilert, D. F. Yost, A. H. Kohn.
Real Estate and Accounting: G. E. Schlegelmilch, D. F. Efird, Croll Keller.
Religious Literature: C. M. Jacobs, A. R. Wentz, A. H. Holthusen.
Secular Literature: S. W. Herman, C. J. Cooper, C. F. Steck.

TERMS EXPIRE AT THIS CONVENTION

Those whose terms expire at this time are: C. F. Steck, N. R. Melhorn, F. P. Manhart, D. F. Efird, George D. Boschen, Geo. E. Schlegelmilch and E. F. Eilert. The Board has placed the above names on the ballot as nominees meriting re-election. They likewise recommend the election of O. W. Osterlund for the unexpired term of the late Dr. Sadtler.

RECOMMENDATIONS

The Board would submit the following for your favorable action:

1. *Resolved,* That the week beginning with the first Sunday in October be designated as "Church Periodical Week," and that the circulation and reading of the periodicals and publications of the Church, and religious literature in general, be particularly stressed during that time.

2. *Resolved,* That the Board of Publication of The United Lutheran Church in America is hereby authorized and empowered, whenever it deems it to be in the best interest of the Church and the Board, to sell, encumber and convey, by its President and attested by its Secretary, the property owned by said Board, commonly known as No. 860 Cass Street in the city of Chicago, Illinois, more particularly described as follows, to wit: Lot Three (3) in Owners' Resubdivision of the East One hundred seventy-three and fifty-three one-hundredths (173.53) feet of Lot Five (5) of the County Clerk's Redivision of Block Fifteen (15) of the Canal Trustees' Subdivision of the South West fractional quarter of Section Three (3), Township Thirty-nine (39) North, Range Fourteen (14), East of the Third (3rd) Principal Meridian, situate in the City of Chicago, County of Cook, in the State of Illinois.

Respectfully submitted,
JOHN M. SNYDER, *Vice-President,*
NATHAN R. MELHORN, *Secretary.*

BOARD OF PUBLICATION BUSINESS MANAGER'S REPORT

CONSOLIDATED PROFIT AND LOSS ACCOUNT

For the Year Ended 30th of June, 1923

Gross Sales of Books, Advertising, etc.	$642,603.48	
Less Returns, Allowances and Discounts	16,053.20	
Net Sales		$626,550.28
Cost of Sales:		
Purchases of Materials, Printing and Binding	$370,423.81	
Printing Department and Editorial Wages and Salaries	65,171.93	
Author and Contributors	8,156.68	
Royalties	1,483.95	

Shipping and Mailing Expenses, including Postage	40,479.07	
Freight, Expressage and Hauling	3,681.86	
Rent	14,100.00	
Power and Light	2,477.39	
General Manufacturing Expense	3,205.94	
Insurance	1,509.72	
Taxes	3,677.20	
Depreciation of Machinery, etc.	5,955.49	

$520,323.04

Deduct:

Increase in Inventories	$9,362.14	
Sales of Waste, etc.	1,958.74	
Discounts on Purchases	2,813.08	
	14,133.96	
		506,189.08

Gross Profit on Sales $120,361.20

Selling, Administrative and General Expenses:

Executive and Office Salaries	$50,258.03	
Office Supplies and Expenses	3,897.67	
Expenses of Board Meetings, etc.	903.30	
Telephone, Telegraph and Messenger	889.07	
Advertising	841.67	
Legal and Auditing	1,963.89	
Memberships	435.00	
Traveling Expenses	2,701.87	
General Expenses	1,093.22	

Branch Office:

Rentals	$6,976.50	
Postage	1,954.11	
Freight, Hauling, Shipping, etc.	1,481.74	
Insurance	733.33	
Taxes and Water Rent	43.10	
Moving Expenses	178.15	
Adjustment of Differences between Branch Office and Philadelphia Office Accounts	703.66	
	12,070.59	

Uncollectible Accounts Written Off	1,145.76	
Reserve for Doubtful Accounts	2,000.00	
Depreciation of Furniture and Fixtures	1,841.71	
Appropriation to the Executive Board of the United Lutheran Church in America	846.00	
		80,887.78
		$39,473.42

Other Income:

Rental from Properties	$5,609.44	
Less Taxes and Expenses of Properties	2,975.76	
	$2,633.68	

Interest:
On Investments $24,420.32
On Bank Balances 1,822.33
                                          26,242.65
                                                        28,876.33

Profit before Interest $68,349.75

Interest:
On Mortgages $6,330.00
On Loans 863.32
                                          7,193.32

Net Profit for the Period $61,156.43

CONSOLIDATED PROFIT AND LOSS ACCOUNT

For the Year Ended 30th of June, 1924.

Gross Sales of Books, Advertising, etc................... $667,130.17
Less Returns, Allowances, and Discounts.......... 15,951.00

Net Sales $651,179.17

Cost of Sales:

Purchases of Materials, Printing and Binding.... $350,351.68
Printing Department and Editorial Wages and
  Salaries 82,060.70
Authors and Contributors 10,612.61
Royalties 1,937.19
Shipping and Mailing Expenses (including
  postage) 41,966.62
Freight, Expressage and Hauling............................ 6,740.37
Rent 12,525.00
Power and Light 2,515.96
General Manufacturing Expense 5,698.12
Insurance 1,400.46
Storage 133.25
Depreciation of Machinery 8,686.08
                                                    $524,628.04

Deduct:

Increase in Inventories $29,670.61
Sales of Waste, etc. 2,505.72
Discounts on Purchases 3,735.38
                                          35,911.71
                                                        488,716.33

Gross Profit on Sales $162,462.84

Selling, Administrative and General Expenses:

Executive and Office Salaries	$55,943.60
Office Supplies and Expenses	5,650.96
Expenses of Board Meetings, etc.	828.57
Telephone, Telegraph and Messenger	1,137.12
Advertising	1,347.41
Legal and Auditing	2,050.97
Memberships	460.00
Traveling Expenses	2,570.60
General Expenses	2,495.72

Branch Office:

Rentals	$7,309.20	
Postage	2,168.56	
Freight, Hauling, Shipping, etc....	1,622.39	
Insurance	343.13	
Taxes and Water Rent	233.88	
Light	83.85	
Adjustment of Differences between Branch Offices and Philadelphia Office Accounts....	103.46	
		11,864.47

Uncollectible Accounts Written Off	533.18	
Depreciation of Furniture and Fixtures	2,290.52	
Appropriations	1,000.00	
Pensions	570.00	
Moving Expenses	9,138.06	
		97,881.18

	$64,581.66
Loss from Operation of Real Estate	19,508.49
	$45,073.17

Other Income:

Interest:

On Investments	$2,389.29	
On Bank Balances	1,278.26	
		3,667.55

Profit before Interest	$48,740.72
Interest on Loans	601.01
Net Profit for the Period	$48,139.71

Respectfully submitted,
GRANT HULTBERG, *Business Manager.*

TREASURER'S REPORT OF JOHN RUNG LEGACY

Cash Balance, July 1, 1922... $977.63

Cash Receipts:

	Year ended June 30, 1923	Year ended June 30, 1924	Totals for the Biennium
Interest on Investments.....................................	$200.00	$220.00	$420.00
Interest on Bank Balances...............................	46.54	6.73	53.27
Bonds Redeemed	....	3,000.00	3,000.00
	$246.54	$3,226.73	$3,473.27
			$4,450.90

Cash Disbursements:

Bonds Purchased	$900.00	$2,980.00	$3,880.00
Accrued Interest on Bonds Purchased	....	51.50	51.50
	$900.00	$3,031.50	$3,931.50

Cash Balance, June 30, 1924 .... $519.40

STATEMENT AT JUNE 30, 1924

ASSETS:

Cash in Bank	$519.40	
Bonds, at Market Values, June 30, 1924.............................	5,063.75	
		$5,583.15

LIABILITIES:

Trust Fund		3,000.00
Surplus on Hand		$2,583.15

Respectfully submitted,
E. G. HOOVER, *Treasurer*.

BUSINESS MANAGER'S REPORT OF ASSETS AND LIABILITIES AS OF JUNE 30, 1924

ASSETS:

Cash in Banks and on Hand...		$23,618.12
Bills, Receivable, for Merchandise............................	$6,269.14	
Accounts Receivable	$162,535.25	
Subscriptions due on *The Lutheran* and *Lutherischer Herold*	5,880.05	
Advertising Accounts	2,116.76	
		170,532.06
	$176,801.20	
Less, Reserve for Doubtful Accounts..............	10,000.00	
		166,801.20

Accrued Interest on Investments	370.17
Merchandise and Stock on Hand in Philadelphia and Branch Houses	236,377.64
Stocks and Bonds, at Market Values, June 30, 1924......................	25,015.25
John Rung Legacy (E. G. Hoover, Treasurer).............................	5,583.15
Prepaid Insurance and Taxes	2,198.30
Land and Buildings, net of depreciation	777,387.45
Machinery and Equipment, net of depreciation..............................	72,181.33
Furniture and Fixtures, net of depreciation	19,773.64
Electrotype Plates, at estimated values...	6,951.12

$1,336,257.37

LIABILITIES:

Accounts Payable	$20,319.83
Accrued Salaries, Interest, Royalties and Taxes...........................	11,232.04
Amount due Subscribers on Subscriptions for Periodicals..........	64,547.05
Mortgages Payable	98,500.00
Trust Fund, John Rung Legacy...	3,000.00

Contingent Liability:

Bills Receivable discounted at Bank......................	$5,350.00	
Net Assets		$1,138,658.45

$1,336,257.37

Respectfully submitted,

GRANT HULTBERG, *Business Manager.*

PHILADELPHIA, August 26, 1924.

We certify that we have examined the accounts of the Board of Publication of the United Lutheran Church in America for the two years ended June 30, 1924, and that the foregoing statements, in our opinion, correctly set forth its financial condition at June 30, 1924, and the results of its operations for the two years ended June 30, 1924.

LYBRAND, ROSS BROS. & MONTGOMERY,
Accountants and Auditors.

In connection with the consideration of this report, Rev. A. R. Wentz, of the Board's Standing Committee on Religious Literature, addressed the Convention. The recommendations 1 and 2 were adopted. The report was adopted as a whole.

The Rev. G. C. Rees presented the report of the Committee on Church Music as follows:

REPORT OF THE COMMITTEE ON CHURCH MUSIC

The committee met at the call of the Convener on January 26, 1923, and organized by electing the Rev. J. F. Ohl, D.D., Mus.D., Chairman, and the Rev. Gomer C. Rees, D.D., Secretary-Treasurer.

1. CONVOCATIONS.

During the last biennium four Convocations were held as follows: At Lancaster, Pa., October 30, 1923, under the joint auspices of the Committee and the Lancaster Conference of the Ministerium of Pennsylvania; at Kitchener, Ontario, November 12, 1923 (the second at this place by special request of the Synods of Canada and Central Canada); at Springfield, Ohio, May 1, 1924, under the joint auspices of the Committee and the Hamma Divinity School; and at Germantown, Philadelphia, May 13, 1924, under the joint auspices of the Committee and the Philadelphia Pastoral Association.

The Committee is convinced that these Convocations, with their instructive papers and practical illustrations by organists and choirs of the best forms of Church Music, are having a wide influence in the regions in which they are held. At the four named above there was a very gratifying attendance of organists, choirmasters, pastors and others interested; large and well-trained choirs had carefully prepared the music called for on the day's program; and for the Choral Vespers at Kitchener the large St. Matthew's Church, holding over a thousand people, was not only packed to the doors, but many failed to gain admittance. As a means of removing prejudices and lack of understanding, and of teaching our people to love and use the best in worship, it is believed that such Convocations would serve a most useful purpose in many more parts of the Church. As Lutherans we are properly solicitous about the faith, and therefore carefully guard the doctrine; but are we equally concerned about the manner in which the faith finds expression in acts of worship? In many of our churches the service music and hymn tunes are sung in such a perfunctory and uninspiring way that they altogether fail to stir the heart to genuine devotion. This is not as it should be. Worship is not, therefore, more spiritual because rendered in an indifferent and slip-shod way. On the contrary, for the greater glory of God as well as for our own edification, we should bring Him the best offering of prayer, praise and thanksgiving of which we are capable. To aid congregations in the attainment of this is the purpose of these Convocations.

We are informed that as a direct result of the Convocation at Springfield, Frederick Lewis Bach, Director of the Wittenberg College Conservatory of Music, has been appointed Professor of Church Music in the Hamma Divinity School. This is a step in the right direction, which could with great profit to the Church be followed by our other theological seminaries. We can hope to improve the music of our churches only as we ourselves train the organists as well as the future ministers to have a correct understanding of the Church's Services and their musical requirements.

During the biennium the Chairman, the Secretary, Dr. Reed, Pastor Trabert and Mr. Lewars lectured on Church and Sunday School Music and demonstrated the Common Service Book at assemblies of various kinds.

An extended notice of the Convocations held by the Committee appeared in *The Diapason,* the official journal of the National Association of Organists.

2. SUNDAY SCHOOL HYMNS AND MUSIC.

In this connection the Committee must again revert to the statements made in its last report regarding the wretched type of hymn books and festival programs used in many of our Sunday schools. It is falsely assumed by pastors and Sunday school leaders that there must be a radical difference between the hymns and music for the adult congregation and the hymns and music for the Sunday school, or, in other words, that children will not sing the Church hymns and music, but only the light stuff that is ground out year after year by men and woman who have neither the poetic gift, nor the spirit of genuine devotion, nor musical ability. The result is the "cheap" hymn, set to music of the jazz and dance-hall variety, "composed" not with a view to training children for the Church and the right kind of a devotional life, but to enrich the "authors," "composers," and, above all, the publishers. Is it any wonder that children lose reverence for sacred things and places when in the Sunday school they are taught to sing "music" reminiscent of the movies and jazz band? Nor is it true that children delight only in this kind of hymnody. It has been the experience of every member of your Committee that they will just as readily learn the best, and that they will love it much more. As we teach children Bible stories, the text of the Catechism, and numerous Scripture passages, so that early in life "the form of sound words" is put into their hearts, precisely so they need to be taught the Church's choicest hymns and melodies at a time when these will become their permanent possession for life. Thus will they learn reverence and how to express themselves in true devotion, and will be trained not *away* from the Church, but *for* the Church. Herein to a great extent also lies the solution of obtaining good congregational singing. As the children grow up into the adult congregation they will be familiar with a large body of the best hymns and tunes, and will at once be able to join in the song of God's house.

3. CHOIR AND ORGAN MUSIC.

As the singing of anthems has become an established feature in our services it is highly important that they should be chosen with discriminating care. Not only should the music be of a kind to excite devotion, and therefore free from profane associations, but the words must suit the day, season or occasion, so that with the rest of the service the anthem will form a harmonious whole as an act of worship. From the catalogues of Novello, Schirmer and other reputable publishers, anthems can be selected that fit every occasion and every part of the Church Year; and, although many of these can be well sung only by capable choirs with a good organist, there are also many others among them sufficiently easy for choirs of very ordinary ability. It is greatly to be desired that choirs of the latter kind should make use of this better type of anthems instead of the very commonplace issues of a number of American publishers. In The Service the anthem may be sung between the Epistle and the Gospel in place of the Gradual, or at the Offertory; and at Matins and Vespers after the Lessons in place of the Responsory or at the Offertory.

For preludes and postludes the organist should likewise be careful to select only that which is appropriate for the house of God. So much of what is published today under the title of organ music is derived from purely secular sources or written in secular style. But music taken from the opera or that reminds one of the concert hall must not be intruded into the services of God's house. The organist may be called the "musical pastor," and by means of judicious selections he can do much to inspire a devotional frame of heart and mind; whereas by the contrary course he can also most effectually destroy it. If he cannot do the former it were better his instrument remained silent.

Another abuse that is beginning to find its way into some of our churches is the playing of soft music during certain spoken parts of the service, even during the prayers. This, too, seems to be derived from the movies, and wherever introduced should be abandoned. It is distracting and if the music is of the flippant type, even irreverent. Stunts of this kind leave a theatrical impression, and cannot possibly minister to devotion.

4. The Influence of the Movies.

In addition to what has already been said this is twofold, first on organs, and second on the organist.

There is no movie theatre of any pretentions that does not have an organ. To meet the demand many builders have made the construction of theatre organs a specialty. These organs have a tone quality of their own, contain many solo stops, and are provided with numerous devices for obtaining unusual effects. Unfortunately some builders no longer seem able to discriminate clearly between the church organ and the movie organ, and get some of the characteristics of the latter into the former; or, perhaps better said, some congregations are fond of having a little of the movie organ in the church organ. The organ, as the pre-eminent instrument for God's house, must, however, have a character of its own. Its tones should be majestic, pervaded by those of the Diapason family, and an unusual number of solo stops together with the fancy devices of the movie organ, should be avoided.

It is the unusual devices in a church organ that here and there prove a temptation to the organist. Finding these handy, and perhaps himself a movie organist, he will use them in church, and instead of church music the congregation is treated to movie music. Congregations contracting for an organ should insist on a *church* organ, and should refuse to accept anything else.

5. INTROITS AND GRADUALS.

Ever since the publication of the Common Service Book the question has been asked, "Where can we get music for the Introits and especially for the Graduals?" The question is now answered, In April of this year the Publication House issued *The Introits and Graduals of the Church Year.* This is Part I, covering the Church Year from Advent to Whitsunday. The music is by H. Alexander Matthews, Mus.D., composer of the well-known Cantata for the Quadri-centennial of the Reformation and numerous other works, large and small. A very instructive Introduction is by Professor Luther D. Reed, D.D. Choirs will find the publication a treasure-house of singable and devotional music. If Part I is favorably received Part II will follow in due time.

6. AN ANNIVERSARY.

This year marks the Four Hundredth Anniversary of the so-called *Acht-Lieder-Buch*, the first hymnological product of the Reformation. Of the eight hymns in this book four were by Luther, three by Paul Speratus, and one by an unknown writer. It was through this book that Luther gave the first powerful impulse toward congregational hymnody and its marvelous development since them. Other books followed in rapid succession, and by 1553 the fifth edition of Babst's hymn book already contained one hundred and thirty-one hymns. This rapid increase of hymns and hymn books continued after Luther's death, and today their number in all lands and languages runs into many thousands.

THE COMMITTEE,

J. F. OHL, *Chairman,*
GOMER C. REES, *Secretary.*

On motion to adopt the report of the Committee, Dr. Rees addressed the Convention, his subject being the 400th Anniversary of the First Protestant Hymnal. The report of the Committee was adopted.

The Rev. Holmes Dysinger led in prayer, and the Convention adjourned until Tuesday morning.

Evening Service

A service was held at eight o'clock P. M., the subject being Home Mission Work.

The Vespers were conducted by the Rev. G. F. Gehr.

The Rev. J. B. Markward presided.

The speakers and their subjects were as follows:

"In Florida and the Southland"—Rev. W. E. Pugh, D.D.

"In Canada's Prairie Provinces"—Rev. G. C. Weidenhammer.

"In Our Growing Cities"—Rev. James Berg.

"Illustrated Talk on Achievements and Possibilities"—Rev. J. S. Herold.

SIXTH MEETING

Morning Session

CONVENTION HALL, EDGEWATER BEACH HOTEL,
Chicago, Ill.

Tuesday, October 28, 8:45 A. M.

Matins were conducted by the Rev. R. D. Wheadon.

The Convention was called to order by the President.

The Minutes of Monday's sessions were read, corrected and approved.

The regular order of business was taken up, and the Rev. E. F. Bachman presented the report of the Inner Mission Board.

REPORT OF THE INNER MISSION BOARD

The Inner Mission is a protest against the traditional practice of the Church which spends most of its energy in the care of the "ninety and nine"—today scarcely forty and nine—who remain within the fold and leaves the lost "one"—today the fifty and one—to perish. Yet these are included in Christ's great commission; for them He shed His blood no less than for the distant Gentiles.

The United Lutheran Church in America by official action has joined this protest against the traditional practice and by the creation of an Inner Mission Board has declared its determination to seek the lost and safeguard the endangered. These are found throughout the entire territory of the Church and can be reached only by the united effort of the entire church from its various boards down to the local congregations, and from the pastors down to the humblest in the pews. Only by the co-operation of every true follower of Jesus within the Church can we hope to fulfill our mission among men far from God, in all conditions of life, and in the social strata from the lowest to the most cultured.

The Inner Mission Board obviously cannot itself assume this great task of the Church, but must by information and inspiration arouse the Church to a full sense of responsibility and by still further information and counsel aim to bring individual and local efforts to such a point of action and co-operation as will lead to the maximum results for the Kingdom of God. This justifies *the Board's policy* of having Inner Mission work done by local or synodical agencies and support, and refusing to assume work of a purely local character. At the same time, however, seeking the lost or safeguarding the endangered may under certain conditions require such measures which cannot well be undertaken by local forces or are so obviously the responsibility of the entire Church that it would be unfair to shift the responsibility on any local group.

Your Board must therefore, under such circumstances act as the authorized instrument of the entire Church and *assume for the entire church the responsibility* for and the support of such work of a general obligation, yes, even to *initiate such work.*

During the past biennium your Board has been called upon twice to exercise the latter phase of the trust imposed upon it by the Church: First, when it agreed to the request of the Executive Board to assume again the responsibility for the care of *Lutheran immigrants at the ports of entry,* and, second, when it consented to co-operate with the Women's Missionary Society of the Church in work among the physically and spiritually destitute *white population in the Southern mountains,* where results can be achieved only by a combination of educational, industrial, and evangelistic features. A fuller statement of both of these Inner Mission activities added to those reported to the last Convention of the United Lutheran Church in America will be found in the proper place in the report.

I. ORGANIZATION

The Buffalo Convention elected the following brethren to membership in the Inner Mission Board:

For the term expiring 1928:

        Rev. G. H. Gerberding, D.D., LL.D.
        Rev. J. F. W. Kitzmeyer
        Rev. J. F. Ohl, D.D.
        Mr. H. W. Bikle
        Mr. C. M. Distler

For the term expiring 1926:
> Rev. H. Brueckner, D.D.

For the term expiring 1924:
> Hon. C. N. Hoover

The Board met for organization on December 7, 1922, and re-elected the same officers for the biennium: Rev. E. F. Bachmann, D.D., president; Mr. I. Searles Runyon, vice-president; Rev. Wm. Freas, secretary and treasurer.

Rev. W. H. Greever, D.D., resigned as a member of the Board because of his election to the Executive Board. Rev. J. J. Scherer, Jr., D.D., was elected by the Executive Board to fill the vacancy until the next Convention.

The Board suffered a great loss during the biennium in the death of Rev. J. F. W. Kitzmeyer. He had been a member of the Board since the first Convention, and previously a member of the Inner Mission Board of the General Synod from its organization. He was a special student of social problems, considering them always from a Christian standpoint. He was a most valuable member both of the Board and of its Executive Committee. Rev. F. B. Clausen was elected by the Executive Board to fill the unexpired term until the next Convention.

II. A Review of the Work During the Biennium

The work of the Board is so ramified and of such variety, that a detailed presentation would go beyond the reasonable limits of this report. We shall therefore aim to make brief reference only to outstanding facts.

1. *Congregational Activities*

The chief activity of the Board must always be the effort to encourage the growth in the congregation of that spirit of service which will always make a ready response to the needs in the community which it serves.

In seeking to develop this spirit the fact was soon established that there were many of our Lutheran people who had been for years without ministration in spiritual things. They were found in almshouse, on poor farms, and in all kinds of institutions managed and maintained by State, county and community. Definite information about them kept coming to the Board.

(a) A *survey* of the entire territory of the United Lutheran Church in America was therefore planned, through our Synodical Inner Mission Committees. The effort was made to discover where all institutions were located. Pastors were asked to visit the institutions and secure information concerning the spiritual care given to those who lived in them, with the view to discovering first of all our Lutheran people. While our own Lutheran people were our first care there was also borne in mind that we have a real responsibility to all, irrespective of faith. In some of our larger Synods key-men have been appointed who now are responsible for regular spiritual care of these folks in the institutions upon their territory.

Two results have by this time, with the survey yet incomplete, made themselves evident. First, it has been discovered, that there are actually thousands of our Lutheran people who have been cut off from the church for many years. It seemed as if nobody cared. Their physical needs were fairly well provided for. Their spiritual needs were largely neglected. Story after story could be told of this sad neglect.

But this condition is slowly being remedied. In one of our Synods 34 men have obligated themselves to minister regularly to these people. Some congregations are interesting themselves in their behalf. We are in a fair way at last to seek out our neglected poor and suffering members.

A second result is cause for great joy. The survey has brought out the fact that many of our pastors and people have been going about quietly in the spirit of Jesus doing good to these neglected folks. While no doubt there are many more of whom we do not know, we do have definite information that 47 pastors or congregations have been doing this quiet service of love for our neglected Lutherans, and for all others who cared for their ministrations.

As the survey goes on it may reasonably be expected that many others will take up such work, and that a vast service will be rendered to the poor and distressed of our church, which will show the mercy of God in the persons of His people.

(b) Another matter of deep concern to our congregations is the number of *migrant groups* which from time to time may be in their community. We have comparatively few congregations near these groups. However there are a few such who are seeking to help these groups— such as berry and hop pickers—who gather near them at certain seasons of the year. This service will be developed as we become conscious of our opportunity.

2. *Institutional Activities*

The local activities of our Institutions of Mercy will be set forth at the end of this report. However it will be necessary to refer here to certain institutional matters which have had the particular attention of the Board.

Tabitha Home. The title to this institution has always rested in the Board of Directors of the institution. Before the merger the institution was supported by the General Synod and its Board of Direcors elected by that body. Since the merger, the title to the institution has been transferred to a Board of Directors elected by the Synods west of the Mississippi River and the Wisconsin Conference of the Synod of the Northwest. Part of the support is still supplied by the budget of the United

Lutheran Church in America. This amount is, however, cut down each biennium, until eventually Tabitha Home will be supported entirely by the Synods upon the territory which she serves. Efforts endorsed by the Board to secure funds for an additional building needed to relieve the overcrowded condition are now being made.

Feghtly Home. Title to this institution still rests in the General Synod, which at its Buffalo Convention elected the Board of Directors for the biennium. Efforts have been made during the biennium to arrange for the transfer of title, preferably to the Ohio Synod, whose territory the institution serves. This has not yet been accomplished, but it is hoped that the matter may be adjusted before the Chicago Convention.

New Institutions An old folks home has been established by our congregations in Los Angeles. A hospital also has been begun. In addition, Unity Lutheran Church of Chicago has established a hospice for girls, which will be dedicated during the Chicago Convention.

New Inner Mission Society. Such a Society, organized in Trenton, N. J., is busily at work developing a local service which promises good things. Chicago will soon be in line with an Inner Mission Society which will give an opportunity for our people there more fully to unite their strength in the service of Christian love.

Proposed Dawson Home. On account of restrictions which it did not seem wise to accept, the proposition of a home on the Dawson property in West Virginia has been abandoned.

Proposed Tuberculosis Sanatorium. A memorial presented to the United Lutheran Church in America at the Buffalo Convention by the Rocky Mountain Synod was referred to the Board for investigation and report. This matter has also been before the Board since its organization in 1918. After thorough investigation the following action was taken by the Board and is recommended to this Convention for adoption:

After a careful study of the subject and consultation with eminent specialists of large experience, conference with other of our Lutheran Church bodies caring for tubercular people, your Board has reached the conclusion that under present conditions it would be very unwise to urge the establishment of a tuberculosis sanatorium upon the church at large, or even upon a single Synod. The following reasons have led to this conclusion:

1. All the authorities consulted agree that climate plays no necessary part in the treatment of tuberculosis, and that it can be properly treated in any climate, if certain other conditions are favorable. It is now generally accepted by the medical profession that rest, fresh air, nourishing food, and a contented mind are the outstanding factors in the treatment of tuberculosis.

2. A sanatorium as far removed as New Mexico, and as expensive to reach, would make it impossible for poor patients to enjoy its benefits, or for relatives to visit patients. Moreover the homesickness thus often

engendered in a patient seriously militates against his improvement and recovery.

3. The cost of erecting, equipping and maintaining a high-grade sanatorium, and providing it with a thoroughly competent staff of physicians and nurses is prohibitive. The physician member of the Board estimates that at present a hundred bed institution could not be satisfactorily built under three thousand dollars a bed, probably not under three thousand five hundred dollars, and that the cost of maintainence in an institution of this size would probably reach from sixty to ninety dollars a month per patient, this without including the interest charge on the cost of building and the salary of a superintendent. In this opinion, Commissioners of Health of several States concur.

4. The superintendents of the Missouri institution at Wheat Ridge, Colo., and the Danish institution at Brush, Colo., advise us not to attempt the founding of a sanatorium, and both inform us that the number of patients coming to their institutions is steadily decreasing. These two institutions offer to take patients of the United Lutheran Church.

5. Where the State or county has established and maintains sanatoria it is the conviction of your Board that these should be utilized by patients, but that the church should make provision for the spiritual care of its members in these, as is already the case in some States.

6. In view of the emergency in which congregations near a sanatorium are sometimes placed in reference to the support of indigent patients of the Lutheran Church, the Inner Mission Board offers its services in the solicitation of funds from the congregations from which such patients come, or with which they may be indirectly affiliated, and other benevolently minded people and congregations who would be glad to respond to this appeal of need.

3. *Educational Activities*

The new series of *"A Message for the Day"* has been prepared by 118 of our pastors and laymen and printed by our Publication House. It is now ready for the use of our people. It is a four-page folder having a complete service for private devotion for "shut-ins" and shut-outs." Its use is a real blessing to many.

A series of Inner Mission *lectures* has been given at all of our Theological Seminaries, except the Pacific Seminary. Our future pastors are thus coming to know more fully of the work. The purpose will, however, not be accomplished until the Inner Mission has been given a more adequate place in the regular curriculum of our Seminaries.

Training Schools for Christian Workers. These schools are being organized throughout the church. In an effort to provide a standard for such schools, the Board has been in conference with the Parish and Church-School and the Deaconess Boards seeking to work out a standard curriculum which will serve as a guide for training schools.

An Inner Mission *Quarterly* is to be issued as soon as the funds of the Board will permit its publication.

III. Two New Activities

1. *Work in the Southern Mountains.* In co-operation with the Women's Missionary Society an important activity in the Southern moun-

tains has been developed. In the summer of 1923 a day school was established in Currin Valley, near Marion, Va. Miss Mary P. Smith is in charge of the school. The mountain children have been gathered in for instruction and services provided for the older folks. The uplifting influence of this work was soon noticed in the homes of the mountain people. It is hoped that a local congregation will eventually assume this work.

Plans are now being made for a school near Konnarock, Va. A fine piece of property has been offered to us by Mr. L. C. Hassinger and the offer accepted. A neighboring house has been rented as temporary quarters so that the school may be opened in September of this year. A school building and dormitory will be erected in the course of the year upon the property thus given to us. The Women's Missionary Society will provide the funds for the erection of the building and the maintainence of the school. Girls only are to be taken at first, but it is hoped that very soon provision may be made to receive boys also. The purpose of the work is to train the children to go back to their own communities as intelligent and progressive Christian boys and girls who will raise the economic and social as well as the religious standards of their people. A Board of nine members, representing the Inner Mission Board, Women's Missionary Society, and the Virginia Synod has been elected and is now working out the details for the school. We trust this will be but the beginning of an important new enterprise of the United Lutheran Church in America.

2. *Port entry Work for Immigrants.* The Executive Board requested your Board to take over the port entry and allied work for immigrants. To this end, the work has been planned, a Secretary for Immigrant Work has been called, and plans made to meet the responsibility of our church to our people of all nationalities coming to our shores. It has been agreed that the task is a five-fold one—(1) work at the port of New York; (2) work at other American ports; (3) work in Canada; (4) establishing contacts at foreign ports from which our people are coming; and (5) follow-up work. The full-time Secretary will develop this field, so that our people will have the ministrations of their church from their embarkation until they have settled in their new homes and connected with a local congregation.

The Women's Missionary Society and the Home Mission Board have made appropriations for this work.

Contact with the Home Missions Council has been established. Foreign representatives have been appointed and are at work in countries from which our people come. Information is gathered by these brethren and forwarded to us so that follow-up work may be well done. Keymen over the country are being selected to follow up those who come to their territory. The Canadian brethren are working with other Lutheran bodies there in the effort to care for Lutheran immigrants. Rev. Sanjek, representative of the Board of Immigrants Missions will co-operate. The prospect is that the church will be able to give better care to all immigrants coming to our shores.

IV. General Matters

1. *Lay Service in the Church.* This matter was presented to the last Convention by the Executive Board. Since that Convention it has been referred to the Inner Mission Board to put into effect the recommendations adopted at that time.

There is some reason for encouragement from the development during the biennium. Some of our young people, well prepared for full-time service in the church have been called by congregations into service and have been doing commendable work. A bulletin will be published from time to time showing those ready for service and the openings for such service. This should help to bring the two together. The Board of Education, especially through its Secretary for Women Students, and also the Superintendent of Instruction at the Baltimore Motherhouse, are deeply concerned in the solution of this problem. Many Conferences of our Synods, at recent meetings, had this subject upon their programs for discussion.

The problem, however, is by no means solved. While there is a real desire to use our young people, yet there are many more offering themselves than can be used in our work at this time. Many are being aroused to the serious loss to the church through the failure to use this consecrated energy of the youth of the church and are working and praying for its solution.

2. *Inner Mission Conference.* Two general Inner Mission conferences have been held. All branches of the Lutheran Church have been represented. Their helpful character has made it evident that they should be continued. The presentation and discussion of common problems has been so rich in inspiration and practical suggestions that your Board has planned to hold similar conferences in our Synods interested in Inner Mission work. Also the Board contemplates the resumption of general conference for all our Synodical Inner Mission Committees and workers.

V. Reports for Institutions

The Constitution of the Board requires that report shall be made to the United Lutheran Church in America at each Convention for the Institutions of Mercy in which our people are interested.

In the effort to represent our work truly a two-fold classification of institutions has been made. Every effort has been made to have this listing correct. It is almost impossible to classify some of them properly. Corrections to the listings will be welcomed.

INNER MISSION INSTITUTIONS AND SOCIETIES

A—United Lutheran Church in America

(Owned, controlled and supported entirely by the United Lutheran Church in America, one or more of its constituent Synods, one or more of its congregations, or by associations within constituent Synods).

I. *Orphans' Homes*

1. St. John's Orphans' Home, Buffalo, N. Y.
2. Tressler Orphans' Home, Loysville, Pa.
3. Lutheran Orphans' Home, Salem, Va.
4. Lutheran Orphans' Home, Topton, Pa.
5. Nachusa Lutheran Orphanage, Nachusa, Ill.
6. Oesterlen Orphans' Home, Route 10, Springfield, Ohio.

II. *Old People's Homes*

1. Mary J. Drexel Home, Philadelphia, Pa.
2. National Lutheran Home for the Aged, Washington, D. C.
3. Lutheran Church Home for the Aged and Infirm, Buffalo, N. Y.
4. Lutheran Home for the Aged, Erie, Pa.
5. Old Peoples' Home of the Pittsburgh Synod, Zelienople, Pa.
6. Feghtly Home, Tippecanoe City, Ohio.
7. Franke Home, Charleston, S. C.
8. Lutheran Home for the Aged, Southbury, Conn.
9. The Lutheran Church Home for the Aged and Infirm of Central New York, Clinton, N. Y.

III. *Orphans' and Old People's Homes*

1. Orphans' Home and Asylum for the Aged, Philadelphia, Pa.
2. Tabitha Home, Lincoln, Neb.

IV. *Institutions for Defectives*

1. Lowman Home for the Aged and Helpless, White Rock, S. C.

V. *Hospices*

1. The Luther Hospice for Young Men, Philadelphia, Pa.
2. The Lutheran Hospice for Young Women, Akron, Ohio.
3. Unity Lutheran Church Home for Girls, Chicago, Ill.

VI. *Hospitals*

1. Children's Hospital, Philadelphia, Pa.

VII. *Miscellaneous Institutions*

1. The Lutheran Settlement, Philadelphia, Pa.

2. Kensington Dispensary for the Treatment of Tuberculosis, Philadelphia, Pa.
3. River Crest Preventorium, Mont Clare, Pa.
4. Spring Garden Neighborhood House, Pittsburgh, Pa.
5. Bethesda Home, Meadville, Pa.
6. Lutheran Children's Bureau, Philadelphia, Pa.
7. Lutheran Bureau, Philadelphia, Pa.
8. St. John's Lutheran Settlement House, Knoxville, Tenn.

VIII. *Seamen's and Immigrant Missions*
1. Seamen's and Immigrant Mission of the Ministerium of Pennsylvania, Port of Philadelphia, Pa.

IX. *Inner Mission Societies and City Missions*
1. The Inner Mission Society of the Evangelical Lutheran Church, Philadelphia, Pa.
2. The Inner Mission Society of the Evangelical Lutheran Church in Brooklyn and vicinity.
3. The Inner Mission Society of the State of Connecticut.
4. Inner Mission Society, Charleston, S. C.
5. The Inner Mission Committee of the Lutheran Alliance, Washington, D. C.
6. The Inner Mission Society of Trenton, N. J.
7. The Philadelphia City Mission.

X. *Deaconess Motherhouses*
1. Lutheran Deaconess Motherhouse, Baltimore, Md.
2. Mary J. Drexel Home and Philadelphia Motherhouse, Philadelphia, Pa.

XI. *Synodical Inner Mission Board*
1. Board of Inner Missions of the Ministerium of Pennsylvania, Philadelphia, Pa.

B—ALLIED TO THE UNITED LUTHERAN CHURCH IN AMERICA

(Not owned, controlled and supported by the United Lutheran Church in America, but in whose ownership, control and support United Lutheran Church congregations have a part).

I. *Orphans' Homes*
1. Emaus Orphans' Home, Middletown, Pa.
2. Orphans' Home and Farm School, Zelienople, Pa.
3. Wartburg Orphans' Home and Farm School, Mt. Vernon, N. Y.
4. Orphan Home of the Children's Friend, Jersey City, N. J.

II. *Old People's Homes*

1. Mary Louise Heins Home for the Aged and Infirm, Mt. Vernon, N. Y.

III. *Institutions for Defectives*

1. Passavant Memorial Home for the Care of Epileptics, Rochester, Pa.
2. Good Shepherd Home, Allentown, Pa.

IV. *Hospices*

1. Trabert Hall (for young women), Minneapolis, Minn.
2. Lutheran Hospice for Young Women, Pittsburgh, Pa.
3. Lutheran Hospice for Girls, Baltimore, Md.
4. Tryon Homestead (for young women), Philadelphia, Pa.
5. The Student House, Pittsburgh, Pa.

V. *Miscellaneous Institutions*

1. Layton Home for Incurables, Milwaukee, Wis.
2. Tabor Home for Children, Doylestown, Pa.
3. Children's Receiving Home, Maywood, Ill.
4. Artman Home for Lutherans, Ambler, Pa.
5. Wilbur A. Herrlich Memorial Home, Towers, N. Y.
6. Inner Mission Center, Brooklyn, N. Y.

VI. *Hospitals*

1. Lutheran Hospital of Manhattan, New York City.
2. Milwaukee Hospital, Milwaukee, Wis.

VII. *Seamen's and Immigrant Missions*

1. Seamen's Mission, Hoboken, N. J.
2. Lutheran Emigrant House Association, Hoboken, N. J.

VIII. *Inner Mission Societies*

1. Lutheran Inner Mission Society of Minnesota.
2. Lutheran Inner Mission Society of Pittsburgh, Pa.
3. Inner Mission Society of the Evangelical Lutheran Church in New York.
4. Inner Mission Society of the Evangelical Lutheran Church of Buffalo, N. Y.
5. Inner Mission Society of the Evangelical Lutheran Church of Baltimore and vicinity.
6. Inner Mission Society of the Evangelical Lutheran Church in Reading, Pa.
7. Inner Mission Society of Milwaukee, Wis.

IX. *Deaconess Motherhouse*

1. The Milwaukee Motherhouse, Milwaukee, Wis.

The Institutions and Societies listed above have sent reports as follows:

I. ORPHANS' HOMES

1. *St. John's Orphan Home, Buffalo, N. Y.*

St. John's Orphan Home was estabished in part to give a home to boys and girls whose fathers died at Lincoln's call. It still is the purpose of the institution to give a good Christian home to all Lutheran orphan boys and girls, also half-orphans, and children whose parents are separated. The children are kept until they are sixteen years old, at which time homes and positions are found for them. The present number of children is 75.

A new building with all up-to-date equipment has been added in the past year, including three schoolrooms, chapel, gymnasium, manual training, domestic science, and sewing rooms.

St. John's exists to give these orphan children a fair show in life. It is the kingdom of childhood ruled by the sole law of childhood: the law of unselfish and devoted love.

2. *Tressler Orphans' Home, Loysville, Pa.*

Tressler Orphans' Home was founded under the direction of the General Synod of the Lutheran Church at Loysville, Pa., in 1868. Then there were a few acres of land, one building and a small number of children. Now there are fifteen substantial buildings on the original grounds, about 700 acres of land in all, a dozen dwellings for employees of the farm and mechanical lines, two mills and an electric system with fifteen miles of line. At the close of the school year, June 5th, 312 children were indentured.

The school course has been extended to include the fourth year of high school work. This will prepare our more apt pupils to enter our first-class colleges.

The Industrial School of the Home has developed a splendid printery where boys learn that trade and which print many bi-pocket envelopes and monthly papers for our churches besides our own publication, the Orphans' Home Echoes.

Mr. C. A. Widle, late Superintendent of the Home suddenly passed to eternal rest April 9, 1923, after faithful service in that capacity for almost one-third of a century. Rev. G. R. Heim was then called upon to act as Superintendent. He was formally installed June 4, 1924. Rev. Heim is a graduate of Millersville State Normal School and of Gettysburg College and Seminary.

A new printery 40x100 is being completed and a trade school is being built as a memorial to Superintendent Widle. A hospital, a dormitory provided by the Alleghany Synod, a heating system provided by the Maryland Synod and a dining hall provided by the Central Pennsylvania Synod and memorializing the Rev. A. H. Spangler, D.D., President of the Board of Trustees, were dedicated during the last biennium.

3. *The Lutheran Orphan Home, Salem, Va.*

The Lutheran Orphan Home of the South, located at Salem, Va., is caring for about ninety-six children. Homeless and dependent children are admitted between the ages of five and twelve and are dismissed at the age of eighteen.

The Home owns a farm of 165 acres which is cultivated by the boys of the institution under the supervision of the Farm Manager. In the administration of its affairs, the Home employs eleven workers, including the Superintendent and Farm Manager. The work is supported by free-will offerings, principally from the Southern church. There is an endowment fund of $34,830, the income from which is used for current expense.

The present building is inadequate and unsuitable. Therefore, the Board has determined to erect new and larger buildings designed in keeping with the most modern idea of orphanage work. For this purpose a general appeal will be presented in November, and it is expected that at least $250,000 will be secured. The Home has a building fund of $40,000. With the fruits of the campaign added to its present building fund together with what may be realized from the sale of its city property, the Home hopes to be able to construct a plant for the care of orphan children more worthy of our beloved Lutheran Church. So may it be!

4. *The Lutheran Orphans' Home, Topton, Pa.*

The Lutheran Orphans' Home at Topton, Pa., was founded twenty-seven years ago. During the past two years, the family averaged 148, 81 boys and 67 girls, coming from congregations of the Ministerium of Pennsylvania.

The Home is continually filled. During the biennium 42 were admitted and 43 released. The majority of those released were placed into private homes. The 256 acres of ground, with its meadows and woodlands, forms an ideal place for the children to play during the summer months.

The work has again been signally blessed. The many friends have been loyal in their support.

The disbursements during the past year were $34,140.48.

Church services and Sunday school are conducted regularly every Lord's day; family worship daily, morning and evening. The week-day schools open with scripture reading and prayer.

The matter of education receives careful study and attention. The aim is to give the children all the school advantages possible. This, with their religious instructions, is their chief asset when they leave the Home. The main object is to prepare them for their life work so that they may become honorable and useful citizens, both as to Church and State.

Children of merit are given the privilege of Normal School and College work, through the kindness of friends.

5. *Nachusa Lutheran Orphanage, Nachusa, Ill.*

The Nachusa Lutheran Orphanage with accommodations for thirty children, has been continuously filled during the biennium. Fifty children were cared for, the average number being thirty-three. There are at present fourteen girls and eighteen boys in the Home.

The finances are in splendid condition. All bills have been paid promptly each month, and the Treasurer reports a good balance on hand.

The greatest handicap to the work at Nachusa has been lack of room to receive worthy applications, and lack of equipment to care for children of all ages.

Plans are under way to remove both these handicaps. The churches on Nachusa territory are now raising funds for the carrying out of a building program. This program calls for the erection of a cottage for girls and one for boys, a school building, a central heating plant and laundry, and other improvements to the building already on the ground, at a total cost of $75,000.

It is planned to begin work on the new buildings as early as possible in 1925.

More than $15,000 in bequests has been given during the biennium.

Valuation of property $41,000. Founded 1904. Endowment $10,000. Employes 6. Boys 18. Girls 14. Total 32. Dismissed 11.

6. *Oesterlen Orphans' Home, Springfield, Ohio.*

The home has cared for 48 children during the past year; 29 boys, 19 girls; 6 attended Senior High School, 4 Junior High and 3 were at Wittenberg Academy; 32 attended the grade school, 3 under school age. All are happily situated and doing nicely. Many applications were turned away during the year because of lack of room. We hope to overcome this feature of the work this year as a new building is planned and bids are being received. The campaign has been on for some time. The building will cost about $200,000. We hope to be able to begin the work very soon. The building will take care of about one hundred more children. Will have four distinct dormitories, hospital ward, dining room, kitchen, auditorium and superintendent and matron suites of rooms. It will be the administration building. Our crops have been very good, and we are getting splendid results from the farm.

II. Old People's Homes

1. *Mary J. Drexel Home for the Aged, Philadelphia, Pa.*

This Home is by its charter limited to residents of Philadelphia who are of German birth and descent. It is always filled to its capacity of 50 men and women, none under 65 years of age, 17 are over 80 years old.

4. *Lutheran Home for the Aged, Erie, Pa.*

The Lutheran Home for the Aged, Erie, Pa., was founded 1906. The pastors and laymen composing its Board of Directors are all members of the Pittsburgh Synod. Two sisters of the Philadelphia Motherhouse are in charge of the institution. Sister Frieda is the directing sister. Its property is valued at $75,000. It has an endowment of $27,850. The receipts for the past year were $11,866.00; the expenditures $9,517.00. It receives aid from the Erie Community Chest. It cared for 35 aged persons during the past year.

The officers are: President, Rev. Gustave A. Benze, D.D.; vice-president, Adam Laver; recording secretary, Charles Beirbach; financial secretary, Adam Leib; treasurer, F. H. Schuette.

5. *The Old People's Home of the Pittsburgh Synod of the Evangelical Lutheran Church, Zelienople, Pa.*

The Home was authorized by the Pittsburgh Synod in 1895, founded in 1904, chartered 1905.

The Synod holds title to all the property, main building, two cottages and 28 acres of valuable land. It conducts the Home through a Board of Managers which it elects. At its recent Convention at Indiana, Pa., it filled two vacancies from nominations made by the Board.

The Home has been called to mourn the loss of its venerable president, Rev. Edmund Belfour, D.D., who died on the evening of July 5, 1923, in the ninetieth year of his age. He entered the Home as house-father 1920 and passed to his heavenly rest amid the beautiful surroundings. He received the ministrations of loving hearts and tender hands through his prolonged sickness. Dr. Belfour was the Chairman of the Committee whose report led the Pittsburgh Synod to consider the founding of the Home in 1894. He took a prominent part in formulating the plans and policies of the Home and gave to the work the full measure of its devotion. He was a wise counselor and readily co-operated with his associates. His delightful optimism was a helpful inspiration. His valuable services unselfishly rendered closed with his eventful life. His memory will be lovingly cherished in the Home.

During the biennium 18 persons have been admitted, 1 dismissed, 8 died and 47 persons cared for, the family now consists of 31 persons. The Board has a waiting list of applications. The regular maintenance expense was $24,222. Indebtedness $1,595. Cash on hand $3,303. Cash in

Building Fund $1,603. General Endowment Fund $24,019. J. S. Seaman, Sr., Endowment Fund $51,439. Additional mortgages and stocks on hand $7,285. Net worth of building, real estate and furnishings is estimated at $129,803.

The foregoing statement shows the institution is in excellent financial condition. Its revenues are increasing. It is growing in favor with its friends. Each year the number of its supporters is becoming larger. Our people are beginning to realize that the Home is their child and as, by visitation and inspection, they learn from personal observation its facilities for caring for the aged and ministering to their comfort, the more liberal are their contributions to its maintenance. With this constant advance in public esteem and the manifest blessings resting upon the work, the Board of Managers are greatly encouraged and feel confident that the future prosperity is assured.

A large addition of an illustrated booklet, "A Few Pleasant Moments," showing the buildings and the activities of the Home, and an attractive souvenir Bible Book Marker were distributed through our congregations during the biennium, doubtless had much to do with acquainting our people with the Home and deepening their interest in its welfare.

The Pittsburgh Synod has authorized a campaign for the fall of 1925 for raising a fund of $103,000 for erecting the south wing to the main building.

The proposed improvement is necessary. The present capacity is utterly inadequate. The rooms are all occupied and many worthy applicants must be turned away. The buildings were lately repainted and other needed improvements were added. The ten-acre grove with its stately oaks, greensward, fine walks, choice shrubbery and well-arranged flower beds, grows more attractive each season and is the admiration of all visitors.

7. Franke Home, Charleston, S. C.

The Franke Home is supported by the five Lutheran churches of Charleston, and is under the control of an organization known as the Lutheran Charities Society.

There is also an auxiliary society composed mostly of women who look after the household affairs.

No admission fee is charged for entrance, but the applicants are required to make a monthly payment according to their means, or that of those who enter them into the home.

In the case of those who have no means to enter, they are taken in and cared for by the Home, but the church from which they come must look after their needs, in the way of clothing and other necessities.

The Home furnishes board and medical attention, but in the case of real illness each guest must provide his or her nurse.

Services are conducted by the Lutheran pastors of the city, and each pastor administers to the spiritual needs of his parishioner.

Devotional services are conducted twice daily by the deaconess in charge.

Entertainment is provided by the Luther Leagues of the city.

The deaconess superintends all departments of the work in th Home, trying to create a spirit of Christianity, and thus make it a real Christian home.

9. *The Lutheran Church Home for the Aged and Infirm of Central New York. Office at Utica, N. Y. Located at Clinton, N. Y.*

The Lutheran Church Home for the Aged and Infirm of Central New York has entered upon the fifth year of operation. The fourth annual report has been printed and distributed. In the providence of God the Home Association has been able to maintain a high standard of Christian care for homeless folks at a minimum cost.

Whereas in the previous report five persons were reported as residents of the Home, it now shelters eleven people, four men and seven women, besides the matron and a cook. Every room is occupied. One member of the family died during the last biennium.

Up to date no superintendent is being employed. The executive and house committee together with the matron are in charge of the management. The board has handled all appeals at minimum expense. The pastors of Utica are in charge of religious services.

The expansion of this Home, however, is greatly needed. A special collection for the building fund has been authorized by the Board to be conducted in the near future with Mr. Chas. Emerich, Treasurer, Chairman of the Committee. May the Lord and Saviour, in whose name we serve, give the increase.

III. ORPHANS' AND OLD PEOPLE'S HOMES

1. *Orphans' Home and Asylum for the Aged, Philadelphia, Pa.*

The Germantown Homes, opened in 1859, have continued their circumspect care of children and aged of the Ministerium of Pennsylvania, during the biennium.

Important developments and extension would enable an extensive report. Careful religious instruction is directed by the Superintendent and the effort made to affiliate the children dismissed, with our churches, has proven very successful. Kindergarten is conducted regularly, while children over six years attend the public school. Wherever possible, boys and girls are continued through the High Schools.

A history, "The Church's Treasures," was published in 1923 and a large edition sold. With the Kiefaber Memorial Hospital dedicated in 1923, our appointments for care of children are unusually complete.

Extensive improvements have been made; especially in the Aged Home kitchen, six baths, etc., and renovation of guest rooms. The cottage system will be further developed by the erection of the Justi Memorial Cottage for Boys, during this summer. This and other buildings projected will be located according to the carefully developed comprehensive plan. A valuable tract of ground at our southeast corner completes available frontage on Germantown Avenue.

The expenses for the year ending April 1, 1923 amounted to $59,218.87. An increased interest is expressed by receipts adequate to our needs, and a goodly number of legacies.

2. Tabitha Home, Lincoln, Neb.

About the same amount of work was done during the past two years as during the biennium preceding. Lack of room did not permit to do more. Sixty-two aged and helpless and 75 children received shelter and care. Forty-three aged and 36 children, a total of 79, are in the Home on this day, July 28, 1924. Fifteen aged died, 4 left or were dismissed.

On account of the financial depression in many of our farming communities the financial support from the territory of the Home was not quite as generous as during the preceding biennium. Five bequests received during the past two years, the total amount of which was $21,000, should all have been added to the New Building Fund. Prevailing circumstances, however, compelled the Executive Committee to use a considerable part of bequest funds to pay current expenses.

The crying need of Tabitha Home is more room. Many applications from churches of Synods outside of the Home territory are being received. There is no Home of the United Lutheran Church for aged men or for helpless and chronic sufferers west of Pittsburgh.

Two buildings are needed, one for aged or for the children, and one for aged, incapacitated pastors of the Church, who without means or family do not have and cannot get the care they need.

Tabitha Home would cheerfully render this service of love if the United Lutheran Church would furnish the funds for the erection of a building of modest size and equipment for that purpose, about $30,000.

Rev. L. Koehler of the Pittsburgh Synod passed away at Tabitha Home in January, 1924. Two other pastors died in the Home a few years ago. The oldest pastor of the United Lutheran Church, 94 years old, who was sent to Nebraska by an Eastern Synod 60 years ago, who has rendered the Church great service, the fruit of whose labors will last forever, is spending the remainder of his life in Tabitha Home. He cannot have a room for himself, which he deserves. Within a few days he will have as a roommate another unfortunate pastor for whom leading men of the Church plead with us for admission. A pastor of an Eastern Synod passed away about two years ago and left his only son suffering from a—well, a sad disease. He is in Tabitha Home of course. He ought not be in a room with others. It cannot be, because there is no room. May our plea find willing ears.

A missionary who labored in Hong Kong 28 years, who has no claim upon any Church of this country and has no fund to return to her home at Berlin, Germany, plead with us until we opened the door to her, this faithful servant of God.

V. Hospices

1. *The Luther Hospice, Philadelphia, Pa.*

The work at the Luther Hospice for Young Men, located at 157 North 20th Street, Philadelphia, progressed in its usual satisfactory manner during the year 1923. The guests were mostly long stayers and hence the total number of men entertained was only about three hundred. However, transient guests were never turned away. There were always accommodations for the new arrivals. In spite of the long service of the Philadelphia Hospice, its transient trade does not warrant the encouragement of the short stayer. Its policy, therefore, is to entertain a guest as long as he wishes to stay even if this period runs into years as it often does. The transient guest it, however, always most cordially invited to stay at the Hospice while in Philadelphia. The Hospice accommodates 65 guests and is continually filled during the winter months. The receipts for room and board for 1923 were more than thirty thousand dollars. The rates for room and board are from $9.50 to $12.50 per week. Those, however, who cannot pay the regular rate are accommodated at a lower rate. This always causes a slight deficit in the work which for 1923 was $300. This amount is made up by contributions. A Christian atmosphere is maintained. Family prayers are conducted and personal and pastoral work is done among the men.

The Hospice offers recreation features, such as reading room, music room, game room, etc. An association is maintained by the men and banquets and special entertainments are features.

The Hospice during its 19 years of existence, has rendered valuable service and in every way is worthy of the support of the church and the patronage of her young men when coming to Philadelphia.

2. *The Lutheran Hospice for Young Women, Akron, Ohio*

The Lutheran Hospice for Young Women, 64 N. Prospect Street, Akron, Ohio, is owned and under the jurisdiction of the Evangelical Lutheran Church of the Holy Trinity, Akron, Ohio. The building adjoins the church property.

The Hospice accommodates 19 young ladies, and during several months of the year, many were turned away because of lack of room. The Christian atmosphere and congenial spirit of the guests make our Hospice family a very happy one. It has proven a refuge for more than one lonely person.

At the end of each year a balance has been shown in the running expenses.

Each year, the first Thursday in November is celebrated as the Hospice birthday, when the Women's Guild of the church conducts open house all day. Liberal donations have been made by members of the congregation.

3. *Lutheran Hospice for Girls, Baltimore, Md.*

Lutheran Hospice for Girls, located at 509 Park Avenue and conducted by the Inner Mission Society has a capacity for 32 girls and has given a home to 68 girls during the past two years.

We aim to make our Hospice as homelike as possible and give personal attention and assistance whenever the girls are sick, out of work, unchurched or whatever help may be needed.

We have devotions every evening following the evening meal and on Sunday morning.

The Hospice Mission Circle composed of 25 members of the Hospice family gave over $200 to benevolence, has sent representatives to summer conferences and assists with Inner Mission activities.

During the year we cared for five girls under 18 years of age who had no parents to give them homes.

Birthdays and holidays are always celebrated in a special way and many other recreations such as picnics, hikes, and camping parties are planned for the girls which they greatly enjoy.

A new heating plant costing $2,600.00 has been installed which the women's auxiliary is paying for.

The value of the property is $30,000. The mortgage has been reduced to $6,000.

4. *Unity Lutheran Church Girls' Home of Edgewater, Chicago, Ill.*

Because of the need for Christian homes for business girls who come from out of town seeking employment in Chicago, in March, 1920, Unity Evangelical Lutheran Church unanimously voted "to establish as may be desirable and possible" a Unity Lutheran Girls' Home. The special Easter offering of the congregation that year which amounted to over $500 was for this project. It was purposed to celebrate Unity's Fifteenth Anniversary on November 12, 1920, by increasing this fund and undertaking to locate a home property. Instead God guided the congregation to successfully inaugurate a movement to cancel the church debt. Following the payment of the debt, extensive improvements were made to the church property. In the meantime the Home Fund was increased, through the contributions of the Ladies' Aid Society and friends, so that in March, 1924, the sum of $3,400 was in hand for this project.

On April 7th, guided of God, two friends promised $1,000 each on condition that the congregation would go forward and purchase a property as a tangible beginning for Unity's proposed home for business girls. Accordingly, under the authority of the congregation the Church Council took title on May 1st to a splendid property, directly opposite the church edifice, at the northwest corner of Balmoral and Magnolia Avenues. The purchase price of the the property which is worth $40,000 was $20,000.

Under the authority of the congregation, the womanhood of the church, through a Board of Managers of twelve women, is undertaking to mother business girls who become residents of the Home. The congregation is enthusiastic over this project and generally giving it hearty support.

In addition to the twelve large rooms which are now available for use there is a third floor which probably will be finished off in order to increase the capacity of the Home. When this alteration is made the Home will accommodate twenty girls. With this number it is believed that more of the surroundings and atmosphere of a real Christian home can be realized than is possible in homes and hospices which accommodate larger numbers and thus come to have something of the nature of a hotel.

The present debt on this Home property is $14,800. From this seemingly small beginning, it is hoped and prayed that there shall develop a far-reaching Inner Mission Work for our United Lutheran Church in Chicago.

VI. HOSPITALS

1. *Children's Hospital of the Mary J. Drexel Home, Philadelphia, Pa.*

Though limited to the first floor in the west wing of the Philadelphia Motherhouse, 1,147 patients were admitted during 1923. The dispensary was visited for treatments more than 20,000 times by 3,225 other children. A need, keenly felt for many years, was met by adding a "sun parlor" for children and a waiting room for parents of private patients. These building operations, completed just in time for the fortieth anniversary observed June 19th, 1924, include also another large treatment room for the dispensary at a total cost of $15,000.

VII. MISCELLANEOUS INSTITUTIONS

1. *The Lutheran Settlement, Philadelphia, Pa.*

The Lutheran Settlement since the fall of 1923 has conducted its activities in a new and well-equipped building, the gift of Philadelphia Lutherans. This building has been dedicated to the works of mercy and to the winning of souls for the Kingdom of God.

In two years over 75 members, adults and young people, have been added to the church. The Sunday school enrollment has reached the 400 mark, with a very good percentage in attendance each Sunday.

Week-day classes in manual arts, gymnasium, story hours, kindergarten, music, Bible and missions, girls' and boys' clubs, and mother's clubs are conducted from October 1st to May 15th. Our savings fund department and library are open throughout the year.

Throughout the summer months outings and picnics are arranged for mothers and children.

One month is given over to the instruction of our children in the D. V. B. S.

Child and family welfare are included in our yearly program.

For the past two years the aggregate attendance at all services and in all classes was over 80,000 men, women and children. 8,100 visits were made in the immediate neighborhood.

The staff consists of four full-time and two part-time workers and is assisted by over sixty volunteers.

3. *River Crest Preventorium, Mont Clare, Pa.*
Purchased July 17, 1911.
Consecrated June 26, 1913.
First children admitted July 17, 1913.
1,350 children admitted to date.
403 during year 1923.
Average length of days present, 32.
Supported by voluntary contributions.
Cost of operation 1923, $12,468.
Minimum 5.00 per week per child.
Very few "pay patients or guests" mostly wholly free or part pay.

Personnel
1. Supervising Deaconess,
   3. helpers.
1 Supervising Deaconess for children's work,
   1 helper.
1 Managing farmer,
   1 helper.

Purpose
As the name suggests, the purpose of the work is prevention of disease, especially tuberculosis. Children of patients of Kensington Dispensary of Philadelphia, who have been exposed to the disease or are predisposed by reason of malnutrition, illness, etc,, are eligible for admission.

A small number of convalescent cases are also admitted.

No active cases of tuberculosis are admitted.

Specific Aim
To build up and repair waste tissue thus increasing resistance to disease.

Method

Fresh air, sunshine, nourishing food, supervised play, exercise and rest. Two hours of school each day adequate for this type of children. *Another definite aim* is to assist the child's mental, moral and spiritual development while his physical needs are being cared for.

Routine work and play in which he participates develop habits of order, cleanliness and good health.

Results

General improvement in health of child shown by gain in weight and improved mental condition.

6. *Lutheran Childrens Bureau, Philadelphia, Pa.*

See under report of the Board of Inner Missions of the Ministerium of Pennsylvania (XI).

7. *Lutheran Bureau, Philadelphia, Pa.*

See under report of the Board of Inner Missions of the Ministerium of Pennsylvania (XI).

8. *St. John's Lutheran Settlement House, Knoxville, Tenn.*

St. John's Lutheran Church of Knoxville, Tenn., has recently taken over a Settlement House, which was founded thirty years ago by a pastor of the Joint Synod of Ohio. The home is intended to receive those who are caught in domestic strife and when the parents separate have nowhere to go. Some of them also are foundlings; others are received on commitment from the Juvenile Court. The home is under the control of a Board of eleven directors, six of whom are elected by St. John's congregation and the other five are business men of the city. The support of the home is received exclusively from the Knoxville Community Chest.

At present there are some twenty children in the home. We can accommodate several more as our capacity is about thirty. The congregation also has thoughts of a Lutheran Girls' Hospice which is one of the crying needs of our community.

VIII. Seamen's and Immigrant Missions

1. *Seamen's and Immigrant Mission of the Ministerium of Pennsylvania, Port of Philadelphia, Pa.*

See under report of Board of Inner Mission of the Ministerium of Pennsylvania (XI).

IX. Inner Mission Societies and City Missions

2. *Inner Mission Society of Brooklyn and Vicinity*

Since the last report made two years ago our society has been incorporated under the laws of New York State. The growth and development of the different branches of our endeavor have been most encouraging. The members of the churches are also beginning to understand the name, purpose and spirit of Inner Missions in a more intelligent manner. The results are seen not only in increased contributions but also in larger access of volunteer workers. The most notable achievement of this society was the acquisition, by puchase, of a splendid property as an Inner Mission Center. In this large building a Tiding Over Home has been operated with increasing success, providing a temporary shelter for small children whose homes have become dislocated. A hospice for girls is also operated in the same building. Two missionaries, one an ordained pastor and the other a lay woman, give all their time to hospital and home visitation. Splendid support accrues to the organization from the Woman's Auxiliary which numbers now more than 500 members. The society is supported, not by individual membership but by congregations and societies within the congregation.

5. *Inner Mission Committee of the Lutheran Alliance, Washington, D. C.*

Work carried on through the Inner Mission Committee of the Lutheran Alliance, Rev. H. Manken, 5106 14th St., N. W., Chairman of the Committee. A full-time Executive Secretary, Miss Bertha A. Heiges, has been working under the direction of this committee since November, 1923, with an office at 820 11th St., N. W. The work is supported by the Maryland Synod, and the Lutherans of Washington. Hospital as well as other institutional visitation has been emphasized. Co-operates with city Rescue Missions in furnishing leaders and speakers for their indoor and street meetings. Works with the Juvenile Court and Juvenile Protective Association. Published a directory of Lutheran churches in Washington to put in the hands of strangers in the city.

6. *Inner Mission Society of Trenton, N. J.*

The Trenton Inner Mission Society was organized December 10, 1922. The following officers were elected: President, Rev. C. W. Diehl; vice-president, Mr. John M. Wolf; secretary, Rev. William Penn Barr; treasurer, Mr. John Eisely. The society was incorporated November 30, 1923.

The society number 111 members and raised $284.25 for its work during the past year.

Four committees are actively at work: Hospice, Institutions, Old Folks and Relief. Cards giving the names and locations of the Lutheran congregations have been placed in the various institutions. *The Lutheran* has been placed in the Y. M. and Y. W. C. A. and a catechetical class has been conducted under the auspices of the Institutional Committee.

The Hospice Committee has distributed tracts, the Gospels and *"A Message for the Day"* to shut-ins and others.

The Relief Committee has extended help to a number of needy persons and on December 28th gave a Christmas dinner to 58 poor children. A "story hour" is conducted weekly in a branch Y. W. C. A.

7. The Philadelphia City Mission

The Philadelphia City Mission, originally established by the Board of Missions of the Ministerium of Pennsylvania, but now affiliated with the Ministerium's new Board of Inner Missions, continues its beneficent work of preaching the Gospel and ministering pastorally to the inmates of hospitals, homes and persons. Three missionaries devote all their time to the work, assisted in the holding of services at conflicting hours by a number of other pastors. One of the missionaries also attends the sessions of the Juvenile Court three mornings of the week in the interest of children from Lutheran families.

Services are held regularly in eighteen institutions, in some of them every Lord's Day, in others two and three times a month; while the visits to persons in these and other institutions average fifteen thousand and more a year. This number, of course, includes many others besides Lutherans. In some of the hospitals the missionaries are the only regular visitors week after week, and so well have they established themselves in the confidence of the authorities that they are always welcome.

Persons and families who have removed to the city, and whose names and addresses have been sent to the Superintendent, are likewise visited, directed to the nearest Lutheran church, and name and address given to the pastor.

The Superintendent is the Rev. J. F. Ohl, D.D., 826 S. St. Bernard St. Office, Room 803, Muhlenberg Building, 13th and Spruce Streets.

X. DEACONESS MOTHERHOUSES

1. Lutheran Deaconess Motherhouse, Baltimore, Md.

The work of the Baltimore Motherhouse continues to enlarge, especially along educational and congregational lines. There has been abundant occupation for the Superintendent of Instruction elected two years ago and the corps of teachers. Class work has been helpfully interspersed with valuable observation and experience in connection with the charitable organizations of the city. Of the sixty deaconesses and probationers, thirty have engaged in parish work, nine new fields having been entered within the biennium. Eight sisters have served in other forms of Inner Mission work; three in Africa and the Virgin Islands. Many testimonials to the efficiency of the services thus rendered have been received and the number of waiting fields is constantly increasing. Three have rendered valuable service in private nursing.

Twelve young women have been in course of preparation for the regular diaconate and thirty-nine have enrolled in the special courses for Christian workers.

A week-day religious school has been conducted by the candidates and students under the supervision of the Superintendent of Instruction and the Training Sister and an evening church school in the Motherhouse for young people of the local churches.

2. *The Philadelphia Motherhouse of Deaconesses*

As an Inner Mission force, the Sisters of this Motherhouse take an important place in the Church. Of its 94 sisters, only 2 are no longer in active service, though 34 have been in the work for 25 years or more. The largest opportunity for Inner Mission work is found in three hospitals served by these sisters, as it annually brings them into contact with fully 5,500 house patients and about 13,000 others visiting the dispensaries. Many of these patients have never heard the gospel and not a few of these are deeply impressed by the morning and evening devotions and prayer before meals in the wards. The Christian atmosphere in these hospitals has frequently evoked comments of agreeable surprise and has helped to open the hearts of patients for the Word preached in the wards at stated times. *"The Message for the Day,"* published by the Inner Mission Board, is distributed every Sunday and eagerly read by many. The singing of hymns by a sisters' choir on Sunday mornings has brought comfort to the dying and encouragement to the convalescent. Nor should the Christian influence on the members of the nurses' training school be overlooked. Of the 42 sisters connected with the hospital work, 12 are in executive positions.

The Motherhouse conducts also the Lankenau School for Girls, offering a Christian education meeting in secular branches the standards of the grammar and high schools. Many of the 90 boarding and 50 day scholars attending last year are not from Lutheran families nor under any religious influences at home; yet all receive religious instruction and none graduate without a systematic course of instruction in Christian fundamentals and in the history of the church. Though usually not so considered, this is Inner Mission work of the highest type, reaching also daughters of the cultured class from the impressionable age of 7 to the critical age of 18-20.

Sisters of this Motherhouse are in charge of the Tabor Home for homeless children, where 70 boys and girls from 3-18 years of age find a home and Christian training. At the Preventorium "River Crest" almost 300 under nourished children in groups of 25-35 recuperate physically and at the same time receive some religious instruction, though necessarily limited. This is a branch of the Kensington Dispensary for the Treatment of Tuberculosis in Philadelphia, in charge of one of the deaconesses, where little less than 200 patients are regularly under treatment and observation. In two Homes for the Aged more than 80 men and women are under the care of the sisters. By no means all of these inmates have been faithful Christians, but now the daily worship and general influence leads many to turn to God before their final summons comes.

To the above Inner Mission opportunities must be added the seven congregations served by sisters of this Motherhouse, every sister conducting either a kindergarten or giving some other form of week-day religious instruction besides her visitation of the sick and destitute and work with young people. A distinct Inner Mission activity is to be added this September when one of the sisters will be placed in charge of the work of the Inner Mission Society of Reading, Pa.

A number of institutions, congregations, and other fields are pleading in vain for sisters, opening up still more Inner Mission opportunities, but these cannot be considered until more of the church's capable young women are ready to give themselves whole heartedly to the Lord in this ministry of mercy.

XI. SYNODICAL INNER MISSION BOARDS

1. *Board of Inner Missions of Ministerium of Pennsylvania*

The erection of a Board of Inner Missions by the Ministerium of Pennsylvania at its 175th Anniversary meeting at Reading, Pa., 1923, was an epoch making event in the history of Inner Missions. Its duties are defined as follows: "It shall superintend, have charge of and administer the Inner Mission work of the Ministerium. . . . . . It shall endeavor to foster and cultivate a true Inner Mission spirit among the congregations of the Ministerium; to promote associations of congregations and of members of the church for the propagation of local Inner Mission work in communities and the co-ordination of the activities of all Inner Mission agencies upon the territory of the Ministerium."

The Board employes five pastors, one of whom is the Executive Secretary, one layman and two women missionaries. The cost of the work is met by an appropriation of $19,,000.00 per annum from the Ministerium. The work of the Board is carried on in four departments:

> The Lutheran City Mission of Philadelphia,
> The Seamen's and Immigrant Mission,
> The Lutheran Children's Bureau,
> The Lutheran Bureau. .

Lutheran City Mission

During the biennium three pastors have given their full time to work in the hospitals, prisons and charitable institutions of the city. 881 services were held by the missionaries aided by pastors and seminarians. 28,500 individual visits were made, 30 communions were administered, and 4 baptisms and 22 funerals were held. One of the pastors of the City Mission also attended the sessions of the Juvenile Court.

Seamen's and Immigrant Mission

The Seamen's and Immigrant Mission has enjoyed great prosperity.

A pastor and lay helper are supported by the Ministerium, the layman acting as housefather of the Seamen's Home. 173 vessels were visited, 59 services were held and over 5,000 periodicals were distributed. In the Seamen's Home additions and renovations were made for which the Ministerium expects to raise $25,000.00. 2,375 lodgers were accommodated, more than 500 of whom were cared for free. 1,500 positions have been found and thousands of dollars were received for forwarding or temporary safe keeping.

Lutheran Children's Bureau

The first synodical agency in the United Lutheran Church for the placement of dependent, orphaned and neglected children, operates in 29 counties in Pennsylvania, 14 counties in New Jersey and the State of Delaware. During the biennium 224 children were received of whom 82 remained in our custody on June 1st. The Bureau is the official agency recognized by the County Courts for the care of Lutheran children for placement in private homes and institutions. A feature of the work is the care of unmarried mothers and family welfare work, supplementing the regular work of the Children's Bureau.

Lutheran Bureau

The Lutheran Bureau provides for the care of Lutherans in public institutions with special reference to tubercular sanatoria and corrective institutions for girls. 35 girls have been confirmed during the past two years. The follow up work is done by one of the missinoaries of the Board. In this department an Inner Mission survey of the whole territory of the Ministerium is now in progress and the Ministerium has authorized the holding of special conferences during the ensuing year for the promotion of this work.

The Bureau also gathers information of an Inner Mission character for the use of the Ministerium.

I. Orphans' Homes

2. *Orphans' Home and Farm School, Zelienople, Pa.*

The Orphans' Home and Farm School, Zelienople, Pa., has experienced a most blessed and prosperous year in caring for orphan and half orphan children of the Pittsburgh Synod. Fifty-five congregations of the Synod are represented here in the Home by dependent children.

The Pittsburgh Synod Board of Directors has co-operated with the Superintendent of the Home and the results are pleasing.

The health of the children was exceptionally good. The churches of the Synod responded liberally to our appeals for maintenance.

The campaign for Zelienople Orphans' Home and Home Missions for $120,000 has not as yet been met. To date we have $84,000. The time during which all subscriptions must be met is September 1st.

The object for which we appeal is a new school building.

The President of the Pittsburgh Synod Board of Directors is the Rev. F. C. Martin, D.D., Greensburg, Pa.   Mr. C. W. Herman Hess, secretary, the Rev. C. W. White, superintendent.

3. *The Wartburg Orphans' Farm School, Mount Vernon, N. Y.*

Begun in 1866 by the Rev. Dr. W. A. Passavant. Has grown to 110 acres and nineteen buildings. Cared for a total of 375 orphans and half orphans in 1923. Governed by a self-perpetuating Board of Trustees of 25 members. Supported entirely from voluntary contributions on the part of individuals and Lutheran congregations irrespective of synodical affiliation. First to have the cottage system. Helpers from training schools in Europe. Private school with religious instruction, church, gymnasium, farm, laundry, dairy with accredited Holstein stock. Fully equipped with modern conveniences. Printing plant, shoemaking establishment and basket weaving are features. Directors: Rev. G. C. Holls, 1866-1885; Rev. Dr. G. C. Berkemeier, 1885-1921; Rev. S. G. von Bosse, 1921.

From annual report for 1923. Receipts $103,470. Expenditures $84,143. In permanent memorial fund $50,000.

Unique year books, profusely illustrated. An annual Easter booklet and a fall greeting. Distribution 18,000 copies. Special for 1924: "In Memoriam" for the late Rev. Dr. G. C. Berkemeier. Airplane views, a "Blue Book," folders and postcards.

A talented musical organization begun in 1899 under the leadership of Professor Robert Steinmetz, has given concerts in the largest auditoriums of seven States and in Canada and has been received by numerous personages of note.

Columbus Day (with an attendance of 10,000) and the third week in May. Board of visitors' day on the second Thursday in May. The Ladies' Volunteers and the Wartburg Men's Club meeting semi-annually. William H. Steinkamp, president; Henry Albers, first vice-president; P. Reppenhagen, second vice-president; Charles H. Dahmer, secretary; Mr. Martin Wulff, treasurer; Rev. S. G. von Bosse, director.

II. Old People's Homes

1. *Mary Louise Heins Memorial Home for the Aged, Mount Vernon, N. Y.*

Begun in 1898. Connected with and under the management of the Wartburg Orphans' Farm School. Capacity 40. Accepts members of Lutheran congregations in New York and vicinity without relatives able and willing to care for them. Admission fee $1,000. Age limit (minimum) 65 years. Superintended by a Lutheran Deaconess. Receipts for 1923, $17,483. Expenditures, $9,246. Memorial fund, $2,000.

III. INSTITUTIONS FOR DEFECTIVES

1. *The Passavant Memorial Homes for the Care of Epileptics, Rochester, Pa.*

June 6, 1924 these homes for the care of epileptics began their thirtieth year. They have sheltered five hundred epileptics who have had mind between seizures to appreciate a home. Of all classes of afflicted, the epileptic is most pitiable. In these homes he is cared for, given useful work and religious privileges.

Sisters from the Milwaukee Lutheran Deaconess Motherhouse are the home makers. They make great sacrifices not only in giving up but in living with and for epileptics.

The money needed comes from the charitable. No one is under legal obligation to give. The Lord has always provided plenty of food and clothing and comfortable dwellings and no debts. His goodness is acknowledged in family and chapel worship.

Dr. Passavant's corporation, the Institution of Protestant Deaconesses, manages the homes and the Auxiliary Board of the Passavant Memorial Homes for the Care of Epileptics is ready to help.

IV. HOSPICES

1. *Trabert Hall, Minneapolis, Minn.*

In 1919 Trabert Hall, formerly called the Hospice for Young Women, was bought by the Lutheran Inner Mission Society of Minnesota. The hall is a three-story brick building large enough to acommodate seventy-eight women. Including the annex we have room for ninety-two residents. The rooms are nearly all single rooms and all of them have lavatories. They are well furnished, steam heated, and electric lighted, a comfortable place for girls to stay who have no home in the city.

We charge the girls three dollars and seventy-five cents a week for three meals a day and from two to three dollars for room.

The charges, we think, are very reasonable, but with careful management, we are able to give the girls good food and clean home-like rooms, and with the proceeds are able to pay all the current expenses besides the interest on $20,900 that we are still owing for the building, and also part of the principal.

We try to make Trabert Hall not a hotel but a home pervaded by a Christian atmosphere and our girls seem to enjoy their stay with us. We often wish we had a larger building to accommodate all who want to come in, and some day we hope to have another building as large as the one we have now.

4. *The Tryon Homestead, Philadelphia, Pa.*

"Tryon Homestead" has now been in operation almost four years, during which time it afforded a home to eighty-eight girls, two-thirds of them

Lutherans, for a period of time from six weeks to three years each.

We accept all applicants between the ages of 15 and 30 years, recommended by pastors or persons known to the committee.

As "Tryon Homestead" becomes more widely known, the number of applicants increases, causing us then to feel that our "Homestead" is too small.

During the winter months the house is filled to capacity, which is 28; in the summer, however, there are vacancies, due to vacations, change of schools, or positions.

"Tryon Homestead" is governed by a committee of 22 women, members of the Woman's Lutheran League. The work of the "Homestead" is directed by a house-mother, who has the welfare of the girls at heart and whose constant aim is to take the place of the absent mother.

This work has been greatly blessed in the past. Hoping for a continuance of this progress, we commit ourselves into the hands of the Almighty, without Whom we can do nothing.

V.   Miscellaneous Institutions

1. *The Layton Home for Invalids, Milwaukee, Wis.*

This institution was built and endowed by Mr. Frederick Layton, of Milwaukee, Wis., "for the benefit of those suffering from incurable diseases and rendered thereby incapable of caring for themselves or being cared for by relatives or friends at home." It was opened in 1907 as an annex to Milwaukee Hospital. Its capacity is 32 patients. Deaconesses of Lutheran Deaconess Motherhouse of Milwaukee are in charge. It receives both men and women. Two-thirds of its work is free. Mr. Frederick Layton provided for an endowment fund of $100,000. Cost of maintainance last year was $14,700. Officers and director, Rev. H. L. Fritschel, D.D., Sister Marie Kern, matron.

2. *Tabor Home for Children, Doylestown, Pa.*

Our official name is Tabor Home for Children. It is in charge of deaconesses. We admit only homeless children (no full orphans) but such where the parents are separated and the children are assigned to us through courts or children's aid societies. We have them from two to sixteen or eighteen years of age according to circumstances. Our children attend the public school of the township. We admit all denominations, not only Lutherans. The Home is not connected with any Ministerium although we have several lady representatives from some of the Lutheran churches in and about Philadelphia.

3. *Children's Receiving Home, Maywood, Ill.*

During the past two years sixty-two (62) children have been admitted to our Home for temporary care. Twenty-seven girls and thirty-five boys. Twenty-six of these were returned to parents and the others have been placed in various institutions. We have some children that are orphans but for various reasons are not placed into other institutions or for adoption. We have at the present time twenty-five children. We are sorry to refuse so many children who ask to be admitted to our Home, but lack of room is our only reason for refusing. The plans for a new dormitory are ready but it has been decided to postpone this another year, due to the high cost of material and labor.

4. *Artman Home for Lutherans, Ambler, Pa.*

With gratitude to God,, we report that the work at the Artman Home moved steadily forward during the past year. Its guests enjoyed the comforts the Home provides and its mailing list is growing.

Quite a few "temporary guests" were entertained throughout the year. One of these came from Ohio. Two of the permanent guests passed into life and three new guests were admitted, making the number of permanent guests ten at this writing. The home was opened in 1915 in a farmhouse on a tract of land at Sellersville, Pa., purchased for that purpose. The location, however, did not offer the necessary requisites for the proper development of the home, and the board considered it advisable to relocate and bring the home nearer to Philadelphia. Through the munificence of Mrs. E. R. Artman the board was enabled to purchase a very suitable property at Ambler, Pa., on December 31, 1923, to which the "Home" was moved on March 26, 1924. The will stipulates that the home be located in either Bucks or Montgomery counties, and Ambler being in Montgomery County, makes it a "legal" location. The newly acquired property is of brown stone, has 18 rooms, is entirely modern in its appointments. The house stands on a beautiful piece of ground containing seven acres. The Board of Directors feel that the future of the home is now assured and that it will receive the support of our Lutheran people as the kind founder hoped it would. Both men and women guests are accommodated. The admission fee for permanent guests is $1,000.00, and transient guests pay a weekly rate.

5. THE *Wilbur A. Herrlich Memorial Farm, Towners, N. Y.*

The Wilbur A. Herrlich Memorial Farm at Towners, N. Y., is beautifully situated on a 40-acre plot of land, including woodland, farmland, and open fields in the foothills of the Berkshires, 900 feet above sea level. The Memorial Farm was presented to the New York Inner Mission Society but in the operation of the Fresh-Air Home for Children each summer the Brooklyn Inner Mission Society co-operates.

A dormitory housing 70 children is supplemented by well-built screened wall tents, making a normal capacity of 80 children at a time. A fully equipped mess hall is in a separate building. A new five-room bungalow has been presented this year as a memorial to departed members by the

Summer Home Guild of Volunteer Workers. This building houses the nurses' clinic and an isolation ward in case of sickness. Modern plumbing and proper sewage, with spring water for drinking secures the approval of the State Board of Health.

The children are selected from among the neediest cases through the churches. Boys and girls between 5 and 12 years are eligible. Each child is given a two weeks' vacation. Every effort is made to improve the children physically and spiritually. A nurse is in constant residence. The food is prepared in accordance with standard dietetics. Christian workers attend the children day and night. Morning and evening prayers and song service, with a Bible hour, are regular events of each day.

Swings and see-saws, hammocks and slides, ball playing, toys and games, hiking, swimming and wading, provide the children's entertainment.

Four hundred children are cared for each summer, during July and August. The work is supported entirely by voluntary contributions. Donations of food supplies, linens, blankets, games and toys and solicited as well as money gifts.

The Superintendent of the Home and Director of the Farm is Rev. C. E. Krumbholz, 412 West 145th Street, New York City.

VI. Hospitals

1. *The Lutheran Hospital of Manhattan, New York City*

Patients treated, 2,198.

Cost of operation, $128,000.

Received from membership dues, $3,937.

Donations, $5,569.

Deficit, $5,000.

Assets, $224,000.

Liabilities, $121,000.

From 40 Lutheran churches of New York and suburbs 274 subscribing members have been enrolled. A Pastors' Committee of 24 aids in the visitation and spiritual care of the patients. The Inner Mission Society conducts the Social Service Department of the hospital and clinic. Visits during the year 3,993. The Medical Service Association has an enrollment of 70 physicians.

The Womens Auxiliary is indispensable to the maintenance of the hospital. The Junior Aid Society pledges its whole-hearted support.

2. *Milwaukee Hospital, Milwaukee, Wis.*

This hospital was founded in 1863 by Rev. Wm. A. Passavant, D.D., and Protestant citizens and pastors of Milwaukee. It completed the fortieth year in August, 1924. It is the first Protestant Church hospital west of Pittsburgh. Its bed capacity is 153. The number of patients cared for during the last year 3,514. The charity work amounted to $42,730. Total expenditures $190,978. A new Nurses' Home, costing $125,000, was built in 1923. Total value of property about $850,000. The hospital is in charge of the Lutheran Deaconesses of the Motherhouse at Milwaukee Hospital. General director H. L. Fritschel, D.D.; directing sister, Deaconess Catherine Dentzer; superintendent of nurses, Sister Emma Lerch; assistant superintendent of nurses, Sister Magdalene Krebs.

VII. Seamen's and Immigrant Missions

1. *Seamen's Mission, Hoboken, N. J.*

An outpost of the Church among our seafaring men, the Seamen's Mission in the port of New York, 64 Hudson Street, Hoboken, N. J. H. Bruckner, D.D., in charge, finds its services eagerly accepted. For over two years there has not been a vacant room in the home. An average of 300 men a day visit the reading rooms. We have an average of fifty callers at the office, and you will trust us that there is "Seelsorge" applied in every case. There are over a thousand who consider themselves members of the family and make us glad by the confidence and true friendship which they show for the Mission. A friend in need to nearly 200 a month sick, destitute, convalescent men and a preacher of the faith by demonstration of the work of love. A considerable extension of our buildings and staff is on the way to make us able to cope with the demand. Letters received for seamen increased to around 35,000 last year. Sailors' savings deposited or forwarded through the home came up to $20,000 a month. We thank God that we are allowed to represent the Lutheran Church in the great work of following our brothers of the sea.

2. *The Emigrant House Association in the Port of New York, Hoboken, N. J.*

Under the changes brought about by the new law governing immigration there has developed as a very important activity the follow-up service for immigrants.

Machinery has been set up in Bremerhaven and Hamburg to get names, dates of arrival and destination of immigrants for distribution to the nearest local church. This service will be done in connection with the Inner Mission Board whose Secretary for Immigrant Work will be in charge of the association. To him too will fall the organization and development of Immigrant Mission work in the Canadian ports. Advice and information about immigration and travel, help to sick or stranded immigrants, providing employment and suitable lodging are among the other branches of the work. If the new law works out according to the intentions of its framers, there should be a minimum of detention at points of entry and hardly any exclusion.

VIII. Inner Mission Societies

2. *Lutheran Inner Mission Society, Pittsburgh, Pa.*

The society maintains a central office in the heart of the city at Sixth and Liberty, 401-405 Pittsburgh Life Building, which serves as a convenient base of operations and general headquarters. Organized 1907, incorporated 1918, the society is governed by an elected Board of fifteen members of which three are women. The following synods are represented: United Lutheran Church, Joint Ohio and Augustana. The general institutional constituency of the society numbers about 4,000 souls scattered through thirty-eight charitable, corrective and penal institutions. Figures given below are for the year ending April 1, 1924.

Lutheran Hospice for Young Women. The second attempt to establish hospice work in Pittsburgh resulted in 1912 in the purchase of the 18-room, 3-story brick dwelling facing North Park at 330 E. North Avenue, North Side. The home has a capacity for 34 guests and last year sheltered 182 guests from nearby towns, rural districts and distant points. Extensive plans for improvements are considered in connection with the Inner Mission Campaign of September, 1924. Annual Hospice Day is observed in November. At an early date field service is to be undertaken in connection with the house. The property is valued at about $35,000. Last year's accounts showed receipts $11,595.66. Expenses $11,385.39.

Student House. At the University and the Carnegie Institute are enrolled over 475 Lutheran students; including other specialized schools, music, expression, chiropractic colleges and nurses' training schools, the total goes beyond 500. To meet the situation the Lutheran Student House was opened January, 1923, as a student boarding home and center for religious inspiration and fellowship. The Lutheran Student Club is enlarging its program. Services and religious discussion groups are conducted and service and social activities maintained. The house is located at 200 Dithridge Street and represents an investment of over $40,000. Income last year $10,017.79. Expenses $9,857.69.

Summer Camp, near Zelienople, Pa., on the beautiful Passavant tract, served 1,339 children and adults and 763 visitors. The camp has a capacity for 130 campers and is equipped with a large dining pavilion with kitchen, 15 pyramid and 10 smaller wall tents with floors, 135 iron cots, canoes, boats and athletic material. A fine Christian atmosphere and a strong religious program have characterized the camp.

The Training School was in session for 30 weeks as a night school and enrolled 83 students from 27 congregations. Six instructors assisted by lectures, offered courses in Bible, Religious Education, Faith, Missions and Field Work.

Institutional Ministrations. A total of 12,625 bedside visits in 19 institutions were reported and 623 public and 518 ward services were conducted. There were 219 communions, 5 baptisms, 1 confirmation, 1 funeral and 1 marriage. The department is in charge of an ordained missionary who is assisted by a group of lay visitors, pastors, Luther League and Sunday school workers.

Literature Distribution. A total of 61 Bibles, 294 New Testaments, 1,430 gospels, 81 devotional books, 7,017 tracts, 33,408 religious and 7,666 secular periodicals in 19 different languages were distributed among institutional inmates. By regular means literature is gathered through church and Sunday school agencies and since New Year the department has been in the hands of a Literature Secretary. *"The Inner Mission Worker,"* the monthly journal of the society, has 4,739 paid up subscribers.

Family Welfare. Christian home service functioned in 223 cases of need involving 742 persons. 71 court sessions were attended. The missionary of the department is in constant touch with court, social agencies, police stations, humane society, traveler's aid, public schools, rescue homes and health authorities. A large number of visitors assist in follow-up work, and full records are kept of all case work. At an early date an additional worker is to be called to take charge of all children's work.

Street Preaching was maintained throughout the summer in one of the crowded districts of the South Side. A total of 1,375 tracts and 70 gospels were distributed. Attendance was estimated over 2,000.

Vacation Bible Schools. While not directing and financing individual schools, the society has vigorously sponsored this week-day religious work. An all-day training institute was conducted, workers were enlisted and congregations aided in the establishment and conduct of schools. 18 schools enrolled over 1,700 children. The term in most instances continued for five weeks.

The entire receipts for the year were $52,337.86. Disbursements $51,491.12. Seven missionaries are employed and the society membership is 5,592. The Woman's Auxiliary has over 200 members and raised about $2,000 besides other help in mission work.

3. *Inner Mission Society of the Evangelical Lutheran Church in New York City*

The work of the Inner Mission Society of New York is divided into four main departments: Institutional, Family Welfare, Social Service Work in Hospital, and Fresh-Air Work in the summer.

Under the first head the work in the city institutions comes first. Services are held in English and German, each Sunday in a Lutheran chapel at the City Homes on Welfare Island. Week-day visitation by pastors and lay workers, supplying needs and comforts, covers many wards in city institutions.

In connection with institutional visitation, a system of referring unchurched persons to the pastors and workers of a church nearest the homes of the persons found, is effecting a connection with the church which has never obtained before. This system is being extended to cover all hospitals.

The Family Welfare Division is only just being developed. The securing of work, attention to physical ailments, abnormal living conditions, etc., are studied and taken into account in dealing with each case. The spiritual element is always recognized as of chief importance.

The society conducts the Social Service Department of the Lutheran Hospital. It arranges for convalescent care, conducts the registration in the clinic and provides spiritual and temporal care and relief wherever possible.

The Fresh-Air Work is conducted at the Wilbur A. Herrlich Memorial Farm and is reported under this separate heading. Four hundred children are given a two weeks' vacation each summer. Good food, wholesome recreation and Christian workers assist to mold young lives into useful citizens of State and Kingdom.

The society maintains an office at 412 West 145th Street. Its staff of workers includes a superintendent, a full-time lay worker, two part-time workers, and eighteen volunteers. Its annual budget is over $10,000, which is raised by voluntary membership contributions only. The society is non-synodical in its scope and work and has no official relation to any body of Lutherans, but is entirely Lutheran in its methods and viewpoint.

5. *Inner Mission Society of the Evangelical Lutheran Church of Baltimore and vicinity.*

The Inner Mission Society of Baltimore City has been very busily engaged during this last year. It is, of course, only a rough sketch of the work that has been done. There has been a wonderful manifestation of helpfulness and a spirit of co-operation in the various Lutheran churches which has been truly refreshing. More and more this Inner Mission work is taking hold in the hearts and lives of our Lutheran people.

We have conducted:

Services	330
Lectures	27
Baptisms	10
Funerals	7
Weddings	2
Communions in Institutions	786
Confirmed	26
Worker's Conferences	70
Special calls, family welfare and others	1,077
Catechetical instruction—hours	56
Our paid and volunteer hospital visitors have made—calls	13,500
Special hospital calls made by the superintendent....	300
Services conducted under the auspices of the Inner Mission by pastors, societies of the various churches and individuals	360

Literature distributed:

Messages for the Day 35,000
Scripture as a whole or in part.................... 12,000
Miscellaneous 53,000
_____
Total 100,000

At present we are in contact with 225 children through our Family Welfare Work.

Fifty-two fallen women and girls have been assisted to a better life. A number of families have been lead back to the church.

Hundreds of out-of-town patients in the hospitals have been given pastoral care.

We have done work in 32 institutions, homes of mercy, hospitals and prisons. The ministry of redeeming love has been applied to the unsaved, those in danger, the afflicted, the court wards, old and young, to the stranger within our gates.

Our society has grown to a membership of over 2,300. Mistakes have been made and many shortcomings can be noted. We can only hope to carry on in a more efficient way in the untried future. To our God, who judges mercifully, belongs the past.

Inner Mission Society of Milwaukee, Wis.

We organized on the 8th of November, 1919, with a charter membership of 200. We have about 370 members in good standing. Next Sunday will be our First Annual Roll Call Sunday and we expect to have 3,000 memberships after that. Our big piece of work has been the Lutheran Girls' Hospice located at 324 12th St., Milwaukee, Wis. The Hospice is self supporting. We have about thirty girls and serve meals to a few more. This is a $25,000 proposition and is debt free. We have furnished hymn books to the home for the friendless, also about 200 Testaments. A number of the pastors connected with the organization are visiting and bringing the Gospel to various hospitals and other institutions. We are trying very hard to do systematic work along these lines at the present time. We are planning to enlarge the Girls' Hospice and establish a Boys' Hospice near the Marquette University (which is a Catholic institution). We issue a quarterly bulletin called "Inner Mission Inklings."

RECOMMENDATIONS

1. *Resolved,* That the plan to conduct Inner Mission Conferences throughout the territory of the United Lutheran Church in co-operation with Synodical authorities be approved.

2. *Resolved,* That under present conditions it would be unwise to establish a general tuberculosis sanatorium in the Southwest.

Respectfully submitted,

E. F. BACHMANN, President.
WM. FREAS, *Secretary.*

INNER MISSION BOARD TREASURER'S REPORT

BALANCE SHEET—July 31, 1924

ASSETS

Cash in Bank and on hand	$3,604.94
Stamps	7.51
Inventory of Salable Literature at cost	1,326.00
Furniture and Fixtures at estimated value	200.00
	$5,138.45

LIABILITIES

Loans due Bank	$700.00
Loans due Individuals	150.00
Accounts Payable	92.00
Advanced Rental	5.00
	$947.00

FUNDS

General Fund	$2,399.92	
Special Fund for Mountain Work	8.47	
Special Fund for Immigrant Work	1,800.00	
		$4,191.45
		$5,138.45

Respectfully submitted,

WM. FREAS, *Treasurer.*

TREASURER'S REPORT FOR YEAR ENDING JULY 31, 1923

RECEIPTS

United Lutheran Church		$8,716.00
United, General and Branch Synods		269.13
Women's Missionary Society, for Mountain Work		150.00
Donations from Individuals		50.25
Donations for specific purposes		167.50
Sales of Literature		389.49
Loans:		
From Bank	$250.00	
From Individuals	950.00	1,200.00
		$10,942.37

DISBURSEMENTS

Salary of Secretary	$3,499.92
Salaries of Clerks, Stenographers, etc.	1,590.00
Expenses of Secretary	1,766.92
Expenses of Board Members, etc.	503.91
Literature purchased	1,589.17
Office Rental, net	691.95
Printing and Stationery	64.09
Postage and Expressage	138.89
Auditing	100.00
Office Supplies and Expenses	135.25

Loans repaid:
To Bank	$250.00	
To Individuals	700.00	950.00
Interest on Bank Loan..................	—	3.23
Donations for specific purposes, disbursed........		157.50
		$11,190.83
Excess of Disbursements....................		$248.46

Respectfully submitted,

WM. FREAS, *Treasurer.*

TREASURER'S REPORT FOR YEAR ENDING JULY 31, 1924

RECEIPTS

	General Work	Mountain Work	Immigrant Work
United Lutheran Church.................	$11,152.40		
United, General & Branch Synods.......	95.00		
Women's Missionary Society for Immigrant Work			$2,000.00
Donations for Mountain Work..........		$1,095.50	
Other Donations	55.85		
Sales of Literature	478.44		
Loans:			
From Bank $1,650.00			
From Individuals 310.00	1,960.00		
	$13,741.69	$1,095.50	$2,000.00

DISBURSEMENTS

	General Work	Mountain Work	Immigrant Work
Salary of Secretary	$3,624.93		
Salaries of Clerks, Stenographers, etc....	1,470.00		
Expenses of Secretary	2,260.62		
Expenses of Board Members, etc.........	663.67		
Literature Purchased	702.96		
Office Rental, net	1,207.92		
Printing and Stationery	144.00		
Postage and Expressage	212.47		
Auditing	100.00		
Office Supplies and Expenses............	335.63		
Office Fixtures	50.00		
Loans repaid:			
To Bank $950.00			
To Individuals 660.00			
	1,610.00		
Interest on Bank Loans.................	19.22		
Donations for specific purposes, disbursed	10.00		
Disbursements from Specific Funds:			
Salaries		880.00	
Expenses		293.97	200.00
	$12,411.42	$1,173.97	$200.00
Excess of Receipts or Disbursements......	1,330.27	$78.47	$1,800.00

Respectfully submitted,

WM. FREAS, *Treasurer.*

Philadelphia, September 10, 1924.

We have audited the accounts of the Board of Inner Missions of the United Lutheran Church in America for the two years ended July 31, 1924, and we certify that, in our opinion, the foregoing Balance Sheet, Receipts and Disbursements, etc., are in accordance with the books of account and are correct.

LYBRAND, ROSS BROS. & MONTGOMERY,
Accountants and Auditors.

The Rev. William Freas, Secretary of the Board, and the Rev. E. A. Sievert, recently called by the Board to take charge of work for immigrants at the ports of entry, addressed the Convention. The Rev. Ernst Walter, Superintendent of Tabitha Home, was introduced and presented the work of that institution.

Recommendations 1 and 2 were adopted.

The question having been raised with regard to the classification of institutions, it was moved and carried, That this question be referred to the Inner Mission Board for consideration.

The report was adopted as a whole.

At this point the President recognized the Rev. N. R. Melhorn, Secretary of the Board of Publication, who announced the death yesterday of the President of that Board, Dr. William C. Stoever. The Secretary was instructed to send the condolences of the United Lutheran Church to Mrs. Stoever.

Thereupon, at the request of the President, the Convention was led in prayer by the Rev. F. P. Manhart.

Dr. Tulloss, Chairman of the Committee of Reference and Counsel, proposed special orders as follows:

1. That the request of members dissenting from the action of the Convention concerning Peace and War be made a special order immediately following the report of the National Lutheran Home for the Aged.

2. That the report of the National Lutheran Council be made a special order immediately following the report of the Committee on Women's Work and the hearing of a representative of the Women's Missionary Society.

3. That in connection with the report of the Committee on Memorials from Constituent Synods, the matter of invitations for the next Convention be the special order.

4. That the session this afternoon begin at 1.30 o'clock, as a special order.

The Rev. John Weidley presented the report of the National Lutheran Home for the Aged.

REPORT OF BOARD OF TRUSTEES OF THE NATIONAL LUTHERAN HOME FOR THE AGED, WASHINGTON, D. C.

Great men of all time have acknowledged their indebtedness to the example and precept of some older man or woman, and sometimes these mentors were very humble. One of the first letters written by President Coolidge when he came to the White House was to James Lucey, a shoemaker, in which the President said, "I would not be here were it not for you." Immediately after the nomination of John W. Davis the newspapers pictured a venerable patriarch, with flowing white whiskers, a comparatively unknown adviser of a man whose character is admired even by those of opposite political opinions.

One of the divine facts about human life is that the effects of personality transcend all institutions, all laws, all the printed pages. Most of the men and women at the Home are humble folk. Who dare say what their contribution to the onflowing stream of human life has been, how much or how little they may have shaped the thought, the acts, and the achievements of their associates through the years?

There are today in the world certain savage tribes where the elder folk, when the working days are done, steal silently away to die. They know no grandparents; they haven't even words for them.

Grandparents were the first agents of civilization. It was not until the elders of certain communities were kept alive to tell their lore, to impart their wisdom to children that the hard-won knowledge of one age was handed down to the next.

The first hospital was on a grandmother's bosom; the first university was at a grandfather's knee.

Universities give honorary degrees to their students who have carried forward their traditions. The country honors its elder statesmen. Those who have come to the Church's Home are our respected honorary elders.

The Jewish churches set a notable example in their tender care of their elders. They literally carry out the Divine promise that never shall the righteous be forsaken nor their children begging bread.

We send missionaries to China to teach the tenets of Christianity. If we fail in the care of our elders the Chinese might justifiably send missionaries to America to teach respect for our aged.

The work of the National Lutheran Home for the Aged is not an expression of a gracious act, or a pretty sentiment for gray hairs, but a prime duty the Church owes to its aged members.

The rooming facilities at the Home are inadequate. The appeals for admission are pitiful. One of the urgent necessities is a new and larger building. We must have it if we are to answer the calls that are coming for admission. It is pleasing to know that of the hundreds of thousands of members in our Church, so few are compelled, when old age is upon them, to knock at the heart of the Church for help. But for the few who call there ought to be a ready response. There happen to be, even in our land so rich and favorable, a few who need the support of their brethren. There are men and women whose strength is gone, who are not able to support themselves, who have no relatives, but depend upon the Church for creature comforts.

We have thirty acres of land, nicely located, in the District of Columbia. In connection with the main building there is a neat and well-furnished chapel with a seating capacity of one hundred and fifty. Services are held regularly every Sunday afternoon in charge of the Lutheran pastors of the City of Washington. Each takes his turn in orderly succession. Other meetings are held from week to week conducted by the Young Peoples' Societies, the Women's Missionary Society, the Inner Mission Society, and other organizations of our city churches. Some civic organizations and individuals, aside from the Church, give gifts in money, and send their automobiles to give excursions to the old folks to historic places in and about the District of Columbia. Kellar Memorial congregation presented a fine radio outfit so that the members of the family can gather in the assembly room, afternoons and evenings, to hear lectures, sermons, and concerts.

The total expenditure for the maintenance of the Home, for all purposes, is one dollar a day per member.

Since rendering our last report to the United Church there has been one death in the Board of Trustees. Mr. George F. Muth departed this life June 5, 1923. He was a member of St. Paul's Lutheran Church, Washington, D. C., the Rev. John T. Huddle, D.D., pastor. The members of the Home family did not have a more sympathetic friend. He was prominent in business in the city of Washington for many years. While we speak of our grief it is mingled with gratitude for this servant who wrought so well for his fellows.

There were a number of deaths in the Home family:

Miss Lizzie Ringer from York, Pa., January 4, 1923.

Mrs. Catherine Minnick, New Philadelphia, Ohio, January 8, 1923.

Mr. Harry Engel, Baltimore, Md., March 8, 1923.

Miss Elizabeth Eschenauer, Middletown, Pa., March 9, 1923.

Miss Catherine Caufman, Philadelphia, Pa., May 16, 1923.

Mrs. Dora Summers, Sunbury, Pa., August 3, 1923.

Mrs. Elizabeth Fair, Manchester, Md., August 23, 1923.

Mr. Abraham Grubb, Liverpool, Pa., January 31, 1924.

ACCESSIONS

Miss Agnes Headington, Washington, D. C., May 6, 1923.

Miss Mary Stockett, Baltimore, Md., Feb. 14, 1923.

Mrs. Elizabeth Hamilton, Washington, D. C., Feb. 19, 1923.

Mrs. Elenora Bowers, Baltimore, Md., Mar. 23 1923.

Rev. William Spangler, Williamsport, Pa., June 16, 1923.

Mrs. Sarah Spangler, Williamsport, Pa., June 16, 1923.

Miss Ada Hill, Williamsport, Pa., Nov. 14, 1923.

There are thirty applicants on the waiting list.

The matron in charge of the Home is Sister Mabel Stanley, a graduate of the Baltimore Deaconess Motherhouse. She has three assistants, two of whom are trained nurses.

There are many visitors from the States. Every one who comes to see the Home seems to be gratified at the good location, the fine building, and the comforts enjoyed by the members of the family. Strangers are coming to Washington in increasing numbers. It is the City Beautiful. Here are noble memorials, imposing public buildings, the Lincoln Memorial, the Washington Monument, the Capitol, which impart reverence for the nation's makers and its present institutions. Here also is the Home, a noteworthy memorial to one of the Church's finest activities. When you come to Washington do not fail to see the Home. It is located on Eighteeth Street near Rhode Island Avenue, N. E.

We receive inquiries from time to time about the legal title of the Home. This would imply that its welfare is being considered by those who are writing wills. Bequests are being made. We are anxious that this information shall come into the possession of the millions of Lutherans in our country. There ought to be an endowment fund sufficiently large to make the Home self-supporting. The Home was founded and maintained by the General Synod by whose aid it was to erect a fine modern building.

BOARD OF TRUSTEES

Rev. John Weidley, Washington, D. C.

Rev. Henry Anstadt, Chambersburg, Pa.

Rev. John T. Huddle, Washington, D. C.

Rev. Richard Schmidt, Washington, D. C.

Rev. F. R Wagner, Martinsburg, W. Va.

Rev. J. L. Frantz, Myersdale, Pa.

Rev. J. E. Harms, Hagerstown, Md.

William H. Finckel, Washington, D. C.

John H. Jones, Hagerstown, Md.

William K. Butler, M.D., Washington, D. C.

Frederick W. Kakel, Baltimore, Md.

Harry T. Domer, Washington, D. C.

L. Russell Alden, Washington, D. C.

H. L. Snyder, Shepherdstown, W. Va.

F. E. Cunningham, Washington, D. C.

The Board meets semi-annually the second Monday in May and November.

The members of the Board resident in the city of Washington constitute the Executive Committee, and have charge of all the details incident to the management of the Home.

There is a Board of Lady Managers consisting of thirty-three members from the Lutheran congregations of Washington. This Board meets every month to consider the welfare of the members of the Home and to support the matron in the conduct of the Home.

Officers of the Board of Trustees

President.—Rev. John Weidley, 233 2d St., S. E., Washington, D. C.

Vice-president.—Rev. J. E. Harms, Hagerstown, Md.

Recording Secretary.—Rev. John T. Huddle, 738 11th Street, N. W., Washington, D. C.

Corresponding Secretary.—William H. Finckel, 918 F Street, N. W., Washington, D. C.

Treasurer.—Harry T. Domer, 727 15th Street, N. W., Washington, D. C.   Respectfully submitted,   JOHN WEIDLEY,
For the Board.

TREASURER'S REPORT OF THE NATIONAL LUTHERAN HOME FOR THE AGED

Harry T. Domer, Treasurer, in account with the Board of Trustees of the National Lutheran Home for the Aged, Washington, D. C., for the fiscal year from August 1, 1922, to July 31, 1923.

1922

Aug. 1 To Cash on Hand as per report to United Lutheran Church:

Columbia National Bank	$1,223.54
Washington Loan & Trust Co.	296.87
Home Savings Bank (Amer. Sec. & Tr. Co.)	2,872.77

Total $4,393.18

Receipts

United Lutheran Church $11,604.07

Donations:

St. Luke's, Baltimore, Md.	$34.31	
A. G. Herrmann, Washington, D. C.	50.00	
John J. Buffington, St. Mark's, Baltimore	25.00	
Memorial Luth. Church, Shippensburg, Pa.	40.50	
Prince of Peace Luth. Ch., Philadelphia	7.33	
Maryland Synod	313.00	
Franklin Nat. Bank, Washington, D. C.	100.00	
Rev. J. H. Turner, D.D., Ruxton, Md.	10.00	
Woman's Miss. Society, Frederick, Md.	20.00	
		600.14

Interest on securities and bank deposits...................... 823.69
Sale of farm products 88.89
Miscellaneous Receipts 16.27
Room renovation account :
   Memorial S. S., Shippensburg, Pa. 25.00
   Waynesboro Luth. Church, Pa. 25.00
   Rev. I. O. Baker and family, Washington,
      D. C. 25.00
   St. Peter's, Riegelsville, Pa. 25.00
                           ——— 100.00
Admission Fee Fund, 5 fees 1,050.00
Legacy and Trust Fund :
   Mrs. Anna M. Lake legacy, Gettysburg,
      Pa. 270.00
   Mrs. Ann M. Tritle legacy, Cheevesville,
      Md. 152.80
   Mrs. L. C. Snyder legacy, Washington,
      D. C. 500.00
   Mrs. H. M. Hankey legacy, New Ken-
      sington, Pa. 452.50
   Mrs. Adah B. Sauer legacy, Washington,
      D. C. ....'.............. 200.00
   Securities paid off 3,100.00
   Received from Inmates 8,182.98
                           ——— 12,858.28
Annuity Fund, Annuity Received 3,000.00

      Total Receipts 30,141.34

      Total to be Accounted for $34,534.52

DISBURSEMENTS

Executive Expenses :
   Board Meetings $36.83
   President's Salary 250.00
   Treasurer's Salary 500.00
   Treasurer's Bond 50.00
   Auditing (Paid under protest) 112.86
   Sundries 21.50
                           ——— $971.19
Board of Lady Managers for domestic expenses...... 6,000.00
Farm :
   Farmer's wages $900.00
   Extra Help and Board 760.50
   Supplies 404.23
   Feed 962.36
   Blacksmithing 32.65
   Cottage :
      Installing water main 485.45
      Repairs, etc. 167.75
                       ——— 653.20
   Veterinary Services 4.75
                           ——— 3,717.69

Professional Services:
Physician 454.00
Dentist 15.00
Architects 20.00
                                                                    489.00
Religious Services at Home 245.00
Deaconess Services 200.00
Nursing and Hospital 1,571.45
Medical Supplies 87.27
Engineer's Wages 900.00
Building Repairs:
Room Renovation 375.00
Various 192.72
                                                                    567.72
Plumbing and Sewer 454.90
Fuel 1,365.66
Electric Current 342.55
Gas 78.75
Telephone Service 158.60
Printing, Stationery and Postage 72.25
Taxes:
Water Rent 60.75
Grundy Co., Tenn. 11.30
                                                                    72.05
Funeral Expenses (4 deaths) 436.74
Interest Disbursements:
To Inmates 1,087.54
Various 325.75
                                                                    1,413.29
Legacy and Trust Fund:
Purchase Wash. Gas-Light Co. Bonds.... 2,000.00
Annuity Fund:
Purchase Wash. Gas-Light Co. Bonds........ 3,000.00
Exhibit:
Cost Buffalo Exhibit 232.20
General Fund Loan Account:
Purchase one share Amer. Tel. & Tel. Stock 102.75
Miscellaneous Disbursements 151.11

       Total Disbursements $24,630.17
Cash on Hand, July 31, 1923:
Columbia National Bank $2,011.63
Washington Loan and Trust Co. 302.82
Home Savings Bank (Amer. Sec. & Tr. Co.)........ 7,589.90

       Total Cash on Hand 9,904.35

       Total Accounted for $34,534.52

Securities: ASSETS
Legacy and Trust Fund 8,810.00
New Building Fund 400.00
General Fund Loan Account 100.00
Annuity Fund 3,000.00
                                                                    12,310.00

Grundy County Tract, assessed valuation	200.00
National Lutheran Home property, D. C., assd. val....	27,598.00
New Building, Cost	91,555.64
Farmer's Cottage, $3.000, Barn, $2,000..........................	5,000.00
Bedford, Pa., share in Fetterly bequest	1,606.83
Cash on hand, July 31, 1923 ....:.....	9,904.35

Total Assets $148,174.82

LIABILITIES

Unpaid bills .... $ 138.15

Respectfully submitted,

HARRY T. DOMER, *Treasurer.*

FOR FISCAL YEAR FROM AUGUST 1, 1923, TO JULY 31, 1924

1923

Aug. 1 To cash on hand as per report to United Lutheran Church:

Columbia National Bank	$ 2,011.63	
Washington Loan and Trust Co.	302.82	
Home Savings Bank (Amer. Sec. & Tr. Co.)........	7,589.90	
Total		$9,904.35

RECEIPTS

United Lutheran Church ....$	13,845.25	
Admission Fee Fund (1 fee)	200.00	
Legacies:		
George F. Muth, Wash., D. C. $200.00		
William C. Rupp, Balto., Md. 300.00		
	500.00	
Trust Fund:		
Proceeds War Savings Stamps 110.00		
Rec'd from Inmates 4,060.50		
	4,170.50	
Sale of Farm Products	54.57	
Interest on Securities and Bank Deposits....	900.39	
Miscellaneous Receipts	19.33	
Annuity Fund, Annuity rec'd	750.00	
Donations:		
Maryland Synod 134.68		
Miss Lelia Ida Gardner, Philada. 25.00		
St. Luke's, Baltimore, Md. 29.14		
Ladies' Aid, First Ch., Altoona, Pa. 10.00		
A. G. Hermann, Wash., D. C. 50.00		
Memorial Bible Sch., Shippensburg, Pa... 62.50		
Rev. J. E. Bittle, Pittsburgh, Pa. 5.00		
	316.32	
Maryland Synod Building Fund:		
Gift from Mrs. Matilda Seifert, Balto., Md.	100.00	
Total Receipts		$20,856.36
Total to be Accounted for		$30,760.71

DISBURSEMENTS

Trust Fund, Purchase Wash. Ry. & Elec. Bonds		4,950.00
Plumbing and Sewer		86.00
Fuel Account		1,455.15
Taxes		439.42
Farm:		
Blacksmithing	38.00	
Veterinary Services	6.00	
Supplies	383.59	
Feed	1,104.11	
Extra Help	560.00	
Farmer's Wages	900.00	
		2,991.70
Religious Services at Home		300.00
Funeral Expenses (5 deaths)		597.41
Medical Supplies		106.56
Deaconess Services		260.83
Gas		109.98
Telephone		146.88
Electric Current		338.30
Printing, Stationery and Postage		87.62
Building Repairs		245.66
Engineer's Wages		900.00
Board of Lady Managers, Domestic Expenses		6,600.00
Professional Services, Physician		450.00
Miscellaneous Disbursements:		
Sibley Hospital (Rebecca Gulick)	$132.30	
Garfield Hospital (Dr. Croll)	234.75	
Sundries	147.97	
		515.02
Nursing (Regular, 1,440; special, 61.00)		1,501.00
Executive Expenses:		
Board Meetings	43.60	
President's Salary	250.00	
Treasurer's Salary	500.00	
Treasurer's Bond	50.00	
Auditing (Paid under protest)	125.72	
Traveling Expenses, President	81.50	
		1,050.82
Interest Disbursements:		
To Inmates	1,288.97	
To Annuitants	407.50	
Various	125.42	
		1,821.89
Annuity Fund, Purchase Amer. Tel. & Tel. Stock		561.50
Total Disbursements		$25,515.74
Cash on hand, July 31, 1924:		
Columbia National Bank	593.66	
Washington Loan & Trust Co.	308.89	
Home Savings Bank (Amer. Sec. & Tr. Co.)	4,342.42	
Total Cash on Hand		5,244.97
Total Accounted for		$30,760.71

Securities: ASSETS

Legacy and Trust Fund	13,700.00	
New Building Fund	400.00	
General Fund Loan Account	100.00	
Annuity Fund	3,500.00	
		17,700.00
Grundy County Tract, assessed valuation		200.00
National Lutheran Home property, D. C., ass'd. val.		27,598.00
New Building, cost		91,555.64
Farmer's Cottage, $3,000; Barn, $2,000		5,000.00
Bedford, Pa., share in Fetterly bequest		1,606.83
Cash on hand, July 31, 1924		5,244.97
Total Assets		$148,905.44

No LIABILITIES

Respectfully submitted,
HARRY T. DOMER, *Treasurer.*

Note.—This statement does not include the July, 1924, apportionment and specials amounting to $1,266, received and deposited as of August 1, 1924.

Philadelphia, September 12, 1924.

We have audited the accounts of the National Lutheran Home for the Aged for the two years ended July 31, 1924, and we certify that in our opinion the attached reports of the treasurer for the years ended July 31, 1923, and July 31, 1924, are in accordance with the books of account and are correct.

LYBRAND, ROSS BROS. & MONTGOMERY,
Accountants and Auditors.

The statement concerning a requested increase of $5,000 a year on the budget of the Home was referred to the Finance Committee and ordered stricken from the report. Thereupon the report was adopted as a whole.

It was ordered that the Secretary remove from any report, in which it may occur, any similar statement.

The matter of dissent of certain members to the action taken on Item 8 of the report of the Committee on Moral and Social Welfare was taken up. The members referred to had attempted to enter their dissent yesterday, stating at the same time the reason for such dissent. The form in which the dissent was stated not being acceptable to the Convention, the dissent was withdrawn for the time being. No record was made of this in the Minutes of the session of Monday afternoon because of the withdrawal of the dissent.

Upon taking up this matter for consideration, the President

stated two processes by which the desire of those dissenting might be recorded, the one involving parliamentary processes which would open the question to debate, the other not. It was found that the matter could not be presented in a form to be acted upon at the time, and it was therefore moved and carried, That a special order be set for the further consideration of the matter immediately after the report of the National Lutheran Council this afternoon.

The Rev. L. M. Zimmerman, President of the Board of Deaconess Work, presented the report of that Board.

REPORT OF THE BOARD OF DEACONESS WORK

Two prominent milestones in the progress of the deaconess cause in America have recently been passed, i. e., the seventy-fifth anniversary of the arrival of Theodore Fliedner and four Kaiserswerth Sisters at Pittsburgh and the fortieth anniversary of the coming seven sisters of the Iserlohn Motherhouse to Philadelphia. The former was celebrated on May 25th in connection with the Sixteenth Biennial Convention of Lutheran Deaconess Motherhouses at Milwaukee. The latter was signalized by a series of services and evening reception in the Philadelphia Motherhouse on June 19th. The enthusiasm manifested upon these occasions was evidence of the vitality of the enterprise and the conviction of its permanent place among the progressive agencies of the Church.

The number of consecrated sisters and probationers now in regular connection with the nine Motherhouses as reported at Milwaukee is 369. The recently established institution of the Missouri Synod at Fort Wayne reports in addition 5 sisters and 19 candidates. The harmonious co-operation of these institutions in the great field of woman's loving ministry is a hopeful prophecy of closer fellowship in all departments of our great Church's activity.

We note with pleasure the increasing interest in the diaconate manifested by the Women's Missionary Society and the Luther Leagues, both of which organizations now include the cause among the annual topics in their courses of study. We are glad also to find prominent mention of the female diaconate in the Life-Service appeals of the Board of Education. The Board has endeavored by all legitimate means to bring the cause to the attention of the Church with a view to increasing the number of candidates. The pastors of the Motherhouses are always ready to respond when possible to invitations for the presentation of the work to congregations and synodical conventions. We have found especially effective the presentation of the work by deaconesses actually engaged in the various forms of service. Their very presence in the assemblies of the church and the simple narrative of their experiences serve to remove foolish prejudices and appeal most strongly to earnest-minded young women. An increasing use has been made of advertisements in the periodicals of the Church and a number of leaflets have been widely distributed. A large edition of an appealing tract written by the president of the Board has been presented by him for general distribution. But above all these efforts, dependence must continue to be placed chiefly upon the intelligent and active interest of the pastors of the church in commending the cause from the pulpit and in personal intercourse with their active membership.

There has been but one change in the personnel of the Board during the biennium. Dr. W. H. Greever, having been elected a member of the Executive Board of the United Lutheran Church, presented his resignation to this Board. The vacancy was filled by the election of Dr. J. F. Crigler, of Charlotte, N. C.

BALTIMORE MOTHERHOUSE
Instruction and Training

The revival of the office of Superintendent of Instruction in the election of Dr. Foster U. Gift to the position has been abundantly justified. Without any curtailment of the regular course for candidates or the one-year course for Christian Workers, it has been possible to add a two-year course, which has already enrolled six students. A model Weekday School of Religion has been conducted in Calvary Lutheran Church with an enrollment of more than 100 under the direct supervision of the Superintendent of Instruction and the Training Sister, the teaching being all done by probationers and students of the Motherhouse. Upon request of the Baltimore Lutheran pastors, evening religious classes have been conducted with great interest in the Motherhouse during the winter attended by young people from twelve churches in the city.

Five students have specialized in kindergarten work, assisting in the care of the children during the morning hours and themselves receiving technical instruction every afternoon.

In addition to the classroom work by the regular staff of the Motherhouse, which includes Rev. Henry Manken, Rev. C. J. Hines, George A. Bawden, M.D., Eugene Zellers, M.D., Prof. A. L. Judefind and the physical director of the Baltimore Young Women's Christian Asociation, special lectures have been given by Dr. E. H. Delk, Dr. A. Pohlman, Dr. U. S. G. Rupp, Dr. F. P. Manhart, Dr. J. F. Ohl, Dr. Chas. F. Steck, Dr. A. D. R. Hancher, Dr. E. K. Bell, Dr. L. M. Zimmerman, Dr. J. C. Bowers, Rev. W. Freas, Dr. L. Kuhlman, Dr. G. Drach, Dr. F. H. Knubel, Dr. A. S. Hartman, Dr. D. E. Benham, Mrs. C. E. Hay, Sister Jennie Christ, Sister Sophia and Miss L. E. McCormick.

Ten probationers have gained practical experience in the Lankenau

Hospital in Philadelphia, the Church Home and Infirmary of Baltimore, and the Maryland General Hospital of Baltimore.

Consecrations

At a special service in the Motherhouse Chapel on April 24, 1923, Sisters Georgia Bushman, Anna Friedrich, Margaret Gundrum, Gladys Kumler, Jessie Peterson and Bertha Schwanewede were in the solemn service of consecration admitted to full membership in the Sisterhood, the sermon being preached by Dr. Elias D. Weigle. At a service on April 29, 1924, Sisters Alma Boarts, Martha Hansen, Kathryn Merkh and Pearle Lyerly were similarly inducted into the full diaconate, the sermon being preached by Dr. J. F. Crigler.

Number of Sisters

The number of consecrated sisters now connected with the Motherhouse is 48 and of probationers 11, a total of 59; 4 having withdrawn within the biennium.

Work of Sisters

Parish work has been done within the biennium of 30 congregations, as follows: Christ, St. John's, Atonement and Advent, New York City; Zion, Syracuse, N. Y.; First, Albany, N. Y.; Reformation, Rochester, N. Y.; St. Luke's, Brooklyn, N. Y.; St. Matthew's, Messiah and Muhlenberg Memorial, Philadelphia, Pa.; Memorial, Harrisburg, Pa.; Zion, York, Pa.; Zion, Sunbury, Pa.; First, St. Stephen's, Pittsburgh, Pa.; First, New Kensington, Pa.; Second, Altoon, Pa.; First, Warren, Pa.; Holy Trinity, Elizabeth, N. J.; Trinity, Hagerstown, Md.; Reformation, Christ and First, Baltimore, Md.; Trinity, Canton, Ohio; Trinity, Akron, Ohio; First, Wheeling, W. Va.; First, Richmond, Va.; St. John's, Charleston, S. C.; St. John's, Salisbury, N. C.; St. John's, Cherryville, N. C.

One of our sisters is laboring in Tabitha Home, Lincoln, Neb.; one in the National Lutheran Home for the Aged, Washington, D. C.; one in the Orphans' Home, Loysville, Pa.; one in the Franke Home for the Aged, Charleston, S. C.; one in the Children's Home, Knoxville, Tenn. One is conducting the Lutheran Settlement House in Philadelphia. One is in charge of the Girls' Hospice, Baltimore. One is visitor of the Inner Mission Society of Baltimore among the hospitals and poor of the city. One is serving in Summerland College, S. C. Three are in Muhlenberg Mission, Africa, and one in the Virgin Islands.

Special Students

The results of the admission of special students to the Training School of the Motherhouse continue to be very gratifying. It has in no way interfered with the course prescribed for candidates and probationers, but on the contrary has been the means of leading a number of very efficient workers to enter the regular course.

More than 150 young women have pursued the special One-Year Course for Christian Workers, which was originally designed merely to prepare for more effective gratuitous service in their home congregations. This end has been accomplished, as testified by many pastors; but many are occpuying positions of great usefulness in wider spheres. Three are laboring under the care of the Inner Mission Society of Philadelphia— two of these as assistants of our deaconess, Sister Martha, in the Lutheran Settlement House, and one as kindergartner in the Martin Luther Neighborhood House. One is serving under the auspices of the Inner Mission Society of Minneapolis and one engaged officially in Inner Mission work in New York City. One has accepted a position under the Women's Missionary of the United Lutheran Church in Philadelphia. One is assistant to our Sister Mabel in the National Lutheran Home for the Aged in Washington, D. C. Two are engaged in the Loysville Orphans' Home, and one in the orphanage at Nachusa, Ill. Five are laboring as pastors' helpers upon salary, i. e., in Lancaster, Ohio; Cobleskill, N. Y.; Roanoke, Va.; York, Pa., and New York City. Fourteen are serving in our Foreign Mission fields, India, Africa and Japan; one is in Porto Rico and one in the Virgin Islands. Fourteen entered the Motherhouse as fiancees of theological students and are now the wives of pastors in our home and foreign fields.

In response to a desire expressed by a number of the students in recent years, the Board now offers also a Two-Year Course, upon which a number have already entered. During the biennium 40 students have been enrolled in these special courses.

Gifts

Legacies have been received from estates of the following friends of the cause: Mrs. Anna M. Lake, $270; Mr. Francis A. Reichard, $100; Mr. Wm. L. Fleagle, $52.22. A number of substantial contributions have been made in cash or provisions by individuals, congregations, and Sunday schools.

THE PHILADELPHIA MOTHERHOUSE

Forty years of deaconess work in Philadelphia were completed on June 19th, of this year. The day was fittingly observed not merely because of its significance in the life of the Motherhouse and the Church, but also because two of the original group of seven sisters who arrived from Iserlohn, Westphalia, on June 19, 1884, are still with with us, one of them in active service. The importance of this successful transplanting of the Female Diaconate can hardly be overestimated. This Motherhouse, like the others founded since, is an open door through which consecrated young women can enter upon a life-service in the Church's ministry of mercy. These Motherhouses have been centers of spiritual power quickening the lives of thousands every year and setting a high standard of consecration and efficiency for all religious workers. The Ministerium of Pennsylvania and Ministerium of New York by official action recognized this anniversary and the presidents of the United Lutheran Church, of the Ministerium of Pennsylvania and of the Board of Deaconess Work delivered inspiring addresses on this day.

The Sisterhood has grown to 95 members, 78 deaconesses and 17 probationers, including two sisters sent us by the West Indies' Mission Board for work among their own race and one sister from a Mother-house in Berlin whose long experience in a line of treatment compara-tively new in this country will be of special value in our Children's Hospital work.   Of the 92 sisters 34 have entered during the past decade, 12 during the past biennium. They came from 14 different synods and other Lutheran bodies, 15 of the sisters from congregations of the Ministerium of Pennsylvania; of the 92 sisters 11, *i. e.,* 12 per cent are from Philadelphia congregations. This leads to the reasonable conclusion that *the deaconess work will continue to gain ground most where it is known best.* This is the basis for our expectation of a fuller development of the diaconate during the fifth decade just begun.

The pleas for deaconesses are growing in numbers and persistence and *the great need is a more widespread and active co-operation by pastors and other leaders in the Church for winning candidates.* Sisters of the Philadelphia Motherhouse are stationed at three hospitals with a total of more than 5,500 patients every year, besides more than three times that number treated in the dispensaries. Our sisters care for 80 men and women in two homes for the aged, for 70 children, mostly from dis-rupted families, for several hundred under-nourished children in danger of tuberculosis sent to a preventorium in groups of 15—25 by a dis-pensary in charge of one of our deaconesses, having about 200 tuberculosis patients regularly on their list. Our sisters also conduct our Lankenau School for Girls, the only Lutheran school admitting children of all ages and the only school in this country conducted by deaconesses. Some children have received their entire education here, from the kindergarten through the high school. The graduating class of 1924 numbered 14 young women from five States and five different denominations. Last, but not least, seven of our sisters are in as many parishes where they devote themselves chiefly to educational work and visitations. Almost 60 deaconesses more are needed now, about half for new fields of labor insistently pleading for help. Teachers, nurses, social workers and others with highly specialized training could soon be sent out as deaconesses to labor directly for Christ.

A Two-Year Course for Christian Workers is offered by this Mother-house, but owing to lack of room only four students at a time can be admitted. The first year includes a full kindergarten course, the second year is devoted to practical training along lines needed by parish workers.

As this course is rather strenuous and is but little advertised, the number of students has at no time exceeded said number.

The Philadelphia Motherhouse has felt for many years the need of additional room and has added a "Sun Parlor" for children and a rest room for their parents; also a room for physiotherapy at a cost of $15,000; other necessary improvements added $7,500 more. To meet these extra expenses a "Donation Day" was held for the first time in the history of this institution on October 26, 1923, which netted over $8,000. The response of the many friends was so encouraging that "Donation Day" will probably become a permanent feature. This Motherhouse is deeply grateful to the United Lutheran Church for the $3,000 received in 1922 and $4,500 in 1923. Without this assistance the Motherhouse would soon face a serious situation, for even with this help the current expenses for 1923 exceeded the income by $2,222.27. The treasurer's accounts are audited annually by the same firm engaged for this service by the United Lutheran Church.

Respectfully submitted,

E. F. BACHMANN.

THE MILWAUKEE MOTHERHOUSE

The Board of Managers of the Institution of Protestant Deaconesses which controls the Milwaukee Motherhouse consists of nine members, five of whom must be members of the Pittsburgh Synod, and four members of other co-operating synods. The present members of the Board are: Rev. H. L. Fritschel, D.D., president, Milwaukee, Wis.; Rev. F. W. Kohler, secretary, Rochester, Pa.; Sister Catharine Dentzer, Milwaukee, Wis.; Mr. H. E. Passavant, Philadelphia, Pa.; Prof. Otto Proehl, Clinton, Iowa; Rev. C. W. White, Zelienople, Pa.; Rev. Ellis B. Burgess, D.D., Crafton, Pa.; Rev. Jesse LeRoy Miller, D.D., Youngstown, Ohio; Mr. William Steinmyer, Pittsburgh, Pa.

The Sisterhood consists of 42 consecrated Deaconesses and 10 probationary Sisters, a total of 52 Sisters. Five Sisters were consecrated in our chapel on the 11th of November, 1923, Pastor H. L. Fritschel, D.D., and A. Gruhn, pastor of the Mothersouse, officiating. The Lord willing, Sister Nanca Schoen, of St. Croix, Virgin Islands, who is here on furlough, will be consecrated on the 14th of September, 1924. After her consecration she will return to her field of labor.

The Sisters serve at the following stations and fields of labor: Motherhouse, Milwaukee, Wis., 3; Milwaukee Hospital, Milwaukee, Wis., 18; Layton Home, Milwaukee, Wis., 3; Passavant Hospital, Pittsburgh, Pa., 6; Home for Epileptics, Rochester, Pa., 6; Orphans' Home, Zelienople, Pa., 4; Orphans' Home, Toledo, Ohio, 3; Old Folks' Home, Toledo, Ohio, 2; Church of the Redeemer, Milwaukee, Wis., 1; Orphans' Home, Waverly, Iowa, 1; St. Croix, Virgin Islands, 1; on furlough, 2.

During the biennium approximately 80 aged men and women were given Christian care in Christian Homes for the aged; 250 orphans and dependent children have been cared for spiritually and bodily.   The sufferings of 40 incurables were relieved by loving hands in a Christian Home.   The souls and bodies of 100 Epileptics were provided for, 14,000 patients have been cared for and nursed in our hospitals, and extensive service has been rendered to the poor by the dispensary.   Parish work has been done in the Church of the Redeemer, Milwaukee, Wis.

The Pittsburgh Synod has successfully conducted a campaign to raise funds for a new school building for the Orphans' Home at Zelienople, Pa. This will be a much needed and valuable addition to that institution. May God continue blessing the efforts of this Synod.   The Milwaukee Hospital has erected a new house for nurses, at the cost of one hundred and twenty-five thousand dollars, which was completed in February, 1924.

The Sixteenth Conference of Lutheran Deaconess Motherhouses in America met in Milwaukee, Wis., May 20-22, 1924. All the Lutheran Motherhouses in America were well represented, except one. The sessions throughout were very inspiring, and much benefit was derived from them by everyone who attended them.   The officers were re-elected, and a committee was appointed to write a history of the diaconate in America.

The Diamond Jubilee of the Deaconess Work in America was celebrated on Sunday, May 25, 1924, with appropriate services. In the morning service the Rev. C. P. MacLaughlin, D.D., of the First Lutheran Church of Pittsburgh, Pa., preached a very impressive anniversary sermon. The Rev. H. L. Fritschel, D.D., and A. Gruhn also officiated. In the afternoon service the speakers were: E. F. Bachmann, D.D., of the Philadelphia Motherhouse; C. G. Chinlund, S.T.D., of the Augustana Motherhouse, Omaha, Neb.; H. B. Kildahl, D.D., Superintendent of the Home Finding Department of the Board of Charities, Minneapolis, Minn.; J. A. Morehead, D.D., Sister Anna of Bethany Motherhouse, Berlin, Germany, Pastor J. F. Fedders of Lake Park Church, Milwaukee, Wis., and H. L. Fritschel, D.D., General Director of the Institution of Protestant Deaconesses. The delegates who attended the Deaconess Conference took part in this celebration, thus nearly every Motherhouse in America was represented.

Respectfully submitted,
A. Gruhn, Pastor.

Resolutions Suggested

1. The United Lutheran Church records its gratitude to God upon the Seventy-fifth Anniversary of the introduction of deaconesses into this country by the late Dr. Wm. A. Passavant, of Pittsburgh, Pa., and congratulates the Institution of Protestant Deaconesses founded by him and now carrying on its work in connection with the Lutheran Motherhouse at Milwaukee.

2. It likewise records its deep appreciation of the services rendered by the deaconesses of the Lutheran motherhouses throughout this country,

and rejoices in the fact that in the female diaconate there has been offered to the consecrated young womanhood of the church an opportunity for life service, so varied in its demands as to utilize every talent, so divergent in its operations as to meet every need, so Christ-like in its spirit as to challenge the devotion of all who love the Lord.

3. In view of the fact that our Sisters are serving in parishes and institutions under the auspices of the various Boards of the Church, we bespeak for our deaconess work the hearty support of our pastors and of the official representatives of the various agencies of the Church.

4. We commend the wisdom of the Baltimore Motherhouse in seeking to establish an endowment fund as provision for the future and approve the application to this purpose of all contributions received upon the annuity plan.

5. We approve the establishment of special courses in the Motherhouses for young women who desire to secure special training for Christian service but are unable to enter the deaconess calling.

Respectfully submitted,
L. M. ZIMMERMAN, President.
C. E. HAY, Secretary.

TREASURER'S REPORT OF CASH RECEIPTS AND DISBURSEMENTS

For the Year Ended 31st July, 1923

RECEIPTS:

	General Fund	Endowment Fund	New Building Fund
United Lutheran Church in America..	$21,809.00		
United, General and Branch Synods..	147.85		
Donations	90.00		$1,044.50
Tuition	2,427.50		
Kindergarten	556.76		
Nursing	753.21		
Stations	7,058.35		
Miscellaneous Refunds	79.79		
Bank Interest	78.41	$14.52	105.94
Interest on Investments			106.25
Discounts earned	102.41		
Proceeds from Sale of Liberty Bonds			4,979.85
	$33,103.23	$14.52	$6,236.54

DISBURSEMENTS

Salaries of Superintendent and Asst.	$4,000.02
Superintendent's Traveling Expenses	545.90
Wages of General and Domestic Help	3,610.00
Expenses of Motherhouse	308.15
Furniture and Fixtures, Purchased....	393.00
Expenses of other Officers and Board Members	516.36
Expenses of Grounds	155.25
Household Expenses	4,500.00
Personal Expenses of Sisters	1,149.75
Sisters' Training Fund	175.00
Professional Services for Sisters	598.25
Sisters' Quarterly Allowance	5,126.10
Sisters' Traveling Allowance	757.59
Wearing Apparel	2,865.18
Lectures and Class Instruction	568.35
Class and Library Books	809.28
Printing and Stationery	906.40
Office Salary and Expenses	133.33
Telephone and Telegraph	82.32
Postage and Expressage	76.13
Fuel and Light	3,268.43
Auditing	100.00
Contribution to Mary J. Drexel Home	2,000.00
Sewing Room Expenses	550.00
Annuity Bond Interest	305.17
Grain, Feed and Garden Supplies	400.12
Expenses of other Buildings owned by Board	1,460.47
New Cottages	5,097.00
General Expenses	1,391.71
	$41,849.26

Excess or Deficit for the Year....	$8,745.98	$14.52	$6,236.54

ANNUITY FUND:

Annuities	$7,000.00
Ground Rents Purchased	3,300.00
Excess	$3,700.00

SUMMARY

Balance, August 1, 1922		$6,585.29
Add, Excess of Receipts:		
Endowment Fund	$14.52	
New Building Fund	6,236.54	
Annuity Fund	3,700.00	
		9,951.06
		$16,536.35
Deduct, Excess of Disbursments: General Fund		8,745.98
		$7,790.37

Respectfully submitted,

FREDERICK J. SINGLEY, *Treasurer.*

PHILADELPHIA, August 28, 1924.

We have audited the accounts of the Board of Deaconess Work of the United Lutheran Church in America for the year ended July 31, 1923, and we certify that, in our opinion, the foregoing statements of Receipts and Disbursements, etc., are in accordance with the books of account and are correct.

LYBRAND, ROSS BROS. & MONTGOMERY,
Accountants and Auditors.

TREASURER'S REPORT OF CASH RECEIPTS AND DISBURSEMENTS
for the year ended 31st July, 1924

RECEIPTS

	General Fund	Endowment Fund	New Building Fund	Annuity Fund
United Lutheran Church in America	$25,796.00			
United, General and Branch Synods	184.97			
Donations	100.00	$220.05	$247.36	
Tuition	3,075.17			
Kindergarten	692.82			
Nursing	878.66			
Stations	6,974.14			
Annuities				$1,000.00
Miscellaneous Refunds	900.71			
Bank Interest	26.96	14.22	73.23	
Discounts Earned	99.96			
Ground Rents	342.62			
	$39,072.01	$234.27	$320.59	$1,000.00

DISBURSEMENTS

Salaries of Superintendent & Asst..	$4,000.00
Superintendent Traveling Expenses	205.25
Wages of General & Domestic Help	4,110.00
Expenses of Motherhouse and Cottages	682.72
Furniture and Fixtures Purchased.	391.75
Expenses of Other Officers and Board Members	581.74
Expenses of Grounds	271.47
Household Expenses	5,000.00
Personal Expenses of Sisters	1,067.57
Sisters' Training Fund	150.00
Professional Service for Sisters..	810.75
Sisters' Quarterly Allowance	4,679.30
Sisters' Traveling Allowance	441.32
Wearing Apparel	2,637.26
Lectures and Class Instruction	737.20
Class and Library Books	405.87
Printing and Stationery	554.05
Office Salary and Expenses	305.53

Fuel and Light....................	3,168.82				
Contribution to Mary J. Drexel Home	4,500.00				
Sewing Room Expenses...........	550.00				
Grain, Feed and Garden Supplies..	411.11				
Advertising in *"Lutheran"*.........	171.86				
Auditing	100.00				
Annuity Bond Interest............	591.75				
Expenses of other Buildings owned by Board	35.12				
Lorraine Park Cemetery Lot Purchased	600.00				
Ground Rents Purchased.........	154.48				4,700.00
General Expenses	779.52				

	$38,094.44			$4,700.00
Excess or Deficit for the year	$977.57	$234.27	$320.59	$3,700.00

Summary

Balance, August 1, 1923.............................		$7,790.37
Add Excess of Receipts:		
General Fund	$977.57	
Endowment Fund	234.27	
New Building Fund	320.59	1,532.43
		$9,322.80
Deduct, Excess of Disbursements:		
Annuity Fund		$3,700.00
		$5,622.80

FREDERICK J. SINGLEY, *Treasurer.*

Philadelphia, August 28, 1924.

We have audited the accounts of the Board of Deaconess Work of the United Lutheran Church in America for the year ended July 31, 1924, and we certify that, in our opinion, the foregoing statements of Receipts and Disbursements, etc., are in accordance with the books of account and are correct.   LYBRAND, ROSS BROS. & MONTGOMERY,
Accountants and Auditors.

The Rev. C. E. Hay, Secretary of the Board and Pastor of the Baltimore Motherhouse, presented the work of that institution, and then introduced successively the Rev. Herman L. Fritschel, President of the Institution of Protestant Deaconesses, Milwaukee, Wis., and the Rev. E. F. Bachmann, Pastor of the Philadelphia Motherhouse, each of whom addressed the Convention.

Resolutions 1, 2, 3, 4 and 5 were adopted. The report was adopted as a whole.

The Rev. A. Pohlman presented the report of the Board of Ministerial Relief.

REPORT OF THE BOARD OF MINISTERIAL RELIEF

The "Keynote" of the Biennial Report of the Board of Ministerial Relief is "Encouraging Progress." There have been days of stress and anxiety, when the Board wondered how it could pay its pension pledges; there was also a rapidly increasing debt which created an alarming problem, but the crisis has been passed and the outlook for the future is brighter than at any time since the establishment of the pension.

The story of the biennium is one of development. The work of the Board is still new to the Church. Due to the fact that pastors show reticence in presenting a cause which will eventually benefit them, in many places it is scarcely known. Publicity has been the Board's great fundamental need and it has sought to attain it through presentation to congregations and at Synodical and other meetings by the Executive Secretary; through articles and advertisements in *The Lutheran* and other Church publications, and through personal letters. It is further seeking this end by securing cooperating committees in every synod who will secure laymen in their various districts to present the cause before congregations, seeking appointments for them in every congregation of the district. To this end a "Speaker's Manual" has been prepared which will provide material for addresses as well as give knowledge of what is being done and planned for the ministers, not only in our own communion, but in the various Churches of the Protestant faith in the United States and Canada, so that the speakers may have a background which will enable them to answer any questions which may be asked.

In some quarters it has been suggested that it might be better if the pension was on a contributory basis, the ministers, in order to participate, making an annual contribution toward its maintenance. This has been rejected because, however small the required amount might be, there would inevitably be some who would feel unable to pay it, and though they would be the ones who would need it most, their failure would bar them and their widows from the pension benefits. The pension is not an insurance, but is the Church's provision for its veterans. As a matter of fact, every minister who is so inclined is free to contribute to the work as much and as often as he may desire.

It has also been suggested that some do not require a pension and that therefore it should be conditioned upon need. This has also been rejected because of the utter inability of any Board to pass justly upon "need." It cannot be measured upon any standard of a given number of dollars of private income. Too many other things enter in. Private resources are usually over-estimated. Such things are judged by a man's manner of life and liberality. Ministers must maintain a scale of living in accord with the congregation which they serve and invariably they are liberal beyond their means. The whole sweetness of the Church's provision for its veterans would be taken away if reception of the pension depended upon a man or woman having to justify to the Board their need of a pension before they could enjoy its benefits. Some who do not need it do not make application. Others give back the entire amount to the Board to be applied to its Endowment or Relief. Still others share it with other agencies of the Church. Some few possibly receive it who might forego their privilege, from the point of view of expediency, but they too have earned it and no one knows either their actual circumstances or what disposition they make of what they receive. It would not be just or right to penalize the entire ministry by any requirement of the statement of need bcause of the few whom local opinion, which may be grossly mistaken, thinks should not be included in the provision. As a matter of fact, the United States Income-tax returns of 1916 show that less than one in 100 had a gross income of $3,000, so that even with the increased salaries since that time, which have not kept up with the cost of living, very few would have income enough when salary ceased, to live without being dependent upon some one. The judgment of the laymen of the Church, in so far as we have been able to gather it, is strongly in favor of the present plan, which is identical, in its application, with that of the great corporations of the land, which give to all, executives as well as the humblest workers, a pension on the basis of service.

The history of the biennium is a story of struggle. The amount received from the apportionment for the three years ending July 31, 1923, averaged $12,000 annually less than the cost of the pensions. For the past two years the Women's Missionary Society has been giving $5,000 a year to the work. Additional gifts and the small income from the Endowment have enabled the Board to meet all running expenses and keep the debt down to $20,000 at the end of that period. In December, 1923, however, the situation became so acute that a special meeting of the Executive Committee had to be called to provide funds before the monthly checks could be sent out. The Church could not break faith with its veterans and a way out was found. With that the crisis was passed. A number of large gifts were received and the Christmas gifts began to pour in, about 50 per cent. of them for the General Fund. With January the new apportionment became effective and the benevolence of the Church showed a decided improvement, so that payments have been made on the debt and the summer shortage provided for. Brighter days seem to have arrived.

The Relief Work of the Board has developed materially during the biennium. For four years Christmas letters have been sent out to a constantly growing mailing list asking for gifts to enable us to dispense the

Christmas spirit through the year to those in need. The first year the appeal brought in $2,600; the second, $6,300; the third, $9,000, and the fourth, between $12,000 and $13,000, half of which was indicated for the debt. During the past two years as a result, the Board has been able to make four grants annually to those who made application for it on the basis of need, and to give help to a number of active pastors into whose lives had come financial crises through sickness or death in their families. The regular grants were made at Christmas, Easter, in July and October— $50.00 at each time to those who had no income on which they could count beyond their pension, and smaller amounts, down to $12.50 to those whose income did not exceed the amount of their pension. The appreciation of even the smallest gifts has been almost pathetic. About $12,000 a year is distributed in this manner.

Nothing of this sort would be possible without special contributions for the purpose, and individuals, churches, Sunday schools, and Church Societies, are asked to support the Relief Fund with contributions at Christmas time and throughout the year.

In securing these extra gifts the cooperation of the pastors is essential in furnishing lists of those to whom letters may be sent with the prospect of arousing interest in the work. In this connection it is well to note that the Board has adopted the policy of reporting to every pastor whose people, as individuals or as societies, have made contributions directly to the Board, the amount received from his church. All blanks for remitting the money have a space for indicating congregational membership, as our card index system is kept by states, cities and congregations. All gifts, too, are acknowledged immediately on receipt. In order that congregational gifts coming through the treasurers of synods may also be acknowledged, blanks have been prepared for their use in order that they may indicate the source of the gifts.

It is gratifying to note that all of the Synods which had funds for the relief of their clergy before the Merger have transferred them to the Board of Ministerial Relief, with the exception of the Ministerium of Pennsylvania and the Synod of Canada. The former indicates its purpose soon to do so. The latter desires to avoid sending its funds across the international border. Both, however, pay the *income* of their funds into the hands of the Board. The Endowment funds of the Pastors' Fund of the General Synod, amounting to about $62,000 (owing to the fact that it was given for the relief of needy ministers and their widows and orphans), has been transferred to the Board of Ministerial Relief as a "Relief Endowment."

During the biennium there have been added to the Endowment Fund of the Board $26,105.46 and Annuity Bonds to the amount of $22,173.00, which will eventually become part of the Endowment. Of the bonds, $14,223 have been taken by ministers, one of whom has given the Board $8,223, $5,223 of which is for Relief Endowment, and another $5,000. The total gifts to the Board during the biennium for all purposes, including the money received from the Women's Missionary Society, but not the annuity bonds, amounts of $63,667.54, which shows decided progress and growth of interest.

The present roll of those receiving pensions (August 1, 1924) includes 168 retired ministers, 20 disabled ministers, 402 widows and 82 children, involving an annual expenditure of $141,000.00. In the two years there have been removed by death 51 retired ministers, 10 disabled ministers, 27 widows; 2 widows have remarried; and 36 children have reached the age of 16. During the same period there have been added 45 retired ministers, 20 disabled ministers, 65 widows and 16 children. A detailed account of those now on the roll and the amounts received by synods follows:

PENSION ROLL BY SYNODS.
August 1, 1924.

Synod	Retired Ministers	Disabled Ministers	Widows	Children	Yearly Pension	Yearly Relief
Alleghany	7	....	10	....	$4,100	$750
California	3	2	6	1	2,750	80
Canada	5	1	6	2	3,100	....
Cen. Canada	....	....	1	2	300	....
East Pa.	8	2	31	2	9,300	800
Georgia	2	1	5	7	2,250	600
German Neb.	6	....	10	12	4,400	150
Illinois	7	....	12*	....	4,500	400
Indiana	1	....	5	....	1,300	80
Iowa	2	....	2	2	1,100	70
Kansas	4	....	10	....	3,200	180
Manitoba	2	6	2	1	2,850	....
Maryland	8	....	21	2	6,700	290
Michigan	4	....	8	....	2,800	....
Mississippi	1	....	....	....	300	....
Nebraska	2	1	5	....	1,900	....
New York	13	1	26	2	9,500	1,360
N. Y. & N. E.	1	....	8	4	2,100	80
N. Y. Min.	9	....	23*	3	7,450	950
N. C.	6	....	24	3	6,750	690
Northwest	1	....	3†	1	1,050	80
Ohio	20	....	31	6	12,500	710
Pacific	1	....	3	1	950	....
Pa. Min.	14	1	55	4	15,700	1,250
Pittsburgh	13	1	29	10	10,500	930
Rocky Mt.	3	....	....	....	900	200
South Car.	1	1	16	9	4,250	710
Susquehanna	7	....	12	3	4,650	380
Texas	2	....	1	....	800	150
Virginia	7	1	9	....	4,200	200
Wartburg	1	1	1	....	800	....
West Pa.	7	1	25	5	7,650	570
West Va.	....	....	2	....	400	....
Totals	168	20	402	82	$141,000	$11,660

* Include daughter of Minister.
† One widow receives $25.00 through special agreement.

The campaign for $3,000,000 endowment, authorized by the Buffalo Convention, has been set by the Executive Board for 1927-1928, culminating in the tenth anniversary of the merger. The Board has been promised right of way until after its collection of pledges is completed. We feel confident of the hearty co-operation of the whole Church.

Certain changes of rules, extending the provision for children of retired and disabled ministers and guarding a little more carefully the matter of widows have been found necessary, as follows:

"The widow of an ordained clergyman of the United Lutheran Church shall be entitled to a minimum pension of $200 per annum, or two-thirds the sum granted or due her husband, provided, if her husband was retired, she had been married at least five years before her husband's retirement. In the case of widows of men who die in active service the right to pension shall be automatic, except that when the husband shall have been received from another ecclesiastical body, he shall have served at least three years in the United Lutheran Church before his wife shall be eligible to a pension. These pensions shall be in effect as long as the recipient remains a widow and in connection with the United Lutheran Church. When the circumstances are such as commend themselves to the Executive Committee, it can, by a unanimous vote, waive the special requirements. A statement concerning continued eligibility shall be required in December of each year."

"Widows shall receive in addition an allowance of $50.00 a year for each child under 16 years of age."

"Retired ministers having children under the age of 16 years shall be allowed $50.00 per annum for each child."

The following resolutions are submitted for your approval:

1. *Resolved,* that in view of the fact that pensions have been made the chief activity of the Board, the corporate title of the Board of Ministerial Relief be changed to the "Board of Ministerial Pensions and Relief of the United Lutheran Church in America."

2. *Whereas,* in accord with the action of the United Lutheran Church in Convention assembled at Buffalo, approving a campaign for $3,000,000 at such time as the Executive Board, in consultation with the Board of Ministerial Relief, should agree upon, these Boards have settled upon the years 1927-1928 as the time for such campaign, making it culminate in the tenth anniversary of the Merger,

Resolved, that the United Lutheran Church in Convention assembled, approve the time set for the Endowment Campaign of the Board of Ministerial Relief, and reaffirm the assurance that it shall have the right of way as given by the Executive Board. Be it further

Resolved, that all the authority and influence of the Church be behind said campaign, that all Boards and organizations of the Church be urged to co-operate in making it a success, and that all pastors and congregations do what they can to prepare the way during the years before the active campaign shall begin.

3. *Resolved,* that the United Lutheran Church in Convention assembled reaffirm its approval of the policy adopted by the Board of Ministerial Relief and approve the modification of the rules as recited above.

4. *Resolved,* further, that it approve the plan for co-operating committees and for their providing lay speakers who shall present the work

of the Board before congregations, and that when such service be not requested, it be offered by the co-operating committees. And finally

5. We request, that the cause of Ministerial Relief be presented once a year by pastor or layman before every congregation in the years preceding the campaign.

It may interest the Convention to know that a number of Synods have set apart the offering of Ordination Night for Ministerial Relief and that one Synod has recommended that an offering for this purpose be taken at every installation service.

Respectfully submitted,
EDGAR GRIM MILLER, *Executive Secretary.*

TREASURER'S REPORT OF THE BOARD OF MINISTERIAL RELIEF

Balance Sheet, July 31, 1924

ASSETS:

Cash in banks and on hand		$35,909.38
Accounts Receivable—due from Sale of Real Estate		690.00
Investments:		
At Ledger Values:		
U. S. Liberty Loan Bonds	$10,104.12	
Other Bonds	132,070.00	
Stocks	300.00	
Notes Receivable	6,000.00	
Mortgages	14,200.00	
Real Estate	1,389.84	
		164,063.96
Office Furniture and Fixtures		860.00
		$201,523.34

LIABILITIES:

Annuity Bonds	$59,023.00

FUNDS:

Pension Endowment	$52,515.63	
Relief Endowment	64,579.97	
Pension General	17,546.32	
Relief Current	7,858.42	
		142,500.34
		$201,523.34

Respectfully submitted,
J. H. BRANDT, *Treasurer.*

STATEMENT OF RECEIPTS AND DISBURSEMENTS

for the Year ended July 31st, 1923

RECEIPTS

	Pension Endowment Fund	Pension General Fund	Relief Endowment Fund	Current Relief Fund
United Lutheran Church		$124,378.00*		
United, General and Branch Synods	$1,770.12	6,432.60		$1,254.70
Women's Missionary Society		3,750.00		1,250.00
Donations	1,109.26	9,213.99		936.55
Interest:				
On Bank Balances	87.39	117.75	$19.57	14.62
On Bills Receivable	480.00			
On Mortgages	685.96		438.30	
On Investments	2,142.81		3,147.33	
Donations Under Annuity Plan	11,900.00			
Loans		1,700.00		
Collections on Mortgages and Notes	2,650.00			
Securities Called for Redemption			7,070.00	
	$20,825.54	$145,592.34	$10,675.20	$3,455.87

DISBURSEMENTS

Pensions:		
Retired Ministers	$52,725.00	$2,691.72
Disabled Ministers	4,658.37	175.00
Widows and Mothers of Ministers	64,862.02	2,871.15
Children of Ministers	15,606.45	600.02
Special Relief	6,737.94	
Annuities	2,618.50	
Salary of Executive Secretary	3,125.04	
Salary of Office Secretary	1,270.00	
Traveling Expenses of Executive Secretary	675.75	
Expenses of Treasurer and Other Board Members	874.28	
Expenses of Property	45.37	
Printing and Stationary	2,083.30	
Office Supplies and Expenses	392.16	
Rental of Office	525.00	
Auditing	195.00	
Advertising	263.41	
Interest on Bills Payable	1.52	

*Includes July, 1923, apportionment of $10,856.24 received and deposited August 3, 1923.

General Expenses	29.97	$2.63	2.35
Purchase of Office Furniture	56.00		
Repayment of Loans	1,700.00		
Taxes Advanced, on Property in Park Co., Mont.	118.01		
Purchase of Real Estate, Staten Island, New York		50.00	
	$158,563.09	$52.63	$6,340.24

RECONCILEMENT OF CASH

Balances, August 1, 1922........	$1,737.63	$11,920.70	$5,409.94	
Receipts, as per first sheet....	20,825.54	145,592.34	10,675.20	$3,455.87
	22,563.17	157,513.04	16,085.14	3,455.87
Disbursements, as per first sheet		158,563.09	52.63	6,340.24
	22,563.17	1,050.05	16,032.51	2,884.37
Transfers between Funds, as of July 31, 1923	15,924.77	19,704.33	15,495.80	11,716.24
Balances, July 31, 1923......	$6,638.40	$18,654.28*	$536.71	$8,831.87*

$34,661.26

J. H. BRANDT, *Treasurer.*

STATEMENT OR RECEIPTS AND DISBURSEMENTS
for the Year ended July 31, 1924

RECEIPTS

	Pension Endowment Fund	Pension General Fund	Relief Endowment Fund	Current Relief Fund
United Lutheran Church		$143,966.20		
United, General and Branch Synods	$2,184.10	9,734.54		$4,714.72
Women's Missionary Society		3,950.00		1,295.00
Donations	1,089.01	8,737.75	$5.00	4,401.90
Bequests	200.00		1,449.55	
Interest:				
On Bank Balances	75.76	195.47	21.43	186.46
On Bills Receivable	330.00		708.00	
On Mortgages	2,172.34		827.38	
On Investments	772.25		3,472.08	
Donations under Annuity Plan	5,150.00		5,223.00	
Loans		8,000.00		
Collections on Mortgages..	3,950.00		4,300.00	
Securities Redeemed or Sold			9,990.63	
Sale of Real Estate..............			830.00	
	$15,923.46	$174,583.96	$26,827.07	$10,598.08

*Includes July, 1923, apportionment of $10,856.24 received and deposited August 3, 1923.

DISBURSEMENTS

Pensions:			
Retired Ministers	$49,508.39		$4,163.41
Disabled Ministers	5,212.58		1,792.53
Widows and Mothers of Ministers....	67,884.17		5,528.81
Children of Ministers	15,292.22		1,037.58
Special Relief	25.00		
Annuity Interest	2,100.10		1,520.00
Salary of Executive Secretary	3,250.08		
Salary of Office Secretary	1,250.00		
Traveling Expenses of Executive Secretary	667.67		
Expenses of Treasurer and Other Board Members	788.91		
Printing and Stationery	952.23		
Office Supplies and Expenses	1,230.86		
Rental of Office	698.50		
Auditing	200.00		
Advertising	72.75		
Interest on Loans	764.00		
General Expenses	211.56		51.01
Purchase of Office Furniture	411.26		
Purchase of Investments...... $20,500.00		33,500.00	
Repayment of Loan	8,000.00		
Expenses of Acquiring Real Estate	70.83		
	$20,570.83 **$158,520.28**	**$33,500.00**	**$14,093.34**

RECONCILEMENT OF CASH

Balances, August 1, 1923....	$6,638.40	$18,654.28	$536.71	$8,831.87
Receipts, as above	15,923.46	174,583.96	26,827.07	10,598.08
	22,561.86	193,238.24	27,363.78	19,429.95
Disbursements, as above........	20,570.83	158,520.28	33,500.00	14,093.34
	1,991.03	34,717.96	*6,136.22*	5,336.61
Transfers between Funds, as of July 31, 1924.............	3,149.65	*12,649.65*	6,978.19	2,521.81
	$5,140.68	$22,068.31	$841.97	$7,858.42
Balance, July 31, 1924		$35,909.38		

PHILADELPHIA, August 28, 1924.

We have audited the accounts of the Board of Ministerial Relief of the United Lutheran Church in America for the two years ended July 31, 1924, and we certify that the foregoing Balance Sheet, July 31, 1924, and Receipts and Disbursements for the two years ended July 31, 1924, are in accordance with the books of account and, in our opinion, are correct.

LYBRAND, ROSS BROS. & MONTGOMERY,
Accountants and Auditors.

Figures in italic indicates deficit.

The Executive Secretary of the Board, the Rev. Edgar Grim Miller, then addressed the Convention.

By general consent the Treasurer, Mr. J. H. Brandt, was given permission to furnish the financial statement for each of the years of the biennium ending July 31, 1924.

Messrs. M. P. Moller, P. P. Hagan, M. B. Buehler, Robbin B. Wolf, George E. Neff and J. H. Brandt addressed the Convention in the interests of the work of this Board.

The resolutions were then considered seriatim. Resolutions 1 and 2 were covered by the action of the Convention on the Executive Board's report IV, B, 9 (a) and (b).

Resolutions 3 and 4 were adopted.

Resolution 5 was amended by striking out the word "resolved" and inserting the words "we request" making the item read: "We request that the cause of Ministerial Relief be presented once a year," etc. The item was adopted as amended.

The report was adopted as a whole.

Under the head of unfinished business the Rev. George H. Schnur presented the report of the Statistical and Church Year Book Committee.

REPORT OF THE STATISTICAL AND CHURCH YEAR BOOK COMMITTEE

The Standard Parochial Blank and Assembly Sheet

The Statistical and Church Year Book Committee of the United Lutheran Church in America during the biennium 1923-24 revised the Pastor's Standard Parochial Blank twice in its effort to arrive at a minimum blank which will effectively aid the securing of accurate, uniform and standard statistics concerning the work of the congregations of the United Lutheran Church. The first revision was used during the biennium 1923-24. The second revision was printed during the summer of 1924, and will be ready for distribution to the Constituent Synods December 1, 1924, for use after January 1, 1925.

The Committee had the fullest co-operation of the Statistical Secretaries of the Constituent Synods in these revisions. In the first place, the Conference of the Statistical Secretaries held in Buffalo at the time of the Buffalo Convention of the United Lutheran Church was attended by representatives of twenty-two Constituent Synods. , These representatives in this conference had gone over the Standard Parochial Blank then in use and had made definite recommendations for revision along the lines of reduction and standardization. The minutes of this conference were sent to all of the Statistical Secretaries of Constituent Synods, and further recommendations were secured. Largely upon these recommendations, your Statistical and Church Year Book Committee acted in the formulation of the Standard Parochial Blank which was used during the last biennium.

Among the men who attended the Buffalo Conference of Statistical Secretaries who were not Statistical Secretaries· of Constituent Synods during the biennium 1923-24, were:

Ministerium of Pennsylvania..Rev. D. H. Frederick
Synod of South Carolina.....Mr. B. M. Hare, of Saluda, S. C., State
                             Statistician of S. C.
Indiana Synod ....Rev. J. B. Gardner, Missionary Supt.
Illinois Synod ....Rev. C. J. Rockey, Secretary of Synod
Susquehanna Synod ....Rev. F. R. Greninger
Synod of West Virginia......Rev. S. S. Adams
Synod of Nebraska..........Rev. W. I. Guss

The following Constituent Synods were represented by their Statistical Secretaries:

Ministerium of Pennsylvania   Texas Synod
Ministerium of New York   Synod of Central Pennsylvania
United Synod of North Carolina   Mississippi Synod
Synod of Maryland   Synod of Canada
Synod of West Pennsylvania   Susquehanna Synod
Synod of Virginia   Synod of California
East Pennsylvania Synod   Rocky Mountain Synod
Alleghany Synod   New York and New England Synod
Pittsburgh Synod   Synod of West Virginia
Illinois Synod

The following served as Statistical Secretaries of the Constituent Synods of the United Lutheran Church in America during the biennium 1923-24:

	1923	1924
Ministerium of Pa.	Rev. Ira. F. Frankenfield	Rev. Ira F. Frankenfield
Ministerium of N. Y.	Rev. B. Mehrtens	Rev. B. Mehrtens
United Synod of N. C.	Rev. E. H. Kohn, Ph.D.	Rev. E. H. Kohn, Ph.D.
Synod of Maryland	Rev. W. G. Minnick	Rev. W. G. Minnick
Synod of S. C.	Rev. H. S. Petrea	Rev. H. S. Petrea
Synod of West Pa.	Rev. D. S. Martin	Rev. D. S. Martin
Synod of Virginia	Mr. Harry E. Pugh	Mr. Harry E. Pugh, 105 Lancaster Road, Richmond, Va.
Synod of Ohio	Mr. Amor W. Ulrici	Mr. Amor W. Ulrici, 3747 Elsmere Ave., Cincinnati, Ohio
East Pa. Synod	Rev. J. D. Krout	Rev. J. D. Krout
Alleghany Synod	Rev. C. P. Bastian	Rev. C. P. Bastian
Pittsburgh Synod	Rev. George H. Schnur, D.D.	Rev. George H. Schnur, D.D.
Indiana Synod	Mr. H. D. C. Loemker	Mr. H. D. C. Loemker, 1257 S. Floyd Street, Louisville, Ky.

Illinois Synod ....Mr. Frederick Sachse...........Mr. Frederick Sachse, 5510
        •   Magnolia Ave., Chicago,
                                                                         Ill.
Texas Synod ....Rev. J. C. A. Pfenninger......Rev. F. F. Eberhardt
*Susquehanna Synod of
   Central Pa. ....   Rev. C. S. Bottiger
Mississippi Synod ....Rev. M. D. Huddle...................Rev. M. D. Huddle
Synod of Iowa....................Rev. L. H. Lesher.................Rev. L. H. Lesher
Michigan Synod ....Rev. L. F. Gunderman.......Rev. L. F. Gunderman
Synod of Georgia................Rev. W. P. Cline, Jr........Rev. H. E. Henning
Synod of Canada.................Rev. O. Stockmann ....Rev. O. Stockmann
Synod of Kansas.................Rev. R. J. Wolf....................Rev. R. J. Wolf
Synod of Nebraska...........Rev. George Dorn ....Rev. George Dorn
Wartburg Synod ....Rev. F. W. Schneider...........Rev. F. W. Schneider
German Nebraska Synod..Rev. F. Rabe ....Rev. F. Rabe
Synod of California...........Rev. J. E. Hoick..................Rev. J. E. Hoick
Rocky Mountain Synod.....Rev. H. I. Kohler.................Rev. M. F. Troxell, D.D.
Synod of the Northwest....Rev. L. F. Gruber, D.D......Rev. L. F. Gruber, D.D.
Manitoba Synod ....Rev. E. Tuerkheim .... Rev. E. Tuerkheim
Pacific Synod ....Rev. W. R. Kraxberger.......Rev. W. I. Eck
N. Y. and N. E. Synod....Rev. E. M. Grahn................Rev. E. M. Grahn
Nova Scotia Synod...........Rev. S. W. Hirtle.................Rev. A. G. Jacobi
Synod of New York...........Rev. W. G. Boomhower......Rev. W. G. Boomhower
Central Canada Synod.....Rev. A. C. E. Grotke...........Rev. A. C. E. Grotke
Synod of West Va............Rev. C. E. Butler.................Rev. C. E. Butler
Slovak "Zion" Synod........Rev. John M. Bellan.............Rev. George Roh
*Synod of Central Pa........Rev. J. F. Harkins.................Rev. J. F. Harkins (up until
                                                                         May 1, 1924)
Susquehanna Synod ....Rev. C. S. Bottiger.................Rev. C. S. Bottiger (up until
                                                                         May 1, 1924)

Before making the second revision of the Standard Parochial Blank
which is to be used beginning 1925, your Committee secured further
recommendations of all of the Statistical Secretaries of the Constituent
Synods. The new blank had been in use for one year. Further changes
and corrections were found advisable. The recommendations of the Statistical Secretaries of the Constituent Synods were again considered by
the Committee in the preparation of the new Standard Parochial Blank,
which your Committee believes now conforms to the ideas of the Statistical Secretaries of the Constituent Synods, and will prove satisfactory
and effective in the gathering of minimum, correct, and standard statistics of the congregations of the United Lutheran Church. Your Committee have therefore authorized the printing of three years' supply of
blanks which will make it possible for each succeeding Statistical and
Church Year Book Committee to consider the blank at their first meeting
in the biennium, and if any corrections are found necessary, to incorporate
these corrections for the second year of the biennium.

The Standard Assembly Sheet used by the Statistical Secretaries of the
Constituent Synods in assembling the statistics of the congregations was
revised and numbered according to the rubrics of the Standard Parochial
Blank, and at the same time, proportionate spaces for the various rubrics
were arranged. At the beginning of the biennium a supply of blanks
sufficient for a period of five years was printed.

THE COMMITTEE

Your Committee held two meetings during the biennium. Both were
held in the office of the United Lutheran Church in America, 437 Fifth

Avenue, New York, N. Y., the first, January 24, 1923, and the second, May 5, 1924. The following members of the Committee attended both meetings: Dr. George H. Schnur, Dr. M. G. G. Scherer, Rev. C. W. Cassell, Dr. M. G. L. Reitz, and Rev. G. L. Kieffer. Rev. W. M. Kopenhaver attended the first meeting. Rev. J. D. Krout attended the second meeting. The other member of the Committee, Mr. George Hemsing, Milwaukee, Wis., was unable to attend either of the meetings.

At the first meeting, Dr. George H. Schnur was elected Chairman of the Committee, and Rev. G. L. Kieffer was elected Secretary-Treasurer. Rev. W. M. Kopenhaver was unanimously nominated as editor of the *"United Lutheran Church Year Book,"* and the nomination was forwarded to the United Lutheran Publication House.

HELPING THE STATISTICAL SECRETARIES

During the biennium, the following information was sent to the Statistical Secretaries of the Constituent Synods: A letter calling their attention to the recommendations as found on pages 335-6 of the Buffalo Minutes; the Minutes of the two Statistical Committee meetings; the Minutes of the Statistical Conference held at the time of the Buffalo Convention; a copy of the Minutes of the Pittsburgh Synod as a sample of how to print the congregational parochial statistics 41 lines to the page; a copy of the Synodical Bulletin of the Indiana Synod containing statistical information for the congregations of the Indiana Synod; a copy of Rev. D. H. Frederick's release on "A Salary Survey of the Wilkes-Barre Conference of the Pennsylvania Ministerium, 1923;" a tabulation showing the ending of the fiscal years of the Constituent Synods; a sheet of instructions concerning the gathering of uniform statistics, especially where the returns have missing rubrics concerning "Membership" and "Church Property," and the clarion call concerning "Confirmed Membership."

PROGRESS IN UNIFORMITY AND STANDARDIZATION

The 1923 Minutes of the 36 Constituent Synods of the United Lutheran Church show the following progress having been made in uniformity in printing the Minutes and in printing the parochial statistics:

All but 12 Synods had 41 lines on their page; all but 14 Synods made comparisons of totals; only 1 Synod did not give totals; only 1 Synod used four pages instead of two to place the rubric headings of the parochial statistics; only 1 Synod used three pages instead of two; all but 10 Synods printed the Minutes correctly lengthwise across the page, five of the ten printed the rubric headings across the width of the page, and five printed the parochial statistics on separate sheets. This last is entirely inexcusable in view of the great possibility of losing these separate sheets and thus to that extent making the Minutes valueless. As to the printing and arranging of the parochial statistics, the rest conform to the standard. It is to be hoped that all will conform before the end of another biennium.

As to the size of the Minutes, the standard remains the same, 6x9 inches. Of the 36 Synods, 30 conform, 5 printed their Minutes in smaller form, and one Synod does not have printed minutes.

WORK OF THE COMMITTEE AND OF THE STATISTICAL SECRETARY

1. *The Tools Used by the Statistical Secretaries*

The tools used by the Statistical Secretaries of the Constituent Synods are the Pastor's Standard Parochial Blank and the Standard Assembly Sheet. Without the Pastor's Standard Parochial Blank, the Statistical Secretaries could not gather the congregational statistics. Without the Standard Assembly Sheet, the Statistical Secretaries could not assemble the statistics and report totals for their Synod to the Statistical Secretary of the United Lutheran Church. And, wihout the Assembly Sheet, the Statistical Secretary of the United Lutheran Church could not report the totals and make the comparisons of the parochial statistics of the United Lutheran Church in America. This may seem trite, and you may say obvious. Nevertheless, it shows the importance of the tools.

Your Committee made a survey as to the needs of the Statistical Secretaries of the Constituent Synods in regard to these tools, and during the biennium supplied them with 17,310 Standard Parochial Blanks, and 825 Standard Assembly Sheets.

2. *The United Lutheran Church Year Book*

The "Year Book of the United Lutheran Church" for 1923 and 1924 were issued during the biennium. They were edited by a member of the Committee, Rev. W. M. Kopenhaver.

The Statistical Secretary of the United Lutheran Church supplied the following to the editor, for inclusion in the year books: the Parochial Statistics of the United Lutheran Church in United States and Canada for 1922 and 1923; the Parochial Statistics of the United Lutheran Church outside the United States and Canada for 1922 and 1923; the Comparative Parochial Statistics of the United Lutheran Church; Dr. H. K. Carroll's statistics on Religious Denominations, as printed in the "Christian Herald" in 1923 and 1924; the Parochial Statistics of the Lutherans in United States and Canada for 1922 and 1923; the Comparative Parochial Statistics of the Lutherans in America as of January 1, 1922 and January 1, 1923; corrections for the Ministerial Directory; names of officers of the Constituent Synods; the Necrology table; statistics of all the Educational and Inner Mission institutions, both of the United Lutheran Church and other Lutheran bodies for the years 1923 and 1924.

3. *Releases Through the National Lutheran Council*

The Statistical Secretary supplied the United Lutheran Church statistics to the National Lutheran Council, for their releases to: Dr. H. K.

Carroll, for his article, "Religious Denominations in the United States," as published in the "Christian Herald" for 1923 and 1924; Dr. E. O. Watson, for the "Year Book of the Churches" for the years 1923 and 1924; Dr. C. L. Goodell, of the Commission on Evangelism of the Federal Council of Churches, the accession statistics; Dr. H. S. Myers, of the United Stewardship Council, the per capita contribution statistics; the Home Missions Council, the Home Missions statistics; and, for other releases made by the National Lutheran Council.

4. Incomplete Parochial Statistical Reports

Your Committee are glad to note the steady improvement in the completeness and the uniform conformity to the Standard Parochial Blank as indicated by the congregational statistical reports as they appear in the Minutes of the Constituent Synods during the biennium 1922-23. There are still, however, many blank spaces that are to be regretted and prove one or more of several things—incomplete parish records, undervaluation by the pastors of the importance of making complete parochial reports to the Constituent Synods, or downright carelessness or indifference of the pastors in filling out the Standard Parochial Blank. That this information is important and of value to the United Lutheran Church, and to the Lutheran Church at large, hardly needs to be argued here. Full co-operation of all of the pastors should be had and is to be expected at all times in the filling out of the Standard Parochial Blank. The Statistical Secretaries of the Constituent Synods as good advocates for the Constituent Synods, and indirectly for the United Lutheran Church and the Lutheran Church at large, will use every means to have as few blank spaces appear in their assembly sheets for each congregation as is humanly possible.

Your Commitee have thought this matter of enough importance to instruct the Secretary of the Committee to call the attention of the Presidents of the Constituent Synods to any incomplete statistical reports that may appear in the printed Minutes of the Constituent Synods. The Executive Board of the United Lutheran Church have thought it of enough importance to authorize the Statistical Secretary to complete incomplete reports that may reach him by estimation if necessary, in order that the standing and position of the United Lutheran Church and the Lutheran Church at large may not be lost as a consequence of incomplete reports supplied by pastors. The statistician of the National Lutheran Council called special attention to the danger of the Lutheran Church in United States losing its position as the third largest Protestant Church in the United States, largely as the result of incomplete parochial reports supplied by the pastors. This subject, therefore, is vital and requires the earnest consideration of every pastor in the United Lutheran Church.

5. *Juggling the "Confirmed Membership"*

Your Committee regrets to note that in the case of some congregations, there seems to be a conscious adjusting of the "Confirmed Membership" by somebody so as to avoid something, be it apportionment, or the more refined term, quota, or whatever the term may be in the Constituent Synod. There has come to the attention of your Committee, an instance where after the total of "Confirmed Membership" was honestly arrived at, in some way or other 600 members were automatically not reported. In another instance, a Constituent Synod carried upon the cover page of the printed Minutes, the definition of "Confirmed Members" as "all the confirmed members, (1) who have used the Means of Grace, and (2) who have contributed to Church expenses." This is a new definition. We will now compare it with the definition as found on the Standard Parochial Bank, No. 7, under Notes to Pastors, "The confirmed membership includes all who have been admitted to communion, and who have not been removed by certificate, death or excommunication." In view of this attitude on the part of some of the members of the United Lutheran Church, and a second consideration which we now present, your Committee raises the question as to the advisability of the United Lutheran Church using the "Confirmed Membership" as a part of the basis for arriving at the apportionment or quota. The second consideration is the fact that the "Confirmed Membership" with the definition "the right to commune," is the rubric which corresponds to the rubric "Communicant Members" used by the denominations in arriving at comparative religious statistics. If the Lutherans in America lose their place as the third largest Protestant Church in the United States, one of the chief reasons for it will be the juggling of the "Confirmed Membership" in order to avoid congregational financial responsibility.

No one will deny the fact that the "Confirmed Membership" as reported by the congregations, Synods, and even the United Lutheran Church, in no wise represents the total "Confirmed Membership" which has the "right to go to communion" in the congregations of the Constituent Synods of the United Lutheran Church. A comparison with the "Accessions" and "Losses" (see the table of comparison for 1923, and the years from 1919 to 1923 as printed in this Bulletin) will easily prove that the actual gains in "Confirmed Membership" are not included in the rubric "Confirmed Membership" as reported. This whole matter was gone into in the report to the Buffalo Convention under "Summary," page 334 following. The "Accessions" reported by the congregations to the "Lutheran" are evidently in many instances absorbed by losses in some way or other, when the "Confirmed Membership" rubric is arrived at. Let it not be forgotten by anyone who would juggle, that there are statistical rules that enable a Statistical Secretary to tell in an instant whether the "Confirmed Membership" of a congregation as reported is what it should be under normal conditions. Of course abnormal conditions do exist some times, and there are always exceptions to the rule. But the exceptions dare not be permitted to become the rule.

Perhaps if the "Communing Membership" rubric were used, being related as it is to the use of one of the Means of Grace (the Sacrament of the Altar), in arriving at the apportionment, there would be less juggling and honesty would become more the policy of all concerned. Your Committee, therefore, has a recommendation to submit for this for the consideration of the Convention. It follows this report.

6. *Statistics Supplied to the Treasurer of the United Lutheran Church*

The Treasurer of the United Lutheran Church depends upon your Committee for accurate and up-to-date statistics concerning "Confirmed Membership" and "Current Expenses" totals for the Constituent Synods of the United Lutheran Church in America. The Statistical Secretary supplied the Treasurer, Dr. E. Clarence Miller, with two tables, one for 1922 and one for 1923, showing the "Confirmed Membership" total and the "Current Expenses" total for each of the Constituent Synods of the United Lutheran Church, as well as the grand total for the United Lutheran Church in United States and Canada.

7. *End of the Fiscal Years*

A survey was made during this biennium concerning the ending of the fiscal years of the Constituent Synods. The result is as follows: Five Synods end their fiscal years April 30th; three May 1st; one June 15th; one August 15th; one September 1st; one September 15th; eleven September 30th; one October 31st, and eleven December 31st.

This information was reported to the Executive Board of the United Lutheran Church.

8. *State of the Church Blank*

A survey was made of the blanks used by the different Constituent Synods for reporting facts concerning the state of the church. The results were tabulated and compared with the Standard Parochial Blank so as to avoid all duplication. With the help of Rev. E. Victor Ehrhart, of 46 Foster Street, New Haven, Conn., the efficient chairman of the Committee on the State of the Church of the Synod of New York, the Committee is able to report on the basis of its survey, the following as a model blank for use of the Committees on the State of the Church in the Constituent Synods of the United Lutheran Church.

STANDARD BLANK
STATE OF THE CHURCH
For the use of Congregations of
THE UNITED LUTHERAN CHURCH IN AMERICA

Name of Congregation..

Location or address ....

Synodical ....

Non-Synodical .... Conference......................

Pastor .... Address.........................

This blank is instituted to gather such facts relative to each congregation as do not appear in the parochial reports, in order that this Committee may make a survey of the spiritual conditions as well as of the parochial and financial conditions. Please answer *all* questions accurately, avoiding round numbers.

Three copies are sent, one for the work of the Committee; one to be placed in the archives of your church—to note progress in future years; and, one is to be handed to the lay delegate to the meeting of the convention of the Constituent Synod.

PUBLIC WORSHIP

Is average attendance increasing, stationary or decreasing?..............

How many services do you hold on a Sunday?.......... When?.........

What is your average attendance, Matin?.... the Service.... Vesper ....

What proportion of your confirmed membership are men?..............

What is the nature of your evening service?..........................

Do you hold a mid-week service?........ Give average attendance.......

Have you difficulty in keeping the young people from drifting?..........

What solution can you offer?..

Is Family Worship observed extensively in your church?................

Percentage of families..

What languages are used in your services?............................

Do you use the Common Service?.......................................

If not, why not?..

FESTIVAL SEASONS

What Festival days of the church year do you observe?................

....

Do you stress and observe Lent and Holy Week?......................

State the objective of the Lenten Period this year....................

LUTHERAN PRACTICE

How many Communion Seasons do you observe? .... When? ......
....
Do you hold separate Preparatory Services? .... When? ....
Do you instruct non-Lutherans before receiving into the church? ....
How do you receive them? ....
Do you plan for a two years' course in catechetical instruction? ....

SUNDAY SCHOOL

Do you use Lutheran Literature throughout the Sunday School? ....
State number of Adult Bible classes .... Enrollment ....
What proportion of the Sunday school attend public worship? ....
Do you use the small duplex envelope in the Sunday school? ....
How many councilmen are members of the Sunday school? ....
What part does the pastor take in the work of the Sunday school?
....
How many Sunday school scholars were received into the church this
   year by baptism? ....
How many Sunday school scholars were confirmed? ....
What proportion of the Sunday school are non-members, or children of
   non-members? ....
How many baptized members of your congregation attend other Sunday
   schools? ....

CHURCH SOCIETIES

Are any of your Young Peoples Societies entirely social in character?
....
Which ones? ....
What is the membership of your Brotherhood? ...... Is it affiliated? ......
With what? ....
Do you consider it a successful organization? ....
Is any organization connected with your congregation that does not exist
   for the church first? ....

CHURCH FINANCES

What methods do you use to raise money for current expenses and
   benevolences? ....
Do you use the Duplex Envelopes? ....

Do your contributions from this source meet current expenses?..........
Did you conduct a thorough Every Member Canvass this year?..........
Name any direct benefits derived from this canvass......................
Give the number of actual contributors for Current Expenses............
For Benevolence ....
Have you a separate Benevolence Treasurer?..........................
If not, give the reason...
Is Benevolence money remitted to Synod monthly?......................
If not, why not?..
State the amount of the pastor's salary?...............................
If you have no parsonage, state amount of congregational assistance in
    paying rent ....
Does the congregation pay for the telephone and office supplies of the
    pastor? ....
Does the congregation furnish an automobile?.........................
Is the pastor's salary paid regularly?..................................
If NOT MET, what excuse does the Council and congregation give for
    failure to meet their Benevolence Quota?..........................
Give amount of cost of improvements for the year......................
Does this amount add to the valuation of your property?...............
What does the congregation budget for the Teaching Work of the
    congregation? ....
    Amount for Sunday School......Amount for Week-Day School......
    Amount for Vacation Bible School...............................

Church Records

How is provision made for the preservation of church records? (safe,
    etc.) ....
Are your records in good order?......................................
Do they cover the history of the church?..............................

Miscellaneous

How many churches in your Parish?..................................
Name them ....
State which are Missions and the amount of aid each receives............
....
Is your church property adequately insured?........ Just what proportion
    of the valuation is the total amount of insurance carried?............
What is the general condition of the property?........................
What neighborhood Home Mission work is your congregation doing or
    assisting? ....
How many neighborhood Sunday schools are conducted by members of
    your congregation? ....

....
What Inner Mission Work is your congregation doing or assisting?
Have you a Parish house?........ State benefits, or otherwise........
....
State the number of leaders in your church, Male....... Female.......
Do you issue a weekly bulletin or parish paper?......................
    (If possible submit a sample of the same).
Is your work becoming more or less difficult? (State which, and reasons
    apparent) ....
....
....

Add any other information of interest to the church at large in this space.

                 Signed ....

                                Pastor

                       ....

                      Secretary of Congregation

Date ....
The resolution concerning this blank is herewith appended.

9. *Are More Men Needed for the Ministry*

    During 1924, a survey was made of the Constituent Synods of the
United Lutheran Church to ascertain the number of ministers on the
roll of the Synod, the number of pastors in active charge of a congregation or mission, the number of parishes, the number of congregations that
are synodical, and, the number of congregations that are non-synodical.
The following is the result:

STATISTICS CONCERNING PASTORS, PARISHES AND CONGREGATIONS OF THE CONSTITUENT SYNODS OF THE UNITED LUTHERAN CHURCH IN AMERICA

Name of Synod	No. of Ministers on the roll	No. of Pastors in Active Charge of Congregations or Missions	No. of Parishes in the Synod	Congregations Synodical	Congregations Non-Synodical
Ministerium of Pa.........	425	350	354	570	4
Ministerium of N. Y.......	145	125	134	130	13
United Synod of N. C.....	110	91	87	193	...
Synod of Maryland........	123	91	103	139	2
Synod of S. C.............	58	45	54	109	...
Synod of West Pa.........	112	79	89	158	...
Synod of Virginia.........	79	52	67	148	...

Name of Synod	No. of Ministers on the roll	No. of Pastors in Active Charge of Congregations or Missions	No. of Parishes in the Synod	Congregations Synodical	Non-Synodical
Synod of Ohio............	221	192	191	287	...
East Pa. Synod...........	144	111	120	156	...
Alleghany Synod	81	66	71	149	...
Pittsburgh Synod	260	205	217	307	10
Indiana Synod	53	38	36	72	5
Illinois Synod	130	99	102	135	1
Texas Synod	15	13	14	18	5
Synod of Central Pa.......	35	32	34	87	...
Mississippi Synod	8	4	5	14	...
Synod of Iowa............	29	23	28	29	...
Michigan Synod	61	45	54	85	...
Synod of Georgia.........	16	16	23	35	...
Synod of Canada..........	46	40	44	68	7
Susquehanna Synod	47	41	47	79	...
Synod of Kansas..........	46	30	35	41	...
Synod of Nebraska........	44	38	49	57	...
Wartburg Synod	49	48	51	25	26
German Nebraska Synod...	84	73	112	67	55
Synod of California........	55	31	35	34	1
Rocky Mountain Synod....	19	12	18	14	4
Synod of the Northwest...	77	61	65	73	...
Manitoba Synod	35	29	31	58	...
Pacific Synod	31	23	26	27	2
N. Y. and N. E. Synod....	79	67	68	71	...
Nova Scotia Synod........	6	5	8	29	...
Synod of New York.......	144	111	156	150	6
Central Canada Synod.....	15	12	12	15	2
Synod of West Va.........	14	14	22	36	...
Slovak Zion Synod.........	23	23	28	16	18
U. L. C. in A. Total....	2,919	2,335	2,590	3,681	161

In 1919 there were 314 vacant congregations in the Constituent Synods of the United Lutheran Church, and in 1923 there were 450 vacant congregations. A study of the following two tables compiled from the Minutes for those years will show the character of the vacant congregations.

VACANT CONGREGATIONS—1919

Synod	No. of Vacant Congregations	10 or less	Confirmed Membership 11-50	51-100	101-250	251-500	501-1000
Ministerium of Pa...........	32	..	6	6	13	5	2
Ministerium of N. Y.........	1	1	...	..	..	..	..
North Carolina	8	2	...	2	4	..	..
Tennessee	6	..	3	1	2	..	..
Maryland	9	..	3	1	2	1	2
South Carolina	7	1	3	2	1	..	..
West Pa.	8	..	1	..	6	1	..

Synod	No. of Vacant Congregations	10 or less	Confirmed Membership 11-50	51-100	101-250	251-500	501-1000
Synod of Virginia	4	2	2	..		..	..
East Ohio	8	4	..	2	2	..	..
East Pa.	18	..	3	6	5	..	4
Alleghany	10	1	5	1	2	1	..
Southwestern Va.	11	..	5	5	1		..
Miami	10	..		3	6	1	..
Pittsburgh G. C.	8	..	2	2	..	2	2
Pittsburgh G. S.	19	1	8	2	7	..	1
Wittenberg	7	..	3	4	..	..	..
Olive Branch	8	1	2	3	..	..	2
Northern Ill.	11	2	2	1	4	1	1
Central Pa.	...	..	...	..			
Northern Ind.	10	1	7	2	..	..	..
Iowa	1	..	1	..			
Mississippi	1	..			1	..	..
District Synod of Ohio	6	2	..	2	2	..	..
Georgia and Adjacent States.	7	..	3	2	2	..	..
Holston	...	..	...				
Southern Ill.	2	..	...	2	..		..
Canada	3	..	2	1	..		..
Central Ill.	6	..	3	2	1	..	..
Susquehanna	4	..	1	2	1	..	..
Kansas	11	..	4	3	3	1	..
Nebraska	8	1	2	4	1	..	..
Chicago	11	..	7	2	1	..	1
Wartburg	1	1	...	..			
German Neb.	3	1	2	..	..		..
California	6	..	3	2	1	..	..
Rocky Mountain	4	..	2	1	1	..	..
Manitoba	...	..					
Northwest	4	..	2	2	..		..
Pacific	3	..	2	1	..		..
N. Y. and N. Eng.	...	..					
Nova Scotia	1	..	1	..	..	..	..
Texas	...	..	...	..			
New York	28	1	10	3	12	1	1
Central Canada	3	2	1	..	..		..
West Va.	6	5	1	..	..		..
Slovak "Zion"	...	..	...	..	..	..	..
U. L. C. in A. Total	314	29	102	72	81	14	16

VACANT CONGREGATIONS—1923

Synod	No. of Vacant Congregations	10 or less	11-50	51-100	101-250	251-500	501-1000
Ministerium of Pa.	43	1	4	8	22	8	..
Ministerium of N. Y.	4	2	...	1	1	..	..
United Synod of N. C.	16	3	5	2	4	2	..
Synod of Maryland	9	1	2	3	1	1	1
Synod of S. C.	18	..	6	1	8	3	..
Synod of West Pa.	18	..	4	6	5	3	..
Synod of Virginia	41	3	20	9	9	..	..
Synod of Ohio	47	..	20	14	8	4	1

Synod	No. of Congregations	Vacant 10 or less	Confirmed Membership				
			11-50	51-100	101-250	251-500	501-1000
East Pa. Synod	15	..	3	5	5	1	1
Alleghany Synod	26	..	11	5	9	1	..
Pittsburgh Synod	29	2	12	5	10	..	..
Indiana Synod	14	..	8	3	3	..	..
Illinois Synod	27	8	9	5	5	..	..
Texas Synod	...	..	...	..	..	..	..
Synod of Central Pa.	10	..	5	3	2	..	..
Mississippi Synod	...	..	...	..	..	..	..
Synod of Iowa	4	..	2	2	..	..	..
Michigan Synod	12	2	8	..	1	1	..
Synod of Georgia	16	1	8	4	3	..	..
Synod of Canada	7	..	1	1	2	2	1
Susquehanna Synod	12	..	4	4	2	1	1
Synod of Kansas	4	1	1	1	1	..	..
Synod of Nebraska	13	..	4	4	5	..	..
Wartburg Synod	3	2	...	..	1	..	..
German Nebraska Synod	8	7	1	..	..	..	..
Synod of California	2	..	1	..	1	..	..
Rocky Mountain Synod	5	..	4	1	..	..	..
Synod of the Northwest	...	..	...	..	..	..	..
Manitoba Synod	...	..	...	..	..	..	..
Pacific Synod	1	..	1	..	..	..	..
N. Y. and N. E. Synod	3	1	...	..	..	2	..
Nova Scotia Synod	1	..	...	..	..	1	..
Synod of New York	23	3	8	6	3	2	1
Central Canada Synod	4	..	1	1	2	..	..
Synod of West Va.	14	5	4	1	4	..	..
Slovak "Zion" Synod	1	..	...	1	..	..	..
U. L. C. in A. Total	450	42	157	96	117	32	6

Along with these surveys, the following facts will help to show the relationship of the number of ministers and the number of congregations of the United Lutheran Church, and the need of more men for the ministry.

In 1919 there were 3,473 congregations in the United Lutheran Church. In 1924, there were 3,842 congregations, an increase of 369.

In 1919, there were 2,843 ministers on the rolls of the Synods. In 1924, there were 2,919, a gain of 76 ministers.

A survey of the number of active pastors not having been made in 1919, we cannot make the comparison here. This is likewise true of the number of parishes. But this can be said that in 1919 there were 1.2215 plus, and in 1924, 1.3162 plus congregations for every minister on the rolls of the Constituent Synods of the United Lutheran Church. Or expressing it in another way, the ratio of the number of ministers to the number of congregations—in 1919 there was .818 plus, and in 1924, .759 plus part of a minister for every congregation.

Since 1919, 286 ministers that were on the rolls of the Constituent

Synods of the United Lutheran Church have died. According to the *"United Lutheran Church Year Book for 1924,"* there are 69 retired ministers, 11 pastors emeritus in the United Lutheran Church, and 34 professors teaching in the educational institutions who are without congregations. Comparatively speaking, the survey shows there are 584 Lutheran ministers on the rolls of the Constituent Synods of the United Lutheran Church who are not pastors in active charge of congregations or missions. There are 255 more parishes than active pastors. There are 1,507 more congregations in the United Lutheran Church than there are active pastors. It further shows that there are 329 more Lutheran ministers than there are parishes, but these 329 include the retired ministers, the pastors emeritus, the professors teaching in the educational institution, officers, the secretaries of boards, societies, organizations, officers of Constituent Synods etc., who are without congregations.

A special questionnaire was sent to the theological seminaries of the United Lutheran Church, and the following table of graduates for the years 1919 to 1924 inclusive, showing a total of 482 graduates gives an idea as to how the demand for ministers and active pastors is being met by the supply.

THEOLOGICAL SEMINARY GRADUATES FOR THE
YEARS 1919-1924

Seminary	Graduates						
	1919	1920	1921	1922	1923	1924	Tot.
Hartwick Sem., N. Y., Hartwick	3	2	2	2	3	2	14
Gettysburg, Pa., Theol. Sem. of G. S.	14	15	11	15	15	15	85
Columbia, S. C., Southern	8	6	7	7	5	0	33
Springfield, Ohio, Hamma Divinity	13	6	8	13	9	10	59
Selinsgrove, Pa., Theol Sem., Susquehanna. Univ.	5	3	6	8	6	9	37
Philadelphia, Pa., Mt. Airy	10	19	24	27	19	23	122
Fremont, Neb., Western	5	6	2	2	2	4	21
Maywood, Ill., Theol. Sem	10	10	4	7	5	10	46
Waterloo, Ont., Can., Theol. Sem	2	2	6	1	4	3	18
Seattle Wash., Pacific	..	1	..	2	4	1	8
Saskatoon, Sask., Can., Saskatoon	..	..	..	..	..	2	2
Lincoln, Neb., Martin Luther	2	5	..	2	2	5	16
Minneapolis Minn., Northwestern	..	..	..	8	6	7	21
Total U. L. C. in A	72	75	70	94	80	91	482

Adding the number of new congregations organized since 1919, 369, to the number of pastors who died, 286, the total is 655. New congregations need a pastor, and preachers who die have to be replaced. The necessary replacement figure for the years 1919-1924 for new congregations and preachers who died, totals 655. During this time the Lutheran Theological Seminaries of the United Lutheran Church graduated 482.

10. *United States Religious Census*

Your Committee during the biennium have had under consideration, the recommendations to the United States Census Bureau, as printed on page 333 of the Buffalo Convention Minutes. Nothing new can be reported at this time. This matter is of vital importance to the United Lutheran Church and to the congregations of the United Lutheran Church, in view of the proposed United States Religious Census in 1926, and the regular census in 1930. Your Committee have noted that the Roman Catholic publications are carrying on a consistent campaign on the necessity of more accurate statistics concerning the Roman Catholic Church as reported by the United States Government, and are openly advocating a census of the Roman Catholics in America. Our Lutheran Church can hardly consistently afford to ask for less. A recommendation is submitted with this report.

11. *A Statistical Year Book of the United Lutheran Church*

The possibility and desirability of the publication of a statistical year book which would give statistical information not now included in the *"Year Book of the United Lutheran Church,"* was considered by your Committee, and was referred to a Committee. This Committee has as yet not met, and there is therefore, no recommendation to be made at this time.

The one distinct gain such a statistical year book would provide would be the listing of the congregations of all of the Constituent Synods in a single volume, together with rubrics on membership, education, ministerial acts, property, and finances. This information at the present time is only to be found in the separate Minutes of the Constituent Synods of the United Lutheran Church in America.

12. *The Statistical Secretary and the Theological Seminaries of the United Lutheran Church in America*

Your Committee have had under consideration for some time, the question as to how the importance of full and accurate parochial statistics could be brought home to the pastors. The Committee believes that once the pastors fully understand the need, the value, and the importance of full and accurate parochial statistics, they will see that such are supplied for their congregations. To this end, the Committee has desired the Statistical Secretary to visit the theological seminaries of the United Lutheran Church, to speak upon the subject of United Lutheran Church Parochial Statistics and the Lutheran Statistics in general, and the relation of the pastor and congregation thereto. Such visitation was recommended by the Buffalo Conference of Statistical Secretaries.

To date this recommendation has not been carried out largely due to the fact that the Statistical Secretary met with a serious accident in an elevator, May 1, 1923. This accident made extended travel by the Statistical Secretary practically impossible. It is to be hoped that while in the West in attendance at the United Lutheran Church Convention, the theological seminaries in Springfield, Ohio, Chicago, Minneapolis, Fremont, Lincoln, and Waterloo, Canada, can be visited by the Statistical Secretary and the seminaries in Gettysburg, Selinsgrove, Mt. Airy, Hartwick, and Columbia, during the month of December.

13. A Four-Page Folder for the Pastors

Your Committee have had under consideration the preparation of a four-page folder, showing the importance of parochial statistics, and parish records. It is the purpose of your Committee to release this folder through the Statistical Secretaries of the Constituent Synods. This folder has been delayed, in the first place, because the Pastor's Standard Parochial Blank was in the process of formulation and in the period of being tried out; and, in the second place, because the parish records, kind and character, are even now the subject of discussion. It is to be hoped that it will be possible to release this folder so that the Statistical Secretaries can enclose it, with the Pastor's Standard Parochial Blanks during 1926.

14. Complete and Uniform Systems for Parish Records and Congregational Activities

The Buffalo Convention of the United Lutheran Church, when they received the report of the Committee on Proceedings of Constituent Synods, adopted the following recommendation:

"That the Statistical and Church Year Book Committee be instructed to prepare complete and uniform systems for Parish Records and congregational activities to facilitate the keeping and the reporting of adequate and accurate congregational statistics."

By this action of the Buffalo Convention, this work was definitely put in the hands of your Committee, paralleling it with the recommendation of the Statistical Conference held at the time of the Buffalo Convention as follows:

"That we recommend to the Statistical and Church Year Book Committee that they prepare a uniform system for use in keeping of parish records."

Ever since your Committee has been at work standardizing parochial statistics, it has been evident to your Committee that the crux of success lies finally in complete and uniform systems for parish records and congregational activities. Without these the pastor will always have difficulty in filling out any kind of a statistical blank for he will not have the information necessary, and it will be necessary to blame something or somebody. But with complete and uniform systems for parish records and congregational activities before him, it will be very simple to fill out any kind of a blank, be it ever so complicated, and the pastor, the congregation, church council, trustees, etc., will annually have a truer conception of the actual status of the life of the congregation.

Your Committee have considered and surveyed many of the parish record systems now in use, and as yet are unable to recommend complete and uniform systems for parish records and congregational activities for use in the congregations of the United Lutheran Church. The best that your Committee can say at present is the following: We have examined the Standard System designed by Mr. C. H. Weller, and find it the most complete system of keeping church records that we have seen, and believe that if our Synods and congregations can be induced to adopt it, it would give us a great amount of invaluable information in regard to the individual members of our congregations, and would, at the same time, conserve the membership of our churches. But it must be said that this system is far from complete and needs additions and revisions in parts to conform to the rubrics of the Standard Parochial Blank of the United Lutheran Church. All that we can say is, that it is the best that we have seen. It should also be said that it is a loose-leaf system, and in many of the States, no doubt, a bound congregational record would have to be kept together with this system to meet legal requirements.

Your Committee is still at work, and hopes, during the next biennium, to prepare complete and uniform systems for parish records and congregational activities for the United Lutheran Church. The Committee is glad for the co-operation of the Board of Publication, who have put to work the chairman of the Committee surveying their parish record systems. His findings, of course, will be at the service of the Committee. The survey that the Committee has made thus far will be presented to the Conference of the Statistical Secretaries at their meeting in Chicago, for the consideration of the Statistical Secretaries and their recommendations to the Statistical and Church Year Book Committee of the United Lutheran Church.

15. *Blanks for Assembling the Reports for Organizations, Societies, and Congregational Activities Within the Congregation*

One of the difficulties every pastor finds when he goes to fill out the Standard Parochial Blank is that it is necessary to have before him, not only the record of his ministerial acts, but also the reports for all of the organizations, societies, and congregational activities carried on by the congregation in order that his report as submitted on the Standard Parochial Blank may represent a full congregational report. Your Committee has, therefore, worked on the preparation of possible blanks which every pastor can use in gathering (1) the reports of the Church Schools—Sunday Schools, Weekday Schools, Parochial Schools; (2) the reports of the organizations and societies, such as, Luther League, Ladies' Aid, Women's Missionary Society, Brotherhood, and Young People's Societies of whatever name; and (3) the Church Council report. Your Statistical Secretary has tried out such blanks for the gathering of the statistics for Christ Lutheran Church, Rosedale, L. I. He has used such blanks for the past three years and has made the evident necessary revisions each year. Your Committee will now submit these blanks to the Conference of Statistical Secretaries at the time of the Convention at Chicago for their consideration and recommendation to the Statistical and Church Year Book Committee of the United Lutheran Church. The experience of the Statistical Secretary is that where the Church Schools, organizations, and societies, and the Church Council have faithfully filled out these blank forms, it is relatively an easy matter with his record of his ministerial acts at hand, for the pastor to fill out the Standard Parochial Blank.

16. *Statistical Conference*

In conformity with the recommendation adopted by the Buffalo Convention of the United Lutheran Church as found on page 336 of the Minutes, namely, "That the Constituent Synods of the United Lutheran Church in America be requested to make provision for the presence of their Statistical Secretaries at future Conventions of the United Lutheran Church in order that they may attend the conference of the Statistical Secretaries at the time of the Convention," your Committee has made preparation for a conference of the Statistical Secretaries at the time of the Chicago Convention, to be held Wednesday, October 22d, at 7. P. M., in the Edgewater Beach Hotel. Under the date of May 21, 1924, the Secretary, as requested by the Statistical and Church Year Book Committee, wrote to the Presidents of the Constituent Synods of the United Lutheran Church, calling their attention to the above-quoted action of the Buffalo Convention of the United Lutheran Church.

This conference will again give your Committee an opportunity of meeting the Statistical Secretaries face to face, and with them, to go over the problems incident to the gathering of the parochial statistics of the United Lutheran Church. Practically all of the time of the last conference was spent on the revision of the Standard Parochial Blank and Assembly Sheet. We believe that not as much time will be required for these at the coming conference. The tools are fairly well standardized and agreed upon, but considerable time will be required to go over the blanks that the pastor can use in gathering before him the reports of the Church Schools, organizations, societies and Church Council, as he goes to filling out the Standard Parochial Blank. Such blanks appear necessary. Before release, they must be satisfactory to the Statistical Secretaries of the Constituent Synods.

The larger task and perhaps the most important question that will come before the Statistical Conference will be the consideration of the various surveys as made of the various systems of parish records by your Committee and its members, in order that there may be an agreement among the Statistical Secretaries as to what are considered the most complete and uniform systems for parish records and congregational activities for use in the United Lutheran Church congregations.

The Statistical Secretaries of the Constituent Synods have suggested topics for discussion at the statistical conference.

17. *The 1922 and 1923 Parochial Statistics of the United Lutheran Church in America*

The table showing the totals for the parochial statistics of the Constituent Synods as well as the totals of the United Lutheran Church for the year 1923 is herewith appended, also a table of comparative statistics for five years, 1919, 1920, 1921, 1922 and 1923. It is to be hoped that the 1924 statistics will be available for inclusion in the Minutes of this Convention. This, however, may not be possible in view of the number of Synods ending their fiscal years on December 31st, and the statistics not being available until about the middle of January at the earliest. If the 1924 statistics cannot be included in the Minutes of this Convention, it will be possible for the Bulletin for the next biennium to contain the statistical reports for the years 1924 and 1925.

RECOMMENDATIONS

1. That all Constituent Synods of the United Lutheran Church be again requested to have their Minutes printed in uniform size and style.

2. That those Constituent Synods which have modified the Standard Parochial Assembly Sheet be requested to conform their practice to the Standard.

3. We request that the fiscal years of all congregational organizations, congregations, Synods of the United Lutheran Church be made concurrent with the calendar year—ending December 31st each year, and that all published reports and statistics be of the date of December 31st of the previous year, thereby aiding the effort for uniform and accurate statistics in the United Lutheran Church.

4. That the Constituent Synods again be requested to print their parochial reports crosswise on the page, and not vertically, using only two pages for all the rubrics, thereby having opportunity to make use of 41 lines to a page; and that all parochial reports contain a summary in which a total is given for the Synod for the year covered by the report together with a total for the preceding year and a comparative statement of increase and decrease under all rubrics.

5. That the Constituent Synods again be requested to make provision for the presence of their Statistical Secretaries at future Conventions of the United Lutheran Church in order that they may attend the conference of the Statistical Secretaries at the time of the Convention.

6. That, in view of the approach of the United States census years, the Committee be authorized to negotiate with the United States Census Bureau

and the necessary authorities for the following corrections and additions:
A. As to the 1926 United States Religious Census:

1. The re-classification of the churches along denominational lines, with subdivisions for separate corporate bodies in all the printed reports of the 1926 Religious Census.

2. The placing upon the questionnaire blanks used in making the 1926 census of the churches, the question concerning both "Baptized" and "Confirmed" or "Communicant" membership, with subdivisions "Male" and "Female" in each case, and

3. The addition of rubrics covering the educational work of the churches, with the subdivisions—"Sunday Schools," "Parochial Schools," "Weekday Schools," "Summer Schools" and "Saturday Schools."

B. As to the 1930 United States Regular Census:
That the questions be added to the census questionnaire blank:

1. What religious denomination do you belong to?
2. What religious denomination did your father belong to?
3. What religious denomination did your mother belong to?
4. If not a member, what religious denomination do you prefer?

7. That, in view of the desirability of having the rubric "Confirmed Membership" unencumbered in order that a true representation of the strength of the United Lutheran Church may be put forth when the religious statistics of the United States are gathered, the "Communing Membership" rubric be used instead of the "Confirmed Membership" rubric in the system used for arriving at the United Lutheran Church, synodical and congregational apportionments or quotas.

8. That the model blank for the "State of the Church" as revised according to the recommendations of the Statistical Conference held at the time of the Chicago Convention, and subsequently acted upon by the Statistical and Church Year Book Committee, be referred to the Statistical and Church Year Book Committee in co-operation with the Stewardship Committee for preparation of a final form of standard blank on the "State of the Church" for use in the Constituent Synods of the United Lutheran Church in America.

Respectfully submitted,

GEORGE H. SCHNUR, *Chairman,*

GEO. LINN KIEFFER, *Secretary-Treasurer,*

W. M. KOPENHAVER,

M. G. G. SCHERER,

C. W. CASSELL,

M. G. L. RIETZ,

GEORGE HEMSING,

J. D. KROUT.

The report of the Statistical Secretary of the United Lutheran Church in America is embodied in the report of the Statistical and Church Year Book Committee.

Respectfully,

G. L. KIEFFER,

Statistical Secretary of the United Lutheran Church in America.

PAROCHIAL REPORT OF THE UNITED LUTHERAN CHURCH IN AMERICA (1923)

Compiled by Rev. G. L. Kieffer, Statistical Secretary.

Index No.	Synods	When Organized	Pastors	Parishes	Congregations	Membership: Baptized	Membership: Confirmed	Membership: Communing	Accessions Children: Baptism	Accessions Children: Otherwise	Accessions Adult: Baptism	Accessions Adult: Confirmation	Accessions Adult: Certificate	Accessions Adult: Otherwise	Losses Children: Death	Losses Children: Otherwise	Losses Adult: Death	Losses Adult: Certificate	Losses Adult: Otherwise
1	Ministerium of Pa.	Aug. 15, 1748	424	351	574	254,073	176,956	134,989	7,843	2,507	399	6,299	3,364	2,214	682	2,088	2,925	2,200	3,981
2	Ministerium of N. Y.	Oct. 23, 1786	148	132	141	*107,448	*67,155	*49,456	2,333	786	121	1,666	257	1,106	130	296	1,213	185	431
3	United Synod of N. C.	Oct. 11, 1803	110	91	193	34,396	24,312	18,989	1,030	225	125	863	630	762	63	166	626	494	241
4	Synod of Maryland	Oct. 11, 1820	123	102	140	54,365	41,701	29,151	1,722	366	204	1,499	660	785	110	379	626	473	652
5	Synod of S. C.	Jan. 14, 1824	59	56	109	23,827	12,935	12,935	635	128	96	1,233	34	71	27	53	162	290	252
6	Synod of West Pa.	Sept. 5, 1825	112	89	158	51,554	39,190	33,313	1,331	336	212	1,307	812	923	106	169	616	606	1,022
7	Synod of Virginia	Aug. 10, 1829	79	67	149	17,276	13,541	9,963	346	160	166	447	71	756	29	41	189	208	351
8	Synod of Ohio	Nov. 7, 1836	216	194	287	68,933	51,792	31,212	1,882	515	728	1,655	1,351	2,536	111	323	796	951	2,924
9	East Pennsylvania Synod	May 9, 1842	148	128	156	58,168	43,198	21,389	1,601	491	264	1,359	474	282	120	392	597	684	989
10	Allegheny Synod	Sept. 2, 1842	81	71	148	37,536	28,739		861	324	221	1,169	1,475	843	58	228	337	524	428
11	Pittsburgh Synod	Jan. 15, 1845	259	216	316	103,354	70,603	49,960	3,012	1,628	352	2,640	645	2,536	251	1,093	880	1,239	2,604
12	Indiana Synod	Sept. 8, 1848	53	51	77	13,177	9,066	7,515	339	155	117	167	15	79	18	64	138	158	640
13	Illinois Synod	Sept. 28, 1851	126	102	135	35,874	25,429	20,553	1,198	577	277	2,322	236	843	49	395	271	438	1,901
14	Texas Synod	Nov. 21, 1851	15	18	23	5,435	3,338	2,736	163	32	10	199		79	34	73	41	158	70
15	Synod of Central Pa.	Feb. 25, 1855	38	35	87	17,226	12,619	9,393	330	89	37	1,285	190	55		69	176	215	184
16	Mississippi Synod	Sept. 3, 1855	5	5	14	765	624	391	16			16				14	7	10	58
17	Synod of Iowa	Oct. 27, 1855	26	28	30	8,676	5,357	4,808	375	107	6	317	296	145	15	79	85	155	379
18	Michigan Synod	July 20, 1860	60	54	85	16,422	11,902	8,131	450	137	103	384	99	362	17	256	147	163	739
19	Synod of Georgia	July 21, 1861	22	23	37	6,715	4,643	3,212	76	61	116	76	69	76	10	13	185	33	52
20	Synod of Canada	Nov. 5, 1867	48	44	75	22,390	15,240	12,493	471	147	26	391	203	261	48	102	155	71	190
21	†Susquehanna Synod	Nov. 1, 1868	47	47	79	29,375	22,164	16,459	317	65	19	206	235	110	24	65	81	157	213
22	Synod of Kansas	1871	46	35	41	8,211	5,768	4,513	344	108	35	554	237	221	8	86	155	161	391
23	Synod of Nebraska	July 1, 1875	49	52	57	15,355	11,047	7,530	646	97	119	297	41	221	18	215	77	190	610
24	Wartburg Synod	April 24, 1890	46	42	50	15,593	9,671	6,254	421	119	193	331	200	225	34	124	100	40	193
25	German Nebraska Synod	May 6, 1891	84	77	95	17,924	10,392	9,264	508	48	18	229	95	236	29	75	105	77	65
26	Synod of California	Sept. 22, 1891	54	34	34	8,863	4,583	4,703	324	105	9	58		82	20	168	66	96	421
27	Rocky Mountain Synod	July 16, 1897	14	17	18	2,598	1,910	1,374	95	25						39	20	36	219
28	Synod of the Northwest	Sept. 26, 1901	82	65	72	30,981	19,823	14,547	1,095	1,002	134	1,053	157	1,155	61	1,195	127	339	1,075
29	Manitoba Synod	Sept. 23, 1902	36	31	58	10,168	5,364	4,777	483			320					141		
30	Pacific Synod	July 10, 1903	32	26	30	4,392	2,461	1,919	163	247	24	198	87	157	4	186	31	71	261
31	N. Y. and N. E. Synod	Oct. 7, 1908	77	66	67	41,792	28,630	25,080	1,180	793	116	1,109	506	876	47	331	266	310	959
32	Nova Scotia Synod	Nov. 11, 1908	7	8	30	5,258	2,834	1,493	116	18	3	74	4		18	48	56	21	166
33	Synod of New York	April 17, 1912	143	148	157	52,850	37,415	25,080	1,387	879	143	1,284	641	1,052	77	921	474	319	2,481
34	Central Canada Synod	June 10, 1919	14	14	17	3,280	2,052	1,388	86	95	12	65	21	44	5	20	14	16	58
35	Synod of West Virginia		23	19	39	6,326	4,254	3,287	208	47	44	140	101	106	14	22	59	79	236
36	Slovak "Zion" Synod			28	34	10,825	7,161	5,413									99		
38	1923 Totals U. L. C. in A., Synods in U. S. and Canada.		2,924	2,566	3,812	1,201,401	839,279	633,184	33,387	12,419	4,472	28,188	15,600	16,125	2,244	9,788	11,518	11,016	25,436
39	1922 Totals U. L. C. in A., 2 Congs. in Harlem, N. Y. C., and outside U. S. and Canada.		43		1,541	127,502	79,428	48,300	4,480		3,538	2,112	133	3,121	28		2,722	145	4,341
40	Grand Total U. L. C. in A.		2,967	2,566	5,353	1,328,903	918,707	681,484	37,867	12,419	8,010	30,300	15,733	19,246	2,272	9,788	14,240	11,161	29,777

INDEX NUMBER	PAROCHIAL																						FINANCIAL		
	CHURCH PAPERS			*CHURCH SCHOOLS								STUDENTS				CHURCH SOCIETIES						VALUATION CHURCH PROPERTY		School and Parish Houses
				SUNDAY					WEEKDAY								MEN'S		WOMEN'S		YOUNG P.				
	No. Sub. to Official Papers	No. S. S. Papers Distributed	No. Sub. to Oth'r Ch. Prs.	Number	Officers and Teachers	Scholars	Home Dep't	Cradle Roll	Number	Teachers	Scholars	Catechumens	Ministry	Deaconess	In Lutheran Institutions	In Non-Luth. Institutions	Number	Members	Number	Members	Number	Members	Church Edifices	Parsonages	
	20	21	22	23	24	25	26	27	28	29	30	31	32	33	34	35	36	37	38	39	40	41	42	43	44
1	7,522	14,681	3,887	574	10,934	107,801	4,324	11,512	63	247	4,529	7,620	86	15	242	867	191	9,835	577	30,587	475	21,385	12,821,446	1,506,542	672,300
2	920	3,540	862	127	2,138	19,077	601	2,521	45	60	1,291	347	27		29	90	86	6,023	165	11,375	150	7,285	4,237,275	687,425	373,270
3	2,277	3,011	1,842	142	1,559	20,124	224	602	31	108	1,834	2,360	48	3	282	314	20	740	145	3,484	144	4,171	1,546,410	358,587	62,000
4	2,116	4,845	1,085	143	3,169	21,908	2,168	3,890	12	68	878	2,483	12	26	54	252	47	2,628	191	9,778	161	6,710	4,066,700	573,810	199,500
5	1,284	1,918	757	107	1,148	12,298	299	961	15	91	1,061	1,468	14	2	246	140	16	2,392	108	3,713	95	2,880	2,944,950	177,510	81,000
6	2,134	5,604	959	160	1,198	39,435	2,010	3,939	11	36	826	3,922	50	4	164	189	13	1,373	190	8,673	161	7,943	1,304,900	466,500	21,050
7	1,818	3,111	1,793	101	1,198	48,166	651	866	5	16	144	469	14	3	93	111	13	713	107	3,268	81	2,818	6,164,650	294,075	36,450
8	3,899	20,047	1,399	277	4,667	35,982	1,479	4,398	29	108	2,148	2,922	54	6	291	478	117	4,850	388	16,170	224	6,976	4,263,450	777,800	80,100
9	2,585	8,900	2,056	156	3,539	22,355	3,821	3,795	22	98	1,255	2,599	54	4	106	315	75	1,360	230	10,201	175	6,327	2,485,800	773,500	221,500
10	2,145	8,686	2,393	118	2,194	47,651	1,372	2,316	14	57	1,462	2,243	29	3	80	235	16	4,786	128	5,143	90	3,384	5,980,300	346,138	4,500
11	4,064	20,728	6,459	301	4,916	24,070	3,349	7,049	34	167	2,466	4,404	68	6	171	454	107	4,539	403	14,915	305	10,529	5,980,300	937,210	174,850
12	2,709	3,711	260	70	1,009	8,482	507	861	5	11	118	1,677	13		40	110	21	1,759	98	3,030	51	1,466	964,900	163,300	3,000
13	2,057	11,637	1,358	122	2,308	1,256	615	2,785	2	4	65	108	36	3	111	184	63	101	200	7,100	149	4,396	2,688,475	436,250	55,900
14	148	2,981	30	20	130	12,215	702	93	5	6	65	19	3	1			3	565	17	642	13	566	97,177	33,750	6,100
15	686	311	269	87	1,375	349	12	1,302	2	24	335	764	21	1	61	109	16		70	2,277	62	2,113	860,425	139,100	
16	58	24		8	50	4,346	56	2	9				1				3	25	6	56	3	33	11,150		13,000
17	401	2,619	214	29	522	9,799	253	852		5	20	311	12	3	33	166	15	496	55	2,009	47	1,347	803,533	132,700	10,000
18	1,187	4,671	436	76	1,065	1,784		1,088	2	26	335	429	12	3	45	92	15	1,041	103	3,718	56	1,411	1,436,226	184,617	
19	319	360	25	18	230	4,647		92	10	13	139	71	4		12	26	7	170	20	739	12	470	544,900	73,500	6,400
20	747	453	504	61	633	18,144	1,261	427	13	28	625	336	17	1	20	26	5	286	36	2,179	11	1,429	768,450	147,675	3,500
21	998	1,312	1,490	79	1,652	4,929	174	1,683	29	76	917	941	11	3	43	140	32	2,144	98	4,447	69	2,853	1,752,100	194,250	4,000
22	759	2,634	196	40	634	6,788	468	560	14	28	407	392	14	1	98	98	15	497	64	2,316	44	1,099	812,685	149,450	15,000
23	673	4,022	791	57	834	4,215	260	831	6	2	22	1,122	17		66	208	18	615	76	2,389	53	1,538	993,200	145,700	44,800
24	886	1,250	174	35	353	3,297	108	314	12	13	231	358	11	1	16	20	14	500	47	2,068	25	993	604,700	112,800	21,050
25	620	1,109	155	60	337	2,636	134	294	32	31	704	416	10	1	24	55	14		40	1,005	22	712	520,800	212,600	8,000
26	172	1,529	202	31	348	1,252	172	167		35	559	253	5	2	5	30	12	320	51	1,520	30	614	932,050	38,800	
27	887	775	41	18	173	1,860		1,578	5	20	163	110	3		1	55	7	152	24	573	17	359	136,500	22,000	102,500
28		3,617	843	66	1,197	5,557			4	26	455	1,690	21	1	29	196	32	1,396	93	3,778	91	2,590	263,835	187,150	
29				46	152		108	181	7	40	1,365	171		5						134		238	2,126,250		2,500
30	433	1,020	257	28	201	1,740	595	3,284	39	4	92	972	6		6	41	11	206	5	821	26	556	261,162	48,000	129,000
31	999	3,321	1,837	68	1,774	19,116	1,435	16	4	88	1,540	131	21		23	126	47	2,406	34	5,638	111	3,617	2,670,164	287,000	
32	9	145	432	16	154	1,226		3,003	19			2,067	1	1	3			18	98	632	6		185,025		112,700
33	2,403	8,024	1,365	140	2,241	19,116			22	84	1,144	78	30	5	48	242	74	2,741	8	8,612	174	258	3,716,300	598,575	
34	323	640	202	17	167	1,131	241	241		12	44	326	7	3	13	13	3	65	219	449	16	5,372	175,780	46,000	
35	770	1,495	135	31	428	3,418	82	358	2	3	1,199	113	8		9	29	4	135	20	1,096	30	455	483,100	105,300	
36				11	11	555			15	15			14										388,000		
37																									
38	47,618	152,731	34,708	3,440	56,863	552,872	27,164	61,995	523	1,638	28,438	45,038	746	67	2,381	5,402	1,137	53,706	4,151	174,535	3,200	115,726	70,971,368	10,415,614	2,463,970
39	376	440	10	989	2,055	43,569		9	997	1,540	34,136	18,223	169	1			408	7,017	441	9,258	27	664	260,701	50,300	23,300
40	47,994	153,171	34,718	4,429	58,918	596,441	27,164	62,004	1,520	3,178	62,574	63,261	915	68	2,381	5,402	1,545	60,723	4,592	183,793	3,227	116,390	71,232,069	10,465,914	2,487,270

PAROCHIAL REPORT OF THE UNITED LUTHERAN CHURCH OF AMERICA (1923)—(Continued.)

FINANCIAL

INDEX NUMBER	VALUATION OF CHURCH PROPERTY				CONGREGATIONAL EXPENSES			CONGREGATIONAL BENEVOLENCE									SUMMARY		
								APPORTIONED			UNAPPORTIONED								
	Endowment	Other Property	Total Valuation	Indebtedness	Current	Unusual	Total	Paid	Excess	Deficit	Education	Foreign Missions	Home Missions	Inner Missions	Other Benevolence	Total Un-apportioned Benevolence	Total Benevolence	Total Expenditures
	45	46	47	48	49	50	51	52	53	54	55	56	57	58	59	60	61	62
1	727,576	645,456	16,373,320	1,334,577	1,177,103	938,161	2,115,266	295,308	1,808	113,569	5,553	19,583	4,683	51,817	104,270	185,906	481,214	2,596,480
2	154,137	1,001,944	6,454,051	427,616	*439,583	*210,963	*650,546	51,468			17,305	2,923	1,537	7,553	33,133	62,481	113,949	764,495
3	9,932	195,734	2,172,663	165,176	192,786	100,322	293,108	38,218	251	1,336	34,874	11,391	6,367	4,639	18,045	75,316	113,534	406,642
4	62,173	180,938	5,083,121	467,542	349,153	324,020	673,173	82,594	5,327	11,239	10,270	11,758	5,643	17,837	39,410	84,908	167,502	840,675
5	42,800	19,073	1,274,983	88,455	104,886	51,308	156,194	29,833	40	10,757	11,327	10,555	3,815	5,173	7,805	38,675	68,508	224,702
6	231,253	274,673	3,938,426	114,688	393,860	121,607	515,467	88,036	5,605	19,654	4,379	17,356	1,975	6,023	33,381	63,114	151,150	666,617
7	39,280	60,586	1,735,291	130,460	118,767	56,991	175,758	28,879	582	19,513	11,607	5,673	1,832	5,219	11,679	36,010	64,889	240,647
8	67,921	390,811	7,481,282	575,758	634,609	355,977	990,586	165,773	5,974	28,623	43,743	33,650	9,056	12,367	43,184	142,000	307,773	1,298,359
9	136,840	288,015	5,683,305	547,020	518,835	174,941	693,776	112,729	10,477	21,271	11,664	21,250	4,920	30,896	42,475	111,205	223,934	917,710
10	36,257	63,300	2,935,995	282,346	526,737	139,931	366,668	69,785	6,610	34,822	11,710	16,659	2,663	3,971	23,716	58,719	128,504	495,172
11	171,807	480,760	7,744,927	770,871	650,027	488,484	1,138,511	157,715	1,353	4,286	41,146	16,659	12,272	55,235	62,281	187,593	345,308	1,483,819
12	19,766	58,507	1,209,473	66,438	123,119	63,025	186,144	28,369	1,681	4,107	14,751	9,723	3,499	2,706	7,978	32,109	60,478	246,622
13	25,551	94,688	3,300,864	281,108	328,758	349,850	678,608	70,383		4,476	519	85	3,686	29	21,691	58,920	129,303	807,911
14	1,150	14,300	152,477	10,877	19,320	5,966	25,286	2,263	1,981	4,099	2,555		823	3,859	1,835	3,291	5,554	30,940
15	17,800	14,875	1,041,200	6,850	81,201	25,310	106,511	27,607	23	628	123	3,629	733	59	8,162	18,938	46,545	153,056
16		5,569	18,919	500	2,117	625	2,742	598	1,168	6,867		797	199	605	239	704	1,302	4,044
17	5,000	42,000	996,233	187,370	101,385	57,298	158,683	14,361	220	10,616	2,639	3,456	1,210	527	3,965	9,216	23,577	182,260
18	2,850	113,300	1,746,993	207,476	149,426	73,904	223,330	24,917	2	588	10,998	1,184	496	167	3,221	19,605	44,522	267,852
19	10,000	43,400	671,800	162,614	89,328	31,075	90,058	12,234		23,488	423	814	232	260	5,708	7,978	20,212	110,270
20	1,325	56,300	952,050	29,015	129,741	175,496	120,403	20,820	1,775	5,008	4,336	3,710	785	729	6,303	11,945	32,765	153,168
21	39,250	41,950	2,045,000	216,357	97,997	31,259	305,237	30,487	28	1,725	4,689	1,844	407	2,226	18,093	28,006	58,493	363,730
22	11,600	127,700	1,019,685	72,265	114,431	72,265	129,256	17,234	262	4,020	2,382	2,621	1,126	2,860	4,730	11,589	28,823	158,079
23	1,100	29,570	1,282,700	68,310	54,510	17,571	149,555	22,947	545	180	5,079	975	687	687	6,677	25,600	48,547	198,102
24		13,970	791,870	63,920	67,325	13,317	72,081	9,504	1,243	26,459	768	763	509	1,126	2,917	6,473	15,977	88,058
25	4,700	46,358	1,032,708	17,765	67,325	45,479	80,642	10,246	4	3,855	11,479	1,212	695	975	11,476	25,239	35,485	116,127
26	7,500	50,275	773,120	68,726	68,726	20,563	114,205	12,201	66	1,209	95	677	509	763	7,712	9,831	22,032	136,237
27		41,641	2,208,775	17,765	28,521	20,563	49,084	5,236			645	3,713	107	396	2,009	3,834	9,070	58,154
28	3,798		2,461,339	37,429	157,140	211,336	368,476	34,689			9,845	693	1,588	2,690	1,911	29,747	64,436	432,912
29			264,833	86,170	39,241	39,241	39,241	371	719		1,866	602	152	303	1,445	4,732	5,103	44,344
30	10,133	10,133	341,795	383,277	32,967	22,360	55,327	7,226	17	670	518	354	15	728	3,585	5,227	12,453	67,780
31	33,833	325,570	3,445,567	383,725	335,500	202,677	538,277	60,499		2,042	20,331	8,865	3,868	11,623	20,498	65,185	125,684	663,961
32		1,400	232,225	23,360	32,967	7,415	22,500	2,344		2,156	848	5,070	1,502		608	5,227	4,169	26,669
33	113,328	145,436	4,686,339	390,275	176,148	179,011	555,159	56,962	299	4,605	11,404	354	848	10,100	19,687	47,763	104,725	659,884
34	28,000	15,500	265,280	75,280	23,455	6,775	30,230	9,223		3,454	99	226	278	80	2,435	3,118	6,874	37,104
35	500	51,300	640,200	98,983	48,468	24,403	72,871	9,223			1,427	4,166	323	1,132	2,768	9,816	19,039	91,910
36			383,000		80,355		80,355	475							1,856	1,856	2,331	82,686
37																		
38					7,387,593	4,635,721	12,023,314	1,605,290	48,060	378,486	316,056	227,718	86,762	261,050	596,888	1,488,474	3,093,764	15,117,078
39	2,007,027 / 25,000	4,973,232 / 53,072	90,831,211 / 1,442,373	7,441,246 / 50,000	99,831 / 1,500		101,331	78				78			11,811	11,889	11,889	113,220
40	2,032,027	5,026,304	92,273,584	7,491,246	7,487,424	4,637,221	12,124,645	1,605,290	48,060	378,486	316,056	227,796	86,762	261,050	608,699	1,500,363	3,105,653	15,230,298

COMPARATIVE PAROCHIAL STATISTICS OF THE UNITED LUTHERAN CHURCH IN AMERICA FOR 1919-1920-1921-1922 AND 1923

Compiled by Rev. G. L. Kieffer, Statistical Secretary.

PAROCHIAL

Index	YEAR	Pastors (2)	Parishes (3)	Congregations (4)	MEMBERSHIP Baptized (5)	Confirmed (6)	Communing (7)	ACCESSIONS CHILDREN Baptism (8)	Otherwise (9)	ADULT Baptism (10)	Confirmation (11)	Certificate (12)	Otherwise (13)	LOSSES CHILDREN Death (14)	Otherwise (15)	ADULT Death (16)	Certificate (17)	Otherwise (18)	CHURCH PAPER No. Sub. to Official Papers (19)	No. S. S. Papers Distributed (20)	No. Sub. to Oth'r Ch. Pr's. (21)
1	1923	2,924	2,566	3,812	1,201,401	839,279	633,184	33,387	12,419	4,472	28,188	15,600	16,125	2,244	9,788	11,518	11,016	25,436	47,618	152,731	34,708
2	1922	2,900	2,501	3,732	1,164,550	819,063	621,123	36,016	12,704	5,599	30,954	16,345	16,445	2,334	9,370	11,741	10,934	25,650	49,267	144,631	33,867
3	1 Year Gain	24	65	80	36,851	20,216	12,061								418		82			8,100	841
4	1 Year Decrease							2,629	285	1,127	2,766	745	320	90		223		214	1,649		
5	1923	2,924	2,566	3,812	1,201,401	839,279	633,184	33,387	12,419	4,472	28,188	15,600	16,125	2,244	9,788	11,518	11,016	25,436	47,618	152,731	34,708
6	1921	2,887	2,492	3,803	1,147,007	801,250	597,768	37,403	11,773	5,302	30,467	16,456	16,500	2,392	8,921	11,051	11,475	25,485	36,969	118,139	21,454
7	2 Years' Gain	37	74	9	54,394	38,029	35,416		646						867				10,649	34,592	13,254
8	2 Years' Decrease							4,016		830	2,279	856	375	148		467	459	49			
9	1923	2,924	2,566	3,812	1,201,401	839,279	633,184	33,387	12,419	4,472	28,188	15,600	16,125	2,244	9,788	11,518	11,016	25,436	47,618	152,731	34,708
10	1920	2,812		3,775	1,117,938	791,400	580,018	36,438		4,834	29,380	15,214	14,571			11,554	11,610	26,550			
11	3 Years' Gain	112		37	83,463	47,879	53,166					386	1,554								
12	3 Years' Decrease							3,051		362	1,192					36	594	1,114			
13	1923	2,924	2,566	3,812	1,201,401	839,279	633,184	33,387	12,419	4,472	28,188	15,600	16,125	2,244	9,788	11,518	11,016	25,436	47,618	152,731	34,708
14	1919	2,843		3,473	1,094,153	776,582	474,553	34,785		4,400	27,645	13,915	9,235			14,073	10,664	23,467			
15	4 Years' Gain	81		339	107,248	62,697	158,631				543	1,685	6,890								
16	4 Years' Decrease							1,398		72						2,555	352	1,969			

PAROCHIAL

Index	*CHURCH SCHOOLS SUNDAY Number (22)	Officers and Teachers (23)	Scholars (24)	Home Dep't (25)	Cradle Roll (26)	WEEKDAY Number (27)	Teachers (28)	Scholars (29)	Catechu-mens (30)	STUDENTS Ministry (31)	Deaconess (32)	In Lutheran Institutions (33)	In Non-Luth. Institutions (34)	CHURCH SOCIETIES MEN'S Number (35)	Members (36)	WOMEN'S Number (37)	Members (38)	YOUNG P Number (39)	Members (40)	FINANCIAL Valuation of Church Property Church Edifices (41)	Parsonages (42)	School and Parish Houses (43)
1	3,440	56,863	552,872	27,164	61,995	523	1,638	28,438	45,238	746	67	2,381	5,402	1,137	53,706	4,151	174,535	3,200	115,726	70,971,368	10,415,614	2,463,970
2	3,465	55,330	555,510	28,446	59,264	490	1,453	25,149	35,311	717	59	2,015	4,520	1,102	52,525	4,013	173,270	3,132	115,234	65,598,841	9,237,584	1,584,150
3	25	1,533			2,731	33	185	3,289	9,927	29	8	366	882	35	1,181	138	1,265	68	492	5,372,527	1,178,030	879,820
4			2,638	1,282																		
5	3,440	56,863	552,872	27,164	61,995	523	1,638	28,438	45,238	746	67	2,381	5,402	1,137	53,706	4,151	174,535	3,200	115,726	70,971,368	10,415,614	2,463,970
6	3,682	54,268	522,691	26,142	52,148	375	954	17,534	34,034	582	85	1,712	4,292	967	47,052	3,618	154,089	2,694	106,842	63,193,694	8,138,433	878,400
7	242	2,595	30,181	1,022	9,847	148	684	10,904	11,204	164	22	669	1,110	170	6,654	533	20,446	506	8,884	7,777,674	2,277,181	1,585,570
8																						
9	3,440	56,863	552,872	27,164	61,995	523	1,638	28,438	45,238	746	67	2,381	5,402	1,137	53,706	4,151	174,535	3,200	115,726	70,971,368	10,415,614	2,463,970
10	3,399	52,939	515,815	23,506	46,300	190	326	7,070	44,334	577	46	1,833	4,316	892	39,426	3,547	139,205	2,367	92,822		6,928,456	
11	41	3,924	37,057	3,658	15,695	333	1,312	21,368	904	169	21	548	1,086	245	14,280	604	35,330	833	22,905		3,487,158	
12																						
13	3,440	56,863	552,872	27,164	61,995	523	1,638	28,438	45,238	746	67	2,381	5,402	1,137	53,706	4,151	174,535	3,200	115,726	70,971,368	10,415,614	2,463,970
14	3,412	53,524	514,924	19,019	32,228	109	130	4,779	36,689	526	14	233	611	708	32,550	2,811	104,760	2,114	81,746		2,071,193	
15	28	3,339	37,948	8,145	29,767	414	1,508	23,659	8,549	220	53	2,148	4,791	429	21,156	1,340	69,775	1,086	33,981		8,344,421	
16																						

COMPARATIVE PAROCHIAL STATISTICS OF THE UNITED LUTHERAN CHURCH IN AMERICA FOR 1919-1920-1921 AND 1923—(Continued)

FINANCIAL

Column groups: **VALUATION OF CHURCH PROPERTY** (44–47) · **CONGREGATIONAL EXPENSES** (48–50) · **CONGREGATIONAL BENEVOLENCE** — APPORTIONED (51–53), UNAPPORTIONED (54–59) · **SUMMARY** (60–61)

Index	44 Endowment	45 Other Property	46 Total Valuation	47 Indebtedness	48 Current	49 Unusual	50 Total	51 Paid	52 Excess	53 Deficit	54 Education	55 Foreign Missions	56 Home Missions	57 Inner Missions	58 Other Benevolence	59 Total Un-apportioned Benevolence	60 Total Benevolence	61 Total Expenditures
1	2,007,027	4,973,232	90,831,211	7,441,246	7,387,593	4,635,721	12,023,314	1,605,290	48,060	378,486	316,056	227,718	86,762	261,050	596,888	1,488,474	3,093,764	15,117,078
2	1,851,134	3,701,544	81,973,253	7,047,140	6,816,399	4,009,146	10,825,545	1,513,077	45,328	368,687	292,682	155,599	72,287	233,324	777,002	1,530,894	3,043,971	13,869,516
3	155,893	1,271,688	8,857,958	394,106	571,194	626,575	1,197,769	92,213	2,732	9,799	23,374	72,119	14,475	27,726	180,114	42,420	49,793	1,247,562
4																		
5	2,007,027	4,973,232	90,831,211	7,441,246	7,387,593	4,635,721	12,023,314	1,605,290	48,060	378,486	316,056	227,718	86,762	261,050	596,888	1,488,474	3,093,764	15,117,078
6	1,895,798	2,400,790	76,507,115	6,011,472	6,621,298	3,835,135	10,456,403	1,440,132	62,601	342,307	509,521	140,190	66,369	240,027	884,653	1,901,660	3,341,792	13,798,195
7	111,229	2,572,442	14,324,096	1,429,774	766,325	800,586	1,566,911	165,158		36,179	253,465	87,528	20,333	20,123	287,765	413,186	248,028	1,318,883
8																		
9	2,007,027	4,973,232	90,831,211	7,441,246	7,387,593	4,635,721	12,023,314	1,605,290	48,060	378,486	316,056	227,718	86,762	261,050	596,888	1,488,474	3,093,764	15,117,078
10	2,065,974		70,142,813	5,581,845	5,630,943	2,968,750	8,599,663	1,206,115	14,541		612,129		36,017	233,909	983,743	1,805,798	3,071,913	11,671,606
11	58,947		20,688,398	1,859,401	1,756,650	1,666,971	3,423,621	399,175			296,073		50,745	27,141	386,855	377,324	21,851	3,445,472
12																		
13	2,007,027	4,973,232	90,831,211	7,441,246	7,387,593	4,635,721	12,023,314	1,605,290	48,060	378,486	316,056	227,718	86,762	261,050	596,888	1,488,474	3,093,764	15,117,078
14	1,032,292		42,383,332	4,527,913	4,984,705	1,916,749	6,901,544	1,344,202			315,980		5,459	70	902,981	908,586	2,252,788	9,154,332
15	974,735		48,447,879	2,913,333	2,402,798	2,718,972	5,121,770	261,088			76		81,303	260,980	306,003	579,888	840,976	5,962,746
16																		

TOTAL OF ACCESSIONS AND LOSSES COMPARED

			Current Exp.	Unusual Exp.	Total Cong. Exp.	Appor. Benev. Paid	Total Benevolence	Total Expenditures
1923	Total losses............	60,002	$8.80	$5.52	$14.33	1.91	$3.52	$18.00
1922	Total losses............	60,029	8.32	4.89	13.21	1.84	3.71	16.93
1923	Gain in losses.........	27	.48	.63	1.12	.07	.19	1.07
1923	Total accessions......	110,191						
1922	Total accessions......	118,063						
1923	Decrease in accessions...	7,872						
1923	Ascessions gain over losses....	50,189	8.26	4.79	13.05	1.79	4.17	17.22
1922	Accessions gain over losses....	58,034	7.15	3.75	10.90	1.52	3.88	14.78
1923	Decrease Accessions over losses.	7,845	6.42	2.46	8.88	1.73	2.90	11.78

1923 per capita (839,279 cf. m.)	
1922 per capita (819,063 cf. m.)	
1923 gain over 1922 per capita.	
1923 decrease over 1922 per capita.	
1921 per capita (801,250 cf. m.)	
1920 per capita (791,400 cf. m.)	
1919 per capita (776,582 cf. m.)	

1923 net valuation......	$83,389,965
1922 net valuation......	74,926,113
1923 gain net valuation...	8,463,852
1921 net valuation......	70,495,643
1920 net valuation......	64,560,968
1919 net valuation......	37,855,419

Recommendations 1 and 2 were adopted.

Recommendation 3 was amended by the insertion of the words "we request" at the beginning, the insertion of the word "congregational" before "organizations" and the striking out of the words "boards and committees." Resolution 3 was adopted as amended.

Resolutions 4 and 5 were adopted.

Pending discussion of recommendation 6 the Convention adjourned until 1 : 30 o'clock.

Closing prayer was offered by the Rev. A. S. Hardy.

Afternoon Session

Tuesday, October 28, 1 : 30 P. M.

The President called the Convention to order.

Prayer was offered by the Rev. J. A. Huffard.

The Chairman of the Committee of Reference and Counsel reported that the Danish Church had appointed the Rev. P. Gotke as their representative to bring fraternal greetings to this Convention, but that he had been detained on account of illness. The Committee recommended that the Secretary be instructed to send greetings to the proper authorities, and an expression of our appreciation of their appointment of a representative. The recommendation was approved.

On motion of the Chairman, the action taken yesterday instructing the Executive Board to publish a booklet was reconsidered. The Committee moved to amend by inserting in the resolution the words "at their discretion." The amendment was adopted, and the resolution as amended was adopted.

Following the special order of business, namely, the report of the Committee on Women's Work and the hearing of the representative of the Women's Missionary Society, the Rev. W. D. C. Keiter presented the report of the Committee and introduced Mrs. Sydney R. Kepner, President of the Society.

REPORT OF THE COMMITTEE ON WOMEN'S WORK

The report of the Committee on Women's Work must of necessity be limited to a report on the work and activities of the Women's Missionary Society of the United Lutheran Church in America, as the only women's organization coming within the Committee's jurisdiction. During the past biennium the Committee functioned regularly and in accordance with its prerogatives as a co-ordinating agency of the Church, has maintained that cordial organic relationship which has ever existed between the United Lutheran Church and its strongest and most efficient auxiliary organization. At the same time, the Committee has held itself in readiness to render every service within its power to promote the interest of the Society.

By virtue of a courteous resolution adopted by the Women's Missionary Society, a representative of the Committee on Women's Work was present at most of the meetings of the Executive Board of the Society, where every facility was offered him to become acquainted with every phase of the Society's large and far-reaching operations.

The committee feels that in every way the Society has conducted its work in harmony with the constitution, principles and polity of the Church, and is convinced that the best report it can render on the work of the organization is to present the report of the Society itself.

This report sets forth clearly the really marvellous work which the Society has accomplished and the new record it has made for itself during the past biennium. Without attempting to discuss specific items in the report, your Committee, nevertheless, would avail itself of its privilege merely in a general way to call attention to a few outstanding features.

In the first place we would point to the expansion of the organization itself, evidence by the large increase in its numerical strength, in the number of congregational societies established and by the addition of at least three or more synodical organizations which have united with the General Body since the last Convention. Equally remarkable is the work which is being done along the same line of organizing the children of the Church.

Special attention is directed to the Society's educational activities, to the splendid and varied character of the literature published (probably the best in the country), and to its far-reaching program for the training of workers for the Church. In like manner we would stress the fine achievements of every departmental organization, and last, but not least, call the attention of the Church to the astonishing sum of money raised by the Society through various channels for the support and development of the manifold operations of the Church. Almost every Board and every cause has participated in the generous aid vouchsafed by the Missionary Society.

True to the high purpose for which the Society exists, the organization has indeed proved itself a faithful handmaiden of the Church and of her Lord and Master. The secret of this large measure of success which has attended the work of the Society undoubtedly lies in the zeal, in the consecration and in the spirit of self-denial which has permeated the organization from center to circumference. Nor must we overlook the just and business-like management with which the affairs of the Society have been conducted. With a keen sense of their responsibility the officers and the Executive Board, often at great personal sacrifice, have labored unceasingly to administer the affairs of the Society carefully, economically and for the best interest of the work of the Church.

Before closing this report, the Committee would refer to the sad experience which the Society met in the death of Mrs. Helen Beegle, who had served as the Executive Secretary of the organization ever since the merger in 1918. Mrs. Beegle had but one interest in her life and that was the work and welfare of the Women's Missionary Society of the United Lutheran Church. Her noble Christian character and her consecrated labors have left a lasting impression for good upon the entire organization. A representative of the Committee participated in a memorial service held at Pittsburgh, Pa., in May, 1924.

Respectfully submitted,

COMMITTEE.

F. A. KAEHLER,
J. B. MARKWARD,
W. H. SHEPFER,
M. J. BIEBER,
D. A. DAVY,
S. J. McDOWELL,
W. D. C KEITER, <i>Chairman.</i>

REPORT OF THE WOMEN'S MISSIONARY SOCIETY

To the United Lutheran Church in America. Greetings:

This report is submitted with the feeling that the attainments of the biennium are due alone to divine guidance throughout the biennium and to the consecration of the women of the United Lutheran Church in the activities that they have tried to carry on.

ORGANIZATION

The Board met for its first meeting of the biennium at the Fort Pitt Hotel, Pittsburgh, Pa., September 30, 1922, the following officers and members constituting the Board: Mrs. S. R. Kepner, President; Mrs. W. F. Morehead, Vice-President; Mrs. Horace D. Becker, Recording Secretary; Mrs. S. F. Jensen, Statistical Secretary, and Mrs. W. C. Weier,

Treasurer; Mrs. H. C. Bell, Mrs. W. E. Black, Mrs. F. F. Fry, Mrs. J. E. Hoick, Mrs. H. D. Hoover, Mrs. J. B. Markward, Mrs. G. W. McClanahan, Mrs. H. C. Michael, Miss Flora Prince, Mrs. J. W. Richards, Mrs. P. M. Rossman, Mrs. F. W. Seeger, Mrs. H. C. Ter Vehn, Mrs. J. G. Traver, Mrs. N. Willison. Mrs. Helen C. Beegle was elected Executive Secretary

Administrative Committee.—The following officers and members were appointed on the Administrative Committee: Mrs. S. R. Kepner, President; Mrs. F. E. Jensen, Vice-President; Mrs. Horace D. Becker, Recording Secretary; Mrs. Walter C. Weier, Treasurer; Mrs. J. B. Markward, Mrs. H. C. Michael and Miss Flora Prince.

BOARD OF TRUSTEES

The Board of Trustees elected the following officers: Mrs. F. F. Fry, President; Mrs. J. B. Markward, Vice-President; Mrs. F. E. Jensen, Recording Secretary; Miss Flora Prince, Treasurer.

MEETINGS

The Executive Board held eight quarterly meetings, all of these meetings being held at the headquarters in Pittsburgh except the March, 1924, meeting, which was held in Philadelphia at the new Muhlenberg Building, the meeting being held there at the invitation of the Literature Committee.

Besides the Board members the following representatives were present at Board meetings: A member of the Literature Committee, the Editor of *Lutheran Woman's Work,* the Chairman of the Committee on Woman's Work of the United Lutheran Church, representatives from the Foreign and Home Boards, home missionaries, foreign missionaries and Department Secretaries. The President of the United Lutheran Church was present at one of the quarterly meetings. The Administrative Committee held ad interim meetings between the meetings of the Executive Board for the transaction of important business and to present recommendations to the Executive Board.

The Board of Trustees held two meetings during the biennium.

APPOINTMENTS BY THE EXECUTIVE BOARD

Advisory members were appointed by the Executive Board to attend the meetings of the following Boards of the Church: Deaconess, Foreign Missions, Home Mission and Church Extension, Inner Mission, Immigrant Missions, Ministerial Relief, West Indies and Board of Education. The advantage of having advisory members on these Boards has been of great value to the Executive Board of the Women's Missionary Society, in bringing them into closer touch with the work of the Church.

Department Secretaries were appointed to carry on the various departments of the work in the Society and to stimulate greater interest throughout Synodical, Conference and Congregational Societies.

INTERDENOMINATIONAL AFFILIATION

The outstanding work of our interdenominational affiliation in this biennium has been the funds raised for the Women's Christian Colleges of the Orient, we have a part in two schools, the one at Madras and the other at Vellore, India. Also our affiliations in the Mission Study books and contact with workers of other denominations.

FULFILLMENT OF POLICY

The fulfillment of the Society's policy has been given prominence throughout the biennium, effort having been exerted "to stimulate and promote interest in mission work, by disseminating missionary information, by promoting missionary education and by aiding financially the missionary activities of the Church, through its regularly established Boards."

Also great care has been taken in the endeavor "to co-ordinate the work of the Society with that of the Church, and likewise to co-ordinate and unite the work of the Synodical Societies composing the Women's Missionary Society." The further aim "to maintain and extend organization, until in every congregation of the United Lutheran Church there shall be a Women's Missionary Society" has brought forth great effort to extend organization in Conference and Synodical Societies.

CO-OPERATION

Co-operation with the Executive Board of the United Lutheran Church and with the Boards of the Church with which the Society has affiliated has continued most happily throughout the biennium.

Synodical and Conference Societies have also worked most harmoniously with all the plans and recommendations of the Executive Board.

SPECIAL ACHIEVEMENTS DURING THE BIENNIUM

The effort to raise $175,000 for the Japan School and the opening of a school in the mountains of North Carolina have been the most outstanding achievements for the year, and have been entered into most heartily by the members and friends of the Women's Missionary Society.

SPECIAL APPOINTMENTS DURING THE BIENNIUM

A Secretary who could do visitation work amongst the Young Women of the Church and organize Young Women's Societies, and a Field Secretary were two new appointees during the biennium.

THE RECEIPTS FOR THE BIENNIUM TOTALED

The receipts for the biennium were $889,081.40 which, together with the balance from the last biennium of $122,864.66, makes a total of $1,011,946.06.

The sources of this income were the regular monthly membership contributions, constituting the General Fund, and voluntary contributions from members and friends of the Society. Chief among the latter offerings have been the annual Thank Offering, the Christmas Offering, the Lenten Offering, the Life Membership and In Memoriam fees, bequests and annuities, also the support of missionaries, of Bible women and scholarships has been an appreciable addition to the Society's funds.

SUPPORT OF FOREIGN MISSIONARIES

By Synodical Societies, etc., Assumed During the Biennium

Miss Mary Baer, M.D. ....Maryland
Miss Agnes E. Christenson ....Kansas Conference
Augustana Society
Miss Katharine Fahs ....Susquehanna-Central
Sr. Laura Gilliland ....Pittsburgh
Miss Reba Hendrickson ....Missonary Union, Washington, D. C.
Miss Anna Kugler, M.D., Sc.D. ....East Pennsylvania
Miss Bertha Klein, R.N. ....East Pennsylvania
Sr. Jennie Larmonth ....Ohio
Miss Marie C. Martens ....Illinois
Miss Betty A. Nilsson, M.D. ....Augustana Society
Miss Elsie R. Otto ....West Virginia
Sr. Ruth Robeson ....Alleghany
Miss Agnes I. Schade ....Pittsburgh
Miss Lillith Schwab ....Kansas
Miss Florence M. Welty ....Indiana
Miss Pauline E. Whittaker, R.N. ....Friends, Lancaster Conference Society,
Ministerium of Pennsylvania
Miss Emilie L. Weiskotten..................................Ministerium of Pennsylvania

By Congregations

Miss Metta K. Blair.... ....Kountze Memorial Church, Omaha, Nebr.
Rev. O. D. Baltzly, D.D., Pastor
Miss Mary S. Borthwick............................Holy Communion, Philadelphia, Pa.
Rev. J. Henry Harms, D.D., Pastor
Mrs. C. E. Buschman...............................Temple Church, Philadelphia, Pa.
Rev. A. V. Pohlman, D.D., Pastor
Miss Edith Eykamp...Unity Church, Chicago, Ill.
Rev. D. A. Davy, Pastor
Miss Florence M. Hines.......... ....Dr. and Mrs. A. V. Pohlman,
Temple Church, Philadelphia, Pa
Miss Emma Johnson......Young Women's Missionary Society, Trinity Church,
Rockford, Ill., Rev. H. M. Bannen, D.D., Pastor
Miss Bertha Koenig..Messiah, Williamsport, Pa.
Rev. R. G. Bannen, D.D., Pastor
Miss Eleanor Lange..Emmanuel, Souderton, Pa.
Rev. Warren Nickel, Pastor
Miss Clara J. Leaman..St. Paul's, Carlisle, Pa.
Rev. H. B. Stock, D.D., Pastor
Miss Lottie L. Martin ....Temple Church, Philadelphia, Pa.
Rev. A. V. Pohlman, D.D., Pastor
Miss Alice J. Nickel..............Church of the Good Shepherd, Brooklyn, N. Y.
Rev. C. D. Trexler, D.D., Pastor
Miss Miriam Treon...Zion Church, Sunbury, Pa.
Rev. C. R. Bowers, D.D., Pastor
Miss Agatha Tatge.. ....Advent, New York City
Rev. A. Steimle, D.D., Pastor

By Young Women's Department

Miss Louise A. Miller ....India
Miss Martha B. Akard ....Japan
Miss Mabel Dysinger ....Africa

By Light Brigade Department

Miss Mary Bauer, R.N. ....Africa
Miss Christina E. Eriksson, R.N. ....India
Miss Annie Powlas ....Japan

PATRONS AND PROTEGES

Assuming the support of Bible women in the Foreign Fields has become more generally and favorably understood, as affording special objects for such organizations and individuals as desire to have a feature of the work of the Society distinctly their own, likewise the support of girl students in the schools conducted by our women missionaries has been assumed, such contributions increasing the appropriations for the schools and making the Christian education of more of India's girls and young women possible. Then, too, as many patrons testify, supporting a Bible woman or a girl-student becomes a personal link with the worker or the student in a foreign field.

At present the list of our proteges include 136 Bible women and teachers in India, three in Japan, and the support of the entire staff of women workers in Africa.

One hundred and four scholarships in India and 34 in Africa. Several scholarships for Vellore Medical College have been assumed.

The Luther League of the Synod of Virginia is continuing the support of Miss Minnie Moses, Stall School, Guntur, and Miss Dhanamma Joshua, Dr. Kugler's Indian assistant, is being supported by the group of six who formerly supported Miss M. Paru, N. P.

HOME MISSIONS

Thirty-five Missions were receiving appropriations toward their support at the opening of the biennium. Four have assumed self-support and seven new missions have been added to our list; three in the Rocky Mountain Synod, three in the Pacific Synod and one in the South Carolina Synod.

Monthly appropriations to home missions were $1960 until the month of March, 1924, when the monthly appropriation was increased to $2350. Church Extension appropriations have been special.

The entire or partial support of the following Home Missions has been contributed:

Support of Home Missions

Clarksburg, W. Va. ....Maryland Synodical Society
Kalamazoo, Mich. ....Michigan Synodical Society
Butler, Pa., (Trinity) ....Pittsburgh Synodical Society
Columbus, Ohio, (Indianola Ave.) ....Ohio Synodical Society
Lynchburg, Va., (Holy Trinity) ....Virginia Synodical Society
New Salem, N. D. ....Alleghany Synodical Society
Belmont Park, Chicago, Ill. ....Illinois Synodical Society

Waukesha, Wis. ....Wisconsin Conf. Society, Synod of Northwest
Philadelphia, Pa., (Gloria Dei) ....Ministerium of Penna.
Rock Hill, S. C. ....S. C. Synodical Society
Watauga, N. C., (Support of Parish Worker)................Light Brigade Dept.
Spring Garden Valley, Pittsburgh, Pa. (Settlement Work),
Pittsburgh Synodical Society

Assumed Self-Support

Riverside, Calif. ....Rev. H. S. Weaver, D.D., Pastor
Pasadena, Calif. ....Rev. W. H. Derr, Pastor
North Austin, Chicago, Ill. ....Rev. F. W. Otterbein, Pastor
Indianola, Columbus ....Rev. E. Clyde Xander, Pastor

IMMIGRANT MISSION

The extent of the work of the Society for Immigrant work has been the contribution of funds for the support of Italian, Slavic, etc., students for the ministry of their own people.

INNER MISSION

Settlement work in Pittsburgh has been one of the specials of the Pittsburgh Synodical Society in the Spring Garden Mission, and Port Work in New York City have been the features of Inner Mission Work, besides the great amount of gifts for the orphans' and old people's homes.

JEWISH MISSION

The support of a woman assistant in Messiah Hebrew Lutheran Mission, Philadelphia, has been the extent of the Society's work.

EDUCATION

The Society has worked in conjunction with the Board of Education in having two young women secretaries in the field, looking after the girls in not only our own institutions but also in other educational institutions. The work has been invaluable both from the standpoint of the girls and of our Society.

WEST INDIES

Our work in the West Indies has been the support of two missionaries, one in Porto Rico and the other in the Virgin Islands, and the maintenance of two homes for children in the Virgin Islands.

FOREIGN MISSIONS

The work of our Foreign Fields and the consecrated efforts of all our missionaries has been a real source of inspiration to all of us. Our four hospitals, Guntur, Rajahmundry and Chirala, India, and Phoebe Hospital, Africa, have been overcrowded, but have been a source of blessing to thousands of patients.

The educational, Bible training schools, lace industry, the nurses' training schools, kindergartens and zenana work have all been important parts of our work and have shown great advance during the biennium. In Africa advance steps have been taken in sending women missionaries into the interior stations.

We would like to pay tribute to each one of our missionaries, who has had a part in the furtherance of our work, and we take this opportunity in doing so.

OUR MISSIONARIES

New missionaries commissioned and sent to India during the biennium were: Miss Verna A. Lofgren, R.N., Miss Clara J. Leaman, B.A., and Miss Lottie L. Martin, R.N.

To Africa—Miss Bertha Dierolf, R.N., Miss Bertha Klein, R.N., Miss Miriam Treon, and Miss Dora Hahn.

Under Appointment—To India, Miss Rose Brummer, R.N., Miss Ethel Viele, R.N., Miss Emma Johnson, Miss Edith Eykamp and Miss Ruth Hildegarde Swanson.

Missionaries Deceased—Miss Jessie Brewer.

Missionaries Retired—Miss Marion Eyster, now Mrs. August Schmitt- henner; Miss Isie Weygandt, now Mrs. Clarence Swavely; Miss Viola Steigerwalt, now Mrs. Leon E. L. Irschick; Miss Bertha Dierolf, now Mrs. Paul M. Counts; Dr. Elizabeth Reese-Wilkens, Miss Barbara E. DeRemer, and Mrs. Anna H. Mueller.

OUR PUBLICATIONS AND OUR LITERATURE

With a great deal of pride we point to the work of our Literature Com- mittee and the material that they are putting before our women for their use and for their education. *Lutheran Woman's Work* also meets with the heart- iest appreciation not only amongst our own membership but amongst women of other denominations. To the Literature Committee and Mrs. J. F. Seebach, editor of *Lutheran Woman's Work,* we owe much as a Society.

MRS. HELEN C. BEEGLE

We cannot close this report without a word of appreciation being given to Mrs. Helen C. Beegle, the Executive Secretary of the Executive Board of the Women's Missionary Society of the United Lutheran Church in America. Mrs. Beegle became the Executive Secretary at the time of the merger in 1918, and served until her death in March, 1924. We feel that to her comprehensive knowledge of the work of the entire Church and her sympathy in the work of the three merging bodies, there arose within our Society a feeling of interest and confidence in all that we were trying to do and we are glad that we had for so many years her wise counsel and guidance.

We take this opportunity also in introducing to the Church the new Executive Secretary of our Women's Executive Board, Miss Amelia D. Kemp, formerly of Baltimore, Maryland, who will enter upon her duties August 1, 1924.

OUTLOOK FOR THE NEW BIENNIUM

In reviewing the past biennium with all its achievements we are looking forward to the new biennium with renewed hopes that our aim and our desire for greater and enlarged work may be the desire of all the women of the Church.

We submit therefore the following Budget for the next biennium.

PROPOSED BUDGET FOR THE BIENNIUM
HOME FIELD

Appropriations, Support of Home Missions	$80,000
Appropriations, Church Extension	75,000
Immigrant Missions, Education of Students	10,000
Inner Missions, Settlement Work, Pittsburgh	4,800
Inner Missions, Port Work (for one year)	2,000
Jewish Work, Woman Assistant, Philadelphia, Pa.	2,400
Board of Education, Salary Women Students' Secretaries	6,000
West Indies, Support of Missionaries and Children's Homes	18,200
Board of Ministerial Relief	10,000
Total for Home Field	$224,320

FOREIGN FIELDS

Africa:

Salaries	$16,000
Budget	10,000
Travel Appropriation	7,000
Building	15,000
	$48,000

India:

Salaries	$55,000
Budget	110,000
Travel Appropriation	18,000
Building, including a Memorial for Mrs. Helen C. Beegle	50,000
India Colleges, Madras and Vellore	4,000
Training School, Madras	1,000
	$238,000

Japan:

Salaries	$15,000
Budget	30,000
Travel Appropriations	3,000
Building	50,000
	$98,000

South America:

Salaries and Budget	$14,000
Total Budget for Foreign Field	$398,000

GENERAL APPROPRIATIONS

Literature Committee	$41,724
Departments	15,000
Biennial Convention	12,000
Medical Education	10,000
Administration: Office, Salaries, Executive Board	30,000
Contingent Fund	18,956
Total	$127,680

SUMMARY

Home Missions $224,320
Foreign Missions 398,000
General Appropriations 127,680
                                                                                                              _____
    Total $750,000

Respectfully submitted,
MISS FLORA PRINCE,
MRS. H. C. MICHAEL.

Mrs. Kepner addressed the Convention, bringing the greetings of the Society, and giving a brief resume of the varied and extensive activities of the Society during the past biennium. She spoke of two memorials, one asking the Church to deliver an opinion against war, the other memorializing the Convention to take account of the whole status of religious instruction as related to the public school system of education, with a provision for a survey. She requested that the Rev. W. C. Schaeffer be called upon to give the resolution relating to the second matter.

The Rev. C. A. Freed made response to Mrs. Kepner on behalf of the Convention.

Miss Amelia Kemp, the new Executive Secretary of the Women's Missionary Society, was introduced.

The report of the Committee on Women's Work, incorporating that of the Women's Missionary Society, was then adopted.

The President stated that the matter contained in the first memorial of the Women's Missionary Society had already been acted upon by the Convention, and that the second matter might be presented.

Thereupon the Chairman of the Committee of Reference and Counsel submitted the following resolution prepared by the Rev. W. C. Schaeffer summarizing the memorial:

Be it resolved:

1. That we take cognizance of the fact that in many of the States in which our United Lutheran Church has congregations and schools, both in legislative assemblies and by State Departments of Education, rulings and decisions vitally affecting the cause of Christian education are in process of consideration and enactment.

2. That we propose as a minimum program for practical operation that

   (a) Congregations everywhere endeavor to qualify for educational efficiency in religious instruction, and

(b) That where congregations thus qualify request be preferred to the public school authorities for an allotment of time for the withdrawal of children for religious instruction; and

3. That a commission be appointed to make a survey of the rulings, decisions and legislative enactments in the States represented among the constituency of the United Lutheran Church in America, and that this commission be authorized to offer suggestive and helpful counsel looking to favorable enactment, in the centers where sentiment is crystalizing.

The Committee recommended that this matter be referred to the Parish and Church-School Board with power to appoint the commission suggested in Item 3, said commission to be under the Parish and Church-School Board. The recommendation was adopted.

The next special order for the afternoon was taken up, and the Rev. H. A. Weller presented the report of the Commissioners to the National Lutheran Council.

REPORT OF COMMISSION TO THE NATIONAL LUTHERAN COUNCIL

With regret that the support of the participating bodies to The National Lutheran Council's administrative fund has made it unwise to publish the Annual Reports of the Council for general distribution, your Commissioners feel the necessity of entering at some length upon their biennial report to the Convention.

Closely following the last biennial convention of the United Lutheran Church, and while The National Lutheran Council was continuing and extending its great relief work in Russia, Dr. Lauritz Larsen, its President, was called to his eternal reward, January 28, 1923. Dr. Larsen's abilities to sustain high relations, and his labors in the cause of relief to the famine-stricken peoples in Europe, may best be summed up in the message of the Honorable Herbert Hoover to Mrs. Larsen:

"In my long association with men who have devoted themselves to the relief of innocent sufferers from the errors of peoples and the brutalities of war, no one name stands out more nobly than that of your husband. He was faithful, wise and just. The American Relief Administration was happy in association with him. My fellow-workers and I crave the privilege of sharing in your grief at his loss and in your pride that he was one of the finest type of an American citizen."

Dr. Larsen's death put The National Lutheran Council to a severe test. The workman had gone; but the work for which he gave his life dared not falter nor stop. At an extra meeting of the Council, called by the Vice-

President, suitable resolutions were adopted seeking to give expression to our sorrow, our prayers, and our appreciation of the ability and devotion which made this man give up his life that others might live.

At the extra meeting, held in Chicago, Ill., February 16, 1923, it was determined to divide the duties of the office of President, and to elect an Executive Director. The Reverend Dr. C. H. L. Schuette, of the Joint Synod of Ohio, was elected to the presidency, and the Reverend Dr. John A. Morehead was called to the office of Executive Director.

It is but right, in passing, that official cognizance should be taken of the devotion and sacrifices which Reverend O. C. Mees brought to the office of the secretariat of the Council during Dr. Larsen's absences in Europe, and in the interim between the demise of President Larsen and the reorganization of The National Lutheran Council.

With the creation of the office of Executive Director, apart from the office of the presidency of the Council, it became necessary to define particularly the scope and duties of the office so created. This was done under the following resolutions:

Defining the Authority and Duties of the Executive Director

With the understanding that this new office created under the name of Executive Director of the National Lutheran Council comprise the duties and authority previously vested in the two offices, namely, that of the presidency of The National Lutheran Council and that of the chairmanship of the European Commission, be it therefore

Resolved, That the Executive Director have complete executive authority in all matters pertaining to The National Lutheran Council, both here and abroad under the Articles of Agreement of the Council.

Resolved, That in matters of major importance, especially in matters which involve new action, extraordinary expenditures, or changes and modifications of policy, the Executive Director shall consult with and secure the consent of the Executive Committee of The National Lutheran Council.

Those who come in touch with the acute needs that present themselves from time to time, only through official reports, can scarcely conceive what this change in administration meant in the face of the constructive action and special relief immediately necessary, particularly in Russia and the Central Powers. Though the necessity for reorganization of the work for the accomplishment of the domestic ends of the Council, aside from provision for the heavy office work and the completion of Relief activities, was pressing, the urgent need in Europe made it necessary to send the Executive Director immediately to Europe to be in personal contact with the Russian unit of the American Relief Administration in Moscow, and, through that agency, with the Soviet Government. The months of labor and thought which the Executive Director had to devote in personally working out the business engagements with the American Relief Association and the Soviet Government resulted not only in opening the way, but in the saving of literally hundreds of thousands of dollars to The National Lutheran Council, or, otherwise expressed, in doing with the money we had a relief work that literally represented these hundreds of thousands of dollars.

Not only in Russia, but the immediate need in Central Europe demanded almost superhuman devotion and sacrifice on the part of the Executive Director in organization, planning and execution. In this connection too much cannot be said of the relief the Executive Director obtained through the commissioning and sending of the Reverend Dr. C. Theodore Benze upon the ground. Had not such excellent relief been found through Dr. Benze's devotions, thousands upon thousands of dollars would have had to be expended to accomplish the work which has been done, under the grace of God, through statesmanlike administration and agreements with governments, communities and institutions.

RE-ORIENTATION OF THE COUNCIL

At the Buffalo Convention of the United Lutheran Church a series of resolutions concerning the activities of The National Lutheran Council, together with the necessities for reorganization which came upon the Council, as above detailed, The National Lutheran Council put into effect the following:

A. In accordance with the Regulations Governing The National Lutheran Council, it is not a federation, but only a representative agency of the general bodies supporting it and exists for specific purposes.
   1. It is recommended that the term "constituent bodies" in the first sentence in Article II of the Regulations Governing The National Lutheran Council be understood as meaning nothing more than "participating" bodies.
   2. It is recommended that the letter heads and literature of The National Lutheran Council carry the following statement: "An Agency for," to be followed by an alphabetical list of the participating bodies.
   3. The National Lutheran Council should use the regular Commissioners on all its committees. In an emergency, however, committees may be appointed outside of the Commissioners, but with the consent and approval of the president of the participating bodies.
   4. It is recommended that The National Lutheran Council shall not hold formal membership in other agencies of the general bodies.

B. The work of the Council properly falls into two divisions, viz., Regular Work and Emergency Work.

C. Regular Work.
   1. Representation of the Lutheran Church in its attitude towards
      a. The National Government whenever needed. This is not to exclude direct approach to the government which any general body may wish to make.
      b. Organized bodies and movements outside of the Lutheran Church that may require common action. This is to be undertaken only after consultation with the authorities of the general bodies.
   2. Statistics: includes the Year Book (The Lutheran World Almanac and Annual Encyclopedia). It is to be directed by the Council itself in consultation with the statistical authorities of the general bodies. With reference to general bodies not supporting The National Lutheran Council it may seek cooperation with their statistical authorities.
   3. Reference Library: A center of valuable information for the Church in general.

4. Publicity: (Note: This includes publicity not primarily for The National Lutheran Council, but for the whole Lutheran Church and for the general bodies in particular; also the development of the idea of publicity among the Lutheran congregations, the publication of literature designed not to teach but to promote knowledge of the Lutheran Church, the supervision of general Lutheran anniversaries and similar occasions in which the general bodies are interested.)

5. Additional items of regular work may be undertaken only with the specific consent of the general bodies which support The National Lutheran Council.

D. Emergency Work.

1. To bring physical help to Lutherans in countries affected by war, famine and other calamities.

2. As far as possible to grant to groups, which, according to their confession, are true Lutherans, the material aid which is essential to the reconstruction of their Church work.

3. In cooperation with the Foreign Missions Conference to sustain by gifts and loans Lutheran missionary societies in different countries which without this help from America would be ruined or at least be essentially hampered in their mission. For the purpose of this emergency work, The National Lutheran Council may, until the emergency has passed, hold membership in the Lutheran Foreign Missions Conference.

4. To operate for the general bodies in any new emergencies which may arise. This may be done, however, only with the consent of the *ad interim* executive authorities of the general bodies.

5. Whenever any emergency work is to be conducted it shall be carried on by a separate emergency department of The National Lutheran Council in case it cannot be conducted by the executive office itself. This special department is to be discontinued as soon as the emergency ceases.

E. Finances of Regular Work.

It is estimated that the cost of this service to the Church will be $30,000 per year. In accordance with the articles of agreement (XV) this amount shall be apportioned on the general bodies which support The National Lutheran Council, beginning January 1, 1923.

F. Finances of Emergency Work.

1. The present emergency shall be arranged as soon as possible so that it will be carried on to its conclusion entirely by a special department of The National Lutheran Council. The National Lutheran Council expresses its conviction that the relief work in Europe should be continued and recommends to the participating bodies that an appeal for funds be made.

2. All new emergencies which may arise and which are to be cared for by The National Lutheran Council, in accordance with D-4 and 5 above, shall be financed by special methods which are to be consented to by the *ad interim* executive authorities of the general bodies.

G. *Resolved,* That the president and treasurer of The National Lutheran Council present to the presidents of the participating bodies an itemized statement of the expenses that enter into the $30,000 budget and also suggestions for the proposed appeal for the continuance of the relief work.

FOREIGN MISSION AND EUROPEAN RELIEF

It needs not that we detail further than to append a statement showing

a. Funds raised for European and Foreign Mission Relief up to August 22, 1924;

b. Sources of these contributions in a synodical sense;
c. Expenditures for all purposes to August 22, 1924.

Nevertheless, it must not be forgotten that during the biennium the call for relief to Foreign Missions of European Societies in China, India and Africa has not abated. While in the main this work must go steadily on for a considerable number of years, if it is to be saved from irreparable loss, the Council is active in permanent disposition of former mission fields of European Societies. Part of the Leipsic Society's field in South Africa will probably be permanently occupied by the Augustana Synod; part of the China field of the Berlin Society has been taken over by the Board of Foreign Missions of our United Lutheran Church. It is clear that many such fields have been saved to the Lutheran Church through The National Lutheran Council.

While the Council has continued a measure of relief to fellow-believers in the smaller countries of Europe during the past biennium, its vital activities have been concentrated first in Russia, and, during the last year, in Germany.

Russia.—To the present time the value of at least *one million dollars* in money, food and clothing, has been expended in Russia. This relief can scarcely be estimated in its physical value; but greater than that has been the moral and spiritual force and rehabilitation which such relief has brought to our brethren in Russia. We would not burden this report, but we deem it essential to a better understanding of what we mean when we speak of moral and spiritual support, that we call attention to the recent organization of the Evangelical Lutheran General Synod of Russia, as an indication how worth while and fruitful this work has been in the promotion of the kingdom of Christ.

For the first time since the existence of Lutheran congregations in Russia, clerical and lay representatives from all parts of the country, stretching from the East of Siberia to the Crimea, gathered in Moscow, June 21-26, 1924, to discover a *modus vivendi* for the Evangelical Lutheran Church, under entirely new political conditions, to form an organization entirely separate from the State, and to lay broadly and truly the foundation for future development in order that the Church of the Reformation may accomplish its divine mission in Russia. Surely, the policy of the Lutherans in America and other parts of the world who extended fraternal help to their brethren in Russia during the utter distress of the famine, stands more than justified. Hitherto no Evangelical faith enjoyed the right of organized expression in Russia. True, a general consistory was established by the government during the reign of Nicholas I in 1832; but this in effect made the Czar to be the head of the Church, even where organization of congregations was permitted in the Empire within limits of particular races concerned. Though synods and consistories were permitted for Lutheran people who immigrated from Germany, Sweden, Norway, Denmark, Finland, Esthonia, and Latvia, the government of the Church was from above downward, and had a civil, centralized, if not autocratic, character.

Surely it is an event without parallel in the life of the Church that, since the foundation of Evangelical Lutheran congregations in Russia in the sixteenth century, the constitution of the union of Soviet republics has guaranteed freedom of faith by law. It promises not to swerve from the principle of liberty of conscience, and the permission to all believers to engage in the exercise of their religion without let or hindrance.

It will not be amiss to note in this report, for the sake of exemplifying the influence which brought itself to bear for reconstruction in the Church in Russia through the activities of our relief agencies, especially our National Lutheran Council, how, in the adoption of a constitution for the General Synod of the Evangelical Lutheran Church in Russia, two conceptions became prominent. On the one side were those who contended for the centralization of authority in the interest of avoiding the evils of "unrestrained parliamentarianism with its elections, intrigues, and party quarrels."

The advocates of this view also contended for the election of the higher clerical officers for life in the interest of the quiet and orderly development of the life of the Church. On the other side were those who contended strenuously for the absolute right of the congregations to participate actively in the management of the affairs of the Church in their districts, and through local constituent synods in the general Church administration by the General Synod. The advocates of this contention insisted that the preservation of the congregational and synodical principles is the imperative demand of the present time. In how far they profited in the organization of the General Synod by what had been told them concerning our organization in America may be gathered from the fact that the Evangelical Lutheran Church in Russia is now organized upon the following bases: (a) Individual congregations with the Church Council, or pastorates with their Church Council; (b) District Synods with their presidents; (c) The General Synod with its Superior Church Council. We of the United Lutheran Church, who have a real understanding for such administration, may well rejoice in our hope that, independent of exterior situation, the Lutheran Church in Russia is now organized upon a basis which promises the largest development. It remains for the Superior Church Council, on the basis of the decree of separation of Church and State, to obtain from the United Soviet Government permission to give public catechetical instruction with a view to confirmation at any time and in any place. This also it is prayerfully hoped may be attained.

We of the United Lutheran Church in America, through the agency of The National Lutheran Council, have contributed what we could; and we will be deeply moved with gratitude to God on account of all that He has enabled our brethren to accomplish in the first convention of the General

Synod of the Evangelical Lutheran Church of Russia. Well might we join our voices with those of the delegates to that Synod who, at three important points of that first convention, sang, "A Mighty Fortress is Our God." The Lutherans of Russia have won a great victory over historical tradition and untoward circumstances, by the development of an organization out of the principles of the Gospel, for the service of the Gospel, without leaning on any human arm.

Germany.—In Germany, during the past year, a very large sum of money has been expended for the relief of needy Inner Mission institutions, thousands of pastors, and hundreds of thousands of children and other needy people of the congregations. Since last November about five hundred thousand pounds of clothing, new and old, has been distributed to needy institutions, families and individuals in Germany, through organized Church Committees under The National Lutheran Council's initiative. A food package department has been established, as a part of the relief machinery of the Council, with great success, as the appended statement will show. The Church free table plan has resulted in the strengthening of the moral position of the Evangelical Lutheran Church in Germany, as well as in feeding the hungry and saving and rescuing the lives and faith of thousands more.

From the beginning 2,964,016 pounds of clothing have been given by the Lutherans of America for whom The National Lutheran Council is the common agency for relief in Europe. At the time of the writing of this report (August 25, 1924) the sum of $2,712,048.09 in money has been contributed for European and Foreign Mission relief. The total value of all these gifts in clothing, food and money amounts to at least six and a half million dollars. It must be noted, however, that our method of administration, the stimulation of local giving among the Lutherans of Europe, and the cooperation received in this work of Christian mercy has resulted in a far larger sum contributed to relief and moral and spiritual blessings which none but the Lord Himself will measure, through the abundance of His grace added to our gifts. Well may we thank God for what He has wrought through the agency of The National Lutheran Council.

National Lutheran Council

Expenditures for Relief and Reconstruction to August 22, 1924.
European and Other Countries:

France	$114,821.63
Germany	767,910.55
Poland	305,245.54
Austria	86,547.14
Czecho-Slovakia	49,963.75
Roumania	84,216.54
Finland	49,838.00
Esthonia	32,873.20
Hungary	78,013.06
Lithuania	4,342.59
Latvia	50,116.90

Bulgaria	100.00
Danzig	3,898.21
Jugo-Slavia	14,450.79
Ukraine	12,500.00
Italy	1,492.00
Siberia	2,015.14
Russian Refugees	8,000.00
Russia	346,201.02
Spain	2,776.64
Turkey	204.00
Switzerland	25.00
South America	476.93
American Friends Relief	204.00
Near East Relief	6,448.45
China Famine Fund	14,536.00
Emergency Relief	1,151.25
Clothing Relief	198,984.17
Industrial Relief	1,795.00
European Relief Council	952.07
Orient Mission Society	12.00
Japanese Emergency Relief	2,337.48

Foreign Missions:

China	227,366.81
India	134,951.98
Japan	12,299.25
Persia	55.00
Africa	94,926.00
	$2,712,048.09

STATEMENT OF FOOD PACKAGE DEPARTMENT

Cost of Food, Operation etc.:
Market Value of Food Packages Purchase to August 22, 1924.

8000—No. 1000 @	$10.00	$80,000.00	
2000—No. 2000 @	10.00	20,000.00	
510—No. 3000 @	7.75	3,952.50	
			$103,952.50

Cost of Food Packages:

4000—No. 1000 @	$7.60	$30,400.00		
4000—No. 1000 @	8.40	33,600.00		
			$64,000.00	
2000—No. 2000 @	7.80		15,600.00	
500—No. 3000 @	5.55	2,775.00		
10—No. 3000 @	5.75	57.50		
			2,832.50	
				$82,432.50

Incidental Expenses:

Printing and Postage	$343.48	
Expenses in connection with delivery in Germany reported to date	26.26	
	369.74	
		82,802.24

Total savings and profit for use in general relief.............. $21,150.26

Business Exhibit in Detail:

Market Value of Food Packages donated at various dates since December, 1923:

```
7845—No. 1000 @ $10.00...... $78,450.00
1903—No. 2000 @  10.00......  19,030.00
 384—No. 3000 @   7.75......   2,976.00
                            ————————$100,456.00
```

Cost of Food Packages Donated:

```
3978—No. 1000 @ $8.40...... $33,415.20
3867—No. 1000 @  7.60......  29,389.20
1903—No. 2000 @  7.80......  14,843.40
 384—No. 3000 @  5.55......  .2,131.20
                          ———————— 79,779.00
                                    ———————— $20,677.00
```

Packages sold and delivered for individuals and congregations:

```
153—No. 1000 @ $10.00...... $1,530.00
 93—No. 2000 @  10.00......    930.00
112—No. 3000 @   7.75......    868.00
                          ———————— $3,328.00
```

Cost of Packages sold:

```
131—No. 1000 @ $7.60...... $995.60
 22—No. 1000 @  8.40......  184.80
 93—No. 2000 @  7.80......  725.40
112—No. 3000 @  5.55......  621.60
                          ———————— 2,527.40
                                    ———————— $800.60
```

Market Value of Food Packages on Hand in Hamburg:

```
 2—No. 1000 @ $10.00...... $20.00
 4—No. 2000 @  10.00......  40.00
14—No. 3000 @   7.75...... 108.50
                         ———————— $168.50
```

Cost of Packages on Hand:

```
 2—No. 1000 @ $7.60...... $15.20
 4—No. 2000 @  7.80......  31.20
 4—No. 3000 @  5.55....|   22.20
10—No. 3000 @  5.75......  57.50
                        ———————— 126.10
                                  ———————— $42.40
```

Gross savings and profit of Food Package
   Department $21,520.00
Less incidental expenses 369.74

Total savings and profit for use in general
   relief $21,150.26

RECEIPTS OF CAMPAIGNS OF THE NATIONAL LUTHERAN COUNCIL

Synod	Reconstruction ($500,000)	Clothing (@ 25c. a lb.)	1920 Appeal ($1,800,000)	1921 Appeal ($1,250,000)	1922 Appeal ($850,000)	(Aug. 20th) 1923-1924 Appeal ($1,500,000)	Total
United Lutheran Church	$258,973.13	$103,778.96	$585,404.43	$285,173.91	$232,071.43	$371,211.87	$1,836,613.73
Joint Synod of Ohio	99,690.90	28,031.90	179,615.51	45,165.60	62,857.21	132,061.71	547,422.83
Iowa Synod	53,822.98	16,418.05	6,500.65	8,499.89	1,288.16	48.50	86,573.23
Buffalo Synod	1,826.30	666.63	3,461.41	1,759.55	1,472.51	3,794.67	12,971.07
Immanuel Synod	153.38		27.00	20.69			201.06
Jehovah Conference	85.50	214.25	457.00	356.26	382.50	120.00	1,615.51
Augustana Synod	43,052.07	20,316.95	141,683.24	35,569.95	40,050.13	43,470.73	324,143.07
Norwegian Synod	183,409.68	66,055.76	191,793.17	73,142.93	42,777.45	71,286.79	578,465.78
Lutheran Free Church	3,376.78	3,517.41	12,018.75	2,755.76	967.82	4,533.08	27,169.60
Eielsen Synod	169.35	1.00	259.88	115.27	168.05	354.93	1,059.43
Lutheran Brethren	18.00	240.63	342.60	57.17	60.42	43.00	762.82
United Danish Synod	5,979.96	6,513.30	17,702.88	5,629.78	2,955.33	4,731.35	43,512.60
Danish Synod	959.37	1,540.42	4,225.95	1,418.64	2,185.44	2,728.09	13,011.91
Icelandic Synod	241.20	259.07	601.41	1,365.02	31.45	329.70	2,831.85
Suomi Synod	586.69	544.44	1,985.62	1,352.07	320.68	297.91	5,060.41
Finnish National Church	124.92	30.25	992.17	788.21		7.40	1,942.95
Finnish Apostolic Church	28.55	216.07	158.65	49.10	16.00	9.10	477.47
Synodical Conference	13.00	581.63	163.39	1,552.60	105.58	84.49	2,500.69
Independent	881.50	100.00	3,044.91	135.35	913.00	560.00	5,634.66
Unknown	24,839.38	30,300.68	55,823.80	106,321.93	14,207.96	10,642.91	242,136.66
Totals	$628,232.64	$279,327.40	$1,206,252.87	$571,202.57	$402,781.12	$646,311.23	$3,734,107.33
					* 3,424.36	4,946.11	8,370.47
						Grand Total	$3,742,477.80

* Christmas Seals.

Continuation of Relief Work Essential

Grateful as we may be for the privileges of the past, we must not blind ourselves into an idea that the work is done. We have helped out of the deep waters into a floating canoe; but all the work of the past will have been but in vain if we stop short of furnishing the rescued with the means for propelling the canoe to the sure foundations of the shore. The reliable reports from Germany point out that while the form or objects receiving help will be somewhat different this fall and winter, the measure of the help required to serve vital' purposes of relief and reconstruction will be almost as great as last winter. The homeless children, the impoverished people of the upper classes, including pastors, have permanently lost their savings and, if old, or if able to work, are not receiving enough income to support them. The Church press, the Predigerseminare, students and professors, and poor families of the congregations, will be, if possible, more needy the coming winter than they were last winter.

In Russia the Church is organized, but *on faith.* They have not the means to maintain their pastors or even their new church organization. From reliable sources comes clear information that famine exists in Siberia and is beginning again, on account of the failing of harvests, in the Volga Valley. Into the office of The National Lutheran Council pitiful appeals are pouring from Russia. At this critical time in the history of our Russian Church the Lutherans of America must and will stand loyally by their brethren there.

In order to preserve the property and people of the orphaned mission stations of the Church, the continuation of Foreign Mission Relief is absolutely essential.

Reference to the reports of campaigns printed above will show that though perhaps a little less enthusiastically than before and because of industrial conditions in America, our people of the supporting bodies of the Church have not grown blind nor deaf to the cries and needs of their brethren of the Church in European lands and Foreign Mission countries. High pressure, war-drive methods, have given and must give way to the regular machinery of the Church in all participating bodies for the gathering of the people's gifts for benevolence synodically. Such was the method employed under the direction of the general appeal manager, Rev. O. C. Mees, in the appeal of 1923-24. The results of that method are eloquent. From a further statement appended, showing the World Service expenditures from December 1, 1923, to August 20, 1924, it will appear that the balance in the treasury of the Council for all purposes, August 20, 1924, is $258,145.51.

World Service Expenditures from December 1, 1923-August 20, 1924.

Russia	$8,863.90
Germany	417,880.14
Poland	1,467.00
Austria	11,473.00
Roumania	5,050.00
Latvia	14.00
Esthonia	50.00

```
*Czecho-Slovakia .........................................................................   4,333.00
 Danzig .........................................................................................   1,056.00
 Jerusalem ....................................................................................      25.00
 Jugo-Slavia ................................................................................     200.00
 Bulgaria ......................................................................................     200.00
 Hungary .....................................................................................     100.00
 France .........................................................................................   3,000.00
 India ............................................................................................      30.00
 China ...........................................................................................  28,342.70
 Africa ..........................................................................................  27,801.25
 Japan Emergency ......................................................................  14,062.50
 Armenian Relief (Special) .......................................................     664.28
 European Commission Expense ..............................................      30.00
 Lutheran World Convention ...................................................   4,444.08
 Lutheran World Almanac .........................................................       5.97
                                                                                                   47.96
World Service Appeal:
 Salaries .......................................................................................
 Postage .......................................................................................   6,445.25
 Printing ......................................................................................  11,519.03
 Appeal Expense .......................................................................  20,912.83
 General Expense .......................................................................   2,338.61
 Christmas Seals .......................................................................  11,455.80
                                                                                                  477.25
                                                                                     —————————
                                                                                     $582,089.55
```

Total balance in the treasury of the Council for all purposes, August 20 1924, $258,145.51.

In the application of its relief work, and its contacts with Lutherans of many countries, there was born, in The National Lutheran Council, a conviction which was suggested to its participating bodies and accepted by them as being good, that the time had come in the progress of the Church of the Reformation in the world for a closer conference and a more intimate understanding of one another among the leaders and people of the Church hitherto influenced and led by national or geographical circumstantialities. Naturally, The National Lutheran Council had to confine its activities in this respect to the initiation of such a movement, and an invitation to American constituent bodies to appoint the American Committee which should bring about what has now passed into history as the Lutheran World Convention at Eisenach. Such is the beginning of a history which is in the making by the direct activities of the Evangelical Lutheran Church bodies all over the world who participated in the convention at Eisenach in 1923, the report of which will be brought to this convention at length by the delegates of the United Lutheran Church. It is meet, however, that this record be inscribed in this report; and that the prayers of the Church unitedly promote this work. Not a little matter of congratulation is it that the Executive Director of The National Lutheran Council has been chosen with great confidence as the chairman of the Executive Commission of the

* Since the above statement was made out, $2,000.00 has been sent to Bishop Georg Janoska for the help of retired pastors, widows and orphans of pastors and inner mission institutions of our brethren in Czecho-Slovakia.

Lutheran World Convention. His work and his contacts, made possible through his office in the Council, have, under God, made him the logical presiding officer of that important body.

The Work at Home

When it is kept in mind that all the detail of the work of relief of Foreign Missions and European countries is practically burdened upon the heart, mind and hands of the Executive Director of The National Lutheran Council; and when to this is added upon him the detailed work of the office, entailing large correspondence of great moment, now specially multiplied by the return of the last responsible American agent in Europe for the Council, it will be understood that the work at home, for which the Council was conceived and exists as a common agency for its participating bodies is still largely before us.

So far as humanly possible the home work has not been neglected. Little can be published of the frequent representations of our Lutheran bodies, through the Exectuive Director of the Council, at our government headquarters where the securing of information and counsel as to wise action in matters of relief, both in Russia and in Germany, is a matter of no little moment. Little may be known, but much has been accomplished by personal contact in regard to the safety and welfare of Lutheran missionaries in bandit-ridden China. It is not a mean matter to consider what patience and statesmanship was required to approach the French government, through the American Embassy in Paris, to secure the official assurance of freedom to conduct relief work unmolested in the Ruhr district; or, through the American Embassy in Berlin, to secure the free use of warehouses and free transportation for our relief supplies on the German railways. For the sake of the largest possible assistance toward the needy Foreign Missions, it has been necessary to keep in constant touch with the International Foreign Missions Council, whose secretaries have cooperated with our National Lutheran Council most cordially and helpfully, to safeguard the interests of the Evangelical Lutheran Church. Such negotiations, often too delicate to be made public, have been and are of the greatest importance to the Church. Aside from these, The National Lutheran Council and its Executive Director have stood ready and been almost constantly engaged in serving special interests of individual bodies participant in the membership of the Council.

The Publicity Bureau of The National Lutheran Council has furnished seventy Church papers, together with many news workers, regularly a weekly bulletin, giving outstanding domestic and international Lutheran news. Editors of Church papers express high appreciation of this service. Thousands of these news items have found their way into the columns of the papers; and a broader and truer Lutheran consciousness is developing thus in our Lutheran Church public. To the dailies and weeklies of the country Lutheran news stories and items of public interest are sent regularly by the thousands, and an encouraging percentage of these find welcome publication.

The Reference and Statistical Departments have contributed, in an important way, to the Church's Publicity Service, and are ever ready to supply correct and complete statements of facts. In this way they have been specially helpful in preparing material concerning the Lutheran Church, both in America and in the world, for the Year Books of the Churches, Encyclopedias and other source-books of public information concerning Lutherans. Beside this general service of statistics, references and publicity, special service has been undertaken under proper conditions for participating bodies especially. As an example of such may be cited the fact that the Executive Director of The National Lutheran Council is the coordinating agent for the news bureau, which sends out the authentic reports of the present convention of the United Lutheran Church.

It is due to say that the accumulation of work which is entailed upon the Executive Director of the Council, with many details which could as well have been performed by employees, has become necessary because of the shortcoming of the participating Lutheran bodies in meeting the budget for administration. Our own United Lutheran Church may feel in enviable position, yet it remains true that it also has fallen short of meeting its entire budget undertaken toward The National Lutheran Council. This can be corrected, and when the United Lutheran Church realizes what the budget system, reported regularly to its Executive Board, entails, it will arise to meet its small obligation, comparatively, and enable the Council to perform its work of administration without constant fear of inadequate financial support, and without burdening every detail upon the mind and hands of one man whose services are far more valuable and will be far more effective in the great work of our Lutheran Church in the world if unhampered by such unreadiness to meet budgeted apportionments. We submit the question whether, for the good of each participating body, including our own United Lutheran Church, it will not be better that the budgeted amount of $30,000, together with the slight necessary increase, as exhibited in the appended statement, be appropriated from our treasuries instead of apportioned to the synods. The matter of increase in the budget for The National Lutheran Council has been presented to the Executive Board of our United Lutheran Church, and will come before the convention under its report.

Synod	Share 1923 Budget	Amount Paid	Share 1924 Budget	Amount Paid	Share Proposed Increase	Amount Paid
United Luth.	$16,127.60	$14,037.60	$16,127.60	$8,426.00	$2,094.79	
Norwegian	5,292.07	5,292.00	5,292.07		687.38	
Augustana	4,080.87	2,020.87	4,080.87		530.06	
Joint Ohio	3,023.73	3,023.73	3,023.73		392.75	
United Danish	326.95	326.96	326.95		42.47	
Lutheran Free	611.35		611.35		79.41	
Danish	297.08	297.08	297.08	297.03	38.59	
Icelandic	105.03		105.03		13.64	
Buffalo	135.32	135.32	135.32		17.57	
	$30,000.00	$25,193.56	$30,000.00	$8,723.08	$3,896.66	$37.92

RECOMMENDATIONS

(a) We recommend that the United Lutheran Church continue its participation in The National Lutheran Council, and appoint a commission to again
represent it in said Council.

(b) We recommend that the United Lutheran Church pledge its continued generous support of the relief and reconstruction work of The
National Lutheran Council, so long as our fellow-believers abroad are in
actual need thereof, with the understanding that, as in the past, such future
appeals shall be properly recommended by the Council and approved by the
participating bodies.

Respectfully submitted for the Commission,

H. A. WELLER, Chairman.

The Rev. C. T. Benze addressed the Convention on the state
of the Church in Europe, especially in Russia and Germany.

Recommendations (a) and (b) were adopted.

Dr. Weller presented the supplementary report of the Commissioners as follows:

SUPPLEMENTARY REPORT OF COMMISSION TO THE NATIONAL LUTHERAN COUNCIL

Exigencies in the relief task of the National Lutheran Council rendered
it imperative that a special meeting of the Council be held October 20, 1924.

The cruel conditions to which our relief work is applied for amelioration
still exist in varied forms and countries.

The appeal, sanctioned by the participating bodies in America for funds,
etc., in 1924, has failed of any adequate realization for the relief treasury.
Our own body fell short of its rightfully expected quota by $374,788.13
for the current year.

It profits nothing to speculate as to causes for this, but the Council and
its participating bodies face the result, as they are in Christian fidelity
bound to complete the work so nobly begun, so blessedly continued, and
not yet ended. Our Church and her people, in prosperous America, do not
desire it to fail or fall now. They will betray no Christian trust nor turn
deaf ears and folded hands toward the call of the Saviour through the dire
needs that have befallen our European brethren, their institutions and other
causes of the Church.

With such convictions, and in faith voting a practical depletion of the
relief fund balance of $188,455.72 for all foreign relief in its treasury on
September 30, 1924, until additional funds be quickly contributed, the

Council took the following action and submits it to the United Lutheran Church for approval and participation:

1. *Resolved*: That another appeal to the Church be made.

2. That the Council request its participating bodies to authorize another World Service Appeal for $500,000 for relief and construction to be administered on a flexible basis in re foreign mission relief and physical relief to individuals, institutions and other causes of the Church in the several countries in need.

3. That, on account of the pressing immediate need of funds for European relief, reconstruction, and foreign mission support, January 15, 1925, be set as the official date for the beginning of the next World Service Appeal and that funds be collected as expeditiously as possible, so that the entire amount may be gathered by April 1, 1925.

4. That this appeal, which shall not have the nature of a drive or campaign in any sense, be conducted along Synodical lines, the central agency of the Council acting uniformly but in complete harmony with and through the executive authority of each participating body.

5. That the Council immediately authorize, with the consent of the participating bodies, and as a supplementary measure of relief, a general appeal for the gift of used clothing, accompanied by sufficient donations of cash to cover the cost of transportation and distribution, with a view to the extension of aid in this form, mainly, but not exclusively, in Germany, and if possible in Russia.

Remark: While particular countries or objects of relief are mentioned to indicate the practical basis of these recommendations for the gathering of resources for relief and reconstruction, it is felt that the time has come when no particular country should be featured in the appeal, although facts about many and specific needs in various countries are to be detailed. It seems important, for the sake of the true information of the people at home, and for the sake of a true representation of the challenge of actual conditions abroad, that the thought of the conservation of menaced persons or families, constituencies, institutions, and missions of the Evangelical Lutheran Church throughout the world in the presence of many adversaries should be emphasized more and more.

6. That, as a further supplementary measure of relief, the National Lutheran Council shall authorize the continuance of its Food Package Department in order to have the machinery available to purchase food at wholesale prices for gift in relief work, and in order to be in a position to offer to the people of our American congregations the opportunity of helping their relatives and friends abroad, by the gift of Food Packages.

Your commission craves the privilege also to correct an oversight in its report to this body. During the biennium, beside the other faithful servants mentioned, the Rev. W. L. Scheding, who, for more than a year, rendered faithful services with great personal sacrifice and devotion in Russia, during most trying times, returned home in the fall of 1923. What these servants of the Church have rendered and suffered, none but the Great Head of the Church will appreciate.

Respectfully submitted,

THE COMMISSIONERS,

H. A. WELLER, *Chairman.*

Recommendations 1, 2, 3, 4, 5 and 6 were adopted.

The report of the Commission was adopted as a whole.

The President having called for the special order concerning the dissent from yesterday's action on Item 8 of the report of the Committee on Moral and Social Welfare, he requested that by unanimous consent the Convention hear such statement as those dissenting might wish to make.

Thereupon the Rev. Paul Scherer submitted the following:

Feeling that at the present time we should avoid all reference to the right of war, we desire to record our dissent from the action taken by the Convention on Item 8 of the resolutions proposed by the Committee on Moral and Social Welfare.

Signed:

John A. W. Haas	L. B. Wolf
A. H. Holthusen	W. H. Stutts
Herman Brezing	S. J. McDowell
A. H. Durboraw	Holmes Dysinger
Geo. W. Nicely	Oscar Krauch
A. Steimle	Wm. J. Miller, Jr.
Paul W. Roth	Luther De Yoe
Frisby D. Smith	Edwin Heyl Delk
A. Pohlman	C. N. Swihart
W. P. Elson	S. M. Lesher
S. G. von Bosse	S. P. Long
Theo. O. Posselt	W. H. Greever
Fred H. Bosch	E. C. Harris
W. C. Schaeffer	Wm. G. Boomhower
C. P. MacLaughlin	J. B. Guiney
Henry H. Bagger	E. A. Sievert
Behrend Mehrtens	E. E. Stauffer
M. F. Troxell	Paul Scherer

The President thereupon requested unanimous consent that those asserting their conscientious objection might have the privilege of entering their dissent with the statement just read. The President hearing no objection, ordered the statement to be printed in the minutes.

The Rev. William M. Horn offered the following resolution:

Resolved, That we request the National Lutheran Council, through our Commissioners, to arrange for the publication for 1925 of a Lutheran World Almanac similar to those which it had before distributed.

The resolution was adopted.

The Rev. Paul W. Roth, Chairman of the Committee on the President's Report, reported for the Committee as follows:

REPORT OF COMMITTEE ON PRESIDENT'S REPORT

We find that the report consists of (1) a statement of the work of the President with the explanation that the largest part of his activities finds report in the proceedings of the Executive Board; (2) a summary of the general situation of our Church, its recognition by the public, its organization and the functioning of its parts, its relationships with both Lutheran and non-Lutheran groups, and its inner spiritual life; (3) the suggestion that a volume be prepared for the help and inspiration of our Constituency under the title, "The Ideal Congregation"; and (4) three recommendations: (a) that at a stated time this Convention engage in special memorial thought of our fallen leaders, Rev. Dr. V. G. A. Tressler and the Rev. Dr. M. M. Kinard; (b) that steps be taken toward a fitting commemoration of the four hundredth anniversary of the Augsburg Confession; (c) that the editors of our official Church papers be instructed to give full publicity to certain new developments in our work.

The recommendation concerning memorial thought of our sainted brethren, the Rev. Dr. V. G. A. Tressler and the Rev. Dr. M. M. Kinard, has already been carried out.

We offer four recommendations:

1. In accordance with the suggestion of our President, we recommend that the Executive Board be authorized directly or through a suitable committee, to arrange for a proper observance in 1930 of the four hundredth anniversary of the presentation of the Augsburg Confession, the plans and program for the same to be submitted to the next convention of the United Lutheran Church for approval.

2. Frankly conceding the fact that the full message of the Gospel is not finding adequate expression in the educational and merciful operations of our Church, and particularly among the individual congregations, we recommend that under the auspices of the Committee on Boards and Committees, joint meetings be arranged among representatives and agencies in these departments, looking to a more complete survey of the situation and the suggestion of practical plans of advance and improvement.

3. We recommend that the editors of our official Church papers be instructed to prepare an itemized statement of the new developments in the work of the Church listed by the President, and to give full publicity to the same as an encouragement and a stimulus to the entire Church.

4. Deeply grateful to our President for having brought the timely and vital subject of "The Ideal Congregation" to our attention, we recommend the practical worth of such a publication be realized in a continuation of the series of study books begun under the title, "The Key Books"; and since nobody is better qualified to put a vision into concrete form than he who sees it, we therefore recommend further that the President be petitioned by this Convention to undertake the supervision or editing of such publication as he in his own judgment may deem most satisfactory.

In conclusion, your committee commends the President's report to the careful study of every pastor and layman in the Church, not only for the sake of the gratifying information which it brings concerning our progress and achievements during the biennium, but also because such careful study is sure to issue, under the divine blessing, in a better understanding of our Church and in more ideally working congregations.

Respectfully submitted,

PAUL W. ROTH, *Chairman*,
ARTHUR S. HARDY, *Recording Secretary*,
F. R. WAGNER,
H. C. BRILLHART,
W. J. SHOWALTER,
A. J. HARTER,
GEORGE N. LAUFFER,
R. NEUMANN,
H. M. M. RICHARDS,
C. E. BUTLER,
W. C. SCHAEFFER,
S. G. VON BOSSE,
O. STOCKMANN,
J. B. FRANKE,
J. W. KAHLER.

Recommendations 1, 2, 3 and 4 were adopted. The report of the Committee was adopted as a whole.

The Rev. F. P. Manhart, Chairman of the Committee on Memorials from Constituent Synods, reported for the Committee as follows:

REPORT OF COMMITTEE ON MEMORIALS FROM CONSTITUENT SYNODS

I. Invitations were received from four cities to hold the next Convention of the United Lutheran Church in America in them; namely, Erie, Pa.; Detroit, Mich.; Richmond, Va.; and Philadelphia, Pa.

The committee recommends that the next biennial convention of the United Lutheran Church in America be held in Philadelphia or Richmond.

II. *Apportionment.* The Synod of the Northwest, the East Pennsylvania and Rocky Mountain Synods request that communicant rather than confirmed membership be the basis; the Synod of Illinois asks that current expenses be ignored as a basis; the Synod of Kansas states that its apportionment is proportionately too large and asks for a more just basis.

(1) It should be kept in mind that the United Lutheran Church assigns definite amounts to the Constituent Synods, while the method of distributing these amounts to the pastorates is left entirely to the Synods themselves.

(2) That the whole question of the basis of apportionment to the Synods be given further study in the light of all pertinent facts and the experiences of our bodies, and possibly, also, of the methods and experiences of other Christian bodies.

RECOMMENDATION. That the Executive Board appoint a special committee which shall study this problem as above indicated, and furnish a report to the Synods for information in time for the meetings of the Synods to be held in 1925, if possible.

III. (1) *Tabitha Home.* There are requests from the Rocky Mountain and Nebraska Synods that the annual appropriation to Tabitha Home be $15,000.

Answer. The appropriation has been made $13,000.

(2) The Synod of New York asks for certain changes in the Constitution of the United Lutheran Church.

Answer. Action has been taken covering the question of amendments to the Constitution.

(3) The Pittsburgh Synod requests that the United Lutheran Church "print the Occasional Services in German."

Answer. That this be referred to the Common Service Book Committee and the Board of Publication with power to act.

IV. *Iowa Synod.* The Iowa Synod "petitions that a sufficient apportionment be given to the carrying on of the work of the Luther League of the United Lutheran Church."

Answer. That this be referred to the Finance Committee of the Executive Board with power.

V. *Indiana Synod.* The Indiana Synod resolved "That it is the sense of the Indiana Synod that it is not obligated by the actions of the United

Lutheran Church until such actions have been approved by this Synod."

Answer. Constitution, Article III, Section 6: "Congregations repre-sentatively constituting the various Synods may elect delegates through those Synods to represent them in a general body, all decisions of which, when made in accordance with the Constitution, bind, so far as the terms of mutual agreement make them binding, those congregations and Synods which consent to be represented in the general body."

VI. The Susquehanna Synod of Central Pennsylvania requests that the United Lutheran Church arrange to "affiliate and co-operate with the International Council of Religious Education."

Answer. Action concerning this has been taken at this Convention. (See Executive Board's Report, IV, B, 10, and action thereon.)

VII. The Synod of New York and New England memorializes the United Lutheran Church concerning the presentation of causes in the Con-stituent Synods.

Answer. Action concerning this has been taken.

VIII. The Synod of New York and New England memorializes the United Lutheran Church to "put into effect a larger and continuous pro-gram of publicity and advertising and appropriate to its Committee on Publicity $4,000 for the biennium following the Convention in October."

Answer. Resolved, That this be referred to the Budget Committee for an appropriation.

IX. *Memorials Concerning War*:

1. The Synod of New York and New England memorializes as follows:

(a) That the United Lutheran Church decide on using its Committee on Moral and Social Welfare, its Board of Education, its Parish and Church-School Board and other agencies to create a better understanding of the causes and consequences of war and to indicate the methods whereby peace may be maintained.

(b) That the United Lutheran Church declare in favor of a permanent International Court of Justice.

(c) That the United Lutheran Church "recommend to the next Luth-eran World Conference to adopt a program of education and action so that the 80,000,000 of Lutherans throughout the world may be enlisted and led in a campaign against war."

(d) That the United Lutheran Church, at its convention in October, consider the advisability of co-operating with other Church bodies in a world-wide and determined endeavor to banish war and substitute peaceful means of settling international controversies.

2. The Iowa Synod "suggests that a definition of a 'just war' shall be sent forth to the world from the United Lutheran Church in America, for the sake of safeguarding the principles of the Gospel of our Lord as held and preached by our Church.

3. The Ministerium of Pennsylvania made the following declaration:

(a) Wars between nations are the result of human sinfulness and a manifestation of the presence of evil that has not yet been overcome by the power of the Gospel of Christ.

(b) That the only influence in the world that can put an end to war is the power of God the Holy Spirit spread abroad in the hearts of men, through the preaching of the Gospel of Jesus Christ and bringing the world to repentance, faith and righteousness.

(c) That under the guidance of the Spirit, the leaders of the nation should earnestly resist political, economic and commercial incitements to war; foster international understanding, sympathy and good will; suppress militarism and national selfishness; seek to adjust disputes between the nations by arbitration rather than by the use of force; and apply the ideals of Jesus to foreign as well as to domestic policies.

Answer. Action covering all of the memorials concerning war has been taken by this Convention of the United Lutheran Church.

X. The West Pennsylvania Synod requests that there be a study of the whole question of the re-marriage of divorced persons and of the rights and duties of pastors in relation thereto, and report to the Convention in 1926.

Answer. That this subject of divorce and re-marriage be referred to the Committee on Moral and Social Welfare to formulate a deliverance on the subject to be presented to the next Convention of the United Lutheran Church.

XI. The New York and New England Synod memorializes the United Lutheran Church to instruct its Parish and Church-School Board (1) to prepare special literature for the Weekday Religious School and the Daily Vacation Bible School, and (2) to prepare a unified religious program for the congregation.

Answer. That the United Lutheran Church hereby instructs the Parish and Church-School Board to comply with these requests.

XII. Time for Conventions of the United Lutheran Church. The Texas Synod prefers September; the Wartburg Synod, June; the California Synod, early summer.

Answer. That these preferences be kept in mind for future consideration.

XIII. The Wartburg Synod memorializes the United Lutheran Church to meet once every three years.

Answer. The Constitution (Article VII, Section 1) provides that a Convention shall be held at least once every two years.

The consideration of Item I was deferred until the representatives of the various cities extending invitations should be heard.

Item II being taken up, a division was made, and the first section (1) was received as information. The second section (2) was adopted. The recommendation under section (2) was amended so as to read:

"That the Executive Board appoint a special committee which shall study this problem as above indicated and furnish a report to the Synods for information in time for the meetings of the Synods to be held in 1925, if possible."

The recommendation was adopted as amended.

The answers given by the Committee (III, (1), (2), (3)) to the memorials concerning Tabitha Home, changes in the Constitution of the United Lutheran Church and Occasional Services in German were approved by common consent.

The recommendation (IV) referring the petition of the Iowa Synod for an apportionment for the Luther League to the Finance Committee of the Executive Board was approved.

The answer (V) to the resolution of the Indiana Synod was approved.

The answer (VI) to the memorial of the Susquehanna Synod of Central Pennsylvania concerning International Council of Religious Education was approved.

The answer (VII) to the Synod of New York and New England concerning presentation of causes was approved.

The answer (VIII) to the memorial of the Synod of New York and New England concerning program of publicity, advertising, etc., was referred to the Finance Committee of the Executive Board.

The answer (IX) to the memorials of the New York and New England Synod, the Iowa Synod and the Ministerium of Pennsylvania concerning war, approved.

The answer (X) to the memorial from the West Pennsylvania Synod concerning the re-marriage of divorced persons, etc., was referred to the Committee on Moral and Social Welfare, with the understanding that the information as furnished by the West

Pennsylvania Synod be also referred to that Committee. (The information referred to is to be found in the Minutes of the West Pennsylvania Synod for 1904, page 47, and 1923, page 81, and in the Minutes of the General Synod for 1907, pages 63 and 64.—Secy.)

Reverting to Item I of the report of the Committee, the Convention heard invitations from representatives from the cities of Erie, Detroit, Richmond and Philadelphia.

As a substitute for the recommendation of the Committee, Dr. Burgess moved that the Convention proceed to take a ballot. The motion was carried.

Dr. F. M. Riter and Messrs. W. H. Hager, P. A. Elsesser, G. E. Neff and W. L. Gladfelter were appointed as tellers.

The Committee of Reference and Counsel reported that it had received the following proposal:

"In order that the President of this body may be enabled to act as he may find most advisable under circumstances as they arise, the following is offered as an amendment to the By-Laws, Section VII, B, 14, which reads 'Committee on Necrology.' Add the words 'or Necrologist and such assistants as may be desirable.' "

The Committee recommended the following amendment to Section VII, B, 14, that the item be made to read: "A Committee on Necrology, the Chairman of which shall be recognized as the Necrologist of the United Lutheran Church for the biennium."

The amendment to be acted upon tomorrow.

On motion to adopt the report of the Committee on Moral and Social Welfare, the Convention was reminded that Item 5 had been referred back to the Committee for possible revision.

The Committee moved to amend the item by the striking out of the word "enforcement" and inserting the words "constant inculcation."

The item was adopted as amended.

The report was adopted as a whole.

Resuming consideration of the report of the Statistical and Church Year Book Committee, recommendation 6 was adopted.

Recommendation 7 is covered by a former action of this Convention.

Recommendation 8 adopted.

The report was adopted as a whole.

Mr. P. A. Elsesser reported for the tellers appointed to take the ballot for the place of the next Convention:

Total number of votes cast, 293; necessary for a choice, 147.

Baltimore	1
Erie	20
Detroit	31
Philadelphia	46
Richmond	195

The President announced that Richmond had been chosen.

The Rev. C. K. Fegley presented the report of the Committee on Publicity, together with recommendation.

REPORT OF COMMITTEE ON PUBLICITY

The Committee notes with satisfaction the rapidly increasing attention given to church publicity and advertising, both by religious bodies and the public press. The churches have found publicity and advertising proper aids in prosecuting their work nationally and locally and the public press has come to attach a growing value to church activities as news for their readers. The paid advertisement used in a number of ways has become invaluable to a considerable number of local churches.

Other means of giving news or making announcement of events, such as the circular letter, the "house-organ" or parish paper, the bulletin board, the poster, the illuminated sign are more largely used. Public sentiment is formed more than ever before with the aid of reported opinions of church readers or the pronouncements of church bodies.

Like any other worth-while phase of work, effective church publicity and advertising require proper methods and technique, which entail constant study and development. Large church bodies, like our own, that have been carrying on extensive publicity activities report satisfactory results, both in the stimulus that has come to local and general operations of the church, and in the effect that their interpretation of Christian principles in relation to current questions has had upon the general public.

Your Committee's work has been limited almost entirely to publicity for the national conventions, in which the Publicity Department of the National Lutheran Council has cooperated. The publicity for the Chicago Convention is being planned and carried out cooperatively after the general program of the Washington and Buffalo conventions. This means the writing up and sending out to a carefully selected number of newspapers in the United States and Canada of reports by the officers of the church, Boards and Committees in advance of the Convention itself; the enlistment of the pastors of the Church; the making of contacts with newspapers and the general news agencies such as the Associated Press and United Press; the securing in advance of addresses from speakers; and numerous other tasks.

The Chicago sub-committee on publicity will have charge of supplying the local papers with reports of the Convention and is also generously equipping the press-room and furnishing the stenographic assistance. An adequate staff of news workers will obtain the news of the convention and furnish it to the reporters of great dailies that will be in attendance and also to the representatives of the general news agencies.

The radio broadcasting which was introduced at the Buffalo Convention will be carried out on a larger scale at Chicago. This has been arranged for by the Chicago committee, chairman, the Rev. David A. Davy, D.D.

A new feature will be a Convention Daily, which will be in charge of a staff from *The Lutheran,* headed by Dr. N. R. Melhorn, who will take full charge and responsibility of the paper.

The planning and execution of the program for the Convention is in the hands of Dr. John A. Morehead, Executive Director of the National Lutheran Council; Mr. W. P. Elson, Publicity Secretary of the National Lutheran Council, and the Chairman and other members of this Committee.

During the biennium members of the Committee have been active in their several localities.

Believing that the Church is ready for a forward step in the work falling within the scope of your committee we submit again the outline which in the main was formulated by the committee at its meeting subsequent to the Washington Convention.

The program of activity shall include:

(1) Reports of conventions, board meetings, and other gatherings of the United Lutheran Church, its constituent Synods and auxiliary organizations.

(2) A continuous service giving the public press information on any important developments.

(3) Plan for publicity throughout the territory of the United Lutheran Church. This will necessitate a force of local volunteer news workers.

(4) The gathering in a depository or "morgue" of valuable material for special and general publicity.

(5) Giving dignified and adequate publicity to the history, doctrine, cultus and declaration of the Church.

(6) Information to the press of other Church bodies regarding important action of the United Lutheran Church.

(7) A handbook on publicity and advertising, and other material, which will give help and suggestions to pastors.

(8) A large use of the publicity facilities of the National Lutheran Council.

We respectfully recommend that your committee be authorized and given a budget to put the above program into effect.

The Committee:

> HOWARD R. GOLD,
> M. L. CANUP,
> EDWIN HEYL DELK,
> C. K. FEGLEY,
> C. L. FRY,
> W. H. GREEVER,
> JESSE R. HILDEBRAND,
> WILLIAM L. HUNTON,
> HENRY MOEHLING,
> W. H. STUTTS,
> WILLIAM J. SHOWALTER
> A. E. WAGNER.

It was ruled that the portion referring to budget be referred to the Finance Committee of the Executive Board according to a standing resolution. (See Minutes, Wednesday, October 29th, for action.—Secy.)

The recommendation excepting the part referred was adopted.

The Chairman of the Committee on Publicity then presented additional resolutions:

1. We recommend that the Convention ask all the Constituent Synods to co-operate with the National Committee on Publicity through their local synodical committees on publicity.

2. We recommend that the Convention express its hearty appreciation of the uniformly accurate and generous news service rendered the United Lutheran Church in America during this Convention by the various daily newspapers of Chicago and by the principal national wire services through their Chicago representatives, and that the Secretary of the United Lutheran Church in America be instructed to convey this appreciation to the respective newspapers and agencies.

3. We recommend similar action in the case of the Chicago Radio

Broadcasting Stations known as WEBH, KYW, WLS and WMAQ, all of which served the Convention to a greater or less extent.

Items 1, 2 and 3 were adopted. The report was adopted as a whole.

The closing prayer was offered by the Rev. William E. Crouser.

The Convention adjourned until 8:45 o'clock, Wednesday morning.

Evening Service

A Service was held at eight o'clock P. M.

The Vespers were conducted by the Rev. Theo. Posselt.

The Rev. L. M. Zimmerman presided.

The speakers and their subjects were as follows:

"Spirituality and Morality—How Related"—Rev. E. P. Pfatteicher, D.D., Ph.D.

"Seventy-five Years of American Deaconess Service"—Rev. G. A. Getty, D.D.

———————•———————

SEVENTH MEETING

Morning Session

CONVENTION HALL, EDGEWATER BEACH HOTEL,
Chicago, Ill.
Wednesday, October 29, 8:45 A. M.

Matins were conducted by the Rev. H. B. Stock.

The Convention was called to order by the President.

The Minutes for Tuesday morning and afternoon sessions were read and approved.

The Secretary reported that, according to instructions given by the Convention, he had sent to Mrs. W. C. Stoever, of Philadelphia, the following telegram:

"The United Lutheran Church assembled conveys to you its sympathy and prays that God, our Father, may richly comfort you."

Taking up the regular order of business, the Rev. J. W. Kapp presented the report of the Lutheran Brotherhood.

REPORT OF THE COMMITTEE ON THE LUTHERAN BROTHERHOOD

The Brotherhood is steadily growing in strength and efficiency month after month. From its organization it has never had a period of recession. Slowly and steadily it has gone forward.

We note especially evidences of its growth in the past biennium along the following lines:

(a) A better appreciation of the Brotherhood and its work in the local congregations and the Church at large. One of our serious difficulties has been the lack of an understanding by the men of our Church of the aims, purpose and possibilities of the organization. It has been a difficult task to get this information to the laymen in a way that would lead them to form themselves into an organization and connect themselves with the National Organization. We have had also to meet misrepresentation, false and misleading statements, efforts to discredit the work and other forms of hindrance; but in spite of these the laymen are becoming acquainted with the real aims and work of the Brotherhood. Everywhere that this information is given they are ready to co-operate in their local congregations and affiliate themselves with the national program.

(b) The dues system has been a source of a good deal of criticism; but after a careful study and much discussion nothing better or as good has been suggested. Where the plan has been given a fair trial, it has been found acceptable to the men and has developed system and order in the work. The plan is not only feasible, but will ultimately produce great results. If only half the men in our Church would have responded to this plan we could have given Saskatoon College fifty thousand dollars for its work, our Pacific Seminary or some other institution fifty thousand dollars, the new building in our South American work twenty-five thousand dollars, and still have left one hundred thousand dollars to devote to other objects recommended by the Executive Board. To do all this it would have cost each man just ten cents a month. We give this for an illustration, merely, as to what can and will be accomplished. We are happy to report that more Brotherhoods are now paying the dues than at any previous time in our history. A sufficient number have done this, this past year, to enable the officers to appropriate a sum sufficiently large to complete the building fund for the boys' dormitory at Kumamoto, Japan, costing over $5000.00.

(c) State and Synodical organizations are being formed throughout the Church. In this way interest is stimulated and information given at first hand. State or Synodical organizations have in some cases taken up local work and accomplished some fine things. A notable instance is that of Ohio. The State Brotherhood has undertaken the raising of $150,000 for the purpose of erecting a new building for the Oesterlen Orphans' Home at Springfield. The men have gone into this work with enthusiasm and its successful conclusion is assured. This, and others of like character, is an important undertaking, not only because of what is accomplished, but because it gives the men proof of what they can do when they unite their efforts. It certainly emphasizes the wisdom and points to the imperative necessity of combining the men of the United Lutheran Church into one strong efficient organization in which they will not only learn the great needs of the Church but be practically equipped to meet these needs. Organization for service; the elimination of all needless machinery and the reduction of operating expenses to the minimum required for efficiency are sane principles in the Church as well as in the business world.

It has been the policy of the officers to reduce the overhead expenses to the lowest point consistent with efficiency and to avoid plans that would incur an indebtedness. Much as the committee would like to place one or more men in the field, we have not seen our way clear to do this. For the present other lines of propaganda have been adopted. Much has been done in addresses at Synods, Conferences, Conventions and in local congregations. A large correspondence has been carried on through our Central Office, answering many questions and solving many problems in local Brotherhoods. The *Brotherhood Messenger* is an invaluable aid in the work. Each issue carries excellent programs for the quarter and solves in many cases the question as to how to conduct a Brotherhood meeting. The *Messenger* now has a circulation of 8000, and is steadily growing. At the present rate, within a year, it will easily reach 10,000 copies or more. It is the earnest hope to change the paper from a quarterly to a monthly and enlarge it, in order to discuss Brotherhood aims, plans and problems better, and make a more effective plea to the laymen to enroll themselves in this ever-growing host. From the best information obtainable from reports in our office and synodical Minutes, we estimate that about fifty thousand men are now enrolled in over 1100 organizations reported. Many of these are not reported in our Central Office, through neglect or lack of knowledge of the importance of doing this, etc. We still have much to do to make these men see that the real power of the Brotherhood can only be realized when every Brotherhood is enrolled and every man supports the work according to the plan adopted.

We ask for the adoption of the following:

Your Committee finds that the President of the Brotherhood, Mr. Charles J. Driever, and the group of laymen associated with him, with the wise counsel of the Executive Secretary, have conducted the work in a safe and aggressive manner, and ask that this convention commend them for the faithful work done.

We desire to thank *The Lutheran* for its earnest and able support of the Brotherhood and for its readiness to admit articles about the Brotherhood whenever possible.

We earnestly ask that pastors co-operate with the Brotherhood plans; that they make known to the men the aims, plans and objects of the Brotherhood, and that they seek to bring about the organization of the men and their enrollment in the national organization.

That Synodical, Conference and City Unions seek to bring about the organization of a Brotherhood in every church and its enrollment in the national organization.

Respectfully submitted,

S. S. WALTZ, *Executive Director.*

The Rev. S. S. Waltz, Executive Secretary of the Brotherhood, addressed the Convention.

The findings of the Brotherhood were approved and the report was adopted.

Dr. Henry C. Roehner presented the report of the Committee on Young People's Associations.

REPORT OF THE COMMITTEE ON ASSOCIATIONS OF YOUNG PEOPLE

This Committee is in a way a clearing house between the United Lutheran Church and the young people's organization, the Luther League of America, the official young people's society of the United Lutheran Church. It has no prerogatives, or authority for action, it is simply advisory. Permit us to report briefly the following:

The work of the Luther League shows a gratifying progress and efficiency. By those who have been in touch with the life of the Luther League since its inception, it is stated that the organization is in the best condition in its history.

The General Secretary Mr. Harry Hodges, supplies the following statistics of the Luther League:

REPORT OF LAST BIENNIUM

Senior Organizations	674	membership	23,755
Intermediate Organizations	46	membership	1,049
Junior Organizations	148	membership	4,673
	869		29,377

These have contributed:

For local purposes	$29,804.98
For benevolence	15,964.46
	$45,769.44

BENEVOLENCES FOR 1924

Nova Scotia League....Student Fund
Connecticut League.....Student Fund
New York League......Erected Seminary Professor's House in Japan
Philadelphia League....Supports Japanese Student in Seminary
North Carolina League..Home and Foreign Mission Objectives—$3,650
South Carolina League..Home and Foreign Mission Objectives—$4,500
Indiana League.........Weidner Institute Equipment
Ohio League...........Hospital Work in India
Minnesota League......Provide Traveling Missionary for Forest Country
Illinois League.........Furnish room in Japan Girls' School

150 local Leagues support proteges in Indiana

Your Committee sent out a questionnaire to the presidents of Synods for the purpose of gathering information and constructive suggestions on young people's work, to increase the efficiency of our organization. A questionnaire to the presidents of our colleges and seminaries received a hearty and almost unanimous response. As the result of the same, plans are being worked out through the Luther League to follow up the students attending our institutions, and keep them in the young people's work.

It is planned also that young people's work in methods and plans may be presented to the students in the seminaries. Several presidents expressed the thought that definite courses in young people's work should be given in the seminaries.

The result of the investigation has shown that the young people's work is not only growing, but is becoming more and more efficient.

Our Canada League has withdrawn from the Luther League of America because of financial reasons, desiring to use all of its income for its own work. Incidentally it has stated that it desired to select its own topics, having its own special days in mind. Your Committee advised against the step of withdrawal, and trusts that the Canada League will soon ally itself again with the official young people's organization of the United Lutheran Church.

An increasing number of Christian Endeavor Societies are changing to Luther Leagues, and others are affiliating with district and state organizations.

Your Committee endorsed the plan of the Luther League for the raising of a Sustaining Membership Fund.

The ever present problem with your young people's organization, the Luther League, is that of lack of funds properly to carry on its work. It is greatly handicapped because of the lack of money to do its work. It is surprising to see what has been done under tremendous handicaps. Circumscribed and limited by the very nature of its membership, of young people with little or no income, it is expected to do its large work, which is one of the hardest and yet one of the most vitally important works of the Church. We believe we do not overstate when we say that there are more and better results in whole souled, unselfish, serving, Christian lives and in efficient Church workers coming through the young people's organizations than possibly through any one other organization of the Church.

The United Lutheran Church must increasingly see the vital importance of its young people's work. It should and must hold a place of prime importance.

The Luther League requires help to do the work which the Church needs have done. Its possible income is woefully inadequate.

There is no other large Church body that expects its young people's organization to maintain itself and the following figures which have been obtained directly from the respective Boards and general secretaries show not only what the various denominations are doing for their Young People's Societies, but at the same time indicate the importance and necessity which they attach to the work:

Methodist Episcopal, North—to the Epworth League—$75,000 a year.
Presbyterian, North—$30,00 a year.
Methodist Episcopal, South—$47,000 a year.
Church of the Brethren—$6,000 a year.
Southern Presbyterian—about $33,000 a year.
Cumberland Presbyterian—4 per cent of the total budget.
Congregational—2¼ per cent of the total budget.
Reformed Church—1½ per cent of the total budget.

These sums are given by the parent bodies to the young people's organizations.

The United Lutheran Church in America has given nothing.

Every one of the above bodies recognizes the need of help and the vital importance of the work. Accordingly they give the help needed.

Our official organization needs help no less than those young people's organizations. We handicap our organization and cripple its efficiency by doing nothing. We believe we shall be neglectful of our obligations as a Church unless we give the help needed.

Your Committee recommends, therefore, that at least the modest amount of one-half of one per cent of the total budget per year be granted our official young people's organization, the Luther League of America, to carry on and extend its work.

Respectfully submitted,

THE COMMITTEE.

Mr. Harry Hodges, General Secretary of the Luther League of America, addressed the Convention.

The Rev. A. G. Voigt and the Rev. L. B. Wolf also spoke in support of the work of the Luther League.

The report was adopted.

Moved and carried, That the Executive Board be instructed to consider the advisability of merging the Committee of Work Among Boys and the Committee on Associations of Young People, and report to the next Convention.

The Rev. Paul Mennenoeh, Chairman of the Committee on Necrology, presented the report of that Committee, and read the resolution immediately following the names recorded in the report.

REPORT OF COMMITTEE ON NECROLOGY

Your committee reports that during the past biennium ninety-five ministers have by death been called from the sphere of their earthly labors to their rest and reward in the heavenly kingdom. We have also noted the death of sixteen men and women whose lives have stood out prominently in the larger sphere of the church's activities. They brought to these tasks marked faithfulness, vision, energy and accomplishments.

Deceased Ministers.

Name	Born	Ordained.	Died
Altman, Frank DeGraff	Aug. 7, 1855	1882	Oct. 20, 1922
Atkin, Robert	Dec. 22, 1845	1880	Dec. 2, 1922
Aurand, Frederick	May 16, 1838	1872	April 20, 1923
Bailey, Hugh Estil	Dec. 25, 1848	1878	Sept. 8, 1923
Beates, James Fred	Nov. 17, 1856	1884	Aug. 26, 1923
Beates, William Adam	Feb. 4, 1849	1882	June 2, 1923
Becker, Karl William	July 1, 1887	1917	May 31, 1923
Beiderbecke, C. Henry	April 20, 1879	1901	Mar. 30, 1924
Belfour, Edmund	Aug. 9, 1833	1857	Feb. 5, 1924
Berkemeier, Gottlieb C.			Feb. 10, 1923
Billheimer, Thomas Chas.	Oct. 11, 1842	1867	July 5, 1923
Boyer, Harrison D.	June 16, 1878	1912	Sept. 6, 1922
Brecht, George Heinrich	Feb. 15, 1834	1866	Aug. 15, 1923
Breitenbach, John Wm.		1874	Nov. 20, 1923
Brown, Richard Lewis	Mar. 18, 1842	1871	Aug. 7, 1923
Brubaker, John	Nov. 5, 1848	1875	Oct. 14, 1923
Buehler, Prof. H. G.			
Burgdorf, John E.	Oct. 22, 1880		May 30, 1923
Burkett, J. A.			July 20, 1923
Burkhart, J. A.	May 25, 1873		April 26, 1923
Christy, Van Buren	Jan. 23, 1841	1868	July 7, 1923
Crouse, John Henry	1847	1879	Dec. 20, 1922
Derrick, John Bowman	Sept. 22, 1875		Sept. 6, 1922

Name	Born	Ordained.	Died
Dry, Charles Funk	June 2, 1851	1890	Jan. 26, 1924
Duehrkop, John C. I.	May 14, 1861	1893	May 28, 1924
Efird, Jacob Killian	June 28, 1852	1878	Jan. 9, 1924
Erdman, Asa Edward	June 27, 1852	1877	Aug. 9, 1923
Fahs, William H.	Jan. 3, 1865	1892	Dec. 11, 1923
Finkbiner, J. W.	July 4, 1843	1872	July 11, 1923
Fisher, Oscar W.		1886	May 25, 1922
Focht, John Brown	July 20, 1851	1877	Mar. 10, 1924
Forscht, Augustus C.	May 12, 1859		Nov. 20, 1923
Franke, Ludwig Joseph	April 22, 1862	1886	Jan. 26, 1923
Fulper, Elmer W.	May 1873	1899	Nov. 3, 1922
Garnes, Samuel A.	Jan. 2, 1859	1902	Nov. 30, 1922
Gaver, Martin Daniel	Nov. 14, 1849	1882	Nov. 28, 1923
Gelwicks, Charles A.	Jan. 7, 1835	1858	Nov. 26, 1922
Genzmer, Werner L.	July 17, 1862	1890	Oct. 2, 1923
Gerberich, David G.	March 1, 1863	1891	Jan. 29, 1924
Gringle, Arthur E.	1870		May 25, 1924
Gutleben, John	June 19, 1847	1870	July 21, 1923
Hall, Henry Hosea	April 9, 1844	1870	May 9, 1924
Hamm, Claus M. H.	Feb. 27, 1863	1892	Jan. 16, 1924
Harsh, George Emerson	1854	1878	June 19, 1923
Hausenfluck, John W.	Feb. 14, 1848	1875	Sept. 26, 1922
Heimann, E. N.			Mar. 24, 1923
Holloway, Henry Clay	Sept. 17, 1838	1863	May 5, 1924
Hoskinson, Winfield S.	Oct. 3, 1852		June 29, 1923
Kinard, Michael M.	Feb. 19, 1856	1887	Mar. 13, 1924
Kissel, Albert J.	Sept. 22, 1844		Mar. 9, 1924
Kitzmeyer, John F. W.	May 3, 1868	1893	June 30, 1923
Kling, John	July 1, 1838	1866	Feb. 2, 1923
Koehler, Leonard Charles	Feb. 5, 1850	1879	Jan. 2, 1924
Koser, J. A.	June 24, 1847		July 6, 1924
Kuder, John Henry	May 1, 1852	1882	April 13, 1923
Kurtz, Daniel S.	Mar. 16, 1860	1889	Jan. 22, 1924
Larsen, Lauritz	Nov. 28, 1883		Jan. 28, 1923
Lecrone, D. W.	Nov. 8, 1859	1898	April 25, 1922
Legum, John		1905	July 22, 1923
Linn, Josephus Adolphus	Jan. 22, 1853		Mar. 25, 1923
Linsz, Adam August	Feb. 26, 1845	1869	Aug. 28, 1922
Ludwig, A. T.			July 25, 1924
Meissner, Elias James	June 18, 1853	1877	Dec. 11, 1923
Minter, Elias	Nov. 28, 1836	1877	Dec. 8, 1922
Mueller, Edward J. H.	Oct. 20, 1875	1902	Nov. 22, 1923
Mueller, Walter	May 3, 1853	1883	June 4, 1923
Neudewitz, Eugene E.	Sept. 10, 1863	1896	May 17, 1924
Ott, Hamilton A.	Feb. 11, 1855	1881	Mar. 28, 1923
Pugh, Booz Franklin	Aug. 4, 1847	1877	Mar. 9, 1923
Rehn, Andrew H.	1844		Oct. 3, 1923
Rickert, William Henry	June 4, 1844	1871	Mar. 29, 1924
Riser, Wilbur H.	Dec. 4, 1868	1898	Mar. 17, 1924
Sahm, M. O. T.	April 11, 1853	1879	May 26, 1924
Schaeffer, A. F.	June 29, 1857	1884	Jan. 18, 1923
Seel, George	Sept. 8, 1858	1883	July 19, 1923
Sell, Amos	Mar. 9, 1843	1878	Mar. 30, 1924
Seyler, Levi Youse	May 27, 1884	1911	Feb. 25, 1923

	Born		Died
Shaeffer, James William	July 19, 1860	1889	Sept. 10, 1923
Sibole, Edward E.	Aug. 11, 1840	1873	Mar. 26, 1923
Snyder, George W.	Sept. 14, 1839	1873	Aug. 4, 1923
Sommer, Gustav	July 10, 1859	1884	May 16, 1923
Sowers, Robert R.		1896	June 7, 1924
Spangler, Alexander H.	Feb. 16, 1852	1882	Feb. 21, 1924
Stelljes, John H. M.	Dec. 2, 1880	1907	Nov. 2, 1922
Straub, Harvey Lyman	June 12, 1875	1903	June 14, 1922
Strubel, Grover C.	1896	1918	June 7, 1924
Taylor, A. R.	May 12, 1844	1899	Dec. 2, 1922
Thomas, Abraham Z.	Aug. 8, 1843	1872	Dec. 30, 1923
Thomas, Jacob W.	May 22, 1850	1880	Oct. 24, 1922
Traub, Frank Milton	Oct. 4, 1873	1903	May 7, 1923
Tressler, Victor G. A.	April 10, 1865	1892	Sept. 1, 1923
Waters, James Quigley	Sept. 16, 1835	1864	April 3, 1924
Waters, John Armstrong	July 18, 1857	1888	Oct. 27, 1922
Weigle, Elias Daniel	Jan. 19, 1848	1878	Aug. 27, 1923
Weiskotten, Samuel G.	Dec. 16, 1863	1887	June 18, 1924
Werth, Paul F.			Dec. 22, 1922
Wickman, Martin Henry	Oct. 24, 1889	1912	Sept. 12, 1923
Wolf, Joseph Bittinger	Jan. 9, 1848	1877	Feb. 16, 1923

Laymen and Laywomen.

	Born	Died
Arbogast, Wilson	Jan. 12, 1851	July 13, 1924
Beegle, Helen C.	Oct. 28, 1849	Mar. 12, 1924
Boyer, Virginia M.	Feb. 23, 1889	May 21, 1922
Brewer, Jessie		Feb. 10, 1924
Chester, Susan Kistler		Feb. 17, 1924
Crabtree, Prof. John T.	May 19, 1846	Nov. 4, 1922
Decker, William	Oct. 15, 1861	May 9, 1924
Gaskell, Robert E.	Feb. 5, 1856	Nov. 24, 1923
Herter, John (Diakon)	July 20, 1875	Jan. 1, 1923
Lantz, Hon. Cyrus R.	Aug. 26, 1842	June 3, 1923
Miller, E. Augustus, Esq	Dec. 11, 1860	Dec. 4, 1922
Monroe, Susan E.	Oct. 22, 1848	May 17, 1923
Myers, Francis E.	Mar. 16, 1849	Dec. 2, 1923
Patton, Hon. Theo B.	May 6, 18947	Dec. 16, 1922
Remaley, Daniel John	Nov. 22, 1842	Mar. 9, 1924
Sadtler, Prof. Samuel P.	1847	Dec. 20, 1923
Widle, Chas. A.		April 10, 1923

We recommend the adoption of the following:

Resolved, That we as representatives of the United Lutheran Church lift our hearts and voices in prayer and thanksgiving unto God for the lives of those men and women who have passed out of our midst during the past two years. We are comforted by the thought that the toil and burden-bearing of these are exchanged for the repose of heaven, that the struggle of many years after the likeness of the Master is now completed by their being brought to see Him as He is and to union eternal with Him whom their souls loved. We remember with gratitude the lives of those who walked as leaders among us, whose usefulness and influence were at their greatest, their wisdom most widely confessed, their words most respected and their services most prized. We give thanks unto Him for the lives of those who served as pastors and missionaries; for the lives of those men and women who gave themselves, their counsel and their gifts to hasten the coming of the Kingdom of God. For their sake, as well as for our own and for Christ's, we rejoice to know that the seed they buried will spring up in rich harvests, that the sacred tones of their teachings will swell into growing harmonies—that the forces they set at work, however subtle and silent, will widen in influence and develop and multiply till countless multitudes are affected by their life-work. "They that be wise shall shine as the brightness of the firmament, and they that turn many to righteousness as the stars for ever and ever."

Your committee met at Atlantic City, N. J., July 8th to 10th, 1924.

Questionnaires sent out by the Secretary of our committee to 2,844 ministers were filled out and returned by 842. When pastors learn to realize what the real purpose of the questionnaire is, we feel certain that they will respond more willingly. Our only object is to compile for the archives of our church a correct and historic sketch of each minister, from which church historians may gather correct information. We urge again the hearty cooperation of the Necrologists of the various Synods with the Secretary of this committee, so that our records may be kept accurate and complete.

Resolved (1), That we request that the necrological report of the various Synods be published on separate sheets, so that they can be readily removed and placed in loose-leaf folders by the Secretary of this committee.

(2) That we request that ten copies of the Synodical reports be sent to the secretary.

Respectfully submitted,

PAUL MENNENOEH, *Chairman,*

J. F. LAMBERT, *Rec. Sec.*

The Convention arose and stood while the Chairman of the Committee read the list of those who had been called home by death during the biennium, and so signified their assent to the resolution. The Convention, while standing, was led in prayer by the Rev. Luther De Yoe, closing with the Lord's Prayer.

On motion the Committee on Necrology was permitted to add other names to the list, submitting the completed list promptly to the Secretary.

Resolution 1 was amended so as to read, "That we request that the necrological reports of the various Synods be published," etc.

The resolution was adopted as amended.

Resolution 2 was amended so as to read: "That we request that ten copies," etc.

The resolution was adopted as amended.

The report was adopted as a whole.

The Rev. G. A. Bierdeman presented the following series of "Convention Resolutions" for the Committee of Reference and Counsel:

1. That we thank the Great Head of the Church, Jesus Christ our Lord, for the harmonious, aggressive and constructive spirit which has pervaded and dominated this, the Fourth Convention of The United Lutheran Church in America, and invoke His blessing upon the execution of the work proposed by this Convention.

2. That this Convention express its admiration for and hearty appreciation of the complete and admirable arrangements on the part of the Chicago Entertainment Committee for the entertainment of this Convention.

3. That we extend our most sincere thanks to the management of the Edgewater Beach Hotel for the hospitable and most satisfactory entertainment which they have provided for this Convention, and that a copy of this resolution be delivered to the management of this hotel.

4. That we record our appreciation of the music rendered during the sessions by the vested choirs of the churches of Chicago and by the Gettysburg quartette.

5. That we gratefully acknowledge the cordiality of the Faculty and Board of Directors of the Theological Seminary of the Evangelical Lutheran Church, Chicago, Ill., in their entertainment of the delegates of this Convention at the grounds of said Seminary on the afternoon of October 25th.

6. That we express our appreciation of the very excellent manner in which the Board of Publication has solved the housing problem, through the erection of the Muhlenberg Publication Building. This magnificent building is a credit to the whole Church and a splendid advertisement of our Church's publication cause; also, for the permanent establishment of our publication cause in Chicago by the purchase of property.

7. That we extend thanks to the following for equipment furnished this Convention:

American Seating Company	A. B. Dick Company
Lyon-Healy Company	Royal Typewriter Company
L. C. Smith Typewriter Company	Woodstock Typewriter Company

E. R. Moore and Company

8. That we express our high appreciation of the presence and address of Governor J. A. O. Preuss, Governor of the State of Minnesota, and a member of the United Norwegian Church in America, on the evening of October 24th.

9. That we extend to the Board of Safety of Chicago our thanks for the faithful and courteous attention, direction and guardianship given to this Convention during our most pleasant stay in this great City of Chicago.

Resolutions 1, 2, 3, 4, 5, 6, 7, 8 and 9 were adopted, and the report was adopted as a whole.

The Rev. Luther D. Reed presented the report of the Committee on Church Architecture.

REPORT OF THE COMMITTEE ON CHURCH ARCHITECTURE

The Committee was called upon during the biennium by many congregations, pastors and architects for counsel on a great variety of subjects connected with church building.

Twenty-four meetings were held in Professor Laird's office at the University of Pennsylvania, and in the office of Mr. George C. Baum, Philadelphia. At the first of these Dr. Ohl was elected Chairman and Dr. Reed, Secretary.

REVIEW OF PLANS.

Fifty-three sets of plans for buildings in eighteen states were considered, and formal reports rendered. Many of these were plans for mission congregations submitted through the offices of the District Superintendents. Many others were from self-supporting congregations which sought the assistance of the Committee. Some idea of the variety of points considered and judgment expressed may be obtained from the following summary of plans reviewed.

Plans for a church building and Sunday school for St. Paul's Church, Collingswood, N. J., the Rev. I. H. Hagedorn, pastor, George C. Baum, Philadelphia, architect, were considered and approved.

Pencil drawings for proposed church for Grace Church, Springfield, Ohio, J. C. Fulton & Son, Uniontown, Pa., architects, were considered and suggestions given concerning the plan, particularly of the chancel, and concerning a number of details in the elevations.

Detailed blue prints for Woodlawn Immanuel Church, Chicago, Ill., Iver, Viehe-Naess & Co., architects, were approved with various suggestions concerning points of design in the interest of economy and of simplicity.

Plans for Grace Church, North Belmore, Long Island, N. Y., S. N. Knara Stoyanoff, N. Y., architect, were approved in general with recommendations concerning rearrangement of the chancel, proper entrances and certain features in the basement, including the windows and location of boiler.

Plans for the Church of the Reformation, New Britain, Conn., Delbert K. Perry, architect, were approved with suggestions concerning elimination of certain features in the plan, the character of stone contemplated, and matters of chancel arrangement.

Plans for the Hollywood Church, Los Angeles, California, prepared by the De Luxe Building Company, were considered and not approved. The treatment of the nave without a centre aisle, and with radiating side aisles, the lack of agreement between the main floor plan and the elevations, etc., were among the objectional features. The congregation was advised that it would be impossible to execute a contract upon these plans as a basis. The Committee also stated its disapproval of the congregation's undertaking to build without the advice and protection afforded by a disinterested and competent architect, whose employment was recommended. Revised plans, while showing improvement, were also not approved as lacking many essentials of good church design. The congregation was again advised to secure the services of a church architect, various names of architects of standing in Los Angeles being suggested.

Plans for Grace Church, East Stroudsburg, Pa., the Rev. C. E. Kistler, pastor, Ritcher & Eiler, Reading, architects, were cordially approved with certain suggestions concerning roof trusses over the auditorium and entrances to the building. The Committee also formulated a series of answers to questions referred to it by the Rev. Mr. Kistler concerning chancel and choir arrangement, location of the font, inclined floors, etc.

In response to the request of Mr. Obenhack, a member of the Committee, for the Committee's suggestions concerning preliminary plans for the Church of Peace, Rochester, N. Y., various suggestions were given.

Plans for St. James' Church, Seattle, Washington, Frederick J. Peters, architect, not including detailed arrangements for the chancel, were approved and commended for good taste.

Plans for Grace Church, River Edge, N. Y., the Rev. Otto Becker, pastor, J. L. Tillack, Hackensack, N. J., architect, were approved in general with recommendations concerning chancel arrangement, exits, and various details in the basement.

Plans for St. Peter's Church, Baldwin, Long Island, the Rev. G. C. Goering, pastor, S. N. Knara Stoyanoff, architect, were approved with minor suggestions concerning chancel details and elimination of windows in the organ chamber. Another plan prepared by a different architect was subsequently laid before the Committee, but was not approved, and the congregation decided to build from the first set of approved plans with a few minor modifications.

Plans for Gloria Dei Church, Philadelphia, the Rev. W. C. Sandt, pastor, C. W. Bolton, Philadelphia, architect, were cordially approved, as insuring a building of dignity and beauty, though the attention of the congregation was particularly directed to the matter of expense.

Plans for a Slovak Church, Pittsburgh, Pa., prepared by the Rev. F. F. Haworth, Baden, Pa., were considered and commended in general with suggestions concerning possible omission of the tower and ventilators in the roof, removal of the heating plant from its position under the organ, and providing an entrance to the pulpit from the chancel as well as from the sacristy.

Plans for Grace Church, Muscatine, Iowa, the Rev. T. F. Weiskotten, pastor, H. W. Zeidler, architect, were considered. Revised plans prepared in accordance with the suggestions of the Committee were also reviewed and numerous further suggestions were made concerning details of the front elevation, matters of roof construction and other features.

Plans for Immanuel Church, Meriden, Conn., the Rev. P. A. Kirsch, pastor, Parish & Schroeder, New York, architects, were heartily commended as possessing unusual excellence. A few minor suggestions were given concerning chancel details, location of the choir, etc. Later, at the request of the Secretary of the Building Committee, the names of several architects were suggested who might be considered to supervise the work of construction.

Floor plans for the Sunday school room of a church at Oklahoma, near Du Bois, Pa., W. H. Overdorf, architect, were considered and were not approved as being deficient in various details of good churchly design. Revised plans were regarded as a great improvement, and various suggestions were made concerning these.

Plans for the First Lutheran Church, Murphysboro, Ill., R. L. Gill, architect, were not approved as designed, as showing confusion of styles and being otherwise inadequate. The Committee suggested the possible omission of the tower as an unnecessary expense, and the employment of an associate architect with experience in the Gothic style.

Plans for the Sunday school unit of Messiah Church, Cleveland, Ohio, R. F. Feegan, architect, were approved and commended, with some minor suggestions.

Plans for proposed extension to Grace Church, Casper, Wyoming, William J. Westfall, architect, were approved with recommendations for the omission of the rudimentary transepts.

Plans for the Church of the Resurrection, Minneapolis, Magney and Tusler, architects, were approved with the suggestion that even in this inexpensive building the chancel be given a complete and proper form, and that the basement rooms be grouped so as to give the assembly-room better proportions.

Plans for the Church of the Ascension, Baltimore, Mr. F. E. Beall, architect, were not approved as deficient in churchly feeling and dignity and in various details of chancel arrangement, as well as being inadequately lighted and ventilated. Later plans for the chapel, to be eventually converted into church offices, parlors, reading rooms, etc., with a future church building in the rear, were approved as having interesting possibilities.

Design for a bungalow chapel for the Church of the Advent, St. Louis, Mo., O. D. Schmidt, architect, were considered and suggestions given for redesigning the exterior so as to make it conform in type to the church edifice to be erected in the future.

Design for Holy Trinity Church, La Crosse, Wis., the Rev. S. H. Roth, pastor, was approved with suggestions for decreasing the width of the piers on each side of the chancel and a different location of the organ console.

Design for chapel and rectory for the Rev. Otto Doering, Chicago, R. G. Schmid & Co., architects, was considered. The arrangements for the living quarters were regarded as satisfactory. The balance was criticised as devoid of churchly feeling in exterior and interior.

Plans for Unity English Church, Detroit, Michigan, Spier & Gehrke, architects, were approved in general with suggestions concerning different arrangement of choir stalls, elimination of chancel windows, etc.

Plans for Calvary Church, Arnold, Pa., drawn by the Rev. F. F. Haworth, Baden, Pa., were approved in general with suggestions concerning more symmetrical treatment of the chancel, location of the choir and details of the entrance.

Plans for St. Barnabas' Church, Howard Beach, Borough of Queens, N. Y., Dietrich and Diemer, architects, suggesting a semi-rural type of building with clapboard sides above stone and concrete foundation, were approved.

A block plan for a church plant, and plans for a parsonage for St. James' Church, Merrick, Long Island, N. Y., the Rev. Ivan Heft, pastor, Louis E. Jallade, New York, architect, were considered and approved.

Plans for a church and parish house at Glendale, Calif., the Rev. H. C. Funk, pastor, Allen Ruoff and Arthur C. Munson, Los Angeles, Calif., architects, were approved in general, with suggestions for restudy of the chancel and choir arrangements.

Plans for a church at Hendersonville, N. C., the Rev. J. D. Mauney, pastor, F. H. & J. C. Cunningham, Inc., Greenville, S. C., architects, were not approved as showing bad proportions of walls and openings in all elevations, and otherwise unsatisfactory.

Pencil sketches for a church at Centralia, Washington, the Rev. F. T. Lucas, pastor, E. Kroner, Portland, Ore., architect, were approved with suggestions for rearrangement of chancel details. The congregation was congratulated upon the possibility of securing an attractive building at a very reasonable figure.

Plans for the First Church, Apollo, Pa., the Rev. Martin T. Clare, pastor, O. M. Topp, Pittsburgh, Pa., architect, were approved, the Committee congratulating the Building Committee and the architect upon what promises to be a fine group, consisting of a church building and a parish house on a corner lot sufficiently large to afford a fine setting. The general plan and arrangement, the proportion and details of. design were commended, the only suggestion offered being in connection with the proposed choir and organ arrangement.

Revised plans for St. John's Church, Ocean City, N. J., Mr. George C. Baum, architect, were approved.

Plans for Grace Church, Gary, Ind., Ivar, Viehe-Naess & Co., Chicago, architects, were approved with suggestions concerning the disposition of the choir, various chancel details and matters of design in the front elevation of the building.

Plans for St. Paul's Church, Missouri Valley, Iowa, A. F. Gauger and Ray R. Ganger, St. Paul, architects, were not regarded satisfactory. In fundamental proportions, chancel and choir arrangements, steps in the tower entrance, and various other features which indicated a building lacking in churchly quality.

Plans for the remodeling of St. Luke's Church, Rochester, N. Y., the Rev. William Trebert, pastor, Erick W. Waemecke, architect, were considered. Various features were criticised unfavorably, and the suggestion was made that the congregation might better consider plans for an entirely new building, or have another study made of plans for remodeling.

The Committee replied to questions asked by the Rev. Mr. Hamsher, pastor of Trinity Church, Mechanicsburg Pa., with respect to proposed alterations.

Plans for Salem Church, Fremont, Neb., the Rev. Carl G. Aue, D.D., pastor, H. F. Gauger and Ray R. Gauger, architects, St. Paul, were considered and approved as satisfactory in general, with suggestions for re-study of the chancel and choir space, and possible omission of one or both towers in the interest of economy and good design; also possible use of open timber ceiling instead of flat ceiling in the nave, etc.

Plans for a building to be used for church services and Sunday school purposes and later for Sunday school and parish purposes only, by the mission at Palmyra, N. J., the Rev. Mr. Saul, pastor, Moses and Morfeld, Camden, architects, were approved with the understanding that the chancel arrangement would be restudied so as to conform to the traditional Lutheran plan, and with suggestions for possible use of open timber ceiling.

Plans for Trinity Church, Appleton, Wis., H. C. Haeuser, Milwaukee, architect, were approved with certain suggestions concerning rearrangement of the main entrance to the nave, and possibly a different location for the tower, and a deepening of the chancel.

A stock design for a church at Fairmount, Jackson County, Mo., the Rev. C. G. Georgi, pastor, was approved with suggestions concerning rearrangement of the chancel and a caution to the congregation with respect to the adaptation of the plans and specifications to local conditions, particularly with reference to the foundations, plumbing requirements, etc.

Plans for Trinity Church, Chambersburg, Pa., the Rev. W. A. Kump, pastor, Horace G. Kilmer, architect, were considered and suggestions given for designing the building in the same general style as that of the parish building adjoining (Romanesque). Suggestions were also given for modification of the plans, if it was decided to build in the Gothic style. These included a different treatment of the vestibule and a restudy of the chancel to conform to the traditional Lutheran arrangement; also concerning better connections between the two buildings and different treatment of the tower.

Plans for Calvary, Hillside, N. J., the Rev. Oscar Brandorff, pastor, Dietrich and Diemer, architects, were approved with suggestions concerning the entrances, certain chancel details, etc.

Plans for St. Paul's Church, Johnson City, N. Y., the Rev. A. G. Marcell, pastor, S. D. Leadbeater, Johnson City, architect, were considered. The floor plan was approved with the exception of the arrangement of the chancel, suggestions for which were given. The elevations were commended for careful drawing but poor composition, and various suggestions were given for a restudy of these.

Plans for St. John's Church (Siebenburger), Cleveland, Ohio, the Rev. John Foisel, pastor, were not approved as being elementary, almost primitive, in character, and possessing many undesirable features. The congregation was counselled to secure the services of a competent architect, inasmuch as the success and influence of even our weakest missions in the larger cities will be imperiled unless they erect a building which will make a favorable impression upon the community, however inexpensive it may be. An entirely different set of plans, subsequently, prepared by the Rev. F. F. Haworth, was cordially approved with minor suggestions concerning features of the tower design.

A block plan for a church plant and detailed plans for a building to be used immediately as a church and Sunday school, but eventually as a school building only by St. Paul's Church, Valley Stream, Long Island, the Rev. C. W. Nutzhorn, pastor, T. W. Craddock, architect, were approved and commended. The Committee recommended further study of the building to be erected immediately with reference to its eventual use for Sunday school work, for which greater width would be very desirable. The omission of the tower was also suggested in the interest of economy.

Plans for Emanuel Church, Rochester, N. Y., the Rev. F. E. Reissig, pastor, C. F. Obenhack, Niagara Falls, N. Y., achitect, were approved with suggestions for the enlargement of the narthex and the possible addition of a front porch and for a redesigning of certain windows.

Plans for St. Paul's Church, Dunton, Long Island, the Rev. C. G. Toebke, pastor, Cherry & Matz, N. Y., architects, were approved with suggestions for an apsidal chancel end for the Romanesque building, and for certain rearrangements of the chancel details. The Committee in this connection expressed the conviction which it has frequently expressed to other congregations, that other things being equal, it is generally advisable, particularly in growing suburbs, to build first of all a parish building which may be used for church services for a time, and then after the congregation has grown to some strength, to undertake the erection of a church building proper.

Plans for St. James' Church, Gerrittsen Beach, Brooklyn, Dietrich & Diemer, New York, architects, were approved with suggestions concerning slight modifications of the chancel arrangement, different location of the organ console, and a redesigning of certain features of the facade.

Plans for Bethany, Springfield Garden, N. Y., J. St. Clair Bousurn, pastor, Dietrich & Diemer, architects, were approved with suggestions concerning minor modifications in the chancel and a possible relocation of chimney flues.

Plans for a proposed parish house unit for Ascension Church, St. Paul, Minn., the Rev. R. H. Gerberding, pastor, were considered. The elevations indicated a rather domestic type of building which would not tie up satisfactorily with a future church building, and the Committee recommended the employment of a competent church architect to block out the entire group of buildings and redesign the parish house.

With reference to plans for a church at South Sioux City, Neb., Beuttler & Arnold, architects, the Committee gave suggestions concerning better proportions in the building, possible omission of the tower, and various features of chancel and choir arrangement. It also requested later submission of elevations and sections, particularly of the chancel and the roof construction.

CONFERENCES AND CORRESPONDENCE.

The Chairman and the Secretary personally held a number of conferences with pastors, and, in some instances, with their Church Councils. They also conducted an extensive correspondence, the Chairman reporting letters from thirty-four pastors and others in thirteen states, Ontario and Japan; and the Secretary, letters from one hundred and nine persons in twenty-eight states and two provinces of Canada. This correspondence covered a wide range of subjects; requests for general information preparatory to building, for assistance in the selection of architects, matter of design and construction of churches, parish houses, parsonages, extensions to existing buildings, etc., questions of lighting arrangements, stained glass, altar appointment, etc.

GENERAL SUGGESTIONS.

An analysis of the criticism of plans and the correspondence of the Committee reveals four subjects which, perhaps more than any other, have been under constant discussion by the Committee.

1. *The Choice of an Architect.*

The fundamental importance of securing a thoroughly competent church architect is evidently not fully appreciated. Architecture is a profession of very broad range. Church architecture is one of its special lines, calling for special knowledge, taste, sympathy and experience. Many congregations, particularly missions, make the fundamental mistake of thinking it unnecessary to secure a specialist, believing that any general architect, or in the case of small buildings, even a draftsman or a builder, will be able to supply them with satisfactory plans. There are but few comparatively good church architects, even in the larger cities, and unless one of these be secured, congregations cannot expect to erect buildings of architectural merit and churchly character. The money of our people is being misspent, and the opportunity of the church for service and influence in our communities is being lost by the very general erection of commonplace, characterless structures designed by men unqualified to do this special work.

The employment of a building company, even though the latter has on its staff men with architectural training, is a particularly specious evil. These draftsmen are rarely qualified to design church buildings, not understanding the first principles of good church design, and being quite ignorant of the chancel requirements of the Lutheran Church. In addition to this, the employment of a building company actually leaves the congregation without adequate protection, as the building contract, in practically all cases, makes the builder the interpreter of the terms of the contract, of which he is a party at interest.

The Committee, therefore, constantly strives to impress upon all pastors and building committees the absolute necessity of securing an architect of standing and capacity, with ample experience in good church work. This the Committee does, not in the interests of the architectural profession, but in the interests of the individual congregations and of the Church as a whole; for the Committee is convinced, after wide observation and experience, that the successful solution of every church building problem depends upon the wise selection of an architect, more than upon any other single factor.

It should be understood that it is entirely possible to secure the services of an able church architect at a distance to prepare plans, specifications and details, arrangements being made with an associated architect or some other competent party for local supervision of erection. Most of the really good churches throughout the country have been designed by architects whose offices are hundreds of miles distant. The abler church architects are constantly doing work throughout a radius of hundreds and even thousands of miles. In any important building, especially, the principal things is to secure the services of the ablest, most gifted man obtainable, and have him prepare the plans, arranging for local supervision of erection.

Too frequently the Committee has no opportunity of impressing these fundamental facts upon pastors and building committees until it is too late. If congregations would consult with the Committee as the first step instead of simply sending finished drawings for criticism at the end of their study, the Committee, in many cases, would be able to offer constructive suggestions which would result in a better type of building, often at less cost, and in some cases, would be able to save the congregation great delay and expense resulting from the preparation of unsatisfactory plans which later must be changed.

So far as it is possible to do so, the Committee will be glad to furnish lists of names of firms of recognized ability in different parts of the country, with the understanding, of course, that plans presented by architects whom they have not suggested will not be discriminated against in any respect, but will be judged fairly upon their merits.

2. *Chancel Appointments.*

Largely because of the general employment of architects unfamiliar with the traditional requirements and appointments of the chancel in the Lutheran Church, a very large number of unsatisfactory chancel plans have come before the Committee. Serious mistakes here are fatal to the success of any church building, and greater attention should be given to this fundamental question by all who contemplate building. The Committee will be glad to counsel with pastors and committees on this important detail, which should be fully determined at the very beginning.

3. *Location of Choir and Organ.*

This is one of the questions most frequently discussed. Final decision must be left to the individual congregation. The Committee has approved plans with the choir and organ in the rear gallery, in the chancel, in a corner of the nave, in a transept, on one side of the chancel, and on a low platform immediately in front of the chancel. It, however, records its deepening conviction that there are only two really satisfactory locations for the choir, viz., in the rear gallery or in the chancel. All other locations are experiments and compromises, more or less undesirable liturgically and architecturally.

4. *The Nave Without a Tower.*

One of the characteristic developments in American Church architecture of the best type is the omission of towers and the erection of naves with highly-developed facades of churchly design. This is a movement in the interest of economy, and often of good design itself, and is to be commended to our congregations, particularly where funds are limited. Where towers or spires of real proportion and merit can be built, they are beautiful and desirable, but towers are in no sense necessary to good churchly design, and they can often be omitted to great advantage, both from the standpoint of cost and appearance.

The publications issued by the Committee ("Practical Suggestions for Pastors and Building Committees," and "Church Principles in Church Architecture," prepared by the Secretary) have been widely distributed upon request and the editions of both are almost exhausted.

The Committee is ready to do all within its power to give advice to congregations, to review plans, make suggestions, etc. It is not organized, however, to prepare plans or undertake extensive revisions of plans. Several other Churches maintain building bureaus which are fully organized to render complete architectural service. Your Committee has been investigating these bureaus and their work, but it is not yet prepared to recommend the establishment of such a work by the United Lutheran Church.

The Committee earnestly offers the suggestions contained in this report for the thoughtful consideration of the entire Church. It presents no specific recommendations.

J. F. OHL, *Chairman*,
LUTHER D. REED, *Secretary*.

The report was adopted as a whole.

The following was adopted:

Resolved, That this Convention, through its Secretary, express to Professor Warren P. Laird its high appreciation of the service which he so freely renders in our work.

The Rev. Luther D. Reed presented the report of the Archivist as follows:

REPORT OF THE ARCHIVIST

The Archivist respectfully reports receipt during the past biennium of the following material:

Certified copy of the Minutes of the United Lutheran Church, 1920.
Selected correspondence of the President of the United Lutheran Church.
Selected correspondence of the Secretary.
Minutes of various Synods.
Original design for the seal of the Church of the Advent, St. Louis, Mo.
Anniversary histories, souvenirs, etc., of Zion Church, Sunbury, Pa., Holy Trinity Church, Minneapolis, Minn., Church of the Holy Communion, Racine, Wis., Trinity Church, Lansford, Pa., Church of the Reformation, Brooklyn, N. Y., St. Peter's Church, Janesville, Wis., Christ Church, Shrewsbury, Pa., St. John's Church, Sterling, Ill.

Considerable work has been done in mounting, binding and cataloguing this and similar material previously reported.

LUTHER D. REED,
Archivist.

The report was adopted.

The Rev. William Freas presented the report of the Committee on Army and Navy Work.

REPORT OF THE COMMITTEE ON ARMY AND NAVY WORK

Your Committee on Army and Navy Work met for organization in Philadelphia on January 5, 1923. The following officers were elected: Chairman, Rev. C. D. Trexler; secretary-treasurer, Rev. William Freas. An Executive Committee was appointed consisting of the officers and Mr. Charles H. Dahmer. Rev. S. T. Nicholas, D.D., was appointed as the Washington representative.

The Committee agreed that the work which it had to do was of a three-fold character.

1. To keep the Church in touch with the men in the Army and Navy.

2. To assist and encourage regular army and navy chaplains in their ministry to the men.

3. Arranging for Lutheran ministrations to men in the Army and Navy, at all posts and stations where possible through the volunteer service of camp pastors and congregations.

Your Committee is glad to report that real progress has been shown in the work done during the past biennium. We present to you the following information concerning the work which has been accomplished.

I. CAMP PASTOR WORK

The most important activity of the Committee has been in connection with the development of local service by pastors to our men in camps and posts of the Army and Navy. In the development of this work the Committee has been in close co-operation with the office of the chief of chaplains of the Army and the Washington office of the Federal Council of Churches, through which the General Committee on Army and Navy Chaplains of that body operates. At the time of the last convention there were three camp pastors, members of the United Lutheran Church, still engaged in this work under the direction of the National Lutheran Commission for Soldiers' and Sailors' Welfare. A brief statement concerning the work of each of these three points is here given.

(a) *Brooklyn Navy Yard.* This work was continued under the directions of Rev. T. G. Hartwig, up to March 1, 1923, at which time it was terminated.

(b) *Hospital at San Francisco, California.* Rev. H. M. Leech continued his service at this point in co-operation with the Y. M. C. A., up to March 1, 1923, at which time his work was terminated. Since that date he has been doing similar work of a purely volunteer character.

(c) *Great Lakes Naval Training Station.* Rev. J. A. St. Clair was in charge of the work at this point. On account of the rapidly decreasing number of men assigned to this station it was felt desirable that he should also work at the hospital just opened at Maywood, Ill. Arrangements were made for activity at the latter post. His work at both of these places is still continuing.

This work was supported by the appropriation provided by the Buffalo Convention. Further funds were sought from the treasury of the Church, but were not available. The importance of continuing this work at the three points was presented to local groups or organizations. In Brooklyn and San Francisco it was impossible to make any arrangements for the local support of the work and it was, therefore, necessary to terminate it as stated in the preceding paragraph. In Chicago, however, the situation is somewhat different. Some of the local laymen are deeply concerned with the activity at Great Lakes and Maywood and made themselves responsible for the securing of funds to carry it on. An appropriation of $874 a year was made by the Norwegian Lutheran Church of America towards this work. The balance needed is being provided by people who are locally interested in the work.

The Committee at its meeting decided to organize the work all over the Church, by seeking properly qualified men and urging them to apply for appointment as chaplains in the Officers' Reserve Corps. These men would then be in a position to find more ready admission to the various camps and posts over the country. Largely, as a result of the Committee's efforts, 39 men have been approved and appointed as chaplains in the Officers' Reserve Corps up to May, 1924. From one man it was necessary to withhold approval. Of the number appointed, 23 are pastors of the United Lutheran Church. Since May, 5 more applications have been approved and forwarded to Washington for action there.

II. CHAPLAINS

The Committee has, during the biennium, kept in touch with regular Army and Navy chaplains. There are at present 7 Lutheran pastors serving as chaplains in the Army and of this number 4 are members of the United Lutheran Church. Chaplains Hall, Miller, Rinard and Weber. Two Lutheran chaplains are serving in the Navy, one of these being a pastor of the United Lutheran Church, Chaplain Moyer. The Committee has sought aid for these chaplains from the synods of which they are members, so that our Lutheran chaplains may have the same assistance from their Church that the chaplains of other denominations are receiving. Such assistance is now being given by two of the synods to the chaplains which hold membership in them.

Your Committee has also sought to have properly qualified men apply for appointment to the regular chaplaincy. This effort, however, has not been successful. There are at present 16 vacancies in army chaplaincies which should be filled by Lutheran pastors.

III. General Matters

Representatives of your Committee have been in conference with those of other denominations who have been concerned about the Army and Navy work. Such a conference was called by the Federal Council of Churches in New York, and matters of common interest discussed. This conference led to the calling of a second one. The Secretary of War invited the representatives of the various denominations to meet with him and some of the regular chaplains of the Army and Navy in Washington. This conference extended over a period of two days and was exceedingly helpful in giving fuller information concerning the needs of the Army and Navy. The predominant note of the conference was the responsibility of the churches to do a truly spiritual work at the various army and navy camps and posts through volunteer service and congregational co-operation with chaplains where they were attached to the post.

The Secretary of the Committee visited the Chaplains' School at Ft. Wayne, Mich., at which two of our Lutheran chaplains were in attendance. He was privileged to give a lecture to the chaplains attending the school.

The regular chaplains and Reserve Corps' chaplains are constantly seeking Army and Navy Service Books for use in their work. The supply of these books has now been practically exhausted so that we have been unable to comply with their requests.

We have comparatively few congregations near regular posts of the Army and Navy. Our pastors, however, have been very ready often to make rather long trips so that they may render a particular service to our Lutheran men in the Army and Navy.

Report of the Treasurer

Receipts from Mr. E. C. Miller, Treasurer..........		$4,500.00
Disbursements		
Rev. H. M. Leech, San Francisco...............	$1,500.00	
Rev. T. G. Hartwig, Brooklyn..................	1,500.00	
Mr. C. H. Boyer, for Rev. J. A. St. Clair, Chicago	1,500.00	
	$4,500.00	$4,500.00

Wm. Freas, *Treasurer.*

Recommendation. The Committee presents the following recommendation:

Resolved, That the United Lutheran Church in America records its earnest conviction that more adequate provision should be made by our Government for the spiritual care of our men in the Army and Navy of the country.

To this end we most respectfully urge that the bill now before the Military Affairs Committees of the Senate and House of Representatives, providing for the increase of the number of Chaplains and the placing of the Chaplain Corps upon an equality in rank with the other service corps of the Army and Navy, be reported favorably to their respective bodies.

Respectfully submitted,

C. D. TREXLER, *Chairman,*

WM. FREAS, *Secretary.*

Upon request permission was granted the Committee to withdraw the resolution containing a request for an appropriation, and to submit the following resolution as a part of the report:

Resolved, That the United Lutheran Church in America records its earnest conviction that more adequate provision should be made by our Government for the spiritual care of our men in the Army and Navy of the country.

"To this end we most respectfully urge that the bill now before the Military Affairs Committees of the Senate and House of Representatives, providing for the increase of the number of Chaplains and the placing of the Chaplain Corps upon an equality in rank with the other service corps of the Army and Navy, be reported favorably to their respective bodies."

The resolution was adopted.

The report was adopted as a whole.

The Rev. F. H. Bosch presented the report of the Committee on Linguistic Interests.

REPORT OF THE COMMITTEE ON LINGUISTIC INTERESTS

The Committee as appointed by the president of the United Lutheran Church elected the Rev. E. C. J. Kraeling, of Brooklyn, N. Y., as chairman and Rev. Fritz O. Evers, of Philadelphia, Pa., as secretary. The Committee was charged with the arrangements for the holding of the third General German Conference of the United Lutheran Church. The Conference convened for a two days' session in Zion Lutheran Church, Johnstown, Pa., the Revs. Ernst A. Tappert, D.D., and Wilfried Tappert, pastors, on October 17th and 18th, 1923. It was attended by more than one hundred pastors and lay delegates from all sections of the Church. The five German synods and three synodical German Conferences within the United Lutheran Church, representing more than 500 congregations, were well represented.

The Conference began with the full morning service and the celebration of the Holy Communion. The Conference sermon was preached by Pastor Otto Kleine, of Philadelphia, Pa. It was a remarkable, frank and loyal call to the peculiar field of labor within the United Lutheran Church which is committed to its large German section. It was published in the *Lutherischer Herold* and also appeared in translation in *The Lutheran*.

The Conference organized for the transaction of business by the election of Rev. E. C. J. Kraeling, of Brooklyn, N. Y., as president; Rev. G. H. Michelman, of Grand Island, Nebr., as vice-president; Rev. H. Arend Kropp, of New York, as secretary; Mr. A. Bendel, of Reading, Pa., as treasurer.

There are three seminaries and two colleges in the United Lutheran Church where men are being especially trained with the bilingual ministry in view. Waterloo Seminary at Waterloo, Ontario, Canada; Martin Luther Seminary at Lincoln, Nebraska; Wagner College on Staten Island, New York; Saskatoon College at Saskatoon, Sask., and the Kropp-Breklum institution in Germany constitute the educational forces of the Church for this particular field of service. Reports were given on all these institutions. The Conference expressed the desire for some practical means to be discovered whereby gifted men could be won from the ranks of German theological students in universities for the ministry in this country. Such eminent leaders as Dr. Moldenke, Dr. Mann and Dr. Spaeth came from these sources. Emphasis was laid upon the necessity of stressing the study of the language of Martin Luther in all the educational institutions of the Church.

The German official organ of the United Lutheran Church, *Lutherischer Herold,* had been ably edited during its first year of publication by the Rev. Ernst E. Ortlepp, D.D., of Greenville, Ohio. Since Dr. Ortlepp could not arrange to change his residence to Philadelphia the Conference unanimously nominated as his successor the Rev. C. Reinhold Tappert, of New Rochelle, N. Y. He was subsequently elected by the Church Paper Committee and entered upon his duties May 1, 1924. The editorial committee is to consist of the presidents of the German synods and conferences. A smaller committee of three located as near to the seat of publication as possible shall keep in close touch with the editor. Greetings were sent to the sickbed of the editor of the former *Deutsche Lutheraner,* Pastor Gottlieb C. Berkemeier, D.D. He has since been called to his heavenly reward. As a fluent writer, a fascinating speaker and a pioneer in Inner Missions he had been an outstanding personality in the Church for more than thirty years. He served as German secretary of the General Council and was closely connected with every one of the many interests of the German part of the Church.

The Home Mission work of the Canada, Wartburg, Nebraska, Manitoba and Texas Synods is carried on under the direction of the Board of Northwestern Missions. General Secretary Rev. Paul Ludwig gave an instructive review of the field and was followed by representatives from every one of these mission territories. The Conference voiced hearty endorsement of the work of this Board and also its regret that the Church does not supply sufficient funds to meet all the needs and to grasp all the opportunities of this important work.

A committee appointed at the former conference at Buffalo for revision of the present Agenda of the Kirchenbuch, so as to enable all the German bodies to use one uniform order of service throughout the Church, submitted a very promising report. This work will be done in conjunction with the Committee on Common Service.

The editing of suitable lesson material to be used in the Sunday schools was committed to a special committee, which is to cooperate with the Board of Publication and the Parish and Church School Board.

This Conference was honored by the presence of the president and the treasurer of the United Lutheran Church and the Executive Director of The National Lutheran Council. Dr. Morehead's appeal, ably supported by a most illuminating report by Dr. J. Neve, a delegate to the Eisenach World Conference, was answered by a solemn pledge of the largest possible support of the efforts to alleviate the sufferings of our Lutheran brethren abroad.

In conclusion we wish to call the attention of the Church to the large influx of Lutheran immigration from Germany and German-speaking parts of other countries. Their number is already being felt in all our congregations, especially in the cities. It will increasingly become the duty of the United Lutheran Church to strengthen this arm of her body in order to provide amply, timely and safely for the souls of these new-comers to our shores. For them, in the near future, as in other periods of her history, the Church must educate a German-speaking ministry, publish devotional literature and a representative church paper, and enlarge her missionary activities. The United Lutheran Church of a generation hence will reap abundantly where we are sowing the seed today.

Respectfully submitted,

E. C. J. KRAELING, *Chairman,*
F. O. EVERS, *Secretary.*

The report was adopted.

The Secretary presented the report of the Committee on Transportation, which was adopted.

REPORT OF COMMITTEE ON TRANSPORTATION

As shown in the report of the Executive Board, the Transportation Committee has given attention, throughout the biennium, to the interests committed to it. The Committee would report the additional information that arrangements were made with all of the Passenger Associations in the United States and Canada for reduced rates on the Certificate Plan for members of the United Lutheran Church attending this Convention. A special train was run over the Pennsylvania Railroad from Washington, D. C., to Chicago, via Harrisburg and Pittsburgh, and arrangements have been made for a Special for the return journey. For this special service all the credit is due to Mr. Harvey C. Miller, Chairman of your Committee.

M. G. G. SCHERER, *Secretary of the Committee.*

The following was adopted:

Resolved, That we express to the railroad companies our appreciation of the facilities provided, and to Mr. Harvey C. Miller our appreciation of his valuable services in this matter.

In the absence of Dr. Alleman, the Secretary presented the report of our representative to the American Bible Society.

REPORT OF REPRESENTATIVE IN THE ADVISORY BOARD OF THE AMERICAN BIBLE SOCIETY

Your representative in the Advisory Board of the American Bible Society begs leave to submit his third biennial report.

The Advisory Board is composed of representatives from twenty-three of the churches in the United States. It meets annually in the month of November at the Bible House, Astor Place, New York City, to consider the recommendations of the Secretaries and the Treasurer of the Society and to submit its findings to the Board of Managers, with whom it is invited to sit throughout their consideration. Your representative was unable to be present at the meetings during the past biennium, but his place was taken by Secretary Scherer, who reported the same cordial welcome which has always been accorded your representative.

An idea of the progress and fortunes of the Society's work during the biennium can best be arrived at by taking the report of 1923 in comparison with that of the preceding year.

The outstanding event in the fortunes of the Society in 1923 was the earthquake in Japan on September 1st, in which the Society's offices in Tokio and the printing plant of the Fukuin Printing Company in Yokohama were totally destroyed. All the Society's plates, not only in the various forms of the Japanese Bible, but of certain editions for China, of a larger number of editions for Siam, and in all the languages and forms of printing for the Philippines were deposited there, so that in a moment there was nothing left but molten metal of the type and plates from which the Scriptures for the Society's work in all the Far East, with the exception of most of its editions in China, were produced. The monetary loss alone exceeded $200,000.00.

Furthermore, the Society's work was hindered by political conditions in Latin America and in the Near and Far East.

In spite of disasters and hindrances, however, a very unusual distribution was accomplished. The issues from the Bible House in New York for circulation in the United States and in Latin America for the year 1923 were 3,154,632, which is 1,321,926 more than in 1922, the circulation in the United States through its Home Agencies and its Auxiliaries and affiliated Societies reaching 2,104,000 volumes as against 1,117,000 in 1922. The largest circulation outside of the United States is the Society's circulation in China, which last year amounted to 2,525,017, an advance of 537,691 over the preceding year. Even in Japan, in spite of the earthquake, 343,588 volumes were circulated, an advance of 134,254 over the preceding year.

The total number of books issued in 1923 was 7,097,950, as against 4,593,067 in 1922. The issues for 1923 are the largest in the history of the Society, with the exception of the centennial year 1916, which is evidence of the abiding popularity of the Bible as the world's best seller and of the energy and efficiency of the management of this great enterprise. The total issues of the Society in the 108 years of its service have been 158,254,877.

Financially the Society has enjoyed an unusually prosperous year, judging from its balance-sheet. The total receipts were $1,804,282.14 with expenditures approximately the same, including the paying off of an indebtedness in the banks of $585,000.00. However, the receipts include a legacy of $549,242.18 from the Sage Estate, an embarrassment of riches in the stability of the Society's budget.

The amount contributed by the churches of the United States in 1923 was $278,574.00, the Methodist Episcopal Church being the largest contributor with $100,000.00. The amount contributed by the Lutheran Church of all branches was $1,826.00. Of that total the Augustana Synod contributed $1,153.00 and the United Lutheran Church $573.00.

For the $200,000.00 loss caused by the earthquake in Japan the Society made an appeal for special contributions. Up to March 1st only $80,000 had been secured. Of that amount $203.94 came from the United Lutheran Church.

It gives your representative great pleasure to report that Dr. E. Clarence Miller, Treasurer of the United Lutheran Church, has been made a Vice-President of the Society.

Your representative recommends:

That the United Lutheran Church continue its representation in the Advisory Board.

Respectfully submitted,

HERBERT C. ALLEMAN,

Representative of the United Lutheran Church.

Dr. Kirkbride, of the American Bible Society, was then introduced, and addressed the Convention.

The recommendation was adopted.

The report was adopted as a whole.

The Rev. A. R. Wentz presented the Minutes of the Lutheran Historical Society as follows:

Lutheran Historical Society

The Historical Society of the Evangelical Lutheran Church in America was called to order at 4.30 o'clock, Tuesday afternoon, October 21, 1924, in Holy Trinity Lutheran Church, Chicago, Illinois. President F. P. Manhart presided.

Dr. H. D. Hoover was appointed Secretary pro tempore.

Dr. A. R. Wentz submitted the report of the Curator as follows:

Nearly three hundred bound volumes have been added to our collection since our last meeting in 1922. These are mostly synodical minutes, Lutheran periodicals and classified pamphlets of Lutheran import.

The Curator now has a complete list of the great number of duplicates in our possession. These duplicates he has been offering in exchange for desirable materials that we lack. In this way much progress has been made towards filling out our files of minutes and periodicals.

Work is now in progress organizing our large collection of Lutheran photographs in order to make them readily accessible.

For the sake of our records it should be reported here that the paper read by Miss Mary E. Markley at the last meeting of the Society on the subject, "Some Chapters on the History of Higher Education of Lutheran Women" was published in the Lutheran quarterly for January, 1923.

The collection of the Society, on the first floor of the Seminary Library at Gettysburg, has been used by scores of persons during the biennium. The work of the Society, now eighty-one years old, is proving its usefulness to the Church in increasing measure each year. From widely distant points and from greatly varied circles, both within and outside the Lutheran Church, inquiries come for information and requests for historical materials concerning the history of our Church in this country.

ABDEL ROSS WENTZ, *Curator.*

The report was adopted.

The report of the Treasurer, Mr. J. Elmer Musselman, was presented together with the report of the Auditing Committee. Both reports were adopted. The report of the Treasurer showed a balance of $306.53.

On motion of Dr. A. Pohlman, the Secretary was instructed to cast the ballot of the Society for the re-election of all the officers.

The minutes were read and approved, and the Society adjourned.

An informal meeting of the Society was held at the Edgewater Beach Hotel, Chicago, on Monday evening, October 27, 1924. Dr. Manhart presented a paper on "Lutherans and Bishops," which was thoroughly discussed.   H. D. HOOVER, Secretary pro tem.

It was moved and carried, That this report be printed in the Minutes of this Convention.

The Rev. G. C. Rees presented the report of the Lutheran Church Book and Literature Society.

REPORT OF THE LUTHERAN CHURCH BOOK AND LITERATURE SOCIETY

This Society occupies a unique and distinctive place in the life of the Church. Its object is the distribution of the Common Service Book and the dissemination of other Lutheran literature, whatever the language or wherever the field. Though this Society is twenty years old, the Church has not been fully aware of its usefulness. All the other religious bodies of the country engage in the systematic distribution of their distinctive literature. The Bishop White Prayer Book Society of the Episcopal Church has an endowment fund of $100,000.00. It has distributed about 1,000,000 prayer books and hymnals printed in many languages. In 1923, it distributed 17,001 books. The New York Bible and Common Prayer Book Society, also of the Episcopal Church, distributed in 1923, 14,000 hymnals and 26,238 prayer books, printed in the English, German, Swedish, Spanish and Indian languages. It has also published portions of the Prayer Book for the use of the blind. The figures of other bodies, notably the Christian Scientists, the Swedenborgians, and the Church of Latter Day Saints, are not at hand, but the amounts expended must be enormous.

The good which this Society has been permitted to do with its limited income is very creditable. With the exception of two years its income has never been over $600 a year, but even with that there have been furnished to institutions and needy missions in the United States, Canada, and the West Indies, more than 4,200 copies of the Common Service Book, and more than 2,000 copies of the Sunday School Hymnals. There have been given to the Free Libraries in New York, Brooklyn, Philadelphia, Milwaukee, and other cities over 500 annual subscriptions to The Lutheran. The Society has also issued nine tracts, some of which have been translated into Spanish. Those tracts have now reached a confirmed circulation of over 1,000,000 copies. They can be secured through the Publication House at a nominal cost.

During the past two years, the Society has furnished 811 copies of the Common Service Book and 363 Sunday School Hymnals to new mission stations.

To illustrate the work of the Society it should be stated that not only does the Society take care of new mission undertakings, but when the head of the theological department of a very large Western University requested an exhibit of Lutheran books setting forth the doctrine, history and life of the Lutheran Church, this Society furnished him with the authorized literature of the Church. It is also a matter of interest to know that when the Government Chapel in Yellowstone Park was offered to a pastor of our Church for weekly services, with an attendance of from 400 to 600, this Society furnished the Common Service Books for their use.

However, the Society has only made a beginning of the large work for which it was founded. There are many places to which the Common Service Book can be donated. Since it contains the Epistles and Gospels its value has been very much enhanced, and if the Society had the income these books could be furnished not only to needy missions but also to many different kinds of institutions, to hotels, ocean liners, particularly those under the Scandinavian flag, etc., etc.

The Society would call attention to the fact that it is an incorporated body and as such may receive gifts and legacies. Such are solicited. The beginning of an endowment fund has been made.

The Society would request that each parish of the United Lutheran Church make an annual donation of $5.00 at least, thus recognizing in a practical way the valuable work which the Society is carrying on.

The present officers and Board of Managers are:

Rev. Arthur C. Carty, President *pro tem*, 256 Farragut Terrace, Philadelphia, Pa.

(Vacant), Vice-President.

Rev. Joseph A. Schantz, Corresponding Secretary, Twentieth and Race Streets, Philadelphia, Pa.

Mr. M. L. Holloway, Recording Secretary, Muhlenberg Building, Philadelphia, Pa.

Mr. C. F. Hassold, Treasurer, 410 Chestnut Street, Philadelphia, Pa.

Board of Managers

Rev. W. L. Hunton, D.D.
Rev. G. W. Sandt, D.D.
Rev. Luther D. Reed, D.D.
Rev. Geo. H. Trabert, D.D.

Rev. P. Z. Strodach, D.D.
Rev. H. Moehling
Carl F. R. Hassold
H. G. Querns

Harry Hodges
William Benbow
Oscar C. Schmidt
Dr. George F. Hayunga
Rev. A. C. Carty
Rev. F. H. Knubel, D.D., LL.D.
Rev. John C. Mattes
Rev. J. S. Schantz

Rev. William Freas
Rev. W. D. C. Keiter, D.D.
E. Clarence Miller
George C. Baum
Charles A. Smith
Howard W. Lewis
L. W. Steeble
M. L. Holloway

Respectfully submitted,

ARTHUR C. CARTY.

It was moved and carried, That this be printed in the Minutes of this Convention.

The Rev. A. J. Traver presented the Report of the Committee on Leave of Absence:

REPORT OF THE COMMITTEE ON LEAVE OF ABSENCE

Your Committee would beg leave to report that the following delegations have made report of absentees through their Chairmen: The Iowa Synod, the North Carolina Synod, the Indiana Synod, the California Synod, the New York Synod, the Pittsburgh Synod, the Michigan Synod, the Synod of the Northwest, the German Nebraska Synod, the Wartburg Synod, and the East Pennsylvania Synod.

Upon recommendation of the Chairmen of these delegations we would respectfully recommend that the following be excused for absence as reported to the Committee:

Rev. C. N. Swihart, Rev. S. M. Lesher, Rev. Holmes Dysinger, Mr. J. S. Sawyer, Mr. L. D. Koser and Mr. J. L. Berger, from the Iowa Synod.

Hon. B. B. Miller, from the North Carolina Synod.

Rev. I. W. Gernert, Mr. A. H. Kornfeld, Mr. J. E. Spiegel and Mr. M. L. Zerkel, from the Indiana Synod.

Hon. E. F. Eilert and Mr. A. J. Gruschow, from the New York Synod.

Hon. W. E. Hirt, Mr. C. L. Herbster, Hon. J. F. Graff, Mr. Peter Graff, Hon. A. E. Reiber, Dr. C. E. Miller, Dr. H. C. Hoffman, Rev. G. A. Benze, Mr. E. R. Sheldon, Rev. John I. Shaud, Prof. O. F. H. Bert, Mr. Wm. E. Yeager and Mr. J. L. Frederick, from the Pittsburgh Synod.

Mr. C. E. Baker, Dr. H. G. Merz, Dr. B. F. Teters and Mr. W. W. Anderson, from the Michigan Synod.

Mr. C. N. Hill, Rev. W. P. Christy, Rev. P. H. Roth, Rev. A. J. Soldan, Rev. L. W. Steckel, Mr. W. E. Black, Mr. J. W. Jouno and Mr. G. Hemsing, from the Synod of the Northwest.

Rev. C. Goede, Rev. O. Hausman, Rev. G. H. Michelmann, Mr. G. F. Beschorner, Mr. G. Hilzen, Mr. John Rohrig, Mr. Carl Goll and Mr. H. Busselman, from the German Nebraska Synod.

Rev. E. Ortlepp, Mr. Hermann Oertel and Mr. Charles Scholz, from the Wartburg Synod.

Rev. Ross H. Stover, Mr. George C. Baum, Mr. H. C. Smeltzer, Rev. William J. Miller, Jr., Rev. William C. Ney, Mr. E. G. Hoover, Mr. J. H. Wagner, Mr. Harvey C. Miller, Mr. Romanus Esterly, from the East Pennsylvania Synod.

The California Synod reported every member present at every session.

Your Committee would recommend that the method used at this Convention be continued, namely, that the Chairmen of Synodical Delegations shall be responsible for keeping the roll of their delegations and shall return a report of absentees to the Committee on Leave of Absence.

Respectfully submitted,

A. J. Traver, *Chairman.*
For the Committee.

The recommendation was adopted.

The report was adopted as a whole.

In connection with the foregoing report it was stated that in place of delegates excused, alternates had been seated as follows:

The Rev. J. Earl Spaid, of the Indiana Synod, in the place of the Rev. R. H. Benting from Saturday, October 25th to October 29th.

The Rev. S. W. Herman, of the East Pennsylvania Synod, in the place of the Rev. Ross H. Stover, October 28th and 29th.

The Secretary read the amendment proposed to the By-Laws, Section VII, B, yesterday afternoon by the Committee of Reference and Counsel.

The amendment was adopted.

Under the head of unfinished business the Secretary presented several items of the report of the Executive Board.

Item III, A, 3 (a) was adopted.

Item III, A, 5 was amended by striking out the last line of the first paragraph. The item was adopted.

Item XIII, 4, was adopted.

The Secretary presented Item 5 of the Supplementary Report of the Executive Board.

SUPPLEMENTARY REPORT OF THE EXECUTIVE BOARD

1. Subsequent to the action of the Executive Board as reported under III, B, 3 of the general report, the following communication was received from the Secretary of the Pacific Synod:

"To the Executive Board of the United Lutheran Church in America:

"Be it resolved, That it is the conviction of the Pacific Synod that the resolutions adopted by the United Lutheran Church at its Convention held at Washington do not fulfill the obligations of the United Lutheran Church entered into with the Pacific Seminary, as set forth in the resolutions passed by the Executive Board at its meeting held in New York City.

"Executive Committee of the Pacific Synod,
"W. I. Eck, *Secretary."*

Thereupon the Executive Board took the following action:

Being still of the conviction that the Executive Board has carried out the instructions of the United Lutheran Church given it at the New York Convention as follows:

"Whereas, The United Lutheran Church in America has heard with gratification of the plans, purposes and desires of the Board of Directors of the Pacific Theological Seminary at Seattle, and of the Pacific and California Synods with reference to their co-operation in that institution; and

"Whereas, We are convinced that the amount asked for endowment and equipment should be supplied as speedily as possible to enable the institution to furnish an adequate and efficient ministry for the present and increasing needs in that far Western section, and in the farther East; therefore, be it

"Resolved, That the matter of ways and means for the securing of such funds be referred to the Executive Board of the United Lutheran Church—,"

We report the action of the Pacific Synod as above stated.

2. The following statement concerning conditions upon which the United Lutheran Church might participate in the World Conference on Faith and Order was approved by the Executive Board:

The Executive Board would call attention in the first place to the Statement approved by the Buffalo Convention (Min. pp. 88-90), especially to the considerations there advanced as counting for and against our taking part in the World Conference on Faith and Order. The facts and considerations there stated remain unchanged by anything that has occurred, and they should be carefully weighed before final action is taken.

The Literature of the World Conference on Faith and Order thus far issued, seems to us to give full assurance that it is to be truly a Free Conference. Upon this understanding the Executive Board is of the opinion that we may participate in the Conference provided:

(1) That our representatives may and shall present in love, yet with all frankness, the view of the Lutheran Church on any and all points that may come under discussion,* and specifically

(2) That our representatives may and shall submit for consideration, at the proper time, the whole or any part of the Doctrinal Basis of the United Lutheran Church in America, and also that there shall be accorded a courteous and respectful hearing to their presentation of the doctrines and principles set forth in the Confessions of the Evangelical Lutheran Church. (See Declaration of Principles adopted at Washington, Section C, IV.)

(3) That our representatives shall not take any action involving inconsistency either with our Doctrinal Basis or with any covenanted obligations of the United Lutheran Church to other Lutheran bodies in this country or throughout the world.

(4) That the United Lutheran Church is ready to provide for an annual appropriation toward the expenses of the Conference and also to pay the expenses of its representatives.

We recommend that if the Convention approves this judgment of the Executive Board and desires representation, it instruct the Executive Board to provide for such representation in this Conference.

3. The following statement of conditions upon which the United Lutheran Church might take part in the Universal Conference on Life and Work was also approved with the same recommendation as made concerning participation in the World Conference on Faith and Order:

As regards the Universal Christian Conference on Life and Work, attention is first called to the statement concerning it in the minutes of the Buffalo Convention, pp. 90-92. In addition we believe it desirable to note that although the Conference declares it will not discuss questions of faith, it does desire to know the "mind of Christ" upon the various social, economic, international, and educational problems to be considered. It would seem that any consideration of the mind of Christ must involve a consideration of those things which enter into our Christian faith. Likewise the opening theme for discussion, "The Church's Obligation in View of

---

*This statement is all the more necessary in view of the following paragraph from Subjects Committee Papers, September, 1923, p. 7:

"Statements of the existing opinions of the different Churches should not be asked for as part of the programme of the Conference, but the Delegates would, of course, speak from the point of view of the Churches which they represented."

God's Purpose for the World," can scarcely be considered without reference to questions of faith.

As a second additional item of information it is to be noted that the final subject on the program is "Methods of Co-operative and Federative Efforts by the Christian Communions." In this connection we ought to recognize that there is a manifest desire on the part of some who are leading in this Conference to bring into existence, as a result of the Conference, some form of international, co-operative Christian committee or other organization for further activity. Further in this connection, it should be noted that the membership of the committees of arrangement consist largely of Church leaders and not of special students of the problems to be considered; it is probable that those who attend the Conference will belong more largely to the first class just mentioned than to the second.

As over against these two additional items it is desirable to remember that no action of the Conference will "be binding upon communions without their explicit consent"; "the resolutions passed by the Conference do not commit any Christian communion before being endorsed by that communion."

Viewing the matter as a whole we believe the United Lutheran Church might take part in the Conference under the following conditions:

(1) Certain circulars from the American Committee of Arrangements have included this statement: "It is clearly understood that the Conference will not in any way affect denominational autonomy either in organization, doctrine or administration, and that no ecclesiastical body will be compromised in its distinctive position by participating in the Conference. It is to be a free Conference for mutual benefit; a Conference only." None of the three official announcements from the International Committee has included such a statement. Unofficially it was made known to the officials of the American Committee that some such statement would be desired by the United Lutheran Church. We recommend the adoption by the Chicago Convention of this condition as a basic necessity for participation by the United Lutheran Church. This would seem to be all the more necessary because the Conference has been divided into geographical, not confessional groups and because the Conference would avoid confessional statements. The condition named above amounts practically to a declaration by those who are planning the Conference that no effort will be made to gloss over the fact that confessional differences exist and that the Conference will not be proclaimed as a manifestation of Christian Unity. For Lutherans Christian unity is primarily oneness in faith and its confession.

(2) That our representatives shall be guided by our Declaration of Principles adopted at Washington, especially Section D, concerning Co-

operative Movements Among the Protestant Churches, and that they shall not assume any attitude or take any action inconsistent therewith.

(3) That the United Lutheran Church will authorize the appointment of four representatives chosen especially in view of their fitness to discuss the problems which will come before the Conference.

(4) That the United Lutheran Church will pay the expenses of these representatives.

4. The Executive Board authorized a further advance (see General Report X, C, 4) of $300 on behalf of the United Lutheran Church toward a budget for the Executive Committee of the Lutheran World Convention.

5. A. At the request of the Board two papers were prepared and submitted to the Executive Board by the Revs. J. A. Clutz, A. G. Voigt, J. A. Morehead, E. C. J. Kraeling and Dr. E. C. Miller, one entitled "A Declaration on the Work of American Protestant Churches in Europe," and the other entitled, "Concerning the Roman Catholic Forward Movement." Paragraph 1 of the first of these papers, with the recommendation contained therein, is presented to the Convention for adoption as follows:

A Declaration on the Work of American Protestant Churches in Europe

"The condition of the Lutheran churches in the countries of Europe still claims the serious concern of Lutherans in America. It is true that great progress has been made in the establishment of a new order out of the dislocations and confusion caused by the World War. The work of reorganization has, for the most part, been successfully accomplished, at least so far as to meet present conditions. The latest instance of such a happy consummation is the recent organization of the first synod of Lutheran churches in Russia. But there is still much to be done for the reconstruction and upbuilding of institutions to meet the demands of a new order of things. The poverty of the churches, the lack of education of congregations in self-support, the insufficiency of ministers and in some places the lack of schools to educate them, these and other weaknesses constitute a strong plea to the Lutherans in America to continue the generous aid which, for several years, they have been extending to their sister churches in Europe to help them to become able to help themselves. Recognizing this claim upon our brotherly love, this Convention of the United Lutheran Church in America heartily reaffirms its purpose to co-operate with other Lutherans the world over, through the National Lutheran Council and the Lutheran World Convention Committee, our own established agencies, in lending further assistance to the Lutheran Churches in Europe to attain to self-support and self-sufficiency for the great work resting upon them."

The Executive Board asks permission of the Convention to withhold the remainder of this declaration for further consideration with the understanding that the Board, in the spirit of Christian courtesy and brotherly love, may take such action in the matter as conditions demand and report its action to the next Convention.

B. The Executive Board recommends the adoption of the following paper "concerning the Roman Catholic Forward Movement."

Concerning the Roman Catholic Forward Movement

"It must be patent to all observers that the Roman Catholic Church has most skillfully and vigorously availed itself of the unsettling turmoil caused by the World War and the reconstruction of Europe that followed, to advance its interests, to strengthen its organization, and to institute a general forward movement looking to large conquests. Characteristically of the Roman Church, it has been making full use of its great political power not only in the nations of Europe but throughout the world for its own ends. Protestantism cannot stand idly by and allow Roman Catholic aggression to have free sweep, lest it lose all that was gained in the Reformation of the sixteenth century. It must gird itself to resist this aggression and defend itself against this well-organized and world-wide propaganda. The Lutheran Church in particular has an urgent duty to perform in European countries in protecting itself against losses of property and members by Roman Catholic intrusion.

We therefore recommend that this Convention of the United Lutheran Church in America earnestly request and urge the Executive Committee of the Lutheran World Convention, at the earliest possible date, to take up the present Roman Catholic forward movement for careful study and for such action as in its judgment will conserve the interests of Lutheranism and of Protestantism in general against it."

6. A conference was held with the Executive Committee of the Board of Foreign Missions in regard to the relation of that Board to the question of the sphere of operation of the Board of Foreign Missions as affected by the proposal that the new Board of Home Missions be given the entire Western Hemisphere as its sphere of operations. The Board of Foreign Missions having taken action adverse to the proposed distribution of spheres of operations, the Executive Board adopted the following recommendations which are herewith submitted:

"That the entire matter involving South America be left undecided until the Proposed Home Mission Board, if approved, becomes an established fact.

"Secondly, That at that time the question of South America be referred to this Home Mission Board and the Board of Foreign Missions for joint consideration under the direction of the Executive Board."

7. Dr. Gotwald, Executive Secretary of the Board of Education, informed the Executive Board that plans have been consummated for edu-

cational co-operation with the Icelandic Synod in the support of their institution at Winnipeg, Canada. The Board of Education desires to appropriate $2,000 a year for their budget. The Executive Board approves this proposition and so recommends to the Convention.

Item 5, A. Adopted.

Item 5, B. Adopted.

Item 7 was adopted.

(For actions on other items of Supplementary Report, see Index, Executive Board, Actions on Report of.—Secy.)

The report of the Executive Board, including the supplementary report, was adopted as a whole.

The Convention resumed consideration of the report of the Committee on Memorials from Constituent Synods.

The answer (XI) to the memorial of the New York and New England Synod concerning literature for the weekday religious schools, etc., was approved.

The answer (XII) in regard to the time for conventions of the United Lutheran Church was adopted.

The answer (XIII) to the memorial of the Wartburg Synod concerning frequency of meetings was adopted.

The report of the Committee on Memorials was adopted as a whole.

Dr. E. Clarence Miller presented the report of the Finance Committee of the Executive Board:

There have been referred to the Finance Committee of the Executive Board the requests for appropriations for the Luther League, the Committee on Army and Navy Work, the Committee on Necrology, and the Committee on Publicity.

We would recommend:

First, That the Executive Board be authorized to pay $5,000 per annum for the apportionment years of 1926 and 1927 out of the United Lutheran Church treasury to the Luther League of America.

Second, That the other requests be referred to the Executive Board for their consideration and action.

The report was adopted as a whole.

The Chairman of the Committee of Reference and Counsel presented the following suggestions in regard to the next Convention:

Resolved, That we present to the officers for consideration in connection with the preparation of the program for the next convention the following suggestions:

1. That one evening session toward the close of the convention be set aside as a business session, for the consideration of such unfinished business as may seem to require special discussion.

2. That the report of the Committee on Memorials from Synods be set early in the convention, in order that the memorials may come promptly before the delegates and when desirable be referred to Boards, Committees or Synodical delegations concerned.

The suggestions were approved.

The Chairman of the Committee then presented the Rev. Richard Kuehne, D.D., of Lincoln, Nebraska, who addressed the Convention on the relief work in Germany.

The approval of the Minutes of the last session of this Convention, Wednesday, October 29th, was referred to the Executive Board.

The Executive Board was authorized to provide for the printing of the Minutes of this Convention.

On motion to adjourn, the order for the Closing of Synods was used, and the President declared the Convention adjourned.

Adjourned at 1: 30 P. M.

M. G. G. SCHERER, *Secretary.*

OTHER MEETINGS

HOME MISSION DINNER AND CONFERENCE

An inspiring Home Mission Conference, in connection with a dinner given to the students of the various seminaries, was held at Unity Church, Wednesday evening, October 22, 1924. One hundred and sixty attended as follows:

Board Members	16
Women's Missionary Society	2
Secretaries and Superintendents	6
Synodical Superintendents and Field Missionaries	16
Missionary Pastors	47
Students	75

Dr. Seibert, General Secretary, presided. The following was the program:

THEME: HOME MISSIONS

Invocation	Rev. J. C. Seegers, D.D.
The Challenge	Rev. H. B. Stock, D.D.
The Opportunities	District Superintendents
The Sacrifice Demanded	..Rev. J. E. Bittle, D.D.
The Joy Experienced	Rev. F. M. Hanes
The Recruits	Pres. S. J. Derrick

The Seminarians' Response—

(Responses were given by representatives of Mount Airy, Gettysburg, Susquehanna, Hamma Divinity, Western and Chicago Seminaries.)

Addresses—

Miss Amelia Kemp, Ex-Secy., W. M. S.; Rev. A. Stewart Hartman, D.D. America.

Prayer and Benediction..Rev. S. J. McDowell, D.D.

THE LUTHERAN BROTHERHOOD

The Lutheran Brotherhood held its eighth convention in Chicago, Illinois, October 20-21, 1924. The program and business sessions were held in the Edgewater Beach Hotel, Monday afternoon and all day Tuesday, Mr. C. J. Driever presiding. The addresses, discussions and conferences on various phases of men's work, as related to the Church, were of such character as to give abundant assurance that the men of the United Lutheran Church in America are thoroughly awake to its great and varied interests and can be depended upon for loyal support in all its plans. The banquet on Monday evening, by far the largest in the history of the Brotherhood, was memorable, not only for attendance and enthusiasm, but for the ability and spirit of the various addresses. The prayer was by Dr. J. E. Whitteker, of the Evangelical Lutheran Seminary at Maywood, Ill. The Welcome to Chicago was by Mr. C. J. Driever, and the Response by Mr. E. F. Eilert, of New York. The Toastmaster was Hon. John L. Zimmerman. The speakers and their subjects were:

"Brotherhood Retrospect and Prospect," H. T. Domer, Esq.
"The Lutheran Church and World Evangelism," Dr. H. W. A. Hanson.
"The Message of the Lutheran Church Answering the World's Present-Day Needs," Dr. J. F. Krueger.
"Our Church and Our Country," George B. Cromer, Esq.

Dr. F. H. Knubel brought the greetings of the United Lutheran Church. The business sessions were all characterized by a purpose and readiness to go forward in the part men can take in the Church. The completion of the fund to build a Brotherhood dormitory for our Boys' School in Kumamoto, Japan, was announced and was followed by deciding on larger things for the future. The plan to raise $300,000 to found a Lutheran College in India in the coming biennium was adopted as the definite objective. Following this, in 1927-28, the Brotherhood objective will be the $3,000,000 endowment fund for the Ministerial Pension and Relief Fund.

The following officers were elected for the ensuing two years:

Mr. Charles J. Driever, Chicago, President.
Mr. George M. Jones, Reading, Pa., Vice-President.
Mr. A. F. Sittloh, Denver, Colo., Vice-President.
Mr. William B. Ahlgren, Atlanta, Ga., Vice-President.
Mr. A. H. Homrighaus, Chicago, Recording Secretary.
Mr. C. W. Howe, Chicago, Treasurer.

The Executive Committee remains the same as in the preceding biennium, with Dr. S. S. Waltz as Executive Secretary.

LIST OF BOARDS AND ELECTIVE COMMITTEES

1. Executive Board.
2. Commission of Adjudication.
3. Board of Foreign Missions.
4. Board of Home Missions and Church Extension.
5. Board of Northwestern Missions.
6. Immigrants Mission Board.

7. West Indies Mission Board.
8. Committee on Jewish Missions.
9. Board of Education.
10. Inner Mission Board.
11. Board of Publication.
12. Board of Ministerial Pensions and Relief.
13. Parish and Church-School Board.
14. Board of Deaconess Work.
15. National Lutheran Home for the Aged.
16. Committee on Church Papers.
17. Executive Committee of the Laymen's Movement.

LIST OF STANDING COMMITTEES, COMMISSIONS, ETC.

1. Statistical and Church Year Book Committee.
2. Committee on Common Service Book.
3. Committee on Church Music.
4. Committee on German Interests.
5. Committee on Lutheran Brotherhoods.
6. Committee on Women's Work.
7. Committee on Associations of Young People.
8. Committee on Work Among Boys.
9. Committee on Army and Navy Work.
10. Committee on Moral and Social Welfare.
11. Committee on Evangelism.
12. Committee on Church Architecture.
13. Committee on Publicity.
14. Committee on Necrology.
15. Committee on Transportation.
16. Archivist.
17. Statistical Secretary.
18. Commissioners to the National Lutheran Council.
19. Representative on the Advisory Committee of the American Bible Society.
20. Consultative Representatives to Commissions of the Federal Council of the Churches.
21. Committee on Conference with Y. M. C. A.

SPECIAL COMMITTEES

1. Committee to conduct the opening and closing services of each session.
2. Committee on Leave of Absence.
3. Committee on Proceedings of District Synods.
4. Committee of Reference and Counsel.
5. Committee to Nominate Executive Committee of Laymen's Movement.
6. Committee to Nominate Members of Boards.
7. Committee to Nominate Members of Executive Board and all elective Commissions or Committees.
8. Committee of Tellers.

BOARDS AND ELECTIVE COMMITTEES
EXECUTIVE BOARD

President—Rev. F. H. Knubel, D.D., LL.D., 437 Fifth Avenue, New York City.

Secretary—Rev. M. G. G. Scherer, D.D., 437 Fifth Avenue, New York City.

Treasurer—E. Clarence Miller, LL.D., 410 Chestnut Street, Philadelphia, Pa.

Term Expires 1928

Rev. F. F. Fry, D.D.; Rev. W. D. C. Keiter, D.D.; Rev. A. R. Wentz, D.D., Ph.D.; Robbin B. Wolf, Esq.; George E. Neff, Esq.; Hon. John F. Kramer.

Term Expires 1926

Rev. E. B. Burgess, D.D.; Rev. W. H. Greever, D.D.; Rev. A. H. Smith, D.D.; Hon. C. M. Efird; Mr. William H. Hager; Mr. Frederick Henrich.

COMMISSION OF ADJUDICATION

President—Rev. H. E. Jacobs, D.D., LL.D., S.T.D., 7301 Germantown Avenue, Mt. Airy, Philadelphia, Pa.

Vice-President—Rev. A. G. Voigt, D.D., LL.D., Columbia, South Carolina.

Secretary—Rev. Holmes Dysinger, D.D., LL.D., 1643 N. Nye Avenue, Fremont, Nebr.

Clerk—Judge E. K. Strong, Columbia City, Ind.

Term Expires 1930

Rev. H. E. Jacobs, D.D., LL.D., S.T.D.; Rev. R. E. Tulloss, Ph.D., D.D.; Hon. H. W. Harter.

Term Expires 1928

Rev. L. A. Fox, D.D., LL.D.; Rev. John A. W. Haas, D.D., LL.D.; Hon. Aaron E. Reiber.

Term Expires 1926

Rev. A. G. Voigt, D.D., LL.D.; Rev. Holmes Dysinger, D.D., LL.D.; Hon. E. K. Strong.

BOARD OF FOREIGN MISSIONS

President—Rev. E. K. Bell, D.D., LL.D., 944 Harlem Avenue, Baltimore, Md.

Vice-President—Rev. C. T. Benze, D.D., 7304 Boyer Street, Mt. Airy, Philadelphia, Pa.

Recording Secretary—Rev. George Drach, D.D., 18 E. Mt. Vernon Place, Baltimore, Md.

Treasurer—Rev. L. B. Wolf, D.D., 18 E. Mt. Vernon Place, Baltimore, Md.

General Secretaries—Rev. L. B. Wolf, D.D., and Rev. George Drach, D.D.

Term Expires 1930

Rev. E. K. Bell, D.D., LL.D.; Rev. J. A. Singmaster, D.D., LL.D.; Rev. M. J. Epting, D.D.; Rev. R. C. G. Bielinski; Rev. C. T. Benze, D.D.; Mr. James M. Snyder; Prof. C. W. Foss.

Term Expires 1928

Rev. A. Steimle, D.D.; Rev. Jacob S. Simon, D.D.; Rev. Lewis C. Manges, D.D.; Rev. P. W. Koller, D.D.; Mr. H. L. Bonham; Mr. Mathias P. Moller; Paul Van Reed Miller, Esq.

Term Expires 1926

Rev. John Edward Byers, D.D.; Rev. George A. Greiss, D.D.; Rev. William E. Frey; Rev. J. Luther Sieber, D.D.; Mr. Wm. H. Menges; Mr. Martin H. Buehler; Mr. Augustus J. Herrlich.

Co-operating Members—Rev. Lars G. Abrahamson, D.D.; Rev. G. A. Brandelle, D.D.; Rev. V. W. Bondo; Rev. E. R. Anderson.

Advisory Members—Mrs. S. R. Kepner; Mrs. J. W. Richards.

BOARD OF HOME MISSIONS AND CHURCH EXTENSION

President—Rev. J. E. Whitteker, D.D., LL.D., Lutheran Theological Seminary, Maywood, Ill.

Vice-President—Rev. J. C. Seegers, D.D., 7301 Germantown Avenue, Philadelphia, Pa.

Recording Secretary—Rev. J. M. Bramkamp, D.D., 860 Cass Street, Chicago, Ill.

General Secretary—Rev. J. F. Seibert, D.D., 860 Cass Street, Chicago, Ill.

Treasurer—Mr. C. J. Driever, 860 Cass Street, Chicago, Ill.

Educational Secretary—Rev. A. Stewart Hartman, D.D., 914 N. Carrollton Avenue, Baltimore, Md.

District Superintendents—East: Rev. I. Chantry Hoffman, D.D., 1228 Spruce Street, Philadelphia, Pa. Central: Rev. J. S. Herold, D.D., 860 Cass Street, Chicago, Ill. South: Rev. A. D. R. Hancher, 1647 W. Grace Street, Richmond, Va. West: Rev. G. H. Hillerman, D.D., 2505 Woolsey Street, Berkeley, Calif.

Term Expires 1930

Rev. H. B. Stock, D.D.; Rev. J. M. Francis, D.D.; Rev. J. E. Whitteker, D.D., LL.D.; Rev. Charles J. Smith, D.D.; Mr. A. Raymond Bard; Prof. S. J. Derrick, LL.D.; Hon. John L. Zimmerman, LL.D.

Term Expires 1928

Rev. G. F. Gehr, D.D.; Rev. O. D. Baltzly, Ph.D., D.D., LL.D.; Rev. C. E. Gardner, D.D.; Rev. O. H. Gruver, D.D.; Mr. C. H. Boyer; Mr. C. J. Driever; Mr. George F. Greiner.

Term Expires 1926

Rev. J. B. Markward, D.D.; Rev. J. C. Seegers, D.D.; Rev. J. M. Bramkamp, D.D.; Rev. G. Keller Rubrecht, D.D.; Mr. J. B. Franke; Mr. F. D. Bittner; Hon. J. F. Kramer.

BOARD OF NORTHWESTERN MISSIONS

President—Rev. Emil C. J. Kraeling, 132 Henry Street, Brooklyn, N. Y.

Vice-President—Rev. Chr. Knudten, 3406 Pierce Avenue, Chicago, Ill.

Secretary—Rev. G. A. Benze, D.D., 118 W. 23d Street, Erie, Pa.

Treasurer—Rev. H. D. E. Siebott, 2502 N. 27th Street, Philadelphia, Pa.

General Secretary—Rev. Paul Ludwig, Barrington, N. J.

Term Expires 1930

Rev. Emil C. J. Kraeling; Rev. G. A. Benze, D.D.; Rev. H. D. E. Siebott; Rev. H. Rembe, Sr.; Rev. C. S. Roberts; Prof. Carl Hausmann; Mr. E. Muncke.

Term Expires 1928

Rev. Theodore Hartig; Rev. O. Krauch; Rev. Chr. Knudten; Rev. O. C. D. Klaehn, D.D.; Rev. C. R. Tappert; Mr. H. Muegge; Mr. M. Wulff.

Term Expires 1926

Rev. E. Klotsche, Ph.D., D.D.; Rev. M. Koolen, D.D.; Rev. G. H. Michelmann; Rev. S. G. von Bosse; Mr. Henry Albers, Sr.; Mr. William Eck; Mr. Aug. Becker.

IMMIGRANTS MISSION BOARD

President—Rev. J. E. Bittle, D.D., 219 Sixth Street, Pittsburgh, Pa.

Vice-President—Rev. E. W. Simon, D.D., 54 N. Prospect Street, Akron, Ohio.

Secretary—Rev. George Gebert, D.D., 111 Schuylkill Avenue, Tamaqua, Pa.

Treasurer—Mr. H. E. Young, Keystone and Glendale Avenues, Bethlehem, Pa.

Superintendents—Slovak and Hungarian Department: Rev. A. L. Ramer, Ph.D., 30 S. Jefferson Street, Allentown, Pa. Italian Department: Rev. F. Scarpitti, 613 Brown Avenue, Erie, Pa. Finnish Department: Rev. V. Koivumaki, Box 908, Ely, Minn.

Term Expires 1930

Rev. Wm. M. Rehrig, Ph.D.; Rev. F. E. Jensen; Mr. H. E. Young; Mr. S. E. Long.

Term Expires 1928

Rev. J. Elmer Bittle, D.D.; Rev. George Gebert, D.D.; Rev. E. W. Simon, D.D.; Mr. Grant Hultberg.

Term Expires 1926

Rev. George H. Rhodes; Rev. S. N. Carpenter, D.D.; Mr. Frank L. Fox; Mr. Joseph Ruzicka.

WEST INDIES MISSION BOARD

President—Rev. H. W. A. Hanson, D.D., Gettysburg College, Gettysburg, Pa.

Vice-President—Rev. C. A. Freed, D.D., Newberry, S. C.

Secretary—Mr. H. F. Heuer, 115 Gowen Avenue, Mt. Airy, Philadelphia, Pa.

Treasurer—Mr. S. F. Telleen, 274 Upper Boulevard, Ridgewood, N. J.

Executive Secretary—Rev. Z. M. Corbe, 3120 N. Park Avenue, Philadelphia, Pa.

Term Expires 1930

Rev. B. F. Hankey; Rev. H. W. A. Hanson, D.D.; Rev. J. H. Meyer; Rev. F. H. Bosch; Mr. H. E. Heuer; Mr. C. W. Fuhr; Mr. J. H. Brandt.

Term Expires 1928

Rev. J. J. Scherer, Jr., D.D.; Rev. W. M. Horn; Rev. S. N. Carpenter, D.D.; Rev. F. U. Gift, D.D.; Mr. A. H. Durboraw; Mr. S. F. Telleen; M. S. Boyer, M D.

Term Expires 1926

Rev. C. A. Freed, D.D.; Rev. F. B. Clausen; Rev. W. C. Schaeffer, Jr., D.D.; Rev. J. A. Eckstrom, D.D.; E. J. Mosser, Esq.; Mr. H. M. Schmitt; George E. Neff, Esq.

Representing the Augustana Synod—Rev. P. J. O. Cornell, D.D.; Rev. J. Alfred Anderson, D.D.

Representing the Women's Missionary Society—Mrs. F. F. Fry; Mrs. L. S. Copenhaver.

COMMITTEE ON JEWISH MISSIONS

President—Rev. F. O. Evers, 228 Franklin Street, Philadelphia, Pa.

Vice-President—Rev. Loyal H. Larimer, D.D., 1107 N. Fountain Avenue, Springfield, Ohio.

Secretary—Rev. Arthur C. Carty, 256 S. Farragut Terrace, Philadelphia, Pa.

Treasurer—Mr. Charles J. Fite, 1301 Farmers' Bank Bldg., Pittsburgh, Pa.

Term Expires 1930

Rev. A. C. Carty; Rev. Loyal H. Larimer, D.D.; Rev. J. F. Heckert; Mr. Charles J. Fite; Mr. Henry F. Heuer.

Term Expires 1928

Rev. F. O. Evers; Rev. J. J. Myers; Rev. E. R. McCauley, D.D.; Rev. M. L. Enders; Mr. H. L. Snyder.

Term Expires 1926

Rev. F. U. Gift, D.D.; Rev. Alvin E. Bell; Rev. Paul L. Yount; Mr. Christian Pflaum, Jr.; Mr. Frank Raup.

BOARD OF EDUCATION

President—Rev. Alonzo J. Turkle, D.D., Stock Avenue and Arch Street, Pittsburgh, Pa.

Vice-President—Rev. George J. Gongaware, D.D., 31 Pitt Street, Charleston, S. C.

Recording Secretary—Rev. H. R. Gold, 2 Winyah Terrace, New Rochelle, N. Y.

Treasurer—Mr. John M. Snyder, Elkins Park, Pa.

Executive Secretary—Rev. F. G. Gotwald, D.D., 47 E. Market Street, York, Pa.

Term Expires 1930

Rev. R. D. Clare, D.D.; Rev. Wm. F. Hoppe, D.D.; Rev. E. P. Pfatteicher, D.D.; Rev. A. Steimle, D.D.; Mr. Wm. H. Stackel; Glenn M. Cummings, Esq.; Mr. J. L. Clark.

Term Expires 1928

Rev. L. F. Gruber, D.D., LL.D.; Rev. J. H. Harms, D.D.; Rev. M. J. Kline, D.D.; Rev. W. M. Horn; Mr. F. W. Albrecht; Mr. John M. Snyder; Wm. J. Showalter, Sc.D.

Term Expires 1926

Rev. Alonzo J. Turkle, D.D.; Rev. C. J. Gongaware, D.D.; Rev. Howard R. Gold; Rev. H. C. M. Wendel, Ph.D.; Mr. Henry Denhart; Hon. Frank M. Riter, LL.D.; W. T. Stauffer, Esq.

Advisory

From Women's Missionary Society—Mrs. S. R. Kepner; Miss Sarah van Gundy.

From Augustana Synod—Prof. D. A. Leonard.

INNER MISSION BOARD

President—Rev. E. F. Bachmann, D.D., 2100 S. College Avenue, Philadelphia, Pa.

Vice-President—Mr. I. Searles Runyon, 502 W. 136th Street, New York City.

Secretary-Treasurer—Rev. Wm. Freas, 437 Fifth Avenue, New York City.

Term Expires 1930

Rev. E. F. Bachmann, D.D.; Rev. Walter Krumwiede; Rev. W. H. Bruce Carney, D.D.; Mr. James Gear; Mr. G. B. Morehead.

Term Expires 1928

Rev. G. H. Gerberding, D.D., LL.D.; Rev. J. F. Ohl, D.D.; Rev. F. B. Clausen; Mr. H. M. Bikle; Mr. C. M. Distler.

Term Expires 1926

Rev. J. J. Scherer, Jr., D.D.; Rev. J. L. Neve, D.D.; Rev. H. Brueckner; Mr. I. Searles Runyon; C. R. Phillips, M.D.

BOARD OF PUBLICATION

President—Hon. E. F. Eilert, C.S.D., 318 W. 39th Street, New York City.

Vice-President—Mr. John M. Snyder, Elkins Park, Pa.

Secretary—Rev. N. R. Melhorn, D.D., 1228 Spruce Street, Philadelphia, Pa.

Treasurer—Mr. E. G. Hoover, 25 N. Third Street, Harrisburg, Pa.

Business Manager—Mr. Grant Hultberg, 1228 Spruce Street, Philadelphia, Pa.

Term Expires 1930

Rev. C. F. Steck, D.D.; Rev. N. R. Melhorn, D.D.; Rev. F. P. Manhart, D.D.; Mr. D. F. Efird; Mr. George D. Boschen; Hon. E. F. Eilert, C.S.D.; George E. Schlegelmilch, Esq.

Term Expires 1928

Rev. A. R. Wentz, Ph.D., D.D.; Rev. S. W. Herman, D.D.; Rev. A. H. Holthusen, Ph.D.; Mr. E. G. Hoover; Mr. A. H. Kohn; Mr. D. F. Yost; Mr. Otto W. Osterlund.

Term Expires 1926

Rev. C. M. Jacobs, D.D.; Rev. C. J. Cooper, D.D.; Rev. George W. Nicely, D.D.; Rev. Stanley Billheimer, D.D.; Mr. Croll Keller; Mr. John M. Snyder; *W. C. Stoever, Litt.D.

BOARD OF MINISTERIAL PENSIONS AND RELIEF

President—Mr. Henry E. Passavant, 1108 Packard Bldg., Philadelphia, Pa.

Vice-President—Rev. E. Luther De Yoe, 5102 Newhall Street, Germantown, Philadelphia, Pa.

Executive Secretary—Rev. Edgar Grim Miller, D.D., 1228 Spruce Street, Philadelphia, Pa.

Treasurer—Mr. Peter P. Hagan, 1103 Prospect Avenue, Philadelphia, Pa.

Term Expires 1930

Rev. M. H. Valentine, D.D.; Rev. C. L. Miller, Rev. Ross H. Stover, D.D.; Mr. George P. Tustin; Mr. J. Harvey Wattles.

Term Expires 1928

Rev. E. Luther De Yoe, D.D.; Rev. M. L. Zweizig, D.D.; Hon. John F. Ficken; Mr. J. H. Brandt; Mr. E. J. Young.

Term Expires 1926

Mr. Henry E. Passavant; Mr. George F. Greiner; Mr. J. Elsie Miller; Mr. William F. Schneider; Mr. Peter P. Hagan.

PARISH AND CHURCH-SCHOOL BOARD

President—Rev. Charles P. Wiles, D.D., 1228 Spruce Street, Philadelphia, Pa.

---

*Deceased.

Vice-President—Rev. S. W. Herman, D.D., 121 State Street, Harrisburg, Pa.

Secretary—Rev. William L. Hunton, Ph.D., D.D., 1228 Spruce Street, Philadelphia, Pa.

Treasurer—H. M. M. Richards, Litt.D., Lebanon, Pa.

Field Secretaries—Rev. D. Burt Smith, D.D., 210 E. Durham Street, Philadelphia, Pa.; Rev. Charles H. B. Lewis, D.D., 535 Elliott Street, Evansville, Ind.

Term Expires 1930

Rev. Wm. L. Hunton, Ph.D., D.D.; Rev. T. B. Birch, Ph.D.; Rev. Charles F. Dapp, Ph.D.; Prof. Gilbert P. Voigt.

Term Expires 1928

Rev. C. P. Wiles, D.D.; Rev. Wm. F. Hoppe, D.D.; Rev. Frank M. Urich; *W. C. Stoever, Litt.D.

Term Expires 1926

Rev. George W. Sandt, D.D.; Rev. S. W. Herman, D.D.; Rev. Fuller Bergstresser, D.D.; H. M. M. Richards, Litt.D.

BOARD OF DEACONESS WORK

President—Rev. L. M. Zimmerman, D.D., 421 Hanover Street, Baltimore, Md.

Vice-President—Rev. G. A. Getty, D.D., 40 S. Duke Street, York, Pa.

Secretary—Rev. Charles E. Hay, D.D., 1905 Thomas Avenue, Baltimore, Md.

Treasurer—Frederick J. Singley, Esq., 215 N. Charles Street, Baltimore, Md.

Term Expires 1930

Rev. J. F. Ohl, D.D.; Rev. E. F. Bachmann, D.D.; Rev. J. F. Crigler; Mr. Frederick C. Hassold; Hon. J. D. Cappelmann.

----

*Deceased.

Term Expires 1928

Rev. E. H. Delk, D.D.; Rev. G. Albert Getty, D.D.; Rev. J. L. Hoffman; Dr. Charles E. Sadtler; Frederick J. Singley, Esq.

Term Expires 1926

Rev. L. M. Zimmerman, D.D.; Rev. U. S. G. Rupp, D.D.; Mr. Frederick W. Kakel; Mr. Pearre E. Crowl; Mr. Frederick H. Wefer.

NATIONAL LUTHERAN HOME FOR THE AGED

President—Rev. John Weidley, D.D., 233 Second Street, S. E., Washington, D. C.

Vice-President—Rev. J. E. Harms, D.D., Hagerstown, Md.

Recording Secretary—Rev. J. T. Huddle, D.D., 738 Eleventh Street, N. W., Washington, D. C.

Corresponding Secretary—Mr. Wm. H. Finckel, 918 F Street, N. W., Washington, D. C.

Treasurer—Harry T. Domer, Litt.D., 727 Fifteenth Street, N. W., Washington, D. C.

Rev. H. Anstadt, D.D.; Rev. J. L. Frantz; Rev. J. E. Harms, D.D.; Rev. John T. Huddle, D.D.; Rev. Richard Schmidt; Rev. F. R. Wagner, D.D.; Rev. John Weidley, D.D.; L. Russell Alden, Esq.; W. K. Butler, M.D.; Mr. F. E. Cunningham; Harry T. Domer, Litt.D.; Mr. Wm. H. Finckel; Mr. John H. Jones; Mr. F. W. Kakel; Mr. Harry L. Snyder.

COMMITTEE ON CHURCH PAPERS

Chairman—Rev. J. A. Singmaster, D.D., LL.D., Gettysburg, Pa.

Secretary—Rev. H. Offermann, D.D., 7206 Boyer Street, Philadelphia, Pa.

Term Expires 1930

Rev. J. A. Singmaster, D.D., LL.D.; Rev. C. E. Gardner, D.D.; William J. Showalter, Sc.D.

Term Expires 1928

Rev. J. A. Morehead, D.D., LL.D.; Rev. J. E. Whitteker, D.D., LL.D.; L. Russell Alden, Esq.

Term Expires 1926

Rev. H. Offermann, D.D.; Rev. H. Anstadt, D.D.; Mr. I. Searles Runyon.

_____

EXECUTIVE COMMITTEE OF THE LAYMEN'S MOVEMENT

Chairman—Mr. J. L. Clark, Ashland, Ohio.

Executive Secretary—C. G. Shatzer, Sc.D., 906 Fairbanks Bldg., Springfield, Ohio.

Associate Secretary—Rev. E. C. Cronk, D.D., 906 Fairbanks Bldg., Springfield, Ohio.

Treasurer—Mr. W. L. Glatfelter, Spring Grove, Pa.

Mr. J. L. Clark; Mr. P. A. Elsesser; Mr. E. Clarence Miller, LL.D.; Mr. F. W. Albrecht; Mr. Harvey C. Miller; Mr. William H. Hager; Mr. W. L. Glatfelter; Mr. P. P. Hagan; Mr. C. J. Driever; Mr. M. P. Moller.

_____

STANDING COMMITTEES
Statistical and Church Year Book Committee

Rev. G. H. Schnur, D.D. (Convener)—Rev. G. L. Kieffer; Rev. W. M. Kopenhaver; Rev. M. G. L. Rietz, D.D.; Rev. C. W. Cassell; Rev. J. D. Krout; Rev. C. J. Rockey; Mr. Harry E. Pugh; also Secretary of the United Lutheran Church in America (ex-officio).

Committee on Common Service Book

Rev. J. A. Singmaster, D.D., LL.D., (Convener)—Rev. H. E. Jacobs, D.D., LL.D., S.T.D.; Rev. L. D. Reed, D.D.; Rev. J. F. Ohl, Mus.D., D.D.; Rev. J. C. Mattes; Rev. A. Steimle, D.D.; Rev. P. Z. Strodach, D.D.; Rev. J. A. Clutz, D.D., LL.D.; Rev. E. K. Bell, D.D., LL.D.; Rev. G. U. Wenner, D.D., L.H.D.;

Rev. M. G. G. Scherer, D.D.; Rev. M. L. Stirewalt; Rev. E. Fischer, D.D.; Rev. C. W. Leitzell, D.D.; Rev. R. M. Smith, Ph.D., D.D.

Committee on Church Music

Rev. J. F. Ohl, Mus.D., D.D. (Convener)—Rev. L. D. Reed, D.D.; Rev. H. K. Lantz; Rev. G. C. Rees, D.D.; Rev. E. F. Krauss, D.D.; Rev. E. A. Trabert; Rev. C. T. Benze, D.D.; Rev. N. R. Melhorn, D.D.; Rev. G. C. F. Haas, D.D.; Rev. J. D. Brown, Litt.D.; Mr. William Benbow; Mr. Harry A. Sykes; Mr. Ralph P. Lewars; Mr. Harold K. Marks; Mr. Henry F. Seibert; Prof. Frederick Lewis Bach.

Committee on German Interests

Rev. H. Offermann, D.D. (Convener)—Rev. G. A. Benze, D.D.; Rev. E. Hoffmann, D.D.; Rev. J. L. Neve, D.D.; Rev. F. E. Oberlander, D.D.; Rev. F. H. Bosch; Rev. J. J. Heischmann, D.D.; Rev. F. O. Evers; Rev. J. A. Weyl; Rev. T. O. Posselt; Rev. S. G. R. von Bosse; Rev. E. A. Tappert, D.D.; Rev. O. Kleine; Rev. J. A. Clutz, D.D., LL.D.; Rev. W. M. Horn.

Corresponding Members—The presidents of the German Nebraska, Manitoba, Texas and Wartburg Synods.

Committee on Lutheran Brotherhoods

Rev. J. W. Kapp, D.D. (Convener)—Hon. John L. Zimmerman, LL.D.; Rev. W. C. Schaeffer, D.D.; Rev. J. E. Heindel, D.D.; Mr. Louis M. Swink; Mr. H. A. Kingsbury; Mr. G. Dalton Meyer; Mr. Rodney T. Martinsen; Mr. Adam H. Bartel; Mr. C. H. Boyer; Mr. W. M. Mearig; Mr. G. Hemsing; Mr. J. K. Jensen; Mr. W. M. Doub; Mr. G. M. Jones.

Committee on Women's Work

Rev. W. D. C. Keiter, D.D. (Convener)—Rev. F. A. Kahler, D.D.; Rev. J. B. Markward, D.D.; Rev. W. H. Shepfer, D.D.; Rev. M. J. Bieber, D.D.; Rev. D. A. Davy, D.D.; Rev. S. J. McDowell, D.D.

Committee on Associations of Young People

Rev. H. C. Roehner, D.D. (Convener)—Rev. J. H. Waidelich, D.D.; Rev. H. A. McCullough, D.D.; Rev. L. M. Kuhns, Litt.D., D.D.; Rev. U. E. Apple; Mr. J. A. Alexander; Mr. William Eck; Hon. E. F. Eilert; Mr. Harry Hodges.

Committee on Work Among Boys

Rev. C. P. Harry (Convener)—Rev. G. H. Bechtold; Rev. L. DeYoe, D.D.; Rev. H. D. Hoover, D.D., Ph.D.; Rev. S. Billheimer, D.D.; Rev. G. Beiswanger; Rev. G. H. Rhodes; Rev. A. B. MacIntosh, D.D.; Rev. C. A. Dennig; Rev. A. E. Deitz, D.D.; Mr. C. J. Driever, Mr. G. M. Jones; Rev. A. T. Michler; Rev. Henry Manken, Jr.; Rev. C. M. Teufel.

Committee on Army and Navy Work

Rev. C. D. Trexler (Convener)—Rev. C. F. Steck, D.D.; Rev. S. T. Nicholas, D.D.; Rev. W. Freas; Rev. P. F. Bloomhardt, Ph.D.; Rev. R. H. Gearhart; Rev. J. Fedders; Rev. A. C. Carty; Mr. C. H. Dahmer; Mr. W. A. G. Lape.

Committee on Moral and Social Welfare

Rev. E. P. Pfatteicher, D.D., Ph.D., (Convener)—Rev. J. W. Horine, D.D.; Rev. L. S. Keyser, D.D.; Rev. E. C. Dinwiddie, D.D.; Rev. G. E. Hipsley, D.D.; L. R. Alden, Esq.; Rev. J. H. Harms, D.D.; E. M. Rabenold, Esq.; Rev. P. H. Heisey; Rev. E. Fischer, D.D.; Rev. E. K. Fretz, Ph.D.; Rev. G. Dorn; Rev. H. W. Tope, D.D.

Committee on Evangelism

Rev. J. C. Seegers, D.D. (Convener)—Rev. F. Wolford, D.D.; Rev. A. Pohlman, D.D., M.D.; Rev. P. W. Roth; Rev. E. A. Tappert, D.D.; Rev. John F. Crigler, D.D.; Rev. C. J. Rockey; Mr. F. Stussy, Jr.; Rev. S. D. Daugherty, D.D.; Rev. Paul Hoh.

Committee on Church Architecture

Rev. J. F. Ohl, Mus.D., D.D. (Convener)—Rev. L. D. Reed, D.D.; Rev. E. F. Krauss, D.D.; Rev. E. A. Trabert; Rev. G. H. Schnur, D.D.; Rev. P. Z. Strodach, D.D.; Rev. H. S. Kidd;

Prof. Warren P. Laird, Sc.D.; Mr. Charles Z. Klauder; Mr. A. A. Ritcher; Mr. G. C. Baum; Mr. J. Horace Frank; Mr. J. A. Dempwolf; Mr. Luther M. Leisenring; Mr. Charles Obenhack.

Committee on Publicity

Rev. H. R. Gold (Convener)—Rev. W. L. Hunton, Ph.D., D.D.; Rev. C. K. Fegley; Rev. M. L. Canup; Rev. W. H. Greever, D.D.; Rev. C. L. Fry, D.D.; Rev. A. E. Wagner, D.D., Ph.D.; Rev. W. H. Stutts, D.D.; Rev. E. H. Delk, D.D.; Rev. H. Moehling; Dr. William Showalter; Mr. Jesse R. Hildebrand.

Committee on Necrology

Rev. James F. Lambert

Committee on Transportation

Mr. Harvey C. Miller; Hon. E. F. Eilert; Mr. W. H. Hager; Rev. J. M. Bramkamp, D.D.; and the Secretary of the United Lutheran Church in America (ex-officio).

Archivist

Rev. L. D. Reed, D.D.

Statistical Secretary

Rev. George L. Kieffer

Commissioners to the National Lutheran Council

Rev. H. A. Weller, D.D. (Convener)—Rev. C. M. Jacobs, D.D.; Rev. C. J. Smith, D.D.; Rev. P. W. Koller, D.D.; Rev. C. A. Freed, D.D.; Rev. M. G. G. Scherer, D.D.; Hon. E. F. Eilert; G. F. Greiner, Esq.

Representative on the Advisory Committee of the American Bible Society

Rev. H. C. Alleman, D.D.

Consultative Representatives to Commissions of the Federal Council of the Churches

Administrative Committee—Rev. G. U. Wenner, D.D., L.H.D.; Rev. A. Steimle, D.D.

Washington Committee—Rev. W. Freas; Rev. S. T. Nicholas, D.D.; Rev. C. F. Steck, D.D.

Commission on International Justice and Good Will—Rev. E. H. Delk, D.D.; Rev. F. H. Knubel, D.D., LL.D.; Rev. A. J. Traver; Rev. L. B. Wolf, D.D.

Committee on Conference With Y. M. C. A.

Rev. P. E. Scherer, D.D. (Chairman); Mr. W. H. Hager; Robbin B. Wolf, Esq.

COMMISSION TO STUDY AND REPORT ON THEOLOGICAL EDUCATION IN THE UNITED LUTHERAN CHURCH IN AMERICA

(Appointed by the Executive Board, December 11th, 1924)

Rev. L. F. Gruber, D.D., LL.D., 1024 Laurel Avenue, St. Paul, Minn.

Rev. A. J. Turkle, D.D., Arch and Stockton Streets, N. E., Pittsburgh, Pa.

Rev. C. M. Jacobs, D.D., 7333 Germantown Avenue, Philadelphia, Pa.

Rev. J. A. Clutz, D.D., LL.D., Gettysburg, Pa.

Rev. A. G. Voigt, D.D., LL.D., Columbia, S. C.

Rev. P. W. Koller, D.D., 68 Sherman Avenue, Mansfield, Ohio.

Rev. J. A. W. Haas, D.D., LL.D., Allentown, Pa.

Rev. E. Hoffman, D.D., Lutheran Seminary, Waterloo, Ont., Canada.

Judge H. W. Harter, 1543 Market Avenue, Canton, Ohio.

Mr. W. H. Stackel, 93 Alliance Avenue, Rochester, New York.

COMMITTEE TO PREPARE A STATEMENT CONCERNING RELATIONS OF CHURCH AND STATE

Rev. C. M. Jacobs, D.D., Rev. J. A. W. Haas, D.D., LL.D., Rev. A. R. Wentz, Ph.D., D.D., Rev. F. K. Fretz, D.D.

SPECIAL SOCIETIES

Historical Society of the Evangelical Lutheran Church in the United States of America

President—Rev. F. P. Manhart, D.D.

Vice-Presidents—Rev. J. A. Singmaster, D.D., LL.D.; Rev. M. G. G. Scherer, D.D.; H. M. M. Richards, Litt.D.; Mr. G. E. Schlegelmilch; Rev. Prof. L. Fuerbringer; Rev. Prof. P. M. Norlie, Litt.D.; Rev. Prof. M. Reu, D.D.; Rev. Prof. George Sverdrup; Rev. P. S. Vig.

Curator—Rev. Prof. A. R. Wentz, Ph.D., D.D.

Secretary—Rev. Prof. H. C. Alleman, D.D.

Treasurer—Mr. J. Elmer Musselman.

The Lutheran Church Book and Literature Society

President pro tem—Rev. A. C. Carty.

Corresponding Secretary—Rev. J. A. Schantz.

Recording Secretary—Mr. M. L. Holloway.

Treasurer—Mr. C. F. Hassold.

PROCEEDINGS OF THE FIFTY-FIRST
CONVENTION

of the

GENERAL SYNOD OF THE EVAN-GELICAL LUTHERAN CHURCH IN THE UNITED STATES OF AMERICA

Chicago, Ill., October 21, 1924.

The Fifty-first Convention of the General Synod of the Evangelical Lutheran Church in the United States of America assembled in Holy Trinity Lutheran Church, Rev. J. A. Leas, D.D., pastor, at 2 P. M.   Rev. Prof. F. P. Manhart, D.D., President, called the members to order and conducted devotional exercises as follows:

Hymn 146.
Scripture, Eph. 4:1-12.
Suitable Collects, Lord's Prayer.

The Secretary announced that he had received properly certified lists of delegates to the number of one hundred and twenty-nine clerical delegates, and an equal number of lay delegates. The President declared Synod officially constituted and ready for the transaction of business.

ROLL OF DELEGATES

1—Maryland

Rev. John Weidley, D.D.
Rev. W. G. Minnick
Rev. J. B. Rupley
Rev. F. R. Wagner, D.D.
Rev. S. J. McDowell, D.D.
Rev. William A. Wade
Rev. M. L. Enders, D.D.
Rev. J. C. Bowers, D.D.
Rev. Prof. A. R. Wentz, Ph.D., D.D.
Rev. J. L. Hoffman

Mr. W. W. Doub
Mr. L. Russell Alden, Esq.
Mr. M. P. Moller
Mr. A. H. Weaver
Mr. E. W. Young, Esq.
Mr. F. W. Kakel
Mr. H. T. Domer, Litt.D.
Mr. E. H. Sharretts
Mr. Wm. J. Showalter, Sc.D.
Mr. M. H. Buehler

2—West Pennsylvania

Rev. Geo. W. Nicely, D.D.
Rev. H. B. Stock, D.D.
Rev. Geo. E. Bowersox
Rev. G. Albert Getty, D.D.
Rev. L. B. Wolf, D.D.
Rev. Luther Kuhlman, D.D.
Rev. Henry Anstadt, D.D.
Rev. S. L. Hench
Rev. W. A. Kump

Mr. Geo. E. Neff, Esq.
Mr. W. L. Gladfelter
Mr. P. A. Elsesser
Hon. E. P. Miller
Mr. W. H. Menges
Mr. A. R. Nissley
Mr. Alex. Diehl
Mr. I. L. Taylor
Mr. Geo. W. Hafer

3—East Ohio

Rev. A. H. Smith, D.D.
Rev. E. C. Herman
Rev. H. C. Brillhart

Mr. J. F. Mellinger
Mr. F. W. Albrecht
Mr. L. F. Palmer

4 Alleghany

Rev. S. N. Carpenter, D.D.
Rev. A. J. Rudisill, D.D.
Rev. L. P. Young, D.D.
Rev. W. I. Good
Rev. John B. Kniseley
Rev. M. S. Kemp, Litt.D.
Rev. George N. Lauffer, D.D.

Prof. H. S. Fleck
Mr. Isaac Harpster
Mr. C. Luther Lowe
Mr. W. E. Dickey
Mr. H. M. Thompson
Mr. S. Z. Miller
Mr. A. J. Harter

5—East Pennsylvania

Rev. Stanley Billheimer, D.D.
Rev. Luther De Yoe, D.D.
Rev. Ross H. Stover, D.D.
Rev. A. Pohlman, M.D., D.D.
Rev. Edwin Heyl Delk, D.D.
Rev. Joseph D. Krout
Rev. E. A. Chamberlin
Rev. Wm. J. Miller, Jr.
Rev. Grayson Z. Stup
Rev. C. E. Rice
Rev. E. E. Schantz
Rev. J. A. Richter
Rev. William C. Ney

Dr. Croll Keller
Mr. Geo. C. Baum
Mr. A. H. Durboraw
Mr. E. G. Hoover
Mr. A. D. Chiquoine
Mr. J. Elsie Miller
Mr. William H. Emhardt
Mr. C. M. Stine, Ph.D.
Mr. Harvey C. Miller
Mr. H. S. Smeltzer
Mr. J. H. Brandt
Mr. J. H. Wagner
Mr. Charles A. Good

6—Miami

Rev. J. W. Kapp, D.D.
Rev. J. B. Birch, D.D.
Rev. Prof. L. H. Larimer, D.D.

Mr. J. W. Kahler
Mr. William Schaus
Mr. A. W. Ulric

7—Pittsburgh

Rev. Ellis B. Burgess, D.D.
Rev. S. G. Dornblaser, D.D.
Rev. E. M. Gearhart, D.D.
Rev. A. J. Turkle, D.D.
Rev. J. B. Baker, D.D.
Rev. G. W. Englar, D.D.
Rev. J. Elmer Bittle, D.D.
Rev. W. H. Hetrick, D.D.

Mr. Robbin B. Wolf, Esq.
Hon. J. Frank Graff
Mr. Chas. F. Stifel
Mr. Harry C. Hoffman, M.D.
Mr. C. J. Mensch
Mr. E. R. Sheldon
Mr. C. E. Miller, M.D.
Mr. Peter Graff, III

8—Wittenberg

Rev. Paul W. Koller, D.D.
Rev. R. E. Tulloss, Ph.D., D.D.
Rev. C. E. Rice. D.D.
Rev. A. J. Hall
Rev. Geo. W. Miley
Rev. B. W. Ziegler, D.D.

Hon. John L. Zimmerman
Mr. M. W. Lutz
Mr. H. A. Sloneker
Mr. R. E. Sawyer

9 Olive Branch

Rev. Frank A. Dressel, D.D.
Rev. John B. Gardner
Rev. R. H. Benting
Rev. I. W. Gernert

Mr. A. H. Kornfeld
Mr. John E. Speigel
Mr. A. G. Renan
Mr. O. W. Cromer

10—Northern Illinois

Rev. J. M. Bramkamp, D.D.
Rev. E. C. Harris, D.D.
Rev. W. F. Rex

Mr. C. J. Driever
Mr. C. W. Howe
Mr. H. J. Kable
Mr. Walter E. White
Mr. Henry Denhart

11—Central Pennsylvania

Rev. L. Stoy Spangler
Rev. M. S. Cressman, D.D.
Rev. J. Grover Knipple
Rev. W. P. Ard

Mr. Joseph Dreese
Hon. C. L. Cramley
Mr. W. E. Benner
Mr. W. C. Garber

12—Iowa

Rev. C. N. Swihart, D.D.
Rev. Prof. Holmes Dysinger, D.D.
Rev. S. M. Lesher, D.D.

Mr. John L. Berger
Mr. J. L. Sawyer
Mr. Lee D. Koser

13—Northern Indiana

Rev. Ralph D. Wheadon
Rev. Prof. L. S. Keyser, D.D.
Rev. David R. Huber, D.D.

Mr. W. W. Anderson
Dr. B. F. Titlers
Mr. O. O. Shafer

14—Central Illinois

15—Susquehanna

Rev. O. E. Sunday
Rev. I. S. Sassaman, D.D.
Rev. B. F. Bieber
Rev. H. W. Miller
Rev. F. P. Manhart, D.D.

Prof. Geo. E. Fisher, Ph.D.
Dr. A. M. Hall
Mr. J. Frank Daugherty
Mr. G. B. Reimensnyder
Mr. David Wardrop

16—Kansas

Rev. Robert J. Wolf
Rev. Wm. E. Wheeler, D.D.
Rev. E. E. Stauffer, D.D.
Rev. J. A. McCulloch, D.D.

Mr. F. A. Isern
Mr. Wm. H. Guenther
Mr. A. B. Zimmerman
Mr. P. F. Bennetzen

17—Nebraska

Rev. W. F. Rangeler, D.D.
Rev. C. G. Aue, D.D.
Rev. George Dorn
Rev. K. de Freese
Rev. M. Koolen, D.D.

Mr. O. A. Keyser
Mr. M. M. Martin
Mr. G. Hahn
Mr. I. N. Augustine
Mr. W. J. Hendy

18—Wartburg

Rev. R. Neumann, D.D., Litt.D.
Rev. Geo. Schulz, D.D.
Rev. R. B. Garten, D.D.
Rev. E. E. Ortlepp, D.D.
Rev. E. T. Finck

Mr. H. Oertel
Mr. Chr. Hummel
Mr. Erich Mueller
Mr. Charles Scholz
Mr. William Buslap

19—California

Rev. Herman Gehrcke
Rev. Wm. E. Crouser, D.D.
Rev. Daniel J. Snyder

Mr. R. A. Kuner
Mr. E. A. Morrison
Mr. W. J. Gram

20 German Nebraska

Rev. C. Goede
Rev. E. Walter
Rev. E. Klotsche
Rev. P. Waldschmidt
Rev. R. Kuehne
Rev. J. A. Bahnsen
Rev. G. H. Michelmann
Rev. G. Duehrkop

Mr. G. F. Beschorner
Mr. Gerhard Hilgen
Mr. Carl Losecke
Mr. John Roehrig
Mr. A. Deichmann
Mr. Carl Goll
Mr. Henry Rohmeiser
Mr. H. Busselmann

21—Rocky Mountain

Rev. M. F. Troxell, D.D.
Rev. J. C. Jacoby, D.D.

Mr. George W. Fogelman
Mr. A. F. Sittloh

22—Southern Illinois

23—New York

Rev. C. W. Leitzell, D.D.
Rev. F. H. Knubel, D.D., LL.D.
Rev. F. E. Oberlander, D.D.
Rev. Carl Zinssmeister, D.D.
Rev. Frank Wolford, D.D.
Rev. A. J. Traver
Rev. A. W. Baker
Rev. W. G. Boomhower
Rev. A. L. Dillenbeck
Rev. A. S. Hardy, D.D.
Rev. T. W. Keller
Rev. E. J. Kueling
Rev. W. E. Pierce
Rev. G. J. Reumann

Mr. A. Albers, Sr.
Hon. E. F. Eilert
Mr. Frank Grumback
Mr. Henry Streibert
Mr. I. S. Runyon
Mr. T. Coon
Mr. W. H. Gomph
Mr. H. Greenwald
Mr. William Horn
Mr. F. J. Keller
Mr. C. H. Wilsnack
Mr. Harry Yarwood
Dr. H. Yeckel
Mr. F. H. Wefer

24—West Virginia

Rev. C. E. Butler   Mr. J. C. Lynch
Rev. Simon Snyder   Mr. W. W. Wolf

TREASURER'S REPORT

JOHN L. ZIMMERMAN, *In' Account With the General Synod of The Lutheran Church*

1924
Sept. 9—Received of Executor of Charles Crivel Estate.......... ....$200.00
For Tressler Orphans' Home
Oct. 30—Paid George E. Neff, Treasurer $200.00

Philadelphia, Pa., October 19, 1924.

To the General Synod of the Lutheran Church in the United States of America:

As Treasurer of the Pastors' Fund Society of the General Synod, and as the Committee of One appointed by the Board of Ministerial Relief of the United Lutheran Church in America to ascertain how best to bring about the transfer of the Pastors' Fund Society moneys and securities to the Board of Ministerial Relief, I presented at your meeting in Buffalo in 1922 a plan to bring about this end. The plan was adopted by this Synod and in due time the tender was made in accord with that plan, and accepted, which plan provided that the cash and securities of the Pastors' Fund Society be made a "trust fund," the income only to be used for the "relief of need" of superannuated ministers and their widows.

This tender was promptly accepted by the Board of Ministerial Relief and it is now known as the Relief Endowment Fund of the Board. The income of this Endowment, together with the special contributions received from individuals, churches, Sunday schools, missionary and other Church societies, has enabled the Board to do some real meritorious relief work, supplementing the pension checks where urgent need existed or special distress overtook some pensioner.

Contributions in any amount will be received and placed in the Endowment Fund, or in the Relief Current Fund, which is the "income" fund from which all relief disbursements are made.

According to our ledger as of July 31, 1924, the Relief Endowment Fund now amounts to $90,402.97, $25,823.00 of which amount represents Annuities on which the Board is still paying interest. There was also $7,858.42 in cash in the Relief Current account. Something over $3,000.00 was distributed this month to those in greatest need, in amounts ranging from $12.50 to $50.00.

We are now making four distributions a year—at Christmas, Easter, July (vacation time), and October (cold weather preparation season).

There are still some bequests due this Pastors' Fund Society that we have record of, the latest one appearing in the newspapers just as I was leaving Philadelphia to attend this Convention. The amount was given as $2,500.00, and when received it will be added to the Endowment Fund.

Very respectfully yours,

J. H. BRANDT, *Treasurer.*

The foregoing report was adopted, subject to the following resolution:

Resolved, That the Board of Ministerial Relief be requested to return to this body for cancellation the deed of trust from the Pastors' Fund Society conveying certain funds, and to declare itself seized of these funds now in its hands, received from the Pastors' Fund Society, subject to the trusts on them originally impressed.

The President appointed the following as Trustees of the Pastors' Fund Society, namely: Rev. M. H. Valentine, D.D., Rev. A. Pohlman, D.D., Rev. Edgar Grim Miller, D.D., Mr. J. H. Brandt, and Mr. J. P. Tustin.

Feghtly Home

Substituting the name of Rev. E. R. Capewell for that of Rev. Dr. Guard, the Trustees of the Home were re-elected as follows:

Rev. E. R. Capewell   Mrs. W. H. Bitner
Rev. D. Frank Garland, D.D.   Mrs. C. B. Herr
Rev. C. J. Kiefer, D.D.   Mrs. A. R. Garver
Leonard H. Shipman, Esq.   Mrs. E. L. Crane
Eric J. Weaver, Esq.   Mrs. Salina Belmer
Mr. A. L. Harshberger   Mrs. C. U. Briggs

It was moved that the Feghtly Home be referred to the Synod of Ohio for action, and report to this body.

Reformation Diamond Jubilee Advance Fund

Touching this Fund, Rev. L. B. Wolf, D.D., Secretary-Treasurer of the Board of Foreign Missions, presented the following statement:

Amount in cash, at the last Convention prior to the merger, was....$88,930.80
Whole amount of cash received $257,011.37
Amount invested for higher education, one-third of cash received....$85,670.00
Amount expended, to date, on all projects in India and Africa......$79,627.52
Balance in Fund $91,713.85

Upon motion the ballot was cast for the re-election of the present officers of the General Synod, as follows:

President—Rev. Prof. Frank P. Manhart, D.D.
Secretary—Rev. Luther Kuhlman, D.D.
Treasurer—Hon. John L. Zimmerman, LL.D.

It was moved and carried that the General Synod hereby appoints and constitutes the Boards, Commissions, Committees and other agencies of the United Lutheran Church to be also its Boards, Commissions, Committees and other agencies, to administer its work represented in and by these several Boards, Commissions, Committees and other agencies of the United Lutheran Church and under the direction and authority of the said United Lutheran Church.

The Minutes of the Convention were read and approved.

Adjournment

The President then requested the Rev. Harlan K. Fenner, D.D., to pronounce the benediction, whereupon the President declared the General Synod adjourned, to meet at the time and place selected by the Executive Board of the United Lutheran Church in America.

LUTHER KUHLMAN, *Secretary.*

MINUTES OF THE THIRTY-NINTH CONVENTION

of the

GENERAL COUNCIL OF THE EVAN-GELICAL LUTHERAN CHURCH IN NORTH AMERICA

UNITY LUTHERAN CHURCH, CORNER BALMORAL AND MAGNOLIA AVENUES, CHICAGO, ILL.

Tuesday, October 21, 1924, 2.00 P. M.

The Thirty-ninth Convention of the General Council of the Evangelical Lutheran Church in North America was called to order by the President, the Rev. Fred. H. Bosch.

The opening devotional service was conducted by the Rev. Theo. Posselt. The hymn was 224 and the Scripture lesson was Matt. 16: 13-19.

The Minutes of the Thirty-eighth Annual Convention were approved as printed.

The President presented the following report:

Chicago, Ill., October 21, 1924.

To the Members of the General Council, GREETING:

MY DEAR BRETHREN : Grace be unto you and peace from God our Father and from our Lord and Saviour, Jesus Christ. Amen.

This meeting of the General Council of the Evangelical Lutheran Church in North America is called in accordance with the wish and direction of the Executive Board of the United Lutheran Church in America.

It is self-evident that since the merger and the organization of the United Lutheran Church, the General Council as a separate body does not carry on the work of our beloved Church as formerly, inasmuch as the United Lutheran Church has undertaken the various spheres of activity formerly occupied by the General Council. The members of the General Council, pastors and congregations have, I am sure, taken the same active part in the work of the Kingdom with the same zeal as when the General

Council had its own particular work to do, separate and apart from the General Synod and the United Synod in the South. Consequently there is practically nothing to report concerning the separate activity of the General Council.

I feel it to be my sacred duty to call to the attention of the General Council that God, in His wisdom and love, has, during the past biennium, called from the spheres of their respective labors many tried and trusted servants who have been active and influential in our body, men consecrated to our Master and His Church, ever zealous in the discharge of their exalted office, devoted to the service of the Church. I refer to E. Augustus Miller, Esq., Hon. William H. Staake, Rev. Dr. G. C. Berkemeier, Rev. Dr. E. Balfour, Mr. Robert E. Gaskell, Prof. S. P. Sadtler, Ph.D., LL.D. I am sure the General Council will not fail to give expression of its gratitude to God for His grace bestowed upon our beloved Church through the service of these men.

At the last meeting of the General Council it was resolved to request the United Lutheran Church to apply the money paid over by the Treasurer of the General Council to a memorial to the late Rev. T. E. Schmauk, D.D., LL.D. It would interest the General Council to learn whether the United Lutheran Church has acceded to the request of the General Council, and if so, in what manner our wishes were carried out.

The Board of Trustees of the General Council has nothing to report, as no meetings of the Board were held. At two separate times I caused a call to be issued for a meeting of the Board, but only two or three members appeared and no meeting was held. As a consequence, no successor to the late E. Augustus Miller, Esq., Secretary of the Board, could be elected.

As the General Council is a corporate and legal body, whose existence must be continued indefinitely, it will be necessary to elect officers and members of the various Boards at this meeting. It might be advisable to extend the time for the expiration of the terms of members on the various Boards, whose term of office expires next year, 1925.

May the Holy Spirit direct us in our deliberations and add His divine blessing.

Respectfully submitted,

FRED. H. BOSCH, President.

The above report was received.

On motion the Secretary was instructed to cast the ballot of the Convention for the present officers. The following were declared elected:

Rev. Fred. H. Bosch, President.
Rev. W. L. Stough, D.D., Secretary.
Rev. E. A. Tappert, German Secretary.
Rev. F. A. Kaehler, D.D., English Corresponding Secretary.
Rev. Prof. H. Offermann, D.D., German Corresponding Secretary.
Mr. J. B. Franke, Treasurer.

On motion the Secretary cast the ballot for the following:

Foreign Mission Board

Term Expiring in 1926—Rev. Prof. C. Theo. Benze, D.D.;
Rev. R. C. G. Bielinski; Rev. E. P. Pfatteicher, Ph.D., D.D.;
Rev. J. A. Dewald; Rev. A. Steimle, D.D.; Mr. H. G. G. Querns;
Mr. James M. Snyder.

The Trustees of the General Council were authorized to fill
all existing vacancies in Boards until the time of the next regular election.

On motion the President was instructed to appoint a committee on nominations to fill vacancies in the Board of Trustees,
said committee to withdraw at once and report before adjournment of this body. The following committee was appointed:
Rev. P. Geo. Sieger, D.D., Mr. Harry Hodges, and Rev. G. W.
Sandt, D.D., LL.D.

The report made by the committee was as follows: For the
unexpired term of Mr. R. E. Gaskell, one year, Robert Bowe, of
New York, N. Y.; for the vacancies created by the death of the
Hon. William H. Staake and E. Aug. Miller, Esq., term to expire in 1926, the Hon. F. M. Riter and Mr. R. Anderman, both
of Philadelphia, Pa.; for the term expiring in 1927, the Rev.
Prof. H. Offermann and George M. Jones, Esq., of Reading, Pa.
The report was received and the Secretary, on motion, cast the
ballot of the Convention for the above nominees.

The matter of the proposed memorial to the Rev. T. E.
Schmauk, D.D., LL.D., referred to in the report of the Presi-

dent, was committed to the following committee to formulate a suitable resolution: Rev. W. D. C. Keiter, D.D., Rev. W. M. Horn, Rev. F. M. Urich, D.D. The following report was pre‑ sented by the committee and adopted by the Convention:

Resolved, That in the matter of the request made of the United Luth‑ eran Church in America to establish a suitable memorial for the Rev. Dr. T. E. Schmauk, the General Council pledges itself to heartily support the proposition; and we recommend that a committee be appointed to take charge of the work and in consultation with the committee of the Executive Board of the United Lutheran Church in America, report a definite plan to the next convention of the General Council.

The item in the report of the President referring to deceased brethren was adopted by a rising vote and a brief silent medi‑ tation.

Regret was expressed at the absence from this Convention of the Rev. Prof. H. E. Jacobs, D.D., LL.D., S.T.D., and the Secre‑ tary was instructed so to advise him. In this same connection, the President was instructed to convey to Dr. Jacobs on the occa‑ sion of his 80th birthday anniversary, November 10th, the greet‑ ings, congratulations and appreciative regard of this convention.

With reference to possible property transfers in the Virgin Islands, it was

Resolved, That in the absence of the Trustees of this body, its officers be and hereby are authorized and empowered to execute deeds or other necessary legal documents.

The Convention extended a vote of thanks to the pastor, church council and congregation of Unity Lutheran Church for the use of their church for this meeting.

The following delegates reported their presence:

I. The Evangelical Lutheran Ministerium of Pennsylvania and the Adjacent States.

Organized August 15 (New Style, 26) A. D., 1748

Clerical	Lay
Rev. H. A. Weller, D.D.	D. D. Fritch, M.D.
Rev. W. D. C. Keiter, D.D.	Mr. James M. Snyder
Rev. G. W. Sandt, D.D., LL.D.	John L. Potteiger, Esq.
Rev. W. L. Stough, D.D.	Mr. Harry Hodges
Rev. I. B. Kurtz, D.D.	Mr. Charles H. Esser
Rev. John C. Mattes	Mr. H. G. G. Querns
Rev. P. Geo. Sieger, D.D.	J. F. Trexler, M.D.
Rev. L. D. Ulrich	Mr. P. J. Laubach
Rev. Preston A. Laury, D.D.	
Rev. Gomer C. Rees, D.D.	
Rev. W. C. Schaeffer, D.D.	
Rev. R. B. Lynch	
Rev. Frank M. Urich, D.D.	
Rev. James F. Lambert, D.D.	
Rev. H. S. Kidd	
Rev. Adolph Hellwege	
Rev. Zenan M. Corbe	
Rev. W. L. Hunton, Ph.D., D.D.	

II. The Evangelical Lutheran Ministerium of the State of New York and Adjacent States and Countries.

Organized October 23, A. D. 1784

Clerical	Lay
Rev. Fred. H. Bosch	Mr. Geo. Bohrer
Rev. Theo. O. Posselt	Mr. Henry D. Brandes
Rev. J. A. W. Kirsch	Mr. Ernest C. Muncke
Rev. G. A. Bierdeman, D.D.	Mr. Theo. Roehrs
Rev. Justus F. Holstein, Ph.D.	Mr. Martin Wulff
Rev. S. G. von Bosse	Mr. Jacob Schantz
Rev. H. C. Wasmund	Mr. William Intemann
	Mr. Henry Kruse

III. Pittsburgh Synod of the Evangelical Lutheran Church.

Organized January 15, A. D. 1845

Clerical	Lay
Rev. Charles P. McLaughlin, D.D.	Hon. Charles Young
Rev. John J. Myers	Mr. J. Louis Frederick
Rev. B. F. Hankey	Mr. William E. Yeager
Rev. G. A. Benze, D.D.	Mr. J. Warren Hemte
Rev. Ernest A. Tappert, D.D.	
Rev. F. W. Kohler	
Rev. Henry H. Bagger	
Rev. C. A. Dennig	
Rev. A. P. Lentz	
Rev. John Jay Hill	
Rev. J. S. Shaud	

IV. Texas Synod.

Organized November 10, A. D. 1851

Clerical   *Lay*

Rev. E. A. Sievert

V. Synod of Canada.

Organized July 21, A. D. 1861

Clerical   *Lay*

Rev. Otto C. D. Klaehn, D.D.   Mr. Louis Peine
                                     Mr. H. Pauli

VI. Chicago Synod.

Organized A. D. 1896

Clerical   *Lay*

Rev. S. P. Long, D.D.

VII. Manitoba Synod.

Organized July 16, A. D. 1897

Clerical   *Lay*

Rev. H. W. Harms
Rev. E. Tuerkheim

IX. New York and New England Synod.

Organized September 23, A. D. 1902

Clerical   *Lay*

Rev. Samuel Trexler, D.D.   Mr. H. W. Ungerer
                                     Mr. Frederick Henrich

X. Central Canada Synod.

Organized November 11, A. D. 1908

Clerical   *Lay*

Rev. J. Maurer, D.D.   Mr. J. C. Klaehn

The following visitors reported their presence:

Rev. M. R. Kunkelman   Rev. A. C. E. Grotke
Rev. Arnold F. Keller   Rev. C. R. Tappert

The Convention adjourned at 4.15 P. M., with the Lord's Prayer and the Benediction.

WILLIAM L. STOUGH, *Secretary.*

MINUTES OF THE UNITED SYNOD OF THE EVANGELICAL LUTHERAN CHURCH IN THE SOUTH

ROGERS PARK LUTHERAN CHURCH

Chicago, Illinois, October 21, 1924.

At the call of the Executive Board of the United Lutheran Church in America, the Nineteenth Biennial Convention of the United Synod of the Evangelical Lutheran Church in the South met in Rogers Park Lutheran Church, Chicago, Ill., at 2 P. M., October 21, 1924. Owing to the death of the President, the Rev. M. M. Kinard, Ph.D., D.D., and the absence of the Vice-President, the Rev. Wm. Hoppe, D.D., the Secretary, the Rev. C. W. Cassell, called the Convention to order and presided until the election of a President. After singing Hymn No. 164, the Convention was formally opened with the use of the Order for the Opening of Synod. Mr. W. B. Clark was elected Secretary pro tem. The official roll of the Convention as presented by the Secretary of the United Lutheran Church in America was called and the absentees noted.

Roll of Synods and Delegates

Synod of North Carolina

Clerical—Rev. J. L. Morgan, D.D., Rev. A. G. Voigt, D.D., LL.D., Rev. J. F. Crigler, D.D., Rev. J. C. Dietz, Rev. E. H. Kohn, Ph.D., *Rev. L. A. Thomas, *Rev. A. R. Beck, Rev. W. J. Finck, D.D., Rev. P. J. Bane.

Lay—*James D. Heilig, *W. L. Dixon, *W. K. Mauney, *Hon. B. B. Miller, *A. R. Rhyne, *Dr. R. W. Leiby, *Prof. George F. McAllister, *Hon. L. M. Swink, J. V. Sutton.

Synod of South Carolina

Clerical—Rev. H. J. Black, *Rev. M. G. G. Scherer, D.D., Rev. C. A. Freed, D.D., Rev. H. A. McCullough, D.D., Rev. W. H. Greever, D.D., Rev. P. D. Brown.

*Absent.

Lay—*Prof. J. S. Derrick, LL.D., *Hon. C. M. Efird, R. C. Counts, *Hon. George B. Cromer, LL.D., *Prof. James C. Kinard, *B. B. Hare, Esq.

Synod of Virginia

Clerical—Rev. C. Brown Cox, D.D., *Rev. J. J. Scherer, Jr., D.D., Rev. R. H. Anderson, Rev. J. L. Sieber, D.D., Rev. George H. Rhodes, Rev. C. L. Miller, D.D., Rev. J. A. Huffard, D.D.

Lay—*A. B. Greiner, M.D., *W. T. Stauffer, Esq., *Hon. H. L. Bonham, *Harry E. Pugh, *J. A. Alexander, Esq., *A. D. Smith, *E. L. Keiser.

Synod of Georgia

Clerical—*Rev. W. E. Pugh, Rev. T. W. Shealy.

Lay—*H. C. Lorick, W. B. Clark.

Synod of Mississippi

Clerical—Rev. J. B. Guiney.

Lay—Ed. Kreucher.

On motion of the Chairman of the South Carolina Synod delegation the names of Messrs. F. W. Seegars and H. B. Snyder were substituted for the names of Prof. Jas. C. Kinard and B. B. Hare, Esq.

On motion of the Chairman of the Virginia Synod delegation the name of the Rev. C. W. Cassell was substituted for that of the Rev. J. A. Huffard, and the name of Mr. H. L. Snyder was substituted for that of J. A. Alexander, Esq.

The Convention now went into the election of President. After the second ballot a motion prevailed instructing the Secretary to cast the unanimous ballot for the Rev. A. G. Voigt for President, he having led in each of the two ballots. The Secretary having cast the ballot the newly elected President took the chair.

The Convention suspended business for a brief period for an informal conference.

---

*Absent.

Upon resuming business the Treasurer, Mr. J. D. Cappelman, read his report which was received and referred to the Auditing Committee, consisting of Messrs. J. V. Sutton, H. L. Snyder, and H. B. Snyder.

Treasurer's Report
REPORT OF J. D. CAPPELMANN
Treasurer, United Synod of the Evangelical Lutheran Church in the South
Charleston, S. C., October 16, 1924

(For next previous report see Minutes U. L. C. Buffalo Convention, pages 564 *et seq.* October 12, 1922.)

Receipts

Balance on hand per last account	$3,394.65
Interest Hotel Huffry Bonds, payable March, 1923, September, 1923, March, 1924	647.25
Interest on Bank balances	.49
Interest Hotel Huffry Bonds September, 1924, less exchange	216.00
Total receipts	$4,258.39

Disbursements

November, 1922, Paid Orphan Home, Salem, Va., Lown Legacy		$2,000.00	
November, 1922, Paid Foreign Mission Board, Lown Legacy		500.00	
November, 1922, Paid Home Mission Board, Lown Legacy		500.00	
November, 1922, Paid Treasurer's expenses to Buffalo to Convention	$94.01		
Refund from U. L. C.	40.01		
		54.02	
November, 1922, Paid Orphan Home, share interest		113.54	
November, 1922, Paid Foreign Board, share interest		113.54	
November, 1922, Paid Home Board, share interest		113.54	
April, 1924, Paid Orphan Home, share interest		215.75	
April, 1924, Paid Foreign Board, share interest		215.75	
April, 1924, Paid Home Board, share interest		215.75	
			4,041.89
Balance on hand			$216.50

Distributable

One-third to Orphan Home	$72.17
One-third to Foreign Board	72.17
One-third to Home Board	72.16
	216.50

The Treasurer surrendered the $7,200 of Bonds of the Hotel Huffry Company at Hickory, N. C., bearing 6 per cent interest, semi-annually, Nos. 1 to 72, each for $100 and received in return Bonds of same Company, Nos. 24, 25, 26, 27, 28, 29 and 30, each for $1,000, and No. 50 for $500, total $7,500, next coupon being payable March 1, 1925, the interest being 6 per cent. The exchange so made effectuates what is equal to a 7 per cent investment. The Trust Deed securing this issue is made to Security Trust Company, of Hickory, N. C., regarded as efficient and responsible from whose letter of September 13, 1924, is quoted the following:

"The method of making a 6 per cent bond a 7 per cent investment is done by selling the bonds below par. This is expressly authorized by statute. In this case a $100 five-year 6 per cent Bond is sold for $95.84 and will net 7 per cent. For your $7,200 old bonds you will get in exchange $7,500 par value new Bonds and $12 in cash."

The Treasurer personally investigated the property mortgaged and estimates it worth easily double the amount of the $40,000 loan made thereon in the issue of bonds of which the Bonds so received are a part, the will of Mr. Huffman requiring that in all loans of funds given by him, the Treasurer of the United Synod should be satisfied that the property mortgaged is worth double the amount to be loaned thereon.

The Treasurer holds the written opinion of Messrs. Self, Bagby and Aiken, Attorneys of Hickory, N. C., who are the attorneys employed by the Trust Company, by which it appears that all requirements of law have been complied with and the Trust Company has reported that the old mortgage securing the old issue has been duly canceled of record.

The Treasurer acted in this matter on consultation with the Executive Committee, Secretary Cassell of Synod, and with Hon. C. M. Efird, as counsel. The President of the Synod, Dr. M. M. Kinard, being deceased, he applied to Vice-President Dr. William Hoppe, who, being about to leave for Europe, directed the Treasurer to confer with the Executive Committee and Secretary Cassell.

Under Mr. Huffman's will one-third of the above bonds and the $12 in cash is investment for the Foreign Mission Work, one-third for Home Mission Work and one-third for Lutheran Orphan Home.

Hon. C. M. Efird, acting as counsel for United Synod, will probably report to Synod the progress being made in having the United Lutheran Church of America substituted as Trustee in place of the United Synod.

Respectfully submitted,

JOHN D. CAPPELMANN, *Treasurer.*

Chicago, Ill., October 20, 1924.

The Rev. J. L. Morgan read the report of the Executive Committee, which was adopted.

Report of Executive Committee

The only business claiming the attention of the Executive Committee during the past biennium was a request from Mr. J. D. Cappelmann, Treasurer of this body, for an opinion as to the advisability of reinvesting the Huffman will funds, in first mortgage bonds of the Huffry Hotel Company, of Hickory, N. C. After inquiring into the matter, it was given as the opinion of the Committee that such an investment would be satisfactory.

Respectfully submitted,

J. L. MORGAN, *Chairman.*

The Rev. C. A. Freed reported for the Board of Home Missions and Church Extension, saying that all matters pertaining to the Board had been handled by the Board of Home Missions and Church Extension of the United Lutheran Church in America. The report was adopted.

Revs. P. D. Brown, W. J. Finck and R. H. Anderson were appointed a committee to nominate members for Boards and an Executive Committee.

The following resolution offered by the Rev. C. A. Freed was adopted:

Resolved, That the Executive Committee be authorized to examine the representation of District Synods in the Boards of the Theological Seminary, the Orphan Home and the Lowman Home, and that the Committee report its findings to the next Convention of this body.

The following report of the Board of Foreign Missions was read by the Secretary, and was received and adopted:

Report of the Board of Foreign Missions

(For the Biennium, October 17, 1922, to October 17, 1924)

Members of the Board—The following were elected by the United Synod of the Evangelical Lutheran Church in the South during its Eighteenth Biennial Convention held at Buffalo, N. Y., October 17, 1922: Revs. M. J. Epting, D.D., W. Hoppe, D.D., George J. Gongaware, D.D., T. W. Shealy, D. B. Groseclose, and Messrs. J. H. Paulsen and S. H. Schirmer. The Board was convened immediately after the adjournment of the United Synod and was organized by the election of officers. No necessity arose for subsequent meetings.

A matter requiring official attention during the biennium was a transaction in connection with the estate of the late Mr. J. E. Cooper, of Winchester, Va. After zealous and faithful service during a period of thirteen years on the Board of Missions and Church Extension and eight years on the Board of Foreign Missions, Mr. Cooper was received into the glory of the Church Triumphant in heaven, March 26, 1922. Under his will, this Board, jointly with the Board of Home Missions and Church Extension, became a residuary legatee by the following bequest:

"All the rest and residue of my estate, after the foregoing specific bequests have been paid or set aside, I give, devise and bequest absolutely to the Board of Foreign Missions of the United Synod of the Evangelical Lutheran Church in the South, and the Board of Home Missions and Church Extension of the United Synod of the Evangelical Lutheran Church in the South, both of which Boards have been incorporated under the laws of the State of South Carolina, said estate to be divided *share and share alike* between said Boards, and to be used by them at their discretion in prosecution of the Foreign and Home Missionary work for which they were organized. I charge the said Boards faithfully to employ these funds in promulgation of the doctrine of the Holy Gospel as held and taught by the Evangelical Lutheran Church. If investments from this bequest are made in property I charge the Board to use the utmost caution and diligence that the funds so invested will not be jeopardized or become unprofitable, but that they may remain a constant source of blessing to the Church. I further request the Board to make the reading of my will a regular item of the order of business at each of the meetings when disposition of these funds is proposed."

In obedience to a citation from the Corporation Court, Winchester, Va., and after consulting the officials of the Board of Foreign Missions of the United Lutheran Church in America, at the request and upon the authority of the said officials, the president of this Board (United Synod) appeared in the Corporation Court, February 18, 1924, and examined the records of the estate of Mr. J. E. Cooper, with special reference to the appraisement as bearing upon the inheritance tax laws of the State of Virginia. The appraisement as filed in the Court shows:

Total assets, real and personal		$115,964.87
Charges against the Estate:		
Specific bequests	$12,000.00	
Debts and cost of administration	2,300.75	
Properties included originally in the appraisement, but subsequently ascertained to have been given by codicil to the sister of the testator	19,000.00	
		33,300.75
Total residue of property		$82,664.12

The residue consists of realty (Lutheran Church site) in the city of Portsmouth, Va., (appraised at $50,000.00), bonds, notes and mortgages. Listed among the assets is a bond charged against the United Synod Board in the sum of $2,500.00 This is the annuity bond given Mr. Cooper by the Foreign Mission Board of the United Synod, said bond taking the place of an agreement between Mr. Cooper and the sainted President Holland, in October, 1915. The conditions of the bond were complied with by the United Synod Board and by the Board of the United Lutheran Church since the merger and up to the time of the death of Mr. Cooper. The bond is, therefore, void and the total residue shown should be reduced by the amount represented by the bond, viz., $2,500.00.

Representing the two Boards of Foreign Missions, the president of the Board of the United Synod experienced no difficulty in arriving at an understanding and effecting an agreement with the executor and his attorney and the Corporation Court that the Board of Foreign Missions of the United Lutheran Church in America is in all respects the legal successor of the Board of Foreign Missions of the Evangelical Lutheran Church in the South. Accordingly, negotiations looking to the final settlement of the estate of Mr. J. E. Cooper, deceased, will be transacted by the Board of Foreign Missions of the United Church and final settlement made with said Board, which Board is already functioning.

Respectfully submitted,

M. J. EPTING,
W. HOPPE,
GEORGE J. GONGAWARE,
T. W. SHEALY,
D. B. GROSECLOSE,
J. H. PAULSEN,
S. H. SCHIRMER.

The Committee on Nominations recommended the following as members of the Board of Home Missions and Church Extension: Revs. C. A. Freed, C. K. Bell, J. F. Crigler, A. D. R. Hancher, and Messrs. A. H. Kohn, John Kellenberg, D. F. Efird.

On motion, the Secretary was instructed to cast the unanimous vote of the Convention for these brethren. This being done, they were declared elected.

The same committee recommended the names of Revs. M. J. Epting, Wm. Hoppe, Geo. J. Gongaware, T. W. Shealy, D. B. Groseclose, and Messrs. J. H. Paulsen and S. H. Shirmer as members of the Foreign Mission Board.

On motion, the Secretary was instructed to cast the unanimous ballot of the Convention for these brethren. This being done, they were declared elected.

The committee further recommended the names of the Revs. J. L. Morgan, J. J. Scherer, Jr., A. G. Voigt, Hon. B. B. Miller and Hon. L. M. Swink as those constituting the Executive Committee. The Secretary was instructed to cast the unanimous vote of the Convention for these brethren. This being done, they were declared elected.

Th Auditing Committee rendered the following report which was adopted:

Report of Auditing Committee

The committee appointed to audit and vouch report of Treasurer of Synod find same correct and properly vouched and recommend the adoption of the following resolution:

Resolved, That the report of John D. Cappelmann, Treasurer, dated October 20th, be received as information and spread on the minutes, that the exchange of bonds reported by him therein is approved and ratified, and that it is hereby directed that there be paid over one-third of the $216.50 reported in hand to the Treasurer of the Home Mission Board of the United Lutheran Church in America as successor to this Board, one-third to the Treasurer of the Foreign Mission Board, and one-third to the Treasurer of the Orphan Home in Salem, Va.

Resolved further, That the transfer and delivery of the said bonds so reported in the hands of the Treasurer of the United Lutheran Church in America is authorized and directed to be made as soon as the counsel of this Synod, Hon. C. M. Efird, (or such other counsel as the Executive Committee of this Synod may indicate), shall advise in writing that the United Lutheran Church in America has been substituted as Trustee in place of this Synod and authorized to assume and execute the trust devolving on this Synod by the last will and testament of the late W. P. Huffman in his lifetime at Hickory, N. C.

J. V. Sutton,
H. B. Snyder,
H. L. Snyder,
Auditing Committee.

The following statement from the Hon. C. M. Efird was read and received as information:

1. The Cover Fund has been transferred to the First National Bank, Salem, Va., as Trustee.

2. The Swygert Fund has been transferred to the Seminary as Trustee.

3. The Huffman Fund will be transferred to the United Lutheran Church as Trustee as soon as practicable.

On motion the Executive Committee was instructed to endeavor to provide for the traveling expenses of Secretary, the Rev. C. W. Cassell, to the Convention.

On motion the Revs. A. G. Voigt and J. L. Morgan were appointed to prepare a memorial to our late President, the Rev. M. M. Kinard, and place it in the hands of the Secretary, to be printed in the Minutes.

Memorial to President Kinard

During the past biennium of the United Synod it fell to us to mourn the death of the President, the Rev. M. M. Kinard, D.D. While we mourn his departure, we take comfort and are thankful to God for the life of useful service he was enabled to give to the Church. This is not the place to record the earnest striving of the ambitious youth to get the necessary education to qualify him for the ministry of the Gospel, nor the years of faithful service of the mature man as a pastor in Columbia, S. C., Knoxville, Tenn., Salisbury, N. C., and Winston-Salem, N. C., nor even the active and distinguished part he took and the high offices he filled in the Synods of which he was successively a member. It is in his long and prominent connection with the United Synod that we here cherish his memory. We recall the faithful and distinguished services he rendered to the Church as a member of many of its conventions, as a member of Committees and Boards, as its vice-president for four years, and as its able president from his election in 1918 until his lamented death on March 13, 1924.

The Lord has called him from his labors in the Church on earth; the memory of his faithful services and his pleasing personality remain with us.

J. L. MORGAN,
A. G. VOIGT,
Committee.

The Secretary pro tem was instructed by the Convention to cast the unanimous ballot for the Rev. C. W. Cassell for Secretary. This being done he was declared elected.

The Secretary was instructed by the Convention to cast the unanimous ballot for the Rev. C. A. Freed for Vice-President. This being done, he was declared elected.

The Secretary was instructed by the Convention to cast the unanimous ballot for Mr. J. D. Cappelman for Treasurer. This being done, he was declared elected.

The following resolution was presented and passed by unani·mous vote:

Resolved, That this Convention hereby expresses its most hearty appreciation to Pastor Hogshead and his congregation for the privilege of meeting in his church for this Convention of the United Synod in the South, and that Pastor Hogshead be requested to inform his congregation of this action on next Sunday.

The Minutes were read and approved.

The Convention was closed with the use of the Order for the Closing of Synod.

C. W. CASSELL, Secretary.

INDEX

PAGE